# 8th Workshop on Asian Translation (WAT 2021)



Held online due to COVID-19

Bangkok, Thailand
5 – 6 August 2021

ISBN: 978-1-7138-3390-1

**Printed from e-media with permission by:**

Curran Associates, Inc.
57 Morehouse Lane
Red Hook, NY 12571

**Some format issues inherent in the e-media version may also appear in this print version.**



Association for Computational Linguistics
209 N. Eighth Street
Stroudsburg, Pennsylvania 18360

Phone: 1-570-476-8006
Fax: 1-570-476-0860

acl@aclweb.org

**Additional copies of this publication are available from:**

Curran Associates, Inc.
57 Morehouse Lane
Red Hook, NY 12571 USA
Phone: 845-758-0400
Fax: 845-758-2633
Email: curran@proceedings.com
Web: www.proceedings.com

WAT 2021

# The 8th Workshop on Asian Translation

## Proceedings of the Workshop

August 5–6, 2021
Bangkok, Thailand (online)

# Preface

Many Asian countries are rapidly growing these days and the importance of communicating and exchanging the information with these countries has intensified. To satisfy the demand for communication among these countries, machine translation technology is essential.

Machine translation technology has rapidly evolved recently and it is seeing practical use especially between European languages. However, the translation quality of Asian languages is not that high compared to that of European languages, and machine translation technology for these languages has not reached a stage of proliferation yet. This is not only due to the lack of the language resources for Asian languages but also due to the lack of techniques to correctly transfer the meaning of sentences from/to Asian languages. Consequently, a place for gathering and sharing the resources and knowledge about Asian language translation is necessary to enhance machine translation research for Asian languages.

The Conference on Machine Translation (WMT), the world's largest machine translation workshop, mainly targets on European language. The International Workshop on Spoken Language Translation (IWSLT) has spoken language translation tasks for some Asian languages using TED talk data, but there is no task for written language. The Workshop on Asian Translation (WAT) is an open machine translation evaluation campaign focusing on Asian languages. WAT gathers and shares the resources and knowledge of Asian language translation to understand the problems to be solved for the practical use of machine translation technologies among all Asian countries. WAT is unique in that it is an "open innovation platform": the test data is fixed and open, so participants can repeat evaluations on the same data and confirm changes in translation accuracy over time. WAT has no deadline for the automatic translation quality evaluation (continuous evaluation), so participants can submit translation results at any time.

Following the success of the previous WAT workshops (WAT2014 – WAT2020), WAT2021 will bring together machine translation researchers and users to try, evaluate, share and discuss brand-new ideas about machine translation. For the 8th WAT, we included several new translation tasks including Malayalam Visual Genome Task, MultiIndicMT, Restricted Translation Task and Ambiguous MSCOCO Task. We had 28 teams participated in the shared tasks and 24 teams submitted their translation results for the human evaluation. About 2,100 translation results were submitted to the automatic evaluation server, and selected submissions were manually evaluated. In addition to the shared tasks, WAT2021 also features research papers on topics related to machine translation, especially for Asian languages. The program committee accepted 5 research papers.

We are grateful to "SunFlare Co., Ltd.", "Kawamura International" and "Asia-Pacific Association for Machine Translation (AAMT)" for partially sponsoring the workshop. We would like to thank all the authors who submitted papers. We express our deepest gratitude to the committee members for their timely reviews. We also thank the ACL-IJCNLP 2021 organizers for their help with administrative matters.

WAT 2021 Organizers

**Organizing Committee:**

Toshiaki Nakazawa, The University of Tokyo, Japan

Hideki Nakayama, The University of Tokyo, Japan

Isao Goto, Japan Broadcasting Corporation (NHK), Japan

Hideya Mino, Japan Broadcasting Corporation (NHK), Japan

Chenchen Ding, National Institute of Information and Communications Technology (NICT), Japan

Raj Dabre, National Institute of Information and Communications Technology (NICT), Japan

Anoop Kunchukuttan, Microsoft AI and Research, India

Shohei Higashiyama, National Institute of Information and Communications Technology (NICT), Japan

Hiroshi Manabe, National Institute of Information and Communications Technology (NICT), Japan

Win Pa Pa, University of Computer Studies, Yangon (UCSY), Myanmar

Shantipriya Parida, Idiap Research Institute, Martigny, Switzerland

Ondřej Bojar, Charles University, Prague, Czech Republic

Chenhui Chu, Kyoto University, Japan

Akiko Eriguchi, Microsoft, USA

Kaori Abe, Tohoku University, Japan

Yusuke Oda, LegalForce, Japan

Katsuhito Sudoh, Nara Institute of Science and Technology (NAIST), Japan

Sadao Kurohashi, Kyoto University, Japan

Pushpak Bhattacharyya, Indian Institute of Technology Bombay (IIT), India

**Program Committee:**

Hailong Cao, Harbin Institute of Technology, China

Michael Carl, Kent State University, USA

Chenhui Chu, Kyoto University, Japan

Fabien Cromières, Free, France

Kenji Imamura, NICT, Japan

Yang Liu, Tsinghua University, China

Takashi Ninomiya, Ehime University, Japan

Masao Utiyama, NICT, Japan

Jiajun Zhang, Chinese Academy of Sciences, China

**Technical Collaborators:**

Luis Fernando D'Haro, Universidad Politécnica de Madrid, Spain
Rafael E. Banchs, Nanyang Technological University, Singapore
Haizhou Li, National University of Singapore, Singapore
Chen Zhang, National University of Singapore, Singapore

# Table of Contents

# Workshop Program

**August 5-6, 2021 [UTC+0]**

**22:00–22:05 Welcome**

*Overview of the 8th Workshop on Asian Translation*
Toshiaki Nakazawa, Hideki Nakayama, Chenchen Ding, Raj Dabre, Shohei Higashiyama, Hideya Mino, Isao Goto, Win Pa Pa, Anoop Kunchukuttan, Shantipriya Parida, Ondřej Bojar, Chenhui Chu, Akiko Eriguchi, Kaori Abe, Yusuke Oda and Sadao Kurohashi

**22:05–22:45 Invited Talk I**

Francisco Guzmán

**22:45–22:50 Short Break**

**22:50–0:30 Shared Task I**

*Task Descriptions and Results (Restricted / ALT+UCSY / NICT-SAP)*
Akiko Eriguchi, Chenchen Ding, and Raj Dabre

*NHK's Lexically-Constrained Neural Machine Translation at WAT 2021*
Hideya Mino, Kazutaka Kinugawa, Hitoshi Ito, Isao Goto, Ichiro Yamada and Takenobu Tokunaga

*Input Augmentation Improves Constrained Beam Search for Neural Machine Translation: NTT at WAT 2021*
Katsuki Chousa and Makoto Morishita

*NICT's Neural Machine Translation Systems for the WAT21 Restricted Translation Task*
Zuchao Li, Masao Utiyama, Eiichiro Sumita and Hai Zhao

*Machine Translation with Pre-specified Target-side Words Using a Semi-autoregressive Model*
Seiichiro Kondo, Aomi Koyama, Tomoshige Kiyuna, Tosho Hirasawa and Mamoru Komachi

*NECTEC's Participation in WAT-2021*
Zar Zar Hlaing, Ye Kyaw Thu, Thazin Myint Oo, Mya Ei San, Sasiporn Usanavasin, Ponrudee Netisopakul and Thepchai Supnithi

**August 5-6, 2021 [UTC+0] (continued)**

*Hybrid Statistical Machine Translation for English-Myanmar: UTYCC Submission to WAT-2021*
Ye Kyaw Thu, Thazin Myint Oo, Hlaing Myat Nwe, Khaing Zar Mon, Nang Aeindray Kyaw, Naing Linn Phyo, Nann Hwan Khun and Hnin Aye Thant

*NICT-2 Translation System at WAT-2021: Applying a Pretrained Multilingual Encoder-Decoder Model to Low-resource Language Pairs*
Kenji Imamura and Eiichiro Sumita

*Rakuten's Participation in WAT 2021: Examining the Effectiveness of Pre-trained Models for Multilingual and Multimodal Machine Translation*
Raymond Hendy Susanto, Dongzhe Wang, Sunil Yadav, Mausam Jain and Ohnmar Htun

**0:30–0:35** **Short Break**

**0:35–1:15** **Invited Talk II**

Graham Neubig

**1:15–1:20** **Short Break**

**1:20–2:40** **Research Paper / Findings I**

*BTS: Back TranScription for Speech-to-Text Post-Processor using Text-to-Speech-to-Text*
chanjun park, Jaehyung Seo, Seolhwa Lee, Chanhee Lee, Hyeonseok Moon, Sugyeong Eo and Heuiseok Lim

*Zero-pronoun Data Augmentation for Japanese-to-English Translation*
Ryokan Ri, Toshiaki Nakazawa and Yoshimasa Tsuruoka

*Evaluation Scheme of Focal Translation for Japanese Partially Amended Statutes*
Takahiro Yamakoshi, Takahiro Komamizu, Yasuhiro Ogawa and Katsuhiko Toyama

*[ACL2021 Findings] Joint Optimization of Tokenization and Downstream Model*
Tatsuya Hiraoka, Sho Takase, Kei Uchiumi, Atsushi Keyaki, and Naoaki Okazaki

**August 5-6, 2021 [UTC+0] (continued)**

**2:40–4:00 Lunch Break (11:40-13:00 UTC+9)**

**4:00–5:40 Shared Task II**

*Task Descriptions and Results (JPC / Hindi&Malayalam Multimodal / Japanese Multimodal)*
Shohei Higashiyama, Shantipriya Parida, Hideki Nakayama, and Chenhui Chu

*TMU NMT System with Japanese BART for the Patent task of WAT 2021*
Hwichan Kim and Mamoru Komachi

*System Description for Transperfect*
Wiktor Stribiżew, Fred Bane, José Conceição and Anna Zaretskaya

*Bering Lab's Submissions on WAT 2021 Shared Task*
Heesoo Park and Dongjun Lee

*NLPHut's Participation at WAT2021*
Shantipriya Parida, Subhadarshi Panda, Ketan Kotwal, Amulya Ratna Dash, Satya Ranjan Dash, Yashvardhan Sharma, Petr Motlicek and Ondřej Bojar

*Improved English to Hindi Multimodal Neural Machine Translation*
Sahinur Rahman Laskar, Abdullah Faiz Ur Rahman Khilji, Darsh Kaushik, Partha Pakray and Sivaji Bandyopadhyay

*IITP at WAT 2021: System description for English-Hindi Multimodal Translation Task*
Baban Gain, Dibyanayan Bandyopadhyay and Asif Ekbal

*ViTA: Visual-Linguistic Translation by Aligning Object Tags*
Kshitij Gupta, Devansh Gautam and Radhika Mamidi

*TMEKU System for the WAT2021 Multimodal Translation Task*
Yuting Zhao, Mamoru Komachi, Tomoyuki Kajiwara and Chenhui Chu

**5:40–4:45** **Short Break**

**5:45–6:45** **Research Paper / Findings II**

*Optimal Word Segmentation for Neural Machine Translation into Dravidian Languages*
Prajit Dhar, Arianna Bisazza and Gertjan van Noord

*Itihasa: A large-scale corpus for Sanskrit to English translation*
Rahul Aralikatte, Miryam de Lhoneux, Anoop Kunchukuttan and Anders Søgaard

*[ACL2021 Findings] IndoCollex: A Testbed for Morphological Transformation of Indonesian Word Colloquialism*
Haryo Akbarianto Wibowo, Made Nindyatama Nityasya, Afra Feyza Akyüek, Suci Fitriany, Alham Fikri Aji, Radityo Eko Prasojo, and Derry Tanti Wijaya

**6:45–6:50** **Short Break**

**6:50–8:20** **Shared Task III**

*Task Descriptions and Results (MultiIndicMT)*
Shantipriya Parida

*NICT-5's Submission To WAT 2021: MBART Pre-training And In-Domain Fine Tuning For Indic Languages*
Raj Dabre and Abhisek Chakrabarty

*How far can we get with one GPU in 100 hours? CoAStaL at MultiIndicMT Shared Task*
Rahul Aralikatte, Héctor Ricardo Murrieta Bello, Daniel Hershcovich, Marcel Bollmann and Anders Søgaard

*IIIT Hyderabad Submission To WAT 2021: Efficient Multilingual NMT systems for Indian languages*
Sourav Kumar, Salil Aggarwal and Dipti Sharma

*Language Relatedness and Lexical Closeness can help Improve Multilingual NMT: IITBombay@MultiIndicNMT WAT2021*
Jyotsana Khatri, Nikhil Saini and Pushpak Bhattacharyya

*Samsung R&D Institute Poland submission to WAT 2021 Indic Language Multilingual Task*
Adam Dobrowolski, Marcin Szymański, Marcin Chochowski and Paweł Przybysz

**August 5-6, 2021 [UTC+0] (continued)**

*Multilingual Machine Translation Systems at WAT 2021: One-to-Many and Many-to-One Transformer based NMT*
Shivam Mhaskar, Aditya Jain, Aakash Banerjee and Pushpak Bhattacharyya

*IITP-MT at WAT2021: Indic-English Multilingual Neural Machine Translation using Romanized Vocabulary*
Ramakrishna Appicharla, Kamal Kumar Gupta, Asif Ekbal and Pushpak Bhattacharyya

*ANVITA Machine Translation System for WAT 2021 MultiIndicMT Shared Task*
Pavanpankaj Vegi, Sivabhavani J, Biswajit Paul, Chitra Viswanathan and Prasanna Kumar K R

**8:20–8:25** **Closing**

# Overview of the 8th Workshop on Asian Translation

**Toshiaki Nakazawa**
The University of Tokyo
nakazawa@logos.t.u-tokyo.ac.jp

**Hideki Nakayama**
The University of Tokyo
nakayama@ci.i.u-tokyo.ac.jp

**Chenchen Ding** and **Raj Dabre** and **Shohei Higashiyama**
National Institute of
Information and Communications Technology
{chenchen.ding, raj.dabre, shohei.higashiyama}@nict.go.jp

**Hideya Mino** and **Isao Goto**
NHK
{mino.h-gq, goto.i-es}@nhk.or.jp

**Win Pa Pa**
University of Conputer Study, Yangon
winpapa@ucsy.edu.mm

**Anoop Kunchukuttan**
Microsoft AI and Research
anoop.kunchukuttan@microsoft.com

**Shantipriya Parida**
Idiap Research Institute
shantipriya.parida@idiap.ch

**Ondřej Bojar**
Charles University, MFF, ÚFAL
bojar@ufal.mff.cuni.cz

**Chenhui Chu**
Kyoto University
chu@i.kyoto-u.ac.jp

**Akiko Eriguchi**
Microsoft
akikoe@microsoft.com

**Kaori Abe**
Tohoku University
abe-k@ecei.tohoku.ac.jp

**Yusuke Oda**
Tohoku University, LegalForce
yusuke.oda.c1@tohoku.ac.jp

**Sadao Kurohashi**
Kyoto University
kuro@i.kyoto-u.ac.jp

## Abstract

This paper presents the results of the shared tasks from the 8th workshop on Asian translation (WAT2021). For the WAT2021, 28 teams participated in the shared tasks and 24 teams submitted their translation results for the human evaluation. We also accepted 5 research papers. About 2,100 translation results were submitted to the automatic evaluation server, and selected submissions were manually evaluated.

## 1 Introduction

The Workshop on Asian Translation (WAT) is an open evaluation campaign focusing on Asian languages. Following the success of the previous workshops WAT2014-WAT2020 (Nakazawa et al., 2020), WAT2021 brings together machine translation researchers and users to try, evaluate, share and discuss brand-new ideas for machine translation. We have been working toward practical use of machine translation among all Asian countries.

For the 8th WAT, we included the following new tasks:

- Malayalam Visual Genome Task: English → Malayalam multi-modal translation
- MultiIndicMT: Bengali / Gujarati / Hindi / Kannada / Malayalam / Marathi / Odia / Punjabi / Tamil / Telugu ↔ English translation
- Restricted Translation Task: Japanese ↔ English translation
- Ambiguous MSCOCO Task: Japanese ↔ English multi-modal translation

All the tasks are explained in Section 2.

WAT is a unique workshop on Asian language translation with the following characteristics:

- Open innovation platform
  Due to the fixed and open test data, we can repeatedly evaluate translation systems on the same dataset over years. WAT receives submissions at any time; i.e., there is no submission deadline of translation results w.r.t automatic evaluation of translation quality.
- Domain and language pairs
  WAT is the world's first workshop that targets scientific paper domain, and Chinese↔Japanese and Korean↔Japanese language pairs.



*Proceedings of the 8th Workshop on Asian Translation*, pages 1–45
Bangkok, Thailand (online), August 5-6, 2021. 

- Evaluation method
  Evaluation is done both automatically and manually. Firstly, all submitted translation results are automatically evaluated using three metrics: BLEU, RIBES and AMFM. Among them, selected translation results are assessed by two kinds of human evaluation: pairwise evaluation and JPO adequacy evaluation.

## 2 Tasks

### 2.1 ASPEC+ParaNatCom Task

Traditional ASPEC translation tasks are sentence-level and the translation quality of them seem to be saturated. We think it's high time to move on to document-level evaluation. For the first year, we use ParaNatCom[1] (Parallel English-Japanese abstract corpus made from Nature Communications articles) for the development and test sets of the Document-level Scientific Paper Translation subtask. We cannot provide document-level training corpus, but you can use ASPEC and any other extra resources.

### 2.2 Document-level Business Scene Dialogue Translation

There are a lot of ready-to-use parallel corpora for training machine translation systems, however, most of them are in written languages such as web crawl, news-commentary, patents, scientific papers and so on. Even though some of the parallel corpora are in spoken language, they are mostly spoken by only one person (TED talks) or contain a lot of noise (OpenSubtitle). Most of other MT evaluation campaigns adopt the written language, monologue or noisy dialogue parallel corpora for their translation tasks. Traditional ASPEC translation tasks are sentence-level and the translation quality of them seem to be saturated. To move to a highly topical setting of translation of dialogues evaluated at the level of documents, WAT uses BSD Corpus[2] (The Business Scene Dialogue corpus) for the dataset including training, development and test data for the first time this year. Participants of this task must get a copy of BSD corpus by themselves.

### 2.3 JPC Task

JPO Patent Corpus (JPC) for the patent tasks was constructed by the Japan Patent Office (JPO) in collaboration with NICT. The corpus consists of Chinese-Japanese, Korean-Japanese and English-Japanese patent descriptions whose International Patent Classification (IPC) sections are chemistry, electricity, mechanical engineering, and physics.

At WAT2021, the patent task has two subtasks: normal subtask and expression pattern subtask. Both subtasks use common training, development and development-test data for each language pair. The normal subtask for three language pairs uses four test datasets with different characteristics:

- test-N: union of the following three sets;
- test-N1: patent documents from patent families published between 2011 and 2013;
- test-N2: patent documents from patent families published between 2016 and 2017; and
- test-N3: patent documents published between 2016 and 2017 where target sentences are manually created by translating source sentences.

| Lang | Train | Dev | DevTest | Test-N |
|---|---|---|---|---|
| zh-ja | 1,000,000 | 2,000 | 2,000 | 5,204 |
| ko-ja | 1,000,000 | 2,000 | 2,000 | 5,230 |
| en-ja | 1,000,000 | 2,000 | 2,000 | 5,668 |

| Lang | Test-N1 | Test-N2 | Test-N3 | Test-EP |
|---|---|---|---|---|
| zh-ja | 2,000 | 3,000 | 204 | 1,151 |
| ko-ja | 2,000 | 3,000 | 230 | – |
| en-ja | 2,000 | 3,000 | 668 | – |

Table 1: Statistics for JPC

The expression pattern subtask for zh→ja pair uses test-EP data. The test-EP data consists of sentences annotated with expression pattern categories: title of invention (TIT), abstract (ABS), scope of claim (CLM) or description (DES). The corpus statistics are shown in Table 1. Note that training, development, development-test and test-N1 data are the same as those used in WAT2017.

### 2.4 Newswire (JIJI) Task

The Japanese ↔ English newswire task uses JIJI Corpus which was constructed by Jiji Press Ltd. in collaboration with NICT and NHK. The corpus consists of news text that comes from Jiji Press news of various categories including politics, economy, nation, business, markets, sports and so on. The corpus is partitioned into training, development, development-test and test data, which con-

[1] `http://www2.nict.go.jp/astrec-att/member/mutiyama/paranatcom/`

[2] `https://github.com/tsuruoka-lab/BSD`

| Training | | 0.2 M sentence pairs |
|---|---|---|
| Test set I | Test | 2,000 sentence pairs |
| | DevTest | 2,000 sentence pairs |
| | Dev | 2,000 sentence pairs |
| Test set II | Test-2 | 1,912 sentence pairs |
| | Dev-2 | 497 sentence pairs |
| | Context for Test-2 | 567 article pairs |
| | Context for Dev-2 | 135 article pairs |

Table 2: Statistics for JIJI Corpus

sists of Japanese-English sentence pairs. In addition to the test set (test set I) that has been provided from WAT 2017, a test set (test set II) with document-level context has also been provided from WAT 2020. These test sets are as follows.

**Test set I** : A pair of test and reference sentences. The references were automatically extracted from English newswire sentences and not manually checked. There are no context data.

**Test set II** : A pair of test and reference sentences and context data that are articles including test sentences. The references were automatically extracted from English newswire sentences and manually selected. Therefore, the quality of the references of test set II is better than that of test set I.

The statistics of JIJI Corpus are shown in Table 2.

The definition of data use is shown in Table 3.

Participants submit the translation results of one or more of the test data.

The sentence pairs in each data are identified in the same manner as that for ASPEC using the method from (Utiyama and Isahara, 2007).

### 2.5 ALT and UCSY Corpus

The parallel data for Myanmar-English translation tasks at WAT2021 consists of two corpora, the ALT corpus and UCSY corpus.

- The ALT corpus is one part from the Asian Language Treebank (ALT) project (Riza et al., 2016), consisting of twenty thousand Myanmar-English parallel sentences from news articles.

- The UCSY corpus (Yi Mon Shwe Sin and Khin Mar Soe, 2018) is constructed by the NLP Lab, University of Computer Studies, Yangon (UCSY), Myanmar. The corpus consists of 200 thousand Myanmar-English parallel sentences collected from different domains, including news articles and textbooks.

The ALT corpus has been manually segmented into words (Ding et al., 2018, 2019), and the UCSY corpus is unsegmented. A script to tokenize the Myanmar data into writing units is released with the data. The automatic evaluation of Myanmar translation results is based on the tokenized writing units, regardless to the segmented words in the ALT data. However, participants can make a use of the segmentation in ALT data in their own manner.

The detailed composition of training, development, and test data of the Myanmar-English translation tasks are listed in Table 4. Notice that both of the corpora have been modified from the data used in WAT2018.

### 2.6 NICT-SAP Task

In WAT2021, we decided to continue the WAT2020 task for joint multi-domain multilingual neural machine translation involving 4 low-resource Asian languages: Thai (Th), Hindi (Hi), Malay (Ms), Indonesian (Id). English (En) is the source or the target language for the translation directions being evaluated. The purpose of this task was to test the feasibility of multi-domain multilingual solutions for extremely low-resource language pairs and domains. Naturally the solutions could be one-to-many, many-to-one or many-to-many NMT models. The domains in question are Wikinews and IT (specifically, Software Documentation). The total number of evaluation directions are 16 (8 for each domain). There is very little clean and publicly available data for these domains and language pairs and thus we encouraged participants to not only utilize the small Asian Language Treebank (ALT) parallel corpora (Thu et al., 2016) but also the parallel corpora from OPUS[3], other WAT tasks (past and present) and WMT[4]. The ALT dataset contains 18,088, 1,000 and 1,018 training, development and testing sentences. As for corpora for the IT domain we only provided evaluation (dev and test sets) corpora[5] (Buschbeck and Exel, 2020) and encouraged participants to consider GNOME, UBUNTU and KDE corpora from OPUS. We

[3] http://opus.nlpl.eu/

[4] http://www.statmt.org/wmt20/

[5] Software Domain Evaluation Splits

| Task | Use | | Content |
|---|---|---|---|
| Japanese to English | Training | | Training, DevTest, Dev, Dev-2, context for Dev2 |
| | Test set I | To be translated | Test in Japanese |
| | | Reference | Test in English |
| | Test set II | Test-2 | Test-2 in Japanese |
| | | Context | Context in Japanese for Test-2 |
| | | Reference | Test-2 in English |
| English to Japanese | Training | | Training, DevTest, Dev, Dev-2, context for Dev2 |
| | Test set I | To be translated | Test in English |
| | | Reference | Test in Japanese |
| | Test set II | To be translated | Test-2 in English |
| | | Context in English for Test-2 | Context in English for Test-2 |
| | | Reference | Test-2 in Japanese |

Table 3: Definition of data use in the Japanese ↔ English newswire task

| Corpus | Train | Dev | Test |
|---|---|---|---|
| ALT | 18,088 | 1,000 | 1,018 |
| UCSY | 204,539 | – | – |
| All | 222,627 | 1,000 | 1,018 |

Table 4: Statistics for the data used in Myanmar-English translation tasks

| Split | Domain | Language Pair | | | |
|---|---|---|---|---|---|
| | | **Hi** | **Id** | **Ms** | **Th** |
| **Train** | **ALT** | 18,088 | | | |
| | **IT** | 254,242 | 158,472 | 506,739 | 74,497 |
| **Dev** | **ALT** | 1,000 | | | |
| | **IT** | 2,016 | 2,023 | 2,050 | 2,049 |
| **Test** | **ALT** | 1,018 | | | |
| | **IT** | 2,073 | 2,037 | 2,050 | 2,050 |

Table 5: The NICT-SAP task corpora splits. The corpora belong to two domains: wikinews (ALT) and software documentation (IT). The Wikinews corpora are N-way parallel.

also encouraged the use of monolingual corpora expecting that it would be for pre-trained NMT models such as BART/MBART (Lewis et al., 2020; Liu et al., 2020). In Table 5 we give statistics of the aforementioned corpora which we used for the organizer's baselines. Note that the evaluation corpora for both domains are created from documents and thus contain document level meta-data. Participants were encouraged to use document level approaches. Note that we do not exhaustively list[6] all available corpora here and participants were not restricted from using any corpora as long as they are freely available.

### 2.7 News Commentary Task

For the Russian↔Japanese task we asked participants to use the JaRuNC corpus[7] (Imankulova et al., 2019) which belongs to the news commentary domain. This dataset was manually aligned and cleaned and is trilingual. It can be used to evaluate Russian↔English translation quality as well but this is beyond the scope of this years sub-task. Refer to Table 6 for the statistics of the in-domain parallel corpora. In addition, we encouraged the participants to use out-of-domain parallel corpora from various sources such as KFTT,[8] JESC,[9] TED,[10] ASPEC,[11] UN,[12] Yandex[13] and Russian↔English news-commentary corpus.[14] This year we also encouraged participants to use any corpora from WMT 2020[15] and WMT 2021[16] involving Japanese, Russian, and English as long as it did not belong to the news commentary domain to prevent any test set sentences from being unintentionally seen during training.

| Lang.pair | Partition | #sent. | #tokens | #types |
|---|---|---|---|---|
| Ja↔Ru | train | 12,356 | 341k / 229k | 22k / 42k |
| | development | 486 | 16k / 11k | 2.9k / 4.3k |
| | test | 600 | 22k / 15k | 3.5k / 5.6k |
| Ja↔En | train | 47,082 | 1.27M / 1.01M | 48k / 55k |
| | development | 589 | 21k / 16k | 3.5k / 3.8k |
| | test | 600 | 22k / 17k | 3.5k / 3.8k |
| Ru↔En | train | 82,072 | 1.61M / 1.83M | 144k / 74k |
| | development | 313 | 7.8k / 8.4k | 3.2k / 2.3k |
| | test | 600 | 15k / 17k | 5.6k / 3.8k |

Table 6: In-Domain data for the Russian–Japanese task.

[6] http://lotus.kuee.kyoto-u.ac.jp/WAT/NICT-SAP-Task

[7] https://github.com/aizhanti/JaRuNC

[8] http://www.phontron.com/kftt/

[9] https://datarepository.wolframcloud.com/resources/Japanese-English-Subtitle-Corpus

[10] https://wit3.fbk.eu/

[11] http://lotus.kuee.kyoto-u.ac.jp/ASPEC/

[12] https://cms.unov.org/UNCorpus/

[13] https://translate.yandex.ru/corpus?lang=en

[14] http://lotus.kuee.kyoto-u.ac.jp/WAT/News-Commentary/news-commentary-v14.en-ru.filtered.tar.gz

[15] http://www.statmt.org/wmt20/translation-task.html

[16] http://www.statmt.org/wmt21/translation-task.html

| source | bn | gu | hi | kn | ml | mr | or | pa | ta | te | Grand Total |
|---|---|---|---|---|---|---|---|---|---|---|---|
| **alt** | 20,106 | | 20,106 | | | | | | | | **40,212** |
| **bibleuedin** | | 15,609 | 62,073 | 61,707 | 61,300 | 60,876 | | | | 62,191 | **323,756** |
| **cvit-pib** | 91,985 | 58,264 | 266,545 | | 43,087 | 114,220 | 94,494 | 101,092 | 115,968 | 44,720 | **930,375** |
| **iitb** | | | 1,603,080 | | | | | | | | **1,603,080** |
| **jw** | 278,307 | 310,094 | 509,594 | 303,991 | 362,816 | 270,346 | | 388,364 | 673,232 | 192,904 | **3,289,648** |
| **mtenglish2odia** | | | | | | | 34,846 | | | | **34,846** |
| **nlpc** | | | | | | | | | 31,373 | | **31,373** |
| **odiencorp** | | | | | | | 90,854 | | | | **90,854** |
| **opensubtitles** | 411,097 | | 92,319 | | 383,313 | | | | 32,140 | 27,063 | **945,932** |
| **pmi** | 23,306 | 41,578 | 50,349 | 28,901 | 26,916 | 28,974 | 31,966 | 28,294 | 32,638 | 33,380 | **326,302** |
| **tanzil** | 187,052 | | 187,080 | | 187,081 | | | | 93,540 | | **654,753** |
| **ted2020** | 10,318 | 15,691 | 46,759 | 2,253 | 5,990 | 22,608 | | 749 | 11,105 | 5,236 | **120,709** |
| **ufal** | | | | | | | | | 166,866 | | **166,866** |
| **urst** | | 65,000 | | | | | | | | | **65,000** |
| **wikimatrix** | 280,566 | | 231,459 | | 71,508 | 124,304 | | | 95,159 | 91,908 | **894,904** |
| **wikititles** | | 11,665 | | | | | | | 102,131 | | **113,796** |
| **Grand Total** | **1,302,737** | **517,901** | **3,069,364** | **396,852** | **1,142,011** | **621,328** | **252,160** | **518,499** | **1,354,152** | **457,402** | **9,632,406** |

Table 7: Statistics of the filtered parallel corpora provided by the organizers. The target language is English.

| Language | #Lines |
|---|---|
| as | 1.39M |
| bn | 39.9M |
| en | 54.3M |
| gu | 41.1M |
| hi | 63.1M |
| kn | 53.3M |
| ml | 50.2M |
| mr | 34.0M |
| or | 6.94M |
| pa | 29.2M |
| ta | 31.5M |
| te | 47.9M |

Table 8: Monolingual corpora statistics.

### 2.8 Indic Multilingual Task

Owing to the increasing interest in Indian language translation and the success of the multilingual Indian languages tasks in 2018 (Nakazawa et al., 2018) and 2020 (Nakazawa et al., 2020), we decided to enlarge the scope of the 2020 task by adding new languages, scouring new data and creating an N-way parallel evaluation set. In 2020, the evaluation data came from the CVIT-PIB dataset[17] but it did not contain sufficient N-way parallel sentences to evaluate on additional languages. To this end, we decided to obtain evaluation corpora from the PMI dataset[18] which contains sufficient N-way parallel corpora spanning 10 Indian languages and English and is similar (domain wise) to the CVIT-PIB dataset.

The evaluation data consists of various articles composed by the Prime Minister of India. The languages involved are Hindi (Hi), Marathi (Mr), Kannada (Kn), Tamil (Ta), Telugu (Te), Gujarati (Gu), Malayalam (Ml), Bengali (Bn), Oriya (Or), Punjabi (Pa) and English (En). Compared to 2020, we have 3 additional languages leading to a total of 10 Indian languages, 4 of which are Dravidian and the rest are Indo-Aryan. English is either the source or the target language during evaluation leading to a total of 20 translation directions. Due to the N-way nature of the evaluation corpus we can also evaluate 90 Indian language to Indian language translation pairs but this may be the focus in future workshops.

The objective of this task, like the Indic languages tasks in 2018 and 2020, was to evaluate the performance of multilingual NMT models. The desired solution could be one-to-many, many-to-one or many-to-many NMT models. We provided a filtered parallel corpus collection spanning all languages[19] which was split into training, development and test sets. This dataset was created by first creating an evaluation set of 3,390 11-way sentences (1,000 for development and 2,390 for testing) and then filtering them out from all parallel corpora we could obtain at the time. Furthermore, we made sure to filter out sentences from the 2020 evaluation set. This way the provided parallel corpus can be safely used for benchmarking the 2020 evaluation set as well. The filtered training parallel corpora came from a variety of sources such as: CVIT-PIB, PMIndia, IITB 3.0,[20] JW,[21]

[17] http://preon.iiit.ac.in/~jerin/resources/datasets/pib_v1.3.tar

[18] http://data.statmt.org/pmindia

[19] http://lotus.kuee.kyoto-u.ac.jp/WAT/indic-multilingual/indic_wat_2021.tar.gz

[20] http://www.cfilt.iitb.ac.in/iitb_parallel/

[21] http://opus.nlpl.eu/JW300.php

NLPC,[22]UFAL EnTam,[23]Uka Tarsadia,[24]Wiki Titles (ta,[25]gu,[26])ALT,[27]OpenSubtitles,[28] Bible-uedin,[29] MTEnglish2Odia,[30]OdiEnCorp 2.0,[31] TED,[32] and WikiMatrix[33]. Additionally we listed the CCAligned corpus[34] to be used despite its poor quality which applies to WikiMatrix as well. We also provided filtered monolingual corpora[35] sourced from PMI and we also encouraged the use of monolingual corpora from the IndicCorp.[36]The statistics of this corpus are given in table 8. We expected that this year, the novel way of using the monolingual corpora would be to pre-train NMT models such as BART/MBART (Lewis et al., 2020; Liu et al., 2020). In general we encouraged participants to focus on multilingual NMT (Dabre et al., 2020) solutions.

Detailed statistics for the aforementioned corpora can be found in Table 7. We also listed additional sources of corpora for participants to use. Our organizer's baselines used the PMI corpora for training as it is the in-domain corpus.

### 2.9 English→Hindi Multi-Modal Task

This task is running successfully in WAT since 2019 and attracted many teams working on multimodal machine translation and image captioning in Indian languages (Nakazawa et al., 2019, 2020).

For English→Hindi multi-modal translation task, we asked the participants to use Hindi Visual Genome 1.1 corpus (HVG, Parida et al., 2019a,b).[37]

| | | Tokens | |
|---|---|---|---|
| Dataset | Items | English | Hindi |
| Training Set | 28,930 | 143,164 | 145,448 |
| D-Test | 998 | 4,922 | 4,978 |
| E-Test (EV) | 1,595 | 7,853 | 7,852 |
| C-Test (CH) | 1,400 | 8,186 | 8,639 |

Table 9: Statistics of Hindi Visual Genome 1.1 used for the English→Hindi Multi-Modal translation task. One item consists of a source English sentence, target Hindi sentence, and a rectangular region within an image. The total number of English and Hindi tokens in the dataset also listed. The abbreviations EV and CH are used in the official task names in WAT scoring tables.

The statistics of HVG 1.1 are given in Table 9. One "item" in HVG consists of an image with a rectangular region highlighting a part of the image, the original English caption of this region and the Hindi reference translation. Depending on the track (see 2.9.1 below), some of these item components are available as the source and some serve as the reference or play the role of a competing candidate solution.

#### 2.9.1 English→Hindi Multi-Modal Task Tracks

1. Text-Only Translation (labeled "TEXT" in WAT official tables): The participants are asked to translate short English captions (text) into Hindi. No visual information can be used. On the other hand, additional text resources are permitted (but they need to be specified in the corresponding system description paper).

2. Hindi Captioning (labeled "HI"): The participants are asked to generate captions in Hindi for the given rectangular region in an input image.

3. Multi-Modal Translation (labeled "MM"): Given an image, a rectangular region in it and an English caption for the rectangular region, the participants are asked to translate the English text into Hindi. Both textual and visual information can be used.

The English→Hindi multi-modal task includes three tracks as illustrated in Figure 1.

[22]https://github.com/nlpc-uom/English-Tamil-Parallel-Corpus
[23]http://ufal.mff.cuni.cz/~ramasamy/parallel/html/
[24]https://github.com/shahparth123/eng_guj_parallel_corpus
[25]http://data.statmt.org/wikititles/v2/wikititles-v2.ta-en.tsv.gz
[26]http://data.statmt.org/wikititles/v1/wikititles-v1.gu-en.tsv.gz
[27]http://www2.nict.go.jp/astrec-att/member/mutiyama/ALT
[28]http://opus.nlpl.eu/OpenSubtitles-v2018.php
[29]http://opus.nlpl.eu/bible-uedin.php
[30]https://github.com/soumendrak/MTEnglish2Odia
[31]https://ufal.mff.cuni.cz/odiencorp
[32]http://lotus.kuee.kyoto-u.ac.jp/WAT/indic-multilingual/
[33]https://github.com/facebookresearch/LASER/tree/master/tasks/WikiMatrix
[34]http://www.statmt.org/cc-aligned/
[35]http://lotus.kuee.kyoto-u.ac.jp/WAT/indic-multilingual/filteredmono.tar.gz
[36]https://indicnlp.ai4bharat.org/corpora
[37]https://lindat.mff.cuni.cz/repository/xmlui/handle/11234/1-3267

| | Text-Only MT | Hindi Captioning | Multi-Modal MT |
|---|---|---|---|
| Image | – |  |  |
| Source Text | The woman is waiting to cross the street | – | A blue wall beside tennis court |
| System Output | महिला सड़क पार करने का इंतजार कर रही है | सड़क पर कार | टेनिस कोर्ट के बगल में एक नीली दीवार |
| Gloss | Woman waiting to cross the street | Car on the road | a blue wall next to the tennis court |
| Reference Solution | एक महिला सड़क पार करने के लिए इं-तजार कर रही है | सड़क के किनारे खड़ी कारें | टेनिस कोर्ट के बगल में एक नीली दीवार |
| Gloss | the woman is waiting to cross the street | Cars parked along the side of the road | A blue wall beside the tennis court |

Figure 1: An illustration of the three tracks of WAT 2021 English→Hindi Multi-Modal Task.

English Text: Two elephants standing in the water.

Malayalam Text: വെള്ളത്തിൽ നിൽക്കുന്ന രണ്ട് ആനകൾ

Figure 2: Sample item from Malayalam Visual Genome (MVG), Image with specific region and its description.

### 2.10 English→Malayalam Multi-Modal Task

This task is introduced this year using the first multimodal machine translation dataset in *Malayalam* language. For English→Malayalam multi-modal translation task we asked the participants to use the Malayalam Visual Genome corpus (MVG for short Parida and Bojar, 2021)[38].

The statistics of MVG are given in Table 10. One "item" in MVG consists of an image with a rectangular region highlighting a part of the image, the original English caption of this region and the Malayalam reference translation as shown in Figure 2. Depending on the track (see 2.10.1 below), some of these item components are available as the source and some serve as the reference or play the role of a competing candidate solution.

#### 2.10.1 English→Malayalam Multi-Modal Task Tracks

1. Text-Only Translation (labeled "TEXT" in WAT official tables): The participants are asked to translate short English captions (text) into Malayalam. No visual information can be used. On the other hand, additional text resources are permitted (but they need to be specified in the corresponding system description paper).

2. Malayalam Captioning (labeled "ML"): The participants are asked to generate captions in Malayalam for the given rectangular region in an input image.

3. Multi-Modal Translation (labeled "MM"): Given an image, a rectangular region in it and an English caption for the rectangular region, the participants are asked to translate the English text into Malayalam. Both textual and visual information can be used.

### 2.11 Flickr30kEnt-JP Japanese↔English Multi-Modal Tasks

The goal of Flickr30kEnt-JP Japanese↔English multi-modal task[39] is to improve translation performance with the help of another modality (images) associated with input sentences. For both English→Japanese and Japanese→English tasks, we use the Flickr30k Entities Japanese (F30kEnt-Jp) dataset (Nakayama et al., 2020). This is an

[38]`https://lindat.mff.cuni.cz/repository/xmlui/handle/11234/1-3533`

[39]https://nlab-mpg.github.io/wat2021-mmt-jp/

| Dataset | Items | Tokens English | Malayalam |
|---|---|---|---|
| Training Set | 28,930 | 143,112 | 107,126 |
| D-Test | 998 | 4,922 | 3,619 |
| E-Test (EV) | 1,595 | 7,853 | 6,689 |
| C-Test (CH) | 1,400 | 8,186 | 6,044 |

Table 10: Statistics of Malayalam Visual Genome used for the English→Malayalam Multi-Modal translation task. One item consists of a source English sentence, target Hindi sentence, and a rectangular region within an image. The total number of English and Malayalam tokens in the dataset also listed. The abbreviations EV and CH are used in the official task names in WAT scoring tables.

| Data | Images | Sentences/Tokens English | Japanese |
|---|---|---|---|
| Train | 29,783 | 148,915/1.99M | 148,910*/2.50M |
| Dev | 1,000 | 5,000/67,288 | 5,000/84,017 |
| Test | 1,000 | 1,000/10,876 | 1,000/16,113 |

Table 11: Statistics of the dataset used for Japanese↔English multi-modal tasks. Here we use the MeCab tokenizer to count Japanese tokens. *Some of the original English sentences are actually broken so we did not provide their translations.

extended dataset of the Flickr30k[40] and Flickr30k Entities[41] datasets where manual Japanese translations are added. Notably, it has the annotations of many-to-many phrase-to-region correspondences in both English and Japanese captions, which are expected to strongly supervise multimodal grounding and provide new research directions.

This year, from the same shared tasks in WAT 2020, we increased the number of parallel sentences for training and validation. We summarize the statistics of the dataset for this year in Table 11. We use the same splits of training, validation and test data specified in Flickr30k Entities. For the training and the validation data, we use the F30kEnt-Jp version 2.0 which is publicly available.[42] The original Flickr30k has five English sentences for each image. While the Japanese set for WAT 2020 had the translations of only the first two sentences, this year we have all five translations for each image. Therefore, we can use five parallel sentences for each image to train and validate the systems. The test data remain exactly the same as in WAT 2020, where phrase-to-region annotation is not included.

There are two settings of submission: with and without resource constraints. In the constrained setting, external resources such as additional data and pre-trained models (with external data) are not allowed, except for pre-trained convolutional neural networks (for visual analysis) and basic linguistic tools such as taggers, parsers, and morphological analyzers.

### 2.12 Ambiguous MS COCO Japanese↔English Multimodal Task

This is another Japanese–English multimodal machine translation task. We provide the Japanese–English Ambiguous MS COCO dataset (Merritt et al., 2020) for validation and testing, which contains ambiguous verbs that may require visual information in images for disambiguation. The validation and testing sets contain 230 and 231 Japanese–English sentence pairs, respectively. The Japanese sentences are translated from the English sentences in the original Ambiguous MS COCO dataset.[43]

Participants can use the constrained and unconstrained training data to train their multimodal machine translation system. In the constrained setting, only the Flickr30kEntities Japanese (F30kEnt-Jp) dataset[44] can be used as training data. In the unconstrained setting, the MS COCO English data[45] and STAIR Japanese image captions[46] can be used as additional training data.

We prepare a baseline using the double attention on image region method following (Zhao et al., 2020) for both Japanese→English and English→Japanese directions.

### 2.13 Restricted Translation Task

Despite recent success of NMT, the MT systems still struggle to generate translation with a consistent terminology. Consistency is the key to clear and accurate translation, especially when translating documents in a specific field, for instance, science or business and marketing contexts, requiring technical terms and proper nouns to get translated into the corresponding unique expressions continuously in the entire documents. To tackle this inconsistent translation issue, we have designed *Restricted Translation task* at WAT 2021.

In the restricted translation task, participants are required to submit a system that translates source

[40] http://shannon.cs.illinois.edu/DenotationGraph/

[41] http://bryanplummer.com/Flickr30kEntities/

[42] https://github.com/nlab-mpg/Flickr30kEnt-JP

[43] http://www.statmt.org/wmt17/multimodal-task.html

[44] https://github.com/nlab-mpg/Flickr30kEnt-JP

[45] https://cocodataset.org/#captions-2015

[46] https://stair-lab-cit.github.io/STAIR-captions-web/

|  | En-Ja (# phrase, # char) | Ja-En (# phrase, # word) |
|---|---|---|
| Dev. | (2.8, 164) | (2.8, 6.6) |
| Devtest | (3.2, 18.2) | (3.2, 7.3) |
| Test | (3.3, 18.1) | (3.2, 7.4) |

Table 12: Statistics of the restricted vocabulary in the evaluation data. We report average number of phrases and characters/words per source sentence.

texts under target vocabulary constraints. At inference time, such a restricted vocabulary is provided as a list of target words, consisting of scientific technical terms in the target language, and the system outputs must contain all these target words. For the English↔Japanese translation tasks, we employ the ASPEC corpus and allow to use other external data source. We built the restricted vocabulary lists by asking 10 bilingual speakers to manually extract the scientific technical terms from the evaluation data sets (*"dev/devtest/test"*). Table 12 reports the data statistics of the restricted vocabulary in the evaluation data.

We evaluate systems with two distinct metrics: 1) BLEU score as a conventional translation accuracy and 2) a consistency score: the ratio of the number of sentences satisfying exact match of given constraints over the whole test corpus. For the "exact match" evaluation, we conduct the following process. In English, we simply lowercase hypotheses and constraints, then judge character-level sequence matching (including whitespaces) for each constraint. In Japanese, we judge character-level sequence matching (including whitespaces) for each constraint without preprocessing. For the final ranking, we also calculate the combined score of both: calculating BLEU with only the exact match sentences. We note that, in this scenario, the brevity score in BLEU does not carry its usual meaning, but the n-gram scores maintain their consistency.

## 3 Participants

Table 13 shows the participants in WAT2021. The table lists 24 organizations from various countries, including Japan, India, USA, Singapore, Myanmar, Thailand, Korea, Poland, Denmark and Switzerland.

2,100 translation results by 28 teams were submitted for automatic evaluation and about 360 translation results by 24 teams were submitted for the human evaluation. Table 14 summarizes the participation of teams across WAT2021 tasks and indicates which tasks included manual evaluation. The human evaluation was conducted only for the tasks with the check marks in "human eval" line.

There were no participants in the Newswire (JIJI) task, BSD task and JaRuNC task.

## 4 Baseline Systems

Human evaluations of most of WAT tasks were conducted as pairwise comparisons between the translation results for a specific baseline system and translation results for each participant's system. That is, the specific baseline system served as the standard for human evaluation. At WAT 2021, we adopted some of neural machine translation (NMT) as baseline systems. The details of the NMT baseline systems are described in this section.

The NMT baseline systems consisted of publicly available software, and the procedures for building the systems and for translating using the systems were published on the WAT web page.[47] We also have SMT baseline systems for the tasks that started at WAT 2017 or before 2017. The baseline systems are shown in Tables 15, 16, and 17. SMT baseline systems are described in the WAT 2017 overview paper (Nakazawa et al., 2017). The commercial RBMT systems and the online translation systems were operated by the organizers. We note that these RBMT companies and online translation companies did not submit their systems. Because our objective is not to compare commercial RBMT systems or online translation systems from companies that did not themselves participate, the system IDs of these systems are anonymous in this paper.

### 4.1 Tokenization

We used the following tools for tokenization.

#### 4.1.1 For ASPEC, JPC, JIJI, and ALT+UCSY

- Juman version 7.0[48] for Japanese segmentation.
- Stanford Word Segmenter version 2014-01-04[49] (Chinese Penn Treebank (CTB) model) for Chinese segmentation.

[47] http://lotus.kuee.kyoto-u.ac.jp/WAT/WAT2021/baseline/baselineSystems.html

[48] http://nlp.ist.i.kyoto-u.ac.jp/EN/index.php?JUMAN

[49] http://nlp.stanford.edu/software/segmenter.shtml

| Team ID | Organization | Country |
|---|---|---|
| TMU | Tokyo Metropolitan University | Japan |
| NTT | NTT Corporation | Japan |
| NICT-2 | NICT | Japan |
| NICT-5 | NICT | Japan |
| NLPHut | Idiap Research Institute Switzerland, IIT BHU, BITS Pilani India, KIIT University India, Silicon Techlab pvt. Ltd India, University of Chicago | Switzerland, India, USA |
| TMEKU | Tokyo Metropolitan University, Ehime University, Kyoto University | Japan |
| *goodjob | Dalian University of Technology | China |
| YCC-MT1 | University of Technology (Yatanarpon Cyber City) | Myanmar |
| YCC-MT2 | University of Technology (Yatanarpon Cyber City) | Myanmar |
| NECTEC | National Electronics and Computer Technology Center (NECTEC) | Thailand |
| mcairt | CAIR | India |
| nictrb | NICT | Japan |
| sakura | Rakuten Institute of Technology Singapore, Rakuten Asia. | Singapore |
| IIT-H | International Institue of Information Technology | India |
| *gauvar | Amazon | Singapore |
| *JBJBJB | Indivisual participant | Korea |
| SRPOL | Samsung R&D Poland | Poland |
| NHK | NHK | Japan |
| CFILT | Computing for Indian Language Technology | India |
| iitp | IIT Patna | India |
| Volta | International Institute of Information Technology Hyderabad | India |
| coastal | University of Copenhagen | Denmark |
| CFILT-IITB | Indian Institute of Technology Bombay | India |
| CNLP-NITS-PP | NIT Silchar | India |
| Bering Lab | Bering Lab | South Korea |
| tpt_wat | Transperfect Translations | USA |

Table 13: List of participants who submitted translations for the human evaluation in WAT2021 (Note: teams with '*' marks did not submit their system description papers, therefore the evaluation results are UNOFFICIAL according to our policy)

| Team ID | ASPEC + ParaNatCom EJ | ASPEC Restricted EJ | ASPEC Restricted JE | ALT + UCSY En-My | ALT + UCSY My-En | NICT-SAP En-Hi/Id/Ms/Th IT | NICT-SAP En-Hi/Id/Ms/Th Wikinews | NICT-SAP Hi/Id/Ms/Th-En IT | NICT-SAP Hi/Id/Ms/Th-En Wikinews |
|---|---|---|---|---|---|---|---|---|---|
| TMU | | | ✓ | | | | | | |
| NTT | | ✓ | ✓ | | | | | | |
| NICT-2 | | | | | | ✓ | ✓ | ✓ | ✓ |
| goodjob | ✓ | | | | | | | | |
| YCC-MT1 | | | | ✓ | | | | | |
| YCC-MT2 | | | | ✓ | | | | | |
| NECTEC | | | | | ✓ | | | | |
| nictrb | | ✓ | ✓ | | | | | | |
| sakura | | | | ✓ | ✓ | ✓ | ✓ | ✓ | ✓ |
| NHK | | ✓ | ✓ | | | | | | |
| human eval | ✓ | ✓ | ✓ | | | ✓ | | ✓ | |

| Team ID | JPC EJ | JPC JE | JPC CJ | JPC JC | JPC KJ | JPC JK | Multimodal En-Hi TX | Multimodal En-Hi HI | Multimodal En-Hi MM | Multimodal En-Ml TX | Multimodal En-Ml HI | Multimodal Flickr EJ | Multimodal Flickr JE | Multimodal MS COCO EJ |
|---|---|---|---|---|---|---|---|---|---|---|---|---|---|---|
| TMU | ✓ | ✓ | | | ✓ | ✓ | | | | | | | | |
| NLPHut | | | | | | | ✓ | ✓ | | ✓ | ✓ | | | |
| TMEKU | | | | | | | | | | | | ✓ | | ✓ |
| sakura | | | | | | | | | | | | ✓ | ✓ | |
| iitp | | | | | | | | | ✓ | | | | | |
| Volta | | | | | | | ✓ | | ✓ | | | | | |
| CNLP-NITS-PP | | | | | | | ✓ | | ✓ | | | | | |
| Bering Lab | ✓ | ✓ | ✓ | ✓ | ✓ | ✓ | | | | | | | | |
| tpt_wat | ✓ | ✓ | ✓ | ✓ | ✓ | ✓ | | | | | | | | |
| human eval | ✓ | ✓ | | | | | ✓ | ✓ | ✓ | ✓ | ✓ | ✓ | ✓ | ✓ |

| Team ID | Indic21 En-X Bn | Kn | Ml | Mr | Or | Hi | Gu | Pa | Ta | Te | Indic21 X-En Bn | Kn | Ml | Mr | Or | Hi | Gu | Pa | Ta | Te |
|---|---|---|---|---|---|---|---|---|---|---|---|---|---|---|---|---|---|---|---|---|
| NICT-5 | ✓ | ✓ | ✓ | ✓ | ✓ | ✓ | ✓ | ✓ | ✓ | ✓ | ✓ | ✓ | ✓ | ✓ | ✓ | ✓ | ✓ | ✓ | ✓ | ✓ |
| NLPHut | ✓ | ✓ | ✓ | ✓ | ✓ | ✓ | ✓ | ✓ | ✓ | ✓ | ✓ | ✓ | ✓ | ✓ | ✓ | ✓ | ✓ | ✓ | ✓ | ✓ |
| mcairt | ✓ | ✓ | ✓ | ✓ | ✓ | ✓ | ✓ | ✓ | ✓ | ✓ | ✓ | ✓ | ✓ | ✓ | ✓ | ✓ | ✓ | ✓ | ✓ | ✓ |
| sakura | ✓ | ✓ | ✓ | ✓ | ✓ | ✓ | ✓ | ✓ | ✓ | ✓ | ✓ | ✓ | ✓ | ✓ | ✓ | ✓ | ✓ | ✓ | ✓ | ✓ |
| IIT-H | ✓ | ✓ | ✓ | ✓ | ✓ | ✓ | ✓ | ✓ | ✓ | ✓ | ✓ | ✓ | ✓ | ✓ | ✓ | ✓ | ✓ | ✓ | ✓ | ✓ |
| gauvar | ✓ | ✓ | ✓ | ✓ | ✓ | ✓ | ✓ | ✓ | ✓ | ✓ | ✓ | ✓ | ✓ | ✓ | ✓ | ✓ | ✓ | ✓ | ✓ | ✓ |
| JBJBJB | ✓ | ✓ | ✓ | ✓ | ✓ | ✓ | ✓ | ✓ | ✓ | ✓ | ✓ | ✓ | ✓ | ✓ | ✓ | ✓ | ✓ | ✓ | ✓ | ✓ |
| SRPOL | ✓ | ✓ | ✓ | ✓ | ✓ | ✓ | ✓ | ✓ | ✓ | ✓ | ✓ | ✓ | ✓ | ✓ | ✓ | ✓ | ✓ | ✓ | ✓ | ✓ |
| CFILT | ✓ | ✓ | ✓ | ✓ | ✓ | ✓ | ✓ | ✓ | ✓ | ✓ | ✓ | ✓ | ✓ | ✓ | ✓ | ✓ | ✓ | ✓ | ✓ | ✓ |
| coastal | ✓ | ✓ | ✓ | ✓ | ✓ | ✓ | ✓ | ✓ | ✓ | ✓ | ✓ | ✓ | ✓ | ✓ | ✓ | ✓ | ✓ | ✓ | ✓ | ✓ |
| CFILT-IITB | | | | | | | | | | | ✓ | ✓ | ✓ | ✓ | ✓ | ✓ | ✓ | ✓ | ✓ | ✓ |
| human eval | ✓ | ✓ | ✓ | ✓ | ✓ | | | | | | ✓ | ✓ | ✓ | ✓ | ✓ | | | | | |

Table 14: Submissions for each task by each team. E and J denote English and Japanese respectively. The human evaluation was conducted only for the tasks with the check marks in "human eval" line.

| System ID | System | Type | ASPEC ja-en | ASPEC en-ja | ASPEC ja-zh | ASPEC zh-ja | JPC ja-en | JPC en-ja | JPC ja-zh | JPC zh-ja | JPC ja↔ko |
|---|---|---|---|---|---|---|---|---|---|---|---|
| NMT | OpenNMT's NMT with attention | NMT | ✓ | ✓ | ✓ | ✓ | ✓ | ✓ | ✓ | ✓ | ✓ |
| SMT Phrase | Moses' Phrase-based SMT | SMT | ✓ | ✓ | ✓ | ✓ | ✓ | ✓ | ✓ | ✓ | ✓ |
| SMT Hiero | Moses' Hierarchical Phrase-based SMT | SMT | ✓ | ✓ | ✓ | ✓ | ✓ | ✓ | ✓ | ✓ | ✓ |
| SMT S2T | Moses' String-to-Tree Syntax-based SMT and Berkeley parser | SMT | ✓ | | ✓ | | ✓ | | ✓ | | |
| SMT T2S | Moses' Tree-to-String Syntax-based SMT and Berkeley parser | SMT | | ✓ | | ✓ | | ✓ | | ✓ | |
| RBMT X | The Honyaku V15 (Commercial system) | RBMT | ✓ | ✓ | | | ✓ | ✓ | | | |
| RBMT X | ATLAS V14 (Commercial system) | RBMT | ✓ | ✓ | | | ✓ | ✓ | | | |
| RBMT X | PAT-Transer 2009 (Commercial system) | RBMT | ✓ | ✓ | | | ✓ | ✓ | | | |
| RBMT X | PC-Transer V13 (Commercial system) | RBMT | | | | | | | | | |
| RBMT X | J-Beijing 7 (Commercial system) | RBMT | | | ✓ | ✓ | | | ✓ | ✓ | |
| RBMT X | Hohrai 2011 (Commercial system) | RBMT | | | ✓ | ✓ | | | | ✓ | |
| RBMT X | J Soul 9 (Commercial system) | RBMT | | | | | | | | | ✓ |
| RBMT X | Korai 2011 (Commercial system) | RBMT | | | | | | | | | ✓ |
| Online X | Google translate | Other | ✓ | ✓ | ✓ | ✓ | ✓ | ✓ | ✓ | ✓ | ✓ |
| Online X | Bing translator | Other | ✓ | ✓ | ✓ | ✓ | ✓ | ✓ | ✓ | ✓ | ✓ |
| AIAYN | Google's implementation of "Attention Is All You Need" | NMT | ✓ | ✓ | | | | | | | |

Table 15: Baseline Systems I

| System ID | System | Type | JIJI ja-en | JIJI en-ja | ALT+UCSY my↔en | ALT+UCSY km↔en |
|---|---|---|---|---|---|---|
| NMT | OpenNMT's NMT with attention | NMT | ✓ | ✓ | ✓ | ✓ |
| SMT Phrase | Moses' Phrase-based SMT | SMT | ✓ | ✓ | | |
| SMT Hiero | Moses' Hierarchical Phrase-based SMT | SMT | ✓ | ✓ | | |
| SMT S2T | Moses' String-to-Tree Syntax-based SMT and Berkeley parser | SMT | ✓ | | | |
| SMT T2S | Moses' Tree-to-String Syntax-based SMT and Berkeley parser | SMT | | ✓ | | |
| RBMT X | The Honyaku V15 (Commercial system) | RBMT | ✓ | ✓ | | |
| RBMT X | PC-Transer V13 (Commercial system) | RBMT | ✓ | ✓ | | |
| Online X | Google translate | Other | ✓ | ✓ | ✓ | ✓ |
| Online X | Bing translator | Other | ✓ | ✓ | | |

Table 16: Baseline Systems II

| System ID | System | Type | NewsCommentary | NICT+SAP IT&Wikinews | Indic | Multimodal | | | |
|---|---|---|---|---|---|---|---|---|---|
| | | | | | | | | Flickr | MS COCO |
| | | | ru↔ja | {hi,id,ms,th}↔en | {bn,gu,hi,kn,ml,mr,or,pa,ta,te}↔en | en-hi | en-ml | ja↔en | ja↔en |
| NMT | OpenNMT's NMT with attention | NMT | | | | | | | |
| NMT T2T | Tensor2Tensor's Transformer | NMT | ✓ | ✓ | ✓ | | | | |
| NMT OT | OpenNMT-py's Transformer | NMT | | | | ✓ | ✓ | | |
| MNMT | Multimodal NMT | NMT | | | | | | ✓ | |
| MNMT2 | Double-attention based Multimodal NMT | NMT | | | | | | | ✓ |

Table 17: Baseline Systems III

- The Moses toolkit for English and Indonesian tokenization.
- Mecab-ko[50] for Korean segmentation.
- Indic NLP Library[51] (Kunchukuttan, 2020) for Indic language segmentation.
- The tools included in the ALT corpus for Myanmar and Khmer segmentation.
- subword-nmt[52] for all languages.

When we built BPE-codes, we merged source and target sentences and we used 100,000 for -s option. We used 10 for vocabulary-threshold when subword-nmt applied BPE.

#### 4.1.2 For News Commentary

- The Moses toolkit for English and Russian only for the News Commentary data.
- Mecab[53] for Japanese segmentation.
- Corpora are further processed by tensor2tensor's internal pre/post-processing which includes sub-word segmentation.

#### 4.1.3 For Indic and NICT-SAP Tasks

- For the Indic task we did not perform any explicit tokenization of the raw data.
- For the NICT-SAP task we only character segmented the Thai corpora as it was the only language for which character level BLEU was to be computed. Other languages corpora were not preprocessed in any way.
- Any subword segmentation or tokenization was handled by the internal mechanisms of tensor2tensor.

#### 4.1.4 For English→Hindi Multi-Modal and English→Malayalam Tasks

- Hindi Visual Genome 1.1 and Malayalam Visual Genome comes untokenized and we did not use or recommend any specific external tokenizer.
- The standard OpenNMT-py sub-word segmentation was used for pre/post-processing for the baseline system and each participant used what they wanted.

[50]https://bitbucket.org/eunjeon/mecab-ko/

[51]https://github.com/anoopkunchukuttan/indic_nlp_library

[52]https://github.com/rsennrich/subword-nmt

[53]https://taku910.github.io/mecab/

#### 4.1.5 For English↔Japanese Multi-Modal Tasks

- For English sentences, we applied lowercase, punctuation normalization, and the Moses tokenizer.
- For Japanese sentences, we used KyTea for word segmentation.

### 4.2 Baseline NMT Methods

We used the NMT models for all tasks. Unless mentioned otherwise we use the Transformer model (Vaswani et al., 2017). We used OpenNMT (Klein et al., 2017) (RNN-model) for ASPEC, JPC, JIJI, and ALT tasks, tensor2tensor[54] for the News Commentary (JaRuNC), NICT-SAP and MultiIndicMT tasks and OpenNMT-py[55] for other tasks.

#### 4.2.1 NMT with Attention (OpenNMT)

For ASPEC, JPC, JIJI, and ALT tasks, we used OpenNMT (Klein et al., 2017) as the implementation of the baseline NMT systems of NMT with attention (System ID: NMT). We used the following OpenNMT configuration.

- encoder_type = brnn
- brnn_merge = concat
- src_seq_length = 150
- tgt_seq_length = 150
- src_vocab_size = 100000
- tgt_vocab_size = 100000
- src_words_min_frequency = 1
- tgt_words_min_frequency = 1

The default values were used for the other system parameters.

We used the following data for training the NMT baseline systems of NMT with attention.

- All of the training data mentioned in Section 2 were used for training except for the ASPEC Japanese–English task. For the ASPEC Japanese–English task, we only used train-1.txt, which consists of one million parallel sentence pairs with high similarity scores.
- All of the development data for each task was used for validation.

[54]https://github.com/tensorflow/tensor2tensor

[55]https://github.com/OpenNMT/OpenNMT-py

#### 4.2.2 Transformer (Tensor2Tensor)

For the News Commentary task, we used tensor2tensor's[56] implementation of the Transformer (Vaswani et al., 2017) and used default hyperparameter settings corresponding to the "base" model for all baseline models. The baseline for the News Commentary task is a multilingual model as described in Imankulova et al. (2019) which is trained using only the in-domain parallel corpora. We use the token trick proposed by Johnson et al. (2017) to train the multilingual model.

For the NICT-SAP task, we used tensor2tensor to train many-to-one and one-to-many models where the latter were trained with the aforementioned token trick. We used default hyperparameter settings corresponding to the "big" model. Since the NICT-SAP task involves two domains for evaluation (Wikinews and IT) we used a modification of the token trick technique for domain adaptation to distinguish between corpora for different domains. In our case we used tokens such as $2alt$ and $2it$ to indicate whether the sentences belonged to the Wikinews or IT domain, respectively. For both tasks we used 32,000 separate sub-word vocabularies. We trained our models on 1 GPU till convergence on the development set BLEU scores, averaged the last 10 checkpoints (separated by 1000 batches) and performed decoding with a beam of size 4 and a length penalty of 0.6.

For the MultiIndicMT task we trained unidirectional models using only the PMI corpus instead of the entire training data. We intentionally used the PMI corpus because its domain is the same as that of the evaluation set. Due to lack of time and resources we did not train multilingual models nor did we use additional data. We trained "transformer_base" models with shared vocabularies of 8,000 subwords. We trained our models on 1 GPU till convergence on the development set BLEU scores, chose the model with the best development set BLEU and performed decoding with a beam of size 4 and a length penalty of 0.6.

#### 4.2.3 Transformer (OpenNMT-py)

For the English→Hindi Multimodal and English→Malayalam Multimodal tasks, we used the Transformer model (Vaswani et al., 2018) as implemented in OpenNMT-py (Klein et al., 2017) and used the "base" model with default parameters for the multi-modal task baseline. We have generated the vocabulary of 32k sub-word types jointly for both the source and target languages. The vocabulary is shared between the encoder and decoder.

## 5 Automatic Evaluation

### 5.1 Procedure for Calculating Automatic Evaluation Score

We evaluated translation results by three metrics: BLEU (Papineni et al., 2002), RIBES (Isozaki et al., 2010) and AMFM (Banchs et al., 2015a). BLEU scores were calculated using `multi-bleu.perl` in the Moses toolkit (Koehn et al., 2007). RIBES scores were calculated using `RIBES.py` version 1.02.4.[57] AMFM scores were calculated using scripts created by the technical collaborators listed in the WAT2021 web page.[58] All scores for each task were calculated using the corresponding reference translations.

Before the calculation of the automatic evaluation scores, the translation results were tokenized or segmented with tokenization/segmentation tools for each language. For Japanese segmentation, we used three different tools: Juman version 7.0 (Kurohashi et al., 1994), KyTea 0.4.6 (Neubig et al., 2011) with full SVM model[59] and MeCab 0.996 (Kudo, 2005) with IPA dictionary 2.7.0.[60] For Chinese segmentation, we used two different tools: KyTea 0.4.6 with full SVM Model in MSR model and Stanford Word Segmenter (Tseng, 2005) version 2014-06-16 with Chinese Penn Treebank (CTB) and Peking University (PKU) model.[61] For Korean segmentation, we used mecab-ko.[62] For Myanmar and Khmer segmentations, we used `myseg.py`[63] and `kmseg.py`[64]. For English and Russian tokenizations, we used `tokenizer.perl`[65] in the Moses toolkit. For

[56] https://github.com/tensorflow/tensor2tensor

[57] http://www.kecl.ntt.co.jp/icl/lirg/ribes/index.html

[58] lotus.kuee.kyoto-u.ac.jp/WAT/WAT2021/

[59] http://www.phontron.com/kytea/model.html

[60] http://code.google.com/p/mecab/downloads/detail?name=mecab-ipadic-2.7.0-20070801.tar.gz

[61] http://nlp.stanford.edu/software/segmenter.shtml

[62] https://bitbucket.org/eunjeon/mecab-ko/

[63] http://lotus.kuee.kyoto-u.ac.jp/WAT/my-en-data/wat2020.my-en.zip

[64] http://lotus.kuee.kyoto-u.ac.jp/WAT/km-en-data/km-en.zip

[65] https://github.com/moses-smt/mosesdecoder/tree/RELEASE-2.1.1/scripts/tokenizer/tokenizer.perl

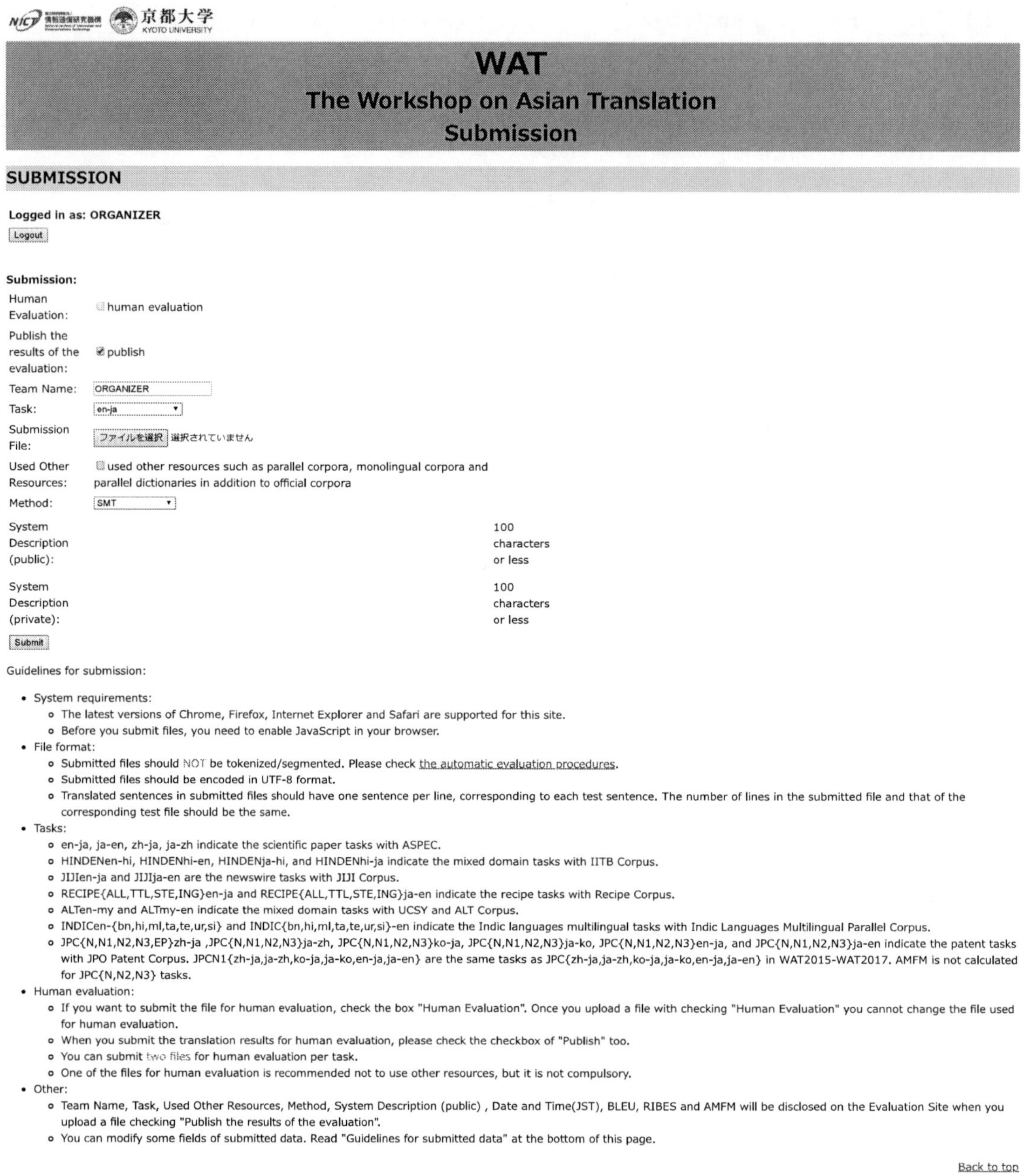


Figure 3: The interface for translation results submission

Indonesian and Malay tokenizations, we used `tokenizer.perl` actually sticking to the English tokenization settings. For Thai tokenization, we segmented the text at each individual character. For Bengali, Gujarati, Hindi, Kannada, Malayalam, Marathi, Odia, Punjabi, Tamil, and Telugu tokenizations, we used Indic NLP Library[66] (Kunchukuttan, 2020). The detailed procedures for the automatic evaluation are shown on the WAT evaluation web page.[67]

### 5.2 Automatic Evaluation System

The automatic evaluation system receives translation results by participants and automatically gives

[66] `https://github.com/anoopkunchukuttan/indic_nlp_library`

[67] `http://lotus.kuee.kyoto-u.ac.jp/WAT/evaluation/index.html`

evaluation scores to the uploaded results. As shown in Figure 3, the system requires participants to provide the following information for each submission:

- Human Evaluation: whether or not they submit the results for human evaluation;
- Publish the results of the evaluation: whether or not they permit to publish automatic evaluation scores on the WAT2021 web page;
- Task: the task you submit the results for;
- Used Other Resources: whether or not they used additional resources; and
- Method: the type of the method including SMT, RBMT, SMT and RBMT, EBMT, NMT and Other.

Evaluation scores of translation results that participants permit to be published are disclosed via the WAT2021 evaluation web page. Participants can also submit the results for human evaluation using the same web interface.

This automatic evaluation system will remain available even after WAT2021. Anybody can register an account for the system by the procedures described in the application site.[68]

### 5.3 A Note on AMFM Scores

Up until WAT 2020, we used an older generation AMFM evaluation approach which did not use deep neural networks. Given the advances in multilingual pre-trained models, this year, our collaborators provided us with deep AMFM models. With the exception of ASPEC and restricted translation tasks we used the provided deep AMFM models to compute AMFM scores. Given that these deep models need GPUs to run quickly, we have not yet integrated it into our evaluation server as it is not equipped with GPUs. Instead, we compute the AMFM scores offline and add them to the evaluation scoreboard. For readers interested in AMFM and recent advances we refer readers to the following literature: Zhang et al. (2021b,a); D'Haro et al. (2019); Banchs et al. (2015b).

## 6 Human Evaluation

In WAT2021, we conducted *JPO adequacy evaluation* (other than En-Hi and En-Ml multi-modal task, Section 6.1).

[68] http://lotus.kuee.kyoto-u.ac.jp/WAT/WAT2021/application/index.html

| | |
|---|---|
| 5 | All important information is transmitted correctly. (100%) |
| 4 | Almost all important information is transmitted correctly. (80%–) |
| 3 | More than half of important information is transmitted correctly. (50%–) |
| 2 | Some of important information is transmitted correctly. (20%–) |
| 1 | Almost all important information is NOT transmitted correctly. (–20%) |

Table 18: The JPO adequacy criterion

### 6.1 JPO Adequacy Evaluation

We conducted JPO adequacy evaluation for the top two or three participants' systems of pairwise evaluation for each subtask.[69] The evaluation was carried out by translation experts based on the JPO adequacy evaluation criterion, which is originally defined by JPO to assess the quality of translated patent documents.

#### 6.1.1 Sentence Selection and Evaluation

For the JPO adequacy evaluation, the 200 test sentences were randomly selected from the test sentences.

For each test sentence, input source sentence, translation by participants' system, and reference translation were shown to the annotators. To guarantee the quality of the evaluation, each sentence was evaluated by two annotators. Note that the selected sentences are basically the same as those used in the previous workshop.

#### 6.1.2 Evaluation Criterion

Table 18 shows the JPO adequacy criterion from 5 to 1. The evaluation is performed subjectively. "Important information" represents the technical factors and their relationships. The degree of importance of each element is also considered to evaluate. The percentages in each grade are rough indications for the transmission degree of the source sentence meanings. The detailed criterion is described in the JPO document (in Japanese).[70]

## 7 Evaluation Results

In this section, the evaluation results for WAT2021 are reported from several perspectives. Some of the results for both automatic and human evaluations are also accessible at the WAT2021 web-

[69] The number of systems varies depending on the subtasks.

[70] http://www.jpo.go.jp/shiryou/toushin/chousa/tokkyohonyaku_hyouka.htm

site.[71]

### 7.1 Official Evaluation Results

Figures 4 and 5 show those of JPC subtasks, Figures 6 and 7 show those of MMT subtasks, Figures 8, 9, 10, 11, 12, 13, 14, 15, 16, and 17 show those of Indic Multilingual subtasks and Figures 18 and 19 show those of . Each figure contains the JPO adequacy evaluation result and evaluation summary of top systems.

The detailed automatic evaluation results are shown in Appendix A. The detailed JPO adequacy evaluation results for the selected submissions are shown in Table 19. The weights for the weighted $\kappa$ (Cohen, 1968) is defined as $|Evaluation1 - Evaluation2|/4$.

## 8 Findings

### 8.1 JPC Task

Three teams participated in JPC task. Bering Lab and tpt_wat submitted results for all language pairs and TMU submitted results for J↔K and J↔E pairs. Similarly to WAT 2020, participants' systems were transformer-based or BART-based. Bering Lab trained Transformer models with additional corpora, which were crawled patent document pairs aligned by a sentence encoding method and contained more than 13M sentences for each language pair. Their system achieved the best BLEU, RIBES, and AMFM scores for J→C/K/E and the best BLEU and RIBES scores for K→J among the past and this year's systems. tpt_wat used Transformer and back-translation with a single setting for six language pairs. TMU used fine-tuned Japanese BART models and achieved the best AMFM score for K→J. As for human adequacy evaluation, the evaluated system TMU did not show superior performance to past years' systems for J↔E, while the results cannot be directly compared.

Among the top-performing systems, Bering Lab's systems obtained large BLEU improvements around two points over the past years' systems for J↔K. The improvements were probably due to their additional corpora, because their model without the additional corpus ranked second for J→K. Another finding by TMU was that pretrained Japanese BART brought gains for all J↔K/E directions.

[71] http://lotus.kuee.kyoto-u.ac.jp/WAT/evaluation/

### 8.2 NICT-SAP Task

In contrast to 2020 where we had only 1 submission, this year we received submissions from 5 teams, 4 of which submitted system description papers. The submitted models were trained using a variety of techniques such as domain adaptation, corpora selection and weighing, MBART pretraining and multilingual NMT training. All submissions significantly outperformed the organizers baselines as well as the best submission in 2020. The gains showed by this year's submissions range from approximately 14 to 30 BLEU (depending on the task) compared to the baselines. The main reason was that this year's submission rely on high quality data selection as well as on massively multilingual pre-trained models. Out of the 4 teams that submitted system description papers, only one relied on data selection and surprisingly obtained the best results for some language pairs. For other language pairs, this team obtained cometitive results. Regardless, is is clear that models like MBART are extremely useful in extremely low-resource domains such as Wikinews and software documentation.

Regarding, human evaluation we did JPO adequacy evaluation for English to Indonesian and English to Malay for the Software Documentation domain. Kindly refer to Figure 18 and 19 for the results of human evaluation. For both translation directions, team "sakura" had the highest JPO as well as BLEU scores but the scores for team "NICT-2" were not that far behind. They were certainly significantly better than the organizer scores who only developed models using parallel corpora without any pre-training. We can certainly say that at high enough BLEU score levels (higher than 40), the large differences in BLEU do not necessarily correlate with large differences in human evaluation scores. To be specific, the gap between "sakura" and "NICT-2" in terms of BLEU for English to Indonesian is 2.14 and for English to Malay is 1.5 BLEU. However, the corresponding gaps in human evaluation are 0.08 and 0.15 which is not significant. Human evaluation on a larger scale might be needed but we were unable to do so due to budgetary limitations.

#### 8.2.1 News Commentary (JaRuNC) task

Unfortunately we did not receive any submissions this year.

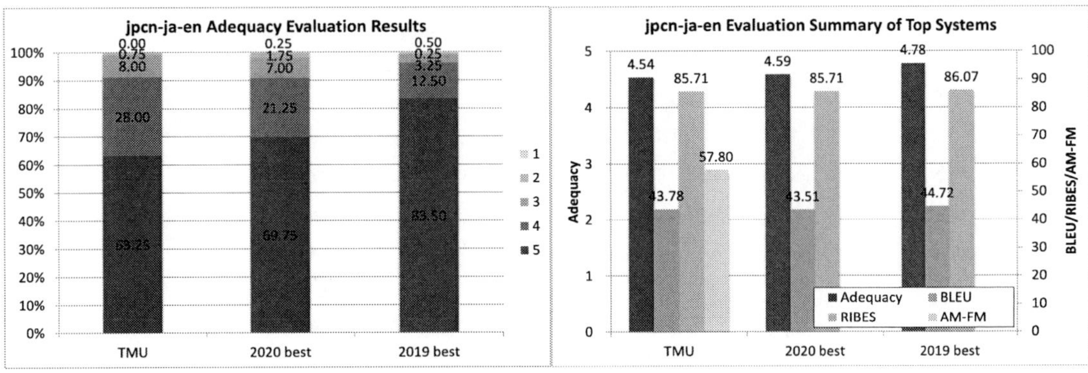


Figure 4: Official evaluation results of jpcn-ja-en.

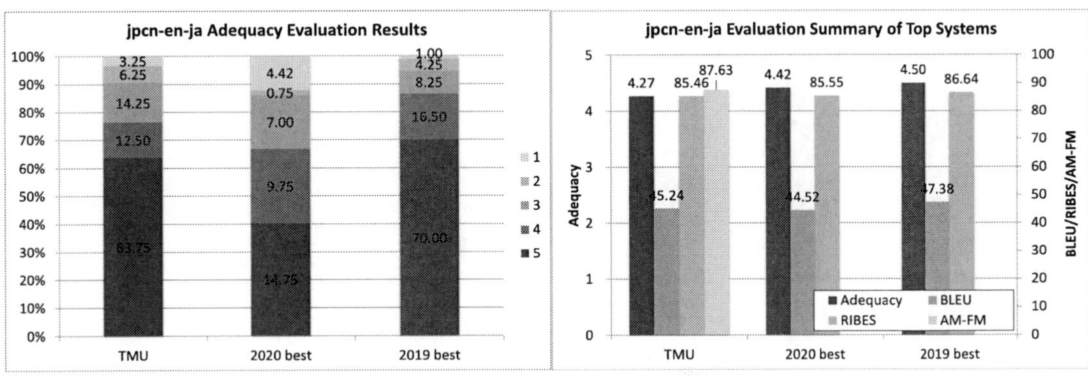


Figure 5: Official evaluation results of jpcn-en-ja.

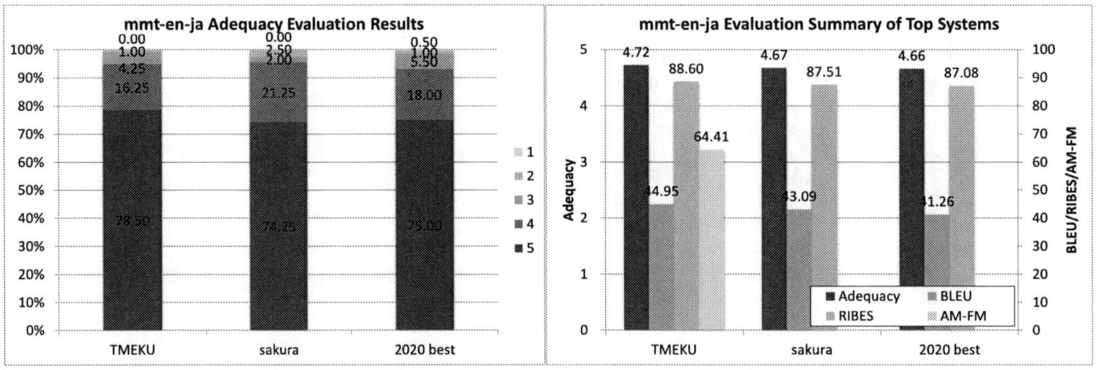


Figure 6: Official evaluation results of mmt-en-ja.

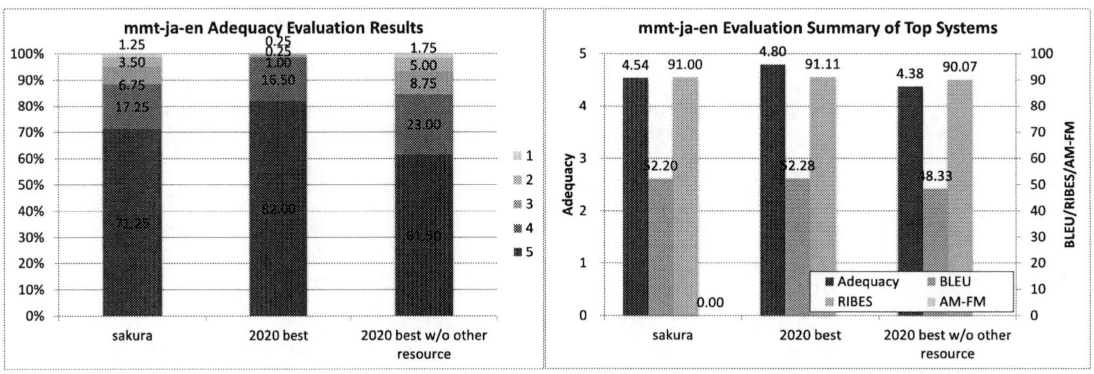


Figure 7: Official evaluation results of mmt-ja-en.

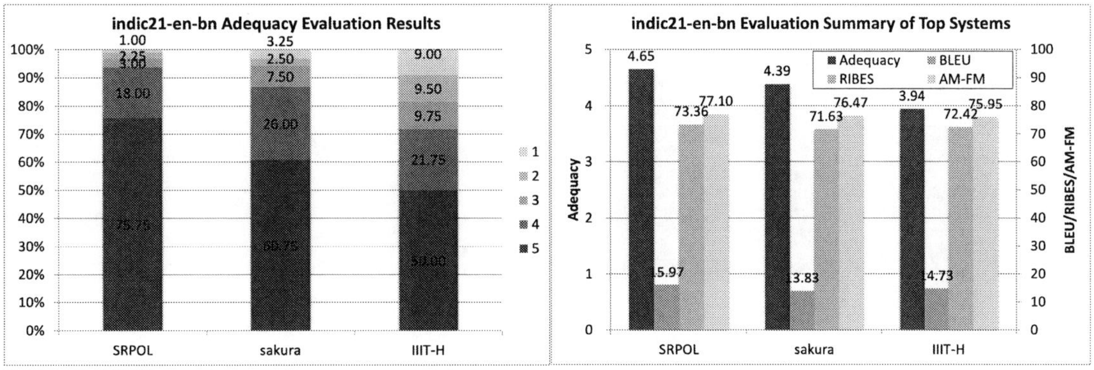


Figure 8: Official evaluation results of indic21-en-bn.

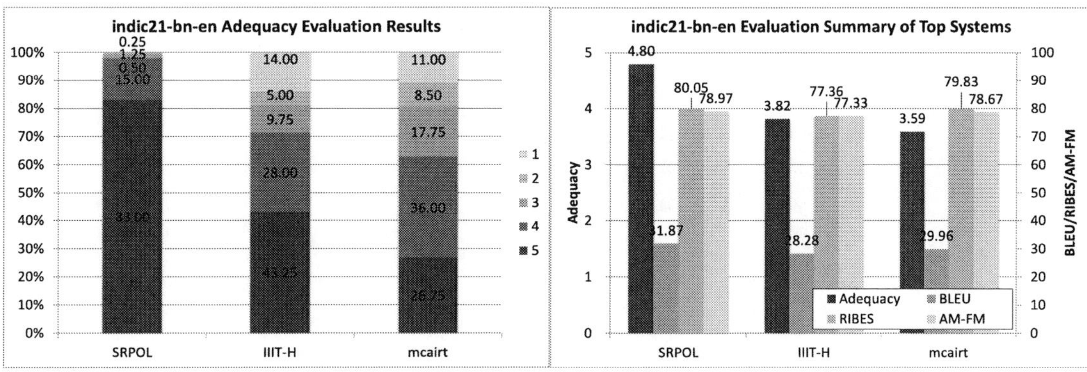


Figure 9: Official evaluation results of indic21-bn-en.

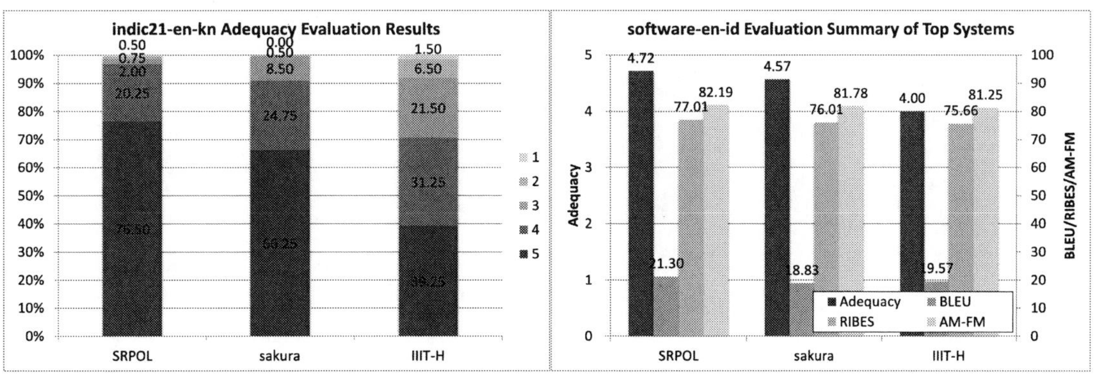


Figure 10: Official evaluation results of indic21-en-kn.

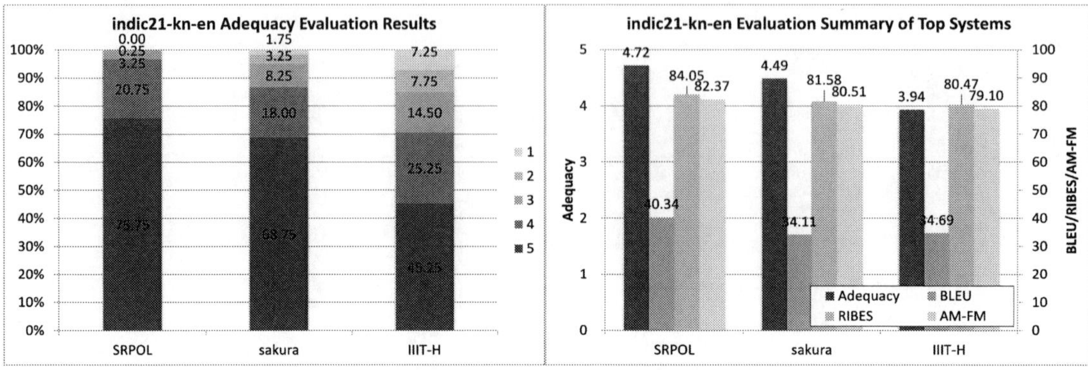


Figure 11: Official evaluation results of indic21-kn-en.

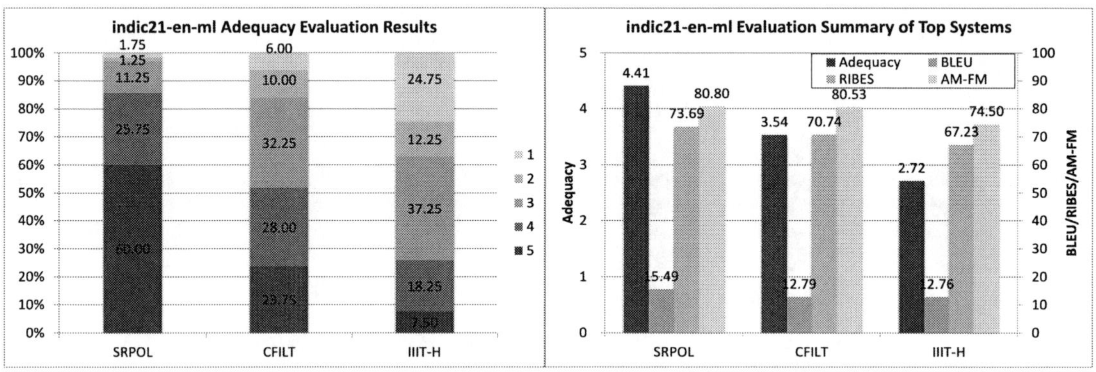


Figure 12: Official evaluation results of indic21-en-ml.

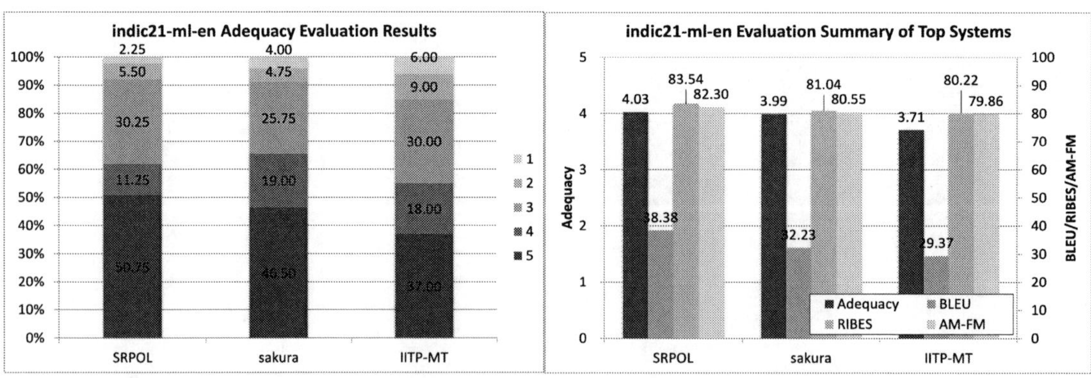


Figure 13: Official evaluation results of indic21-ml-en.

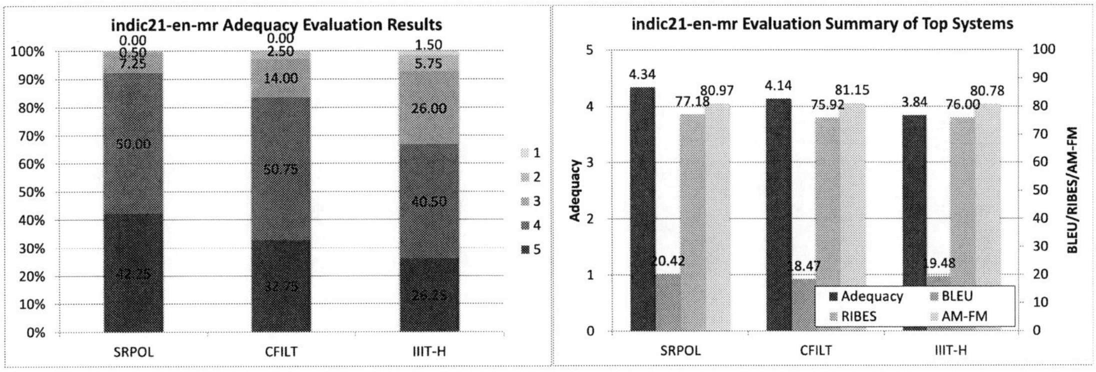


Figure 14: Official evaluation results of indic21-en-mr.

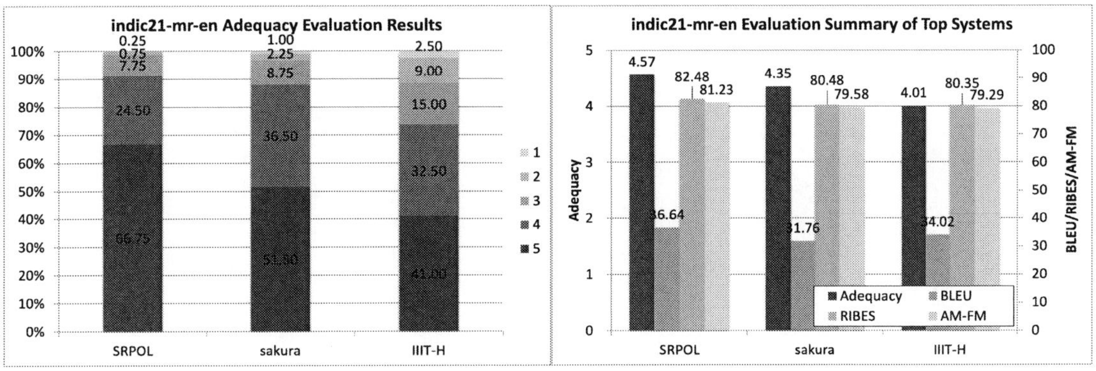


Figure 15: Official evaluation results of indic21-mr-en.

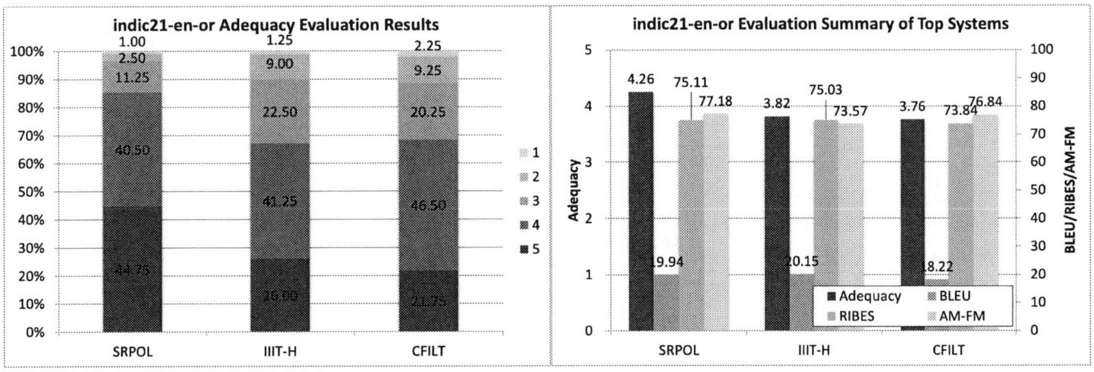


Figure 16: Official evaluation results of indic21-en-or.

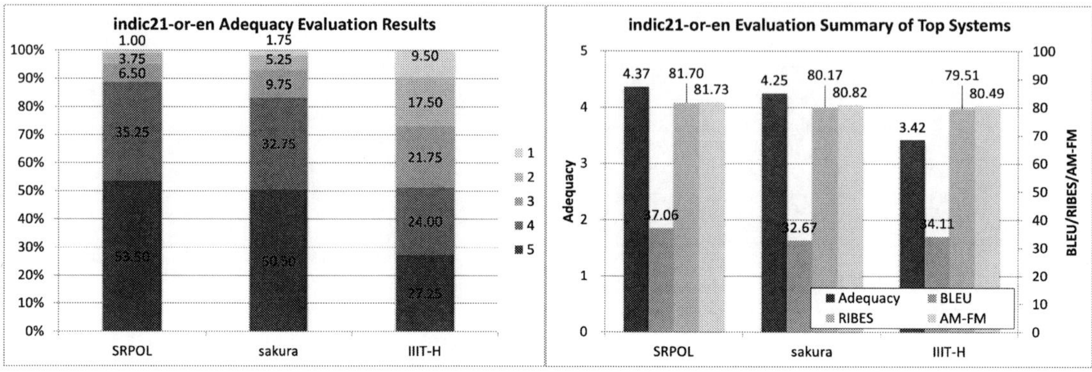


Figure 17: Official evaluation results of indic21-or-en.

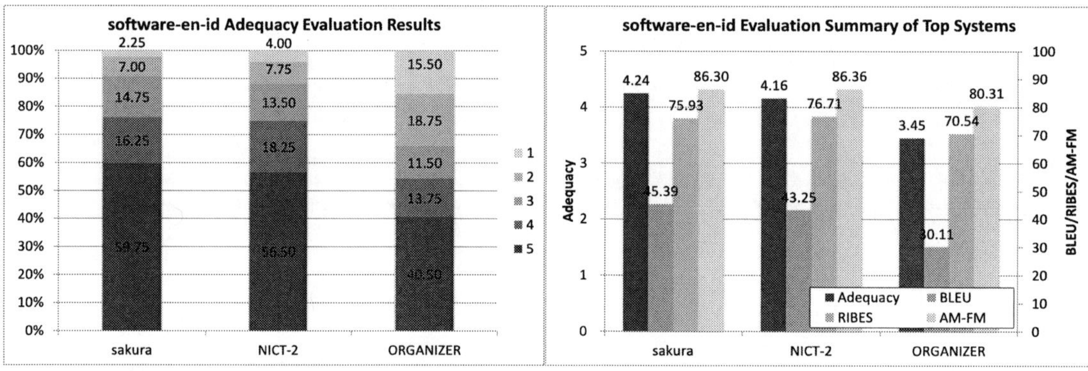


Figure 18: Official evaluation results of software-en-id.

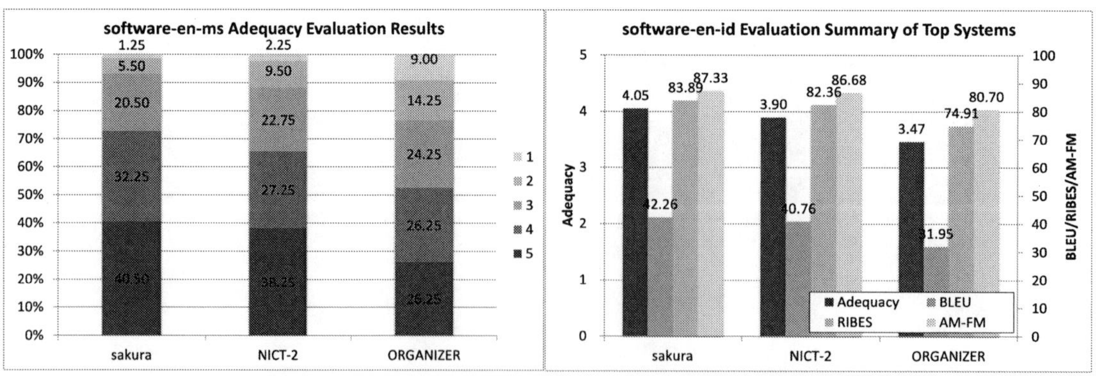


Figure 19: Official evaluation results of software-en-ms.

| Subtask | SYSTEM ID | DATA ID | Annotator A average | Annotator A variance | Annotator B average | Annotator B variance | all average | κ | weighted κ |
|---|---|---|---|---|---|---|---|---|---|
| jpcn-ja-en | TMU | 5187 | 4.34 | 0.52 | 4.74 | 0.30 | 4.54 | 0.09 | 0.20 |
| jpcn-en-ja | TMU | 5347 | 4.21 | 1.34 | 4.34 | 1.14 | 4.27 | 0.33 | 0.53 |
| indic21-en-bn | SRPOL | 6232 | 4.57 | 0.71 | 4.74 | 0.36 | 4.65 | 0.30 | 0.36 |
| | sakura | 6150 | 4.32 | 1.25 | 4.46 | 0.60 | 4.38 | 0.20 | 0.34 |
| | IIIT-H | 6005 | 3.89 | 2.01 | 4.00 | 1.55 | 3.94 | 0.27 | 0.52 |
| indic21-bn-en | SRPOL | 6242 | 4.79 | 0.31 | 4.80 | 0.18 | 4.80 | 0.14 | 0.18 |
| | IIIT-H | 6015 | 3.67 | 2.38 | 3.96 | 1.49 | 3.81 | 0.31 | 0.54 |
| | mcairt | 6332 | 3.33 | 1.82 | 3.85 | 1.26 | 3.59 | 0.19 | 0.34 |
| indic21-en-kn | SRPOL | 6235 | 4.70 | 0.28 | 4.74 | 0.41 | 4.71 | 0.23 | 0.29 |
| | sakura | 6153 | 4.73 | 0.20 | 4.41 | 0.64 | 4.57 | 0.15 | 0.22 |
| | IIIT-H | 6008 | 4.11 | 0.63 | 3.90 | 1.35 | 4.00 | 0.33 | 0.48 |
| indic21-kn-en | SRPOL | 6245 | 4.63 | 0.29 | 4.81 | 0.25 | 4.72 | 0.25 | 0.30 |
| | sakura | 5873 | 4.62 | 0.38 | 4.36 | 1.23 | 4.49 | 0.21 | 0.32 |
| | IIIT-H | 6018 | 4.17 | 0.77 | 3.70 | 2.23 | 3.94 | 0.21 | 0.40 |
| indic21-en-ml | SRPOL | 6236 | 4.26 | 1.09 | 4.56 | 0.37 | 4.41 | 0.20 | 0.30 |
| | CFILT | 6046 | 3.46 | 1.30 | 3.60 | 1.26 | 3.54 | 0.16 | 0.30 |
| | IIIT-H | 6009 | 2.24 | 1.99 | 3.19 | 0.58 | 2.71 | 0.04 | 0.11 |
| indic21-ml-en | SRPOL | 6246 | 3.27 | 0.90 | 4.78 | 0.43 | 4.03 | 0.05 | 0.05 |
| | sakura | 5874 | 3.57 | 0.86 | 4.42 | 1.33 | 3.99 | 0.03 | 0.10 |
| | IITP-MT | 6289 | 3.31 | 1.23 | 4.12 | 1.41 | 3.71 | 0.11 | 0.21 |
| indic21-en-mr | SRPOL | 6237 | 4.26 | 0.34 | 4.42 | 0.44 | 4.34 | 0.05 | 0.04 |
| | CFILT | 6047 | 4.08 | 0.44 | 4.20 | 0.65 | 4.14 | 0.01 | 0.01 |
| | IIIT-H | 6010 | 3.63 | 0.71 | 4.05 | 0.93 | 3.84 | 0.09 | 0.18 |
| indic21-mr-en | SRPOL | 6247 | 4.34 | 0.55 | 4.79 | 0.31 | 4.57 | 0.07 | 0.11 |
| | sakura | 5875 | 4.14 | 0.70 | 4.56 | 0.53 | 4.35 | 0.12 | 0.18 |
| | IIIT-H | 6021 | 3.86 | 1.26 | 4.15 | 0.99 | 4.00 | 0.05 | 0.15 |
| indic21-en-or | SRPOL | 6238 | 4.12 | 0.65 | 4.38 | 0.69 | 4.25 | 0.31 | 0.49 |
| | IIIT-H | 6011 | 3.80 | 0.77 | 3.83 | 1.08 | 3.82 | 0.63 | 0.75 |
| | CFILT | 6048 | 3.75 | 0.90 | 3.77 | 0.97 | 3.76 | 0.77 | 0.85 |
| indic21-or-en | SRPOL | 6248 | 4.36 | 0.85 | 4.38 | 0.56 | 4.37 | 0.14 | 0.35 |
| | sakura | 5876 | 4.24 | 1.06 | 4.26 | 0.75 | 4.25 | 0.26 | 0.49 |
| | IIIT-H | 6022 | 3.34 | 2.08 | 3.50 | 1.32 | 3.42 | 0.32 | 0.63 |
| software-en-id | sakura | 5799 | 4.86 | 0.20 | 3.62 | 1.37 | 4.24 | 0.02 | 0.07 |
| | NICT-2 | 5902 | 4.74 | 0.45 | 3.58 | 1.56 | 4.16 | 0.07 | 0.15 |
| | organizer | 3609 | 4.17 | 1.66 | 2.73 | 2.04 | 3.45 | 0.13 | 0.25 |
| software-en-ms | sakura | 5818 | 3.44 | 0.76 | 4.66 | 0.38 | 4.05 | 0.01 | 0.08 |
| | NICT-2 | 5904 | 3.25 | 0.93 | 4.54 | 0.61 | 3.90 | -0.03 | 0.09 |
| | organizer | 3610 | 2.88 | 1.18 | 4.05 | 1.34 | 3.46 | 0.06 | 0.27 |

Table 19: JPO adequacy evaluation results in detail.

### 8.3 Indic Multilingual Task

In WAT 2021, we received an overwhelming participation from 11 teams, 10 of which submitted system description papers. In contrast, in WAT 2020 there were only 4 system description papers. All participants trained multilingual NMT models. Some teams focused on leveraging monolingual corpora for pre-training MBART models or for backtranslation whereas other teams focused on script mapping to increase the similarity between the Indian languages and other teams focused on language family specific (Indo-Aryan vs Dravidian) models. Compared to the previous years, it is clear that backtranslation needs to be supplemented with pre-training as well as data selection for the best translation quality. The best performing team, "SRPOL", used back-translation, pre-training, data selection and domain adaptation. Following "SRPOL" teams such as "sakura", "CFILT", "IIIT-H", "IITP-MT" and "mcairt" performed the best with ranks varying depending on the translation direction. One important observation we made was that "SRPOL" results for Indian to English translation were far higher than those of the other teams. In general their submission were 2 to 5 BLEU higher than the second best team. We suppose that this is due to their detailed experimentation with data selection and back-translation. On the other hand, for English to Indian language translation, although "SRPOL" had the highest BLEU for most directions, the gap between "SRPOL" and other participants was not that high. In a number of cases the differences were less than 0.5 BLEU which is not significant.

In general, we observed that translation into English had substantially high BLEU scores with most participants obtaining higher than 25 BLEU for most directions. This makes sense because Indian languages are similar to each other and when the target language is the same, the increase in the target language data and transfer learning on the source side will lead to a large improvement in translation quality. In most cases, the scores for Indo-Aryan (Hindi, Marathi, Oriya, Punjabi, Gujarati and Bengali) to English translation were much higher than the scores for Dravidian (Tamil Telugu, Kannada and Malayalam) to English translation.

On the other hand, for translation into Indian languages, BLEU scores were relatively lower. This is due to the morphological richness of Indian languages as well as the fact that multilingual English to Indian language translation does not benefit from the abundance of target language corpus like multilingual Indian language to English translation does. The BLEU scores for translation into Indo-Aryan languages such as Hindi and Punjabi showed the best translation quality exceeding 30 BLEU. This makes sense because Hindi and Punjabi are very similar and Hindi is the most resource rich among all Indian languages. It is certain that Punjabi benefits from the Hindi parallel data via transfer learning despite not sharing the same script. Script sharing, a technique used by some participants, could help enhance the amount of transfer learning taking place even further. For other Indo-Aryan languages the translation quality was a bit lower where English to Bengali exhibited the least translation quality compared to the other Indo-Aryan languages. This shows that linguistic similarity is not enough to lead to a high amount of transfer. In the case of translation into Dravidian languages we observed the lowest BLEU scores, usually around 15 BLEU or lower, with the exception of English to Kannada. Despite having larger corpora than some Indo-Aryan languages, translation into Dravidian languages is very hard as they are significantly morphologically richer than Indo-Aryan languages. Simply leveraging large monolingual corpora may not be enough and methods that take Dravidian linguistics into account may be necessary.

With regards to human evaluation, we observed that differences in BLEU scores do not always correspond to differences in human evaluation scores. For example, take the case of English to Malayalam translation where the gap between "SRPOL" and "CFILT" in terms of BLEU is 2.7 and in terms of JPO scores is 0.87. For the same teams in case of English to Marathi, the gap in BLEU and JPO scores are 1.95 and 0.2 respectively. The difference between a gap of 2.7 and 1.95 is not very large as it is on a scale of 100[72] but the difference between 0.87 and 0.2 on a scale of 5[73] is quite large. In previous editions of this workshop we have always insisted that BLEU scores should not always be trusted in order to decide if translations truly are the best and this year's human evaluation results show that this is still the case. Multi-metric evaluation helps us better understand different aspects of translation and we recommend readers to adopt the same even if automatic metrics are used. Although we are limited by budgetary constraints we hope to conduct larger scale human evaluation in the future.

### 8.4 English→Hindi Multi-Modal Task

This year four teams participated in the different sub-tasks (TEXT, MM, and HI) of the English→Hindi Multi-Modal task. The WAT2021 automatic evaluation scores for the participating teams are shown in Tables 63, 60, 62, 58, 55, 57. The team "Volta" obtained the highest BLEU score for the text-only translation (TEXT) for both the evaluation (E-Test) and challenge (C-Test) test set. The best performance is obtained by fine-tuned *mBART* using IITB Corpus as an additional resource. For the captioning sub-task (HI) one team "NLPHut" participated and able to obtained better results compared to previous years' best results based on region-specific image caption generation. For the multimodal sub-task (MM), we received three submissions from the teams "Volta", "iitp" and "CNLP-NITS-PP", respectively. The team "Volta" obtained the highest BLEU score for the multimodal translation (MM) for both the evaluation (E-Test) and challenge (C-Test) test set. They extracted object tags from images using visual information to enhance the textual input and achieve the BLEU score of *51.60* on the challenge test set, also the translation output able to resolve ambiguity as compared with text-only translation.

Due to constraints, no human evaluation was made this year for the English→Hindi Multi-Modal Task.

[72]BLEU scores go from 0 to 100.

[73]Human evaluation scores go from 1 to 5.

### 8.5 English→Malayalam Multi-Modal Task

This year one team "NLPHut" participated in the different sub-tasks text-only translation (TEXT) and Malayalam captioning (ML) sub-tasks of the English→ Multi-Modal task. The WAT2021 automatic evaluation scores are shown in the Table 64, 61, 59, 56.

For English to Malayalam text-only translation the team "NLPHut" using the *Transformer* model obtained a BLEU score of *34.83* as compared to baseline of *30.49* on the evaluation test set and for the challenge test set obtained *12.15* compared to the baseline *12.98*. For Malayalam image captioning, the team "NLPHut" used the region-specific approach by extracting image features for the given specific region (bounding box) along with the whole image features and concatenating both to pass into an LSTM decoder to obtained the captions.

Due to constraints, no human evaluation was made this year for the English→Malayalam Multi-Modal Task.

### 8.6 Flickr30kEnt-JP Japanese↔English Multi-Modal Tasks

This year, two teams participated in the English→Japanese task, and one team participated in the Japanese→English task, respectively. It is notable that all submissions outperformed the best scores in WAT 2020, probably because of the increased size of the training dataset as well as the novel techniques introduced by the participants.

Overall, we observe the similar trend as in the last year. In the English→Japanese task, MMT systems constantly outperformed text-only NMT models including unconstrained ones, while in the Japanese→English task, unconstrained NMT model achieved the best performance. This is perhaps because the Flickr30kEnt-JP dataset itself is indeed constructed by English to Japanese human translation where images were actually referred to resolve ambiguity. One team developed an elegant method for soft alignment of word–region to realize better grounding of multimodal information, which is shown to achieve a favorable performance gain. This result again indicates the importance of text–image grounding in MMT, and we believe that we still have much room for improvements.

### 8.7 Ambiguous MS COCO Japanese↔English Multimodal Task

This year only one team participated in the English→Japanese task. Their system was based on a word-region alignment method to enhance the interaction between source tokens and image regions and then integrating aligned information to the visual features during decoding (Zhao et al., 2021). We observe that their system outperformed the organizer's system, which is based on double attention to both source tokens and image regions. It verified that it is important to integrate visual information in a proper way for this task and multimodal MT in general that text is a strong clue for translation, but visual information can further improve translation if it is used properly.

Unfortunately, there is no team participating the Japanese→English task. We hope that we can have more participates next year for the tasks in both directions.

### 8.8 Restricted Translation Task

We received 3 systems for the English→ Japanese translation task and 4 systems for the Japanese→ English.[74] On the whole, all the submitted systems are basically lexical-constraint-aware NMT models with lexically constrained decoding method, where the restricted target vocabulary is concatenated into source sentences and, during the beam search at inference time, the models generate translation outputs containing the target vocabulary. We observed that these techniques boost the final translation performance of the NMT models in the restricted translation task.

For human evaluation, we conducted the source-based direct assessment (Cettolo et al., 2017; Federmann, 2018) and source-based contrastive assessment (Sakaguchi and Van Durme, 2018; Federmann, 2018), to have the top-ranked systems of each team appraised by bilingual human annotators. In the human evaluation campaign, we also include the human reference data. Table 20 reports the final automatic evaluation score and the human evaluation results. In both tasks, the systems from the team "NTT" are the most highly evaluated in all the submitted systems in the final score and the human evaluation, consistently. We also note that our designed automation metric is well correlated

[74] We discuss 3 submitted systems from the teams "NTT", "NHK", and "NICTRB" teams, as we do not have a system description paper from the team "TMU".

| En-Ja | | Human Eval. | |
|---|---|---|---|
| Team | final | src-based DA | src-based CA |
| NTT | **57.2** | **77.5** | **79.7** |
| NHK | 33.9 | 74.1 | 77.2 |
| NICTRB | 28.8 | 73.6 | 77.1 |
| (human ref.) | — | 73.4 | 76.4 |
| Ja-En | | Human Eval. | |
| Team | final | src-based DA | src-based CA |
| NTT | **44.1** | **75.6** | **74.4** |
| NHK | 37.5 | 73.9 | 73.5 |
| NICTRB | 31.8 | 72.1 | 71.8 |
| TMU | 22.6 | 50.2 | 48.3 |
| (human ref.) | — | 74.1 | 72.9 |

Table 20: Human evaluation results of source-based direct assessment (src-based DA) and source-based contrastive assessment (src-based CA), ranging 0 to 100. TThe column of "final" reports the final score of the automatic evaluation metric described in Section 2.13

with the human evaluation results. Besides that, we found that the ASPEC human reference data might have a quality issue, consisting of low-quality examples that are annotated with a score of [0, 50], with the ratio of (En-Ja, Ja-En)=(13.30%, 12.43%). This is why a few systems are shown to surpass the original human reference data in the human evaluation.

## 9 Conclusion and Future Perspective

This paper summarizes the shared tasks of WAT2021. We had 24 participants worldwide who submitted their translation results for the human evaluation, and collected a large number of useful submissions for improving the current machine translation systems by analyzing the submissions and identifying the issues.

For the next WAT workshop, we will try to add more Indic languages to our MultiIndicMT task along with newer evaluation sets. Also, we will add a new English→Bengali Multi-Modal task into the Multimodal translation tasks.

## Acknowledgement

The English→Hindi and English→Malayalam Multi-Modal shared tasks were supported by the following grants at Idiap Research Institute and Charles University. The authors do not see any significant ethical or privacy concerns that would prevent the processing of the data used in the study. The datasets do contain personal data, and these are processed in compliance with the GDPR and national law.

- At Idiap Research Institute, the work was supported by the EU H2020 project "Real-time network, text, and speaker analytics for combating organized crime" (ROXANNE), grant agreement: 833635.
- At Charles University, the work was supported by the grant 19-26934X (NEUREM3) of the Czech Science Foundation and using language resources distributed by the LINDAT/CLARIN project of the Ministry of Education, Youth and Sports of the Czech Republic (projects LM2015071 and OP VVV VI CZ.02.1.01/0.0/0.0/16013/0001781).

## References

Rafael E. Banchs, Luis F. D'Haro, and Haizhou Li. 2015a. Adequacy-fluency metrics: Evaluating mt in the continuous space model framework. *IEEE/ACM Trans. Audio, Speech and Lang. Proc.*, 23(3):472–482.

Rafael E. Banchs, Luis F. D'Haro, and Haizhou Li. 2015b. Adequacy–fluency metrics: Evaluating mt in the continuous space model framework. *IEEE/ACM Transactions on Audio, Speech, and Language Processing*, 23(3):472–482.

Bianka Buschbeck and Miriam Exel. 2020. A parallel evaluation data set of software documentation with document structure annotation.

M. Cettolo, Marcello Federico, L. Bentivogli, Niehues Jan, Stüker Sebastian, Sudoh Katsuitho, Yoshino Koichiro, and Federmann Christian. 2017. Overview of the iwslt 2017 evaluation campaign.

Jacob Cohen. 1968. Weighted kappa: Nominal scale agreement with provision for scaled disagreement or partial credit. *Psychological Bulletin*, 70(4):213 – 220.

Raj Dabre, Chenhui Chu, and Anoop Kunchukuttan. 2020. A survey of multilingual neural machine translation. *ACM Comput. Surv.*, 53(5).

Luis Fernando D'Haro, Rafael E. Banchs, Chiori Hori, and Haizhou Li. 2019. Automatic evaluation of end-to-end dialog systems with adequacy-fluency metrics. *Computer Speech and Language*, 55:200–215.

Chenchen Ding, Hnin Thu Zar Aye, Win Pa Pa, Khin Thandar Nwet, Khin Mar Soe, Masao Utiyama, and Eiichiro Sumita. 2019. Towards Burmese (Myanmar) morphological analysis: Syllable-based tokenization and part-of-speech tagging. *ACM Transactions on Asian and Low-Resource Language Information Processing (TALLIP)*, 19(1):5.

Chenchen Ding, Masao Utiyama, and Eiichiro Sumita. 2018. NOVA: A feasible and flexible annotation system for joint tokenization and part-of-speech tagging. *ACM Transactions on Asian and Low-Resource Language Information Processing (TALLIP)*, 18(2):17.

Christian Federmann. 2018. Appraise evaluation framework for machine translation. In *Proceedings of the 27th International Conference on Computational Linguistics: System Demonstrations*, pages 86–88, Santa Fe, New Mexico. Association for Computational Linguistics.

Aizhan Imankulova, Raj Dabre, Atsushi Fujita, and Kenji Imamura. 2019. Exploiting out-of-domain parallel data through multilingual transfer learning for low-resource neural machine translation. In *Proceedings of Machine Translation Summit XVII Volume 1: Research Track*, pages 128–139, Dublin, Ireland. European Association for Machine Translation.

Hideki Isozaki, Tsutomu Hirao, Kevin Duh, Katsuhito Sudoh, and Hajime Tsukada. 2010. Automatic evaluation of translation quality for distant language pairs. In *Proceedings of the 2010 Conference on Empirical Methods in Natural Language Processing*, EMNLP '10, pages 944–952, Stroudsburg, PA, USA. Association for Computational Linguistics.

Melvin Johnson, Mike Schuster, Quoc V. Le, Maxim Krikun, Yonghui Wu, Zhifeng Chen, Nikhil Thorat, Fernanda Viégas, Martin Wattenberg, Greg Corrado, Macduff Hughes, and Jeffrey Dean. 2017. Google's multilingual neural machine translation system: Enabling zero-shot translation. *Transactions of the Association for Computational Linguistics*, 5:339–351.

Guillaume Klein, Yoon Kim, Yuntian Deng, Jean Senellart, and Alexander Rush. 2017. Opennmt: Open-source toolkit for neural machine translation. In *Proceedings of ACL 2017, System Demonstrations*, pages 67–72. Association for Computational Linguistics.

Philipp Koehn, Hieu Hoang, Alexandra Birch, Chris Callison-Burch, Marcello Federico, Nicola Bertoldi, Brooke Cowan, Wade Shen, Christine Moran, Richard Zens, Chris Dyer, Ondrej Bojar, Alexandra Constantin, and Evan Herbst. 2007. Moses: Open source toolkit for statistical machine translation. In *Annual Meeting of the Association for Computational Linguistics (ACL), demonstration session*.

T. Kudo. 2005. Mecab : Yet another part-of-speech and morphological analyzer. *http://mecab.sourceforge.net/*.

Anoop Kunchukuttan. 2020. The IndicNLP Library. `https://github.com/anoopkunchukuttan/indic_nlp_library/blob/master/docs/indicnlp.pdf`.

Sadao Kurohashi, Toshihisa Nakamura, Yuji Matsumoto, and Makoto Nagao. 1994. Improvements of Japanese morphological analyzer JUMAN. In *Proceedings of The International Workshop on Sharable Natural Language*, pages 22–28.

Mike Lewis, Yinhan Liu, Naman Goyal, Marjan Ghazvininejad, Abdelrahman Mohamed, Omer Levy, Veselin Stoyanov, and Luke Zettlemoyer. 2020. BART: Denoising sequence-to-sequence pretraining for natural language generation, translation, and comprehension. In *Proceedings of the 58th Annual Meeting of the Association for Computational Linguistics*, pages 7871–7880, Online. Association for Computational Linguistics.

Yinhan Liu, Jiatao Gu, Naman Goyal, Xian Li, Sergey Edunov, Marjan Ghazvininejad, Mike Lewis, and Luke Zettlemoyer. 2020. Multilingual denoising pretraining for neural machine translation. *Transactions of the Association for Computational Linguistics*, 8:726–742.

Andrew Merritt, Chenhui Chu, and Yuki Arase. 2020. A corpus for english-japanese multimodal neural machine translation with comparable sentences.

Hideki Nakayama, Akihiro Tamura, and Takashi Ninomiya. 2020. A visually-grounded parallel corpus with phrase-to-region linking. In *Proceedings of the 12th Language Resources and Evaluation Conference*.

Toshiaki Nakazawa, Nobushige Doi, Shohei Higashiyama, Chenchen Ding, Raj Dabre, Hideya Mino, Isao Goto, Win Pa Pa, Anoop Kunchukuttan, Yusuke Oda, Shantipriya Parida, Ondřej Bojar, and Sadao Kurohashi. 2019. Overview of the 6th workshop on Asian translation. In *Proceedings of the 6th Workshop on Asian Translation*, pages 1–35, Hong Kong, China. Association for Computational Linguistics.

Toshiaki Nakazawa, Shohei Higashiyama, Chenchen Ding, Hideya Mino, Isao Goto, Hideto Kazawa, Yusuke Oda, Graham Neubig, and Sadao Kurohashi. 2017. Overview of the 4th workshop on asian translation. In *Proceedings of the 4th Workshop on Asian Translation (WAT2017)*, pages 1–54. Asian Federation of Natural Language Processing.

Toshiaki Nakazawa, Hideki Nakayama, Chenchen Ding, Raj Dabre, Shohei Higashiyama, Hideya Mino, Isao Goto, Win Pa Pa, Anoop Kunchukuttan, Shantipriya Parida, Ondřej Bojar, and Sadao Kurohashi. 2020. Overview of the 7th workshop on Asian translation. In *Proceedings of the 7th Workshop on Asian Translation*, pages 1–44, Suzhou, China. Association for Computational Linguistics.

Toshiaki Nakazawa, Katsuhito Sudoh, Shohei Higashiyama, Chenchen Ding, Raj Dabre, Hideya Mino, Isao Goto, Win Pa Pa, Anoop Kunchukuttan, and Sadao Kurohashi. 2018. Overview of the 5th workshop on Asian translation. In *Proceedings of the 32nd Pacific Asia Conference on Language, Information and Computation: 5th Workshop on Asian Translation: 5th Workshop on Asian Translation*, Hong Kong. Association for Computational Linguistics.

Graham Neubig, Yosuke Nakata, and Shinsuke Mori. 2011. Pointwise prediction for robust, adaptable japanese morphological analysis. In *Proceedings of the 49th Annual Meeting of the Association for Computational Linguistics: Human Language Technologies: Short Papers - Volume 2*, HLT '11, pages 529–533, Stroudsburg, PA, USA. Association for Computational Linguistics.

Kishore Papineni, Salim Roukos, Todd Ward, and Wei-Jing Zhu. 2002. Bleu: a method for automatic evaluation of machine translation. In *ACL*, pages 311–318.

Shantipriya Parida and Ondřej Bojar. 2021. Malayalam visual genome 1.0. LINDAT/CLARIAH-CZ digital library at the Institute of Formal and Applied Linguistics (ÚFAL), Faculty of Mathematics and Physics, Charles University.

Shantipriya Parida, Ondřej Bojar, and Satya Ranjan Dash. 2019a. Hindi visual genome: A dataset for multimodal english-to-hindi machine translation. *arXiv preprint arXiv:1907.08948*.

Shantipriya Parida, Ondřej Bojar, and Satya Ranjan Dash. 2019b. Hindi Visual Genome: A Dataset for Multimodal English-to-Hindi Machine Translation. *Computación y Sistemas*. In print. Presented at CICLing 2019, La Rochelle, France.

Hammam Riza, Michael Purwoadi, Teduh Uliniansyah, Aw Ai Ti, Sharifah Mahani Aljunied, Luong Chi Mai, Vu Tat Thang, Nguyen Phuong Thai, Vichet Chea, Sethserey Sam, Sopheap Seng, Khin Mar Soe, Khin Thandar Nwet, Masao Utiyama, and Chenchen Ding. 2016. Introduction of the asian language treebank. In *In Proc. of O-COCOSDA*, pages 1–6.

Keisuke Sakaguchi and Benjamin Van Durme. 2018. Efficient online scalar annotation with bounded support. In *Proceedings of the 56th Annual Meeting of the Association for Computational Linguistics (Volume 1: Long Papers)*, pages 208–218, Melbourne, Australia. Association for Computational Linguistics.

Ye Kyaw Thu, Win Pa Pa, Masao Utiyama, Andrew Finch, and Eiichiro Sumita. 2016. Introducing the Asian language treebank (ALT). In *Proceedings of the Tenth International Conference on Language Resources and Evaluation (LREC'16)*, pages 1574–1578, Portorož, Slovenia. European Language Resources Association (ELRA).

Huihsin Tseng. 2005. A conditional random field word segmenter. In *In Fourth SIGHAN Workshop on Chinese Language Processing*.

Masao Utiyama and Hitoshi Isahara. 2007. A japanese-english patent parallel corpus. In *MT summit XI*, pages 475–482.

Ashish Vaswani, Samy Bengio, Eugene Brevdo, Francois Chollet, Aidan Gomez, Stephan Gouws, Llion Jones, Łukasz Kaiser, Nal Kalchbrenner, Niki Parmar, Ryan Sepassi, Noam Shazeer, and Jakob Uszkoreit. 2018. Tensor2tensor for neural machine translation. In *Proceedings of the 13th Conference of the Association for Machine Translation in the Americas (Volume 1: Research Papers)*, pages 193–199. Association for Machine Translation in the Americas.

Ashish Vaswani, Noam Shazeer, Niki Parmar, Jakob Uszkoreit, Llion Jones, Aidan N. Gomez, Lukasz Kaiser, and Illia Polosukhin. 2017. Attention is all you need. *CoRR*, abs/1706.03762.

Yi Mon Shwe Sin and Khin Mar Soe. 2018. Syllable-based myanmar-english neural machine translation. In *In Proc. of ICCA*, pages 228–233.

Chen Zhang, Luis Fernando D'Haro, Rafael E. Banchs, Thomas Friedrichs, and Haizhou Li. 2021a. *Deep AM-FM: Toolkit for Automatic Dialogue Evaluation*, pages 53–69. Springer Singapore, Singapore.

Chen Zhang, Grandee Lee, Luis Fernando D'Haro, and Haizhou Li. 2021b. D-score: Holistic dialogue evaluation without reference. *IEEE/ACM Transactions on Audio, Speech, and Language Processing*, pages 1–1.

Yuting Zhao, Mamoru Komachi, Tomoyuki Kajiwara, and Chenhui Chu. 2020. Double attention-based multimodal neural machine translation with semantic image regions. In *EAMT*, pages 105–114.

Yuting Zhao, Mamoru Komachi, Tomoyuki Kajiwara, and Chenhui Chu. 2021. Neural machine translation with semantically relevant image regions. In *NLP*.

## Appendix A Submissions

Tables 21 to 76 summarize translation results submitted to WAT2021. Type and RSRC columns indicate type of method and use of other resources.

| System | ID | Type | RSRC | BLEU | RIBES | AMFM |
|---|---|---|---|---|---|---|
| NICT-2 | 5916 | NMT | YES | 34.970000 | 0.822350 | 0.839182 |
| sakura | 5791 | NMT | NO | 34.250000 | 0.820590 | 0.849202 |

Table 21: ALT20 en-hi submissions

| System | ID | Type | RSRC | BLEU | RIBES | AMFM |
|---|---|---|---|---|---|---|
| NICT-2 | 5918 | NMT | YES | 41.15 | 0.901974 | 0.867678 |
| sakura | 5798 | NMT | NO | 41.57 | 0.901977 | 0.868025 |

Table 22: ALT20 en-id submissions

| System | ID | Type | RSRC | BLEU | RIBES | AMFM |
|---|---|---|---|---|---|---|
| NICT-2 | 5920 | NMT | YES | 45.17 | 0.912195 | 0.873476 |
| sakura | 5816 | NMT | NO | 44.01 | 0.908439 | 0.871875 |

Table 23: ALT20 en-ms submissions

| System | ID | Type | RSRC | BLEU | RIBES | AMFM |
|---|---|---|---|---|---|---|
| NICT-2 | 5922 | NMT | YES | 55.690000 | 0.815863 | 0.832513 |
| sakura | 5843 | NMT | NO | 55.980000 | 0.818307 | 0.837062 |

Table 24: ALT20 en-th submissions

| System | ID | Type | RSRC | BLEU | RIBES | AMFM |
|---|---|---|---|---|---|---|
| NICT-2 | 5917 | NMT | YES | 35.21 | 0.834649 | 0.814594 |
| sakura | 5793 | NMT | NO | 36.17 | 0.835220 | 0.832895 |

Table 25: ALT20 hi-en submissions

| System | ID | Type | RSRC | BLEU | RIBES | AMFM |
|---|---|---|---|---|---|---|
| NICT-2 | 5919 | NMT | YES | 43.90 | 0.898700 | 0.844199 |
| sakura | 5800 | NMT | NO | 44.72 | 0.897314 | 0.850998 |

Table 26: ALT20 id-en submissions

| System | ID | Type | RSRC | BLEU | RIBES | AMFM |
|---|---|---|---|---|---|---|
| NICT-2 | 5921 | NMT | YES | 44.53 | 0.904478 | 0.841632 |
| sakura | 5821 | NMT | NO | 45.70 | 0.901696 | 0.851471 |

Table 27: ALT20 ms-en submissions

| System | ID | Type | RSRC | BLEU | RIBES | AMFM |
|---|---|---|---|---|---|---|
| NICT-2 | 5923 | NMT | YES | 28.96 | 0.829525 | 0.817972 |
| sakura | 5845 | NMT | NO | 30.10 | 0.832399 | 0.822585 |

Table 28: ALT20 th-en submissions

| System | ID | Type | RSRC | BLEU | RIBES | AMFM |
|---|---|---|---|---|---|---|
| YCC-MT1 | 6195 | SMT | NO | 20.880000 | 0.553319 | 0.655310 |
| YCC-MT1 | 6201 | SMT | NO | 20.130000 | 0.545962 | 0.654820 |
| YCC-MT2 | 6175 | NMT | NO | 14.820000 | 0.659582 | 0.663840 |
| YCC-MT2 | 6178 | NMT | NO | 14.020000 | 0.639593 | 0.645470 |
| sakura | 6031 | NMT | NO | 29.620000 | 0.739320 | 0.752340 |

Table 29: ALT2 en-my submissions

| System | ID | Type | RSRC | BLEU | RIBES | AMFM |
|---|---|---|---|---|---|---|
| NECTEC | 6188 | NMT | NO | 6.24 | 0.620840 | 0.424640 |
| NECTEC | 6192 | NMT | NO | 4.62 | 0.587155 | 0.391710 |
| sakura | 5230 | NMT | NO | 19.75 | 0.742698 | 0.562680 |
| sakura | 5990 | NMT | NO | 18.70 | 0.736523 | 0.550430 |

Table 30: ALT2 my-en submissions

| System | ID | Type | RSRC | BLEU | | | RIBES | | | AMFM |
|---|---|---|---|---|---|---|---|---|---|---|
| | | | | juman | kytea | mecab | juman | kytea | mecab | |
| NTT | 5368 | NMT | NO | 56.39 | 56.87 | 56.57 | 0.882454 | 0.882322 | 0.887104 | 0.817290 |
| NTT | 5616 | NMT | YES | 56.20 | 56.67 | 56.47 | 0.885308 | 0.885612 | 0.889831 | 0.818190 |
| nictrb | 5591 | NMT | YES | 51.07 | 51.32 | 51.36 | 0.836874 | 0.839934 | 0.844141 | 0.799950 |
| NHK | 5502 | NMT | NO | 52.07 | 52.69 | 52.33 | 0.815612 | 0.823084 | 0.827300 | 0.801660 |

Table 31: ASPECRT en-ja submissions

| System | ID | Type | RSRC | BLEU | RIBES | AMFM |
|---|---|---|---|---|---|---|
| TMU | 5994 | NMT | NO | 25.29 | 0.653597 | 0.612290 |
| NTT | 5209 | NMT | NO | 44.34 | 0.811700 | 0.672320 |
| NTT | 5615 | NMT | YES | 44.28 | 0.813155 | 0.676670 |
| nictrb | 5592 | NMT | YES | 37.01 | 0.753823 | 0.651570 |
| NHK | 5505 | NMT | NO | 42.94 | 0.801015 | 0.661560 |

Table 32: ASPECRT ja-en submissions

| System | ID | Type | RSRC | BLEU | RIBES | AMFM |
|---|---|---|---|---|---|---|
| ORGANIZER | 4789 | NMT | NO | 11.27 | 0.638781 | 0.613093 |
| NICT-5 | 5274 | NMT | NO | 21.37 | 0.747435 | 0.744400 |
| NICT-5 | 5349 | NMT | NO | 23.89 | 0.754772 | 0.758921 |
| NLPHut | 4583 | NMT | NO | 13.88 | 0.669588 | 0.657119 |
| mcairt | 6026 | NMT | NO | 25.22 | 0.773387 | 0.778620 |
| mcairt | 6332 | NMT | NO | 29.96 | 0.798326 | 0.786717 |
| sakura | 5870 | NMT | NO | 26.69 | 0.776808 | 0.772365 |
| IIIT-H | 6015 | NMT | NO | 28.28 | 0.773574 | 0.773292 |
| gaurvar | 5556 | NMT | NO | 11.33 | 0.634088 | 0.673457 |
| gaurvar | 5565 | NMT | NO | 11.83 | 0.629932 | 0.674034 |
| IITP-MT | 6280 | NMT | NO | 25.77 | 0.774004 | 0.777377 |
| SRPOL | 6242 | NMT | NO | 31.87 | 0.800501 | 0.789735 |
| SRPOL | 6268 | NMT | NO | 31.82 | 0.800145 | 0.792364 |
| CFILT | 6052 | NMT | NO | 25.98 | 0.760268 | 0.766461 |
| coastal | 6162 | NMT | NO | 24.39 | 0.772190 | 0.778356 |
| CFILT-IITB | 6112 | NMT | NO | 18.48 | 0.721176 | 0.730379 |
| CFILT-IITB | 6124 | NMT | NO | 20.18 | 0.732342 | 0.734491 |

Table 33: HINDEN21 bn-en submissions

| System | ID | Type | RSRC | BLEU | RIBES | AMFM |
|---|---|---|---|---|---|---|
| ORGANIZER | 4788 | NMT | NO | 5.580000 | 0.573377 | 0.701527 |
| NICT-5 | 5273 | NMT | NO | 10.590000 | 0.677858 | 0.755363 |
| NICT-5 | 5348 | NMT | NO | 12.840000 | 0.704620 | 0.767497 |
| NLPHut | 4582 | NMT | NO | 8.130000 | 0.645895 | 0.735005 |
| mcairt | 6000 | NMT | NO | 13.020000 | 0.715490 | 0.779592 |
| sakura | 6150 | NMT | NO | 13.830000 | 0.716347 | 0.764714 |
| IIIT-H | 6005 | NMT | NO | 14.730000 | 0.724245 | 0.759513 |
| gaurvar | 5588 | NMT | NO | 3.230000 | 0.452631 | 0.628707 |
| gaurvar | 5938 | NMT | NO | 2.950000 | 0.465755 | 0.641712 |
| IITP-MT | 6278 | NMT | NO | 11.040000 | 0.703372 | 0.731181 |
| SRPOL | 6232 | NMT | NO | 15.970000 | 0.733646 | 0.771033 |
| SRPOL | 6258 | NMT | NO | 15.580000 | 0.732792 | 0.772309 |
| CFILT | 6041 | NMT | NO | 13.240000 | 0.710664 | 0.777074 |
| coastal | 6074 | NMT | NO | 11.090000 | 0.694142 | 0.763665 |

Table 34: HINDEN21 en-bn submissions

| System | ID | Type | RSRC | BLEU | RIBES | AMFM |
|---|---|---|---|---|---|---|
| ORGANIZER | 4790 | NMT | NO | 16.380000 | 0.748273 | 0.757069 |
| NICT-5 | 5275 | NMT | NO | 23.040000 | 0.797371 | 0.801466 |
| NICT-5 | 5350 | NMT | NO | 24.260000 | 0.806181 | 0.811717 |
| NLPHut | 4585 | NMT | NO | 17.760000 | 0.763222 | 0.768177 |
| mcairt | 6003 | NMT | NO | 23.210000 | 0.809389 | 0.816739 |
| sakura | 6151 | NMT | NO | 25.270000 | 0.814798 | 0.813350 |
| IIIT-H | 6006 | NMT | NO | 26.970000 | 0.820249 | 0.820127 |
| gaurvar | 5580 | NMT | NO | 6.810000 | 0.586360 | 0.628529 |
| gaurvar | 5927 | NMT | NO | 6.920000 | 0.599337 | 0.645669 |
| IITP-MT | 6281 | NMT | NO | 20.460000 | 0.750935 | 0.808824 |
| SRPOL | 6233 | NMT | NO | 27.800000 | 0.824866 | 0.821221 |
| SRPOL | 6259 | NMT | NO | 27.310000 | 0.822329 | 0.819923 |
| CFILT | 6042 | NMT | NO | 24.560000 | 0.806649 | 0.817681 |
| coastal | 6078 | NMT | NO | 20.420000 | 0.795314 | 0.809795 |

Table 35: HINDEN21 en-gu submissions

| System | ID | Type | RSRC | BLEU | RIBES | AMFM |
|---|---|---|---|---|---|---|
| ORGANIZER | 4792 | NMT | NO | 23.310000 | 0.778841 | 0.759679 |
| NICT-5 | 5277 | NMT | NO | 29.590000 | 0.817892 | 0.800234 |
| NICT-5 | 5352 | NMT | NO | 30.180000 | 0.820984 | 0.801680 |
| NLPHut | 5987 | NMT | NO | 25.370000 | 0.788001 | 0.747598 |
| mcairt | 6004 | NMT | NO | 35.850000 | 0.846656 | 0.822626 |
| sakura | 6152 | NMT | NO | 36.920000 | 0.848042 | 0.816999 |
| IIIT-H | 6007 | NMT | NO | 38.250000 | 0.854192 | 0.822836 |
| gaurvar | 5578 | NMT | NO | 17.020000 | 0.681760 | 0.676601 |
| gaurvar | 5928 | NMT | NO | 15.860000 | 0.647511 | 0.681511 |
| IITP-MT | 6283 | NMT | NO | 34.480000 | 0.844721 | 0.820543 |
| SRPOL | 6254 | NMT | NO | 38.650000 | 0.855879 | 0.824649 |
| SRPOL | 6260 | NMT | NO | 38.040000 | 0.852496 | 0.822371 |
| CFILT | 6043 | NMT | NO | 35.390000 | 0.843969 | 0.821713 |
| coastal | 6079 | NMT | NO | 31.750000 | 0.829731 | 0.801179 |

Table 36: HINDEN21 en-hi submissions

| System | ID | Type | RSRC | BLEU | RIBES | AMFM |
|---|---|---|---|---|---|---|
| ORGANIZER | 4794 | NMT | NO | 10.110000 | 0.651048 | 0.741873 |
| NICT-5 | 5279 | NMT | NO | 16.130000 | 0.732794 | 0.798654 |
| NICT-5 | 5354 | NMT | NO | 18.220000 | 0.746230 | 0.813658 |
| NLPHut | 4591 | NMT | NO | 11.840000 | 0.689612 | 0.762931 |
| mcairt | 5998 | NMT | NO | 14.580000 | 0.726259 | 0.805963 |
| sakura | 6153 | NMT | NO | 18.830000 | 0.760100 | 0.817831 |
| IIIT-H | 6008 | NMT | NO | 19.570000 | 0.756613 | 0.812490 |
| gaurvar | 5581 | NMT | NO | 4.350000 | 0.477922 | 0.658271 |
| gaurvar | 5929 | NMT | NO | 3.900000 | 0.469815 | 0.657091 |
| IITP-MT | 6285 | NMT | NO | 13.220000 | 0.635288 | 0.791821 |
| SRPOL | 6235 | NMT | NO | 21.300000 | 0.770110 | 0.821941 |
| SRPOL | 6261 | NMT | NO | 20.910000 | 0.771246 | 0.821329 |
| CFILT | 6044 | NMT | NO | 17.980000 | 0.747233 | 0.816981 |
| coastal | 6113 | NMT | NO | 16.110000 | 0.736528 | 0.809687 |

Table 37: HINDEN21 en-kn submissions

| System | ID | Type | RSRC | BLEU | RIBES | AMFM |
|---|---|---|---|---|---|---|
| ORGANIZER | 4796 | NMT | NO | 3.340000 | 0.475441 | 0.706782 |
| NICT-5 | 5281 | NMT | NO | 5.980000 | 0.605053 | 0.764924 |
| NICT-5 | 5356 | NMT | NO | 6.510000 | 0.623301 | 0.789337 |
| NLPHut | 4590 | NMT | NO | 4.570000 | 0.554478 | 0.740136 |
| mcairt | 6002 | NMT | NO | 6.170000 | 0.622598 | 0.793308 |
| sakura | 5886 | NMT | NO | 10.940000 | 0.686534 | 0.794481 |
| IIIT-H | 6009 | NMT | NO | 12.760000 | 0.672331 | 0.745043 |
| gaurvar | 5582 | NMT | NO | 1.790000 | 0.338533 | 0.666547 |
| gaurvar | 5930 | NMT | NO | 1.480000 | 0.306966 | 0.656847 |
| IITP-MT | 6287 | NMT | NO | 3.790000 | 0.437679 | 0.758960 |
| SRPOL | 6236 | NMT | NO | 15.490000 | 0.736915 | 0.807998 |
| SRPOL | 6262 | NMT | NO | 15.430000 | 0.734111 | 0.808089 |
| CFILT | 6046 | NMT | NO | 12.790000 | 0.707437 | 0.805291 |
| coastal | 6081 | NMT | NO | 6.270000 | 0.619774 | 0.784292 |

Table 38: HINDEN21 en-ml submissions

| System | ID | Type | RSRC | BLEU | RIBES | AMFM |
|---|---|---|---|---|---|---|
| ORGANIZER | 4798 | NMT | NO | 8.820000 | 0.652134 | 0.730656 |
| NICT-5 | 5283 | NMT | NO | 14.690000 | 0.720677 | 0.785952 |
| NICT-5 | 5358 | NMT | NO | 16.380000 | 0.739171 | 0.800357 |
| NLPHut | 4594 | NMT | NO | 10.410000 | 0.684554 | 0.745915 |
| mcairt | 5999 | NMT | NO | 14.900000 | 0.740079 | 0.791850 |
| sakura | 6156 | NMT | NO | 17.870000 | 0.752439 | 0.803566 |
| IIIT-H | 6010 | NMT | NO | 19.480000 | 0.760009 | 0.807758 |
| gaurvar | 5583 | NMT | NO | 5.100000 | 0.482727 | 0.654698 |
| gaurvar | 5931 | NMT | NO | 4.490000 | 0.467281 | 0.658104 |
| IITP-MT | 6291 | NMT | NO | 13.950000 | 0.665934 | 0.798673 |
| SRPOL | 6237 | NMT | NO | 20.420000 | 0.771845 | 0.809721 |
| SRPOL | 6263 | NMT | NO | 19.930000 | 0.766897 | 0.810757 |
| CFILT | 6047 | NMT | NO | 18.470000 | 0.759182 | 0.811499 |
| coastal | 6082 | NMT | NO | 14.480000 | 0.727647 | 0.799538 |

Table 39: HINDEN21 en-mr submissions

| System | ID | Type | RSRC | BLEU | RIBES | AMFM |
|---|---|---|---|---|---|---|
| ORGANIZER | 4800 | NMT | NO | 9.080000 | 0.638520 | 0.714530 |
| NICT-5 | 5285 | NMT | NO | 15.010000 | 0.716665 | 0.748319 |
| NICT-5 | 5360 | NMT | NO | 16.690000 | 0.734028 | 0.757804 |
| NLPHut | 4596 | NMT | NO | 12.810000 | 0.693696 | 0.736638 |
| mcairt | 5996 | NMT | NO | 17.710000 | 0.743984 | 0.763064 |
| sakura | 6157 | NMT | NO | 17.880000 | 0.740263 | 0.769884 |
| IIIT-H | 6011 | NMT | NO | 20.150000 | 0.750260 | 0.735718 |
| gaurvar | 5584 | NMT | NO | 2.200000 | 0.380253 | 0.591864 |
| gaurvar | 5932 | NMT | NO | 2.600000 | 0.431373 | 0.611704 |
| IITP-MT | 6293 | NMT | NO | 12.570000 | 0.714731 | 0.737576 |
| SRPOL | 6238 | NMT | NO | 19.940000 | 0.751086 | 0.771831 |
| SRPOL | 6264 | NMT | NO | 19.150000 | 0.749740 | 0.771493 |
| CFILT | 6048 | NMT | NO | 18.220000 | 0.738397 | 0.768399 |
| coastal | 6084 | NMT | NO | 15.660000 | 0.727477 | 0.758199 |

Table 40: HINDEN21 en-or submissions

| System | ID | Type | RSRC | BLEU | RIBES | AMFM |
|---|---|---|---|---|---|---|
| ORGANIZER | 4802 | NMT | NO | 21.770000 | 0.765216 | 0.762364 |
| NICT-5 | 5287 | NMT | NO | 26.940000 | 0.808173 | 0.794023 |
| NICT-5 | 5362 | NMT | NO | 29.150000 | 0.820085 | 0.803326 |
| NLPHut | 4598 | NMT | NO | 22.600000 | 0.785047 | 0.778215 |
| mcairt | 6001 | NMT | NO | 30.560000 | 0.830405 | 0.810106 |
| sakura | 6158 | NMT | NO | 30.930000 | 0.829019 | 0.802223 |
| IIIT-H | 6012 | NMT | NO | 33.350000 | 0.837603 | 0.810972 |
| gaurvar | 5585 | NMT | NO | 9.350000 | 0.633937 | 0.620318 |
| gaurvar | 5933 | NMT | NO | 10.020000 | 0.632319 | 0.643473 |
| IITP-MT | 6298 | NMT | NO | 16.810000 | 0.785680 | 0.663206 |
| SRPOL | 6239 | NMT | NO | 33.430000 | 0.837542 | 0.814115 |
| SRPOL | 6265 | NMT | NO | 32.880000 | 0.835465 | 0.813158 |
| CFILT | 6049 | NMT | NO | 31.160000 | 0.826367 | 0.813658 |
| coastal | 6085 | NMT | NO | 27.250000 | 0.816792 | 0.803382 |

Table 41: HINDEN21 en-pa submissions

| System | ID | Type | RSRC | BLEU | RIBES | AMFM |
|---|---|---|---|---|---|---|
| ORGANIZER | 4804 | NMT | NO | 6.380000 | 0.588286 | 0.723160 |
| NICT-5 | 5289 | NMT | NO | 10.330000 | 0.675039 | 0.776138 |
| NICT-5 | 5364 | NMT | NO | 11.420000 | 0.701210 | 0.792622 |
| NLPHut | 4616 | NMT | NO | 7.680000 | 0.630830 | 0.739011 |
| mcairt | 5995 | NMT | NO | 11.980000 | 0.707054 | 0.801632 |
| sakura | 6159 | NMT | NO | 13.250000 | 0.721520 | 0.795712 |
| IIIT-H | 6013 | NMT | NO | 14.430000 | 0.711995 | 0.778991 |
| gaurvar | 5586 | NMT | NO | 4.090000 | 0.452271 | 0.694376 |
| gaurvar | 5934 | NMT | NO | 3.600000 | 0.431281 | 0.684232 |
| IITP-MT | 6303 | NMT | NO | 8.510000 | 0.578195 | 0.756693 |
| SRPOL | 6240 | NMT | NO | 14.150000 | 0.730705 | 0.798837 |
| SRPOL | 6266 | NMT | NO | 13.890000 | 0.728770 | 0.799382 |
| CFILT | 6050 | NMT | NO | 12.990000 | 0.715699 | 0.802920 |
| coastal | 6086 | NMT | NO | 9.990000 | 0.682220 | 0.788022 |

Table 42: HINDEN21 en-ta submissions

| System | ID | Type | RSRC | BLEU | RIBES | AMFM |
|---|---|---|---|---|---|---|
| ORGANIZER | 4806 | NMT | NO | 2.800000 | 0.479896 | 0.708086 |
| NICT-5 | 5291 | NMT | NO | 4.590000 | 0.569735 | 0.754015 |
| NICT-5 | 5366 | NMT | NO | 4.200000 | 0.576863 | 0.752068 |
| NLPHut | 5986 | NMT | NO | 4.880000 | 0.570112 | 0.713960 |
| mcairt | 5997 | NMT | NO | 11.170000 | 0.702337 | 0.783647 |
| sakura | 6160 | NMT | NO | 15.480000 | 0.725543 | 0.785055 |
| IIIT-H | 6014 | NMT | NO | 15.610000 | 0.728432 | 0.780218 |
| gaurvar | 5587 | NMT | NO | 2.310000 | 0.414016 | 0.634376 |
| gaurvar | 5935 | NMT | NO | 2.310000 | 0.389727 | 0.642502 |
| IITP-MT | 6305 | NMT | NO | 6.250000 | 0.530898 | 0.764977 |
| SRPOL | 6241 | NMT | NO | 16.850000 | 0.739835 | 0.791085 |
| SRPOL | 6267 | NMT | NO | 16.820000 | 0.734483 | 0.792970 |
| CFILT | 6051 | NMT | NO | 15.520000 | 0.725496 | 0.789820 |
| coastal | 6088 | NMT | NO | 12.860000 | 0.707817 | 0.778251 |

Table 43: HINDEN21 en-te submissions

| System | ID | Type | RSRC | BLEU | RIBES | AMFM |
|---|---|---|---|---|---|---|
| ORGANIZER | 4791 | NMT | NO | 26.21 | 0.764569 | 0.726576 |
| NICT-5 | 5276 | NMT | NO | 33.65 | 0.810918 | 0.793874 |
| NICT-5 | 5351 | NMT | NO | 33.53 | 0.811609 | 0.796604 |
| NLPHut | 4633 | NMT | NO | 23.10 | 0.755101 | 0.713984 |
| mcairt | 6334 | NMT | NO | 36.77 | 0.829389 | 0.819546 |
| sakura | 5871 | NMT | NO | 38.73 | 0.834934 | 0.820654 |
| IIIT-H | 6016 | NMT | NO | 39.39 | 0.830158 | 0.806061 |
| gaurvar | 5557 | NMT | NO | 16.79 | 0.715044 | 0.696879 |
| gaurvar | 5566 | NMT | NO | 17.50 | 0.712002 | 0.698257 |
| IITP-MT | 6282 | NMT | NO | 36.49 | 0.827301 | 0.814556 |
| SRPOL | 6243 | NMT | NO | 43.98 | 0.853263 | 0.835789 |
| SRPOL | 6269 | NMT | NO | 42.87 | 0.849734 | 0.833146 |
| CFILT | 6053 | NMT | NO | 35.31 | 0.807849 | 0.797069 |
| coastal | 6163 | NMT | NO | 34.60 | 0.824060 | 0.814168 |
| CFILT-IITB | 6114 | NMT | NO | 28.79 | 0.786408 | 0.765441 |
| CFILT-IITB | 6125 | NMT | NO | 31.02 | 0.795199 | 0.776935 |

Table 44: HINDEN21 gu-en submissions

| System | ID | Type | RSRC | BLEU | RIBES | AMFM |
|---|---|---|---|---|---|---|
| ORGANIZER | 4793 | NMT | NO | 28.21 | 0.782146 | 0.736131 |
| NICT-5 | 5278 | NMT | NO | 35.80 | 0.828390 | 0.808180 |
| NICT-5 | 5353 | NMT | NO | 36.20 | 0.832916 | 0.805716 |
| NLPHut | 5985 | NMT | NO | 24.55 | 0.785027 | 0.721805 |
| mcairt | 6333 | NMT | NO | 40.05 | 0.850322 | 0.832119 |
| sakura | 5872 | NMT | NO | 41.58 | 0.856469 | 0.834172 |
| IIIT-H | 6017 | NMT | NO | 43.23 | 0.853267 | 0.823007 |
| gaurvar | 5532 | NMT | NO | 20.90 | 0.729188 | 0.714649 |
| gaurvar | 5567 | NMT | NO | 21.33 | 0.759034 | 0.722822 |
| IITP-MT | 6284 | NMT | NO | 40.08 | 0.851601 | 0.831265 |
| SRPOL | 6244 | NMT | NO | 46.93 | 0.872874 | 0.847064 |
| SRPOL | 6270 | NMT | NO | 45.61 | 0.867712 | 0.843456 |
| CFILT | 6054 | NMT | NO | 39.71 | 0.837668 | 0.822034 |
| coastal | 6164 | NMT | NO | 36.47 | 0.840014 | 0.824040 |
| CFILT-IITB | 6115 | NMT | NO | 30.90 | 0.807304 | 0.775032 |
| CFILT-IITB | 6126 | NMT | NO | 33.70 | 0.820716 | 0.791408 |

Table 45: HINDEN21 hi-en submissions

| System | ID | Type | RSRC | BLEU | RIBES | AMFM |
|---|---|---|---|---|---|---|
| ORGANIZER | 4795 | NMT | NO | 20.33 | 0.717654 | 0.692019 |
| NICT-5 | 5280 | NMT | NO | 29.29 | 0.793521 | 0.782087 |
| NICT-5 | 5355 | NMT | NO | 30.87 | 0.796119 | 0.792622 |
| NLPHut | 4593 | NMT | NO | 17.72 | 0.710551 | 0.679617 |
| mcairt | 6374 | NMT | NO | 31.16 | 0.803525 | 0.799216 |
| sakura | 5873 | NMT | NO | 34.11 | 0.815837 | 0.805112 |
| IIIT-H | 6018 | NMT | NO | 34.69 | 0.804694 | 0.790977 |
| gaurvar | 5558 | NMT | NO | 13.45 | 0.683906 | 0.687726 |
| gaurvar | 5568 | NMT | NO | 13.86 | 0.674282 | 0.687810 |
| IITP-MT | 6286 | NMT | NO | 31.24 | 0.806170 | 0.798540 |
| SRPOL | 6245 | NMT | NO | 40.34 | 0.840458 | 0.823730 |
| SRPOL | 6271 | NMT | NO | 39.01 | 0.837287 | 0.820355 |
| CFILT | 6055 | NMT | NO | 30.23 | 0.772913 | 0.778602 |
| coastal | 6165 | NMT | NO | 31.04 | 0.811950 | 0.806951 |
| CFILT-IITB | 6121 | NMT | NO | 24.01 | 0.758489 | 0.751223 |
| CFILT-IITB | 6131 | NMT | NO | 24.18 | 0.759045 | 0.744802 |

Table 46: HINDEN21 kn-en submissions

| System | ID | Type | RSRC | BLEU | RIBES | AMFM |
|---|---|---|---|---|---|---|
| ORGANIZER | 4797 | NMT | NO | 13.64 | 0.673109 | 0.646559 |
| NICT-5 | 5282 | NMT | NO | 26.55 | 0.780019 | 0.772691 |
| NICT-5 | 5357 | NMT | NO | 28.23 | 0.786269 | 0.786909 |
| NLPHut | 4634 | NMT | NO | 15.47 | 0.700957 | 0.668778 |
| mcairt | 6344 | NMT | NO | 28.07 | 0.792884 | 0.794932 |
| sakura | 5874 | NMT | NO | 32.23 | 0.810429 | 0.805450 |
| IIIT-H | 6020 | NMT | NO | 29.19 | 0.780463 | 0.748518 |
| gaurvar | 5559 | NMT | NO | 12.99 | 0.678961 | 0.684370 |
| gaurvar | 5569 | NMT | NO | 13.64 | 0.657440 | 0.684483 |
| IITP-MT | 6289 | NMT | NO | 29.37 | 0.802153 | 0.798550 |
| SRPOL | 6246 | NMT | NO | 38.38 | 0.835444 | 0.823006 |
| SRPOL | 6272 | NMT | NO | 37.04 | 0.830449 | 0.820716 |
| CFILT | 6056 | NMT | NO | 29.28 | 0.784424 | 0.789095 |
| coastal | 6166 | NMT | NO | 28.55 | 0.803090 | 0.805091 |
| CFILT-IITB | 6117 | NMT | NO | 22.10 | 0.751437 | 0.744459 |
| CFILT-IITB | 6130 | NMT | NO | 22.84 | 0.763162 | 0.745908 |

Table 47: HINDEN21 ml-en submissions

| System | ID | Type | RSRC | BLEU | RIBES | AMFM |
|---|---|---|---|---|---|---|
| ORGANIZER | 4799 | NMT | NO | 15.10 | 0.676716 | 0.658130 |
| NICT-5 | 5284 | NMT | NO | 25.45 | 0.771352 | 0.764852 |
| NICT-5 | 5359 | NMT | NO | 27.88 | 0.783012 | 0.779746 |
| NLPHut | 5983 | NMT | NO | 17.07 | 0.706399 | 0.696839 |
| mcairt | 6335 | NMT | NO | 27.29 | 0.785579 | 0.780231 |
| sakura | 5875 | NMT | NO | 31.76 | 0.804834 | 0.795844 |
| IIIT-H | 6021 | NMT | NO | 34.02 | 0.803479 | 0.792878 |
| gaurvar | 5560 | NMT | NO | 13.38 | 0.679550 | 0.692897 |
| gaurvar | 5570 | NMT | NO | 13.96 | 0.669879 | 0.693109 |
| IITP-MT | 6292 | NMT | NO | 29.96 | 0.799383 | 0.797333 |
| SRPOL | 6247 | NMT | NO | 36.64 | 0.824831 | 0.812258 |
| SRPOL | 6273 | NMT | NO | 35.68 | 0.821164 | 0.810290 |
| CFILT | 6057 | NMT | NO | 29.71 | 0.786570 | 0.789075 |
| coastal | 6167 | NMT | NO | 27.71 | 0.795729 | 0.791157 |
| CFILT-IITB | 6118 | NMT | NO | 23.57 | 0.752476 | 0.751917 |
| CFILT-IITB | 6127 | NMT | NO | 25.40 | 0.765200 | 0.767347 |

Table 48: HINDEN21 mr-en submissions

| System | ID | Type | RSRC | BLEU | RIBES | AMFM |
|---|---|---|---|---|---|---|
| ORGANIZER | 4801 | NMT | NO | 16.35 | 0.679781 | 0.730819 |
| NICT-5 | 5286 | NMT | NO | 25.81 | 0.762604 | 0.780431 |
| NICT-5 | 5361 | NMT | NO | 27.93 | 0.769634 | 0.782917 |
| NLPHut | 4597 | NMT | NO | 18.92 | 0.720916 | 0.740606 |
| mcairt | 6338 | NMT | NO | 29.96 | 0.798326 | 0.795586 |
| sakura | 5876 | NMT | NO | 32.67 | 0.801734 | 0.808239 |
| IIIT-H | 6022 | NMT | NO | 34.11 | 0.795132 | 0.804930 |
| gaurvar | 5550 | NMT | NO | 13.71 | 0.634313 | 0.725121 |
| gaurvar | 5571 | NMT | NO | 13.69 | 0.662493 | 0.721531 |
| IITP-MT | 6294 | NMT | NO | 31.19 | 0.794791 | 0.803226 |
| SRPOL | 6248 | NMT | NO | 37.06 | 0.816956 | 0.817318 |
| SRPOL | 6274 | NMT | NO | 36.04 | 0.812816 | 0.814871 |
| CFILT | 6058 | NMT | NO | 30.46 | 0.772850 | 0.793769 |
| coastal | 6107 | NMT | NO | 19.61 | 0.737380 | 0.727657 |
| CFILT-IITB | 6119 | NMT | NO | 25.05 | 0.754313 | 0.770941 |
| CFILT-IITB | 6128 | NMT | NO | 26.34 | 0.761082 | 0.780009 |

Table 49: HINDEN21 or-en submissions

| System | ID | Type | RSRC | BLEU | RIBES | AMFM |
|---|---|---|---|---|---|---|
| ORGANIZER | 4803 | NMT | NO | 23.66 | 0.749459 | 0.701483 |
| NICT-5 | 5288 | NMT | NO | 34.34 | 0.816975 | 0.792541 |
| NICT-5 | 5363 | NMT | NO | 35.81 | 0.827528 | 0.800753 |
| NLPHut | 4615 | NMT | NO | 24.35 | 0.766047 | 0.717322 |
| mcairt | 6342 | NMT | NO | 38.42 | 0.840360 | 0.818332 |
| sakura | 5877 | NMT | NO | 40.38 | 0.844351 | 0.823464 |
| IIIT-H | 6023 | NMT | NO | 41.24 | 0.837608 | 0.811169 |
| gaurvar | 5551 | NMT | NO | 18.61 | 0.703876 | 0.693631 |
| gaurvar | 5572 | NMT | NO | 18.59 | 0.730487 | 0.694658 |
| IITP-MT | 6301 | NMT | NO | 38.41 | 0.839598 | 0.815989 |
| SRPOL | 6249 | NMT | NO | 46.39 | 0.865765 | 0.841641 |
| SRPOL | 6275 | NMT | NO | 44.87 | 0.861389 | 0.836440 |
| CFILT | 6059 | NMT | NO | 38.01 | 0.818396 | 0.804561 |
| coastal | 6168 | NMT | NO | 35.90 | 0.835327 | 0.814440 |
| CFILT-IITB | 6123 | NMT | NO | 29.87 | 0.795413 | 0.772655 |
| CFILT-IITB | 6129 | NMT | NO | 32.34 | 0.805722 | 0.782112 |

Table 50: HINDEN21 pa-en submissions

| System | ID | Type | RSRC | BLEU | RIBES | AMFM |
|---|---|---|---|---|---|---|
| ORGANIZER | 4805 | NMT | NO | 16.07 | 0.690144 | 0.675969 |
| NICT-5 | 5290 | NMT | NO | 24.72 | 0.766631 | 0.758282 |
| NICT-5 | 5365 | NMT | NO | 26.90 | 0.780120 | 0.772249 |
| NLPHut | 5984 | NMT | NO | 15.40 | 0.702428 | 0.669984 |
| mcairt | 6346 | NMT | NO | 28.04 | 0.793839 | 0.790184 |
| sakura | 5878 | NMT | NO | 31.09 | 0.806993 | 0.796074 |
| IIIT-H | 6024 | NMT | NO | 29.61 | 0.785332 | 0.750297 |
| gaurvar | 5563 | NMT | NO | 13.36 | 0.677433 | 0.687892 |
| gaurvar | 5573 | NMT | NO | 13.77 | 0.660037 | 0.688325 |
| IITP-MT | 6304 | NMT | NO | 27.76 | 0.788181 | 0.786587 |
| SRPOL | 6250 | NMT | NO | 36.13 | 0.822312 | 0.806540 |
| SRPOL | 6276 | NMT | NO | 35.06 | 0.815951 | 0.803595 |
| CFILT | 6060 | NMT | NO | 29.34 | 0.784291 | 0.785098 |
| coastal | 6169 | NMT | NO | 26.69 | 0.794380 | 0.786098 |
| CFILT-IITB | 6122 | NMT | NO | 21.37 | 0.747748 | 0.742311 |
| CFILT-IITB | 6132 | NMT | NO | 22.75 | 0.756364 | 0.745090 |

Table 51: HINDEN21 ta-en submissions

| System | ID | Type | RSRC | BLEU | RIBES | AMFM |
|---|---|---|---|---|---|---|
| ORGANIZER | 4807 | NMT | NO | 14.70 | 0.665774 | 0.636031 |
| NICT-5 | 5292 | NMT | NO | 27.76 | 0.777383 | 0.771109 |
| NICT-5 | 5367 | NMT | NO | 28.77 | 0.782427 | 0.779053 |
| NLPHut | 4619 | NMT | NO | 16.48 | 0.695348 | 0.674821 |
| mcairt | 6348 | NMT | NO | 29.26 | 0.790319 | 0.786396 |
| sakura | 5879 | NMT | NO | 33.87 | 0.810630 | 0.802030 |
| IIIT-H | 6025 | NMT | NO | 30.44 | 0.783709 | 0.754690 |
| gaurvar | 5564 | NMT | NO | 12.14 | 0.652408 | 0.668328 |
| gaurvar | 5574 | NMT | NO | 12.44 | 0.629617 | 0.666143 |
| IITP-MT | 6306 | NMT | NO | 28.13 | 0.784897 | 0.776964 |
| SRPOL | 6251 | NMT | NO | 39.80 | 0.836433 | 0.820889 |
| SRPOL | 6277 | NMT | NO | 38.57 | 0.831502 | 0.820360 |
| CFILT | 6061 | NMT | NO | 30.10 | 0.778981 | 0.783349 |
| coastal | 6170 | NMT | NO | 30.50 | 0.806646 | 0.799696 |
| CFILT-IITB | 6120 | NMT | NO | 22.37 | 0.746368 | 0.743435 |
| CFILT-IITB | 6133 | NMT | NO | 24.02 | 0.757702 | 0.745885 |

Table 52: HINDEN21 te-en submissions

| System | ID | Type | RSRC | BLEU | | | RIBES | | | AMFM |
|---|---|---|---|---|---|---|---|---|---|---|
| | | | | juman | kytea | mecab | juman | kytea | mecab | |
| TMU | 5347 | NMT | NO | 45.24 | 47.12 | 45.27 | 0.854558 | 0.853335 | 0.854298 | 0.876323 |

Table 53: JPCN en-ja submissions

| System | ID | Type | RSRC | BLEU | RIBES | AMFM |
|---|---|---|---|---|---|---|
| TMU | 5187 | NMT | NO | 43.78 | 0.857054 | 0.578009 |

Table 54: JPCN ja-en submissions

| System | ID | Type | RSRC | BLEU | RIBES | AMFM |
|---|---|---|---|---|---|---|
| NLPHut | 5231 | NMT | NO | 1.690000 | 0.095373 | 0.385495 |

Table 55: MMCHHI21 en-hi submissions

| System | ID | Type | RSRC | BLEU | RIBES | AMFM |
|---|---|---|---|---|---|---|
| NLPHut | 5439 | OTHER | NO | 0.990000 | 0.024940 | 0.383880 |

Table 56: MMCHHI21 en-ml submissions

| System | ID | Type | RSRC | BLEU | RIBES | AMFM |
|---|---|---|---|---|---|---|
| Volta | 6430 | NMT | YES | 51.600000 | 0.859645 | 0.877000 |
| CNLP-NITS-PP | 5730 | NMT | YES | 39.280000 | 0.792097 | 0.817356 |
| iitp | 5942 | NMT | NO | 37.500000 | 0.790809 | 0.823429 |

Table 57: MMCHMM21 en-hi submissions

| System | ID | Type | RSRC | BLEU | RIBES | AMFM |
|---|---|---|---|---|---|---|
| Volta | 6429 | NMT | YES | 51.660000 | 0.855410 | 0.876300 |
| NLPHut | 4623 | NMT | YES | 43.290000 | 0.824521 | 0.841544 |
| CNLP-NITS-PP | 5732 | NMT | YES | 37.160000 | 0.770621 | 0.797409 |

Table 58: MMCHTEXT21 en-hi submissions

| System | ID | Type | RSRC | BLEU | RIBES | AMFM |
|---|---|---|---|---|---|---|
| ORGANIZER | 6146 | NMT | NO | 12.980000 | 0.378045 | 0.603143 |
| NLPHut | 4621 | NMT | NO | 12.150000 | 0.373986 | 0.649550 |

Table 59: MMCHTEXT21 en-ml submissions

| System | ID | Type | RSRC | BLEU | RIBES | AMFM |
|---|---|---|---|---|---|---|
| NLPHut | 5400 | OTHER | NO | 1.300000 | 0.093243 | 0.333490 |

Table 60: MMEVHI21 en-hi submissions

| System | ID | Type | RSRC | BLEU | RIBES | AMFM |
|---|---|---|---|---|---|---|
| NLPHut | 5438 | OTHER | NO | 0.970000 | 0.047566 | 0.405275 |

Table 61: MMEVHI21 en-ml submissions

| System | ID | Type | RSRC | BLEU | RIBES | AMFM |
|---|---|---|---|---|---|---|
| Volta | 6428 | NMT | YES | 44.640000 | 0.823319 | 0.839100 |
| iitp | 5941 | NMT | NO | 42.470000 | 0.807123 | 0.629444 |
| CNLP-NITS-PP | 5731 | NMT | YES | 39.460000 | 0.802055 | 0.641430 |

Table 62: MMEVMM21 en-hi submissions

| System | ID | Type | RSRC | BLEU | RIBES | AMFM |
|---|---|---|---|---|---|---|
| Volta | 6427 | NMT | YES | 44.120000 | 0.821469 | 0.838180 |
| NLPHut | 4622 | NMT | YES | 42.110000 | 0.813837 | 0.634481 |
| CNLP-NITS-PP | 5733 | NMT | YES | 37.010000 | 0.795302 | 0.642785 |

Table 63: MMEVTEXT21 en-hi submissions

| System | ID | Type | RSRC | BLEU | RIBES | AMFM |
|---|---|---|---|---|---|---|
| ORGANIZER | 6145 | NMT | NO | 30.490000 | 0.580807 | 0.726976 |
| NLPHut | 4620 | NMT | NO | 34.830000 | 0.636404 | 0.798859 |

Table 64: MMEVTEXT21 en-ml submissions

| System | ID | Type | RSRC | BLEU | | | RIBES | | | AMFM |
|---|---|---|---|---|---|---|---|---|---|---|
| | | | | juman | kytea | mecab | juman | kytea | mecab | |
| TMEKU | 4730 | NMT | NO | 44.95 | 53.50 | 48.57 | 0.886046 | 0.890507 | 0.886316 | 0.644124 |
| TMEKU | 5452 | NMT | NO | 43.40 | 51.81 | 47.02 | 0.874392 | 0.880350 | 0.874700 | 0.644113 |
| sakura | 6313 | NMT | NO | 43.09 | 51.17 | 46.32 | 0.875110 | 0.879799 | 0.875825 | 0.644507 |

Table 65: MMT en-ja submissions

| System | ID | Type | RSRC | BLEU | RIBES | AMFM |
|---|---|---|---|---|---|---|
| sakura | 6349 | NMT | NO | 52.20 | 0.909991 | 0.577316 |

Table 66: MMT ja-en submissions

| System | ID | Type | RSRC | BLEU | | | RIBES | | | AMFM |
|---|---|---|---|---|---|---|---|---|---|---|
| | | | | juman | kytea | mecab | juman | kytea | mecab | |
| ORGANIZER | 4403 | NMT | NO | 22.65 | 28.16 | 24.75 | 0.781797 | 0.784997 | 0.778157 | 0.790050 |
| ORGANIZER | 4423 | NMT | NO | 25.73 | 31.46 | 27.77 | 0.804437 | 0.806973 | 0.801715 | 0.806910 |
| TMEKU | 4731 | NMT | NO | 28.79 | 34.33 | 31.04 | 0.809852 | 0.813066 | 0.810293 | 0.821745 |
| TMEKU | 5451 | NMT | NO | 28.23 | 33.71 | 30.23 | 0.806312 | 0.808009 | 0.800428 | 0.815016 |

Table 67: MSCOCO en-ja submissions

| System | ID | Type | RSRC | BLEU | RIBES | AMFM |
|---|---|---|---|---|---|---|
| ORGANIZER | 4404 | NMT | NO | 30.04 | 0.800134 | 0.757189 |
| ORGANIZER | 4422 | NMT | NO | 30.70 | 0.798426 | 0.755753 |

Table 68: MSCOCO ja-en submissions

| System | ID | Type | RSRC | BLEU | RIBES | AMFM |
|---|---|---|---|---|---|---|
| NICT-2 | 5900 | NMT | YES | 29.050000 | 0.651775 | 0.821077 |
| sakura | 5792 | NMT | NO | 28.500000 | 0.663932 | 0.826771 |

Table 69: SOFTWARE en-hi submissions

| System | ID | Type | RSRC | BLEU | RIBES | AMFM |
|---|---|---|---|---|---|---|
| NICT-2 | 5902 | NMT | YES | 43.25 | 0.767124 | 0.863589 |
| sakura | 5799 | NMT | NO | 45.39 | 0.759304 | 0.863010 |

Table 70: SOFTWARE en-id submissions

| System | ID | Type | RSRC | BLEU | RIBES | AMFM |
|---|---|---|---|---|---|---|
| NICT-2 | 5904 | NMT | YES | 40.76 | 0.823552 | 0.866766 |
| sakura | 5818 | NMT | NO | 42.26 | 0.838933 | 0.873296 |

Table 71: SOFTWARE en-ms submissions

| System | ID | Type | RSRC | BLEU | RIBES | AMFM |
|---|---|---|---|---|---|---|
| NICT-2 | 5906 | NMT | YES | 50.910000 | 0.770522 | 0.809907 |
| sakura | 5844 | NMT | NO | 55.640000 | 0.813347 | 0.829860 |

Table 72: SOFTWARE en-th submissions

| System | ID | Type | RSRC | BLEU | RIBES | AMFM |
|---|---|---|---|---|---|---|
| NICT-2 | 5901 | NMT | YES | 35.32 | 0.712675 | 0.843388 |
| sakura | 5795 | NMT | NO | 40.17 | 0.726708 | 0.861348 |

Table 73: SOFTWARE hi-en submissions

| System | ID | Type | RSRC | BLEU | RIBES | AMFM |
|---|---|---|---|---|---|---|
| NICT-2 | 5903 | NMT | YES | 40.69 | 0.745225 | 0.852173 |
| sakura | 5810 | NMT | NO | 44.70 | 0.759751 | 0.862999 |

Table 74: SOFTWARE id-en submissions

| System | ID | Type | RSRC | BLEU | RIBES | AMFM |
|---|---|---|---|---|---|---|
| NICT-2 | 5905 | NMT | YES | 38.42 | 0.818175 | 0.843418 |
| sakura | 5823 | NMT | NO | 40.97 | 0.819980 | 0.849354 |

Table 75: SOFTWARE ms-en submissions

| System | ID | Type | RSRC | BLEU | RIBES | AMFM |
|---|---|---|---|---|---|---|
| NICT-2 | 5907 | NMT | YES | 21.89 | 0.673464 | 0.787909 |
| sakura | 5846 | NMT | NO | 26.30 | 0.694253 | 0.809105 |

Table 76: SOFTWARE th-en submissions

# NHK's Lexically-Constrained Neural Machine Translation at WAT 2021

**Hideya Mino** [1,2] **Kazutaka Kinugawa** [1] **Hitoshi Ito** [1]
**Isao Goto** [1] **Ichiro Yamada** [1] **Takenobu Tokunaga** [2]
[1] NHK Science & Technology Research Laboratories
1-10-11 Kinuta, Setagaya-ku, Tokyo 157-8510, Japan
{mino.h-gq,kinugawa.k-jg,itou.h-ce,
goto.i-es,yamada.i-hy}@nhk.or.jp
[2] Tokyo Institute of Technology
2-12-1 Ookayama, Meguro-ku, Tokyo 152-8550, Japan
take@c.titech.ac.jp

## Abstract

This paper describes the system of our team (NHK) for the WAT 2021 Japanese↔English restricted machine translation task. In this task, the aim is to improve quality while maintaining consistent terminology for scientific paper translation. This task has a unique feature, where some words in a target sentence are given in addition to a source sentence. In this paper, we use a lexically-constrained neural machine translation (NMT), which concatenates the source sentence and constrained words with a special token to input them into the encoder of NMT. The key to the successful lexically-constrained NMT is the way to extract constraints from a target sentence of training data. We propose two extraction methods: proper-noun constraint and mistranslated-word constraint. These two methods consider the importance of words and fallibility of NMT, respectively. The evaluation results demonstrate the effectiveness of our lexical-constraint method.

## 1 Introduction

Our team (NHK) participated in the restricted machine translation task[1] using the Japanese-English dataset of the Asian scientific paper excerpt corpus (ASPEC-JE) (Nakazawa et al., 2016) at WAT 2021 (Nakazawa et al., 2021). In this task, the aim is to improve translation quality while preserving consistent terminology for translating scientific papers that include technical terms and proper nouns. In this task, a list of target words is given for each source sentence to appear in a target sentence. Figure 1 shows the overview of this task. There are two evaluation criteria: the translation accuracy via bilingual evaluation understudy (Papineni et al., 2002) (BLEU score) and the consistency score of the ratio of sentences satisfying an exact match of given constraints (consistency score). The final ranking is determined by the combined score of both: calculating BLEU with only the exact match sentences[2].

**Input**
**Source sentence**: この回路は，入力信号位相の変化により共振周波数がシフトする帰還回路であり，２基のコイルの中央にある物体の磁気特性の変化を，高い感度と分解能で検出することができる。

**Target-vocabulary list**: {magnetic features, resonance frequency, feedback circuit, resolution}

**Requirement for output**
Output sentence is required to contain all the target words in each target-vocabulary list.

**Reference**
This is a feedback circuit shifting resonance frequency by change of input signal phase, which can detect change of magnetic features of an object present at a center of two coils on high sensitivity and resolution.

Figure 1: Overview of the restricted translation task (Japanese→English).

In related work (Chen et al., 2020a; Song et al., 2019; Wang et al., 2019; Post and Vilar, 2018; Hokamp and Liu, 2017), since it does not require higher computational complexity than the other methods using the grid beam search (GBS) decoding algorithm (Hokamp and Liu, 2017; Post and Vilar, 2018), we use the lexical-constraint method of Chen et al. (2020a). This method concatenates a source sentence and constrained words with a special token to input them into an encoder of the neural machine translation

[1]https://sites.google.com/view/restricted-translation-task/

[2]If the translation does not satisfy the constraint, replace the translation with an empty string.



*Proceedings of the 8th Workshop on Asian Translation*, pages 46–52
Bangkok, Thailand (online), August 5-6, 2021. 

(NMT). In addition to the merit of reducing the computational cost compared with GBS decoding, this method has two other merits: no need to modify the architecture of the NMT system or prepare any word alignment data. In this method for this task, one of the main problems is how to extract constraints from training data since only constrained word lists for dev, devtest, and test sets are provided to participants.

In this paper, we propose extracting constraints from target sentences on the basis of proper-noun and mistranslated-word constraints considering the importance of words and fallibility of NMT. The former constraint is a list of proper nouns extracted with named-entity recognition. The latter constraint is a list of words mistranslated or under-translated with vanilla NMT compared with a target sentence. We conducted experiments to evaluate the NMT using the proposed method and found that the proposed method outperformed a baseline lexical-constraint method.

## 2 Restricted Translation Task Description

### 2.1 Official Dataset

The main dataset of the restricted translation task is the Japanese-English paper abstract corpus (ASPEC-JE) and the target vocabulary list as constraints. In addition to the main dataset, participants can use any other resources by mentioning their details. The ASPEC-JE dataset consists of training, dev, devtest, and test data. The training data contains 3.0 million bilingual pairs provided with similarity scores automatically calculated by DP matching (Utiyama and Isahara, 2007). The target vocabulary list for restricted translation is attached to the dev, devtest, and test data dedicated for this task. Participants are not told the detailed way to select constraints. Table 1 shows statistics of each data.

### 2.2 Official Evaluation

In this task, four distinct metrics are calculated: BLEU, RIBES (Isozaki et al., 2010), AMFM (Banchs et al., 2015), and consistency scores. The BLEU, RIBES, and AMFM scores are calculated in accordance with the WAT convention. The consistency score is the ratio of the number of sentences satisfying the exact match of given constrained words over the whole test corpus. The final score is calculated using both BLEU

| Language | Number of sentences | | | |
|---|---|---|---|---|
| pair | Train | Dev | Devtest | Test |
| JA-EN | 3.0M | 1,790 | 1,784 | 1,812 |
| | | (2.8/2.9) | (3.2/3.2) | (3.2/3.3) |

Table 1: Statistics of official data including ASPEC-JE and target vocabulary lists. Average numbers of constrained words per sentence (Left:Japanese / Right:English) are shown for the dev, devtest, and test data. There are no vocabulary lists for the training data.

and consistency scores by WAT 2021 organizers as below:

1. Check whether the translation satisfies the given constraints or not.
2. If the translation does not satisfy the constraint, replace the translation with an empty string.
3. Calculate BLEU with modified translations.

Furthermore, bilingual human annotators evaluate the top-ranked submitted systems based on source-based direct assessment (Federmann, 2018; Cettolo et al., 2017) and source-based contrastive assessment (Federmann, 2018; Sakaguchi and Van Durme, 2018).

## 3 NMT with Lexical Constraint

Borrowing Chen et al. (2020a)'s idea, we implemented a lexically-constrained NMT with encoder and decoder modules. We concatenated a source sentence and constrained words with a special token to input into the encoder, as illustrated in Figure 2. The key to the successful lexically-constrained NMT is the way to extract constraints from a target sentence. Though the constraints are given for the dev, devtest, and test data, they are not given for the training data. In this paper, we focus on the way to extract a constraint from the target sentence in training data for the training phase.

The simplest method of extracting a lexical constraint is randomly sampling words from the target sentence, as Chen et al. (2020a) did. Beyond the random sampling method, we propose two other directions with a focus on proper nouns and mistranslated words to extract the constrained words automatically from the target sentence.

- **Proper-Noun Constraint.** Though participants were not told the detailed way to se-

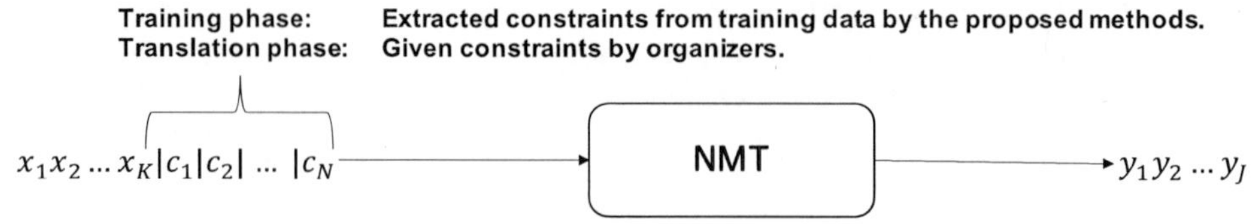


Figure 2: Overview of NMT using lexical-constraint method. $\boldsymbol{x} = (x_1, x_2, ..., x_K)$, $\boldsymbol{c} = (c_1, c_2, ..., c_N)$, and $\boldsymbol{t} = (y_1, y_2, ..., y_J)$ show source-, constraint-, and predicted-sequences, respectively. $K$ and $J$ are the lengths of source and target sentences. $N$ is a number of constrained words. "|" is a special token for delimiter. During the training phase, constraints are extracted from training data by the proposed methods. During the translation phase, constraints are given by WAT 2021 organizers.

lect constraints, we found that the vocabulary list in dev data includes many technical terms and proper nouns. Supposing that the important words such as technical terms and proper nouns tend to be selected as constraints, we extract proper nouns on the basis of the named-entity recognition.

- **Mistranslated-Word Constraint.** The proper-noun constraint is not enough to be sufficient to cover all constraints in this task. Given constrained words including the proper-noun constraints accounted for 21% of the Japanese dev data. To increase the number of appropriate constrained words, we extract mistranslated or dropped words by NMT as constraints. First, we trained an NMT model on parallel training data, and translated the source sentences in training data with this model. We then picked out the words that do not appear in the translated sentence but appear in the target sentence. Both proper-noun and mistranslated-word constraints could cover 38% of constraints for the dev data. The remaining 62% constrained words could be translated correctly without adding them as constraints.

- **Both the Proper-Noun and Mistranslated-Word Constraints.** Both constraints are made by concatenating the proper-noun and mistranslated-word constraints and removing duplicates.

## 4 Experiments

### 4.1 Data

In this paper, we used only the first 2.0 million bilingual pairs[3] in the official dataset, i.e., ASPEC-JE, with high similarity scores for training the models. We did not use any other resources.

### 4.2 System Setup

We used the KyTea (Neubig et al., 2011) to tokenize Japanese sentences and the Moses toolkit[4] to clean and tokenize English sentences. We then used a vocabulary of 48K tokens on the basis of joint byte-pair encoding (BPE) (Sennrich et al., 2016) for the source and target. We used the encoder and decoder of the transformer model (Vaswani et al., 2017), which is a state-of-the-art NMT model. The encoder converts a source sentence into a sequence of continuous representations, and the decoder generates a target sentence. We implemented this system with the Sockeye 2 toolkit (Hieber et al., 2020). All models were trained within at most three days on four Nvidia V100 Tesla GPUs with 16-GB memory in parallel. In training the model, we applied stochastic gradient descent with Adam (Kingma and Ba, 2015) as the optimizer, using a learning rate of 0.0002, multiplied by 0.7 after every 8 checkpoints. We set the batch size to 5000 tokens and the maximum sentence length to 150 BPE tokens. We applied early stopping with a patience of 32. Dropout was set to 0.1 for encoder, decoder, attention layer, and feed-forward layer after testing with 0.1, 0.3, and 0.5 using development data. For the other hyperparameters of the models, we used the default Sockeye 2 parameters[5].

Translation was carried out through a beam search with a beam size of 30, and we used an ensemble of 5 models with different seeds.

We used three types of constraints for the pro-

[3]The remaining 1.0 million bilingual pairs were often noisy as described in Neubig (2014). We found the performance degraded when using all data in this work.

[4]https://github.com/moses-smt/mosesdecoder

[5] Sockeye 2 uses a transformer model with 6 encoder and decoder layers, 8 parallel attention heads, model dimensionality of 512, and a feed-forward layer size of 2048 as default.

| Task | Method | Average of constrained words | Consistency rate (word) | BLEU |
|---|---|---|---|---|
| Japanese→English | Baseline | N/A | 52.3 | 29.3 |
| | Random-word | 4.99 | 78.6 | 29.5 |
| | Proper-noun | 1.25 | 78.8 | 36.3 |
| | Mistranslated-word | 4.68 | 86.1 | 39.2 |
| | Prop. & Mistrans. | 5.63 | **96.0** | **43.9** |
| English→Japanese | Baseline | N/A | 61.7 | 45.9 |
| | Random-word | 4.89 | 77.8 | 37.4 |
| | Proper-noun | 1.91 | 96.2 | 48.2 |
| | Mistranslated-word | 2.74 | 85.7 | 48.3 |
| | Prop. & Mistrans. | 4.48 | **97.4** | **53.2** |

Table 2: Experimental results for each task. Baseline is trained without any constraint, Random-word is trained with the randomly extracted constraint, Proper-noun is trained with the proper-noun constraint, Mistranslated-word is trained with the mistranslated-word constraint, and Prop. & Mistrans. is trained with both the proper-noun and mistranslated-word constraints. "Average of constrained word" shows the average number of constrained words per sentence.

posed method: the proper-noun constraint, the mistranslated-word constraint, and both, called "Proper-noun," "Mistranslated-word," and "Prop. & Mistrans.," respectively. For extracting the proper nouns from the target sentence, we used GiNZA 4.0[6] for Japanese and *en_core_web_sm* model of spaCy 2.3[7] for English. We used at most five words from candidates sorted on the basis of term-frequency inverse document frequency (TF-IDF) scores (Chen et al., 2020b) in each constraint.

To evaluate translation quality separately from the official evaluation, we calculated case-insensitive BLEU (Papineni et al., 2002) scores by using multi-bleu.perl[8] and a consistency rate of words, which is the ratio of the number of words appearing in the output of given constrained words.

### 4.3 Baselines

We trained two types of baselines using the transformer model.

1. **Baseline**: The model trained on the parallel data (2.0 million bilingual pairs) without any constraint.

2. **Random-word**: The model trained on the parallel data with constraints of five words randomly extracted from the target sentence. We extracted different constraints randomly for each epoch.

[6]https://megagonlabs.github.io/ginza/

[7]https://spacy.io/usage/v2-3

[8]https://github.com/moses-smt/mosesdecoder/blob/master/scripts/generic/multi-bleu-detok.perl

### 4.4 Experimental Results

Table 2 shows the experimental results for Japanese↔English tasks. Compared with the Baseline method, our proposed methods improved both consistency rates of words and BLEU scores for Japanese↔English tasks.

Though models using the Random-word method improved the consistency rate compared with Baseline, there is no or little improvement in BLEU scores. For the Japanese→English task, though the consistency rates of the Random-word and Proper-noun methods are almost same, the BLEU scores of the Proper-noun performed better than the Random-word method. The average number of constrained words of the Random-word method is higher than the Proper-noun method. This result indicates that translation quality highly depends on the way to extract constraints rather than the number of constraints.

From comparing among the versions of our proposed method using three types of constraints, the model using the Prop. & Mistrans. method performed the best for both the Japanese↔English tasks.

From comparing the use of the proper-noun and mistranslated-word constraints, the "Mistranslated-word" method performed better for Japanese→English, whereas the "Proper-noun" method performed better for

| Task | Method | BLEU | RIBES | AMFM | HUMAN DA | HUMAN CA | Final score |
|---|---|---|---|---|---|---|---|
| Japanese→English | Baseline | 29.25 | 0.77 | 0.62 | N/A | N/A | N/A |
| | Random-word | 29.49 | 0.68 | 0.52 | N/A | N/A | N/A |
| | Prop. & Mistrans. + rule | 42.94 | 0.80 | 0.66 | 74.1 | 77.2 | 33.9 |
| English→Japanese | Baseline | 45.93 | 0.85 | 0.76 | N/A | N/A | N/A |
| | Random-word | 37.43 | 0.80 | 0.70 | N/A | N/A | N/A |
| | Prop. & Mistrans. + rule | 52.69 | 0.82 | 0.80 | 73.9 | 73.5 | 37.5 |

Table 3: Official results (Japanese tokenizer:KyTea and English tokenizer:moses). HUMAN DA and CA is source-based direct assessment and source-based contrastive assessment. See 2.2 for the details of each evaluation criterion.

English→Japanese. In addition, there is no significant difference in the consistency rate of the mistranslated-word constraint between English→Japanese and Japanese→English. The proper-noun constraint for English→Japanese appears likely to be more similar to constraints of the test data than that for Japanese→English.

For the average number of constrained words, though the Random-word method has the most constrained words, it did not perform the best for either the consistency rate or BLEU score. The results indicate that the quality of the model using constraints relies on whether constraints are suitable for the task or not.

As a whole, we found that the using both the proper-noun and mistranslated-word constraints is effective for the restricted machine translation task.

### 4.5 Official Results

Table 3 lists the official results. For "Prop. & Mistrans. + rule" method, we input the unsatisfied constrained word, which does not appear in the output with the following procedure:

1. extracts unsatisfied words, which do not appear in the output, from the constrained words.
2. calculates Levenshtein distance between each unsatisfied word and each word in the output.
3. swaps the word of the output with the closest distance for the unsatisfied word.

The outputs of the "Prop. & Mistrans. + rule" method satisfy all given constraints. The official results indicate the effectiveness of using the proposed constraints in terms of the human evaluation since the rankings of "BLEU," "HUMAN DA," "HUMAN CA," and "Final score" are the same as among participants of this task at WAT 2021.

## 5 Conclusion

We described our proposed method using lexical constraints for a Japanese↔English restricted machine translation task with the Asian scientific paper excerpt corpus (ASPEC). We proposed a method to extract appropriate constraints of the lexically-constrained neural machine translation (NMT) for this task. Our proposed method using the proper-noun and mistranslated-word constraints improved translation performance compared with random-word constraint.

For future work, we plan to apply the proposed constraints into NMT with a grid beam search decoding algorithm (Hokamp and Liu, 2017; Post and Vilar, 2018) to compare the performance.

## References


Rafael E. Banchs, Luis F. D'Haro, and Haizhou Li. 2015. Adequacy-fluency metrics: Evaluating MT in the continuous space model framework. *IEEE ACM Trans. Audio Speech Lang. Process.*, 23(3):472–482.

Mauro Cettolo, Marcello Federico, Luisa Bentivogli, Jan Niehues, Sebastian Stüker, Katsuhito Sudoh, Koichiro Yoshino, and Christian Federmann. 2017. Overview of the IWSLT 2017 evaluation campaign. In *2017 International Workshop on Spoken Language Translation, IWSLT 2017, Tokyo, Japan*, pages 2–14.

Guanhua Chen, Yun Chen, Yong Wang, and Victor O.K. Li. 2020a. Lexical-constraint-aware neural machine translation via data augmentation. In *Proceedings of the Twenty-Ninth International Joint Conference on Artificial Intelligence, IJCAI-20*, pages 3587–3593. International Joint Conferences on Artificial Intelligence Organization. Main track.

Kehai Chen, Rui Wang, Masao Utiyama, and Eiichiro Sumita. 2020b. Content word aware neural machine translation. In *Proceedings of the 58th Annual Meeting of the Association for Computational Linguistics*, pages 358–364, Online. Association for Computational Linguistics.

Christian Federmann. 2018. Appraise evaluation framework for machine translation. In *Proceedings of the 27th International Conference on Computational Linguistics: System Demonstrations*, pages 86–88, Santa Fe, New Mexico. Association for Computational Linguistics.

Felix Hieber, Tobias Domhan, Michael Denkowski, and David Vilar. 2020. Sockeye 2: A toolkit for neural machine translation. In *Proceedings of the 22nd Annual Conference of the European Association for Machine Translation*, pages 457–458, Lisboa, Portugal. European Association for Machine Translation.

Chris Hokamp and Qun Liu. 2017. Lexically constrained decoding for sequence generation using grid beam search. In *Proceedings of the 55th Annual Meeting of the Association for Computational Linguistics (Volume 1: Long Papers)*, pages 1535–1546, Vancouver, Canada. Association for Computational Linguistics.

Hideki Isozaki, Tsutomu Hirao, Kevin Duh, Katsuhito Sudoh, and Hajime Tsukada. 2010. Automatic evaluation of translation quality for distant language pairs. In *Proceedings of the 2010 Conference on Empirical Methods in Natural Language Processing*, pages 944–952, Cambridge, MA. Association for Computational Linguistics.

Diederick P Kingma and Jimmy Ba. 2015. Adam: A method for stochastic optimization. In *International Conference on Learning Representations (ICLR)*.

Toshiaki Nakazawa, Hideki Nakayama, Chenchen Ding, Raj Dabre, Shohei Higashiyama, Hideya Mino, Isao Goto, Win Pa Pa, Anoop Kunchukuttan, Shantipriya Parida, Ondřej Bojar, Chenhui Chu, Akiko Eriguchi, Kaori Abe, Yusuke Oda, and Sadao Kurohashi. 2021. Overview of the 8th workshop on Asian translation. In *Proceedings of the 8th Workshop on Asian Translation*, Bangkok, Thailand. Association for Computational Linguistics.

Toshiaki Nakazawa, Manabu Yaguchi, Kiyotaka Uchimoto, Masao Utiyama, Eiichiro Sumita, Sadao Kurohashi, and Hitoshi Isahara. 2016. ASPEC: Asian scientific paper excerpt corpus. In *Proceedings of the Tenth International Conference on Language Resources and Evaluation (LREC'16)*, pages 2204–2208, Portorož, Slovenia. European Language Resources Association (ELRA).

Graham Neubig. 2014. Forest-to-string SMT for Asian language translation: NAIST at WAT 2014. In *Proceedings of the 1st Workshop on Asian Translation (WAT2014)*, pages 20–25, Tokyo, Japan. Workshop on Asian Translation.

Graham Neubig, Yosuke Nakata, and Shinsuke Mori. 2011. Pointwise prediction for robust, adaptable Japanese morphological analysis. In *Proceedings of the 49th Annual Meeting of the Association for Computational Linguistics: Human Language Technologies*, pages 529–533, Portland, Oregon, USA. Association for Computational Linguistics.

Kishore Papineni, Salim Roukos, Todd Ward, and Wei-Jing Zhu. 2002. Bleu: a method for automatic evaluation of machine translation. In *Proceedings of the 40th Annual Meeting of the Association for Computational Linguistics*, pages 311–318, Philadelphia, Pennsylvania, USA. Association for Computational Linguistics.

Matt Post and David Vilar. 2018. Fast lexically constrained decoding with dynamic beam allocation for neural machine translation. In *Proceedings of the 2018 Conference of the North American Chapter of the Association for Computational Linguistics: Human Language Technologies, Volume 1 (Long Papers)*, pages 1314–1324, New Orleans, Louisiana. Association for Computational Linguistics.

Keisuke Sakaguchi and Benjamin Van Durme. 2018. Efficient online scalar annotation with bounded support. In *Proceedings of the 56th Annual Meeting of the Association for Computational Linguistics (Volume 1: Long Papers)*, pages 208–218, Melbourne, Australia. Association for Computational Linguistics.

Rico Sennrich, Barry Haddow, and Alexandra Birch. 2016. Neural machine translation of rare words with subword units. In *Proceedings of the 54th Annual Meeting of the Association for Computational Linguistics (Volume 1: Long Papers)*, pages 1715–1725, Berlin, Germany. Association for Computational Linguistics.

Kai Song, Yue Zhang, Heng Yu, Weihua Luo, Kun Wang, and Min Zhang. 2019. Code-switching for enhancing NMT with pre-specified translation. In *Proceedings of the 2019 Conference of the North American Chapter of the Association for Computational Linguistics: Human Language Technologies, Volume 1 (Long and Short Papers)*, pages 449–459, Minneapolis, Minnesota. Association for Computational Linguistics.

Masao Utiyama and Hitoshi Isahara. 2007. A Japanese-English patent parallel corpus. *Proceedings of Machine Translation Summit XI, Copenhagen, Denmark, 2007*, pages 457–482.

Ashish Vaswani, Noam Shazeer, Niki Parmar, Jakob Uszkoreit, Llion Jones, Aidan N Gomez, Ł ukasz Kaiser, and Illia Polosukhin. 2017. Attention is all you need. In I. Guyon, U. V. Luxburg, S. Bengio, H. Wallach, R. Fergus, S. Vishwanathan, and R. Garnett, editors, *Advances in Neural Information Processing Systems 30*, pages 5998–6008. Curran Associates, Inc.

Longyue Wang, Zhaopeng Tu, Xing Wang, and Shuming Shi. 2019. One model to learn both: Zero pronoun prediction and translation. In *Proceedings of the 2019 Conference on Empirical Methods in Natural Language Processing and the 9th International Joint Conference on Natural Language Processing (EMNLP-IJCNLP)*, pages 921–930, Hong Kong, China. Association for Computational Linguistics.

# Input Augmentation Improves Constrained Beam Search for Neural Machine Translation: NTT at WAT 2021

**Katsuki Chousa*** and **Makoto Morishita***
NTT Communication Science Laboratories, NTT Corporation
2-4, Hikaridai, Seika-cho, Soraku-gun, Kyoto, 619-0237, Japan
{katsuki.chousa.bg, makoto.morishita.gr}@hco.ntt.co.jp

## Abstract

This paper describes our systems that were submitted to the restricted translation task at WAT 2021. In this task, the systems are required to output translated sentences that contain all given word constraints. Our system combined input augmentation and constrained beam search algorithms. Through experiments, we found that this combination significantly improves translation accuracy and can save inference time while containing all the constraints in the output. For both En→Ja and Ja→En, our systems obtained the best translation performances in both automatic and human evaluations.

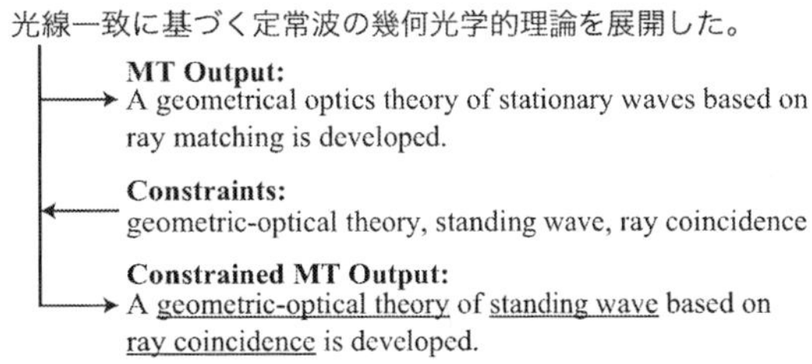


Figure 1: Overview of the restricted translation task

## 1 Introduction

This year, we participated in the restricted translation task at WAT 2021 (Nakazawa et al., 2021), in which we were asked to control a model so that the translation output would contain specified terms. Although the recent neural machine translation (NMT) model achieves excellent performance, controlling its output is still a challenging task. Figure 1 shows an overview of the task. Each sentence includes the target words (constraints) that must be contained in the output. We believe this task reflects a critical function, especially in practical applications. For example, users may want to control the translation of technical terms or proper nouns.

Several works have tried to control the NMT outputs, and these works can be divided into two categories: *hard* and *soft* methods. The hard lexically constrained method guarantees that all the target words are in the output. Current works achieve this by modifying the beam search algorithm to find the hypothesis that contains all of the target words (Hokamp and Liu, 2017; Post and Vilar, 2018). The hard method guarantees all constraints are satisfied, but its translation performance is sometimes lower than the conventional NMT. This is because it requires all given target words to be contained in the decoding step, which may disrupt the model inference.

The soft lexically constrained method, on the other hand, does not guarantee that all target words are contained in the output. These methods usually modify or augment the input of the NMT model and try to output the given target words without changing the decoding algorithm (Song et al., 2019; Chen et al., 2020). Its decoding speed is usually faster than the hard method, but some of the constraints may not be satisfied.

Our submission aims to contain all of the specified target words with high translation accuracy. To achieve this goal, we applied both input augmentation and constrained beam search algorithms. To the best of our knowledge, this is the first work that combines these two methods. Through experiments, we found that this combination achieves quite high translation performance while containing all target words in the output and saving inference time. We submitted the systems to the English-to-Japanese (En→Ja) and Japanese-to-English (Ja→En) tasks, and we were ranked first in both language pairs in terms of BLEU scores and human evaluations.

*Equal contribution.



*Proceedings of the 8th Workshop on Asian Translation*, pages 53–61
Bangkok, Thailand (online), August 5-6, 2021. 

## 2 Task Definition

Suppose we have a source sentence $X = (x_1, x_2, \ldots, x_S)$ with $S$ tokens and a target sentence $Y = (y_1, y_2, \ldots, y_T)$ with $T$ tokens. In a conventional machine translation approach, the problem of translation from $X$ to $Y$ can be solved by finding the best target sentence that maximizes the conditional probability

$$p(Y \mid X) = \prod_{t=1}^{T} p(y_t \mid y_{<t}, X). \quad (1)$$

In the restricted translation task, lists of target words are provided to represent word restrictions, and systems are required to output translations that contain all of the target words in each list. Here, the problem of translation with word constraints can be defined as

$$p(Y \mid X, C) = \prod_{t=1}^{T} p(y_t \mid y_{<t}, X, C), \quad (2)$$

where $C = (C_1, C_2, \ldots, C_N)$ is the provided word constraints with $N$ phrases, and the constraints are given in random order.

The performance of systems in this task is evaluated through two metrics:

- Translation accuracy: BLEU (Papineni et al., 2002) is used for evaluation in this task.
- Consistency score: The percentage of sentences that correctly contain the given constraints over the entire test set.

For the final ranking, the combined score of the above metrics is calculated as follows:

1. If the translation does not contain all of the constraints based on exact matching, replace the translation with an empty string.
2. Calculate BLEU scores with modified translations.

## 3 Data

### 3.1 Provided Data

In this task, we were asked to translate an English/Japanese scientific paper. As the in-domain training data, organizers provided ASPEC (Nakazawa et al., 2016), which contains three million parallel sentences. Since this corpus is

| | |
|---|---|
| Architecture | Transformer (big) |
| Tied-embeddings | Tied the encoder/decoder embeddings and the decoder output layer |
| Optimizer | Adam ($\beta_1 = 0.9, \beta_2 = 0.98, \epsilon = 1 \times 10^{-8}$) (Kingma and Ba, 2015) |
| Learning Rate Schedule | Inverse square root decay |
| Warmup Steps | 4,000 |
| Max Learning Rate | 0.001 |
| Dropout | 0.3 |
| Gradient Clipping | 1.0 |
| Label Smoothing | $\epsilon_{ls} = 0.1$ (Szegedy et al., 2016) |
| Mini-batch Size | 512,000 tokens (Ott et al., 2018) |
| Number of Updates | 8,000 steps |
| Averaging | Save checkpoint for every 100 steps and take an average of last 8 checkpoints |

Table 1: List of hyperparameters

ordered by the sentence-alignment quality, the sentences at the end might be noisy. Following a previous work (Morishita et al., 2017), we used only the first two million sentences as parallel sentences. We treated the final one million sentences as monolingual data and created a synthetic corpus (Sennrich et al., 2016). Based on a previous analysis (Morishita et al., 2019), we forward-translated it for the Japanese-English task and back-translated it for the English-Japanese task.

### 3.2 Other Resources

We also trained the model with additional resources. As an additional parallel corpus, we used JParaCrawl (Morishita et al., 2020), which contains 10 million sentence pairs.

We also used CommonCrawl provided by the WMT 2020 news shared task (Barrault et al., 2020) as additional monolingual data. For CommonCrawl data, we chose the ten million English and Japanese sentences that are similar to the scientific domain based on the language model trained with ASPEC (Moore and Lewis, 2010). Then we further filtered out the following noisy sentences: (1) non-English/Japanese sentences with CLD2 [1], (2) excessively long sentences (more than 250 subwords), (3) sentences that contain out-of-vocabulary characters. After cleaning, we kept 7.9 million English and 9.2 million Japanese sentences. We then back-translated these sentences with the NMT model trained with ASPEC to make a synthetic corpus.

| Setting | BLEU | Term% | Sent% |
|---|---|---|---|
| BASE | 29.4 | 50.80 | 23.3 |
| + LCD (beam=60) | 24.0 | 94.40 | 85.3 |
| LeCA | 42.2 | 87.64 | 72.02 |
| + LCD (beam=30) | 43.9 | 94.34 | 85.21 |

Table 2: Comparison of translation accuracy and consistency score for each setting on Ja→En.

## 4 System Details

### 4.1 Base Model and Hyperparameters

As a baseline system, we employed the Transformer model with the big setting (Vaswani et al., 2017). Table 1 shows the detailed settings and hyperparameters. As an NMT implementation, we used `fairseq` (Ott et al., 2019), and modified it in the following experiments.

### 4.2 Lexically Constrained Decoding

We used the lexically constrained decoding (LCD) technique (Hokamp and Liu, 2017; Post and Vilar, 2018) to incorporate constraints at decoding time. In this task, the translations that do not satisfy the constraints lead to a substantial decrease in the final score. This technique is a hard lexically constrained method that uses grid beam search algorithm, and it guarantees that all word constraints appear in the target sentence.

To evaluate the effectiveness of this technique, we compared the baseline model (BASE) and the baseline with LCD (BASE+LCD). Here, we used two metrics for the consistency score: term% is the percentage of constraints that are correctly generated in the translations, and sent% is the percentage of sentences that contain all given constraints. Table 2 shows that the BASE+LCD significantly improves both term% and sent% on Ja→En. The reason why the two consistency scores of BASE+LCD are not 100% is due to the normalization on the tokenization, and this can be addressed by post-processing (§4.7).

However, BASE+LCD decreased the translation accuracy of the model. In preliminary experiments with the baseline models, we also found that the beam size needs to be larger than 60 to successfully generate all the constraints in this task. This is because the translations contain much repetition and the model never finishes generation before reaching the maximum output length.

[1]`https://github.com/CLD2Owners/cld2`

### 4.3 LExical-Constraint-Aware NMT

To ease the problem in LCD, we used the Lexical-Constraint-Aware NMT (LeCA) model (Chen et al., 2020), whose input is augmented by concatenating constraints and the source sentence together. This method can inform the model of what constraints are given before decoding time, and thus the model can properly decide where to output a constraint. LeCA is a one of the soft lexically constrained methods, which do not guarantee all constraints are in the output. However, in combination with LCD, we can guarantee the model always satisfies the constraints while keeping or improving the translation performance.

The input is constructed by concatenating the source sentence $X$ and each phrase $C_i$ in the constraints $C$ with a separator symbol $\langle \texttt{sep} \rangle$, as follows:

$$[X, \langle \texttt{sep} \rangle, C_1, \langle \texttt{sep} \rangle, C_2, \ldots, C_N, \langle \texttt{eos} \rangle], \quad (3)$$

where $\langle \texttt{eos} \rangle$ is the symbol indicating the end of the sentence.

To construct the input at training time, Chen et al. (2020) proposed a method that dynamically samples constraints from a reference sentence. They first sampled the number of constrained words $k$, and then they randomly sampled $k$ target words (not subwords) as constraints from the reference. Here, we sampled the number of constrained words $k$ from 0 to 14 following the distribution that is $p = 0.4$ for 0 and $p = 0.6/14 (= 0.04)$ for the other ones. The high probability for no constraint is to maintain the translation performance for unconstrained settings.

To handle such a source sequence, this method modifies the input representation of the encoder to distinguish the source sentence and each constraint. This representation is composed of three types of learned embeddings: token embeddings, positional embeddings, and segment embeddings, as shown in Fig. 2. The position of each constraint starts from the maximum length of the source sentences to avoid overlapping with the sentence. We assigned different values for the source sentence and each constraint and fed it to the model with the segment embeddings. This method also introduces a pointer network architecture(Vinyals et al., 2015; See et al., 2017) that helps to generate constraints by copying from the source sequence. Finally, we updated the models with 10,000 steps for Ja→En and 12,000 steps for En→Ja and set the beam size to 30 for

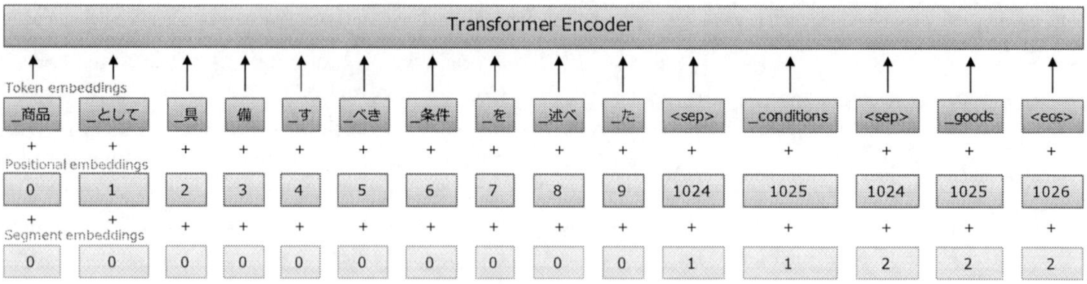


Figure 2: Input representation of the LeCA model.

| Tokenizer | BLEU | Term% | Sent% |
|---|---|---|---|
| MeCab + ipadic | 44.8 | 68.67 | 43.87 |
| MeCab + NEologd | 46.5 | 72.35 | 49.39 |

Table 3: Comparison of translation performance when changing the dictionary of tokenizer on En→Ja. The model setting is LeCA with a few updates.

LCD.

We evaluated the effectiveness of LeCA and LeCA with LCD (LeCA+LCD). Table 2 shows that LeCA achieved high translation accuracy and consistency scores. The input of both LeCA and BASE+LCD are the same, but the translation accuracy of LeCA is significantly better than that of BASE+LCD. Moreover, LeCA+LCD with a small beam size improves the translation accuracy and satisfies all of the constraints. This implies that inputting both a source sentence and constraints as source sequence is very effective for improving the performance in this task.

### 4.4 Pre-process

Since constraints that are sampled from the reference are given as not a subword but a word, we need to separate the sentence into words. To do this, we first tokenized both the input and output sentences. For English, we simply applied the tokenizer scripts available in the `Moses` toolkit (Koehn et al., 2007). We used the Moses `truecaser` when the target language is English. For Japanese, we use the `MeCab` tokenizer (Kudo, 2006) with the `mecab-ipadic-NEologd` (Sato, 2015) dictionary. This dictionary contains many neologisms and thus it helps in handling named entities or technical terms, which are included in ASPEC but cannot be tokenized correctly using the default system dictionary. We compared the LeCA performance of `mecab-ipadic-NEologd` with the default system dictionary on an En→Ja task. Table 3 shows that `mecab-ipadic-NEologd` significantly improved translation accuracy and consistency scores. We confirmed that using `mecab-ipadic-NEologd` is the best option for LeCA on this task.

Then, we trained subword encoding models using the `sentencepiece` implementation (Kudo and Richardson, 2018). According to an earlier work (Morishita et al., 2019), a smaller vocabulary size (e.g., 4,000) is empirically superior to the commonly used ones (e.g., 32,000). On the other hand, larger vocabulary size is preferred for an LCD to keep the number of constraint tokens small. This is because a large number of tokens requires a large beam size of the LCD and increases the inference time. Finally, we found in a preliminary experiment that a vocabulary size of 32,000 achieved the best results, so we used a joint subword vocabulary with 32,000 tokens. For training data, we applied the Moses `clean-corpus-n` scripts to remove sentence pairs that are either too long or too different int their lengths[2].

### 4.5 Fine-Tuning and Data Selection

The synthetic corpora (e.g., ASPEC last 1M and CommonCrawl) contain noisy sentence pairs, and the domain of JParaCrawl is different from that of ASPEC, a scientific paper domain. We used these corpora to make the translations more fluent. The model was initially pre-trained with these corpora and the first 2M sentence pairs of ASPEC for 12,000 updates. We then fine-tuned the pre-trained model using only the first 2M sentence pairs of ASPEC for 2,000 steps. For the pre-training, we oversampled ASPEC three-times to keep roughly the same number of sentences as the synthetic cor-

[2] We set the minimum length to 1, the maximum length to 250, and the maximum ratio of lengths to 9.

| Setting | BLEU Ja→En | En→Ja |
|---|---|---|
| ASPEC 2M | 44.34 | —[3] |
| + synth 1M | 44.26 | 56.57 |
| after pre-training | 44.28 | 56.47 |

Table 4: Effectiveness of fine-tuning. The model settings are LeCA+LCD.

| Model type | BLEU En→Ja | Ja→En |
|---|---|---|
| Single model | 55.49 | 43.44 |
| 8 Ensemble | 56.57 | 44.34 |

Table 5: Effectiveness of ensembling models. The model settings are LeCA+LCD.

pora.

We searched for an effective setting to use the training data. Table 4 shows the results. The model using only ASPEC 2M for En→Ja and the model using ASPEC 2M and forward-translated ASPEC last 1M for Ja→En achieved the highest translation accuracies. For both En→Ja and Ja→En, the models trained on ASPEC 2M after pre-training achieved comparable results to the best ones. Since these models are trained on large amounts of parallel sentence pairs, they might be expected to produce more natural output than the best ones and thus be preferred by humans. Therefore, we decided to submit these four models for human evaluation.

### 4.6 Ensemble

We applied a model ensemble technique to improve the translation accuracy. First, eight models were trained with different random seeds. We then computed the average scores of these models and generated hypotheses based on these scores using beam search decoding.

Table 5 shows the effectiveness of ensembling models. Ensembling the eight models shows a significant improvement over the single model.

### 4.7 Post-processing

For the submission, we need to match the tokenization to the reference constraints. To achieve this, we fixed the terms that are not matched to the constraints due to tokenization issues. Specifically, for each unmatched constraint, we removed spaces in both the output and the constraint, and then replaced the constraint in the output with the reference-spaced constraint. In some cases, we found that constraints may contain out-of-vocabulary (OOV) characters, resulting in translation failure[4]. The model outputs the special OOV tokens for these sentence, and thus we replaced them with correct characters in the reference constraint.

## 5 Official Results

Table 6 shows the automatic evaluated performance of our systems on the test set. These scores were measured in the evaluation server[5]. The best systems improved the BLEU score by +11.93 pts for En→Ja and +15.04 pts for Ja→En against the BASE. Our systems achieved the best BLEU score for both En→Ja and Ja→En subtasks.

Table 7 shows the official results of our systems[6]. For both En→Ja and Ja→En, our systems achieved the best scores in the final ranking. Our submissions did not drop the scores from the BLEU, while the other participants dropped it. This means that our team only succeeded in implementing systems whose translation output could contain all the specified terms. Our systems also achieved the best performance in terms of human evaluations for both En→Ja and Ja→En. Notably, our scores are better than the reference ones even for Ja→En. This implies that constrained translation can yield human-parity performance when the system can receive appropriate terms in the target language.

## 6 Analysis

Figure 3 shows the example translation of the baseline and LeCA with lexically constrained decoding. Underlines in Figure 3 show the terms that match the constraints. Obviously, the baseline model generated the same term repeatedly and failed to translate while all of the constraints were satisfied. The baseline model appears to struggle with generating

[3] In a preliminary experiment on En→Ja, we found that a model using synthetic data was superior to that using only ASPEC 2M. However, we did not compare the three settings under the same conditions.

[4] We found that two percent of the lines in the test set include OOV characters.

[5] http://lotus.kuee.kyoto-u.ac.jp/WAT/evaluation/index.html

[6] The results of all participants are reported in https://sites.google.com/view/restricted-translation-task/#h.g3vfoh2oljpq

| ID | Setting | BLEU En→Ja | BLEU Ja→En |
|---|---|---|---|
| (a) | BASE (§4.1) | 44.64 | 29.30 |
| (b) | BASE + LCD (§4.2) | 45.38 | 23.22 |
| (c) | LeCA (§4.3) | 53.79 | 41.88 |
| (d) | LeCA + LCD | 55.49 | 43.33 |
| (e) | (d) × 8 ensemble (§4.6) | **56.57** | **44.34** |
| (f) | [(d) + fine-tuning (§4.5)] × 8 | 56.47 | 44.28 |

Table 6: The performance of the submitted systems. According to §4.5, we used only ASPEC 2M for En→Ja and ASPEC 2M + synth 2M for Ja→En. For En→Ja, we show BLEU scores with `MeCab` tokenizer. Bold values indicate the highest score in each column.

| | Automatic Eval. | | Human Eval. | | | |
|---|---|---|---|---|---|---|
| **Language pair** | **Final score** | **(Rank)** | **DA** | **(Rank)** | **CA** | **(Rank)** |
| En→Ja | 57.2 | (1) | 77.5 | (1) | 79.7 | (1) |
| Ja→En | 44.1 | (1) | 75.6 | (1) | 74.4 | (1) |

Table 7: Official results of our team. The definition of the final score is described in §2. Human evaluations are based on source-based direct assessment (DA) (Cettolo et al., 2017; Federmann, 2018) and source-based contrastive assessment (CA) (Sakaguchi and Van Durme, 2018; Federmann, 2018).

the constraint "superconductivity single phase autotransformer." One likely reason for this is that the baseline model generated a phrase that was quite similar to the constraint in the early phase (marked with a wavy line in Figure 3), and thus the model considered the constraint as translated.

In contrast, LeCA+LCD successfully translated the sentence with the constraints. We believe this is because the LeCA model correctly gives higher scores to the constraint phrases compared to the baselines, helping to generate a sentence with constraints.

Figure 4 shows the BLEU scores of En→Ja translation decoding with various beam sizes. As mentioned in §4.2, the beam size of BASE+LCD needs to be larger than 60 to successfully generate all of the constraints. In contrast, LeCA+LCD can generate all of the constraints and improve the translation accuracy even when their beam size is quite small. This result indicates that the output of LeCA is helpful for LCD to score the candidates and that LeCA can save inference time.

## 7 Related Work

Hokamp and Liu (2017) proposed Grid Beam Search (GBS), an extended beam search algorithm that forces the NMT model to output pre-specified lexical constraints of words or phrases. At each decoding step, a beam is allocated to each number of constraints, and the top-k candidates that contain $n$ constraints are selected for the $n^{\text{th}}$ beam. Translations that satisfy the constraints appear in the beam corresponding to the number of constraints. The beam size changes depending on the number of constraints for each sentence, which makes batch decoding difficult. Post and Vilar (2018) proposed Dynamic Beam Allocation (DBA), which dynamically allocates the beam with a fixed size and improves decoding more efficiently. However, the distribution of the number of constraint tokens in the experiments of these papers was much smaller than that of this task, and we found these methods did not perform well on this task.

Song et al. (2020) and Chen et al. (2021) proposed lexically constrained decoding given explicit alignment guidance between the constraints and the source text. Alignments were induced from an additional alignment head or attention weights (Garg et al., 2019), but these methods assumed that gold alignments are given as constraints. To apply these methods to this task, we would have to use an automatic alignment method (e.g., GIZA++, Fast-Align) to obtain the alignments, and the translation accuracy might suffer due to alignment error.

Susanto et al. (2020) proposed non-autoregressive NMT for lexically constrained

| **Source** | 分路巻線のみに補助巻線を持つ超電導単相単巻変圧器を試作した。 |
|---|---|
| **Reference** | Superconductivity single phase auto-transformer with auxiliary winding only at the shunt winding was produced experimentally. |
| **Constraints** | shunt winding, auxiliary winding, superconductivity single phase auto-transformer |
| **Base+LCD** | We have developed a superconducting single - phase transformer with auxiliary windings only in the shunt windings, in which the auxiliary windings are connected to the shunt windings of the single - phase transformer, and the auxiliary windings are connected to the shunt windings of the single - phase transformer with auxiliary windings of the auxiliary windings of the auxiliary windings of the auxiliary windings of the auxiliary windings of the auxiliary windings of the auxiliary windings of the auxiliary windings of the auxiliary windings of the auxiliary windings. Superconductivity single phase auto - transformer is assisted by the auxiliary windings of the auxiliary windings. |
| **LeCA+LCD** | A superconductivity single phase auto-transformer with auxiliary winding only in the shunt winding was produced experimentally. |

Figure 3: Example translation: Underlines show the matched constraints, and wavy lines show the phrases that the models fail to match.

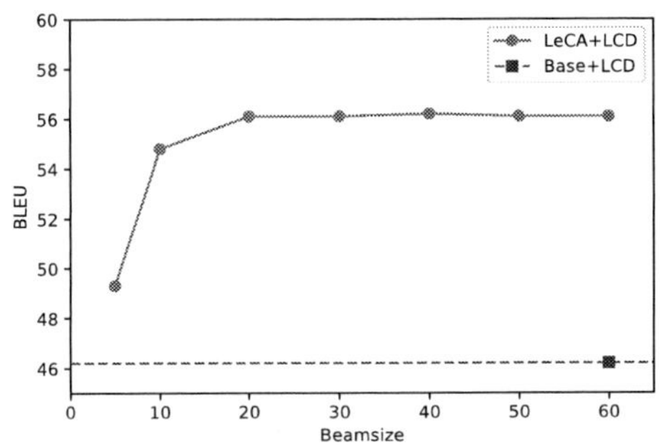


Figure 4: BLEU scores of En→Ja translation decoding with various beam sizes. The BLEU scores are calculated with `sacreblue` (Post, 2018)

translation. They used the Levenshtein Transformer (Gu et al., 2019), which inserts and deletes tokens at each time step, starting from the given constraints as the initial state. They assumed that the order of the given constraints is the same as the order in the reference, but the given constraints in this task appear in random order. Furthermore, they have not achieved comparable translation accuracy to the auto-regressive approaches.

Some works augment the input sequence with constraints. Song et al. (2019) augmented the source sentence by replacing or appending constraints with its corresponding source phrase through leveraging an SMT phrase table. Chen et al. (2020) proposed a simple yet effective augmentation method that appends constraints after the source sentence. Although the decoding speed is fast, Song et al. (2019) relied on the quality of the SMT phrase table. Furthermore, neither of the works could guarantee that the translation would contains all constraints.

## 8 Conclusion

This paper described the systems that were submitted to the WAT 2021 restricted translation task. We submitted systems for both En→Ja and Ja→En, and both of our systems won the best translation accuracy as assessed by BLEU, the consistency score, and human evaluations. We also confirmed that the data augmentation method makes lexically constrained decoding more effective and, furthermore, that combining data augmentation and constrained decoding significantly improves translation accuracy.

## References


Loïc Barrault, Magdalena Biesialska, Ondřej Bojar, Marta R. Costa-jussà, Christian Federmann, Yvette Graham, Roman Grundkiewicz, Barry Haddow, Matthias Huck, Eric Joanis, Tom Kocmi, Philipp Koehn, Chi-kiu Lo, Nikola Ljubešić, Christof Monz, Makoto Morishita, Masaaki Nagata, Toshiaki Nakazawa, Santanu Pal, Matt Post, and Marcos Zampieri. 2020. Findings of the 2020 conference on machine translation (WMT20). In *Proceedings of the 5th Conference on Machine Translation (WMT)*, pages 1–55.

Mauro Cettolo, Marcello Federico, Luisa Bentivogli, Jan Niehues, Sebastian Stüker, Katsuitho Sudoh, Koichiro Yoshino, and Christian Federmann. 2017. Overview of the IWSLT 2017 evaluation campaign. In *Proceedings of the International Workshop on Spoken Language Translation (IWSLT)*, pages 2–14.

Guanhua Chen, Yun Chen, and Victor OK Li. 2021. Lexically constrained neural machine translation with explicit alignment guidance. *Proceedings of the AAAI Conference on Artificial Intelligence*.

Guanhua Chen, Yun Chen, Yong Wang, and Victor O.K. Li. 2020. Lexical-constraint-aware neural machine translation via data augmentation. In *Proceedings of the Twenty-Ninth International Joint Conference on Artificial Intelligence, IJCAI-20*, pages 3587–3593. International Joint Conferences on Artificial Intelligence Organization. Main track.

Christian Federmann. 2018. Appraise evaluation framework for machine translation. In *Proceedings of the 27th International Conference on Computational Linguistics: System Demonstrations*, pages 86–88, Santa Fe, New Mexico. Association for Computational Linguistics.

Sarthak Garg, Stephan Peitz, Udhyakumar Nallasamy, and Matthias Paulik. 2019. Jointly learning to align and translate with transformer models. In *Proceedings of the 2019 Conference on Empirical Methods in Natural Language Processing and the 9th International Joint Conference on Natural Language Processing (EMNLP-IJCNLP)*, pages 4453–4462, Hong Kong, China. Association for Computational Linguistics.

Jiatao Gu, Changhan Wang, and Junbo Zhao. 2019. Levenshtein transformer. In H. Wallach, H. Larochelle, A. Beygelzimer, F. d'Alché-Buc, E. Fox, and R. Garnett, editors, *Advances in Neural Information Processing Systems 32*, pages 11179–11189. Curran Associates, Inc.

Chris Hokamp and Qun Liu. 2017. Lexically constrained decoding for sequence generation using grid beam search. In *Proceedings of the 55th Annual Meeting of the Association for Computational Linguistics (Volume 1: Long Papers)*, pages 1535–1546, Vancouver, Canada. Association for Computational Linguistics.

Diederik Kingma and Jimmy Ba. 2015. Adam: A method for stochastic optimization. In *Proceedings of the 3rd International Conference on Learning Representations (ICLR)*.

Philipp Koehn, Hieu Hoang, Alexandra Birch, Chris Callison-Burch, Marcello Federico, Nicola Bertoldi, Brooke Cowan, Wade Shen, Christine Moran, Richard Zens, Chris Dyer, Ondrej Bojar, Alexandra Constantin, and Evan Herbst. 2007. Moses: Open source toolkit for statistical machine translation. In *Proceedings of the 45th Annual Meeting of the Association for Computational Linguistics (ACL)*, pages 177–180.

Taku Kudo. 2006. MeCab: yet another part-of-speech and morphological analyzer. http://mecab.sourceforge.net.

Taku Kudo and John Richardson. 2018. SentencePiece: A simple and language independent subword tokenizer and detokenizer for Neural Text Processing. In *Proceedings of the 2018 Conference on Empirical Methods in Natural Language Processing: System Demonstrations*, pages 66–71.

Robert C. Moore and William Lewis. 2010. Intelligent selection of language model training data. In *Proceedings of the 48th Annual Meeting of the Association for Computational Linguistics (ACL)*, pages 220–224.

Makoto Morishita, Jun Suzuki, and Masaaki Nagata. 2017. NTT neural machine translation systems at WAT 2017. In *Proceedings of the 4th Workshop on Asian Translation (WAT)*, pages 89–94.

Makoto Morishita, Jun Suzuki, and Masaaki Nagata. 2019. NTT Neural Machine Translation Systems at WAT 2019. In *Proceedings of the 6th Workshop on Asian Translation (WAT 2019)*, pages 99–105.

Makoto Morishita, Jun Suzuki, and Masaaki Nagata. 2020. JParaCrawl: A large scale web-based English-Japanese parallel corpus. In *Proceedings of the 12th International Conference on Language Resources and Evaluation (LREC)*, pages 3603–3609.

Toshiaki Nakazawa, Hideki Nakayama, Chenchen Ding, Raj Dabre, Shohei Higashiyama, Hideya Mino, Isao Goto, Win Pa Pa, Anoop Kunchukuttan, Shantipriya Parida, Ondřej Bojar, Chenhui Chu, Akiko Eriguchi, Kaori Abe, and Sadao Oda, Yusuke Kurohashi. 2021. Overview of the 8th workshop on Asian translation. In *Proceedings of the 8th Workshop on Asian Translation*, Bangkok, Thailand. Association for Computational Linguistics.

Toshiaki Nakazawa, Manabu Yaguchi, Kiyotaka Uchimoto, Masao Utiyama, Eiichiro Sumita, Sadao Kurohashi, and Hitoshi Isahara. 2016. ASPEC: Asian scientific paper excerpt corpus. In *Proceedings of the 10th International Conference on Language Resources and Evaluation (LREC)*.

Myle Ott, Sergey Edunov, Alexei Baevski, Angela Fan, Sam Gross, Nathan Ng, David Grangier, and Michael Auli. 2019. fairseq: A fast, extensible toolkit for sequence modeling. In *Proceedings of the 2019 Conference of the North American Chapter of the Association for Computational Linguistics: Human Language Technologies (NAACL HLT)*, pages 48–53.

Myle Ott, Sergey Edunov, David Grangier, and Michael Auli. 2018. Scaling neural machine translation. In *Proceedings of the 3rd Conference on Machine Translation (WMT)*, pages 1–9.

Kishore Papineni, Salim Roukos, Todd Ward, and Wei-Jing Zhu. 2002. Bleu: a method for automatic evaluation of machine translation. In *Proceedings of 40th Annual Meeting of the Association for Computational Linguistics*, pages 311–318, Philadelphia, Pennsylvania, USA. Association for Computational Linguistics.

Matt Post. 2018. A call for clarity in reporting BLEU scores. In *Proceedings of the 3rd Conference on Machine Translation (WMT)*, pages 186–191.

Matt Post and David Vilar. 2018. Fast lexically constrained decoding with dynamic beam allocation for neural machine translation. In *Proceedings of the 2018 Conference of the North American Chapter of the Association for Computational Linguistics: Human Language Technologies, Volume 1 (Long Papers)*, pages 1314–1324, New Orleans, Louisiana. Association for Computational Linguistics.

Keisuke Sakaguchi and Benjamin Van Durme. 2018. Efficient online scalar annotation with bounded support. In *Proceedings of the 56th Annual Meeting of the Association for Computational Linguistics (Volume 1: Long Papers)*, pages 208–218, Melbourne, Australia. Association for Computational Linguistics.

Toshinori Sato. 2015. Neologism dictionary based on the language resources on the web for mecab.

Abigail See, Peter J. Liu, and Christopher D. Manning. 2017. Get to the point: Summarization with pointer-generator networks. In *Proceedings of the 55th Annual Meeting of the Association for Computational Linguistics (Volume 1: Long Papers)*, pages 1073–1083, Vancouver, Canada. Association for Computational Linguistics.

Rico Sennrich, Barry Haddow, and Alexandra Birch. 2016. Improving neural machine translation models with monolingual data. In *Proceedings of the 54th Annual Meeting of the Association for Computational Linguistics (ACL)*, pages 86–96.

Kai Song, Kun Wang, Heng Yu, Yue Zhang, Zhongqiang Huang, Weihua Luo, Xiangyu Duan, and Min Zhang. 2020. Alignment-enhanced transformer for constraining nmt with pre-specified translations. In *Proceedings of the AAAI Conference on Artificial Intelligence*, volume 34, pages 8886–8893.

Kai Song, Yue Zhang, Heng Yu, Weihua Luo, Kun Wang, and Min Zhang. 2019. Code-switching for enhancing NMT with pre-specified translation. In *Proceedings of the 2019 Conference of the North American Chapter of the Association for Computational Linguistics: Human Language Technologies, Volume 1 (Long and Short Papers)*, pages 449–459, Minneapolis, Minnesota. Association for Computational Linguistics.

Raymond Hendy Susanto, Shamil Chollampatt, and Liling Tan. 2020. Lexically constrained neural machine translation with Levenshtein transformer. In *Proceedings of the 58th Annual Meeting of the Association for Computational Linguistics*, pages 3536–3543, Online. Association for Computational Linguistics.

Christian Szegedy, Vincent Vanhoucke, Sergey Ioffe, Jon Shlens, and Zbigniew Wojna. 2016. Rethinking the Inception Architecture for Computer Vision. In *2016 IEEE Conference on Computer Vision and Pattern Recognition (CVPR 2016)*, pages 2818–2826.

Ashish Vaswani, Noam Shazeer, Niki Parmar, Jakob Uszkoreit, Llion Jones, Aidan N. Gomez, Lukasz Kaiser, and Illia Polosukhin. 2017. Attention is all you need. In *Proceedings of the 31st Annual Conference on Neural Information Processing Systems (NeurIPS)*, pages 6000–6010.

Oriol Vinyals, Meire Fortunato, and Navdeep Jaitly. 2015. Pointer networks. In *Advances in Neural Information Processing Systems*, volume 28. Curran Associates, Inc.

# NICT's Neural Machine Translation Systems for the WAT21 Restricted Translation Task

**Zuchao Li**[1,2,3], **Masao Utiyama**[4,*], **Eiichiro Sumita**[4], **and Hai Zhao**[1,2,3*]
[1]Department of Computer Science and Engineering, Shanghai Jiao Tong University
[2]Key Laboratory of Shanghai Education Commission for Intelligent Interaction and Cognitive Engineering, Shanghai Jiao Tong University, Shanghai, China
[3]MoE Key Lab of Artificial Intelligence, AI Institute, Shanghai Jiao Tong University
[4]National Institute of Information and Communications Technology (NICT), Kyoto, Japan
charlee@sjtu.edu.cn, {mutiyama, eiichiro.sumita}, zhaohai@cs.sjtu.edu.cn

## Abstract

This paper describes our system (Team ID: nictrb) for participating in the WAT'21 restricted machine translation task. In our submitted system, we designed a new training approach for restricted machine translation. By sampling from the translation target, we can solve the problem that ordinary training data does not have a restricted vocabulary. With the further help of constrained decoding in the inference phase, we achieved better results than the baseline, confirming the effectiveness of our solution. In addition, we also tried the vanilla and sparse Transformer as the backbone network of the model, as well as model ensembling, which further improved the final translation performance.

## 1 Introduction

The performance of machine translation has been greatly improved since it entered the era of Neural Machine Translation (NMT) (Bahdanau et al., 2015; Sutskever et al., 2014; Wu et al., 2016). Different from traditional statistical machine translation (SMT) (Koehn et al., 2003), NMT models are trained end-to-end with contextualized representations to alleviate the locality problem and dense representations to mitigate the sparsity issue. The incorporation of novel structures such as CNN (Gehring et al., 2017) and Transformer (Vaswani et al., 2017) into NMT has brought the performance one step closer to practical translation.

Though NMT can more effectively exploit large parallel corpora, the performance is still insufficient to meet the requirements in some special translation scenarios. The end-to-end NMT models remove many approaches in the SMT paradigm for manually guiding the translation process. One attractiveness of the SMT method is that it provides explicit control over translation output, which is effective in a variety of translation settings, including interactive machine translation (Peris et al., 2017) and domain adaptation (Chu and Wang, 2018), which is also crucial for the practical application of NMT.

Since there is still a need for manual interventions for the new NMT paradigm, much effort is spent in studying how to incorporate this explicit control into the end-to-end neural translation (Arthur et al., 2016). Among these efforts, Constrained Decoding (CD) has gained a lot of attention in this research field, which is a modification to commonly adopted beam search in ordinary NMT models. Hokamp and Liu (2017) proposed *grid beam search*, which expands beam search to include pre-specified lexical constraints. Anderson et al. (2017) used *constrained beam search* to force the inclusion of restricted words in the output, and employed fixed pre-trained word embeddings to facilitate vocabulary expansion to unseen words in training.

While these works accomplish the goal of explicit translation control, the time complexity of their decoding algorithm and resultant decoding speed falls short of the expectations. The complexity of *grid beam search* and *constrained beam search* is linear and exponential to the number of constraints, respectively. These algorithms are thus too inefficient to be practical for large-scale use. To alleviate the shortcomings in constrained decoding, Post and Vilar (2018) proposed a new constrained decoding algorithm with a claimed complexity of $O(1)$ in the number of constraints - *dynamic beam allocation* which allocates the slots in a fixed-size beam. However, their approach still processes sentence constraints sequentially rather than batch processing, limiting the GPU's parallel processing capabilities. Based on Post and Vilar (2018), a *vectorized dynamic beam allocation* approach was proposed in Hu et al. (2019), which which vector-

*Corresponding author. This work was completed when Zuchao Li was a fixed-term technical researcher at NICT.



*Proceedings of the 8th Workshop on Asian Translation*, pages 62–67
Bangkok, Thailand (online), August 5-6, 2021. 

izes the *dynamic beam allocation* for batching and thus leading to improvement in throughput with parallelization. Based on Post and Vilar (2018), Hu et al. (2019) proposed a *vectorized dynamic beam allocation* approach, which vectorizes the *dynamic beam allocation* for batching, resulting in increased throughput with parallelization.

Constrained decoding is a very general method for incorporating additional translation knowledge into the output without modifying the model parameters or training data. However, the model's prediction distribution can be skewed during the decoding process with hard constraints, resulting in poor translation results. When the model is exposed to the restricted translation paradigm during training, the gap between training and inference can be reduced, potentially improving performance. Therefore, in this paper, we propose a training method of *Sampled Constraints as Concentration* (SCC). In this method, training data is the same as the ordinary NMT; only minor modifications on the loss calculation are required to adapt the model to restricted translation.

In our submission to WAT'21 (Nakazawa et al., 2021) restricted translation task, we chose Transformer (Vaswani et al., 2017) as our baseline because of its high performance and scalability. Although there are some variants, our previous experiments have shown there are not too many approaches that can be both concise and effective. At the same time, though multi-head self-attention in Transformer can model extremely long dependencies, deep layer attention tends to overconcentrate on a single token, resulting in inadequate use of local information and difficulty representing long sequences. To address this disadvantage, we employ the PRIME Transformer (Zhao et al., 2019) with a multi-scale sparse attention mechanism as a second baseline. The models in the two architectures are ensembled to improve the overall results. Our final system uses a combination of the SCC training method and the constrained decoding of Hu et al. (2019), which makes our system leverages soft constrained (inside the model) and benefit from hard restrictions (external decoding).

## 2 Our System

In this section, we describe the methods used in our system in detail. Our system is made up of four components: the Transformer model, the Sparse Transformer model, the SCC training approach, and the constrained decoding algorithm. In translation, given the source input sequence $X = \{w_1, w_2, ..., w_m\}$, its target translation is $Y = \{y_1, y_2, ..., y_n\}$, the parameter of the NMT model is $\theta$, then the probability form of the translation process can be written as:

$$P(Y|X, \theta) = \prod_{i=1}^{n} P(y_i|y_{<i}, X, \theta),$$

where $y_{<i}$ denotes the tokens generated before time step $i$.

### 2.1 Transformer Model

Transformer model (Li et al., 2021) is a encoder-decoder architecture entirely built on multi-head self-attention which is responsible for learning representations of global context. With an input representation $H$, a multi-head self-attention (MHA) layer first projects $H$ into three representations, key $K$, query $Q$, and value $V$. Then, it uses a self-attention mechanism to get the output representation:

$$head_k = \text{Attn}(H) = \sigma(QW^Q, KW^K, VW^V)W^O$$
$$\text{MHA}(H) = \text{Concat}(head_1, \cdots, head_{\mathcal{K}})W^O,$$

where $Q = \text{Linear}_Q(H)$, $K = \text{Linear}_K(H)$, $V = \text{Linear}_V(H)$, $W^O$, $W^Q$, $W^K$, and $W^V$ are projection parameters. The self-attention operation $\sigma$ is the dot-production between key, query, and value pairs:

$$\sigma(Q_1, K_1, V_1) = \text{Softmax}(\frac{Q_1 K_1^T}{\sqrt{d_k}})V_1,$$

where $d_k = d_{model}/\mathcal{K}$ is the dimension of each head. The encoder of the Transformer model consists of a stack of multiple layers with MHA structure (Self-MHA$_{enc}$) where the residual mechanism and layer normalization are used to connect two adjacent layers. Similar to the encoder, each decoder layer decoder is composed of two MHA structures: Self-MHA$_{dec}$ and Cross-MHA, since it not only encodes the input sequence but also incorporates the source representation. Then the processing flow of the model can be written as:

$$H_{enc} = \text{Self-MHA}_{enc}(X),$$

$$H_{dec} = \text{Self-MHA}_{dec}(\text{IncMask}([\text{BOS}, y_1, \cdots, y_{n-1}])),$$

$$P(Y|X) = \text{Softmax}(\text{Linear}(\text{Cross-MHA}(H_{dec}, H_{enc}))),$$

where IncMask$(\cdot)$ represents the incremental masking strategy.

### 2.2 Sparse Transformer Model

According to the evaluation in recent research (Tang et al., 2018), it has shown that the vanilla Transformer has surprising shortcomings in long sequence encoding even the Transformer is designed to modeling long dependencies. Vanilla Transformer works well for short sequence translation, but performance drops as the source sentence length increases because only a small number of tokens are represented by self-attention, resulting in difficulty for translation. Replacing the dense self-attention mechanism with a sparse attention mechanism will alleviate the difficulties in long sentence translation; we chose the PRIME Transformer (Zhao et al., 2019) as our another base model. Compared to vanilla Transformer, PRIME Transformer generates the output representation of layer $i$ in a fusion way:

$$\begin{aligned} H^i = H^{i-1} &+ \text{MHA}(H^{i-1}) \\ &+ \text{Conv}(H^{i-1}) + \text{Pointwise}(H^{i-1}), \end{aligned}$$

where $H^{i-1}$ is the output of layer $i-1$. $\text{Conv}(\cdot)$ refers to dynamic convolution with multiple kernel sizes, which is employed to capture local context:

$$\begin{aligned} \text{Conv}_k(H) &= \text{DepthConv}_k(HW^V)W^{out} \\ \text{DepthConv}_k(H) &= \sum_{j=1}^{k} (\text{Softmax}(\sum_{c=1}^{d} W^Q_{j,c} H_{i,c}) \\ &\quad \cdot H_{i+j-\lceil \frac{k+1}{2} \rceil, c}), \\ \text{Conv}(H) &= \sum_{i=1}^{\mathcal{K}} \frac{\exp(\alpha_i)}{\sum_{j=1}^{n} \exp(\alpha_j)} \text{Conv}_{k_i}(X) \end{aligned}$$

in which $\text{DepthConv}(\cdot)$ is the depth convolution structure proposed in Wu et al. (2019). And $\text{Pointwise}(\cdot)$ refers to a position-wise feed-forward network:

$$\text{Pointwise}(H) = max(0, HW_1 + b_1)W_2 + b_2.$$

where $W_1$, $b_1$, $W_2$, and $b_2$ are learnable parameters.

### 2.3 Sampled Constraints as Concentration Training

The predicted probability in ordinary NMT is $y_i \sim P(y_i|X, \theta)$. Because of the inclusion of the constrained word sequence $C$ in restricted translation, the probability distribution becomes $y_i \sim P(y_i|X, C, \theta)$. To adapt the restricted translation for the NMT model rather than just influencing the search process, we expose the constrained word sequence $C$ as additional context like source input.

Since the parallel training data only contains the source and target language sequences, we obtain the constrained word sequence for training via random dynamic sampling from the reference target translation. This not only alleviates the burden of constrained word annotation but also has the potential to minimize overfitting.

Specifically, in the model, we use the Self-$\text{MHA}_{dec}$ to encode the input constrained sequence to obtain its representation:

$$H_{cst} = \text{Self-MHA}_{dec}(C).$$

It is worth noting that we remove the positional encoding of constrained sequence since the order of restricted word sequence is usually inconsistent with the target translation; additionally, we also remove the incremental mask because the whole sequence is exposed to the decoder as an additional context at the same time. The probabilistic form of restricted translation accordingly changes to:

$$\begin{aligned} P(Y|X) = \text{Softmax}(\text{Linear}(&\text{Cross-MHA}(H_{dec}, H_{enc}) + \\ &\text{Cross-MHA}(H_{dec}, H_{cst})))). \end{aligned}$$

Because sampled constrained words are exposed to the decoder, to enforce the inclusion of these words in the translation, we place additional penalties on the loss of these sampled positions to achieve the goal of restrict translation with soft constraints on the model:

$$\begin{aligned} \mathcal{L}_{\text{SCC}} = -\sum_{i=1}^{m} &((1 + \gamma \mathbb{1}(y_i \in C)) \\ &logP(y_i|X; C; y_{<i}; \theta)), \end{aligned}$$

where $\mathbb{1}(\cdot)$ is the indicator function and $\gamma$ is the penalty factor.

### 2.4 Lexically Constrained Decoding

Beam search (Koehn, 2010) is a common approximate search algorithm for sequence generation task. Lexically constrained decoding is a modification to the beam search algorithm, which is proposed to enforce hard constraints that force a given constrained sequence to appear in the generated sequence. Specifically, beam search maintains a beam $B_t$ on time step $t$, which contains only the $b$ most likely partial sequences, where $b$ is known as the beam size. The beam $B_t$ is updated by retaining the $b$ most likely sequences in the candidate set $E_t$ generated by considering all possible next word predictions:

$$E_t = \{(\hat{Y}_{t-1}, w) \mid \hat{Y}_{t-1} \in B_{t-1}, w \in \mathcal{V}\},$$

| Model | BLEU | | | RIBES | | | AMFM |
|---|---|---|---|---|---|---|---|
| | *jum* | *kyt* | *mec* | *jum* | *kyt* | *mec* | – |
| Transformer-big | 41.67 | 41.82 | 41.84 | 81.05 | 81.32 | 81.50 | 74.95 |
| Transformer-big + SCC + CD* | 48.92 | 49.24 | 49.25 | 82.79 | 83.15 | 83.57 | 79.15 |
| Sparse Transformer-big + SCC + CD* | 50.93 | 51.18 | 51.21 | 83.27 | 83.52 | 84.00 | 79.91 |
| Ensemble* | 51.07 | 51.32 | 51.36 | 83.68 | 83.99 | 84.41 | 79.99 |

Table 1: Results on ASPECT En→Ja test sets. $*$ indicates that the official evaluation results are reported.

| Dataset | Sentences |
|---|---|
| ParaCrawl-v5.1 | 10.12M |
| Wiki Titles v2 | 3.64M |
| ASPEC | 3.01M |

Table 2: Training data statistics.

| Model | BLEU | RIBES | AMFM |
|---|---|---|---|
| Transformer-big | 28.18 | 67.79 | 58.69 |
| Transformer-big + SCC + CD* | 35.26 | 74.44 | 64.16 |
| Sparse Transformer-big + SCC + CD* | 36.83 | 75.84 | 65.29 |
| Ensemble* | 37.01 | 75.38 | 65.15 |

Table 3: Results on ASPECT Ja→En test sets. $*$ indicates that the official evaluation results are reported.

where $\hat{Y}_{t-1}$ is the generated sequence in time step $t-1$ and $\mathcal{V}$ is the target vocabulary.

In lexically constrained decoding, a finite-state machine (FSM) is used to impose the constraints. For each state $s \in S$ in the FSM, a corresponding search beam $B^s$ is maintained similar to the beam search:

$$E_t^s = \bigcup_{s' \in S} \{(\hat{Y}_{t-1}, w) \mid \hat{Y}_{t-1} \in B_{t-1}^{s'}, w \in V, \delta(s', w) = s\},$$

where $\delta : S \times V \mapsto S$ is the FSM state-transition function that maps states and predicted words to states.

### 2.5 System Details

Our implementation of the Transformer models and lexically constrained decoding algorithm are based on the Fairseq toolkit[1]. We follow the settings and pre-processing methods in our previous models and systems (He et al., 2018; Li et al., 2018; He et al., 2019; Li et al., 2019; Zhou et al., 2020; Li et al., 2020b,d,c; Zhang et al., 2020). We use Transformer-big as our basic model, which has 6 layers in both the encoder and decoder, respectively. For each layer, it consists of a multi-head attention sublayer with 16 heads and a feed-forward sublayer with an inner dimension 4096. The word embedding dimensions and the hidden state dimensions are set to 1024 for both the encoder and decoder. In the training phase, the dropout rate is set to 0.1.

Our model training consists of two phases. In the first NMT pre-training phase, the ParaCrawl-v5.1 (Esplà et al., 2019) and Wiki Titles v2 datasets are used. Then we finetune the model using the ASPEC training data in the second domain finetune phase. Table 2 shows the data statistics for each dataset. In both phases, cross-entropy with label smoothing of 0.1 and D2GPo (Li et al., 2020a) are employed as the training loss criterions. We use Adam (Kingma and Ba, 2015) as our optimizer, with parameters settings $\beta_1 = 0.9$, $\beta_2 = 0.98$ and $\epsilon = 10^{-8}$. The initial learning rate is set to $10^{-4}$ for NMT pre-training and $10^{-5}$ for domain finetuning. The models are trained on 8 GPUs for about 500,000 steps. In our systems, we follow standard practice and learn a subword (Sennrich et al., 2016) encoding with 40K joint merge operations.

## 3 Results

Table 1 shows the official results evaluated on ASPEC En→Ja test set. Comparing the results of the vanilla Transformer-big model and Transformer-big+SCC+CD, restricted translation under +SCC+CD has brought a very large performance improvement, which illustrates the performance advantage of restricted translation. Similar to ordinary NMT, sparse Transformer achieves better results than Transformer-big in restricted translation, which demonstrates that Sparse Transformer is a general model structure. A further increase in performance is achieved after ensembling on these two models. This benefits from the models of the distinct architectures of the two models. In general, the improvement brought about by the same architecture is less. We show the results of ASPEC En→Ja test set in Table 3. By comparison, the conclusion is essentially consistent with Table 2.

[1]https://github.com/pytorch/fairseq

## 4 Conclusion

In this paper, we present our NMT systems for WAT21 restricted translation shared tasks in English $\leftrightarrow$ English. By integrating the following techniques: Sparse Transformer, Sampled Constraints as Concentration, and Lexically Constrained Decoding, our final system achieves substantial improvement over baseline systems which show the effectiveness of our approaches.

## References


Peter Anderson, Basura Fernando, Mark Johnson, and Stephen Gould. 2017. Guided open vocabulary image captioning with constrained beam search. In *Proceedings of the 2017 Conference on Empirical Methods in Natural Language Processing*, pages 936–945, Copenhagen, Denmark. Association for Computational Linguistics.

Philip Arthur, Graham Neubig, and Satoshi Nakamura. 2016. Incorporating discrete translation lexicons into neural machine translation. In *Proceedings of the 2016 Conference on Empirical Methods in Natural Language Processing*, pages 1557–1567, Austin, Texas. Association for Computational Linguistics.

Dzmitry Bahdanau, Kyunghyun Cho, and Yoshua Bengio. 2015. Neural machine translation by jointly learning to align and translate. In *3rd International Conference on Learning Representations, ICLR 2015, San Diego, CA, USA, May 7-9, 2015, Conference Track Proceedings*.

Chenhui Chu and Rui Wang. 2018. A survey of domain adaptation for neural machine translation. In *Proceedings of the 27th International Conference on Computational Linguistics*, pages 1304–1319, Santa Fe, New Mexico, USA. Association for Computational Linguistics.

Miquel Esplà, Mikel Forcada, Gema Ramírez-Sánchez, and Hieu Hoang. 2019. ParaCrawl: Web-scale parallel corpora for the languages of the EU. In *Proceedings of Machine Translation Summit XVII Volume 2: Translator, Project and User Tracks*, pages 118–119, Dublin, Ireland. European Association for Machine Translation.

Jonas Gehring, Michael Auli, David Grangier, Denis Yarats, and Yann N. Dauphin. 2017. Convolutional sequence to sequence learning. In *Proceedings of the 34th International Conference on Machine Learning, ICML 2017, Sydney, NSW, Australia, 6-11 August 2017*, volume 70 of *Proceedings of Machine Learning Research*, pages 1243–1252. PMLR.

Shexia He, Zuchao Li, and Hai Zhao. 2019. Syntax-aware multilingual semantic role labeling. In *Proceedings of the 2019 Conference on Empirical Methods in Natural Language Processing and the 9th International Joint Conference on Natural Language Processing (EMNLP-IJCNLP)*, pages 5350–5359, Hong Kong, China. Association for Computational Linguistics.

Shexia He, Zuchao Li, Hai Zhao, and Hongxiao Bai. 2018. Syntax for semantic role labeling, to be, or not to be. In *Proceedings of the 56th Annual Meeting of the Association for Computational Linguistics (Volume 1: Long Papers)*, pages 2061–2071, Melbourne, Australia. Association for Computational Linguistics.

Chris Hokamp and Qun Liu. 2017. Lexically constrained decoding for sequence generation using grid beam search. In *Proceedings of the 55th Annual Meeting of the Association for Computational Linguistics (Volume 1: Long Papers)*, pages 1535–1546, Vancouver, Canada. Association for Computational Linguistics.

J. Edward Hu, Huda Khayrallah, Ryan Culkin, Patrick Xia, Tongfei Chen, Matt Post, and Benjamin Van Durme. 2019. Improved lexically constrained decoding for translation and monolingual rewriting. In *Proceedings of the 2019 Conference of the North American Chapter of the Association for Computational Linguistics: Human Language Technologies, Volume 1 (Long and Short Papers)*, pages 839–850, Minneapolis, Minnesota. Association for Computational Linguistics.

Diederik P. Kingma and Jimmy Ba. 2015. Adam: A method for stochastic optimization. In *3rd International Conference on Learning Representations, ICLR 2015, San Diego, CA, USA, May 7-9, 2015, Conference Track Proceedings*.

Philipp Koehn. 2010. *Statistical Machine Translation*. Cambridge University Press.

Philipp Koehn, Franz J. Och, and Daniel Marcu. 2003. Statistical phrase-based translation. In *Proceedings of the 2003 Human Language Technology Conference of the North American Chapter of the Association for Computational Linguistics*, pages 127–133.

Zuchao Li, Shexia He, Jiaxun Cai, Zhuosheng Zhang, Hai Zhao, Gongshen Liu, Linlin Li, and Luo Si. 2018. A unified syntax-aware framework for semantic role labeling. In *Proceedings of the 2018 Conference on Empirical Methods in Natural Language Processing*, pages 2401–2411, Brussels, Belgium. Association for Computational Linguistics.

Zuchao Li, Rui Wang, Kehai Chen, Masao Utiyama, Eiichiro Sumita, Zhuosheng Zhang, and Hai Zhao. 2020a. Data-dependent gaussian prior objective for language generation. In *8th International Conference on Learning Representations, ICLR 2020, Addis Ababa, Ethiopia, April 26-30, 2020*. OpenReview.net.

Zuchao Li, Rui Wang, Kehai Chen, Masao Utiyama, Eiichiro Sumita, Zhuosheng Zhang, and Hai Zhao.

2020b. Explicit sentence compression for neural machine translation. In *The Thirty-Fourth AAAI Conference on Artificial Intelligence, AAAI 2020, The Thirty-Second Innovative Applications of Artificial Intelligence Conference, IAAI 2020, The Tenth AAAI Symposium on Educational Advances in Artificial Intelligence, EAAI 2020, New York, NY, USA, February 7-12, 2020*, pages 8311–8318. AAAI Press.

Zuchao Li, Zhuosheng Zhang, Hai Zhao, Rui Wang, Kehai Chen, Masao Utiyama, and Eiichiro Sumita. 2021. Text compression-aided transformer encoding. *IEEE Transactions on Pattern Analysis and Machine Intelligence*.

Zuchao Li, Hai Zhao, Rui Wang, Kehai Chen, Masao Utiyama, and Eiichiro Sumita. 2020c. SJTU-NICT's supervised and unsupervised neural machine translation systems for the WMT20 news translation task. In *Proceedings of the Fifth Conference on Machine Translation*, pages 218–229, Online. Association for Computational Linguistics.

Zuchao Li, Hai Zhao, Rui Wang, Masao Utiyama, and Eiichiro Sumita. 2020d. Reference language based unsupervised neural machine translation. In *Findings of the Association for Computational Linguistics: EMNLP 2020*, pages 4151–4162, Online. Association for Computational Linguistics.

Zuchao Li, Hai Zhao, Zhuosheng Zhang, Rui Wang, Masao Utiyama, and Eiichiro Sumita. 2019. SJTU-NICT at MRP 2019: Multi-task learning for end-to-end uniform semantic graph parsing. In *Proceedings of the Shared Task on Cross-Framework Meaning Representation Parsing at the 2019 Conference on Natural Language Learning*, pages 45–54, Hong Kong. Association for Computational Linguistics.

Toshiaki Nakazawa, Hideki Nakayama, Chenchen Ding, Raj Dabre, Shohei Higashiyama, Hideya Mino, Isao Goto, Win Pa Pa, Anoop Kunchukuttan, Shantipriya Parida, Ondřej Bojar, Chenhui Chu, Akiko Eriguchi, Kaori Abe, and Sadao Oda, Yusuke Kurohashi. 2021. Overview of the 8th workshop on Asian translation. In *Proceedings of the 8th Workshop on Asian Translation*, Bangkok, Thailand. Association for Computational Linguistics.

Álvaro Peris, Miguel Domingo, and Francisco Casacuberta. 2017. Interactive neural machine translation. *Comput. Speech Lang.*, 45:201–220.

Matt Post and David Vilar. 2018. Fast lexically constrained decoding with dynamic beam allocation for neural machine translation. In *Proceedings of the 2018 Conference of the North American Chapter of the Association for Computational Linguistics: Human Language Technologies, Volume 1 (Long Papers)*, pages 1314–1324, New Orleans, Louisiana. Association for Computational Linguistics.

Rico Sennrich, Barry Haddow, and Alexandra Birch. 2016. Neural machine translation of rare words with subword units. In *Proceedings of the 54th Annual Meeting of the Association for Computational Linguistics (Volume 1: Long Papers)*, pages 1715–1725, Berlin, Germany. Association for Computational Linguistics.

Ilya Sutskever, Oriol Vinyals, and Quoc V. Le. 2014. Sequence to sequence learning with neural networks. In *Advances in Neural Information Processing Systems 27: Annual Conference on Neural Information Processing Systems 2014, December 8-13 2014, Montreal, Quebec, Canada*, pages 3104–3112.

Gongbo Tang, Mathias Müller, Annette Rios, and Rico Sennrich. 2018. Why self-attention? a targeted evaluation of neural machine translation architectures. In *Proceedings of the 2018 Conference on Empirical Methods in Natural Language Processing*, pages 4263–4272, Brussels, Belgium. Association for Computational Linguistics.

Ashish Vaswani, Noam Shazeer, Niki Parmar, Jakob Uszkoreit, Llion Jones, Aidan N. Gomez, Lukasz Kaiser, and Illia Polosukhin. 2017. Attention is all you need. In *Advances in Neural Information Processing Systems 30: Annual Conference on Neural Information Processing Systems 2017, December 4-9, 2017, Long Beach, CA, USA*, pages 5998–6008.

Felix Wu, Angela Fan, Alexei Baevski, Yann N. Dauphin, and Michael Auli. 2019. Pay less attention with lightweight and dynamic convolutions. In *7th International Conference on Learning Representations, ICLR 2019, New Orleans, LA, USA, May 6-9, 2019*. OpenReview.net.

Yonghui Wu, Mike Schuster, Zhifeng Chen, Quoc V. Le, Mohammad Norouzi, Wolfgang Macherey, Maxim Krikun, Yuan Cao, Qin Gao, Klaus Macherey, Jeff Klingner, Apurva Shah, Melvin Johnson, Xiaobing Liu, Lukasz Kaiser, Stephan Gouws, Yoshikiyo Kato, Taku Kudo, Hideto Kazawa, Keith Stevens, George Kurian, Nishant Patil, Wei Wang, Cliff Young, Jason Smith, Jason Riesa, Alex Rudnick, Oriol Vinyals, Greg Corrado, Macduff Hughes, and Jeffrey Dean. 2016. Google's neural machine translation system: Bridging the gap between human and machine translation. *CoRR*, abs/1609.08144.

Zhuosheng Zhang, Yuwei Wu, Hai Zhao, Zuchao Li, Shuailiang Zhang, Xi Zhou, and Xiang Zhou. 2020. Semantics-aware bert for language understanding. In *Proceedings of the AAAI Conference on Artificial Intelligence*, volume 34, pages 9628–9635.

Guangxiang Zhao, Xu Sun, Jingjing Xu, Zhiyuan Zhang, and Liangchen Luo. 2019. MUSE: parallel multi-scale attention for sequence to sequence learning. *CoRR*, abs/1911.09483.

Junru Zhou, Zuchao Li, and Hai Zhao. 2020. Parsing all: Syntax and semantics, dependencies and spans. In *Findings of the Association for Computational Linguistics: EMNLP 2020*, pages 4438–4449, Online. Association for Computational Linguistics.

# Machine Translation with Pre-specified Target-side Words Using a Semi-autoregressive Model

**Seiichiro Kondo** **Aomi Koyama** **Tomoshige Kiyuna**
**Tosho Hirasawa** **Mamoru Komachi**
Tokyo Metropolitan University
kondo-seiichiro@ed.tmu.ac.jp, koyama-aomi@ed.tmu.ac.jp
kiyuna-tomoshige@ed.tmu.ac.jp, hirasawa-tosho@ed.tmu.ac.jp
komachi@tmu.ac.jp

## Abstract

We introduce our TMU Japanese-to-English system, which employs a semi-autoregressive model, to tackle the WAT 2021 (Nakazawa et al., 2021) restricted translation task. In this task, we translate an input sentence with the constraint that some words, called restricted target vocabularies (RTVs), must be contained in the output sentence. To satisfy this constraint, we use a semi-autoregressive model, namely, RecoverSAT (Ran et al., 2020), due to its ability (known as "forced translation") to insert specified words into the output sentence. When using "forced translation," the order of inserting RTVs is a critical problem. In our system, we obtain word alignment between a source sentence and the corresponding RTVs and then sort the RTVs in the order of their corresponding words or phrases in the source sentence. Using the model with sorted order RTVs, we succeeded in inserting all the RTVs into output sentences in more than 96% of the test sentences. Moreover, we confirmed that sorting RTVs improved the BLEU score compared with random order RTVs.

## 1 Introduction

In this study, we tackle a machine translation task called "restricted translation." This task requires the output sentence to contain all the pre-specified restricted target vocabularies (RTVs)[1]. In other words, we are given a source sentence and a set of RTVs, and we are supposed to generate an output sentence that contains all the RTVs in the set[2].

Since the emergence of neural machine translation (NMT) models (Sutskever et al., 2014; Bahdanau et al., 2015; Vaswani et al., 2017), several studies have been conducted to explore NMT systems capable of decoding translations under terminological constraints (Hasler et al., 2018; Dinu et al., 2019; Chen et al., 2020; Song et al., 2020). However, these previous studies were conducted under the condition that a bilingual dictionary is given. Moreover, these challenges are limited to autoregressive NMT systems, and scant research has been conducted on non-autoregressive or semi-autoregressive NMT systems, which have received more attention recently.

To accomplish restricted translation, where only target terminologies are given, we used a semi-autoregressive model called RecoverSAT (Ran et al., 2020), which generates a sentence as a sequence of segments. In this model, the segments are generated simultaneously, and each segment is predicted token-by-token. Ran et al. (2020) also attempted to force the model to generate a certain token at the beginning of a segment and showed that the model could generate valid sentences under the constraint. Then, we considered whether this model could be applied to generate sentences containing RTVs.

When tackling this task using this model, the insertion order of RTVs is a critical issue. To address this issue, we used GIZA++ (Och and Ney, 2003) to obtain word alignments and then identify the source position corresponding to the RTVs. Subsequently, we inserted them in the order in which their corresponding source tokens appear. We confirmed that sorting RTVs with GIZA++ improved the BLEU (Papineni et al., 2002) score. Finally, by using this model, we achieved all the RTVs outputs in more than 96% of the test sentences.

## 2 System Overview

### 2.1 Corpus Refinement

Morishita et al. (2019) reported that the synthetic

[1] Each RTV is either a word or a phrase.

[2] For details of the task description, see https://sites.google.com/view/restricted-translation-task/.



*Proceedings of the 8th Workshop on Asian Translation*, pages 68–73
Bangkok, Thailand (online), August 5-6, 2021. ©2021 Association for Computational Linguistics

data generated by back-translation (Sennrich et al., 2016) degraded the performance in the Japanese-to-English translation setting. The reason for this phenomenon was that the ASPEC (Nakazawa et al., 2016) training sentences are ordered by sentence alignment scores, and so the sentences with lower scores are considered relatively noisy data. Therefore, Morishita et al. (2019) attempted to generate synthetic data using forward-translation instead of standard back-translation and confirmed that forward-translation improved the performance of the Japanese-to-English translation setting.

Following Morishita et al. (2019), we used forward-translation to refine the latter half of the ASPEC training data. In the same manner as their method, we first trained a Japanese-to-English translation model on the first 1.5M sentences of the ASPEC training data. Subsequently, we used the trained model to translate the latter 1.5M Japanese sentences of the ASPEC training data and obtained refined English sentences. Finally, we combined the first 1.5M training data and the refined 1.5M training data and trained a Japanese-to-English translation model.

### 2.2 RecoverSAT

RecoverSAT (Ran et al., 2020) is a semi-autoregressive model that performs generation autoregressively in local and non-autoregressively in global. At each decoding step, the model generates a token in each segment, with paying attention to not only all the previous tokens in the segment but also those in all the other segments. The model continues decoding in each segment until either a special token, EOS or DEL, is generated, or the length of the generated token reaches the maximum token number. The final translation is a concatenation of all the segments except those that end with DEL.

RecoverSAT is also known for its capability to generate a translation under a word constraint (Ran et al., 2020), which is called the "forced translation" approach. In this approach, the model generates the constraint word (or phrases) at the beginning of an arbitrary segment. Once the constraint word (or phrase) has been generated, the model predicts the remainder of the segment in a semi-autoregressive manner.

In contrast to the original "forced translation," which only takes one constrained word (or phrase), we are required to place multiple RTVs in a translation. To compensate for this gap, we place the $i$-th RTV at the $P_i$-th segment as follows[3]:

$$P_i = \lfloor \frac{N_S}{N_V} \rfloor \cdot i \quad (1)$$

where $N_S$ is the number of segments and $N_V$ is the number of RTVs. When the RTVs have more phrases than segments during inference, we cut off phrases in the RTVs from the tail to fit the placeholder.

### 2.3 Sorting RTVs Using Source Alignment

RecoverSAT outputs RTVs in the order where they are inserted, so the order of inserting RTVs is important for accurate translation. We determined the order of the RTVs under the assumption that it correlated with the order of the aligned words in the input sentence.

We used GIZA++ to align each RTV with a word in the input sentence and sorted the RTVs in the order of their corresponding input words. When the RTV was a phrase, we first obtained a source word that was most aligned with each word in the RTV and then selected the source word with the highest alignment score as the aligned word for the entire RTV. If there was a tie, the first aligned word in the input sentence was selected as the corresponding word.

## 3 Experimental Setup

### 3.1 Dataset

We used the ASPEC (Nakazawa et al., 2016) dataset for Japanese-to-English translation. This dataset contains 3M sentences as training data, 1,790 sentences as validation data, and 1,812 sentences as test data. As explained in Section 2.1, we refined the latter half of the training data using forward-translation.

We used SentencePiece (Kudo and Richardson, 2018) to tokenize the training data for both the source and target sentences, where the vocabulary size was set to 4K. Note that we used SentencePiece models obtained from the first 1.5M training data through all the experiments. When determining the insertion order of RTVs using GIZA++, we used MeCab[4] with IPADIC to tokenize Japanese sentences before computing the alignment.

[3]Note that both $P_i$ and $i$ start from 0.

[4]`https://taku910.github.io/mecab/`

### 3.2 Evaluation

We evaluated system outputs using the following two distinct metrics.

**BLEU score.** The BLEU score is a metric evaluated by the n-gram matching rate with the reference. We calculated it using `multi-bleu.perl` in the Moses toolkit (Koehn et al., 2007).

**Consistency score.** The consistency score is the ratio of translations that satisfy the exact match of all the given constraints over the entire test corpus. The exact match is determined as follows. We simply lowercased hypotheses and constraints and then judged character-level sequence matching (including whitespaces) for each constraint.

For the final score, we calculated the BLEU score using only the translations that exactly matched their RTVs. In other words, first, we calculated the exact match, and then, we replaced the translations that did not satisfy the constraint with an empty string. Subsequently, we calculated the BLEU score with the modified translations.

### 3.3 Model

**Transformer.** We used "Transformer (base)" (Vaswani et al., 2017) for forward-translation and a baseline model. The hyperparameter settings were the same as described in Vaswani et al. (2017).

In the baseline model, we inserted the RTVs at the tail of the output sentence without sorting.

**RecoverSAT.** We use the encoder of the Transformer to initialize the encoder of RecoverSAT, and share the parameters of the embedding layers and the pre-softmax linear layer in the same way as Ran et al. (2020). We adopted the same model and hyperparameters that were used in the previous study (Ran et al., 2020)[5], where $d_{\text{model}} = 512$, $d_{\text{hidden}} = 512$, $n_{\text{layer}} = 6$, and $n_{\text{head}} = 8$. However, we did not share the source and target vocabularies.

Moreover, we changed the number of segments from the original paper (i.e., 10) because some examples had more than 10 (up to 14) RTVs in the test data. We also expanded the length of a segment to be able to insert all the tokens of the RTV if the RTV has more tokens than allowed by default. We examined four RecoverSAT models with different numbers of segments: 10 is the default value in Ran et al. (2020) and 14 is the maximum number of RTVs among the development data. The models with 21 and 29 segments have more free segments than the previous models, which are supposed to be lubricating segments to improve the overall output.

[5] We used the implementation at `https://github.com/ranqiu92/RecoverSAT` and minimally modified it for inserting RTVs.

| | BLEU | RIBES | AMFM |
|---|---|---|---|
| RecoverSAT | 25.29 | 0.653597 | 0.612290 |

Table 1: Results of the official score using RecoverSAT with 14 segments and forced translation with sorted order.

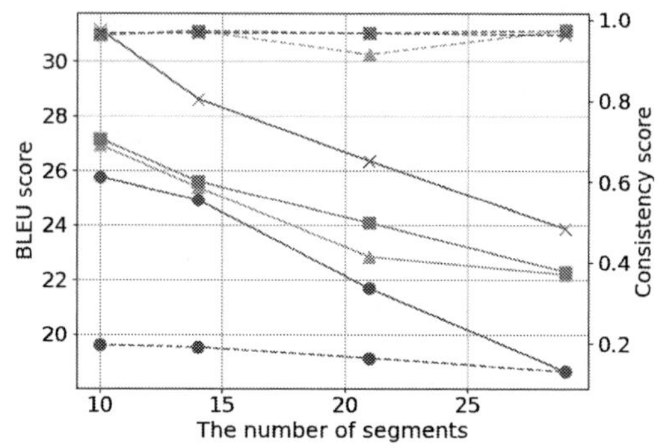


Figure 1: Results of our experiments using RecoverSAT. The solid line represents the BLEU score, and the dotted line represents the consistency score. The dot marker represents RecoverSAT without RTVs. The triangle marker represents forced translation without sorting RTVs. The square marker represents forced translation with sorted order. The cross marker represents forced translation with oracle order.

## 4 Results

### 4.1 Official Evaluation

Table 1 presents the official BLEU, RIBES (Isozaki et al., 2010), and AMFM (Banchs et al., 2015) scores, calculated in the evaluation server, for the model in which the number of segments is 14. As shown in Table 1, the BLEU, RIBES, and AMFM scores were 25.29, 0.653597, and 0.612290 points, respectively.

### 4.2 Our Evaluation

Table 2 presents the scores obtained in our evaluation. Moreover, Figure 1 shows the BLEU score and consistency scores for different numbers of segments $\{10, 14, 21, 29\}$.

**BLEU score.** Figure 1 shows that the translation accuracy decreases as the number of segments in-

| Model | BLEU score | Consistency score | Final score |
|---|---|---|---|
| Transformer | 27.78 | 0.220 | 0.27 |
| + Append RTVs | 25.57 | **1.000** | 26.75 |
| RecoverSAT | 25.76 | 0.197 | 0.16 |
| + Forced translation with random order | 26.93 | 0.962 | 26.98 |
| + Forced translation with sorted order | 27.16 | 0.961 | 27.10 |
| + Forced translation with oracle order | **31.14** | 0.966 | **31.02** |

Table 2: Results of the experiments in our evaluation. The number of segments of RecoverSAT is 10. The consistency score is the ratio of sentences satisfying the exact match of the given constraints. The final score is the constraint-aware BLEU score. "random order": we insert RTVs without sorting. "sorted order": we insert RTVs in the order of the corresponding source words. "oracle order": we insert RTVs in the same order as that in the reference.

creases, similar to the previous study (Ran et al., 2020). This may be because the model predicts the target tokens more independently as the number of segments increases. As the number of segments increases, the length of each segment becomes shorter, and the model becomes closer to the non-autoregressive model.

Table 2 shows that sorting the RTVs using GIZA++ improves the BLEU score. However, there is still a significant gap in the scores compared with those obtained using the oracle order. This is because the word order between Japanese and English is different.

**Consistency score.** Figure 1 shows that RecoverSAT with forced translation reliably outputs RTVs in almost all the cases. When the number of segments was 10, we could not insert all the RTVs in some test sentences with more than 10 RTVs[6]. On the other hand, when the number of segments was 14 or more, it was expected that all the RTVs could be inserted into all the test sentences. However, some output sentences did not contain all the RTVs, even if the number of segments was 14 or more. This result indicates that the model generates a special token, DEL, to delete segments beginning with the RTVs.

The final BLEU score of the model with 10 segments, which gives up to generate some RTVs on occasion, was the highest. This is because it is rare to have more than 10 RTVs for a single sentence[7]. Additionally, we confirmed that the insertion of RTVs was effective in improving not only the consistency score but also the BLEU score.

[6]As mentioned in Section 3.3, the maximum number of RTVs in the test set was 14.

[7]Only 14 out of 1,812 (0.8%) sentences were given more than 10 RTVs in the test data.

## 5 Related Work

Previously, some NMT with terminology constraints have been studied (Hasler et al., 2018; Alkhouli et al., 2018; Dinu et al., 2019; Chen et al., 2020; Song et al., 2020). For example, Song et al. (2020) proposed a dedicated head in a multi-head Transformer architecture to learn explicit word alignment and use it to guide the constrained decoding process. When the source-aligned word matches a dictionary, the model outputs the corresponding target word. However, these models are not available for the "restricted translation" task because we can only access the target-side vocabularies.

In this study, we used the semi-autoregressive model RecoverSAT (Ran et al., 2020). Originally, this model was not intended to output forcibly more than one constrained word. A non-autoregressive model can decode target tokens simultaneously, resulting in faster decoding. However, its output sentence suffers from the multi-modality problem causing token repetitions or missing by not using the dependency between the output words (Gu et al., 2018; Ran et al., 2020). Thus, Ran et al. (2020) proposed RecoverSAT to alleviate this problem. Their model could maintain the accuracy of the autoregressive model while achieving a faster processing speed. They also mentioned that, as the number of segments increases, the closer the model becomes to a non-autoregressive model. In other words, when the number of segments increases, the decoding process is faster, but the accuracy is lower. Moreover, they attempted to force the model to generate a pre-specified token at the beginning of a segment and showed that the model could avoid repetitive output and translate properly.

## 6 Conclusions

We introduced a semi-autoregressive approach to tackle the restricted translation task. In our experiments, we showed that RecoverSAT could output almost all the RTVs. Additionally, we used source sentence alignment to determine the insertion position and observed that it improved the BLEU score. Moreover, the importance of the order of the RTVs was confirmed by the fact that the score was considerably improved by inserting RTVs in the order in which they appear in the reference translations. However, there is still room for improvement in determining the insertion order. In future work, investigating how to determine the best order to insert RTVs will be necessary.

## References


Tamer Alkhouli, Gabriel Bretschner, and Hermann Ney. 2018. On the alignment problem in multi-head attention-based neural machine translation. In *Proceedings of the Third Conference on Machine Translation: Research Papers*, pages 177–185, Brussels, Belgium. Association for Computational Linguistics.

Dzmitry Bahdanau, Kyunghyun Cho, and Yoshua Bengio. 2015. Neural machine translation by jointly learning to align and translate. In *Proceedings of the 3rd International Conference on Learning Representations*, San Diego, California.

Rafael E. Banchs, Luis F. D'Haro, and Haizhou Li. 2015. Adequacy–fluency metrics: Evaluating MT in the continuous space model framework. *IEEE/ACM Transactions on Audio, Speech, and Language Processing*, 23(3):472–482.

Guanhua Chen, Yun Chen, Yong Wang, and Victor O.K. Li. 2020. Lexical-constraint-aware neural machine translation via data augmentation. In *Proceedings of the Twenty-Ninth International Joint Conference on Artificial Intelligence*, pages 3587–3593. International Joint Conferences on Artificial Intelligence Organization.

Georgiana Dinu, Prashant Mathur, Marcello Federico, and Yaser Al-Onaizan. 2019. Training neural machine translation to apply terminology constraints. In *Proceedings of the 57th Annual Meeting of the Association for Computational Linguistics*, pages 3063–3068, Florence, Italy. Association for Computational Linguistics.

Jiatao Gu, James Bradbury, Caiming Xiong, Victor O.K. Li, and Richard Socher. 2018. Non-autoregressive neural machine translation. In *Proceedings of the 6th International Conference on Learning Representations*, Vancouver, Canada. OpenReview.net.

Eva Hasler, Adrià de Gispert, Gonzalo Iglesias, and Bill Byrne. 2018. Neural machine translation decoding with terminology constraints. In *Proceedings of the 2018 Conference of the North American Chapter of the Association for Computational Linguistics: Human Language Technologies, Volume 2 (Short Papers)*, pages 506–512, New Orleans, Louisiana. Association for Computational Linguistics.

Hideki Isozaki, Tsutomu Hirao, Kevin Duh, Katsuhito Sudoh, and Hajime Tsukada. 2010. Automatic evaluation of translation quality for distant language pairs. In *Proceedings of the 2010 Conference on Empirical Methods in Natural Language Processing*, pages 944–952, Cambridge, MA. Association for Computational Linguistics.

Philipp Koehn, Hieu Hoang, Alexandra Birch, Chris Callison-Burch, Marcello Federico, Nicola Bertoldi, Brooke Cowan, Wade Shen, Christine Moran, Richard Zens, Chris Dyer, Ondřej Bojar, Alexandra Constantin, and Evan Herbst. 2007. Moses: Open source toolkit for statistical machine translation. In *Proceedings of the 45th Annual Meeting of the Association for Computational Linguistics Companion Volume Proceedings of the Demo and Poster Sessions*, pages 177–180, Prague, Czech Republic. Association for Computational Linguistics.

Taku Kudo and John Richardson. 2018. SentencePiece: A simple and language independent subword tokenizer and detokenizer for neural text processing. In *Proceedings of the 2018 Conference on Empirical Methods in Natural Language Processing: System Demonstrations*, pages 66–71, Brussels, Belgium. Association for Computational Linguistics.

Makoto Morishita, Jun Suzuki, and Masaaki Nagata. 2019. NTT neural machine translation systems at WAT 2019. In *Proceedings of the 6th Workshop on Asian Translation*, pages 99–105, Hong Kong, China. Association for Computational Linguistics.

Toshiaki Nakazawa, Hideki Nakayama, Chenchen Ding, Raj Dabre, Shohei Higashiyama, Hideya Mino, Isao Goto, Win Pa Pa, Anoop Kunchukuttan, Shantipriya Parida, Ondřej Bojar, Chenhui Chu, Akiko Eriguchi, Kaori Abe, and Sadao Oda, Yusuke Kurohashi. 2021. Overview of the 8th workshop on Asian translation. In *Proceedings of the 8th Workshop on Asian Translation*, Bangkok, Thailand. Association for Computational Linguistics.

Toshiaki Nakazawa, Manabu Yaguchi, Kiyotaka Uchimoto, Masao Utiyama, Eiichiro Sumita, Sadao Kurohashi, and Hitoshi Isahara. 2016. ASPEC: Asian scientific paper excerpt corpus. In *Proceedings of the Tenth International Conference on Language Resources and Evaluation (LREC'16)*, pages 2204–2208, Portorož, Slovenia. European Language Resources Association (ELRA).

Franz Josef Och and Hermann Ney. 2003. A systematic comparison of various statistical alignment models. *Computational Linguistics*, 29(1):19–51.

Kishore Papineni, Salim Roukos, Todd Ward, and Wei-Jing Zhu. 2002. Bleu: a method for automatic evaluation of machine translation. In *Proceedings of the 40th Annual Meeting of the Association for Computational Linguistics*, pages 311–318, Philadelphia, Pennsylvania, USA. Association for Computational Linguistics.

Qiu Ran, Yankai Lin, Peng Li, and Jie Zhou. 2020. Learning to recover from multi-modality errors for non-autoregressive neural machine translation. In *Proceedings of the 58th Annual Meeting of the Association for Computational Linguistics*, pages 3059–3069, Online. Association for Computational Linguistics.

Rico Sennrich, Barry Haddow, and Alexandra Birch. 2016. Improving neural machine translation models with monolingual data. In *Proceedings of the 54th Annual Meeting of the Association for Computational Linguistics (Volume 1: Long Papers)*, pages 86–96, Berlin, Germany. Association for Computational Linguistics.

Kai Song, Kun Wang, Heng Yu, Yue Zhang, Zhongqiang Huang, Weihua Luo, Xiangyu Duan, and Min Zhang. 2020. Alignment-enhanced transformer for constraining NMT with pre-specified translations. In *Proceedings of the Thirty-Fourth AAAI Conference on Artificial Intelligence*, pages 8886–8893, New York City, New York. Association for the Advancement of Artificial Intelligence.

Ilya Sutskever, Oriol Vinyals, and Quoc V Le. 2014. Sequence to sequence learning with neural networks. In *Advances in Neural Information Processing Systems 27*, pages 3104–3112, Montreal, Canada. Curran Associates, Inc.

Ashish Vaswani, Noam Shazeer, Niki Parmar, Jakob Uszkoreit, Llion Jones, Aidan N Gomez, Łukasz Kaiser, and Illia Polosukhin. 2017. Attention is all you need. In *Advances in Neural Information Processing Systems 30*, pages 5998–6008, Long Beach, California. Curran Associates, Inc.

# NECTEC's Participation in WAT-2021

**Zar Zar Hlaing[1], Ye Kyaw Thu[2,3], Thazin Myint Oo[2], Mya Ei San[4], Sasiporn Usanavasin[4], Ponrudee Netisopakul[1], Thepchai Supnithi[3]**
[1]King Mongkut's Institute of Technology Ladkrabang, Thailand
[2]Language Understanding Lab., Myanmar
[3]NECTEC, Thailand
[4]Sirindhorn International Institute of Technology (SIIT), Thammasat University, Thailand
{zarzarhlaing.it,yktnlp,queenofthazin,myaeisan1995}@gmail.com
sasiporn.us@siit.tu.ac.th, ponrudee@it.kmitl.ac.th,
thepchai.supnithi@nectec.or.th

## Abstract

In this paper, we report the experimental results of Machine Translation models conducted by a NECTEC team (Team-ID: NECTEC) for the WAT-2021 Myanmar-English translation task (Nakazawa et al., 2021). Basically, our models are based on neural methods for both directions of English-Myanmar and Myanmar-English language pairs. Most of the existing Neural Machine Translation (NMT) models mainly focus on the conversion of sequential data and do not directly use syntactic information. However, we conduct multi-source neural machine translation (NMT) models using the multilingual corpora such as string data corpus, tree data corpus, or POS-tagged data corpus. The multi-source translation is an approach to exploit multiple inputs (e.g. in two different formats) to increase translation accuracy. The RNN-based encoder-decoder model with attention mechanism and transformer architectures have been carried out for our experiment. The experimental results showed that the proposed models of RNN-based architecture outperform the baseline model for the English-to-Myanmar translation task, and the multi-source and shared-multi-source transformer models yield better translation results than the baseline.

## 1 Introduction

Machine translation (MT) is a quick and very effective way to communicate one language to another. MT consists of the automatic translation of human languages by using computers. The first machine translation systems were rule-based built only using linguistic information. The translation rules were manually created by experts. Although the rules are well defined, this process is very expensive and cannot translate well for all domains and languages. Currently, many researchers had successfully built the most popular machine translations such as SMT (Statistical Machine Translation) and NMT (Neural Machine Translation) for various languages instead of rule-based translation.

NMT has become the state-of-the-art approach compared to the previously dominant phrase-based statistical machine translation (SMT) approaches. However, the existing NMT models do not directly use syntactic information. Therefore, we propose tree-to-string and pos-to-string NMT systems by the multi-source translation models. We conducted these multi-source translation models with Myanmar-English and English-Myanmar in both directions. The multi-source translation models conducted in our experiments are based on the multi-source and shared-multi-source approaches of the previous research work (Junczys-Dowmunt and Grundkiewicz, 2017). Figure 1 and Figure 2 show the architecture of multi-source translation models. For doing the training processes of proposed models by the transformer and s2s architectures, word-level segmentation and tree-format on the English corpus side and syllable-level segmentation on the Myanmar corpus side are applied in English-to-Myanmar translation. In addition, we used the syllable-level segmentation and POS-tagged word on the Myanmar corpus side, and word-level segmentation on the English side for conducting the Myanmar-to-English translation.

In this paper, section 2 will describe our MT systems. The experimental setup will be proposed in section 3. In section 4, the results of our experiments will be reported, and section 5 will present the error analysis on translated outputs. Finally, section 6 will conclude the report.



*Proceedings of the 8th Workshop on Asian Translation*, pages 74–82
Bangkok, Thailand (online), August 5-6, 2021. 

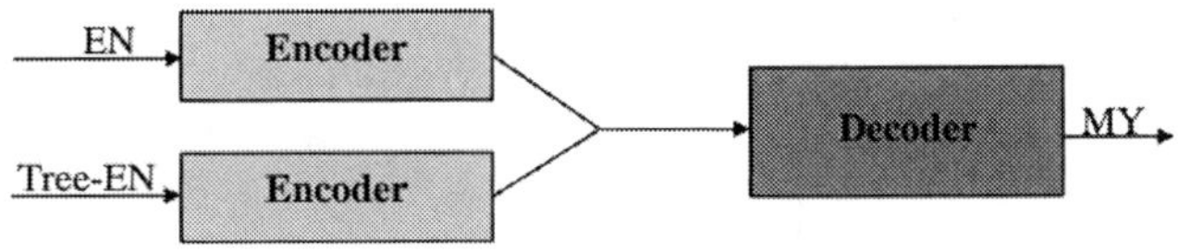


Figure 1: The basic idea of multi-source translation model for English-to-Myanmar translation

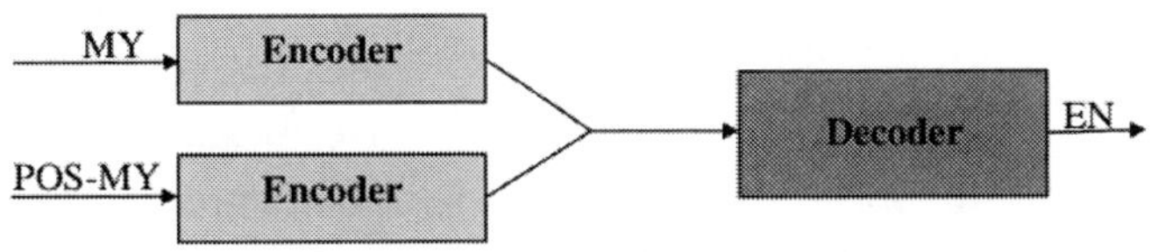


Figure 2: The basic idea of multi-source translation model for Myanmar-to-English translation

## 2 System Description

In this section, we describe the methodology used in our experiments for this paper. To build NMT systems, we chose the Marian framework[1] (Junczys-Dowmunt et al., 2018) with the architectures of Transformer and RNN based encoder-decoder model with attention mechanism (s2s). Marian is a self-contained neural machine translation toolkit focus on efficiency and research. This framework, the reimplementation of Nematus (Sennrich et al., 2017), is an efficient Neural Machine Translation framework written in pure C++ with minimal dependencies.

The main features of Marian are pure C++ implementation, one engine for GPU/CPU training and decoding, fast multi-GPU training and batched translation on GPU/CPU, minimal dependencies on external software (CUDA or MKL, and Boost), the static compilation (i.e., compile once, copy the binary and use anywhere), and permissive open-source MIT license. There are several model types supported by the Marian framework. Among them, we used ***transformer***, ***multi-transformer***, ***shared-multi-transformer***, ***s2s*** (RNN-based encoder-decoder model with attention mechanism), ***multi-s2s***, and ***shared-multi-s2s*** models for our experiment.

***transformer***: a model originally proposed by Google (Vaswani et al., 2017) based on attention mechanisms. ***multi-transformer***: a transformer model but uses multiple encoders. ***shared-multi-transformer***: is the same as multi-transformer but the difference is that the two encoders in shared-multi-transformer share parameters during training. ***s2s***: an RNN-based encoder-decoder model with attention mechanism. The architecture is equivalent to the Nematus models (Sennrich et al., 2017). ***multi-s2s***: s2s model but uses two or more encoders allowing multi-source neural machine translation. ***shared-multi-s2s***: is the same as multi-s2s but the difference is that the two encoders in shared-multi-s2s share parameters during training.

In our experiments, two baseline models (transformer and RNN based attention: s2s) are used for the translation tasks of English-to-Myanmar and Myanmar-to-English. For the first translation task, the baseline models take single input of English tree data {tree-en} and produce the output of Myanmar string {my}. The multi-transformer, shared-multi-transformer, multi-s2s, and shared-multi-s2s models use two inputs of English string data and tree data {en, tree-en} and produce the output of Myanmar string {my}. For the second translation task, the input of Myanmar POS data {pos-my} is taken by the baseline models and produces the output of English string {en}. The multi-source and shared multi-source models take two inputs of Myanmar sting data and Myanmar POS data {my, pos-my} and yield the output of English string {en}. The baseline models, the multi-source and shared-multi-source models do the same action as the first translation task with different inputs and outputs.

## 3 Experimental Setup

### 3.1 Parallel Data

The parallel data for Myanmar-English and English-Myanmar translation tasks was provided by the organizers of the competition and consists of two corpora: the ALT corpus and the UCSY corpus. The ALT cor-

[1] https://github.com/marian-nmt/marian

pus is one part of the Asian Language Treebank (ALT) Project (Riza et al., 2016) which consists of twenty thousand Myanmar-English parallel sentences from the Wikinews. The UCSY corpus (Yi Mon ShweSin et al., 2018) contains 238,014 sentences from various domains, including news articles and textbooks. The UCSY corpus for WAT-2021 is not identical to those used in WAT 2020 due to the extension of corpus size. Unlike the ALT corpus, Myanmar text in the UCSY corpus is not segmented. ALT corpus size is extremely small. And thus, the development data and test data were chosen from the ALT corpus. Moreover, we planned to do the experimental settings in training data with and without ALT training data because the test data are retrieved only from the ALT corpus. Due to the very limited hardware (only 2 GPUs and 8 GB memory workstation), the training time took very long and also crush several times, and we couldn't manage to finish both of the experiments. Therefore, in this paper, we present the experimental results with the training data only using the UCSY corpus that contained around 238,000 lines. Table 1 shows data statistics used for the experiments.

### 3.2 Data Preprocessing

In this section, we describe the preprocessing steps before doing the training processes. Proper syllable segmentation or word segmentation is essential for the quality improvement of machine translation in the Myanmar language because this language has no clear definition of word boundaries. Although Myanmar text data in the ALT corpus are manual word segmentation data, those in the UCSY corpus are not segmented. Thus, we need to segment these data. We prepared both syllable and word segmentation for Myanmar language data. We used in-house **myWord**[2] segmenter for Myanmar word segmentation and Myanmar **sylbreak**[3] segmenter for syllable segmentation. The myWord segmenter is a useful tool that can make the syllable segmentation, word segmentation, and phrase segmentation for the Myanmar language. In this paper, we used this tool only for word segmentation. The myWord segmenter tool will be released soon.

After doing the word segmentation process, we need to apply POS tagging to the segmented Myanmar data. In addition, for the English tree data, we also need to parse the English data. There are some reasons that we had implemented a multi-source NMT system for this paper. To the best of our knowledge, no experiments have been conducted for the multi-source NMT system using POS data and syntactic tree information. In particular, this multi-source NMT system has not been developed in the Myanmar language. There is only one Factored SMT paper (Ye Kyaw Thu et al., 2014) using Myanmar POS data. Thus, we had implemented a multi-source NMT system for Myanmar-to-English and English-to-Myanmar translations in this paper. To implement this system, we need to apply the POS tagging on the Myanmar data side and the tree data format on the English side. Although we desired to use the tree format on the Myanmar side, Myanmar data cannot be currently built like the English syntactic tree data format. And thus, we can only use Myanmar POS(Part-of-speech) data and English tree data format for implementing the multi-source translation models. Part-of-speech tagging and the parser that we used in our experiment will be described in the following sections.

#### 3.2.1 Part-of-speech Tagging

For the part-of-speech (POS) Myanmar data, the segmented data obtained by the myWord segmenter was tagged by using the RDR model built-in **myPOS** version 2.0[4] (Zar Zar Hlaing et al., 2020). 16 POS Tag-sets (Khin War War Htike et al., 2017) were used in myPOS version 2.0. These POS tag-sets are ***abb*** (Abbreviation), ***adj*** (Adjective), ***adv*** (Adverb), ***conj*** (Conjunction), ***fw*** (Foreign word), ***int*** (Interjection), ***n*** (Noun), ***num*** (Number), ***part*** (Particle), ***part_neg*** (Negative particle), ***ppm*** (Post-positional Marker), ***pron*** (Pronoun), ***punc*** (Punctuation), ***sb*** (Symbol), ***tn*** (Text Number) and ***v*** (Verb). Supervised tagging algorithms, namely, Conditional Random Fields (CRFs), Hidden Markov Model (HMM), Ripple Down Rules-based (RDR), and neural sequence labeling approach of Conditional Random Fields (NCRF++) were used to compare the tagging accuracies of the original myPOS version 1.0 (Khin War War Htike et al., 2017) and myPOS version 2.0. Among these four tagging methods, the RDR model gave the best tagging accuracy. Thus, we chose the RDR model for tagging the Myanmar data for our experiment. The example of POS-tagged

[2] `https://github.com/ye-kyaw-thu/myWord`

[3] `https://github.com/ye-kyaw-thu/sylbreak`

[4] `https://github.com/ye-kyaw-thu/myPOS`

Table 1: English-Myanmar Parallel Dataset

| Data Type | File Name | Number of Sentence |
|---|---|---|
| **TRAIN** | train.ucsy.[my \| en] | 238,014 |
| **DEV** | dev.alt.[my \| en] | 1,000 |
| **TEST** | test.alt.[my \| en] | 1,018 |

data for the sentence **“ကျွန်တော် က သုတေသီ တစ် ယောက် ပါ ။” (I am a researcher.)** is described in the following:

`ကျွန်တော်/pron က/ppm သုတေသီ/n တစ်/tn ယောက်/part ပါ/part ။/punc`

We also evaluated the accuracy of the RDR model. To evaluate this model, 1,300 Myanmar sentences were retrieved from the UCSY corpus, and these sentences were tagged by the selected RDR model. On the other hand, we manually tagged these Myanmar sentences. Finally, we evaluated the accuracy of the RDR model by comparing these two tagged data. We found that the RDR model provides the tagging accuracy of 77% Precision, 81% Recall, and 79% F-Measure.

#### 3.2.2 RegexpParser

Word-level segmentation and tree data format were used on the English side for the experiment. English data given by the WAT-2021 are already segmented. Thus, no segmentation process is needed to do for the English side. For parsing the English data, some parsers such as English PCFG (Probabilistic Context-Free Grammar) parser from Stanford Parser[5], BLLIP Parser[6], Berkeley Neural Parser[7], and RegexpParser[8] were tested with our experiment data of English side. **PCFG Parser** is used to parse the English sentence into tree data format. This parser cannot parse long sentences of more than 70 words. The longest sentence in our experiment data contains approximately 1,000 words. And thus, this PCFG parser cannot be used for parsing our experiment data. **BLLIP Parser** is a statistical natural language parser that includes a generative constituent parser and discriminative maximum entropy re-ranker. It can be used as Python version or Java version. This parser cannot parse the long sentences in our experiment data although it can accept more sentence length 853 than the PCFG parser.

**Berkeley Neural Parser** is a high-accuracy parser with models for 11 languages which is implemented by Python. It is based on constituency parsing with a self-attentive encoder, with additional changes in multilingual constituency parsing with self-attention and pre-training. Although this parser can parse the long sentences in our experiment data, training time takes a lot more than the **RegexpParser[9] (grammar-based chunk parser)** from **nltk** package. By comparing the aforementioned parsers, RegexpParser can parse the longest sentences and all the experiment data within a few minutes. Moreover, this RegexpParser is the simplest parser for generating the parse tree data. Thus, we chose the RegexpParser for the tree data format of the English side of our experiment data.

A grammar-based chunk parser **RegexpParser** uses a set of regular expression patterns to specify the behavior of the parser. The chunking of the text is encoded by using a ChunkString, and each rule performs by modifying the chunking in the ChunkString. The rules are implemented by using regular expression matching and substitution. A grammar contains one or more clauses in the following form:

$\{< DT \mid JJ >\}$ #chunk determiners and adjectives

$\} < [\backslash \cdot VI] \cdot * > +\{$ #strip any tag beginning with V, I, or .

$< \cdot * >\}\{< DT >$ #split a chunk at a determiner

$< DT \mid JJ > \{\} < NN \cdot * >$ #merge chunk ending with det /adj with one starting with a noun

The clauses of a grammar are also executed in order. A cascaded chunk parser is one having more than one clause. The maximum depth of a parse tree generated by RegexpParser is the same as the number of clauses in the gram-

[5] https://nlp.stanford.edu/software/lex-parser.shtml

[6] https://github.com/BLLIP/bllip-parser

[7] https://github.com/nikitakit/self-attentive-parser

[8] https://www.programcreek.com/python/example/91255/nltk.RegexpParser

[9] https://www.programcreek.com/python/example/91255/nltk.RegexpParser

mar. To parse a sentence, firstly, we need to create the chunker by using the RegexpParser function with the built grammar. Secondly, an input sentence is needed to tokenize and the tokenized sentence will need to be tagged by using the functions from **nltk** package. After tagging the tokenized sentence, the chunker calls the parse function with the tagged string parameter. Later, we will get the parse tree format output and need to convert this tree format to the tree format string. These procedures were used for parsing the English side of our experiment data. The example of English parse tree produced by this Regexp-Parser is shown as follow:

**(S I/PRP (VP (V love/VBP)) (VP (V programming/VBG)) ./.)**

### 3.3 Training

All our NMT systems were trained on 2 GPUs with the following parameters for Marian framework. Two architectures such as ***transformer*** and ***s2s*** (RNN-based encoder-decoder model with attention mechanism) are applied in our experiment. For the first architecture, we used the different model types (`--type transformer` for Transformer Model, `--type multi-transformer` for Multi-Transformer Model, and `--type shared-multi-transformer` for Shared-Multi-Transformer Model) with the following parameters:

```
--max-length 500 --maxi-batch
 100 --valid-freq 5000
--valid-metrics cross-entropy
 perplexity bleu --save-freq
 5000 --disp-freq 500
--valid-mini-batch 64
--beam-size
 6 --normalize 0.6 --enc-depth 2
--mini-batch-fit -w 1000
--dec-depth 2 --transformer-heads
 8 --transformer-dropout 0.3
--label-smoothing 0.1
--early-stopping 10
--tied-embeddings
--exponential-smoothing
--learn-rate 0.0003 --lr-warmup 0
--lr-decay-inv-sqrt 16000
--clip-norm 5 --devices 0 1
--sync-sgd --seed 1111
```

For the second architecture, we also used the different model types (`--type s2s` for RNN with attention Model, `--type multi-s2s` for Multi-s2s Model, and `--type shared-multi-s2s` for Shared-Multi-s2s Model) with the following parameters:

```
--max-length 500 --workspace
 500 --enc-depth 2 --enc-type
 alternating --enc-cell
 lstm --enc-cell-depth 2
--dec-depth 2 --dec-cell
 lstm --dec-cell-base-depth
 2 --dec-cell-high-depth
 2 --mini-batch-fit
--valid-mini-batch 16
--valid-metrics cross-entropy
 perplexity translation
 bleu --valid-freq 5000
--save-freq 5000 --disp-freq
 500 --dropout-rnn
 0.3 --early-stopping
 10 --tied-embeddings
--mini-batch-fit --dropout-src
 0.3 --devices 0 1 --sync-sgd
--seed 1111
```

## 4 Evaluation Results

Our systems are evaluated on the ALT test set and the evaluation results are shown in Table 2. For the evaluation of Myanmar-to-English and English-to-Myanmar translation pairs, we used the different evaluation metrics such as Bilingual Evaluation Understudy (BLEU) (Papineni et al., 2002), Rank-based Intuitive Bilingual Evaluation Score (RIBES) (Isozaki et al., 2010), and Adequacy-Fluency Metrics (AMFM) (Banchs et al., 2015).

The BLEU score measures the precision of n-gram (overall $n \leq 4$ in our case) with respect to a reference translation with a penalty for short translations. Intuitively, the BLEU score measures the adequacy of the translation and a larger BLEU score indicates a better translation quality. RIBES is an automatic evaluation metric based on rank correlation coefficients modified with precision and special care is paid to the word order of the translation results. The RIBES score is suitable for distance language pairs such as Myanmar and English. Larger RIBES scores indicate better translation quality. AM-FM is a two-dimensional automatic evaluation metric for machine translation, which is used to evaluate the machine translation systems. The evaluation metric designed to address independently the semantic and syntactic aspects of the translation. The larger the AMFM scores, the better the trans-

Table 2: BLEU, RIBES and AMFM scores for English-to-Myanmar and Myanmar-to-English translations

| Models | English-to-Myanmar | | | Myanmar-to-English | | |
|---|---|---|---|---|---|---|
| | BLEU | RIBES | AMFM | BLEU | RIBES | AMFM |
| transformer | 12.72 | **0.610951** | 0.645760 | **6.24** | **0.620840** | **0.424640** |
| multi-transformer | 12.94 | 0.598012 | **0.654780** | 4.44 | 0.577247 | 0.393760 |
| shared-multi-transformer | **13.90** | 0.608810 | 0.645260 | 4.62 | 0.587155 | 0.391710 |
| s2s | 12.35 | 0.620377 | 0.618420 | **6.72** | **0.616469** | **0.395310** |
| multi-s2s | **12.82** | 0.625476 | **0.638870** | 4.73 | 0.578146 | 0.357150 |
| shared-multi-s2s | 12.11 | **0.626460** | 0.631630 | 6.13 | 0.609560 | 0.376140 |

lation quality. Experiments are conducted by tuning different parameter settings for the proposed models. The best scores among those of the experimental results are submitted in this description. The highest scores of the proposed models are indicated as bold numbers. Since the UCSY corpus is updated annually, we cannot directly compare the official baseline results of WAT-2020 and our experimental results of WAT-2021. Thus, the experimental results are compared only with our baseline model results.

Table 2 shows the experimental results of the first and second architectures. The first part of the table consists of English-to-Myanmar translation scores and the second part consists of Myanmar-to-English translation scores. For the first architecture (i.e., transformer) in the first part of the table, the shared-multi-transformer model achieves higher BLEU scores (+1.18) than the baseline transformer model. Furthermore, the multi-transformer model performs better than the baseline transformer in terms of AMFM scores. However, RIBES scores of multi-transformer and shared-multi-transformer models are lower than the baseline transformer model. For the second architecture (i.e., s2s or RNN-based Attention), the multi-s2s model outperforms the baseline s2s model and shared-multi-s2s in terms of BLEU and AMFM scores. The shared-multi-s2s model provides better RIBES scores (0.626460). The highest BLEU scores (13.90) of the shared-multi-transformer model and the highest AMFM scores (0.654780) of the multi-transformer model are produced by the first architecture while the highest RIBES scores (0.625476) are achieved by the multi-s2s model of the second architecture.

Myanmar-to-English translation results are shown in the second part of the Table 2. For Myanmar to English translation, the two baseline models (i.e., transformer and s2s) outperform the other models in terms of BLEU, RIBES, and AMFM scores. No improvements occur in this translation task. On the other hand, from English to Myanmar translation, the multi-transformer model is better than the baseline transformer model in terms of AMFM score, and the shared-multi-transformer model performs better than the baseline in terms of BLEU score. Moreover, the multi-s2s and shared-multi-s2s models also provide better translation results compared with the baseline model.

## 5 Error Analysis

For both English-to-Myanmar and Myanmar-to-English translation models, we analyzed the translated outputs by using Word Error Rate[10]. For doing the error analysis, we used SCLITE (score speech recognition system output) program from the NIST scoring toolkit SCTK[11] version 2.4.10 for making dynamic programming based alignments between reference (ref) and hypothesis (hyp) and calculation of WER. The WER formula can be described as the following equation:

$$WER = \frac{(I + D + S)100}{N} \quad (1)$$

where $S$ is the number of substitutions, $D$ is the number of deletions, $I$ is the number of insertions, $C$ is the number of correct words and N is the number of words in the reference ($N = S + D + C$). The percentage of WER can be greater than 100% when the number of insertions is very high.

[10] https://en.wikipedia.org/wiki/Word_error_rate

[11] https://github.com/usnistgov/SCTK

Table 3: WER scores for English-to-Myanmar and Myanmar-to-English translation models (Generally, lower WER indicates better translation performance)

| Models | English-to-Myanmar | Myanmar-to-English |
|---|---|---|
| | WER(%) | WER(%) |
| **transformer** | **81.3%** | **82.6%** |
| **multi-transformer** | 83.9% | 90.0% |
| **shared-multi-transformer** | 83.5% | 88.2% |
| **s2s** | 84.2% | **85.1%** |
| **multi-s2s** | 82.7% | 91.8% |
| **shared-multi-s2s** | **82.5%** | 86.0% |

Table 3 shows the WER scores of English-to-Myanmar and Myanmar-to-English translation models. In this table, lower WER scores are highlighted as bold numbers. The lower the WER scores, the better the translation models. For the first architecture of English-to-Myanmar translation, the baseline transformer model gives lower WER scores (81.3%) than the multi-transformer and shared-multi-transformer models. However, in the second architecture, the shared-multi-s2s model provides lower WER scores (82.5%) compared with the baseline (s2s) and multi-s2s models. In Myanmar-to-English translation, the multi-transformer and shared-multi-transformer models yield greater WER scores (90.0% and 88.2%) than the baseline transformer model of the first architecture. In addition, the multi-s2s and shared-multi-s2s model also give higher WER scores (91.8% and 86.0%) than the baseline s2s models (85.1%). Due to the higher WER scores in Myanmar-to-English translation models, the multi-transformer and shared-multi-transformer models couldn't provide better translation results than the baseline transformer model, and the multi-s2s and shared-multi-s2s models couldn't also yield the improvements than the baseline s2s model.

After we analyzed the confusion pairs of English-to-Myanmar and Myanmar-to-English translation models in detail, we found that most of the confusion pairs in the translations are caused by (1) the nature of the Myanmar language (written or speaking form), (2) the incorrect word segmentation or data cleaning errors of English language, (3) the Myanmar language with no articles (i.e., **a**, **an**, and **the**), and (4) the different nature and language gaps of Myanmar and English languages. The top 10 confusion pairs of English-to-Myanmar and Myanmar-to-English translations of the model transformer are shown in Table 4. In this table, the first column is the reference and hypothesis pair (i.e., output of the translation model) for English-to-Myanmar translation. The third one is for that of Myanmar-to-English translation.

All of the confusion pairs in the first column are caused by the nature of the Myanmar language. For example, in Myanmar written or speaking form, the word "သည် ("is" in English)" are the same as the word "တယ် ("is" in English)". Moreover, the words "၏ ("of or 's" in English)" and "ရဲ့ ("of or 's" in English)" in the possessive place and the words "များ ("plural form" in English)" and "တွေ ("plural form" in English)" are the same meanings. In other words, these hypotheses are synonyms of the reference words. In the third column of the Table 4, for the Myanmar-to-English translation, the confusion pairs of "apos → quot", "quot → apos", "the → &amp", ", → the" and "the → s" are caused by the incorrect word segmentation or data cleaning errors of English language. Furthermore, we found that the confusion pairs of "the → a" and "a → the" are caused by the Myanmar language with no articles (i.e., **a**, **an**, and **the**). The confusion pairs of "in → of", "to → of" and "with → and" are caused due to the different nature and language gaps of Myanmar and English languages. Occasionally, most of the Myanmar people misused the usage of the words "**in, of,** and **with**" in English writing.

For instance, for the Myanmar sentence "သူ

Table 4: An example of confusion pairs of the model Transformer

| **EN-MY Ref→Hyp** | **Freq** | **MY-EN Ref→Hyp** | **Freq** |
|---|---|---|---|
| သည် → တယ် | 371 | apos→ quot | 30 |
| များ → တွေ | 63 | the → a | 29 |
| ၏ → ရဲ့ | 33 | quot → apos | 24 |
| တယ် → သည် | 36 | , → the | 23 |
| သော → တဲ့ | 17 | the → &amp | 23 |
| ရန် → ဖို့ | 9 | in → of | 18 |
| ယောက် → ဦး | 9 | a → the | 17 |
| မည် → မယ် | 8 | the → s | 14 |
| တို့ → များ | 7 | to → of | 10 |
| ၎င်း → ဒါ | 3 | with → and | 6 |

က အတန်း ထဲ မှာ အတော်ဆုံး ကျောင်းသား ဖြစ်တယ်။", they translate this sentence to the English sentence "He is the most clever student **of** the class.". In this case, they misused the word "**of**" instead of the word "**in**". The correct English sentence is "He is the most clever student **in** the class." For another example of Myanmar sentence "စားပွဲ ကို သစ်သား ဖြင့် ပြုလုပ် ထားတယ်။", they translate to English sentence "The table is made **with** wooden." with the misused of the word "**with**" instead of "**of**". The correct sentence for this example is "The table is made **of** wooden." When the prepositions "**in**, **of**, and **with**" are combined with the main verbs, the prepositions "**in** and **of**" and "**with** and **of**" have generally same meanings in Myanmar language. These may cause the Myanmar-to-English translation models hard to learn well during the training processes compared with the English-to-Myanmar translation models.

## 6 Conclusion

In this system description for WAT-2021, we submitted our NMT systems with two architectures such as transformer and RNN with attention. We evaluated our proposed models in both directions of Myanmar-English and English-Myanmar translations at WAT-2021. In this paper, for English to Myanmar translation, multi-source and shared-multi-source models outperform the baseline models in terms of BLEU, RIBES, and AMFM scores. In the Myanmar-to-English translation task, the proposed models could not provide better translation quality than the baselines. The top 10 frequent errors in the model's hypothesis could be clearly found from our error analysis. For examples, the confusion pairs of "သည် → တယ် 371", "များ → တွေ 63", "၏ → ရဲ့ 33", and so on. Moreover, our study also made a contribution to the fact that if these errors can be cleaned up, the translation performance of the shared task will improve. In the future, we intend to apply post-editing techniques in Myanmar to English translation to improve the translation quality. Furthermore, we intend to extend string-to-tree and string-to-pos translation approaches for under-resourced languages such as Myanmar and Thai.

## Acknowledgments

This work was supported by King Mongkut's Institute of Technology Ladkrabang (KMITL) and in collaboration with Artificial Intelligence Research Group, National Electronics and Computer Technology Center (NECTEC), Thailand.

## References

Rafael E. Banchs, Luis F. D'Haro, and Haizhou Li. 2015. Adequacy–fluency metrics: Evaluating mt in the continuous space model framework.

*IEEE/ACM Transactions on Audio, Speech, and Language Processing*, 23(3):472–482.

Hideki Isozaki, Tsutomu Hirao, Kevin Duh, Katsuhito Sudoh, and Hajime Tsukada. 2010. Automatic evaluation of translation quality for distant language pairs. In *Proceedings of the 2010 Conference on Empirical Methods in Natural Language Processing*, pages 944–952, Cambridge, MA. Association for Computational Linguistics.

Marcin Junczys-Dowmunt and Roman Grundkiewicz. 2017. An exploration of neural sequence-to-sequence architectures for automatic post-editing.

Marcin Junczys-Dowmunt, Roman Grundkiewicz, Tomasz Dwojak, Hieu Hoang, Kenneth Heafield, Tom Neckermann, Frank Seide, Ulrich Germann, Alham Fikri Aji, Nikolay Bogoychev, André F. T. Martins, and Alexandra Birch. 2018. Marian: Fast neural machine translation in C++. In *Proceedings of ACL 2018, System Demonstrations*, pages 116–121, Melbourne, Australia. Association for Computational Linguistics.

Khin War War Htike, Ye Kyaw Thu, Zuping Zhang, and Win Pa Pa. 2017. Comparison of six pos tagging methods on10k sentences myanmar language (burmese) pos tagged corpus. In *18th International Conference on Computational Linguistics and Intelligent Text Processing (CICLing 2017)*.

Toshiaki Nakazawa, Hideki Nakayama, Chenchen Ding, Raj Dabre, Shohei Higashiyama, Hideya Mino, Isao Goto, Win Pa Pa, Anoop Kunchukuttan, Shantipriya Parida, Ondřej Bojar, Chenhui Chu, Akiko Eriguchi, Kaori Abe, and Sadao Oda, Yusuke Kurohashi. 2021. Overview of the 8th workshop on Asian translation. In *Proceedings of the 8th Workshop on Asian Translation*, Bangkok, Thailand. Association for Computational Linguistics.

Kishore Papineni, Salim Roukos, Todd Ward, and Wei-Jing Zhu. 2002. Bleu: a method for automatic evaluation of machine translation. In *Proceedings of the 40th Annual Meeting of the Association for Computational Linguistics*, pages 311–318, Philadelphia, Pennsylvania, USA. Association for Computational Linguistics.

Hammam Riza, Michael Purwoadi, Gunarso, Teduh Uliniansyah, Aw Ai Ti, Sharifah Mahani Aljunied, L. C. Mai, Vu Tat Thang, N. Thai, Vichet Chea, Rapid Sun, Sethserey Sam, Sopheap Seng, K. Soe, K. Nwet, M. Utiyama, and Chenchen Ding. 2016. Introduction of the asian language treebank. *2016 Conference of The Oriental Chapter of International Committee for Coordination and Standardization of Speech Databases and Assessment Techniques (O-COCOSDA)*, pages 1–6.

Rico Sennrich, Orhan Firat, Kyunghyun Cho, Alexandra Birch, Barry Haddow, Julian Hitschler, Marcin Junczys-Dowmunt, Samuel Läubli, Antonio Valerio Miceli Barone, Jozef Mokry, and Maria Nădejde. 2017. Nematus: a toolkit for neural machine translation. In *Proceedings of the Software Demonstrations of the 15th Conference of the European Chapter of the Association for Computational Linguistics*, pages 65–68, Valencia, Spain. Association for Computational Linguistics.

Ashish Vaswani, Noam Shazeer, Niki Parmar, Jakob Uszkoreit, Llion Jones, Aidan N Gomez, Ł ukasz Kaiser, and Illia Polosukhin. 2017. Attention is all you need. In *Advances in Neural Information Processing Systems*, volume 30. Curran Associates, Inc.

Ye Kyaw Thu, Andrew Finch, Akihiro Tamura, Eiichiro Sumita, and Yoshinori Sagisaka. 2014. Factored machine translation for myanmar to english, japanese and vice versa. In *Proceedings of the 12th International Conference on Computer Applications (ICCA 2014)*, pages 171–177, Yangon, Myanmar. Association for Computational Linguistics.

Yi Mon ShweSin, Khin Mar Soe, and Khin Yadanar Htwe. 2018. Large scale myanmar to english neural machine translation system. In *2018 IEEE 7th Global Conference on Consumer Electronics (GCCE)*, pages 464–465.

Zar Zar Hlaing, Ye Kyaw Thu, Myat Myo Nwe Wai, Thepchai Supnithi, and Ponrudee Netisopakul. 2020. Myanmar pos resource extension effects on automatic tagging methods. In *2020 15th International Joint Symposium on Artificial Intelligence and Natural Language Processing (iSAI-NLP)*, pages 1–6.

# Hybrid Statistical Machine Translation for English-Myanmar: UTYCC Submission to WAT-2021

**Ye Kyaw Thu[1,2], Thazin Myint Oo[2], Hlaing Myat Nwe[1], Khaing Zar Mon[1], Nang Aeindray Kyaw[1], Naing Linn Phyo[1], Nann Hwan Khun[1], Hnin Aye Thant[1]**
[1]University of Technology (Yatanarpon Cyber City), Myanmar
[2]Language Understanding Lab., Myanmar
{yekyawthu,hlaingmyatnwe,khaingzarmon,nangaeindraykyaw}@utycc.edu.mm,
{nainglinphyo,nannhwankhun, hninayethant}@utyccc.edu.mm,
queenofthazin@gmail.com

## Abstract

In this paper we describe our submissions to WAT-2021 (Nakazawa et al., 2021) for English-to-Myanmar language (Burmese) task. Our team, ID: "YCC-MT1", focused on bringing transliteration knowledge to the decoder without changing the model. We manually extracted the transliteration word/phrase pairs from the ALT corpus and applying XML markup feature of Moses decoder (i.e. `-xml-input exclusive`, `-xml-input inclusive`). We demonstrate that hybrid translation technique can significantly improve (*around 6 BLEU scores*) the baseline of three well-known "Phrase-based SMT", "Operation Sequence Model" and "Hierarchical Phrase-based SMT". Moreover, this simple hybrid method achieved the second highest results among the submitted MT systems for English-to-Myanmar WAT2021 translation share task according to BLEU (Papineni et al., 2002) and AMFM scores (Banchs et al., 2015).

## 1 Introduction

While both statistical machine translation (SMT) and neural machine translation (NMT) have proven successful for high resource language, it is still an open research question how to make it work well especially for the low resource and long distance reordering language pairs such as English and Burmese (Duh et al., 2020), (Kolachina et al., 2012), (Trieu et al., 2019), (Win Pa Pa et al., 2016). To the best of our knowledge there are only two publicly available English-Myanmar parallel corpora; ALT Corpus (Ding et al., 2020) and UCSY Corpus (Yi Mon Shwe Sin and Khin Mar Soe, 2019) for research purpose, and the size of the corpora are around 20K and 200K respectively. The parallel data for Myanmar-English machine translation share task at Workshop on Asian Translation (WAT) using combination of that two corpora and thus it is a good chance for the NLP researchers who are working on low resource machine translation. Motivated by this challenge, we represented the University of Technology, Yatanarpon Cyber City (UTYCC) and participated in the English-Myanmar (en-my) share task of WAT2021 (Nakazawa et al., 2021).

In this paper, we propose one hybrid system based on plugging XML markup translation knowledge to the SMT decoder. The translation rules for transliteration and borrowed words, and direct usage of English words in the target language are constructed by using a parallel word dictionary. The English-Myanmar transliteration dictionary was built by manual extracting parallel words/phrases from the whole ALT corpus. This simple hybrid method outperformed the three baselines and achieved the second highest results among the submitted MT systems for English-to-Myanmar WAT2021 translation share task according to BLEU (Papineni et al., 2002) and AMFM scores (Banchs et al., 2015).

The remainder of this paper is organized as follows. In Section 2, we introduce the data preprocessing, including word segmentation and cleaning steps. In Section 3, we describe the details of our three SMT systems. The machine translation evaluation metrics are presented in Section 4. The manual extraction process of transliteration word/phrase pairs from the ALT English-Myanmar parallel data is described in Section 5. Then, the SMT decoding with XML markup technique is described in Section 6. In Section 7, we present hybrid translation results achieved by all our systems. Section 8 concludes this paper.

## 2 Data preprocessing

### 2.1 Preprocessing for English and Myanmar

We tokenized and escaping English data respectively with the tokenizer and escaping perl script (`escape-special-chars.perl`) of Moses (Koehn et al., 2007). For Myanmar, although provided training data of ALT was already segmented, word segmentation was not provided for the UCSY corpus. And thus, we did syllable segmentation by using `sylbreak.pl` (Ye Kyaw Thu, 2017).

### 2.2 Parallel Data Statistic

The corpus for the English-Myanmar share task contained two separate corpora and they are UCSY corpus and ALT corpus. The domain of the UCSY corpus is general and the



*Proceedings of the 8th Workshop on Asian Translation*, pages 83–89
Bangkok, Thailand (online), August 5-6, 2021. 

Table 1: Statistics of our preprocessed parallel data

| Data Type | # of Sentences | # of Myanmar Syllables | # of English Words |
|---|---|---|---|
| **TRAIN (UCSY)** | 238,014 | 6,285,996 | 3,357,260 |
| **TRAIN (ALT)** | 18,088 | 1,038,640 | 413,000 |
| **DEV** | 1,000 | 57,709 | 27,318 |
| **TEST** | 1,018 | 58,895 | 27,929 |

original English sentences of the ALT corpus was extracted from the Wikinews (Ye Kyaw Thu et al., 2016). The size of the UCSY parallel corpus is about 238K sentence pairs and it is also a part of the training data of the WAT2021 share task. The size of the English-Myanmar ALT parallel corpus is about 20K sentence pairs and splitted into 18,088 sentences for training, 1,000 sentences for development and 1,018 sentences for test data respectively (see Table 1). While the number of development and test set sentences are the same, we implemented phrase-based, operating sequence model and hiero systems with the UCSY training corpus only and the combination of the UCSY and the ALT training sets. The statistics of our preprocessed parallel data are shown in Table1.

## 3 SMT Systems

In this section, we describe the methodology used in the machine translation experiments for this share task.

### 3.1 Phrase-based Statistical Machine Translation

A PBSMT translation model is based on phrasal units (Koehn et al., 2003). Here, a phrase is simply a contiguous sequence of words and generally, not a linguistically motivated phrase. A phrase-based translation model typically gives better translation performance than word-based models. We can describe a simple phrase-based translation model consisting of phrase-pair probabilities extracted from corpus and a basic reordering model, and an algorithm to extract the phrases to build a phrase-table (Specia, 2011). The phrase translation model is based on noisy channel model. To find best translation $\hat{e}$ that maximizes the translation probability $\mathbf{P}(f)$ given the source sentences; mathematically. Here, the source language is French and the target language is an English. The translation of a French sentence into an English sentence is modeled as equation 1.

$$\hat{e} = argmax_e \mathbf{P}(e|f) \quad (1)$$

Applying the Bayes' rule, we can factorized into three parts.

$$P(e|f) = \frac{\mathbf{P}(e)}{\mathbf{P}(f)} \mathbf{P}(f|e) \quad (2)$$

The final mathematical formulation of phrase-based model is as follows:

$$argmax_e \mathbf{P}(e|f) = argmax_e \mathbf{P}(f|e) \mathbf{P}(e) \quad (3)$$

### 3.2 Operation Sequence Model

The operation sequence model which combines the benefits of two state-of-the-art SMT frameworks named n-gram-based SMT and phrase-based SMT. This model simultaneously generate source and target units and does not have spurious ambiguity that is based on minimal translation units (Durrani et al., 2011) (Durrani et al., 2015). It is a bilingual language model that also integrates reordering information. OSM motivates better reordering mechanism that uniformly handles local and non-local reordering and strong coupling of lexical generation and reordering. It means that OSM can handle both short and long distance reordering. The operation types are such as generate, insert gap, jump back and jump forward which perform the actual reordering.

### 3.3 Hierarchical Phrase-based Statistical Machine Translation

The hierarchical phrase-based SMT approach is a model based on synchronous context-free grammar (Specia, 2011). The model is able to be learned from a corpus of unannotated parallel text. The advantage this technique offers over the phrase-based approach is that the hierarchical structure is able to represent the word re-ordering process. The re-ordering is represented explicitly rather than encoded into a lexicalized re-ordering model (commonly used in purely phrase-based approaches). This makes the approach particularly applicable to language pairs that require long-distance re-ordering during the translation process (Braune et al., 2012).

### 3.4 Moses SMT System

We used the PBSMT, HPBSMT and OSM system provided by the Moses toolkit (Koehn et al., 2007) for training the PBSMT, HPBSMT and OSM statistical machine translation systems. The word segmented source language was aligned with the word segmented target language using GIZA++ (Och and Ney, 2000). The alignment was symmetrized by grow-diag-final and heuristic (Koehn et al., 2003). The lexicalized reordering model was trained with the msd-bidirectional-fe option (Tillmann, 2004). We use KenLM (Heafield, 2011) for training the 5-gram language model with modified Kneser-Ney discounting (Chen and Goodman, 1996). Minimum error rate training (MERT) (Och, 2003) was used to tune the decoder parameters and the decoding was done using the Moses decoder (version 2.1.1). We used default settings of Moses for all experiments.

## 4 Evaluation

Our systems are evaluated on the ALT test set and we used the different evaluation metrics such as Bilingual Evaluation Understudy (BLEU) (Papineni et al., 2002), Rank-based Intuitive Bilingual Evaluation Score (RIBES) (Isozaki et al., 2010), and Adequacy-Fluency Metrics (AMFM) (Banchs et al., 2015). For the official evaluation of English-to-Myanmar share task, we uploaded our hypothesis files to the WAT2021 evaluation server and sub-syllable (almost same with sylbreak toolkit's syllable units) segmentation was used for Myanmar language. We submitted "hybrid PBSMT with XML markup (inclusive)" and "hybrid OSM with XML markup (inclusive)" systems training only with UCSY corpus for human evaluation.

## 5 Manual Extraction of Parallel Transliteration Words

When we studied on the Myanmar language corpus provided by the WAT2021, we found that many sentences are very long, containing spelling errors, unnaturalness of translation (i.e. translation from English to Myanmar) and many transliteration words (i.e. word-by-word, phrase-by-phrase, compound word transliteration). Moreover, the ALT corpus was extracted from the English Wikinews (Ye Kyaw Thu et al., 2016) and it contains many named entity words such as person names, organizations, locations. See three example English-Myanmar parallel sentences of the ALT test data that contained several transliteration words. This paper tackling the problem of machine translation on transliteration word/phrase pairs by hybrid translation approach.

[ဆစ် ဒ နီ][1] က [ရ န့် ဝစ်ခ်][2] မြင်း ပြိုင် ကွင်း မှ မျိုး သ န့် ပြိုင် မြင်း ရှစ် ကောင် ဟာ မြင်း တုတ် ကွေး ရော ဂါ ကူး စက် ခံ ခဲ့ ရ တယ် ဆို တာ အ တည် ပြု ခဲ့ ပါ တယ် ။ (It has been confirmed that eight thoroughbred race horses at [Randwick][2] Racecourse in [Sydney][1] have been infected with equine influenza .)

ဒီ စ နေ တ နင်္ဂ နွေ မှာ [အန် အက်စ် ဒ ဗ လျူ][1] နှ င့် [ကွင်း စ် လန်း ဒ်][2] မှ လွဲ ၍ [ဩ စ တြေး လျ][3] တိုက် ပြည် နယ် များ အား လုံး တွင် မြင်း ပွဲ ပြန် စ ဖို့ မျှော် လ င့် ပါ တယ် ။ (Racing is expected to resume in all [Australian][3] states except [NSW][1] and [Queensland][2] on the weekend .)

[ဘ ရစ် တ နီ စ ပီး ယား][1] သူ မ ၏ နေ အိမ် သို့ အ ပြန် ကို နောက် ယောင် ခံ လိုက် ပြီး နောက် [ကယ် လီ ဖိုး နီး ယား][2] ပြည် နယ် [မစ် ရှင်း][3] တောင် ကုန်း များ အ တွင်း ၊ အ တား အ ဆီး မဲ့ စွာ မောင်း နှင် ခြင်း အ တွက် ဗုဒ္ဓ ဟူး နေ့ တွင် သ တင်း ထောက် အ ဖွဲ့ ဝင် အ မျိုး သား လေး ယောက် အ ဖမ်း ခံ ခဲ့ ရ ပြီး ဒဏ် ငွေ ပေး ဆောင် ခဲ့ ရ သည် ။ (Four male members of the paparazzi were arrested and charged on Wednesday with reckless driving in [Mission][3]1 Hills , [California][2] after following [Britney Spears][1] back to her mansion .)

We manually extracted English-Myanmar transliteration word and phrase pairs from the whole ALT corpus and prepared 14,225 **unique word dictionary**[1]. The main categories are Country/City Names, Demonyms, Personal Names, Month Names, General Nouns, Organization Names, Abbreviations, Units and English-to-English Translation Words (see Table 2).

## 6 Hybrid Translation

Generally, hybrid translation integrates the strengths of rationalism method and empiricist method. (Hunsicker et al., 2012) described how machine learning approaches can be used to improve the phrase substitution component of a hybrid machine translation system. Essential of hybrid translation is to integrate the

[1]https://github.com/ye-kyaw-thu/MTRSS/tree/master/WAT2021/en-my_transliteration-dict

Table 2: Some example of manually extracted transliteration word/phrase pairs.

| **Country/City Names and Demonyms** | |
|---|---|
| Italy | အီတလီ |
| Portugal | ပေါ်တူဂီ |
| Paris | ပြင်သစ် |
| Shanghai | ရှန်ဟိုင်း |
| Australian | သြစတြေးလျ လူမျိုး |
| **Personal Names** | |
| David Bortolussi | ဒေးဗစ် ဘော်တိုလပ်စီ |
| coach William McKenny | ကော့ချ် ဝီလီယမ် အမ်စီကန်နီ |
| Dr. Michel Pellerin | ဒေါက်တာ မီရှဲလ် ပဲလာရီ |
| Liu Jianchao | လျူ ကျန်းချောင် |
| manager Phil Garner | မန်နေဂျာ ဖီး ဂါနာ |
| **Month Names** | |
| January | ဇန်နဝါရီ လ |
| March | မတ် လ |
| May | မေ လ |
| September | စက်တင်ဘာ |
| October | အောက်တိုဘာ |
| **General Nouns** | |
| penalties | ပယ်နယ်လ်တီ |
| theory | သီအိုရီ |
| bowling | ဘိုးလင်း |
| the Yankees | ရန်ကီး |
| baseball | ဘေ့စ်ဘော |
| **Organization Names** | |
| Liberal Democrats | လစ်ဘရယ် ဒီမိုကရက် |
| Scottish Premier League (SPL) | စကော့တလန် ပရီမီယာ လိဂ် ( အက်စ်ပီအယ်လ် ) |
| Walt Disney World's Wide World of Sports | ဝေ့ါ ဒစ္စနေး ဝေါလ် ၏ ဝိုက် ဝါ စ ပေ့ါ |
| Somali Defence Ministry | ဆိုမာလီ ကာကွယ်ရေး ဝန်ကြီး ဌာန |
| Iranian press-agency IRNA | အီရန် စာနယ်ဇင်း-အေဂျင်စီ အာနာ |
| **Abbreviations and Units** | |
| Intel x86 | အင်တဲလ် အိတ်စ်ဧဒ |
| NFL | အန်အက်ဖ်အယ် |
| A.Q.U.S.A | အေ.ကျူ.ယူ.အက်.အေ |
| AC-130 | အေစီ-၁၃၀ |
| km | ကီလိုမီတာ |
| **English-to-English Words** | |
| Big C | Big C |
| iTV | iTV |
| F-16 | F - 16 |
| Khlong Toei | Khlong Toei |
| Na Ranong | Na Ranong |

core of MT engines. Multiple- engine HMT integrates all available MT methods, applying to their benefits, in order to improve qualities of output (Xuan et al., 2012). The popular combinations comprise "rule-based machine translation vs the SMT" and multiple combinations of machine translation engines, for example "SMT vs neural machine translation". Our work in this paper focuses on hybrid machine translation of SMT engine and XML tags inserting (i.e. applying rules) into transliteration words of each source sentence. We used the Moses SMT toolkit and it also supports `-xml-input` flag to activate XML tags inserting feature with one of the five options; `exclusive`, `inclusive`, `constraint`, `ignore` and `pass-through`. Refer manual page of the Moses toolkit [2] for detail explanation. Although we studied all options, we will present the two options that work well for English-Myanmar hybrid translation.

The Moses decoder has an XML markup scheme that allows the specification of translations for parts of the sentence. In its simplest form, we can guide the decoder what to use to translate certain transliteration words or phrases in the source sentence. We wrote a perl script for XML Markup inserting into the source English sentences based on the manually extracted transliteration dictionary. As shown in follows, the XML Markup scheme for HPBSMT is different with PBSMT and OSM. This is because the syntactic annotation of the HPBSMT system also used XML Markup. And thus, we used `--xml-brackets "{{ }}"` option when decoding hybrid HPBSMT system.

**XML Markup Scheme for PBSMT and OSM:**
Tanks of <np translation="အောက် စီ ဂျင်" prob="0.8">oxygen</np> , <np translation="ဟီ လီ ရမ်" prob="0.8">helium</np> and <np translation="အက် ဆီ တ လင်း" prob="0.8">acetylene</np> began to explode after a connector used to join <np translation="အက် ဆီ တ လင်း" prob="0.8">acetylene</np> tanks during the filling process malfunctioned .

**Decoding with XML Markup Scheme for PBSMT and OSM:**
```
$moses -xml-input exclusive -i ./test.xml.en -f ../evaluation/test.filtered.ini.1
> en-my.xml.hyp1
```

**XML Markup Scheme for HPBSMT:**
Tanks of {{np translation="အောက် စီ ဂျင်" prob="0.8"}}oxygen{{/np}} , {{np translation="ဟီ လီ ရမ်" prob="0.8"}}helium{{/np}} and {{np translation="အက် ဆီ တ လင်း" prob="0.8"}}acetylene{{/np}} began to explode after a connector used to join {{np translation="အက် ဆီ တ လင်း" prob="0.8"}}acetylene{{/np}} tanks during the filling process malfunctioned .

**Decoding with XML Markup Scheme for HPBSMT:**
```
$moses_chart -xml-input exclusive --xml-brackets "{{ }}" -i ./test.xml.en -f
../evaluation/test.filtered.ini.1 > en-my.xml.hyp1
```

## 7 Results

Our systems are evaluated on the ALT test set and the results are shown in Table 3. Our observations from the results are as follows:

1. Hybrid translation of SMT with XML Markup scheme showed significant improvement for all three SMT approaches; PBSMT, OSM and HPBSMT.
2. Generally, `-xml-input exclusive` option gives a slightly higher scores than `-xml-input inclusive`.
3. HPBSMT achieved the highest scores especially for training without ALT corpus (i.e. we can assume working well for Out-of-Vocabulary case).
4. The baseline translation performance score difference between training with or without ALT corpus is about 5.0 BLEU score.

## 8 Conclusion

We presented in this paper the UTYCC's participation in the WAT-2021 shared translation task. Our hybrid SMT submission to the task performed the second in English-to-Myanmar translation direction according to several evaluation scores including the de facto BLEU. Our results also confirmed the XML markup technique for transliteration words dramatically increase the translation performance up

[2] `http://www.statmt.org/moses/?n=Advanced.Hybrid`

Table 3: BLEU, RIBES and AMFM scores for English-to-Myanmar translation (Bold number indicate the highest score for each scoring method)

| Experiments | Only UCSY Training Data | | | UCSY+ALT Training Data | | |
|---|---|---|---|---|---|---|
| | **BLEU** | **RIBES** | **AMFM** | **BLEU** | **RIBES** | **AMFM** |
| **Baseline: PBSMT** | 15.01 | 0.519451 | 0.550400 | 20.80 | 0.542406 | 0.617900 |
| **Hybrid: xml-exclusive** | 20.80 | 0.551514 | 0.653850 | 24.54 | 0.563854 | **0.690020** |
| **Hybrid: xml-inclusive** | **20.88** | **0.553319** | **0.655310** | **25.11** | **0.567187** | 0.689400 |
| **Baseline: OSM** | 15.05 | 0.528968 | 0.557240 | 20.33 | 0.550329 | 0.622350 |
| **Hybrid: xml-exclusive** | 19.94 | 0.540820 | 0.651070 | **23.82** | 0.554226 | 0.691450 |
| **Hybrid: xml-inclusive** | **20.13** | **0.545962** | **0.654820** | 23.73 | **0.556381** | **0.691910** |
| **Baseline: Hiero** | 14.83 | 0.555290 | 0.545900 | 20.29 | 0.587136 | 0.612400 |
| **Hybrid: xml-exclusive** | **21.02** | **0.588198** | **0.653840** | **25.48** | **0.60733** | **0.684110** |
| **Hybrid: xml-inclusive** | **21.02** | **0.588198** | **0.653840** | **25.48** | **0.607339** | **0.684110** |

to 6 BLEU scores. Moreover, our results highlighted that hybrid statistical machine translation is easy to implement and we need to explore more for low-resource distant language pairs such as English-Myanmar translation.


## Acknowledgments

We would like to thank Ms. Mya Ei San (School of Information, Computer and Communication Technology, Sirindhorn International Institute of Technology (SIIT), Thammasat University, Bangkok, Thailand) and Ms. Zar Zar Hlaing (Faculty of Information Technology, King Mongkut's Institute of Technology Ladkrabang, Bangkok, Thailand) for helping manual extraction of English-Myanmar transliteration word pairs from the ALT corpus.


## References


Rafael E. Banchs, Luis F. D'Haro, and Haizhou Li. 2015. Adequacy–fluency metrics: Evaluating mt in the continuous space model framework. *IEEE/ACM Transactions on Audio, Speech, and Language Processing*, 23(3):472–482.

Fabienne Braune, Anita Gojun, and Alexander Fraser. 2012. Long-distance reordering during search for hierarchical phrase-based SMT. In *Proceedings of the 16th Annual conference of the European Association for Machine Translation*, pages 177–184, Trento, Italy. European Association for Machine Translation.

Stanley F. Chen and Joshua Goodman. 1996. An empirical study of smoothing techniques for language modeling. In *Proceedings of the 34th Annual Meeting on Association for Computational Linguistics*, ACL '96, page 310–318, USA. Association for Computational Linguistics.

Chenchen Ding, Sann Su Su Yee, Win Pa Pa, Khin Mar Soe, Masao Utiyama, and Eiichiro Sumita. 2020. A Burmese (Myanmar) treebank: Guildline and analysis. *ACM Transactions on Asian and Low-Resource Language Information Processing (TALLIP)*, 19(3):40.

Kevin Duh, Paul McNamee, Matt Post, and Brian Thompson. 2020. Benchmarking neural and statistical machine translation on low-resource African languages. In *Proceedings of the 12th Language Resources and Evaluation Conference*, pages 2667–2675, Marseille, France. European Language Resources Association.

Nadir Durrani, Helmut Schmid, and Alexander Fraser. 2011. A joint sequence translation model with integrated reordering. In *Proceedings of the 49th Annual Meeting of the Association for Computational Linguistics: Human Language Technologies*, pages 1045–1054, Portland, Oregon, USA. Association for Computational Linguistics.

Nadir Durrani, Helmut Schmid, Alexander Fraser, Philipp Koehn, and Hinrich Schütze. 2015. The operation sequence Model—Combining n-gram-based and phrase-based statistical machine translation. *Computational Linguistics*, 41(2):157–186.

Kenneth Heafield. 2011. KenLM: Faster and smaller language model queries. In *Proceedings of the Sixth Workshop on Statistical Machine Translation*, pages 187–197, Edinburgh, Scotland. Association for Computational Linguistics.

Sabine Hunsicker, Yu Chen, and Christian Federmann. 2012. Machine learning for hybrid machine translation. In *Proceedings of the Seventh Workshop on Statistical Machine Translation*, pages 312–316, Montréal, Canada. Association for Computational Linguistics.

Hideki Isozaki, Tsutomu Hirao, Kevin Duh, Katsuhito Sudoh, and Hajime Tsukada. 2010. Automatic evaluation of translation quality for distant language pairs. In *Proceedings of the 2010 Conference on Empirical Methods in Natural Language Processing*, pages 944–952, Cambridge, MA. Association for Computational Linguistics.

Philipp Koehn, Hieu Hoang, Alexandra Birch, Chris Callison-Burch, Marcello Federico, Nicola Bertoldi, Brooke Cowan, Wade Shen, Christine Moran, Richard Zens, Chris Dyer, Ondřej Bojar, Alexandra Constantin, and Evan Herbst. 2007. Moses: Open source toolkit for statistical machine translation. In *Proceedings of the 45th Annual Meeting of the ACL on Interactive Poster and Demonstration Sessions*, ACL '07, pages 177–180, Stroudsburg, PA, USA. Association for Computational Linguistics.

Philipp Koehn, Franz J. Och, and Daniel Marcu. 2003. Statistical phrase-based translation. In *Proceedings of the 2003 Human Language Technology Conference of the North American Chapter of the Association for Computational Linguistics*, pages 127–133.

Prasanth Kolachina, Nicola Cancedda, Marc Dymetman, and Sriram Venkatapathy. 2012. Prediction of learning curves in machine translation. In *Proceedings of the 50th Annual Meeting of the Association for Computational Linguistics (Volume 1: Long Papers)*, pages 22–30, Jeju Island, Korea. Association for Computational Linguistics.

Toshiaki Nakazawa, Hideki Nakayama, Chenchen Ding, Raj Dabre, Shohei Higashiyama, Hideya Mino, Isao Goto, Win Pa Pa, Anoop Kunchukuttan, Shantipriya Parida, Ondřej Bojar, Chenhui Chu, Akiko Eriguchi, Kaori Abe, and Sadao Oda, Yusuke Kurohashi. 2021. Overview of the 8th workshop on Asian translation. In *Proceedings of the 8th Workshop on Asian Translation*, Bangkok, Thailand. Association for Computational Linguistics.

Franz Josef Och. 2003. Minimum error rate training in statistical machine translation. In *Proceedings of the 41st Annual Meeting of the Association for Computational Linguistics*, pages 160–167, Sapporo, Japan. Association for Computational Linguistics.

Franz Josef Och and Hermann Ney. 2000. Improved statistical alignment models. In *Proceedings of the 38th Annual Meeting of the Association for Computational Linguistics*, pages 440–447, Hong Kong. Association for Computational Linguistics.

Kishore Papineni, Salim Roukos, Todd Ward, and Wei-Jing Zhu. 2002. Bleu: a method for automatic evaluation of machine translation. In *Proceedings of the 40th Annual Meeting of the Association for Computational Linguistics*, pages 311–318, Philadelphia, Pennsylvania, USA. Association for Computational Linguistics.

Lucia Specia. 2011. Tutorial, fundamental and new approaches to statistical machine translation. *International Conference Recent Advances in Natural Language Processing*.

Christoph Tillmann. 2004. A unigram orientation model for statistical machine translation. In *Proceedings of HLT-NAACL 2004: Short Papers*, pages 101–104, Boston, Massachusetts, USA. Association for Computational Linguistics.

Hai-Long Trieu, Duc-Vu Tran, Ashwin Ittoo, and Le-Minh Nguyen. 2019. Leveraging additional resources for improving statistical machine translation on asian low-resource languages. *ACM Trans. Asian Low Resour. Lang. Inf. Process.*, 18(3):32:1–32:22.

Win Pa Pa, Ye Kyaw Thu, Andrew Finch, and Eiichiro Sumita. 2016. A study of statistical machine translation methods for under resourced languages. *Procedia Computer Science*, 81:250–257. SLTU-2016 5th Workshop on Spoken Language Technologies for Under-resourced languages 09-12 May 2016 Yogyakarta, Indonesia.

H.W. Xuan, W. Li, and G.Y. Tang. 2012. An advanced review of hybrid machine translation (hmt). *Procedia Engineering*, 29:3017–3022. 2012 International Workshop on Information and Electronics Engineering.

Ye Kyaw Thu. 2017. sylbreak toolkit for burmese (myanmar language). Accessed: 2021-03-06.

Ye Kyaw Thu, Win Pa Pa, Masao Utiyama, Andrew Finch, and Eiichiro Sumita. 2016. Introducing the asian language treebank (alt). In *Proceedings of the Tenth International Conference on Language Resources and Evaluation (LREC 2016)*, Paris, France. European Language Resources Association (ELRA).

Yi Mon Shwe Sin and Khin Mar Soe. 2019. Attention-based syllable level neural machine translation system for myanmar to english language pair. *International Journal on Natural Language Computing*, 8(2):01–11.

# NICT-2 Translation System at WAT-2021: Applying a Pretrained Multilingual Encoder-Decoder Model to Low-resource Language Pairs

**Kenji Imamura** and **Eiichiro Sumita**
National Institute of Information and Communications Technology
3-5 Hikaridai, Seika-cho, Soraku-gun, Kyoto 619-0289, Japan
{kenji.imamura,eiichiro.sumita}@nict.go.jp

## Abstract

In this paper, we present the NICT system (NICT-2) submitted to the NICT-SAP shared task at the 8th Workshop on Asian Translation (WAT-2021). A feature of our system is that we used a pretrained multilingual BART (Bidirectional and Auto-Regressive Transformer; mBART) model. Because publicly available models do not support some languages in the NICT-SAP task, we added these languages to the mBART model and then trained it using monolingual corpora extracted from Wikipedia. We fine-tuned the expanded mBART model using the parallel corpora specified by the NICT-SAP task. The BLEU scores greatly improved in comparison with those of systems without the pretrained model, including the additional languages.

## 1 Introduction

In this paper, we present the NICT system (NICT-2) that we submitted to the NICT-SAP shared task at the 8th Workshop on Asian Translation (WAT-2021) (Nakazawa et al., 2021). Because the NICT-SAP task expects to perform translations with little parallel data, we developed a system to improve translation quality by applying the following models and techniques.

**Pretrained model:** An encoder-decoder model pretrained using huge monolingual corpora was used. We used a multilingual bidirectional auto-regressive Transformer (mBART) (i.e., multilingual sequence-to-sequence denoising auto-encoder (Liu et al., 2020)) model, which supports 25 languages. Because it includes English and Hindi, but does not include Indonesian, Malay, and Thai, we expanded it to include the unsupported languages and additionally pretrained it on these five languages.[1]

**Multilingual models:** We tested multilingual models trained using multiple parallel corpora to increase resources for training.

**Domain adaptation:** We tested two domain adaptation techniques. The first technique is training multi-domain models. Similar to multilingual models, this technique trains a model using the parallel corpora of multiple domains. The domains are identified by domain tags in input sentences. The second technique is adaptation based on fine-tuning. This method fine-tunes each domain model (using its domain corpus) from a model trained by a mixture of multi-domain corpora.

Our experimental results showed that the pretrained encoder-decoder model was effective for translating low-resource language pairs. However, the effects of multilingual models and domain adaptation became low when we applied the pretrained model.

The following sections are organized as follows. We first summarize the NICT-SAP shared task in Section 2, and briefly review the pretrained mBART model in Section 3. Details of our system is explained in Section 4. In Section 5, we present experimental results. Finally, we conclude our paper in Section 6.

## 2 NICT-SAP Shared Task

The NICT-SAP shared task was to translate text between English and four languages, that is, Hindi (Hi), Indonesian (Id), Malay (Ms), and Thai (Th), for which the amount of data in parallel corpora is relatively low. The task contained two domains.

The data in the Asian Language Translation (ALT) domain (Thu et al., 2016) consisted of translations obtained from WikiNews. The ALT

[1] The mBART-50 model (Tang et al., 2020) supports 50 languages including Indonesian and Thai. However, Malay is not supported by either the mBART model or mBART-50 models. Therefore, we applied additional pretraining to the mBART model.



*Proceedings of the 8th Workshop on Asian Translation*, pages 90–95
Bangkok, Thailand (online), August 5-6, 2021. 

| Domain | Set | En-Hi | En-Id | En-Ms | En-Th |
|---|---|---|---|---|---|
| ALT | Train | 18,088 | 18,087 | 18,088 | 18,088 |
| | Dev | 1,000 | | | |
| | Test | 1,018 | | | |
| IT | Train | 252,715 | 158,200 | 504,856 | 73,829 |
| | Dev | 2,016 | 2,023 | 2,050 | 2,049 |
| | Test | 2,073 | 2,037 | 2,050 | 2,050 |

Table 1: Data sizes for the NICT-SAP task after filtering.

data is a multilingual parallel corpus, that is, it contains the same sentences in all languages. The training, development, and test sets were provided from the WAT organizers.

The data in the IT domain consisted of translations of software documents. The WAT organizers provided the development and test sets (Buschbeck and Exel, 2020). For the training set, we obtained GNOME, KDE, and Ubuntu sub-corpora from the OPUS corpus (Tiedemann, 2012). Therefore, the domains for the training and dev/test sets were not identical.

The data sizes are shown in Table 1. There were fewer than 20K training sentences in the ALT domain. Between 73K and 504K training sentences were in the IT domain. Note that there were inadequate sentences in the training sets. We filtered out translations that were longer than 512 tokens, or where source/target sentences were three times longer than the target/source sentences if they had over 20 tokens.

## 3 mBART Model

In this section, we briefly review the pretrained mBART model (Liu et al., 2020).

The mBART model is a multilingual model of bidirectional and auto-regressive Transformers (BART; (Lewis et al., 2020)). The model is based on the encoder-decoder Transformer (Vaswani et al., 2017), in which the decoder uses an auto-regressive method (Figure 1).

Two tasks of BART are trained in the mBART model. One is the token masking task, which restores masked tokens in input sentences. The other is the sentence permutation task, which predicts the original order of permuted sentences. Both tasks learn using monolingual corpora.

To build multilingual models based on BART, mBART supplies language tags (as special tokens) at the tail of the encoder input and head of the decoder input. Using these language tags, a mBART model can learn multiple languages.

| Language | #Sentences | #Tokens |
|---|---|---|
| English (En) | 7,000,000 (*1) | 174M |
| Hindi (Hi) | 1,968,984 | 51M |
| Indonesian (Id) | 6,997,907 | 151M |
| Malay (Ms) | 2,723,230 | 57M |
| Thai (Th) | 2,233,566 (*2) | 60M |

Table 2: Statistics of the training data for the pretrained model. The number of tokens indicates the number of subwords. (*1) The English data were sampled from 150M sentences to fit the number of sentences into the maximum number of the other languages. (*2) Sentences in Thai were detected using an in-house sentence splitter.

The published pretrained mBART model[2] consists of a 12-layer encoder and decoder with a model dimension of 1,024 on 16 heads. This model was trained on 25 languages in the Common Crawl corpus (Wenzek et al., 2019). Of the languages for the NICT-SAP task, English and Hindi are supported by the published mBART model, but Indonesian, Malay, and Thai are not supported.

The tokenizer for the mBART model uses byte-pair encoding (Sennrich et al., 2016) of the SentencePiece model (Kudo and Richardson, 2018)[3]. The vocabulary size is 250K subwords.

## 4 Our System

### 4.1 Language Expansion/Additional Pretraining of mBART

As described above, the published mBART model does not support Indonesian, Malay, and Thai. We expanded the mBART model to support these three languages, and additionally pretrained the model on the five languages in the NICT-SAP task.

The corpus for additional pretraining was extracted from Wikipedia dump files as follows. Unlike the XLM models (Lample and Conneau, 2019), which were also pretrained using Wikipedia corpora, we divided each article into sentences in our corpus, to train the sentence permutation task. Additionally, we applied sentence filtering to clean each language.

1. First, Wikipedia articles were extracted from

[2] `https://dl.fbaipublicfiles.com/fairseq/models/mbart/mbart.cc25.v2.tar.gz`

[3] `https://github.com/google/sentencepiece`

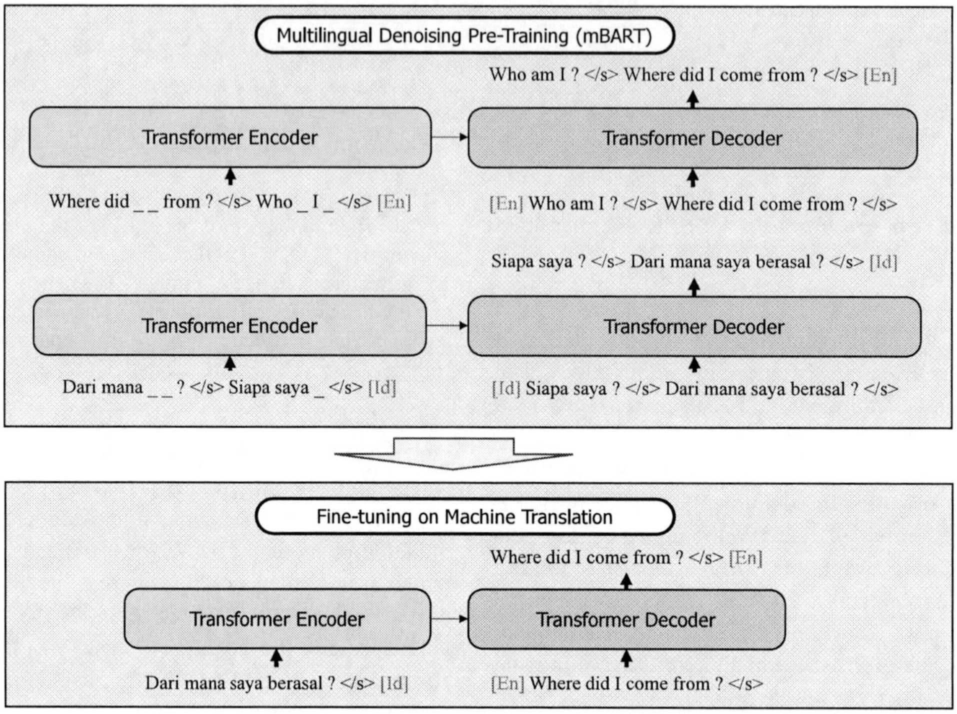


Figure 1: Example of mBART pretraining and fine-tuning for the machine translation task from Indonesian to English (arranged from (Liu et al., 2020)).

the dump files using `WikiExtractor`[4] while applying the NFKC normalization of Unicode.

2. Sentence splitting was performed based on sentence end marks, such as periods and question marks. However, because Thai does not have explicit sentence end marks, we applied a neural network-based sentence splitter (Wang et al., 2019), which was trained using in-house data.

3. We selected valid sentences, which we regarded as sentences that consisted of five to 1,024 letters, where and 80% of the letters were included in the character set of the target language. In the case of Hindi, for example, we regarded a sentence as valid if 80% of the letters were in the set of Devanagari code points, digits, and spaces.

The number of sentences for the mBART additional pretraining is shown in Table 2. We sampled 7M English sentences to balance the sizes of the other languages because the number of English sentences was disproportionately large (about 150M sentences).

We first expanded the word embeddings of the published mBART large model using random initialization and trained it. This is similar to the training procedure for mBART-50 (Tang et al., 2020), except for the corpora and hyperparameters. The settings for the additional pretraining are shown in Table 3.

We conducted the additional pretraining using the Fairseq translator (Ott et al., 2019)[5] on eight NVIDIA V100 GPUs. It took about 15 days.

For the tokenizer, we used the SentencePiece model in the published mBART large model. This model does not support Indonesian, Malay, and Thai. Indonesian and Malay use Latin characters, hence we divert the model to tokenize these languages. Thai uses a special character set. However, we diverted the SentencePiece model because almost all characters in the Thai corpus were included in the vocabulary of the model.

[4] `https://github.com/attardi/wikiextractor`

[5] `https://github.com/pytorch/fairseq`

| Attribute | Value |
|---|---|
| LR | 0.0003 |
| Warm-up | Linear warm-up in 10K updates |
| Decay | Linear decay |
| Tokens per sample | 512 |
| Batch size | 640K tokens |
| # updates | 500K (around 77 epochs) |
| Dropout schedule | 0.10 until 250K updates, 0.05 until 400K updates, and 0.0 until 500K updates |
| Loss function | Cross entropy |
| Token masking | mask=0.3, mask-random=0.1, mask-length=span-poisson, poisson-lambda=3.5, replace-length=1 |
| Sentence permutation | permute-sentence=1.0 |

Table 3: Hyperparameters for the mBART additional pretraining

### 4.2 Other Options

We fine-tuned the pretrained model using the NICT-SAP parallel corpora shown in Table 1. We also used Transformer base models (six layers, the model dimension of 512 on 8 heads) for comparison without the pretrained model. In addition to the effect of the pretrained models, we investigated the effects of multilingual models and domain adaptation.

#### 4.2.1 Multilingual Models

Similar to the multilingual training of mBART, the multilingual model translated all the language pairs using one model by supplying source and target language tags to parallel sentences.

By contrast, bilingual models were trained using the corpora of each language pair. When we use the mBART model, we supplied source and target language tags to parallel sentences, even for the bilingual models.

#### 4.2.2 Domain Adaptation

We tested two domain adaptation methods; multi-domain models and fine-tuning-based methods. Both methods utilize parallel data of the other domains.

Similar to the multilingual models, we trained the multi-domain models by supplying domain tags (this time, we used <__WN__> for the ALT domain and <__IT__> for the IT domain) at the head of sentences in the source language.

The fine-tuning method did not use domain tags. First, a mixture model was trained using a mixture of multiple domain data. Next, domain models were fine-tuned from the mixture model using each set of domain data. Therefore, we created as many domain models as the number of domains.

| Phase | Attribute: Value |
|---|---|
| Fine-tuning | LR: 0.00008,<br>Dropout: 0.3,<br>Batch size: 16K tokens,<br>Loss function: label smoothed cross entropy,<br>Warm-up: linear warm-up in five epochs,<br>Decay: invert square-root,<br>Stopping criterion: early stopping on the dev. set. |
| Translation | Beam width: 10,<br>Length penalty: 1.0. |

Table 4: Hyper-parameters for fine-tuning and translation.

## 5 Experiments

The models and methods described above were fine-tuned and tested using the hyperparameters in Table 4.

Tables 5 and 6 show the official BLEU scores (Papineni et al., 2002) for the test set in the ALT and IT domains, respectively. Similar results were obtained on the development sets, but they were omitted in this paper. We submitted the results using the pretrained mBART model, which were good on the development sets, on average.

The results are summarized as follows;

- For all language pairs in both domains, the BLEU scores with our extended mBART model were better than those under the same conditions without the pretrained models.

  When we focus on Indonesian, Malay, and Thai, which were not supported in the original mBART model, the BLEU scores of the submitted results were increased over 8 points from the baseline results in the ALT domain. We conclude that language expansion and additional pretraining were effective for translating new languages.

  For verification, we checked sentences in the test sets and the corpus for the pretrained model (c.f., Table 2). There were no identical sentences in the two corpora in the ALT domain. (Between 0% and 10% of the test sentences were included in the IT domain.) Therefore, these improvements were not caused by the memorization of the test sentences in the pretrained model.

| Setting | | | Translation Direction | | | | | | | | |
|---|---|---|---|---|---|---|---|---|---|---|---|
| PT | ML | FT/MD | En→Hi | Hi→En | En→Id | Id→En | En→Ms | Ms→En | En→Th | Th→En | Remark |
| | | FT | 12.26 | 8.23 | 24.71 | 23.65 | 31.02 | 27.52 | 13.73 | 2.04 | |
| | | MD | 9.74 | 6.97 | 24.17 | 21.91 | 28.62 | 25.48 | 10.48 | 1.45 | |
| | ✓ | FT | 22.31 | 14.41 | 31.77 | 21.65 | 36.40 | 21.61 | 46.11 | 14.37 | Baseline |
| | ✓ | MD | 15.25 | 12.18 | 29.48 | 22.76 | 29.76 | 23.49 | 43.46 | 14.65 | |
| ✓ | | FT | **34.97** | **35.21** | 41.15 | **43.90** | **45.17** | 44.53 | 55.69 | 28.96 | Submitted |
| ✓ | | MD | 33.31 | 32.71 | **41.80** | 42.35 | 44.09 | 44.03 | 54.21 | 28.92 | |
| ✓ | ✓ | FT | 33.43 | 31.37 | 42.16 | 40.80 | 45.06 | 42.21 | **55.80** | 27.74 | |
| ✓ | ✓ | MD | 28.03 | 33.14 | 41.69 | 43.56 | 43.28 | **45.24** | 55.65 | **29.77** | |

Table 5: Official BLEU scores in the ALT domain. PT, ML, FT, and MD in the setting columns represent pretraining, multilingual models, fine-tuning, and multi-domain models, respectively.

| Setting | | | Translation Direction | | | | | | | | |
|---|---|---|---|---|---|---|---|---|---|---|---|
| PT | ML | FT/MD | En→Hi | Hi→En | En→Id | Id→En | En→Ms | Ms→En | En→Th | Th→En | Remark |
| | | FT | 7.97 | 4.92 | 23.33 | 22.64 | 29.62 | 26.53 | 10.24 | 0.99 | |
| | | MD | 7.01 | 4.37 | 23.63 | 21.40 | 28.43 | 25.01 | 5.60 | 0.59 | |
| | ✓ | FT | 19.77 | 18.09 | 33.47 | 26.15 | 34.75 | 26.48 | 45.66 | 12.73 | Baseline |
| | ✓ | MD | 14.60 | 15.70 | 30.83 | 26.28 | 30.99 | 26.24 | 42.25 | 12.97 | |
| ✓ | | FT | **29.05** | 35.32 | 43.25 | 40.69 | **40.76** | 38.42 | 50.91 | 21.89 | Submitted |
| ✓ | | MD | 28.24 | 34.60 | 43.73 | 40.36 | 40.42 | **39.29** | 50.26 | 23.10 | |
| ✓ | ✓ | FT | 26.54 | 34.82 | 44.19 | 40.45 | 40.56 | 37.79 | 51.34 | 22.22 | |
| ✓ | ✓ | MD | 25.96 | **35.55** | **44.40** | **42.44** | 39.25 | 39.28 | **52.00** | **24.24** | |

Table 6: Official BLEU scores in the IT domain. PT, ML, FT, and MD in the setting columns represent pretraining, multilingual models, fine-tuning, and multi-domain models, respectively.

- The multilingual models were effective only without pretrained models. For example, for English to Hindi translation in the ALT domain, the BLEU scores improved from 12.26 to 22.31 when we used multilingual models without the pretrained model. However, they degraded from 34.97 to 33.43 when we used multilingual models with the pretrained model.

  The multilingual models were effective under low-resource conditions because the size of parallel data increased during training. However, they were ineffective if the models had learned sufficiently in advance, like pretrained models.

- Regarding domain adaptation, the fine-tuning method was better than the multi-domain models in many cases without the pretrained model.

## 6 Conclusions

In this paper, we presented the NICT-2 system submitted to the NICT-SAP task at WAT-2021.

A feature of our system is that it uses the mBART pretrained model. Because the published pretrained model does not support Indonesian, Malay, and Thai, we expanded it to support the above languages using additional training on the Wikipedia corpus. Consequently, the expanded mBART model improved the BLEU scores, regardless of whether multilingual models or domain adaptation methods were applied.

## Acknowledgments

Part of this work was conducted under the commissioned research program 'Research and Development of Advanced Multilingual Translation Technology' in the 'R&D Project for Information and Communications Technology (JPMI00316)' of the Ministry of Internal Affairs and Communications (MIC), Japan.

## References

Bianka Buschbeck and Miriam Exel. 2020. A parallel evaluation data set of software documentation with document structure annotation. arXiv 2008.04550.

Taku Kudo and John Richardson. 2018. SentencePiece: A simple and language independent subword tokenizer and detokenizer for neural text processing. In *Proceedings of the 2018 Conference on Empirical Methods in Natural Language Processing: System Demonstrations*, pages 66–71, Brussels, Belgium.

Guillaume Lample and Alexis Conneau. 2019. Cross-lingual language model pretraining. arXiv 1901.07291.

Mike Lewis, Yinhan Liu, Naman Goyal, Marjan Ghazvininejad, Abdelrahman Mohamed, Omer Levy, Veselin Stoyanov, and Luke Zettlemoyer. 2020. BART: Denoising sequence-to-sequence pre-training for natural language generation, translation, and comprehension. In *Proceedings of the 58th Annual Meeting of the Association for Computational Linguistics*, pages 7871–7880, Online.

Yinhan Liu, Jiatao Gu, Naman Goyal, Xian Li, Sergey Edunov, Marjan Ghazvininejad, Mike Lewis, and Luke Zettlemoyer. 2020. Multilingual denoising pre-training for neural machine translation. arXiv 2001.08210.

Toshiaki Nakazawa, Hideki Nakayama, Chenchen Ding, Raj Dabre, Shohei Higashiyama, Hideya Mino, Isao Goto, Win Pa Pa, Anoop Kunchukuttan, Shantipriya Parida, Ondřej Bojar, Chenhui Chu, Akiko Eriguchi, Kaori Abe, Yusuke Oda, and Sadao Kurohashi. 2021. Overview of the 8th workshop on Asian translation. In *Proceedings of the 8th Workshop on Asian Translation*, Bangkok, Thailand.

Myle Ott, Sergey Edunov, Alexei Baevski, Angela Fan, Sam Gross, Nathan Ng, David Grangier, and Michael Auli. 2019. fairseq: A fast, extensible toolkit for sequence modeling. In *Proceedings of the 2019 Conference of the North American Chapter of the Association for Computational Linguistics (Demonstrations)*, pages 48–53, Minneapolis, Minnesota.

Kishore Papineni, Salim Roukos, Todd Ward, and Wei-Jing Zhu. 2002. Bleu: a method for automatic evaluation of machine translation. In *Proceedings of the 40th Annual Meeting of the Association for Computational Linguistics (ACL)*, pages 311–318, Philadelphia, Pennsylvania, USA.

Rico Sennrich, Barry Haddow, and Alexandra Birch. 2016. Neural machine translation of rare words with subword units. In *Proceedings of the 54th Annual Meeting of the Association for Computational Linguistics (Volume 1: Long Papers)*, pages 1715–1725, Berlin, Germany.

Yuqing Tang, Chau Tran, Xian Li, Peng-Jen Chen, Naman Goyal, Vishrav Chaudhary, Jiatao Gu, and Angela Fan. 2020. Multilingual translation with extensible multilingual pretraining and finetuning. arXiv 2008.00401.

Ye Kyaw Thu, Win Pa Pa, Masao Utiyama, Andrew Finch, and Eiichiro Sumita. 2016. Introducing the Asian language treebank (ALT). In *Proceedings of the Tenth International Conference on Language Resources and Evaluation (LREC'16)*, pages 1574–1578, Portorož, Slovenia.

Jörg Tiedemann. 2012. Parallel data, tools and interfaces in OPUS. In *Proceedings of the Eight International Conference on Language Resources and Evaluation (LREC'12)*, Istanbul, Turkey.

Ashish Vaswani, Noam Shazeer, Niki Parmar, Jakob Uszkoreit, Llion Jones, Aidan N. Gomez, Lukasz Kaiser, and Illia Polosukhin. 2017. Attention is all you need. *CoRR*, abs/1706.03762.

Xiaolin Wang, Masao Utiyama, and Eiichiro Sumita. 2019. Online sentence segmentation for simultaneous interpretation using multi-shifted recurrent neural network. In *Proceedings of Machine Translation Summit XVII Volume 1: Research Track*, pages 1–11, Dublin, Ireland.

Guillaume Wenzek, Marie-Anne Lachaux, Alexis Conneau, Vishrav Chaudhary, Francisco Guzmán, Armand Joulin, and Edouard Grave. 2019. CCNet: Extracting high quality monolingual datasets from web crawl data. arXiv 1911.00359.

# Rakuten's Participation in WAT 2021: Examining the Effectiveness of Pre-trained Models for Multilingual and Multimodal Machine Translation

**Raymond Hendy Susanto, Dongzhe Wang, Sunil Kumar Yadav, Mausam Jain, Ohnmar Htun**
Rakuten Institute of Technology
Rakuten Group, Inc.
{raymond.susanto,dongzhe.wang,sunilkumar.yadav,
mausam.jain,ohnmar.htun}@rakuten.com

## Abstract

This paper introduces our neural machine translation systems' participation in the WAT 2021 shared translation tasks (team ID: *sakura*). We participated in the (i) NICT-SAP, (ii) Japanese-English multimodal translation, (iii) Multilingual Indic, and (iv) Myanmar-English translation tasks. Multilingual approaches such as mBART (Liu et al., 2020) are capable of pre-training a complete, multilingual sequence-to-sequence model through denoising objectives, making it a great starting point for building multilingual translation systems. Our main focus in this work is to investigate the effectiveness of multilingual finetuning on such a multilingual language model on various translation tasks, including low-resource, multimodal, and mixed-domain translation. We further explore a multimodal approach based on universal visual representation (Zhang et al., 2019) and compare its performance against a unimodal approach based on mBART alone.

## 1 Introduction

This paper introduces our neural machine translation (NMT) systems' participation in the 8th Workshop on Asian Translation (WAT-2021) shared translation tasks (Nakazawa et al., 2021). We participated in the (i) NICT-SAP's IT and Wikinews, (ii) Japanese-English multimodal translation, (iii) Multilingual Indic, and (iv) Myanmar-English translation tasks.

Recent advances in language model pre-training have been successful in advancing the state-of-the-art in various natural language processing tasks. Multilingual approaches such as mBART (Liu et al., 2020) are capable of pre-training a full sequence-to-sequence model through multilingual denoising objectives, which leads to significant gains in downstream tasks, such as machine translation. Building upon our success with utilizing mBART25 in the 2020 edition of WAT (Wang and Htun, 2020), we put more focus on multilingual and multimodal translation this year. In particular, instead of performing *bilingual finetuning* on mBART for each language pair, we train a single, multilingual NMT model that is capable of translating multiple languages at once. As first proposed by Tang et al. (2020), we apply *multilingual finetuning* to mBART50 for the NICT-SAP task (involving 4 Asian languages) and Multilingual Indic task (involving 10 Indic languages). Our findings show the remarkable effectiveness of mBART pre-training on these tasks. On the Japanese-English multimodal translation task, we compare a unimodal text-based model, which is initialized based on mBART, with a multimodal approach based on universal visual representation (UVR) (Zhang et al., 2019). Last, we continue our work on Myanmar-English translation by experimenting with more extensive data augmentation approaches. Our main findings for each task are summarized in the following:

- **NICT-SAP task:** We exploited mBART50 to improve low-resource machine translation on news and IT domains by finetuning them to create a mixed-domain, multilingual NMT system.
- **Multimodal translation:** We investigated multimodal NMT based on UVR in the constrained setting, as well as a unimodal text-based approach with the pre-trained mBART model in the unconstrained setting.
- **Multilingual Indic task:** We used the pre-trained mBART50 models, extended them for various Indic languages, and finetuned them on the entire training corpus followed by finetuning on the PMI dataset.



*Proceedings of the 8th Workshop on Asian Translation*, pages 96–105
Bangkok, Thailand (online), August 5-6, 2021. ©2021 Association for Computational Linguistics

| Split | Domain | Language | | | |
|---|---|---|---|---|---|
| | | hi | id | ms | th |
| Train | ALT | 18,088 | | | |
| | IT | 254,242 | 158,472 | 506,739 | 74,497 |
| Dev | ALT | 1,000 | | | |
| | IT | 2,016 | 2,023 | 2,050 | 2,049 |
| Test | ALT | 1,018 | | | |
| | IT | 2,073 | 2,037 | 2,050 | 2,050 |

Table 1: Statistics of the NICT-SAP datasets. Each language is paired with English.

- **Myanmar-English translation:** We designed contrastive experiments with different data combinations for Myanmar↔English translation and validated the effectiveness of data augmentation for low-resource translation tasks.

## 2 NICT-SAP Task

### 2.1 Task Description

This year, we participated in the NICT-SAP translation task, which involves two different domains: IT domain (Software Documentation) and Wikinews domain (ALT). These are considered low-resource domains for Machine Translation, combined with the fact that it involves four low-resource Asian languages: Hindi (hi), Indonesian (id), Malay (ms), and Thai (th).

For training, we use parallel corpora from the Asian Language Treebank (ALT) (Thu et al., 2016) for the Wikinews domain and OPUS[1] (GNOME, KDE4, and Ubuntu) for the IT domain. For development and evaluation, we use the datasets provided by the organizer: SAP software documentation (Buschbeck and Exel, 2020)[2] and ALT corpus.[3] Table 1 shows the statistics of the datasets.

### 2.2 Data Processing

We tokenized our data using the 250,000 SentencePiece model (Kudo and Richardson, 2018) from mBART (Liu et al., 2020), which was a joint vocabulary trained on monolingual data for 100 languages from XLMR (Conneau et al., 2020). Moreover, we prepended each source sentence with a domain indicator token to distinguish the ALT (`<2alt>`) and IT domain (`<2it>`).

[1]https://opus.nlpl.eu/

[2]https://github.com/SAP/software-documentation-data-set-for-machine-translation

[3]http://lotus.kuee.kyoto-u.ac.jp/WAT/NICT-SAP-Task/altsplits-sap-nict.zip

We collect parallel corpora from all the language pairs involved in this task, namely {hi,id,ms,th}↔en. Following mBART, we prepend source and target language tokens to each source and target sentences, respectively. The size of each dataset varies across language pairs. For instance, the size of the Malay training corpus for the IT domain is roughly 5× larger than that of Thai. To address this data imbalance, we train our model with a temperature-based sampling function following Arivazhagan et al. (2019):

$$p_{i,j} \propto \left( \frac{|B_{i,j}|}{\sum_{i,j} |B_{i,j}|} \right)^{1/T}$$

where $B_{i,j}$ corresponds to the parallel corpora for a language pair $(i, j)$ and $T$ the temperature for sampling.

### 2.3 Model

We use the pre-trained mBART50 model (Tang et al., 2020) as our starting point for finetuning our translation systems. Unlike the original mBART work that performed bilingual finetuning (Liu et al., 2020), Tang et al. (2020) proposed *multilingual finetuning* where the mBART model is finetuned on many directions at the same time, resulting in a single model capable of translating many languages to many other languages. In addition to having more efficient and storage maintenance benefits, such an approach greatly helps low-resource language pairs where little to no parallel corpora are available.

While the mBART50 has great coverage of 50 languages, we found that it does not include all languages involved in this task, particularly Malay. Following Tang et al. (2020), who extended mBART25 to create mBART50, we extended mBART50's embedding layers with one additional randomly initialized vector for the Malay language token.[4] We use the same model architecture as mBART50, which is based on Transformer (Vaswani et al., 2017). The model was finetuned for 40,000 steps with Adam (Kingma and Ba, 2015) using $\beta 1 = 0.9$, $\beta 2 = 0.98$, and $\epsilon = 1e^{-6}$. We use a maximum batch size of 512 tokens and gradients were accumulated every 4 mini-batches on each GPU. We ran our experiments on 4 NVIDIA

[4]Our modifications to the original mBART code are accessible at https://github.com/raymondhs/fairseq-extensible-mbart.

| Domain | System | Translation Direction | | | | | | | |
|---|---|---|---|---|---|---|---|---|---|
| | | en→hi | hi→en | en→id | id→en | en→ms | ms→en | en→th | th→en |
| ALT | Dabre and Chakrabarty (2020) | 24.23 | 12.37 | 32.88 | 17.39 | 36.77 | 18.03 | 42.13 | 10.78 |
| | mBART50 - pre-trained | 29.79 | 32.27 | 39.07 | 42.62 | 41.74 | 43.36 | 54.15 | 28.02 |
| | mBART50 - ft.nn | 34.00 | 35.75 | 41.47 | 44.09 | 43.92 | 45.14 | 55.87 | 29.70 |
| | +ensemble of 3* | 34.25 | 36.17 | 41.57 | 44.72 | 44.01 | 45.70 | 55.98 | 30.10 |
| IT | Dabre and Chakrabarty (2020) | 14.03 | 16.89 | 32.52 | 25.95 | 34.62 | 26.33 | 28.24 | 10.00 |
| | mBART50 - pre-trained | 26.03 | 36.38 | 43.97 | 43.17 | 40.15 | 39.37 | 52.67 | 25.06 |
| | mBART50 - ft.nn | 28.43 | 40.30 | 45.01 | 44.41 | 41.92 | 40.92 | 55.60 | 26.05 |
| | +ensemble of 3* | 28.50 | 40.17 | 45.39 | 44.70 | 42.26 | 40.97 | 55.64 | 26.30 |

Table 3: BLEU results on the NICT-SAP task. Our final submission is marked by an asterisk.

| Domain | Translation Direction | | | | | | | |
|---|---|---|---|---|---|---|---|---|
| | en→hi | hi→en | en→id | id→en | en→ms | ms→en | en→th | th→en |
| ALT | 84.92 | 83.29 | 86.80 | 85.10 | 87.19 | 85.15 | 83.71 | 82.26 |
| IT | 82.68 | 86.13 | 86.30 | 86.30 | 87.33 | 84.94 | 82.99 | 80.91 |

Table 4: AMFM results on the NICT-SAP task

| | |
|---|---|
| Vocab size | 250k |
| Embed. dim. | 1024 |
| Tied embed. | Yes |
| FFN dim. | 4096 |
| Attention heads | 16 |
| En/Decoder layers | 12 |
| Label smoothing | 0.2 |
| Dropout | 0.3 |
| Attention dropout | 0.1 |
| FFN dropout | 0.1 |
| Learning rate | $3e^{-5}$ |

Table 2: Models settings for both NICT-SAP and Multilingual Indic tasks

Quadro RTX 6000 GPUs. Table 2 shows the details of our experimental settings.

### 2.4 Results

Table 3 and Table 4 show our experimental results in terms of BLEU (Papineni et al., 2002) and AMFM (Banchs et al., 2015) scores, respectively. We first show our multilingual finetuning results on the released mBART50 model (Tang et al., 2020),[5] which was pre-trained as a denoising autoencoder on the monolingual data from XLMR (Conneau et al., 2020) (*mBART50 - pre-trained*). Compared to one submission from previous year's WAT from Dabre and Chakrabarty (2020), which is a multilingual many-to-many model without any pre-training, we observe a significant improvement from multilingual finetuning across all language pairs for both domains. For instance, we obtain the largest improvement of 25.23 BLEU points for id→en on the ALT domain. These findings clearly show that multilingual models greatly benefit from pre-training as compared to being trained from scratch, and more so for low resource languages.

Second, Tang et al. (2020) released a many-to-many multilingual translation that was finetuned from mBART on publicly available parallel data for 50 languages, including all language pairs in this task, except Malay. We adapt this model by performing a further finetuning on the NICT-SAP dataset (*mBART50 - ft.nn*). On average, this model further improves BLEU by 2.37 points on ALT and 1.98 points on IT.

Finally, we trained three independent models with different random seeds to perform ensemble decoding. This is our final submission, which achieves the first place in AMFM scores on this year's leaderboard for 7 translation directions for ALT (all except en→ms) and 6 directions for IT (all except for en→hi and en→id).

For the human evaluation on the IT task, our systems obtained 4.24 adequacy score for en→id and 4.05 for en→ms, which were the highest among all participants this year. We refer readers to the overview paper (Nakazawa et al., 2021) for the complete evaluation results.

## 3 Japanese↔English Multimodal Task

### 3.1 Task Description

Multimodal neural machine translation (MNMT) has recently received increasing attention in the NLP research fields with the advent of visually-grounded parallel corpora. The motivation of Japanese↔English multimodal task is to improve

[5]https://github.com/pytorch/fairseq/tree/master/examples/multilingual

translation performance with the aid of heterogeneous information (Nakazawa et al., 2020). In particular, we performed the experiments based on the benchmark Flickr30kEnt-JP dataset (Nakayama et al., 2020), where manual Japanese translations are newly provided to the Flickr30k Entities image captioning dataset (Plummer et al., 2015) that consists of 29,783 images for training and 1,000 images for validation, respectively. For each image, the original Flickr30k has five sentences, while the extended Flickr30kEnt-JP has corresponding Japanese translation in parallel[6].

In terms of input sources, this multimodal task has been divided into four sub-tasks: **constrained** and **unconstrained** Japanese↔English translation tasks. In the constrained setting, we investigated the MNMT models with universal visual representation (UVR) (Zhang et al., 2019), which is obtained from the pre-trained bottom-up attention model (Anderson et al., 2018). In contrast, we also explored the capability of unimodal translation (i.e., text modality only) under the unconstrained setting, where the pre-trained mBART25 model (Liu et al., 2020) was employed as the external resource.

### 3.2 Data Processing

**Text preparation** For the constrained setting, we firstly exploited Juman analyzer[7] for Japanese and Moses tokenizer for English. Then, we set the vocabulary size to 40,000 to train the byte-pair encoding (BPE)-based subword-nmt[8] (Sennrich et al., 2016) model. Moreover, we merged the source and target sentences and trained a joint vocabulary for the NMT systems. Under the unconstrained setting, we used the same 250,000 vocabulary as in the pre-trained mBART model for the text input to mBART finetuning, which was automatically tokenized with a SentencePiece model (Kudo and Richardson, 2018) based on BPE method.

**Universal visual retrieval** For the constrained setting particularly, we propose to extract the pre-computed global image features from the raw Flickr30k images using the bottom-up attention Faster-RCNN object detector that is pre-trained on the Visual Genome dataset (Krishna et al., 2017).

| Models | MNMT | mBART |
|---|---|---|
| Vocabulary size | 40k | 250k |
| Embedding dim. | 1024 | 1024 |
| Image dim. | 2048 | - |
| Tied embeddings | Yes | Yes |
| FFN dim. | 4096 | 4096 |
| Attention heads | 16 | 16 |
| En/Decoder layers | 12 | 12 |
| Label smoothing | 0.1 | 0.2 |
| Dropout | 0.3 | 0.3 |
| Attention dropout | 0.1 | 0.1 |
| FFN dropout | 0.1 | 0.1 |
| Learning rate | $5e^{-4}$ | $3e^{-5}$ |

Table 4: Multimodal model parameter settings

Specifically, we adopted the pre-trained model[9] to extract the spatial image features corresponding to 36 bounding boxes regions per image, which were then encoded into a global image feature vector by taking the global average pooling of them. In practice, we followed (Zhang et al., 2019) and presented the UVR relying on image-monolingual annotations (i.e., source sentences). To retrieve the universal visual information from the source sentences, the sentence-image pairs have been transformed into two topic-image lookup tables from the Flickr30kEnt-JP dataset for Japanese→English and English→Japanese tasks, respectively. Note that no image information has been learned in our unconstrained models due to the text-only property.

### 3.3 Model

In this section, we will elaborate on our proposed model architectures for the constrained and unconstrained tasks, respectively.

**Multimodal model with UVR** Following (Zhang et al., 2019), we built the multimodal models based on the standard Transformer (Vaswani et al., 2017) with an additional cross-attention layer in the encoder, followed by a gating mechanism that fused the visual modality and text modality information. In particular, visual representation retrieved from the topic-image lookup table has been encoded by a self-attention network that is in parallel with the source sentence encoder. Then, a cross attention mechanism has been applied to append

[6]During training, we dismissed the 32 out of 29,783 training images having blank Japanese sentences, which ended up with 148,756 lines of Japanese↔English bitext.

[7]`http://nlp.ist.i.kyoto-u.ac.jp/EN/index.php?JUMAN`

[8]`https://github.com/rsennrich/subword-nmt`

[9]Download from `https://storage.googleapis.com/up-down-attention/resnet101_faster_rcnn_final.caffemodel`

the image representation to the text representation. Using a learnable weighting gate $\lambda \in [0, 1)$, we obtained the aggregated multimodal representation corresponding to the significance distribution of either modality, which would be used as input to the decoder for predicting target translations. The hyper-parameter setting is shown in Table 4.

**mBART25 finetuning** Regardless of the image representation, we also finetuned on the Flickr30kEnt-JP corpus using the mBART25 pre-trained model under the unconstrained task setting. Following (Liu et al., 2020), we used the same mBART25-large model[10] and finetuned for 40,000 steps with early stopping control if the validation loss has not been improved for 3 iterations. We used the learning rate schedule of 0.001 and maximum of 4000 tokens in a batch, where the parameters were updated after every 2 epochs. More details of model hyper-parameters setting can be found in Table 4.

We trained the MNMT models and finetuned the mBART25 models using the Fairseq toolkit (Ott et al., 2019) on 4 V100 GPUs. Finally, the best performing models on the validation sets were selected and applied for decoding the test sets. Furthermore, we trained three independent models with different random seeds to perform ensemble decoding.

### 3.4 Results

In Table 5, we show the evaluation scores that the multimodal NMT with universal visual representation and mBART25 finetuning models achieve. In the constrained setting (a.k.a, task (a)), we observed that the MNMT single model (MNMT$_{sin.}$) decoding results unexceptionally lagged behind that of the ensemble decoding (MNMT$_{ens.}$) in both directions. Without any other resources except pre-trained image features, our best submissions of NNMT with UVR win the first place in BLEU as well as human adequacy scores on the WAT leaderboard for the Japanese→English task (a). Moreover, the MNMT$_{ens.}$ model can outperform the mBART25 finetuning model (mBART$_{sin.}$) using external models/embeddings by 0.17 BLEU score in the English→Japanese task (a), which validates the effectiveness of exploring visual information for machine translation.

Under the unconstrained setting, the text-only mBART$_{sin.}$ models achieved significant im-

| Task | Model | BLEU | AMFM | Human |
|---|---|---|---|---|
| en-ja (a) | MNMT$_{sin.}$ | 42.09 | - | - |
| en-ja (a) | MNMT$_{ens.}$ | **43.09** | - | 4.67 |
| en-ja (b) | mBART$_{sin.}$ | 42.92 | 64.83 | - |
| ja-en (a) | MNMT$_{sin.}$ | 51.53 | - | - |
| ja-en (a) | MNMT$_{ens.}$ | 52.20 | - | 4.54 |
| ja-en (b) | mBART$_{sin.}$ | **55.00** | 58.00 | - |

Table 5: Comparisons of MNMT with UVR and mBART25 finetuning best models results in the Japanese↔English multimodal task: (a) constrained setting, (b) unconstrained setting. Note that the human evaluation scores shown in the table are referred to be the adequacy scores.

provement over the MNMT (UVR) single models by 0.83 and 3.47 BLEU scores in the English→Japanese and Japanese→English tasks, respectively. Compared with other submissions, our mBART$_{sin.}$ model decoding achieve the first place in both BLEU scores and AMFM scores on the WAT leaderboard for the Japanese→English (b). It indicates that the advantages of pre-training are substantial in the Flickr30kEnt-JP translation tasks, in spite of the help of another modality (i.e., images) associated to the input sentences.

## 4 Multilingual Indic Task

### 4.1 Task Description

The Multilingual Indic task covers English (en) and 10 Indic (in) Languages: Bengali (bn), Gujarati (gu), Hindi (hi), Kannada (kn), Malayalam (ml), Marathi (mr), Oriya (or), Punjabi (pa), Tamil (ta) and Telugu (te). Multilingual solutions spanning 20 translation directions, en↔in were encouraged in form of many2many, one2many and many2one models. We train one2many for en→in and many2one for in→en directions.

We use the parallel corpora provided by the organizer for training, validation, and evaluation. Table 6 shows the statistics of the entire training data and PMI dataset specific statistics (Haddow and Kirefu, 2020).

### 4.2 Data Processing

We normalize entire Indic language data using Indic NLP Library[11] version 0.71. After that, we use the 250,000-token SentencePiece model from mBART and prepend source and target tokens to

[10] https://github.com/pytorch/fairseq/blob/master/examples/mbart/

[11] https://github.com/anoopkunchukuttan/indic_nlp_library

| | Language | | | | | | | | | |
|---|---|---|---|---|---|---|---|---|---|---|
| | **bn** | **gu** | **hi** | **kn** | **ml** | **mr** | **or** | **pa** | **ta** | **te** |
| Train | 1,756,197 | 518,015 | 3,534,387 | 396,865 | 1,204,503 | 781,872 | 252,160 | 518,508 | 1,499,441 | 686,626 |
| - PMI | 23,306 | 41,578 | 50,349 | 28,901 | 26,916 | 28,974 | 31,966 | 28,294 | 32,638 | 33,380 |
| Dev | 1,000 | 1,000 | 1,000 | 1,000 | 1,000 | 1,000 | 1,000 | 1,000 | 1,000 | 1,000 |
| Test | 2,390 | 2,390 | 2,390 | 2,390 | 2,390 | 2,390 | 2,390 | 2,390 | 2,390 | 2,390 |

Table 6: Statistics of the Multilingual Indic datasets. Each language is paired with English. The PMI dataset is used for adaptation.

| **Direction** | **System** | **Indic Language** | | | | | | | | | |
|---|---|---|---|---|---|---|---|---|---|---|---|
| | | **bn** | **gu** | **hi** | **kn** | **ml** | **mr** | **or** | **pa** | **ta** | **te** |
| en2in | ORGANIZER | 5.58 | 16.38 | 23.31 | 10.11 | 3.34 | 8.82 | 9.08 | 21.77 | 6.38 | 2.80 |
| | mBART50 - ft.1n | 11.09 | 23.25 | 35.57 | 13.57 | 10.94 | 15.99 | 17.81 | 29.37 | 12.58 | 11.86 |
| | +adaptation on PMI | 13.83 | 25.27 | 36.92 | 18.83 | 8.13 | 17.87 | 17.88 | 30.93 | 13.25 | 15.48 |
| in2en | ORGANIZER | 11.27 | 26.21 | 28.21 | 20.33 | 13.64 | 15.10 | 16.35 | 23.66 | 16.07 | 14.70 |
| | mBART50 - ft.nn | 26.69 | 38.73 | 41.58 | 34.11 | 32.23 | 31.76 | 32.67 | 40.38 | 31.09 | 33.87 |
| | +adaptation on PMI | 27.92 | 39.27 | 42.61 | 35.46 | 33.21 | 32.06 | 32.82 | 41.18 | 31.94 | 35.44 |

Table 7: BLEU results on the Multilingual Indic task

each source and target sentence, respectively. We then binarize the data using Fairseq (Ott et al., 2019) framework. Following Section 2.2, we also train with temperature-based sampling to address dataset imbalance.

### 4.3 Model

Similar to our use of the pre-trained mBART50 model from Section 2.3, we use multilingual finetuning and model extension for Oriya, Punjabi, and Kannada using randomly initialized vectors. We use the same model architecture as mBART50 and run Adam optimization using $\beta 1 = 0.9$, $\beta 2 = 0.98$, and $\epsilon = 1e^{-6}$. We use a maximum batch size of 512 tokens and gradients were accumulated every 4 mini-batches on each GPU. We ran our experiments on 8 NVIDIA V100 GPUs. Table 2 shows the details of our experimental settings.

We finetune one2many pre-trained mBART50 (*mBART50 - ft.1n*) for en→in on entire training set for six epochs. We further adapt this model on PMI dataset given as part of the training set for nine epochs. Similarly, we finetune many2many pre-trained mBART50 (*mBART50 - ft.nn*) for in→en on entire training set for six epochs and adaptation on PMI dataset for one epoch.

### 4.4 Results

Table 7 shows our experimental results in terms of BLEU scores. As a baseline, we compare our models with the organizer's bilingual base Transformer model trained on the PMI dataset (*ORGANIZER*). We observe an average improvement of 7.4 BLEU points over this baseline across all en→in pairs by finetuning the *mBART50 - ft.1n* model for 6 epochs. Further adaptation on the PMI dataset for 12 epochs results in an average improvement of 1.6 BLEU points. For en→ml, we observe a drop from 10.94 to 8.13 on adaptation. Similarly, we observe an average improvement of 15.76 BLEU points over baseline across all in→en pairs by finetuning the *mBART50 - ft.nn* model for 4 epochs. Further adaptation on the PMI dataset for a single epoch results in an average improvement of 0.88 BLEU points. Table 8 and 9 show official AMFM and human evaluation results (top three systems for ten translation directions) respectively. Our systems ranked second 6 times out of the 10 directions for which human evaluation results are available, while SRPOL has consistently outperformed all systems. This demonstrates the efficacy of using mBART models for multilingual models. Complete evaluation results are available in the overview paper (Nakazawa et al., 2021).[12]

## 5 Myanmar-English Translation Task

### 5.1 Task Description

In the ALT+ tasks, we conducted experiments on the Myanmar-English parallel data which was provided by the organizers and consist of two corpora, the ALT corpus (Ding et al., 2019, 2020) and UCSY corpus (Yi Mon Shwe Sin and Khin Mar Soe, 2018). The ALT corpus consists of 18,088 training sentences, 1,000 validation sentences, and 1,018 test sentences. The UCSY dataset contains 204,539 training sentences. The quality of the UCSY corpus used in WAT2021 was improved by correcting

[12]Our training scripts are available at `https://github.com/sukuya/indic-mnmt-wat2021-sakura`.

| Direction | System | Indic Language | | | | | | | | | |
|---|---|---|---|---|---|---|---|---|---|---|---|
| | | bn | gu | hi | kn | ml | mr | or | pa | ta | te |
| en2in | ORGANIZER | 70.15 | 75.71 | 75.97 | 74.19 | 70.68 | 73.07 | 71.45 | 76.24 | 72.32 | 70.81 |
| | mBART50 - ft.1n | 73.77 | 81.02 | 81.09 | 80.19 | 79.45 | 79.09 | 76.74 | 80.14 | 79.11 | 77.21 |
| | +adaptation on PMI | 76.47 | 81.34 | 81.70 | 81.78 | 80.19 | 80.36 | 76.99 | 80.22 | 79.57 | 78.51 |
| in2en | ORGANIZER | 61.31 | 72.66 | 73.61 | 69.20 | 64.66 | 65.81 | 73.08 | 70.15 | 67.60 | 63.60 |
| | mBART50 - ft.nn | 77.24 | 82.07 | 83.42 | 80.51 | 80.55 | 79.58 | 80.82 | 82.35 | 79.61 | 80.20 |
| | +adaptation on PMI | 77.29 | 81.86 | 83.45 | 80.97 | 80.68 | 79.55 | 80.60 | 82.34 | 79.04 | 80.40 |

Table 8: AMFM results on the Multilingual Indic task

| Direction | Rank | | |
|---|---|---|---|
| | I | II | III |
| en→bn | 4.65 (SRPOL) | **4.39** (sakura) | 3.94 (IIITH) |
| bn→en | 4.80 (SRPOL) | 3.82 (IIITH) | 3.59 (mcairt) |
| en→kn | 4.72 (SRPOL) | **4.57** (sakura) | 4.00 (IIITH) |
| kn→en | 4.72 (SRPOL) | **4.49** (sakura) | 3.94 (IIITH) |
| en→ml | 4.41 (SRPOL) | 3.54 (CFILT) | 2.72 (IIITH) |
| ml→en | 4.03 (SRPOL) | **3.99** (sakura) | 3.71 (IITP-MT) |
| en→mr | 4.34 (SRPOL) | 4.14 (CFILT) | 3.84 (IIITH) |
| mr→en | 4.57 (SRPOL) | **4.35** (sakura) | 4.01 (IIITH) |
| en→or | 4.26 (SRPOL) | 3.82 (IIITH) | 3.76 (CFILT) |
| or→en | 4.37 (SRPOL) | **4.25** (sakura) | 3.42 (IIITH) |

Table 9: Human evaluation results for the top three systems on the Multilingual Indic task. Bold values represent our system.

| Dataset | English | Myanmar |
|---|---|---|
| $P_1$ | original | original |
| $P_2$ | clean + tokenize | original |
| $P_3$ | clean | clean |
| $P_4$ | clean | clean + word tokenize |
| $P_5$ | clean | clean + syllable tokenize |
| $P_6$ | clean + tokenize | clean + word tokenize |
| $P_7$ | clean + tokenize | clean + syllable tokenize |

Table 10: Preprocessing variations for the Myanmar-English dataset

translation mistakes, spelling errors, and typographical errors.[13] The model was trained and evaluated by using the dataset provided by the organizer, mainly for research around simple hyperparameter tuning of Marian NMT (Junczys-Dowmunt et al., 2018) without any additional data.

### 5.2 Data Processing

For the ALT+ tasks, the ALT and UCSY training datasets were merged first. For cleaning, we removed redundant whitespaces and double quotation marks. We tokenized English sentences using Moses (Koehn et al., 2007) and Myanmar sentences using Pyidaungsu Myanmar Tokenizer[14] with syllable and word level segments, which were then fed into a SentencePiece model to produce subword units. Slightly different from previous approach (Wang and Htun, 2020), we generated three English datasets with different types: (i) original, (ii) clean, and (iii) clean and tokenized versions. For Myanmar, we have four types: (i) original, (ii) clean, (iii) word-level tokenized, and (iv) syllable-level tokenized. Table 10 describes the resulting datasets with different preprocessing steps.

### 5.3 Model

For training, we generated multiple training datasets by using different combinations of the datasets in Table 10:

- $D_1 = \{P_1\}$
- $D_2 = \{P_1, P_2, P_6, P_7\}$
- $D_3 = \{P_1, P_3, P_4, P_6, P_7\}$
- $D_4 = \{P_3, P_4, P_6, P_7\}$

For both directions on each dataset, we trained individual Transformer models using the Marian[15] toolkit. We created two different parameter configurations as shown in Table 11. We used the first configuration (*Config. 1*) on $D_1$ and the second configuration (*Config. 2*) on the rest ($D_2$, $D_3$, and $D_4$). Note that our second configuration has a larger vocabulary size and increased regularization (dropout, label smoothing). All experimental models in this task were trained on 3 GP104 machines with 4 GeForce GTX 1080 GPUs in each, and the experimental results will be shown and analyzed in the following section.

### 5.4 Results

Table 12 presents the results of our experiments on the given ALT test dataset evaluation for two directions. As our baseline, we trained on the original training set ($D_1$) without further preprocessing and using the first model configuration. After using data augmentation, we observed consistent

[13] http://lotus.kuee.kyoto-u.ac.jp/WAT/my-en-data/

[14] https://github.com/kaunghtetsan275/pyidaungsu

[15] https://marian-nmt.github.io

| Models | Config. 1 | Config. 2 |
|---|---|---|
| Vocabulary size | 160k | 380k |
| Embedding dim. | 1024 | 1024 |
| Tied embeddings | Yes | Yes |
| Transformer FFN dim. | 4096 | 4096 |
| Attention heads | 8 | 8 |
| En/Decoder layers | 4 | 4 |
| Label smoothing | 0.1 | 0.2 |
| Dropout | 0.1 | 0.2 |
| Batch size | 12 | 12 |
| Attention weight dropout | 0.1 | 0.2 |
| Transformer FFN dropout | 0.1 | 0.2 |
| Learning rate | $1e^{-3}$ | $1e^{-4}$ |
| Learning rate warmup | 8000 | 16000 |
| Trained positional embeddings | No | Yes |

Table 11: Myanmar-English model parameter settings

improvements in BLEU scores in any combination. This indicates that proper preprocessing steps such as cleaning and tokenization are crucial for this task. On en-my, we obtained the highest BLEU of 29.62 when training on $D_4$, which does not include the original segments $P_1$. On my-en, however, the highest BLEU is achieved on $D_2$, i.e., 19.75. It includes the cleaning and tokenization steps, particularly on the English side. Any forms of tokenization, be it word-level or syllable-level, appear to be helpful for Myanmar. Our best submission obtained the 6[th] place on the en-my leaderboard and the 5[th] place on my-en.

| Task | Dataset | Config. | BLEU |
|---|---|---|---|
| ALT+ en-my | $D_1$ | 1 | 21.70 |
| ALT+ en-my | $D_2$ | 2 | 29.25 |
| ALT+ en-my | $D_3$ | 2 | 29.07 |
| ALT+ en-my | $D_4$ | 2 | **29.62** |
| ALT+ my-en | $D_1$ | 1 | 14.80 |
| ALT+ my-en | $D_2$ | 2 | **19.75** |
| ALT+ my-en | $D_3$ | 2 | 18.70 |
| ALT+ my-en | $D_4$ | 2 | 18.50 |

Table 12: Results on the Myanmar-English translation task

## 6 Conclusion

We presented our submissions (team ID: *sakura*) to the WAT 2021 shared translation tasks in this paper. We showed the remarkable effectiveness of pre-trained models in improving multilingual and multimodal neural machine translation. On multilingual translation, models initialized with mBART50 achieved substantial performance gains on both NICT-SAP and Multilingual Indic tasks. On multimodal translation, a text-only model with mBART25 pre-training improves upon an MNMT model based on UVR. Finally, we extended our data augmentation approaches on the Myanmar-English translation tasks and obtained further improvements.

## References


Peter Anderson, Xiaodong He, Chris Buehler, Damien Teney, Mark Johnson, Stephen Gould, and Lei Zhang. 2018. Bottom-up and top-down attention for image captioning and visual question answering. In *CVPR*.

Naveen Arivazhagan, Ankur Bapna, Orhan Firat, Dmitry Lepikhin, Melvin Johnson, Maxim Krikun, Mia Xu Chen, Yuan Cao, George Foster, Colin Cherry, Wolfgang Macherey, Zhifeng Chen, and Yonghui Wu. 2019. Massively multilingual neural machine translation in the wild: Findings and challenges.

Rafael E. Banchs, Luis F. D'Haro, and Haizhou Li. 2015. Adequacy-fluency metrics: Evaluating mt in the continuous space model framework. *IEEE/ACM Trans. Audio, Speech and Lang. Proc.*, 23(3):472–482.

Bianka Buschbeck and Miriam Exel. 2020. A parallel evaluation data set of software documentation with document structure annotation. In *Proceedings of the 7th Workshop on Asian Translation*, pages 160–169, Suzhou, China. Association for Computational Linguistics.

Alexis Conneau, Kartikay Khandelwal, Naman Goyal, Vishrav Chaudhary, Guillaume Wenzek, Francisco Guzmán, Edouard Grave, Myle Ott, Luke Zettlemoyer, and Veselin Stoyanov. 2020. Unsupervised cross-lingual representation learning at scale. In *Proceedings of the 58th Annual Meeting of the Association for Computational Linguistics*, pages 8440–8451, Online. Association for Computational Linguistics.

Raj Dabre and Abhisek Chakrabarty. 2020. NICT's submission to WAT 2020: How effective are simple many-to-many neural machine translation models? In *Proceedings of the 7th Workshop on Asian Translation*, pages 98–102, Suzhou, China. Association for Computational Linguistics.

Chenchen Ding, Hnin Thu Zar Aye, Win Pa Pa, Khin Thandar Nwet, Khin Mar Soe, Masao Utiyama, and Eiichiro Sumita. 2019. Towards Burmese (Myanmar) morphological analysis: Syllable-based tokenization and part-of-speech tagging. *ACM Transactions on Asian and Low-Resource Language Information Processing (TALLIP)*, 19(1):5.

Chenchen Ding, Sann Su Su Yee, Win Pa Pa, Khin Mar Soe, Masao Utiyama, and Eiichiro Sumita. 2020. A Burmese (Myanmar) treebank: Guildline and analysis. *ACM Transactions on Asian and Low-Resource Language Information Processing (TALLIP)*, 19(3):40.

Barry Haddow and Faheem Kirefu. 2020. PMIndia – A Collection of Parallel Corpora of Languages of India. *arXiv e-prints*, page arXiv:2001.09907.

Marcin Junczys-Dowmunt, Roman Grundkiewicz, Tomasz Dwojak, Hieu Hoang, Kenneth Heafield, Tom Neckermann, Frank Seide, Ulrich Germann, Alham Fikri Aji, Nikolay Bogoychev, André F. T. Martins, and Alexandra Birch. 2018. Marian: Fast neural machine translation in C++. In *Proceedings of ACL 2018, System Demonstrations*, pages 116–121, Melbourne, Australia. Association for Computational Linguistics.

Diederick P Kingma and Jimmy Ba. 2015. Adam: A method for stochastic optimization. In *International Conference on Learning Representations (ICLR)*.

Philipp Koehn, Hieu Hoang, Alexandra Birch, Chris Callison-Burch, Marcello Federico, Nicola Bertoldi, Brooke Cowan, Wade Shen, Christine Moran, Richard Zens, Chris Dyer, Ondřej Bojar, Alexandra Constantin, and Evan Herbst. 2007. Moses: Open source toolkit for statistical machine translation. In *Proceedings of the 45th Annual Meeting of the Association for Computational Linguistics Companion Volume Proceedings of the Demo and Poster Sessions*, pages 177–180, Prague, Czech Republic. Association for Computational Linguistics.

Ranjay Krishna, Yuke Zhu, Oliver Groth, Justin Johnson, Kenji Hata, Joshua Kravitz, Stephanie Chen, Yannis Kalantidis, Li-Jia Li, David A Shamma, Michael Bernstein, and Li Fei-Fei. 2017. Visual genome: Connecting language and vision using crowdsourced dense image annotations. In *IJCV*.

Taku Kudo and John Richardson. 2018. SentencePiece: A simple and language independent subword tokenizer and detokenizer for neural text processing. In *Proceedings of the 2018 Conference on Empirical Methods in Natural Language Processing: System Demonstrations*, pages 66–71, Brussels, Belgium. Association for Computational Linguistics.

Yinhan Liu, Jiatao Gu, Naman Goyal, Xian Li, Sergey Edunov, Marjan Ghazvininejad, Mike Lewis, and Luke Zettlemoyer. 2020. Multilingual denoising pre-training for neural machine translation. *Transactions of the Association for Computational Linguistics*, 8:726–742.

Hideki Nakayama, Akihiro Tamura, and Takashi Ninomiya. 2020. A visually-grounded parallel corpus with phrase-to-region linking. In *Proceedings of The 12th Language Resources and Evaluation Conference*, pages 4204–4210, Marseille, France. European Language Resources Association.

Toshiaki Nakazawa, Hideki Nakayama, Chenchen Ding, Raj Dabre, Shohei Higashiyama, Hideya Mino, Isao Goto, Win Pa Pa, Anoop Kunchukuttan, Shantipriya Parida, OndÅ™ej Bojar, Chenhui Chu, Akiko Eriguchi, Kaori Abe, and Sadao Oda, Yusuke Kurohashi. 2021. Overview of the 8th workshop on Asian translation. In *Proceedings of the 8th Workshop on Asian Translation*, Bangkok, Thailand. Association for Computational Linguistics.

Toshiaki Nakazawa, Hideki Nakayama, Chenchen Ding, Raj Dabre, Shohei Higashiyama, Hideya Mino, Isao Goto, Win Pa Pa, Anoop Kunchukuttan, Shantipriya Parida, et al. 2020. Overview of the 7th workshop on asian translation. In *Proceedings of the 7th Workshop on Asian Translation*, pages 1–44.

Myle Ott, Sergey Edunov, Alexei Baevski, Angela Fan, Sam Gross, Nathan Ng, David Grangier, and Michael Auli. 2019. fairseq: A fast, extensible toolkit for sequence modeling. In *Proceedings of the 2019 Conference of the North American Chapter of the Association for Computational Linguistics (Demonstrations)*, pages 48–53, Minneapolis, Minnesota. Association for Computational Linguistics.

Kishore Papineni, Salim Roukos, Todd Ward, and Wei-Jing Zhu. 2002. Bleu: a method for automatic evaluation of machine translation. In *Proceedings of the 40th annual meeting on association for computational linguistics*, pages 311–318. Association for Computational Linguistics.

Bryan A Plummer, Liwei Wang, Chris M Cervantes, Juan C Caicedo, Julia Hockenmaier, and Svetlana Lazebnik. 2015. Flickr30k entities: Collecting region-to-phrase correspondences for richer image-to-sentence models. In *Proceedings of the IEEE international conference on computer vision*, pages 2641–2649.

Rico Sennrich, Barry Haddow, and Alexandra Birch. 2016. Neural machine translation of rare words with subword units. In *Proceedings of the 54th Annual Meeting of the Association for Computational Linguistics (Volume 1: Long Papers)*, pages 1715–1725, Berlin, Germany. Association for Computational Linguistics.

Yuqing Tang, Chau Tran, Xian Li, Peng-Jen Chen, Naman Goyal, Vishrav Chaudhary, Jiatao Gu, and Angela Fan. 2020. Multilingual translation with extensible multilingual pretraining and finetuning.

Ye Kyaw Thu, Win Pa Pa, Masao Utiyama, Andrew Finch, and Eiichiro Sumita. 2016. Introducing the Asian language treebank (ALT). In *Proceedings of the Tenth International Conference on Language Resources and Evaluation (LREC'16)*, pages 1574–1578, Portorož, Slovenia. European Language Resources Association (ELRA).

Ashish Vaswani, Noam Shazeer, Niki Parmar, Jakob Uszkoreit, Llion Jones, Aidan N Gomez, Łukasz Kaiser, and Illia Polosukhin. 2017. Attention is all you need. In *Advances in neural information processing systems*, pages 5998–6008.

Dongzhe Wang and Ohnmar Htun. 2020. Goku's participation in WAT 2020. In *Proceedings of the 7th Workshop on Asian Translation*, pages 135–141, Suzhou, China. Association for Computational Linguistics.

Yi Mon Shwe Sin and Khin Mar Soe. 2018. Syllable-based myanmar-english neural machine translation. In *Proc. of ICCA*, pages 228–233.

Zhuosheng Zhang, Kehai Chen, Rui Wang, Masao Utiyama, Eiichiro Sumita, Zuchao Li, and Hai Zhao. 2019. Neural machine translation with universal visual representation. In *International Conference on Learning Representations*.

# BTS: Back TranScription for Speech-to-Text Post-Processor using Text-to-Speech-to-Text

**Chanjun Park**[1], **Jaehyung Seo**[1], **Seolhwa Lee**[1], **Chanhee Lee**[1]
**Hyeonseok Moon**[1], **Sugyeong Eo**[1], **Heuiseok Lim**[1†]
[1]Korea University, South Korea
{bcj1210,seojae777,whiteldark, chanhee0222}@korea.ac.kr
{glee889, djtnrud, limhseok}@korea.ac.kr

## Abstract

With the growing popularity of smart speakers, such as Amazon Alexa, speech is becoming one of the most important modes of human-computer interaction. Automatic speech recognition (ASR) is arguably the most critical component of such systems, as errors in speech recognition propagate to the downstream components and drastically degrade the user experience. A simple and effective way to improve the speech recognition accuracy is to apply automatic post-processor to the recognition result. However, training a post-processor requires parallel corpora created by human annotators, which are expensive and not scalable. To alleviate this problem, we propose Back TranScription (BTS), a denoising-based method that can create such corpora without human labor. Using a raw corpus, BTS corrupts the text using Text-to-Speech (TTS) and Speech-to-Text (STT) systems. Then, a post-processing model can be trained to reconstruct the original text given the corrupted input. Quantitative and qualitative evaluations show that a post-processor trained using our approach is highly effective in fixing non-trivial speech recognition errors such as mishandling foreign words. We present the generated parallel corpus and post-processing platform to make our results publicly available.

## 1 Introduction

Automatic speech recognition (ASR) is a technology that converts human voice into text. With the emergence of deep learning, the performance of ASR has been improved considerably. Consequently, many firms are applying ASR to their business models (Kaya et al., 2020).

Although several excellent commercial API systems are available, such as Google Cloud Speech API (Aleksic et al., 2015) and Naver's CLOVA Speech (Chung, 2019), most small- and medium-sized companies are building their own ASR software using open-source tools such as Kaldi (Povey et al., 2011) owing to the need for domain-specific systems as well as security of in-house industrial data (Vajpai and Bora, 2016). In addition, many companies are operating on conventional ASR architectures, such as Gaussian mixture models (GMMs) (Stuttle, 2003) and hidden Markov models (HMMs) (Gales and Young, 2008), which are based on acoustic and language models.

However, a drawback of the above-mentioned method is that words that are not in the dictionary are misrecognized as incorrect words owing to the out-of-vocabulary (OOV) problem. As this method is a statistics-based method, satisfactory performance is achieved only when a massive voice database is available . Probability values for sequences of words that are not present in the training corpus are estimated to be unstable, and it is difficult to sufficiently reflect the context because n values are constrained in n-grams. Moreover, the entry barrier is high because it is difficult for non-professionals to handle the model.

To alleviate these limitations, ASR studies have recently been conducted using pretrained model (PM)-based transfer learning (Baevski et al., 2020; Hjortnæs et al., 2021; Zhang et al., 2021). This methodology shows superior performance compared to methods based on the conventional ASR architecture; however, it has two main limitations in terms of applying it to real-world services.

First, from the data aspect, this methodology requires a large amount of training data for pretraining to service the ASR software. As it is strongly dependent on the data size, it is difficult to apply it to a low-resource language (LRL), such as Korean. Furthermore, as the latest studies are based on a high-resource language (HRL) with sufficient training data, the same performance cannot be achieved

† Corresponding author



*Proceedings of the 8th Workshop on Asian Translation*, pages 106–116
Bangkok, Thailand (online), August 5-6, 2021. ©2021 Association for Computational Linguistics

if the same model is applied to an LRL without any special processing.
Second, from the service environment aspect, this methodology requires service circumstances with sufficient computing power (e.g., GPU) to process large-scale data. It is difficult to establish a sufficient hardware environment to provide services, except for large companies such as Google and Facebook. In other words, as training a model involves many parameters and a large amount of data, companies that do not have sufficient server or GPU environments will find it difficult to configure the service environment and improve performance using the latest model (Park et al., 2020c). Therefore, it is important to ensure that companies with insufficient environments can provide services while performing well against LRLs. To this end, instead of PM-based transfer learning, a new method for improving ASR performance is required.

To alleviate these limitations, some studies have attempted to improve the performance of the ASR model through various pre-processing and post-processing methods without changing the model (Jeong et al., 2003; Jung et al., 2004; Voll et al., 2008; Mani et al., 2020; Liao et al., 2020). This approach does not require a large amount of data for pretraining the model and it can be applied to any model as well as models that can provide sufficient service with a CPU (Klein et al., 2020), such as the vanilla Transformer (Vaswani et al., 2017). In this regard, this method can alleviate the above-mentioned limitations in terms of the data and service environment. Hence, this method is particularly important from the viewpoint of LRLs.

Accordingly, we propose Back TranScription (BTS), a fully automated data construction method for a sequence-to-sequence (S2S)-based post-processor model that does not require human intervention or model modification. The contributions of this study are as follows.

- We propose BTS, a simple and effective method for generating ASR post-processor training corpus without expensive human labor. As this approach does not require human intervention, it can create a vast amount of training data from raw text, which drastically reduces the cost of building such a model.

- We discuss the characteristics and effectiveness of our approach on the basis of extensive quantitative and qualitative evaluations.

- We present the generated parallel data and post-processing platform to make our results publicly available*.

## 2 Related Work

ASR post-processing is a research field that aims to improve performance by correcting the ASR errors rather than changing the model architecture. The two main methodologies for ASR post-processing in the field of speech recognition are the conventional methodology and the sequence-to-sequence (S2S) methodology.

**Conventional Methodology** The conventional methodology is based on rules and statistics. Firms attempt to improve ASR performance by building their own rules while providing ASR services. They apply linguistic rules to improve the quality of the speech recognition results. The drawback of this methodology is that it involves high costs and requires a long time to produce abundant rules. Moreover, conflicts between rules may occur. Furthermore, each component must be implemented independently (Paulik et al., 2008; Škodová et al., 2012). Some post-processing studies have been conducted using the N-gram language model; however, the statistics-based method requires a large amount data and cannot consider the context (Cucu et al., 2013; Bassil and Semaan, 2012).

**Sequence-to-Sequence (S2S) Methodology** The S2S methodology corrects errors in the same way as the machine translation process (Vaswani et al., 2017; Baskar et al., 2019; Park et al., 2020a). Based on the S2S model, the STT result is vectorized using an encoder and the vector is then decoded to generate a human-modified STT sentence. This methodology outperforms the conventional method based on rules and statistics. However, the ASR post-processor based on the S2S methodology has some limitations in terms of data construction and industrial service.

First, from the data construction aspect, no open data are available for training, and a parallel corpus must be manually built for the ASR post-processor. The training data are of the form (speech recognition sentence, human post-edit sentence), and constructing such data involves human intervention to transcribe the speech. In other words, considerable time and effort are required to construct the data. In addition, quality differences may occur depending

*`http://nlplab.iptime.org:32260/`

on the transcriber. Different individuals may transcribe the same sentence differently, resulting in performance degradation of the model. Hence, we aim to alleviate the limitations of S2S-based data construction through BTS using Text-to-Speech-to-Text (TST). This method can reduce the cost and time required for data construction and is free of the quality issues related to human transcription.

Second, from the service aspect, although most recent NLP studies are based on the pretrain-finetuning approach (PFA), small- and medium-sized enterprises lack sufficient hardware; hence, there are many limitations in terms of using the technology to service NLP application software owing to low speed and insufficient memory. Although methods such as XLM (Lample and Conneau, 2019), MASS (Song et al., 2019), and mBART (Liu et al., 2020) show the best current performance, the corresponding models are too large in terms of the number of parameters and model size. Therefore, it is still unreasonable to provide practical services in the industry. Furthermore, as this methodology is dependent on the data size, it can be easily applied to an HRL whereas its application to an LRL is limited.

This study is similar to studies on automatic post-editing (APE) (Chatterjee et al., 2019) and grammar error correction (GEC) (Bryant et al., 2019). However, APE performs post-processing on machine translation results while GEC is designed to correct grammar, i.e., their post-processing targets are different. In addition, these methods are mainly based on an HRL-based pretrained language model (PLM) such as XLM, MASS, or UniLM (Dong et al., 2019). Hence, it is difficult to apply them to services provided by small- and medium-sized enterprises with insufficient environments.

In this study, we use the vanilla Transformer, which can be easily applied to the required service. In contrast to previous studies, we conduct an experiment on the Korean language, which is an LRL, and we make the model constructed in this study freely available.

## 3 Proposed Method

### 3.1 Background

In this study, we introduce four mainstream attributes reflecting the readability and satisfactoriness of ASR service in order to provide high-quality service to end users of our BTS mechanism, which can be used for training the ASR post-processor.

**Spacing** The first limitation is related to segmentation, i.e., the spaces are generally not adequately separated in the speech recognition result. To solve this problem, many studies have investigated an automatic spacing module; however, few studies have focused on ASR (Lee and Kim, 2013; Choi et al., 2021). Thus, the satisfactoriness of ASR service, which is used by end users, is low, and the speech recognition results will lack credibility if this problem is not resolved.

**Foreign Word Conversion** The second limitation is the foreign word conversion problem. For example, for the sentence "`The Lotte tower is on the 123rd floor.`", the ASR service outputs "`The 롯데 타워 is on the 123rd floor.`". In other words, 롯데 타워 is not converted into `Lotte tower`. We refer to this problem as the foreign word conversion problem. Although it is not a critical problem, solving it can improve the readability and satisfactoriness of the ASR system for end users.

**Punctuation** The third limitation is related to punctuation (e.g., period, comma, exclamation and question marks). The correct output of the ASR system should be "`where are you going?`"; however, the general ASR system outputs "`where are you going`" without the question mark. Thus, the lack of punctuation makes it problematic for the end users to understand the purpose of sentence segmentation. This could lead to complex issues in the recognition of end users' utterance intentions in terms of who wants to use the output. Furthermore, commercial ASR systems typically do not use punctuation when they provide services (Ha et al., 2020). Several studies (Yi et al., 2020; Guan, 2020) have attempted to solve these punctuation problems independently.

**Spelling Errors** The fourth limitation is related to spelling errors, which frequently occur in the ASR result. Although previous studies (Kiyono et al., 2019; Choe et al., 2019; Park et al., 2020a) have investigated spelling correction, few have focused on ASR.

### 3.2 Back TranScription (BTS)

BTS is a technique that is integrated with TTS and STT to yield a parallel corpus. The process of building a parallel corpus involves the following steps:

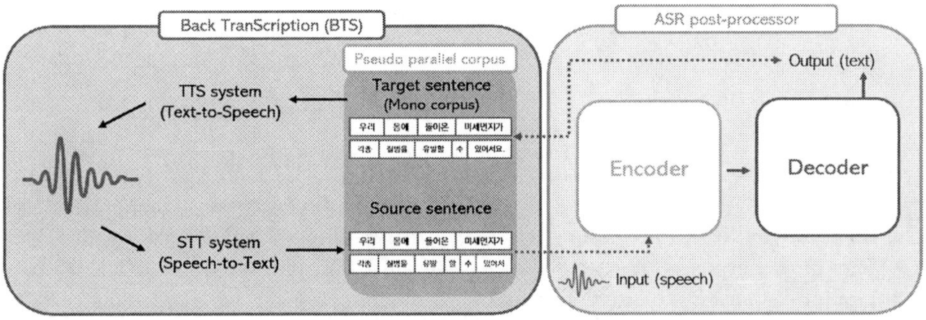


Figure 1: Overall architecture of BTS and ASR post-processor. Note that the red words in the source sentence are ungrammatical words. The source sentence means "Fine dust occurs many diseases when it comes to our bo" and the target sentence means "Fine dust occurs many diseases when it comes to our body.".

| | No Filter | | | | Filter | | | | Test | |
|---|---|---|---|---|---|---|---|---|---|---|
| | Train | | Valid | | Train | | Valid | | | |
| | src | tgt | src | tgt | src | tgt | src | tgt | src | tgt |
| # of sents | 224,987 | 224,987 | 5,000 | 5,000 | 214,318 | 214,318 | 5,000 | 5,000 | 5,000 | 5,000 |
| # of tokens | 7,319,788 | 7,731,924 | 160,773 | 167,888 | 7,117,361 | 7,447,350 | 136,496 | 143,044 | 165,781 | 172,590 |
| # of words | 1,950,669 | 1,900,409 | 42,968 | 41,780 | 1,887,843 | 1,830,500 | 36,655 | 35,961 | 43,482 | 41,472 |
| avg of SL △ | 32.53 | 34.37 | 32.15 | 33.58 | 33.21 | 34.75 | 27.3 | 28.61 | 33.16 | 34.52 |
| avg of WS | 8.67 | 8.45 | 8.59 | 8.36 | 8.81 | 8.54 | 7.33 | 7.19 | 8.7 | 8.29 |
| avg of SS | 7.67 | 7.45 | 7.59 | 7.36 | 7.81 | 7.54 | 6.33 | 6.19 | 7.7 | 7.29 |
| # of K-toks * | 5,503,227 | 5,599,442 | 121,131 | 122,502 | 5,365,092 | 5,420,594 | 103,667 | 104,961 | 123,566 | 124,203 |
| # of E-toks | 32,389 | 61,294 | 504 | 829 | 30,217 | 57,203 | 463 | 724 | 1,162 | 2,262 |
| # of S-toks | 2,181 | 338,459 | 55 | 6,675 | 1,769 | 307,339 | 21 | 5,682 | 74 | 6,873 |

Table 1: Statistics of our parallel corpus results on TST with and without a filter. We define the original colloquial sentences as the target (tgt) and the generated sentences after TST as the source (src). Moreover, we attempt to identify the linguistic features of our parallel corpus, including # of sents/tokens/words (number of sentences/tokens/words); △ avg of SL/WS/SS (average of sentence length/words/spaces per sentence); and $*$ # of K/E/S-toks (number of Korean/English/special-symbol letter tokens).

1) crawling the pre-built mono corpus in a convenient manner; 2) transformation into speech using TTS; and 3) outputting the converted result as text using STT. We aim to apply the BTS mechanism to the mainstream attributes described in Section 3.1.

In other words, we apply TST to the result of TTS (i.e., the original mono corpus) and then create a pseudo-parallel corpus for the ASR post-processor. This can be explained in terms of machine translation as follows: the source sentence is substituted for the output of TST, and the original mono corpus is substituted for the target sentence.

TST is the processor for creating ASR errors from the mono corpus, i.e., the ASR errors can be generated through TST, which is integrated with both the TTS module that provides the data for the STT module and the STT module. The mono corpus is grounded well in space, can handle foreign word conversion and punctuation, and rarely involves spelling errors. We can develop a high-quality ASR post-processor based on S2S training using these processes.

Figure 1 shows the proposed method, including the BTS architecture and ASR post-processor architecture based on S2S training using the pseudo-parallel corpus, which is derived from BTS. The module on the left (BTS) shows the target sentence (ground sentence) converted into speech using the TTS system, which is then converted into the source sentence (error sentence) through the STT system. The module on the right (ASR post-processor) shows the S2S-based ASR post-processor, which uses the speech of the source sentence as the model input and the target sentence as the ground truth. In the BTS module, the pseudo-parallel corpus consists of the target sentence from the mono corpus and the source sentence converted from the TTS output (i.e., speech) into the STT output (i.e., text). The source sentence includes the above-mentioned errors. Finally, we can train the ASR post-processor using the pseudo-parallel corpus.

### 3.3 Why BTS?

The advantages of the BTS method in terms of service can be attributed to five factors.

- First, BTS can build infinite training data for ASR or other purposes. In general, building a parallel corpus is expensive and time-consuming. Moreover, it is difficult to establish a high-quality parallel corpus. However, we can easily build an infinite parallel corpus if we exploit the advantages of the mono corpus through web crawling.

- Second, BTS supports a universal method for integrating solutions to problems such as spacing, foreign word conversion, punctuation, and spelling errors using a single model, as the mono corpus that is used in our method is free of the above-mentioned problems. Previous studies have been conducted independently, whereas our method can resolve these issues simultaneously.

- Third, commercial ASR systems such as Google Cloud Speech API can be converted into domain-specific ASR systems. If a TTS is produced using only a single corpus of the specific domain and a post-processor is created using the constructed parallel corpus, the commercial ASR system can be serviced with a domain-specific ASR. Companies build their own ASR system rather than using commercial systems because of the need for a domain-specific model, which can be built by exploiting the high recognition rate of a commercialized system through BTS. We define these domain corrections.

- Fourth, our method does not require human intervention for building a parallel corpus as it involves automatic generation; therefore, it achieves significant time and cost savings. In addition, it is free of the quality issues that may arise in the case of different human operators.

- Finally, language extension is simple and convenient. The commercial system (Aleksic et al., 2015) provides various TTS and STT language-specific API services. Therefore, we can collect a diverse language dataset for BTS.

In summary, BTS is a practical solution that can enable companies to provide ASR service.

## 4 Experimental Setup

### 4.1 Data Collection

**Build Mono Corpus** The parallel corpus for experimenting with BTS was set to Korean, which is an LRL, and we collected it from two different sources. First, we extracted 129,987 sentences from the business and technology TED provided in a script translated into Korean. Second, we extracted 105,000 sentences from the Korean-English translation corpus in AI-HUB (Park and Lim, 2020)

**TTS** Using the mono corpus, we converted the text into voice data in the mp3 format using Google TTS API. Specifically, 129,987 sentences from TED were divided into 7,969,230 speech tokens and synthesized with 2,081,115 s of voice data. Further, 105,000 sentences from AI-HUB were divided into 3,065,086 speech tokens and synthesized with 1,563,990 s of voice data. The voice data were synthesized using the same WaveNet model (Oord et al., 2016) as that used for Google Assistant, Google Search, and Google Translation, which required less than 36 h and 24 h for the conversion, respectively. The commercialized API system was used to lower the entry barrier, thereby allowing companies that lack a TTS system to use BTS.

**STT** The voice data constructed by TTS use Navers CLOVA Speech Recognition (CSR) API to proceed with the conversion back to text data. The speech recognition API uses the same model as that used for Navers Voice Recognition Notes and Searches, which requires less than 120 h and 72 h for the conversion, respectively. After this process, a parallel corpus of 229,987 sentence pairs, consisting of the target sentences prior to speech synthesis and recognition as well as the translated source sentences, is built for the S2S-based ASR post-processors.

**Parallel Corpus Filtering** Parallel corpus filtering (PCF) (Koehn et al., 2020) is the process of constructing a qualitatively validated parallel corpus. In other words, it is a sub-field of machine translation in which training data are selected to ensure high-quality training to improve the performance of the model.

In the case of the pseudo-parallel corpus built through TST, some source sentences are empty or

| Model | BLEU | GLEU |
|---|---|---|
| Base | 42.19 | N/A |
| Park et al. (2020a) | 50.62 (+8.43) | 31.79 |
| No-Filter | 55.72 (+13.53) | 46.23 |
| Filter | **56.56 (+14.37)** | **46.94** |

Table 2: Overall BTS performance verification results

too short; they are not recognized owing to unintentional errors in the STT and TTS systems. Thus, we use the PCF methodology proposed by Park et al. (2020b) to obtain only high-quality data. A total of 10,669 sentences are filtered, most of which are low-quality data obtained because of poor recognition during STT. In addition, we remove pairs of sentences that are identical or which consist of special symbol tokens comprising more than 50% of the total tokens , as these sentences may not be inconsistent with the learning method.

**Final Constructed Pseudo-Parallel Corpus** We compared the performance of the PCF-driven model with that of the non-progress model to verify the effectiveness of filtering. For models without filtering (No-Filter), the training data included 224,987 sentences and the verification data included 5,000 sentences. For the filtered (Filter) model, the training data included 214,318 sentences and the verification data included 5,000 sentences. In the case of the test set, 5,000 sentences of the No-Filter version were constructed to evaluate the performance changes depending on whether filtering was applied during the training process.

### 4.2 Model

For the post-processor, we trained the vanilla Transformer with the pseudo-parallel corpus, generated by BTS. The hyper-parameter settings were the same as those used by Vaswani et al. (2017). Further, we used SentencePiece (Kudo and Richardson, 2018) for sub-word tokenization and set the vocabulary size to 32,000. Two GTX 1080ti GPUs were used in the experiments.

## 5 Experimental Results

### 5.1 Data statistics and analysis

Using BTS, we constructed a parallel corpus for an S2S-based ASR post-processor with 219,318 sentences that are finally processed by PCF.

We conducted a statistical analysis of the constructed corpus and a comparative analysis with and without PCF. The results are summarized in Table 1.

First, we conducted basic analyses, such as the number of data, number of tokens, and average length of sentences. The lengths of the source sentences built using BTS, regardless of whether the filter was applied, were smaller than those of the target sentences on average 1.69, 1.37, and 1.36 for the training, validation, and test datasets, respectively. However, the average numbers of source sentence words were greater than those of target sentence words on average 0.245, 0.185, and 0.41 for the training, validation, and test datasets, respectively. Considering the average number of blank spaces, these results are attributed to the unnecessary separation of phrases, even though the source sentences have a relatively small total number of tokens.

Second, we analyzed the Korean and English tokens. In the case of K-tokens, 75,859, 1,333, and 672 tokens in the training, validation, and test datasets were lost in the source sentences, respectively. Token loss is the reason for the omission of sentence endings and suffixes, and it is estimated that the model reflects the common characteristics of Korean speakers who pronounce the ending in a slurred manner. In addition, the E-tokens are transformed into Korean tokens as pronounced and suitable phonetic values are not obtained. Consequently, 27,946, 293, and 1,100 E-tokens in the training, validation, and test dataset were lost in the source sentences, respectively.

Third, the most significant loss was in the case of S-tokens. The source sentences in the training, validation, and test datasets lost 320,924, 6,141, and 6,799 special symbol tokens, respectively. For example, periods, commas, exclamation marks, and small brackets, which are added to describe the situation in the transcription of the original data, tend to be lost in the source sentences. Such special symbol tokens may sometimes contain actual colloquial tones or emotions that are not represented by the text adequately. Thus, excessive omission of special symbol tokens is equivalent to the loss of rich representation information of colloquial forms that are different from written ones.

In conclusion, we make the model that we have constructed freely available in order to lower the entry barrier for research institutions and mitigate the cost challenges faced by many small- and medium-sized enterprises that lack sufficient resources.

| Model | Spacing | Word Conversion(KO) | Word Conversion(EN) | Punctuation | Overall |
|---|---|---|---|---|---|
| Base | 89.60 | 46.87 | 4.14 | 0.89 | 61.84 |
| Filter | **91.86 (+2.26)** | **54.41 (+7.54)** | **23.41 (+19.27)** | **61.02 (+60.13)** | **70.73 (+8.89)** |

Table 3: BTS performance classified as Automatic Spacing, Word Conversion, Punctuation, and Overall. The F1 scores are reported for each feature. KO: Korean; EN: English.

| Input Sentence | Output Sentence | Type of Error |
|---|---|---|
| 제가 어렸을 때 우연히 **티비**에서 박지성 선수가 축구 경기를 하는 모습을 보았어요<br>(When I was young, I watched Park Ji-sung playing a soccer on **티비**.) | 제가 어렸을 때 우연히 **TV**에서 박지성 선수가 축구 경기를 하는 모습을 보았어요.<br>(When I was young, I watched Park Ji-sung playing a soccer on **TV**.) | Foreign Word Conversion |
| 참석자 명단을 받으려면 어느 부서에 가야 하나<br>(Which department should I go to receive a list of attendees) | 참석자 명단을 받으려면 어느 부서에 가야 하나**?**<br>(Which department should I go to receive a list of attendees**?**) | Punctuation |
| 너무 보고 싶은데 **볼수가** 없네<br>(I **missyou** so much, but I can't) | 너무 보고 싶은데 **볼 수가** 없네.<br>(I **miss you** so much, but I can't.) | Spacing |
| 가평은 한국의 유명한 관광지<br>(Gapyeong a famous tourist spot in Korea) | 가평은 한국의 유명한 관광지**예요.**<br>(Gapyeong **is** a famous tourist spot in Korea.) | Spelling errors |
| 감자탕은 무료 서비스로 **나온**<br>(Gamjatang is **serv** for free) | 감자탕은 무료 서비스로 **나옵니다.**<br>(Gamjatang is **served** for free.) | Spelling errors |

Table 4: Examples of sentences for qualitative analysis

### 5.2 Quantitative Results

**Spelling Correction** First, we verified the spelling correction performance of the BTS-based ASR post-processor. We employed GLEU (Napoles et al., 2015) and BLEU (Papineni et al., 2002) as the performance evaluation metrics. GLEU is similar to BLEU; the difference is that GLEU also considers the source information and is specialized for spelling error correction systems.

Base refers to the BLEU score between the source and target sentences; we leveraged it as the baseline for assessing the performance improvement. In addition, we compared the performance with that of the Korean spelling error correction model proposed by Park et al. (2020a), who performed ASR post-processing experiments and published the model as a demo system†. This study focused on Korean spelling error correction that is not specialized in ASR post-processing. However, as the experiments were performed with respect to speech recognition error correction, we compared the performance of this model with that of the proposed model. Through this comparison, we could assess the spelling correction performance of our approach. The experimental results are summarized in Table 2.

Our results show that PCF can improve the correction performance. The BLUE and GLEU scores of the No-Filter model were 55.72 and 46.23, respectively. The BLEU score was higher than that of the base model by 13.53. Further, the BLEU and GLEU scores of the Filter model were 56.56 and 46.94, respectively. The BLEU score was higher than that of the base model by 14.37. Thus, PCF can promote performance improvement.

Furthermore, the BLEU and GLEU scores of the Filter model were higher than those of the existing spelling correction model proposed by Park et al. (2020a) by 5.94 and 15.15, respectively. These results show that our post-processor can achieve higher performance in spelling correction.

**Automatic Spacing** Second, we verified the performance of the BTS-based post-processor in automatic spacing. To measure the multi-class accuracy, we used the F1-score to correctly locate the spacing in the target sentences. As the Filter model achieves better performance (see Table 2), further experiments were based on the Filter model. Our results can be found in the Spacing part of Table 3.

Using the post-processor, we achieved a scored that was higher than that of the base model by 2.26. Thus, BTS can promote correct automatic spacing.

**Foreign Word Conversion** Third, we demonstrated the performance of the BTS-based post-processor in foreign word conversion. For the performance evaluation, we used the F1-score to correctly locate Korean and English words in the target sentences. The experimental results are shown in

† http://nlplab.iptime.org:32288/

the Word Conversion part of Table3.

Compared to the base model, our processor yielded scores that were higher by 7.54 and 19.27 for Korean and English word conversion, respectively. From these results, we can conclude that our post-processor facilitates better performance in word conversion.

**Punctuation Attachment** Finally, we verified the performance of the BTS-based post-processor in punctuation attachment. For the performance evaluation, we used the F1-score to correctly locate the punctuation in the target sentences. Our results are presented in the Punctuation part of Table 3.

The performance score of the BTS-based post-processor was 60.13 higher than that of the base model. For the base model, the F1-score of punctuation attachment was 0.89, which indicates that the base model rarely achieves correct punctuation attachment. This represents the limitation of commercial STT systems. For the test set, the base model only attached the period (".") 32 times, the percent sign ("%") 33 times, and the dollar symbol ("$") 1 time. These limitations can be alleviated by applying our method. The BTS-based post-processor facilitates the attachment of the above-mentioned punctuation marks as well as other fundamental punctuation marks, such as the question mark("?"), exclamation mark("!"), and comma(","), in colloquial sentences. Thus, our proposed post-processor can achieve tremendous improvement in punctuation attachment.

Thus, we have shown the performance improvement for the four above-mentioned criteria. Furthermore, the overall F1-score, calculated by considering all these criteria in one step, showed an improvement of 8.89.

### 5.3 Qualitative Analysis

In addition to the quantitative analysis described above, we also performed qualitative analysis. Table 4 lists some examples of source sentences and the corrected output of each sentence, generated by the BTS-based ASR post-processor. As shown in Table 4, the BTS-based ASR post-processor can effectively correct errors arising in ASR models.

First, the post-processor can correct foreign word conversion errors. In Korean sentences, the foreign word "TV" is generally adopted in its original form; however, the ASR system transcribes this word with its Korean pronunciation, "티비". Our results show that the BTS-based post-processor can effectively correct this error.

Second, it is possible to correct punctuation attachment errors and inappropriate spacing, which frequently occur in the ASR model. A period (".") or question mark("?") can be correctly attached to each sentence, and spacing errors such as "missyou" can be corrected as "miss you". Through this revision process, we expect that end users can be provided with clearer sentences.

Third, the BTS-based ASR post-processor can correct spelling errors or improper sentence endings generated by the speech recognition system. In particular, for Korean, improper sentence endings often lead to different interpretations of whole sentences. These issues can be effectively rectified by our method.

For example, in the case of a missing sentence ending, the post-processor can restore the sentence by attaching the omitted part "에요(is)". In addition, the word "serv", which occurs owing to the recognition error of the sentence ending, can be corrected with the appropriate word "나옵니다 (served)".

In summary, by inspecting examples of BTS-based post-processing, we can conclude that BTS is an effective approach for dealing with spelling correction, automatic spacing, foreign word conversion, and punctuation attachment. This study is significant in that errors of ASR systems can be corrected without human-labeled data, which require professional human resources for generation.

## 6 Conclusion and Future Work

We proposed BTS, which can automatically generate a parallel corpus from raw corpora to train ASR post-processors. By combining TTS and STT systems, ASR noise was injected into the raw text, and the post-processing model was trained in a denoising manner. Quantitative and qualitative evaluations showed that our approach can effectively handle challenging ASR errors, such as foreign word conversion.

In the future, we plan to investigate different noising strategies that reflect real-world ASR errors and make the denoising process more challenging. Demonstrating the effectiveness of BTS in additional languages from various language families is another important direction for future research.

## Acknowledgments

This research was supported by the MSIT(Ministry of Science and ICT), Korea, under the ITRC (Information Technology Research Center) support program (IITP-2018-0-01405) supervised by the IITP (Institute for Information & Communications Technology Planning & Evaluation), Institute for Information & communications Technology Planning & Evaluation (IITP), grant funded by the Korean government (MSIT) (No. 2020-0-00368, A Neural-Symbolic Model for Knowledge Acquisition and Inference Techniques) and MSIT(Ministry of Science and ICT), Korea, under the ICT Creative Consilience program(IITP-2021-2020-0-01819) supervised by the IITP(Institute for Information & communications Technology Planning Evaluation).

## References

Petar Aleksic, Mohammadreza Ghodsi, Assaf Michaely, Cyril Allauzen, Keith Hall, Brian Roark, David Rybach, and Pedro Moreno. 2015. Bringing contextual information to google speech recognition.

Alexei Baevski, Henry Zhou, Abdelrahman Mohamed, and Michael Auli. 2020. wav2vec 2.0: A framework for self-supervised learning of speech representations. *arXiv preprint arXiv:2006.11477*.

Murali Karthick Baskar, Shinji Watanabe, Ramon Astudillo, Takaaki Hori, Lukáš Burget, and Jan Černocký. 2019. Semi-supervised sequence-to-sequence asr using unpaired speech and text. *arXiv preprint arXiv:1905.01152*.

Youssef Bassil and Paul Semaan. 2012. Asr context-sensitive error correction based on microsoft n-gram dataset. *arXiv preprint arXiv:1203.5262*.

Christopher Bryant, Mariano Felice, Øistein E Andersen, and Ted Briscoe. 2019. The bea-2019 shared task on grammatical error correction. In *Proceedings of the Fourteenth Workshop on Innovative Use of NLP for Building Educational Applications*, pages 52–75.

Rajen Chatterjee, Christian Federmann, Matteo Negri, and Marco Turchi. 2019. Findings of the wmt 2019 shared task on automatic post-editing. In *Proceedings of the Fourth Conference on Machine Translation (Volume 3: Shared Task Papers, Day 2)*, pages 11–28.

Yo Joong Choe, Jiyeon Ham, Kyubyong Park, and Yeoil Yoon. 2019. A neural grammatical error correction system built on better pre-training and sequential transfer learning. *arXiv preprint arXiv:1907.01256*.

Jeong-Myeong Choi, Jong-Dae Kim, Chan-Young Park, and Yu-Seop Kim. 2021. Automatic word spacing of korean using syllable and morpheme. *Applied Sciences*, 11(2):626.

Joon Son Chung. 2019. Naver at activitynet challenge 2019–task b active speaker detection (ava). *arXiv preprint arXiv:1906.10555*.

Horia Cucu, Andi Buzo, Laurent Besacier, and Corneliu Burileanu. 2013. Statistical error correction methods for domain-specific asr systems. In *International Conference on Statistical Language and Speech Processing*, pages 83–92. Springer.

Li Dong, Nan Yang, Wenhui Wang, Furu Wei, Xiaodong Liu, Yu Wang, Jianfeng Gao, Ming Zhou, and Hsiao-Wuen Hon. 2019. Unified language model pre-training for natural language understanding and generation. *arXiv preprint arXiv:1905.03197*.

Mark Gales and Steve Young. 2008. The application of hidden markov models in speech recognition.

Yushi Guan. 2020. End to end asr system with automatic punctuation insertion. *arXiv preprint arXiv:2012.02012*.

Jung-Woo Ha, Kihyun Nam, Jin Gu Kang, Sang-Woo Lee, Sohee Yang, Hyunhoon Jung, Eunmi Kim, Hyeji Kim, Soojin Kim, Hyun Ah Kim, et al. 2020. Clovacall: Korean goal-oriented dialog speech corpus for automatic speech recognition of contact centers. *arXiv preprint arXiv:2004.09367*.

Nils Hjortnæs, Niko Partanen, Michael Rießler, and Francis M Tyers. 2021. The relevance of the source language in transfer learning for asr. In *Proceedings of the Workshop on Computational Methods for Endangered Languages*, volume 1, pages 63–69.

Minwoo Jeong, Byeongchang Kim, and Gary Geunbae Lee. 2003. Semantic-oriented error correction for spoken query processing. In *2003 IEEE Workshop on Automatic Speech Recognition and Understanding (IEEE Cat. No. 03EX721)*, pages 156–161. IEEE.

Sangkeun Jung, Minwoo Jeong, and Gary Geunbae Lee. 2004. Speech recognition error correction using maximum entropy language model. In *Eighth International Conference on Spoken Language Processing*.

Sema Kayapinar Kaya, Turan Paksoy, and Jose Arturo Garza-Reyes. 2020. The new challenge of industry 4.0. *Logistics 4.0: Digital Transformation of Supply Chain Management*, page 51.

Shun Kiyono, Jun Suzuki, Masato Mita, Tomoya Mizumoto, and Kentaro Inui. 2019. An empirical study of incorporating pseudo data into grammatical error correction. *arXiv preprint arXiv:1909.00502*.

Guillaume Klein, Dakun Zhang, Clément Chouteau, Josep M Crego, and Jean Senellart. 2020. Efficient and high-quality neural machine translation with opennmt. In *Proceedings of the Fourth Workshop on Neural Generation and Translation*, pages 211–217.

Philipp Koehn, Vishrav Chaudhary, Ahmed El-Kishky, Naman Goyal, Peng-Jen Chen, and Francisco Guzmán. 2020. Findings of the wmt 2020 shared task on parallel corpus filtering and alignment. In *Proceedings of the Fifth Conference on Machine Translation*, pages 726–742.

Taku Kudo and John Richardson. 2018. Sentencepiece: A simple and language independent subword tokenizer and detokenizer for neural text processing. *arXiv preprint arXiv:1808.06226*.

Guillaume Lample and Alexis Conneau. 2019. Cross-lingual language model pretraining. *arXiv preprint arXiv:1901.07291*.

Changki Lee and Hyunki Kim. 2013. Automatic korean word spacing using pegasos algorithm. *Information processing & management*, 49(1):370–379.

Junwei Liao, Sefik Emre Eskimez, Liyang Lu, Yu Shi, Ming Gong, Linjun Shou, Hong Qu, and Michael Zeng. 2020. Improving readability for automatic speech recognition transcription. *arXiv preprint arXiv:2004.04438*.

Yinhan Liu, Jiatao Gu, Naman Goyal, Xian Li, Sergey Edunov, Marjan Ghazvininejad, Mike Lewis, and Luke Zettlemoyer. 2020. Multilingual denoising pre-training for neural machine translation. *Transactions of the Association for Computational Linguistics*, 8:726–742.

Anirudh Mani, Shruti Palaskar, Nimshi Venkat Meripo, Sandeep Konam, and Florian Metze. 2020. Asr error correction and domain adaptation using machine translation. In *ICASSP 2020-2020 IEEE International Conference on Acoustics, Speech and Signal Processing (ICASSP)*, pages 6344–6348. IEEE.

Courtney Napoles, Keisuke Sakaguchi, Matt Post, and Joel Tetreault. 2015. Ground truth for grammatical error correction metrics. In *Proceedings of the 53rd Annual Meeting of the Association for Computational Linguistics and the 7th International Joint Conference on Natural Language Processing (Volume 2: Short Papers)*, pages 588–593.

Aaron van den Oord, Sander Dieleman, Heiga Zen, Karen Simonyan, Oriol Vinyals, Alex Graves, Nal Kalchbrenner, Andrew Senior, and Koray Kavukcuoglu. 2016. Wavenet: A generative model for raw audio. *arXiv preprint arXiv:1609.03499*.

Kishore Papineni, Salim Roukos, Todd Ward, and Wei-Jing Zhu. 2002. Bleu: a method for automatic evaluation of machine translation. In *Proceedings of the 40th annual meeting of the Association for Computational Linguistics*, pages 311–318.

Chanjun Park, Kuekyeng Kim, YeongWook Yang, Minho Kang, and Heuiseok Lim. 2020a. Neural spelling correction: translating incorrect sentences to correct sentences for multimedia. *Multimedia Tools and Applications*, pages 1–18.

Chanjun Park, Yeonsu Lee, Chanhee Lee, and Heuiseok Lim. 2020b. Quality, not quantity? : Effect of parallel corpus quantity and quality on neural machine translation. In *The 32st Annual Conference on Human Cognitive Language Technology*, pages 363–368.

Chanjun Park and Heuiseok Lim. 2020. A study on the performance improvement of machine translation using public korean-english parallel corpus. *Journal of Digital Convergence*, 18(6):271–277.

Chanjun Park, Yeongwook Yang, Kinam Park, and Heuiseok Lim. 2020c. Decoding strategies for improving low-resource machine translation. *Electronics*, 9(10):1562.

Matthias Paulik, Sharath Rao, Ian Lane, Stephan Vogel, and Tanja Schultz. 2008. Sentence segmentation and punctuation recovery for spoken language translation. In *2008 IEEE International Conference on Acoustics, Speech and Signal Processing*, pages 5105–5108. IEEE.

Daniel Povey, Arnab Ghoshal, Gilles Boulianne, Lukas Burget, Ondrej Glembek, Nagendra Goel, Mirko Hannemann, Petr Motlicek, Yanmin Qian, Petr Schwarz, et al. 2011. The kaldi speech recognition toolkit. In *IEEE 2011 workshop on automatic speech recognition and understanding*, CONF. IEEE Signal Processing Society.

Svatava Škodová, Michaela Kuchařová, and Ladislav Šeps. 2012. Discretion of speech units for the text post-processing phase of automatic transcription (in the czech language). In *International Conference on Text, Speech and Dialogue*, pages 446–455. Springer.

Kaitao Song, Xu Tan, Tao Qin, Jianfeng Lu, and Tie-Yan Liu. 2019. Mass: Masked sequence to sequence pre-training for language generation. *arXiv preprint arXiv:1905.02450*.

Matthew Nicholas Stuttle. 2003. *A Gaussian mixture model spectral representation for speech recognition*. Ph.D. thesis, University of Cambridge.

Jayashri Vajpai and Avnish Bora. 2016. Industrial applications of automatic speech recognition systems. *International Journal of Engineering Research and Applications*, 6(3):88–95.

Ashish Vaswani, Noam Shazeer, Niki Parmar, Jakob Uszkoreit, Llion Jones, Aidan N Gomez, Lukasz Kaiser, and Illia Polosukhin. 2017. Attention is all you need. *arXiv preprint arXiv:1706.03762*.

Kimberly Voll, Stella Atkins, and Bruce Forster. 2008. Improving the utility of speech recognition through error detection. *Journal of digital imaging*, 21(4):371.

Jiangyan Yi, Jianhua Tao, Ye Bai, Zhengkun Tian, and Cunhang Fan. 2020. Adversarial transfer learning for punctuation restoration. *arXiv preprint arXiv:2004.00248*.

Zi-Qiang Zhang, Yan Song, Ming-Hui Wu, Xin Fang, and Li-Rong Dai. 2021. Xlst: Cross-lingual self-training to learn multilingual representation for low resource speech recognition. *arXiv preprint arXiv:2103.08207*.

# Zero-pronoun Data Augmentation for Japanese-to-English Translation

**Ryokan Ri, Toshiaki Nakazawa and Yoshimasa Tsuruoka**
The University of Tokyo
7-3-1 Hongo, Bunkyo-ku, Tokyo, Japan
`{li0123, nakazawa, tsuruoka}@logos.t.u-tokyo.ac.jp`

## Abstract

For Japanese-to-English translation, zero pronouns in Japanese pose a challenge, since the model needs to infer and produce the corresponding pronoun in the target side of the English sentence. However, although fully resolving zero pronouns often needs discourse context, in some cases, the local context within a sentence gives clues to the inference of the zero pronoun. In this study, we propose a data augmentation method that provides additional training signals for the translation model to learn correlations between local context and zero pronouns. We show that the proposed method significantly improves the accuracy of zero pronoun translation with machine translation experiments in the conversational domain.

## 1 Introduction

While neural machine translation (NMT) has demonstrated high performance in single-sentence translation, it is still challenging to handle linguistic phenomena involving discourse contexts. One such issue is the translation of *zero pronouns* (ZP) in Japanese-to-English translation. In Japanese, subjects and objects are often omitted when the listener can infer them from the context. However, when translating them into English, the omitted words must be explicitly translated in most cases. For example, in the following sentence, the subject omitted in Japanese is the first person, and *I* has to be output in English.

| | |
|---|---|
| うなぎが | 食べたいな |
| unagi-ga | tabe-tai-na |
| eel-OBJ | eat-want-PARTICLE |
| I feel like eating eel. | |

The prediction of ZPs, essentially, requires understanding the topic and old information in the discourse, or referring to the world knowledge. On the other hand, linguistic information within the sentence may provide some clues (Kudo et al., 2015). For example, in the sentence above, the auxiliary verb たい (*want*) suggests that the sentence expresses a subjective statement and thus the missing pronoun is the first person. Here we refer to such information as *local context*.

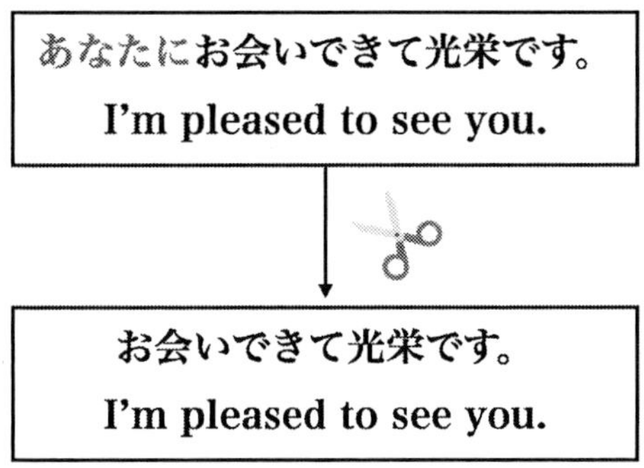


Figure 1: The proposed method: ZP data augmentation

Correlations between local context and ZPs can be learned by the standard single-sentence neural machine translation, but it may not be possible under low-resource conditions. For example, the translation of conversations, which usually contain a large number of ZPs, is currently one of the under-resourced domains.

To address this problem, we propose **zero pronoun data augmentation** to facilitate learning correlations between local context and ZPs (Figure 1). We augment the training data by deleting personal pronouns in the source Japanese sentence. This creates parallel data that include ZPs and provides additional training signals to learn to predict ZPs. Our method is simple yet effective: it does not require any modification to the model architecture nor additional computation at inference time, but significantly improves the accuracy of the ZP translation.



*Proceedings of the 8th Workshop on Asian Translation*, pages 117–123
Bangkok, Thailand (online), August 5-6, 2021. ©2021 Association for Computational Linguistics

## 2 Related Work

### 2.1 Contextual Neural Machine Translation

As the quality of single-sentence machine translation has improved dramatically with the advent of neural machine translation (Sutskever et al., 2014; Vaswani et al., 2017), translation models that take wider contexts into account have seen a surge of interest (Jean et al., 2017; Bawden et al., 2018; Voita et al., 2019b,a; Ma et al., 2020; Saunders et al., 2020). In contrast to the studies trying to incorporate information outside the sentence, in this work, we propose a method to improve zero-pronoun translation by only considering the information within the sentence, but we also explore the effect of combining our method with a contextual machine translation model.

### 2.2 ZP Resolution in Japanese

In some languages, pronouns are sometimes omitted when they are inferable from the context. Such languages are called pro-drop languages and the omitted pronouns are called ZPs.

The translation of ZPs poses a challenge when the corresponding pronoun is syntactically required on the target language side: the model has to infer the omitted pronoun. The task of identifying the omitted pronouns is called ZP resolution and for Japanese, this has been a long-standing problem (Isozaki and Hirao, 2003; Sasano et al., 2008; Imamura et al., 2009; Shibata and Kurohashi, 2018). Japanese is one of the most difficult languages because Japanese words usually do not have any inflectional forms that depend on the omitted pronoun, unlike other pro-drop languages such as Portuguese and Spanish in which ZPs can be inferred from the grammatical case of other words.

Still, Japanese sentences sometimes contain expressions indicative of the missing pronoun. For example, Japanese honorifics naturally indicate the subject is the second person. In this work, we do not explicitly solve ZP resolution but let the translation model learn heuristic relations between ZPs and local context within the sentence (Hangyo et al., 2013; Kudo et al., 2015) and produce appropriate English pronouns.

### 2.3 ZPs in Translation

In the context of statistical machine translation, Japanese ZPs are explicitly predicted by considering verbal semantic attributes (Nakaiwa and Ikehara, 1992), local context in the source and target sentence (Kudo et al., 2015), and incorporated into the resulting translation.

On the other hand, in neural machine translation, the missing pronouns can be automatically inferred by the translation model because of the nature of end-to-end learning, although the correctness cannot be guaranteed. To improve the quality of ZP translation, previous studies have explored a multi-task approach with ZP prediction (Wang et al., 2016, 2019).

In this study, we propose a ZP data augmentation method to provide additional training signals useful to correctly translate ZPs.

## 3 Is Local Context Useful for Predicting Zero Pronouns?

Our proposed method is based on the assumption that local context in Japanese sentences is useful for predicting ZPs. We begin by analyzing to what extent ZPs can be inferred from local context, and what kind of local context is useful.

For the analysis, we use the Business Scene Dialogue Corpus (Rikters et al., 2019), which is a Japanese and English parallel corpus in the conversational domain. Besides the published data, we also use the in-house version of the corpus, which amounts to a total of 104,961 sentence pairs.

### 3.1 Identifying sentence pairs that contain ZPs.

As the corpus does not contain annotations of ZPs, we first identify sentence pairs that contain zero pronouns. We exploit the word alignment information from parallel sentences to detect ZPs. The specific procedure is as follows.

1. We obtain the word alignments of the parallel data with `GIZA++`[1]. We use `Mecab`[2] for Japanese word segmentation, `spaCy`[3] for English.

2. When a pronoun in an English sentence is associated with `NULL`, the pronoun in the English sentence is considered to correspond to a ZP in the Japanese sentence.

The resulting number of pronouns is shown in Figure 2. It can be seen that in the conversational domain, the first person pronoun *I* and the second

[1] https://github.com/moses-smt/giza-pp
[2] https://taku910.github.io/mecab/
[3] https://spacy.io/

|  | I | you | we | they | he | she | us | them | him | her |
|---|---|---|---|---|---|---|---|---|---|---|
| baseline | 35.9 | 25.4 | 11.0 | 3.7 | 2.2 | 0.0 | 2.2 | 1.9 | 1.2 | 0.9 |
| logistic regression | 78.2 | 46.3 | 17.3 | 3.8 | 3.1 | 0.0 | 3.6 | 0.2 | 0.2 | 2.9 |

Table 1: Recall scores of ZP predictions for each pronoun.

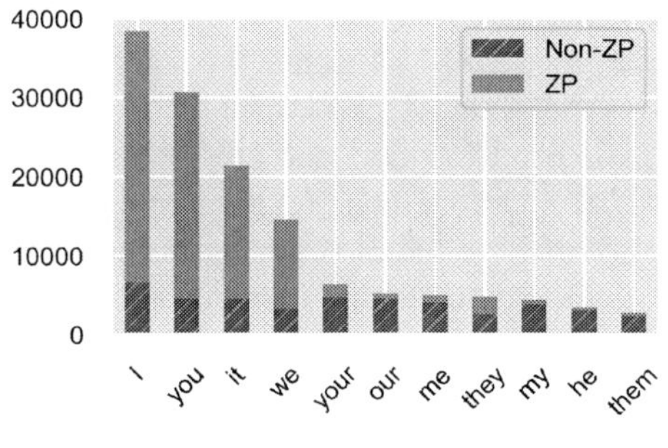


Figure 2: The number of English pronouns in the analyzed data. ZP stands for those whose corresponding pronoun does not appear in the Japanese text.

person pronoun *you* occur frequently and most of them (80% ∼) are omitted in Japanese. More infrequent pronouns are less likely to be ZPs.

### 3.2 Extracting local context that co-occurs with ZPs

To associate the detected ZPs with local context in Japanese sentences, we extract the words that appear in their predicates. We did not use a Japanese syntactic analyzer to detect ZPs but they are associated with the English pronouns by alignment. Therefore, we decided to exploit the alignment information to extract the predicates. We extract the predicates of the English pronoun and the corresponding words in the Japanese sentence. Specifically, the following steps were taken.

3. We obtain the dependency tree of the English sentence with `spaCy` and extract the pronoun's head.

4. The Japanese word aligned to the pronoun's head and its subsequent functional words [4] are extracted as local context.

### 3.3 Predicting ZPs from Local Context

To investigate the extent to which ZPs can be predicted from local context, we conducted an analysis by training a logistic regression classifier [5]. The classifier takes the unigrams, bi-grams, and tri-grams extracted from local context in the Japanese sentence and predicts the associated pronoun in the English sentence.

The recall scores of each pronoun obtained with five-fold cross-validation are shown in Table 1. As a baseline, we adopt the score of random prediction according to the training distribution of pronouns.

One can see that the frequent pronouns such as *I, you, we* can be predicted with significantly higher accuracy than the baseline when local context is used (around 6 to 43 points of improvement). In contrast, the other infrequent pronouns display similar or lower values compared to the baseline. In summary, we can see that local context is predictive of the frequent pronouns but not for the infrequent ones.

To investigate what kind of local context is useful for prediction, for each output label (*i.e.*, pronoun) of the logistic regression classifier, we extracted the input features with higher values in the corresponding weights. As a result, the following words are interpreted to be relevant.

**The first person singular *I*** verbs related to recognition (思う (think), わかる (understand), 感じる (feel)); humble words (申し上げる、存る); and auxiliary verbs expressing desire (たい).

**The second person singular *you*** suffixes expressing questions (かな？, ました？); speculations (でしょ, だろ？), honorifics (仰る, いただける).

**The first person plural *we*** obligations (なきゃ, べき), desire (たい).

For the other pronouns, no local contexts were found to be interpretable as useful for prediction.

## 4 ZP Data Augmentation

In the previous section, we confirmed that local context is useful for predicting ZPs. In this section, we examine the usefulness of ZP data augmentation for machine translation.

[4] In this case, the function words are defined as words with one of the following part of speeches defined in `Mecab`: ["particle", "auxiliary verb", "symbol"].

[5] We use the implementation of the `scikit-learn` library with the default hyperparameters.

| | 1to1 | 2to1 |
|---|---|---|
| baseline | 17.07±0.16 / 83.6±1.1 | 17.07±0.26 / 89.36±0.9 |
| baseline+pro_aug | 17.07±0.19 / 92.32±1.8 | 17.11±0.23 / 92.17±1.1 |

Table 2: Evaluation of the model with ZP data augmentation. The scores on the table are BLEU / ZP evaluation accuracy. The mean and standard deviation of five runs with different random seeds are reported.

The method artificially creates training data containing ZPs by deleting pronouns in the source Japanese sentence along with the following particles. The pronouns to be deleted are detected by string matching with manually created lists (Appendix A). The augmented data is supposed to provide useful training signals for learning correlations between ZPs and local context.

### 4.1 Experimental Setups

**Corpus** We use the Document-aligned Japanese-English Conversation Parallel Corpus (Rikters et al., 2020). We also add an in-house conversational parallel corpus to the training data. The statistics of the corpus are shown in Table 3.

| train | train+pro_aug | dev | test |
|---|---|---|---|
| 246,541 | 282,952 | 2,051 | 2,020 |

Table 3: The number of sentences in the corpus.

**Model** Transformer (Vaswani et al., 2017) was used as the translation model. We adopt the hyperparameters recommended for the corpus of our size in Araabi and Monz (2020) (Appendix B). In addition to the single-sentence translation, we also experimented with the 2to1 setting (Tiedemann and Scherrer, 2017), in which the previous sentence in the document is added to the input.

**Evaluation** We evaluate the overall translation quality on the test set with BLEU (Papineni et al., 2002). We also conduct a targeted evaluation with the ZP evaluation dataset for Japanese-to-English translation (Shimazu et al., 2020). The ZP evaluation dataset contains 724 triples of a source sentence, a target sentence with a correct pronoun, and one with an incorrect pronoun. To evaluate a translation model, we see if the model assigns a lower perplexity to the correct target sentence, and calculate the accuracy.

### 4.2 Results

The results of the experiment are shown in Table 2. We can observe that ZP data augmentation does not improve the BLEU score, but significantly improves the accuracy of ZP evaluation in both the 1to1 (83.6% to 92.3%) and 2to1 settings (89.3% to 92.1%). Our method yields a similar degree of improvement to the 2to1 setting in the ZP evaluation without any computational overhead at the inference time.

We also confirm that adding the previous context (2to1) does not improve BLEU but pronoun translation (83.6% to 89.3%), which conforms to observations in the previous study (Jean et al., 2017; Shimazu et al., 2020). However, this is not the case with the ZP data augmentation (92.3% to 92.1%). We speculate that this is because longer inputs in the 2to1 setting make it more difficult for the model to find correlations between ZPs and local context.

## 5 Conclusion

To address the problem of zero pronoun translation, we proposed zero pronoun data augmentation. Through the analysis with the Japanese-English conversational parallel corpus, we showed that zero pronouns in Japanese sentences can be predicted to some extent from local context within the sentence. In the conversational translation experiment, we compared a translation model trained on the augmented data with the baseline and demonstrate that our method significantly improves the accuracy of zero pronoun translation.

Nevertheless, zero pronoun data augmentation does not solve the cases where the information necessary for zero pronoun translation exists outside the sentence. Also, the analysis suggests that local context is useful for predicting frequent pronouns such as the first and second-person pronouns, but not for the third-person pronouns. An interesting avenue for future work is to explicitly incorporate discourse-level contextual information such as topics or people involved in the conversation into the translation models.

## References


Ali Araabi and Christof Monz. 2020. Optimizing Transformer for Low-Resource Neural Machine Translation. In *Proceedings of the 28th International Conference on Computational Linguistics*.

Rachel Bawden, Rico Sennrich, Alexandra Birch, and Barry Haddow. 2018. Evaluating Discourse Phenomena in Neural Machine Translation. In *Proceedings of the 2018 Conference of the North American Chapter of the Association for Computational Linguistics: Human Language Technologies, Volume 1*.

Masatsugu Hangyo, Daisuke Kawahara, and Sadao Kurohashi. 2013. Japanese Zero Reference Resolution Considering Exophora and Author/Reader Mentions. In *Proceedings of the 2013 Conference on Empirical Methods in Natural Language Processing*.

Kenji Imamura, Kuniko Saito, and Tomoko Izumi. 2009. Discriminative Approach to Predicate-Argument Structure Analysis with Zero-Anaphora Resolution. In *Proceedings of the ACL-IJCNLP 2009 Conference Short Papers*.

Hideki Isozaki and Tsutomu Hirao. 2003. Japanese Zero Pronoun Resolution based on Ranking Rules and Machine Learning. In *Proceedings of the 2003 Conference on Empirical Methods in Natural Language Processing*.

Sébastien Jean, Stanislas Lauly, Orhan Firat, and Kyunghyun Cho. 2017. Does Neural Machine Translation Benefit from Larger Context? *ArXiv*, abs/1704.05135.

Taku Kudo, Hiroshi Ichikawa, and Hideto Kazawa. 2015. Language independent null subject prediction for statistical machine translation. In *Proceedings of the Twenty-first Annual Meeting of the Association for Natural Language Processing*.

Shuming Ma, Dongdong Zhang, and Ming Zhou. 2020. A Simple and Effective Unified Encoder for Document-Level Machine Translation. In *Proceedings of the 58th Annual Meeting of the Association for Computational Linguistics*.

Hiromi Nakaiwa and Satoru Ikehara. 1992. Zero Pronoun Resolution in a Machine Translation System by using Japanese to English Verbal Semantic Attributes. In *Third Conference on Applied Natural Language Processing*.

Kishore Papineni, Salim Roukos, Todd Ward, and Wei-Jing Zhu. 2002. Bleu: a Method for Automatic Evaluation of Machine Translation. In *Proceedings of the 40th Annual Meeting of the Association for Computational Linguistics*.

Matīss Rikters, Ryokan Ri, Tong Li, and Toshiaki Nakazawa. 2019. Designing the Business Conversation Corpus. In *Proceedings of the 6th Workshop on Asian Translation*.

Matīss Rikters, Ryokan Ri, Tong Li, and Toshiaki Nakazawa. 2020. Document-aligned Japanese-English Conversation Parallel Corpus. In *Proceedings of the Fifth Conference on Machine Translation*.

Ryohei Sasano, Daisuke Kawahara, and Sadao Kurohashi. 2008. A Fully-Lexicalized Probabilistic Model for Japanese Zero Anaphora Resolution. In *Proceedings of the 22nd International Conference on Computational Linguistics*.

Danielle Saunders, Felix Stahlberg, and Bill Byrne. 2020. Using Context in Neural Machine Translation Training Objectives. In *Proceedings of the 58th Annual Meeting of the Association for Computational Linguistics*.

Tomohide Shibata and Sadao Kurohashi. 2018. Entity-Centric Joint Modeling of Japanese Coreference Resolution and Predicate Argument Structure Analysis. In *Proceedings of the 56th Annual Meeting of the Association for Computational Linguistics*.

Sho Shimazu, Sho Takase, Toshiaki Nakazawa, and Naoaki Okazaki. 2020. Evaluation Dataset for Zero Pronoun in Japanese to English Translation. In *Proceedings of the 12th Language Resources and Evaluation Conference*.

Ilya Sutskever, Oriol Vinyals, and Quoc V Le. 2014. Sequence to Sequence Learning with Neural Networks. In *Advances in Neural Information Processing Systems*, volume 27.

Jörg Tiedemann and Yves Scherrer. 2017. Neural Machine Translation with Extended Context. In *Proceedings of the Third Workshop on Discourse in Machine Translation*.

Ashish Vaswani, Noam Shazeer, Niki Parmar, Jakob Uszkoreit, Llion Jones, Aidan N Gomez, Ł ukasz Kaiser, and Illia Polosukhin. 2017. Attention is All you Need. In *Advances in Neural Information Processing Systems*, volume 30.

Elena Voita, Rico Sennrich, and Ivan Titov. 2019a. Context-Aware Monolingual Repair for Neural Machine Translation. In *Proceedings of the 2019 Conference on Empirical Methods in Natural Language Processing and the 9th International Joint Conference on Natural Language Processing*.

Elena Voita, Rico Sennrich, and Ivan Titov. 2019b. When a Good Translation is Wrong in Context: Context-Aware Machine Translation Improves on Deixis, Ellipsis, and Lexical Cohesion. In *Proceedings of the 57th Annual Meeting of the Association for Computational Linguistics*.

Longyue Wang, Zhaopeng Tu, Xing Wang, and Shuming Shi. 2019. One Model to Learn Both: Zero Pronoun Prediction and Translation. In *Proceedings of the 2019 Conference on Empirical Methods in Natural Language Processing and the 9th International Joint Conference on Natural Language Processing*.

Longyue Wang, Zhaopeng Tu, Xiaojun Zhang, Hang Li, Andy Way, and Qun Liu. 2016. A Novel Approach to Dropped Pronoun Translation. In *Proceedings of the 2016 Conference of the North American Chapter of the Association for Computational Linguistics: Human Language Technologies*.

## A The pronoun and particle list for pronoun data augmentation

The deletion of pronouns was done by enumerating all combinations from the list of pronouns (Table 4) and particles (Table 5) and deleting strings that correspond to the pattern from the sentence.

| | |
|---|---|
| First person singular | 私, わたし, 僕, ぼく, 俺, おれ, わたくし, オレ, ウチ |
| First person plural | 我々, 僕ら, われわれ, 僕達, 僕たち, 私達 |
| Second person singular | 貴方, 貴女, あなた, お前, おまえ, 君, あんた |
| First person plural | 君たち, みなさま |
| Third person singular | 彼, 彼女, あいつ |
| Third person plural | 彼ら, 彼女ら, みんな, 皆, 皆んな, みなさん, 奴ら |

Table 4: The list of pronouns for pronoun deletion

| | |
|---|---|
| Nominative | は, が |
| Accusative | を |
| Dative | に |
| Possessive | の |
| Others | も, の方から, のほうから, の方に, のほうに, の方で<br>のこと, の事, のほうで, から, 、 |

Table 5: The list of particles for pronoun deletion

## B Hyperparameters for the Machine Translation Experiment

We choose the hyperparameters of the Transformer model recommended in (Araabi and Monz, 2020).

| | |
|---|---|
| layers | 5 |
| model size | 512 |
| feed-forward dimension | 2048 |
| number of attention heads | 4 |
| encoder/decoder layer dropout | 0/0.1 |
| src/tgt word dropout | 0.2/0.2 |
| label_smoothing | 0.3 |
| optimizer | Adam with the Noam Learning rate schedule |
| warmup steps | 8000 |

Table 6: Hyperparameters for the Transformer model.

# Evaluation Scheme of Focal Translation for Japanese Partially Amended Statutes

**Takahiro Yamakoshi**[†], **Takahiro Komamizu**[‡], **Yasuhiro Ogawa**[†♣], and **Katsuhiko Toyama**[†♣]
[†] Graduate School of Informatics, Nagoya University
[‡] Institutes of Innovation for Future Society, Nagoya University
[♣] Information Technology Center, Nagoya University
Furo-cho, Chikusa-ku, Nagoya 464-8601, Japan

## Abstract

For updating the translations of Japanese statutes based on their amendments, we need to consider the translation "focality;" that is, we should only modify expressions that are relevant to the amendment and retain the others to avoid misconstruing its contents. In this paper, we introduce an evaluation metric and a corpus to improve focality evaluations. Our metric is called an Inclusive Score for DIfferential Translation: (*ISDIT*). ISDIT consists of two factors: (1) the $n$-gram recall of expressions unaffected by the amendment and (2) the $n$-gram precision of the output compared to the reference. This metric supersedes an existing one for focality by simultaneously calculating the translation quality of the changed expressions in addition to that of the unchanged expressions. We also newly compile a corpus for Japanese partially amendment translation that secures the focality of the post-amendment translations, while an existing evaluation corpus does not. With the metric and the corpus, we examine the performance of existing translation methods for Japanese partially amendment translations.

## 1 Introduction

In the world's globalized society, governments must quickly announce their statutes worldwide to facilitate international trade, economic investments, legislation support, and so on. The Japanese government addressed this issue in April 2009 by launching the Japanese Law Translation Database System (JLT) (Toyama et al., 2011) where it announces the English translations of Japanese statutes. However, as of January 2020, only 23.4% (163/697) of the translated statutes in JLT correspond to their latest versions (Yamakoshi et al., 2020). After amending a statute, its translation must be promptly updated to avoid creating confusion among international readers. Unfortunately, statutory sentences are much tougher to translate than ordinary sentences because the former are highly technical, complex, and long.

Furthermore, when translating statutory sentences that are partially modified by an amendment, we must consider *focal* translations. That is, we should only modify expressions that are changed by the amendment without changing the others. For example, consider the following sentence: "申立ては、事故の事実を示して、書面でこれをしなければならない。" (The request shall be made in a document stating the facts of the accident.) Its amendment rewrote "事故" (*jiko*; accident) to "海難" (*kainan*; marine accident). The following revision satisfies the focality requirement: "The request shall be made in a document stating the facts of the marine accident" because it contains minimum modifications. On the other hand, although "The petition shall be made in a document describing the facts of the marine accident" is fluent and adequate, it is unsuitable as a revision from the focality perspective because "申立て" (*moshitate*; request) and "示して" (*shimeshite*; stating), which are irrelevant to the amendment, were changed.

Yamakoshi et al. (2020) proposed a machine translation method for Japanese partially amendment translation that generates translation candidates by a Transformer (Vaswani et al., 2017)-based neural machine translation (NMT) model. It selects the best one by comparing the candidates with the output of a template-aware statistical machine translation (SMT) model (e.g., (Koehn and Senellart, 2010; Kozakai et al., 2017)) that only changes the affected expressions. They also proposed an evaluation metric for the focality of the translations.

However, we argue that two matters from their study must be improved: the evaluation metric



*Proceedings of the 8th Workshop on Asian Translation*, pages 124–132
Bangkok, Thailand (online), August 5-6, 2021. 

Amendment sentence in an amendment act (Act No. 34 of 2019)

第百六十四条①第四項を削り、②第三項後段を削り、③同項第一号中「の父母」を「（十五歳以上のものに限る。）」に改め、④同項第二号中「前号に掲げる」を「…に対し親権を行う」に改め、⑤同項第三号を削り、⑥同項を同条第六項とし、⑦同項の次に次の一項を加える。
7　特別養子適格の…（省略）

Translation

In Article 164, ①delete paragraph 4, ②delete the latter part of paragraph 3, ③replace "the parents of" with "(limited to a child of 15 years of age or older)" in item (i) of the same paragraph, ④replace "set forth in the preceding item" with "who exercises parental authority over ···" in item (ii) of the same paragraph, ⑤delete item (iii) of the same paragraph, ⑥regard the same paragraph as paragraph 6 of the same Article, ⑦add the following paragraph next to the same paragraph:
7 ··· of special adoption eligibility ··· (omitted)

Figure 1: Amendment sentence

and the dataset. Their metric consists of two factors: (1) the $n$-gram recall of expressions unaffected by amendments and (2) a redundant penalty for lengthy outputs. Although with this metric we can evaluate how completely the method retained expressions irrelevant to the amendment, we cannot evaluate how adequately it translated expressions relevant to the amendment. The second is the dataset they used for their experiments. Their translation examples of partially amended statutory sentences are from amendment-version-controlled bilingual statutes in JLT. However, translations in JLT are not always focal. Therefore, their reported scores do not seem accurate.

In this paper, we solve these two matters. For the first, we introduce another metric for focality called the Inclusive Score for DIfferential Translation (ISDIT), which incorporates $n$-gram precision between the output and the reference instead of a redundant penalty. With this modification, the metric simultaneously evaluates the translation quality of both the changed and unchanged expressions that indicate the quality of the focal translation. For the second, we compile a corpus that secures focality between pre- and post-amendment translations and achieve it by asking professional human translators to translate focal post-amendment translations.

This paper makes the following contributions to amended statutory sentence translation tasks:

- introduces a new metric that more adequately reflects the focality of translations;
- compiles a translation corpus that ensures the focality of post-amendment translations;
- examines the translation performance of relevant methods with a metric and a corpus.

This paper is organized as follows. In Section 2, we clarify the background of our study. In Section 3, we explain related work. In Section 4, we describe our proposal and present our evaluation experiments and discussions in Section 5. Finally, we summarize and conclude in Section 6.

## 2 Background

In this section, we clarify the background of our study. First, we introduce the partial amendment process in Japanese legislation from the viewpoint of document modification and then we identify our study objective in the process.

### 2.1 Partial Amendments in Japanese Legislation

In Japanese legislation, a partial amendment is created by "patching" modifications to a target statute. Such modifications are prescribed as amendment sentences in an amendment statute. Based on their functions, Ogawa et al. (2008) categorized such modifications as follows:

1. Modification of part of a sentence: (a) replacement, (b) addition, and (c) deletion.
2. Modification of such structural elements as sections, articles, items, sentences, etc.: (a) replacement, (b) addition, and (c) deletion.
3. Modification of element numbers: (a) renumbering, (b) attachment, and (c) shifts.
4. Combined modification of element renumbering and replacement of its title string.

For modifying part of a sentence, Japanese legislation rules (Hoseishitsumu-Kenkyukai, 2018) mandate that the target expressions must be unique and form a chunk of meaning.

Figure 1 shows an example of an amendment sentence prescribed by an amendment act. Any of the seven modifications in the sentence can be assigned to one of the categories described above: Modifications ①, ②, and ⑤ respectively belong to category 2. (c) of a paragraph, a sentence, an item; modifications ③ and ④ belong to category 1. (a); modification ⑥ belongs to category 3. (c); modification ⑦ belongs to category 2. (b).

Most statutes enacted in recent years are amendment statutes. According to Nihon Horei Sakuin (Index of Japanese Statutes) [1], 78% (73/94) of acts enacted in 2019 are amendment ones. After

[1] https://hourei.ndl.go.jp/

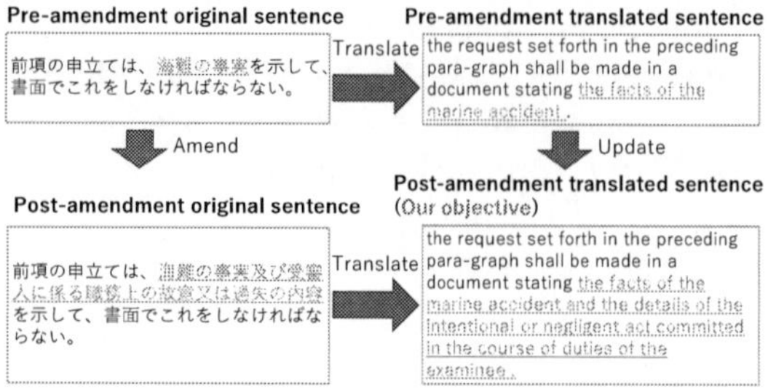


Figure 2: Differential translations in an amended statutory sentence

amending statutes, we should update their translations provided in JLT promptly. However, regarding the discussion in the introduction, many statutes available in JLT are out of date, which can provide wrong legal facts to international readers.

### 2.2 Objective

To solve the problem discussed in the previous section, our study focuses on translating partially amended statutes automatically. More specifically, it adopts a task declared by Yamakoshi et al. (2020). Among the categories described in the previous section, the task focuses on categories that modify the parts of an existing statutory sentence (i.e., category 1). In Fig. 1, modifications ③ and ④ are the targets. It also targets category 2, especially modifications that insert an additional sentence (e.g., a proviso) into an existing element or delete a sentence since such additions and deletions affect the main sentence. Modification ② in Fig. 1, which removes the latter part, is a case.

The task takes a triple of sentences (*a pre-amendment original sentence*, *a post-amendment original sentence*, and *a pre-amendment translated sentence*) as input and generates a translation for the post-amendment original sentence called *a post-amendment translated sentence*. Pre- and post-amendment original sentences are statutory sentences in a statute before and after an amendment, respectively. A pre-amendment translated sentence is a translation of the pre-amendment original sentence. Figure 2 illustrates this task.

In generating post-amendment translated sentences, Yamakoshi et al. advocated the *focality* of translations. This idea argues for only modifying expressions that are changed by the amendment without changing the others based on two reasons from the viewpoint of precise publicization. First, such sentences clearly represent the amendment contents, which helps international readers understand them. On the other hand, non-focal translations contain unnecessary modifications, which blur the amendment contents. Second, since the expressions in the pre-amendment translated sentences are assumed to be reliable, reusing them ensures translation quality.

For example, assume that an amendment statute instructs that we should replace "海難の事実" (*kainan no jijitsu*; the facts of the marine accident) with "海難の事実及び…の内容"(*kainan no jijitsu oyobi ... no naiyo*; the facts of the marine accident and the details of ...)" as depicted in Figure 2. In this case, we should replace "the facts of the marine accident" in the pre-amendment translated sentence with "the facts of the marine accident and the details of ..." and retain the other expressions to comply with the focality.

We define our task as follows:

**Input:**
 Pre-amendment original sentence $W_{\mathrm{PrO}}$;
 Post-amendment original sentence $W_{\mathrm{PoO}}$;
 Pre-amendment translated sentence $W_{\mathrm{PrT}}$.

**Output:** Generated post-amendment translated sentence $\widehat{W}_{\mathrm{PoT}}$.

**Requirements:**

**Focality:** $\widehat{W}_{\mathrm{PoT}}$ should reflect amendment $W_{\mathrm{PrO}}$ to $W_{\mathrm{PoO}}$ and preserve the expressions in $W_{\mathrm{PrT}}$ that are irrelevant to the amendment;

**Fluency:** $\widehat{W}_{\mathrm{PoT}}$ should have natural phrasing and syntax;

**Adequacy:** $\widehat{W}_{\mathrm{PoT}}$ should have $W_{\mathrm{PoO}}$'s contents without excesses or inadequacies.

## 3 Related Work

We describe related work in this section. We overview the suitable machine translation methods for partially amended sentences in Section 3.1. We discuss metrics and data in Sections 3.2 and 3.3.

### 3.1 Method

We consider the focality of translations, which is uncommon in ordinary machine translation tasks. To achieve focal translations, the unchanged expressions must be retained as they appear in the pre-amendment translation. One solution is using a template-aware SMT method. Koehn and Senellart (2010)'s method is a choice, which can retain the unchanged expressions in the pre-amendment translations by copying them to the post-amendment translations.

Kozakai et al. (2017) optimized this method to

Japanese partially amendment translation by applying the following two modifications. First, they used pre-amendment original sentences and their translations instead of a relevant pair from the translation memory. Second, to determine objective expressions, they used the underlined information in a comparative table instead of the edit distance. Such underlined information is more reasonable as a translation unit than edit distance since sentence modification is done by a chunk of meaning in Japanese legislation.

Both methods can meet the focality requirement by copying the unchanged expressions in the pre-amendment translated sentences. However, the translation quality, especially fluency, suffers for the following three reasons. First, they use SMT for the translation model, which is typically outperformed by NMT. Second, their methods completely lock the unchanged expressions, which may strongly restrict the translations. Third, they use word alignment to find English expressions that correspond to Japanese ones, perhaps weakening their performance due to alignment error.

Yamakoshi et al. (2020)'s method solved these problems by incorporating NMT with a template-aware SMT. Their method, which uses an NMT model and a template-aware SMT model, allows the former to output $n$-best translations as candidates by applying Monte Carlo (MC) dropout (Gal and Ghahramani, 2016) to improve the output diversity. It then chooses the candidate that most resembles the *interim* reference translation generated from a template-aware SMT model.

### 3.2 Metrics

Kozakai et al. (2017) used BLEU (Papineni et al., 2002) and RIBES (Hirao et al., 2014) as automatic evaluation metrics in their experiment. BLEU's calculation is based on $n$-gram precision between the system output and references; RIBES's calculation is based on word-order correlation. Therefore, RIBES is more sensitive to drastic structural modifications. However, both metrics are indifferent to whether an expression in the system output is a changed part in the amendment, and thus both fail to indicate the quality of the focality.

Yamakoshi et al. (2020) proposed focality scores to solve this issue. A focality score quantizes the focality of the system output by calculating the recall of the $n$-grams shared by both the pre- and post-amendment translations. With pre-amendment translated sentence $W_{\mathrm{PrT}}$ and actual post-amendment translated sentence $W_{\mathrm{PoT}}$ written by humans, we calculate focality score $\mathrm{Foc}(\widehat{W}_{\mathrm{PoT}}; W_{\mathrm{PrT}}, W_{\mathrm{PoT}})$ of generated sentence $\widehat{W}_{\mathrm{PoT}}$ as follows:

$$\begin{aligned}&\mathrm{Foc}(\widehat{W}_{\mathrm{PoT}}; W_{\mathrm{PrT}}, W_{\mathrm{PoT}}) \qquad (1)\\ &= \mathrm{RP}(W_{\mathrm{PoT}}, \widehat{W}_{\mathrm{PoT}}) \cdot \mathrm{Rec}(\widehat{W}_{\mathrm{PoT}}; W_{\mathrm{PrT}}, W_{\mathrm{PoT}}),\\ &\mathrm{RP}(W_{\mathrm{PoT}}, \widehat{W}_{\mathrm{PoT}})\\ &= \min(1, \exp(1 - |\widehat{W}_{\mathrm{PoT}}|/|W_{\mathrm{PoT}}|)), \qquad (2)\end{aligned}$$

where RP avoids overestimating the scores of the redundant sentences. $|W|$ is the word count of $W$. Rec is the recall of the $n$-grams shared by $W_{\mathrm{PrT}}$ and $W_{\mathrm{PoT}}$, calculated as follows:

$$\mathrm{Rec}(\widehat{W}_{\mathrm{PoT}}; W_{\mathrm{PrT}}, W_{\mathrm{PoT}}) = \qquad (3)$$

$$\frac{\sum_{s \in \mathrm{CN}(\mathcal{W}_1)} \min(c_{\widehat{W}_{\mathrm{PoT}}}(s), c_{W_{\mathrm{PrT}}}(s), c_{W_{\mathrm{PoT}}}(s))}{\sum_{s \in \mathrm{CN}(\mathcal{W}_2)} \min(c_{W_{\mathrm{PrT}}}(s), c_{W_{\mathrm{PoT}}}(s))},$$

$$\mathcal{W}_1 = \{\widehat{W}_{\mathrm{PoT}}, W_{\mathrm{PrT}}, W_{\mathrm{PoT}}\} \qquad (4)$$

$$\mathcal{W}_2 = \{W_{\mathrm{PrT}}, W_{\mathrm{PoT}}\}, \qquad (5)$$

where $c_W(s)$ is the number of occurrences of the $n$-gram $s$ in $W$, and $\mathrm{CN}(\mathcal{W})$, where $\mathcal{W} = \{W_1, W_2, \cdots, W_m\}$, returns common $n$-grams of $W_1, W_2, \cdots, W_m$:

$$\mathrm{CN}(\mathcal{W}) = \left\{ s \;\middle|\; s \in \bigcap_{W_i \in \mathcal{W}} \mathrm{ngrams}(W_i) \right\}, \qquad (6)$$

where $\mathrm{ngrams}(W)$ returns all $n$-grams in $W$ for a given $n$. We use multiple lengths of $n$-grams:

$$\mathrm{ngrams}(W) = \bigcup_{i=1}^{N} i\text{-gram}(W), \qquad (7)$$

where $i\text{-gram}(W)$ returns the $i$-grams of $W$.

### 3.3 Data

Kozakai et al. (2017) used JLT bilingual resources to compile corpora for their experiment. For training data, they gathered 158,928 Japanese-English sentence pairs from 407 statutes provided in JLT. For test data, they selected 17 amendments available in JLT [2] from which they compiled 158 examples of sentence amendments, each of which consists of $W_{\mathrm{PrO}}$, $W_{\mathrm{PrT}}$, $W_{\mathrm{PoO}}$, and $W_{\mathrm{PoT}}$. Yamakoshi et al. (2020) also used this corpus for their experiment.

[2] JLT has a function to browse statutes and the translations of different amendment versions.

| Sort | Content |
|---|---|
| $W_{\mathrm{PrO}}$ | 前項の申立ては、海難の事実を示して、書面でこれをしなければならない。 |
| $W_{\mathrm{PrT}}$ | The request set forth in the preceding paragraph shall be made in a document stating the facts of the marine accident. |
| $W_{\mathrm{PoO}}$ | 前項の申立ては、海難の事実及び受審人に係る職務上の故意又は過失の内容を示して、書面でこれをしなければならない。 |
| $W_{\mathrm{PoT}}$ | The petition set forth in the preceding paragraph shall be made in writing describing the facts of the marine accident and the details of the intentional or negligent act committed in the course of duties of the examinee. |
| Focal $W_{\mathrm{PoT}}$ | The request set forth in the preceding paragraph shall be made in a document stating the facts of the marine accident and the details of the intentional or negligent act committed in the course of duties of the examinee. |

Table 1: Non-focal amendment example

However, some of these examples are not focal because they contain modifications irrelevant the amendment. Table 1 describes such an example. The straight lines in its sentences depict modifications that correspond to the amendment, and the wavy lines depict modifications irrelevant to the amendment. "Request," "a document," and "stating" in $W_{\mathrm{PrT}}$ are replaced with "petition," "writing," and "describing" in $W_{\mathrm{PoT}}$, respectively, although corresponding Japanese expressions "申立て" (*moshitate*), "書面" (*shomen*), and "示して" (*shimeshite*) was retained throughout the amendment. An ideal translation for $W_{\mathrm{PoT}}$ is shown in the table's last row that retains all the expressions irrelevant to the amendment.

## 4 Proposal

In this section, we propose an evaluation scheme for Japanese partially amendment translations. Our evaluation scheme includes a new evaluation metric *ISDIT* and a differential translation corpus that secures the focality of its examples.

### 4.1 ISDIT Scores

The focality score in Section 3.2 assesses only the retention rate of the unchanged expressions in $W_{\mathrm{PrT}}$. That is, it is unaware of the adequacy of expressions that are relevant to the amendment. Therefore, we update the focality scores so that they assess both factors. Our metric, Inclusive Score for DIfferential Translation (*ISDIT*), is calculated as follows:

$$\mathrm{ISDIT}(\widehat{W}_{\mathrm{PoT}}; W_{\mathrm{PrT}}, W_{\mathrm{PoT}}) = \mathrm{Pre}(\widehat{W}_{\mathrm{PoT}}; W_{\mathrm{PoT}}) \cdot \mathrm{Rec}(\widehat{W}_{\mathrm{PoT}}; W_{\mathrm{PrT}}, W_{\mathrm{PoT}}), \quad (8)$$

where Rec is the recall defined in Eq. 3. Pre is the precision of system output $\widehat{W}_{\mathrm{PoT}}$ compared to reference $W_{\mathrm{PoT}}$, which is calculated as follows:

$$\mathrm{Pre}(\widehat{W}_{\mathrm{PoT}}; W_{\mathrm{PoT}}) = \frac{\sum_{s \in \mathrm{CN}(\mathcal{W})} \min(c_{\widehat{W}_{\mathrm{PoT}}}(s), c_{W_{\mathrm{PoT}}}(s))}{\sum_{s \in \mathrm{CN}(\{\widehat{W}_{\mathrm{PoT}}\})} c_{\widehat{W}_{\mathrm{PoT}}}(s)}, \quad (9)$$

$$\mathcal{W} = \{\widehat{W}_{\mathrm{PoT}}, W_{\mathrm{PoT}}\}. \quad (10)$$

For example, we consider the example shown in Table 2. Case 1 contains an unnecessary modification, and Case 2 fails to translate "四十万" (*yonjuman*; four hundred thousand) that is relevant to the amendment. The focality score penalizes the first case, but not the second case. ISDIT penalizes both. From the viewpoint of focal translations that should reflect the amendment contents, penalizing both the unnecessary modification errors and amended phrase translation errors is preferable.

### 4.2 Focal Differential Translation Corpus

As discussed in Section 3.3, the differential translation corpus compiled by Kozakai et al. (2017) includes non-focal examples. To provide a fairer evaluation, we compiled a new corpus that secures the focality of every translation example. We applied the following instructions for the corpus compilation:

1. Compile the versions of statutes provided in JLT;
2. Compile those provided in e-LAWS[3];
3. Compile statutes whose JLT version lags behind its e-LAWS version;

[3] `https://elaws.e-gov.go.jp/` e-LAWS (e-Legislative Activity and Work Support System) provides a governmental open database of national statutes which are original (i.e., written in Japanese) and most recent.

| Sort | Content | ISDIT | Foc. |
|---|---|---|---|
| $W_{\mathrm{PrO}}$ | 解職請求は、八十万人を超える者の連署を要する。 | — | — |
| $W_{\mathrm{PrT}}$ | A request for recall requires joint signatures of more than eight hundred thousand people. | — | — |
| $W_{\mathrm{PoO}}$ | 解職請求は、四十万人を超える者の連署を要する。 | — | — |
| $W_{\mathrm{PoT}}$ | A request for recall requires joint signatures of more than four hundred thousand people. | — | — |
| Case 1 | A petition for recall requires joint signatures of more than four hundred thousand people. | 0.82 | 0.70 |
| Case 2 | A request for recall requires joint signatures of more than forty hundred thousand people. | 0.85 | 1.00 |

Table 2: Example for ISDIT calculation ("Foc." stands for focality score)

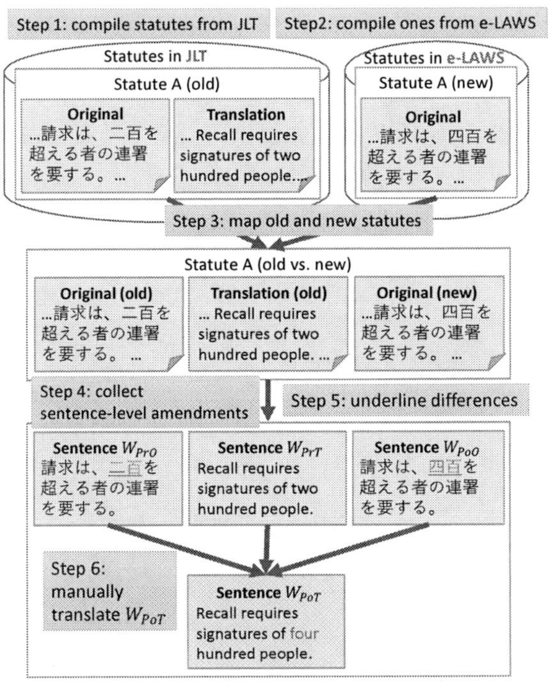


Figure 3: Compilation procedure for a focal corpus

4. Collect sentence-level amendments of such statutes;
5. Underline the modified expressions in $W_{\mathrm{PrO}}$ and $W_{\mathrm{PoO}}$ as if they were highlighted in an actual amendment statute;
6. Manually translate the $W_{\mathrm{PoT}}$ of the amendments by the following instructions:
   (a) Correct $W_{\mathrm{PrT}}$ in advance if it includes inadequate expressions;
   (b) Use $W_{\mathrm{PrT}}$ as a template of $W_{\mathrm{PoT}}$;
   (c) Edit only expressions relevant to the underlining in $W_{\mathrm{PrO}}$ and $W_{\mathrm{PoO}}$.[4]

Figure 3 depicts this procedure.

As of April 2021, we compiled 1,483 differential translation examples from 62 amendment cases. These examples include the following modification instances:

- Phrase-level modifications: 786 replacements, 201 additions, and 89 deletions;
- Sentence-level modifications: 8 replacements, 11 additions, and 2 deletions.

## 5 Experiment

We experimentally evaluated the machine translation methods with our new resources.

### 5.1 Outline

For training data, we mixed two bilingual-statutory sentence corpora. One was made by Kozakai et al. (2017) from JLT. This corpus consists of 158,928 sentence pairs from 407 statutes. We compiled the other one from statutes in JLT that we collected in Step 1 in Section 4.2. Our corpus consists of 232,830 sentence pairs from 462 statutes.

We split our differential translation corpus into development data and test data by the statutes. The development and test data respectively consisted of 745 examples from 30 amendments and 738 examples from 32 amendments.

We used Transformer (Vaswani et al., 2017) for the NMT model under the following settings: six encoder/decoder hidden layers, eight self-attention heads, 512 hidden vectors, a batch size of eight, and an input sequence length of 256. We implemented the training and prediction codes based

[4] We allow grammatical modifications (e.g., number agreement, tense agreement, article selection) in the expressions outside the amendment if they are triggered by it.

| Model | BLEU | RIBES | ISDIT | Focality |
|---|---|---|---|---|
| Naive Moses | 47.93 | 61.75 | 29.32 | 51.54 |
| Naive Koehn model | 83.00 | 92.05 | 77.31 | **91.20** |
| Naive Kozakai model | 82.79 | 92.04 | 77.53 | 90.62 |
| Naive Transformer | 80.72 | 94.16 | 71.32 | 83.64 |
| Transformer + Koehn model | 82.39 | 94.70 | 75.05 | 86.66 |
| Transformer + Kozakai model | 82.46 | 94.75 | 74.69 | 86.42 |
| Transformer + Koehn model + MC dropout | **84.43** | **96.04** | **79.33** | 90.36 |
| Transformer + Kozakai model + MC dropout | 84.37 | 95.80 | 78.31 | 89.45 |
| Transformer + $W_{\mathrm{PoT}}$ + MC dropout | 86.62 | 96.72 | 81.95 | 90.92 |

Table 3: Experimental results

on the TensorFlow official model [5]. We used SentencePiece (Kudo and Richardson, 2018) as a tokenizer and set the vocabulary size to 8,192. We chose a dropout rate of 0.1 for training, which is the default setting of the official Transformer implementation. In the prediction phase, we executed the model with two dropout rates, 0.0 and 0.1, where a 0.0 dropout means that no dropout was applied. We investigated the optimal number of iterations from $\{100\text{k}, 200\text{k}, \cdots, 2{,}000\text{k}\}$ using the development data.

The following are the settings of these template-aware SMTs: GIZA++ (Och and Ney, 2005) for the word alignment, SRILM (Stolcke, 2002) for the language model generation, and Moses (Koehn et al., 2007) for the decoder. We used MeCab (Kudo et al., 2004) for the Japanese tokenizer.

We evaluated the fluency and adequacy with BLEU and RIBES. For the focality evaluation, we utilized the focality scores (Yamakoshi et al., 2020) and our ISDIT. We set the maximum $n$-gram length $N$ to 4 in calculating the focality scores, ISDIT, and BLEU. Using the four metrics, we compared the following translation models:

- Naive Moses (Koehn et al., 2007);
- Naive Koehn model (Koehn and Senellart, 2010);
- Naive Kozakai model (Kozakai et al., 2017);
- Naive Transformer;
- Transformer + Koehn model;
- Transformer + Kozakai model;
- Transformer + Koehn model + MC dropout (Yamakoshi et al., 2020);
- Transformer + Kozakai model + MC dropout (Yamakoshi et al., 2020);
- Transformer + $W_{\mathrm{PoT}}$ + MC dropout.[6]

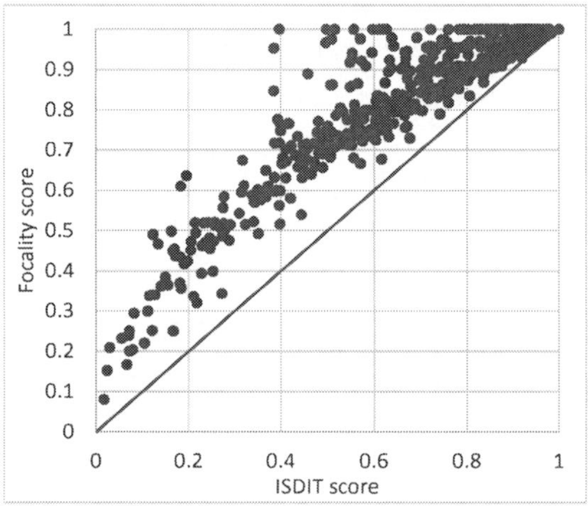


Figure 4: ISDIT and focality scores of each example

| | RIBES | ISDIT | Focality |
|---|---|---|---|
| BLEU | 0.724 | 0.960 | 0.833 |
| RIBES | — | 0.693 | 0.611 |
| ISDIT | — | — | 0.927 |

Table 4: Correlation coefficients between evaluation metrics

"+" expresses a combination of techniques.

### 5.2 Results

Table 3 shows our experimental results. We achieved the same findings as those reported by Yamakoshi et al. (2020). The combination of Transformer, a template-aware SMT model, and MC dropout achieved the best performance in BLEU and RIBES among the comparisons; the naive template-aware SMT methods achieved the best performance in the focality scores; the

[5] https://github.com/tensorflow/models/

[6] We used $W_{\mathrm{PoT}}$ as an "oracular" interim reference.

| Sort | Output |
|---|---|
| $W_{\mathrm{PrO}}$ | （火災共済協同組合の地区） |
| $W_{\mathrm{PrT}}$ | ( district of a fire mutual aid cooperative ) |
| $W_{\mathrm{PoO}}$ | （火災等共済組合等の地区） |
| $W_{\mathrm{PoT}}$ | ( district of a fire and fire-related disaster mutual aid association , etc . ) |
| Output | ( district of a fire mutual aid cooperative , etc . ) |

Table 5: Example with distant ISDIT and focality scores

| Model | Output |
|---|---|
| ($W_{\mathrm{PrO}}$) | 協会及びその子会社から成る集団における業務の適正を確保するための体制 |
| ($W_{\mathrm{PrT}}$) | A system to ensure the appropriateness of the operations in the group forming NHK and its subsidiary company |
| ($W_{\mathrm{PoO}}$) | 次に掲げる体制その他の協会及びその子会社から成る集団の業務の適正を確保するための体制 |
| ($W_{\mathrm{PoT}}$) | The systems listed below and a system to ensure the appropriateness of the operations of a group consisting of NHK and its subsidiary companies |
| Yamakoshi | The following systems and any other system to ensure the appropriateness of the operations of the group comprised of NHK and its subsidiary company: |
| Kozakai | A system to ensure the appropriateness of the operations of the group forming the following systems and any other association and its subsidiary company |

Table 6: Translation example in our corpus

template-aware SMT and MC dropout were also both effective. One different finding from their report is that using the Koehn model generally worked more effectively than the Kozakai model. For our ISDIT metric, the combination methods of Yamakoshi et al. (2020) outperformed the naive template-aware SMT methods.

### 5.3 Discussion

First, we identified the characteristics of ISDIT. The plots in Fig. 4 indicate the focality and ISDIT scores of the Transformer + Kozakai model + MC dropout method (hereinafter "Yamakoshi method") for each translation example. The focality score of every example is higher than or equal to its ISDIT score. This result is natural because both these metrics share $n$-gram recall calculation, and ISDIT introduces $n$-gram precision that is more severe than the redundant penalty in the focality scores. We can observe many examples that have high focality scores but low ISDIT scores. Table 5 shows such an example. Yamakoshi method's output evaluated 100.0 focality scores and 39.74 ISDIT scores. In this example, however, their system failed to translate "等" in "火災等," which denotes a "fire-related disaster." This mistake greatly changed the system output from the reference, which suffered a low ISDIT score. On the other hand, since expressions shared by $W_{\mathrm{PrT}}$ and $W_{\mathrm{PoT}}$ were retained in the system output with no redundant generation, it received the maximum focality score.

Table 4 shows the correlation coefficients among the evaluation metrics. ISDIT and the focality scores have a high correlation coefficient of 0.927. ISDIT has also a strong relationship with BLEU, which is 0.960. High coefficients among them seem to come from a shared calculation strategy that utilizes the $n$-gram match rate.

Next we conducted a short qualitative analysis of our corpus. Table 6 shows a translation example. In this example, we replace "協会" (*kyokai*) with "次に掲げる体制その他の協会" (*tsugi ni kakageru taisei sonotano kyokai*). Its translation is divided into two parts: "the systems listed below and" (corresponding to "次に掲げる体制その他の") and "NHK" (corresponding to "協会"), which generally happens in Japanese partially amendments. The Kozakai method (also the Koehn method) cannot cope with this kind of examples: They put all the translation of the changed expression in $W_{\mathrm{PoO}}$ to the position where such changed expression appears in $W_{\mathrm{PrT}}$.

Another tricky point in this case is the translation of "協会," which generally means "association." However, here it denotes "NHK" (Japan

Broadcasting Corporation). The Kozakai method failed to appropriately translate this word, possibly because it did not use the context of the translation target, "次に掲げる体制その他の協会." On the other hand, the Yamakoshi method successfully placed the new expression and adequately translated "協会." Its success reflects its use of the whole sentence in the translation.

## 6 Summary

We proposed a better evaluation scheme for Japanese partially amendment translations and developed a new metric called ISDIT that assesses the translation quality of both changed and unchanged expressions. We also compiled a corpus that secures the focality of translation. Using our corpus, we observed the characteristics of translation methods and ISDIT.

Our future work will increase the size of our corpus so that it can be used for neural network training, considering the publicization of the corpus. We will also identify the best weighting of the two factors in ISDIT. Third, we will consider applications of ISDIT to other domains of version-controlled documents such as contracts, technical documents, and product manuals.

## Acknowledgments

This work was partly supported by JSPS KAKENHI Grant Number 18H03492 and 21H03772.

## References

Yarin Gal and Zoubin Ghahramani. 2016. Dropout as a Bayesian approximation: Representing model uncertainty in deep learning. In *Proceedings of the 33rd International Conference on Machine Learning*, pages 1–10.

Tsutomu Hirao, Hideki Isozaki, Katsuhito Sudoh, Kevin Duh, Hajime Tsukada, and Masaaki Nagata. 2014. Evaluating translation quality with word order correlations. *Journal of Natural Language Processing*, 21(3):421–444. (In Japanese).

Hoseishitsumu-Kenkyukai. 2018. *Workbook Hoseishitsumu (newly revised second edition)*. Gyosei. In Japanese.

Phillip Koehn, Hieu Hoang, Alexandra Birch, Chris Callison-Burch, Marcello Federico, Nicola Bertoldi, Brooke Cowan, Wade Shen, Christine Moran, Richard Zens, Chris Dyer, Ondřej Bojar, Alexandra Constantin, and Evan Herbst. 2007. Moses: Open source toolkit for statistical machine translation. In *Proceedings of the ACL 2007 Demo and Poster Sessions*, pages 177–180.

Phillip Koehn and Jean Senellart. 2010. Convergence of translation memory and statistical machine translation. In *AMTA Workshop on MT Research and the Translation Industry*, pages 21–31.

Tadao Kozakai, Yasuhiro Ogawa, Tomohiro Ohno, Makoto Nakamura, and Katsuhiko Toyama. 2017. Shinkyutaishohyo no riyo niyoru horei no eiyaku shusei. In *Proceedings of NLP2017*, pages 1–4. (In Japanese).

Taku Kudo and John Richardson. 2018. Sentencepiece: A simple and language independent subword tokenizer and detokenizer for neural text processing. In *Proceedings of the 2018 Conference on Empirical Methods in Natural Language Processing (System Demonstrations)*, pages 66–71.

Taku Kudo, Kaoru Yamamoto, and Yuji Matsumoto. 2004. Applying conditional random fields to Japanese morphological analysis. In *Proceedings of the 2004 Conference on Empirical Methods in Natural Language Processing*, pages 230–237.

Franz Josef Och and Hermann Ney. 2005. A systematic comparison of various statistical alignment models. *Computational Linguistics*, 29(1):19–51.

Yasuhiro Ogawa, Shintaro Inagaki, and Katsuhiko Toyama. 2008. Automatic consolidation of japanese statutes based on formalization of amendment sentences. *New Frontiers in Artificial Intelligence: JSAI 2007 Conference and Workshops, Revised Selected Papers, Lecture Notes in Computer Science*, 4914:363–376.

Kishore Papineni, Salim Roukos, Todd Ward, and Wei Jing Zhu. 2002. BLEU: a method for automatic evaluation of machine translation. In *Proceedings of the 40th Annual Meeting of the Association for Computational Linguistics*, pages 311–318.

Andreas Stolcke. 2002. SRILM — an extensible language modeling toolkit. In *Proceedings of ICSLP 2002*, pages 901–904.

Katsuhiko Toyama, Daichi Saito, Yasuhiro Sekine, Yasuhiro Ogawa, Tokuyasu Kakuta, Tariho Kimura, and Yoshiharu Matsuura. 2011. Design and Development of Japanese Law Translation System. In *Law via the Internet 2011*, pages 1–12.

Ashish Vaswani, Noam Shazeer, Niki Parmar, Jakob Uszkoreit, Llion Jones, Aidan N. Gomez, Lukasz Kaiser, and Illia Polosukhin. 2017. Attention is all you need. In *Proceedings of Advances in Neural Information Processing Systems 30*, pages 6000–6010.

Takahiro Yamakoshi, Takahiro Komamizu, Yasuhiro Ogawa, and Katsuhiko Toyama. 2020. Differential translation for japanese partially amended statutory sentences. In *Proceedings of the Fourteenth International Workshop on Juris-informatics*, pages 1–14.

# TMU NMT System with Japanese BART for the Patent task of WAT 2021

**Hwichan Kim** and **Mamoru Komachi**
Tokyo Metropolitan University
6-6 Asahigaoka, Hino, Tokyo 191-0065, Japan
kim-hwichan@ed.tmu.ac.jp, komachi@tmu.ac.jp

## Abstract

In this paper, we introduce our TMU Neural Machine Translation (NMT) system submitted for the Patent task (Korean⇆Japanese and English⇆Japanese) of 8th Workshop on Asian Translation (Nakazawa et al., 2021). Recently, several studies proposed pre-trained encoder-decoder models using monolingual data. One of the pre-trained models, BART (Lewis et al., 2020), was shown to improve translation accuracy via fine-tuning with bilingual data. However, they experimented only Romanian→English translation using English BART. In this paper, we examine the effectiveness of Japanese BART using Japan Patent Office Corpus 2.0. Our experiments indicate that Japanese BART can also improve translation accuracy in both Korean⇆Japanese and English⇆Japanese translations.

## 1 Introduction

Neural Machine Translation (NMT) has achieved high translation accuracy in large-scale data conditions. However, translation accuracy of NMT drops in the lack of bilingual data (Koehn and Knowles, 2017). There are several approaches such as back-translation (Sennrich et al., 2016) and transfer learning (Zoph et al., 2016) to address this problem. Furthermore, in addition to these methods, there are some approaches to use pre-trained models using only monolingual data.

BERT (Devlin et al., 2019), which is the most typical pre-trained model, can boost the accuracy of many downstream tasks compared to models without BERT via fine-tuning with the task-specific training data. However, applying BERT to NMT in fine-tuning form like the other tasks requires two-stage optimization and does not provide significant improvement (Imamura and Sumita, 2019). Recently, several studies proposed pre-trained encoder-decoder models using a monolingual data. Lewis et al. (2020) proposed BART, which is one of the pre-trained encoder-decoder models. They demonstrated that BART works well for not only comprehension tasks such as GLEU (Wang et al., 2018) and SQuAD (Rajpurkar et al., 2016) but also text generation tasks such as text summarization and translation. However, they reported only the effect of English BART, so they did not investigate BART trained by monolingual data of another language. Furthermore, in the translation task, they experimented with only Romanian→English translation, which have subword overlap. Therefore, the effect in translations between language pairs without subword overlapping is not clear. Furthermore, they did not experiment in translation direction where the source language matches the language of the pre-trained model.

Additionally, we consider that fine-tuning pre-training models such as BART in translation task is similar to transfer learning (Zoph et al., 2016). Transfer learning in NMT is a method that trains the network of the parent language pair (the parent model) as the initial network and then fine-tunes it for the child language pair (the child model). In the terminology of transfer learning, the pre-trained BART and fine-tuned model are the parent model and child model, respectively. Previous studies have shown that transfer learning works most efficiently when the source languages of the parent and child models are syntactically similar (Dabre et al., 2017; Nguyen and Chiang, 2017). Therefore, we hypothesize that BART is more effective when the language pair for fine-tuning is syntactically similar to the pre-training language.

In this study, we examine the effects of Japanese BART on the translation task. We use Korean/Japanese and English/Japanese bilingual data of Japan Patent Office Patent Corpus 2.0 (JPO corpus) for fine-tuning. We also experiment in both translation directions of Ko⇆Ja and En⇆Ja.



*Proceedings of the 8th Workshop on Asian Translation*, pages 133–137
Bangkok, Thailand (online), August 5-6, 2021. 

| Language pair | Partition | Sent. | Tokens |
|---|---|---|---|
| Korean / Japanese | train | 1,000,000 | 31,569,641 / 37,282,300 |
| | dev | 2,000 | 104,493 / 124,871 |
| | test | 5,230 | 271,744 / 320,584 |
| English / Japanese | train | 1,000,000 | 21,071,895 / 25,695,404 |
| | dev | 2,000 | 524,88 / 64,838 |
| | test | 5,668 | 169,023 / 198,039 |

Table 1: Data statistics.

## 2 Related Work

There are some approaches pre-trained encoder models like BERT (Devlin et al., 2019) to the NMT task. Imamura and Sumita (2019) used BERT as an encoder and demonstrated the effectiveness of two-stage optimization, which first trains parameters without BERT encoder, and then fine-tunes all parameters. Zhu et al. (2020) used BERT representations as input embedding and showed more effectiveness than using BERT as the encoder.

Recently, several studies proposed pre-trained encoder-decoder models such as MASS (Song et al., 2019) and BART (Lewis et al., 2020), and these models can improve the translation accuracy via fine-tuning with bilingual data. MASS (Song et al., 2019) uses monolingual data from both the source and target languages for pre-training when applying to the NMT. On the contrary, BART (Lewis et al., 2020) uses only monolingual data of target language, unlike MASS. Liu et al. (2020) trained multilingual BART (mBART) using monolingual data of 25 languages. They indicated that mBART initialization leads significant gains in low resource settings. However, Wang and Htun (2020) showed that mBART cannot obtain improvements in the Patent task.

## 3 Experimental Settings

### 3.1 Implementation

In this study, we use Japanese BART[1] base v1.1 (JaBART) trained using Japanese Wikipedia sentences (18M sentences). For fine-tuning, we do not use an additional encoder like in Lewis et al. (2020)'s method. Instead, we add randomly initialized embeddings for each unknown subword in JaBART to both encoder and decoder. We share the embeddings of characters that match across languages, such as numbers and units. We also train baseline models consisting of the same architecture as that of JaBART. We use the same hyperparameters indicated in Table 2 for both fine-tuning JaBART and training the baseline model. We fine-tune and train the models using the fairseq implementation[2].

| Hyperparameter | Value |
|---|---|
| Embedding dimension | 768 |
| Attention heads | 12 |
| Layers | 6 |
| Feed forward dimension | 3072 |
| Optimizer | Adam |
| Adam betas | 0.9, 0.98 |
| Learning rate | 0.0005 |
| Dropout | 0.1 |
| Label smoothing | 0.1 |
| Max tokens | 4,098 |

Table 2: Hyperparameters.

### 3.2 Data

To train and fin-tune the models, we use Ko–Ja and En–Ja datasets of JPO corpus. Korean and English have almost no subword overlaps with Japanese, because these languages use Hangul, Latin alphabets, and Hiragana/Katakana/Kanji characters, respectively. For Japanese pre-processing, we use JaBART tokenizer. For Korean and English, we tokenize sentences using MeCab-ko[3] and Moses scripts[4], respectively. Then, we apply the SentencePiece (Kudo and Richardson, 2018) with a 32k vocabulary size. Table 1 presents the training, de-

[1] https://github.com/utanaka2000/fairseq/blob/japanese_bart_pretrained_model

[2] https://github.com/utanaka2000/fairseq

[3] https://bitbucket.org/eunjeon/mecab-ko

[4] https://github.com/moses-smt/mosesdecodertree/RELEASE-4.0

| | | Ko→Ja | | Ja→Ko | |
|---|---|---|---|---|---|
| | | dev | test | dev | test |
| Single | Baseline | 67.400±.080 / - | 71.510±.166 / 0.947±.001 | 67.816±.028 / - | 71.103±.144 / 0.942±.001 |
| | JaBART | **68.750±.104** / - | **72.760±.140 / 0.949±.000** | **68.563±.065** / - | **72.116±.060 / 0.946±.001** |
| | Δ | +1.350 / - | +1.250 / +0.002 | +0.746 / - | +1.013 / +0.003 |
| Ensemble | Baseline | 68.770 / - | 73.240 / 0.946 | 68.590 / - | 72.070 / 0.942 |
| | JaBART | **69.570** / - | **73.670 / 0.949** | **69.440** / - | **72.700 / 0.946** |
| | Δ | +0.800 / - | +0.430 / +0.001 | +0.850 / - | +0.630 / +0.002 |
| | | En→Ja | | Ja→En | |
| | | dev | test | dev | test |
| Single | Baseline | 38.706±.083 / - | 42.533±.151 / 0.843±.0.02 | 37.636±.112 / - | 40.873±.231 / 0.843±.001 |
| | JaBART | **39.146±.077** / - | **43.720±.053 / 0.849±.001** | **38.393±.060** / - | **41.943±.084 / 0.851±.001** |
| | Δ | +0.440 / - | +1.187 /+0.005 | +0.757 / - | +1.070 / +0.008 |
| Ensemble | Baseline | **40.360** / - | 45.000 / 0.853 | 39.260 / - | 43.140 / 0.853 |
| | JaBART | 40.270 / - | **45.240 / 0.855** | **39.660** / - | **43.780 / 0.857** |
| | Δ | -0.090 / - | +0.240 / +0.002 | +0.400 / - | +0.640 /+0.004 |

Table 3: BLEU / RIBES scores of each single and ensemble of three models. The scores of single are the average of the three models. We indicate the best scores in bold. The scores of Δ indicate the gains of the fine-tuned JaBART's BLEU score over the baseline model.

velopment, and test[5] data statics.

### 3.3 Results

Table 3 shows that the BLEU and RIBES scores of each single and ensemble model.

In the single model, the fine-tuned JaBART achieves the highest scores for dev and test data in both language pairs and translation directions of Ko⇆Ja and En⇆Ja. Specifically, the BLEU scores of the dev and test data reveal improvements of 0.440-1.350 and 1.013-1.250 from the baseline models, respectively. The RIBES scores also reveal improvements of 0.001-0.007, but there is no significant difference between the fine-tuned BART and baseline models.

In the ensemble model[6], the fine-tuned JaBART improves the BLEU and RIBES scores approximately 0.440-0.850 and 0.001-0.008, respectively, in the dev and test of Ko⇆Ja and Ja→En translations. However, in En→Ja translation, the BLEU score of the fine-tuned JaBART decreases 0.09 in the dev and improves 0.240 in the test data. Thus, in the ensemble scenario, the fine-tuned JaBART model can improve translation accuracy except for En→Ja translation.

[5]In this study, we use test-n data, a union of test-n1, test-n2, and test-n3 data, for evaluation.

[6]We submitted the En⇆Ja ensemble models as the target for human evaluation.

## 4 Discussions

We hypothesize that JaBART is more effective when the language pair for fine-tuning is syntactically similar to the pre-training language, as in transfer learning. In our experimental settings, Korean and English are syntactically similar and different languages with Japanese, respectively [7]. Therefore, we expect that JaBART is more effective in the Ko⇆Ja translations than in the En⇆Ja translations. However, Table 3 shows no significant differences in Δ scores between the Ko⇆Ja and En⇆Ja translations. These results indicate that syntactic similarity does not affect the enhancement in the final BLEU scores.

## 5 Conclusions

In this paper, we described our NMT system submitted to the Patent task (Ko⇆Ja and En⇆Ja) of the 8th Workshop on Asian Translation. We compared the baseline and fine-tuned JaBART models, and demonstrated that the fine-tuned JaBART achieves consistent improvements of BLEU scores in language pairs with no subword overlapping, and irrespective of translation directions.

Contrary to our hypothesis, our experiments indicated no significant difference in the translation accuracy depending on the syntactic similarity. However, we consider that there are some differences in

[7]Japanese and Korean are SOV and agglutinative languages, whereas English is SVO and fusional language (Masayoshi, 1990; Jeong et al., 2007).

another aspect such as training process per epoch and network representations. Therefore, we attempt to analyze BART fine-tuned using language pairs with varying syntactic proximities in detail in the future.

## Acknowledgments

This work has been partly supported by the programs of the Grant-in-Aid for Scientific Research from the Japan Society for the Promotion of Science (JSPS KAKENHI) Grant Number 19K12099.

## References

Raj Dabre, Tetsuji Nakagawa, and Hideto Kazawa. 2017. An empirical study of language relatedness for transfer learning in neural machine translation. In *Proceedings of the 31st Pacific Asia Conference on Language, Information and Computation*, pages 282–286.

Jacob Devlin, Ming-Wei Chang, Kenton Lee, and Kristina Toutanova. 2019. BERT: Pre-training of deep bidirectional transformers for language understanding. In *Proceedings of the 2019 Conference of the North American Chapter of the Association for Computational Linguistics: Human Language Technologies, Volume 1 (Long and Short Papers)*, pages 4171–4186.

Kenji Imamura and Eiichiro Sumita. 2019. Recycling a pre-trained BERT encoder for neural machine translation. In *Proceedings of the 3rd Workshop on Neural Generation and Translation*, pages 23–31.

Hyeonjeong Jeong, Motoaki Sugiura, Yuko Sassa, Tomoki Haji, Nobuo Usui, Masato Taira, Kaoru Horie, Shigeru Sato, and Ryuta Kawashita. 2007. Effect of syntactic similarity on cortical activation during second language processing: a comparison of English and Japanese among native Korean trilinguals. *Human Brain Mapping*, 28(3):195–204.

Philipp Koehn and Rebecca Knowles. 2017. Six challenges for neural machine translation. In *Proceedings of the First Workshop on Neural Machine Translation*, pages 28–39.

Taku Kudo and John Richardson. 2018. SentencePiece: A simple and language independent subword tokenizer and detokenizer for neural text processing. In *Proceedings of the 2018 Conference on Empirical Methods in Natural Language Processing: System Demonstrations*, pages 66–71.

Mike Lewis, Yinhan Liu, Naman Goyal, Marjan Ghazvininejad, Abdelrahman Mohamed, Omer Levy, Veselin Stoyanov, and Luke Zettlemoyer. 2020. BART: Denoising sequence-to-sequence pre-training for natural language generation, translation, and comprehension. In *Proceedings of the 58th Annual Meeting of the Association for Computational Linguistics*, pages 7871–7880.

Yinhan Liu, Jiatao Gu, Naman Goyal, Xian Li, Sergey Edunov, Marjan Ghazvininejad, Mike Lewis, and Luke Zettlemoyer. 2020. Multilingual denoising pre-training for neural machine translation. *Transactions of the Association for Computational Linguistics*, 8:726–742.

Shibatani Masayoshi. 1990. *The Languages of Japan*. Cambridge University Press.

Toshiaki Nakazawa, Hideki Nakayama, Chenchen Ding, Raj Dabre, Shohei Higashiyama, Hideya Mino, Isao Goto, Win Pa Pa, Anoop Kunchukuttan, Shantipriya Parida, Ondřej Bojar, Chenhui Chu, Akiko Eriguchi, Kaori Abe, and Sadao Oda, Yusuke Kurohashi. 2021. Overview of the 8th workshop on Asian translation. In *Proceedings of the 8th Workshop on Asian Translation*.

Toan Q. Nguyen and David Chiang. 2017. Transfer learning across low-resource, related languages for neural machine translation. In *Proceedings of the Eighth International Joint Conference on Natural Language Processing (Volume 2: Short Papers)*, pages 296–301.

Pranav Rajpurkar, Jian Zhang, Konstantin Lopyrev, and Percy Liang. 2016. SQuAD: 100,000+ questions for machine comprehension of text. In *Proceedings of the 2016 Conference on Empirical Methods in Natural Language Processing*, pages 2383–2392. Association for Computational Linguistics.

Rico Sennrich, Barry Haddow, and Alexandra Birch. 2016. Improving neural machine translation models with monolingual data. In *Proceedings of the 54th Annual Meeting of the Association for Computational Linguistics (Volume 1: Long Papers)*, pages 86–96.

Kaitao Song, Xu Tan, Tao Qin, Jianfeng Lu, and Tie-Yan Liu. 2019. MASS: Masked sequence to sequence pre-training for language generation. In *Proceedings of the 36th International Conference on Machine Learning*, pages 5926–5936.

Alex Wang, Amanpreet Singh, Julian Michael, Felix Hill, Omer Levy, and Samuel Bowman. 2018. GLUE: A multi-task benchmark and analysis platform for natural language understanding. In *Proceedings of the 2018 EMNLP Workshop BlackboxNLP: Analyzing and Interpreting Neural Networks for NLP*, pages 353–355. Association for Computational Linguistics.

Dongzhe Wang and Ohnmar Htun. 2020. Goku's participation in WAT 2020. In *Proceedings of the 7th Workshop on Asian Translation*, pages 135–141.

Jinhua Zhu, Yingce Xia, Lijun Wu, Di He, Tao Qin, Wengang Zhou, Houqiang Li, and Tieyan Liu. 2020. Incorporating BERT into neural machine translation.

In *International Conference on Learning Representations*.

Barret Zoph, Deniz Yuret, Jonathan May, and Kevin Knight. 2016. Transfer learning for low-resource neural machine translation. In *Proceedings of the 2016 Conference on Empirical Methods in Natural Language Processing*, pages 1568–1575.

# System Description for Transperfect

**Wiktor Stribiżew** and **Fred Bane** and **José Conceição** and **Anna Zaretskaya**
Transperfect Translations
{wstribizew, fbane, jconceicao, azaretskaya}@translations.com

## Abstract

In this paper, we describe our participation in the 2021 Workshop on Asian Translation (team ID: tpt_wat). We submitted results for all six directions of the JPC2 patent task. As a first-time participant in the task, we attempted to identify a single configuration that provided the best overall results across all language pairs. All our submissions were created using single base transformer models, trained on only the task-specific data, using a consistent configuration of hyperparameters. In contrast to the uniformity of our methods, our results vary widely across the six language pairs.

## 1 Introduction

The field of machine translation has seen rapid innovation in the last few years, with new model architectures, pre-training regimens, and computational algorithms emerging at a dizzying pace. However, translation of these techniques into industry practice occurs more slowly. Companies utilizing these techniques must take into account considerations such as deployment costs (model speed and size), scalability, explainability, the complexity of training regimens (resource constraints limiting independent hyperparameter optimization for all language pairs), and risk management, against which advances yielding performance gains must be weighed.

For our participation in the 2021 Workshop on Asian Translation shared task on patent translation, we have applied a single, standardized data preparation and model training pipeline as a way of benchmarking the performance of this process. We conducted limited experiments to test different parameters, before settling on the approach which provided the best overall results across all language pairs. Our NMT systems are standard base Transformer (Vaswani et al., 2017) models, which were trained using only the data resources provided by the task organizers. These models used shared subword vocabularies created with SentencePiece (Kudo and Richardson, 2018).

In contrast to the uniformity of our methods, our results varied widely across the six language pairs. Different scoring metrics prevent the direct comparison of scores from different language pairs, but relative to the top performing model in each language pair, our scores ranged from 98.84% of the top score for the English → Japanese language pair, to 83.89% of the top score for Korean → Japanese. Below, we describe in detail our system architecture, hyperparameter configuration, hardware resources, and results.

## 2 System Overview

### 2.1 Task Description

The JPC2 patent task consisted of translation in the patent domain between English and Japanese, Korean and Japanese, and Chinese and Japanese. The training data consisted of parallel corpora provided by the Japan Patent Office (JPO), with training sets containing one million sentence pairs for each language pair. The data are drawn from four domains, chemistry, electricity, mechanical engineering, and physics.[1]

### 2.2 Data Processing

The data were encoded using subword encodings learned from the corpora using the unigram model trainer provided by SentencePiece (Kudo and Richardson, 2018). To avoid the added complexity of using different pre-tokenization strategies for

[1] http://lotus.kuee.kyoto-u.ac.jp/WAT/patent/



*Proceedings of the 8th Workshop on Asian Translation*, pages 138–140
Bangkok, Thailand (online), August 5-6, 2021. ©2021 Association for Computational Linguistics

different languages, we did not pre-tokenize the data prior to learning the subword model. We tested vocabulary sizes of 8000 and 32000, as well as using shared or split vocabularies for the source and target languages. Character coverage was set to 0.9995, the recommended value for languages with extensive character sets such as Chinese and Japanese.

For the English → Japanese, Korean → Japanese, and Chinese → Japanese language pairs, we supplemented the corpora with back translation (from Japanese into each language), which is a common data augmentation technique in NMT (Sennrich et al., 2016). The back translations were produced by the NMT systems trained for the other three directions (Japanese → English, Korean, and Chinese).

### 2.3 Models

Our NMT systems were standard base Transformer models trained using the Marian NMT framework (Junczys-Dowmunt et al., 2018). We trained separate, unidirectional models for each language pair. Hyperparameters such as label smoothing, dropout, learning rate, batch size, number of encoder/decoder layers, number of attention heads, embedding dimensionality, etc., were held fixed across all language pairs. The validation frequency was every 500 updates, and training was continued for 50 epochs or until the primary validation metric (ce-mean-words, or mean word cross-entropy score) failed to improve for five consecutive checkpoints. Our models were trained on AWS P3 instances using 4 NVIDIA Tesla V100 GPUs.

## 3 Results

Our results show that for most language pairs, a shared vocabulary of size 8,000 achieved the best performance. For the Korean → Japanese and Japanese → Korean language pairs, using a vocabulary size of 32,000 produced better results. Using a split vocabulary for these language pairs also resulted in better performance, whereas a shared vocabulary was advantageous for all other language pairs. In all cases, the inclusion of back translated training data resulted in higher validation scores. Table 1 shows our results in terms of BLEU scores (Papineni et al., 2002) as calculated on our local machines. Due to differences in processing, these scores do not match the scores reported by the Organizers.

## 4 Discussion

In this shared task, we set out to identify a single configuration of hyperparameters that provided the best overall performance across all six language pairs. While this approach precluded the possibility of obtaining optimal performance for all language pairs, it afforded the opportunity to investigate which hyperparameters have similar effects on different language pairs, and which have varied effects on different language pairs. As different language pairs require different hyperparameters, any parameter that can be held fixed during the experimentation stage can create significant savings for companies training their own machine translation models.

For instance, variation in parameters such as learning rate, dropout, embedding dimensions, and tying the weights of the source and target embedding layers seemed to have similar effects on performance across all language pairs that we tested. Using back translated data to augment the training sets also appeared to be universally beneficial. However, the size of the vocabulary seemed to have quite different effects in different language pairs. We are not aware of any theoretical framework for explaining how the various

| Language Pair | Split 32K | Split 32K + BT | Shared 32K | Shared 8K | Shared 8K + BT |
|---|---|---|---|---|---|
| EN → JA | 23.2 | 26.6 | 23.8 | 23.8 | **27.1** |
| JA → EN | 38.9 | - | 39.4 | **40.2** | - |
| KO → JA | 46.6 | **46.8** | 46.7 | 45.6 | 45.6 |
| JA → KO | **52.0** | - | 50.8 | - | - |
| ZH → JA | 30.6 | 31.6 | 31.8 | 31.9 | **32.9** |
| JA → ZH | 46.2 | - | 37.6 | **47.5** | - |

Table 1: BLEU scores for different language pairs and different vocabulary configurations

hyperparameters interact to produce such different results, nor do we know of any way of predicting the optimal hyperparameters for a given language pair other than iterative experimentation.

If additional resources are used, several additional steps have also been shown to be effective at boosting performance, but were not employed in these experiments in order to maintain maximum simplicity. These additional steps include using an ensemble of models for decoding, using larger model sizes, performing word segmentation prior to creating the vocabularies, ordering the training data using the output of a language model (a technique referred to as curriculum learning), and employing an additional model for right-to-left re-ranking.

With minimal manual intervention, our models achieved results ranging from fair to excellent. The large variance in the relative performance of these systems shows that no "one-size-fits-all" yet exists for the problem of machine translation. Despite monumental advances in the field over the past several years, achieving optimal performance requires careful selection of hyperparameters, and different configurations are required for different languages.

## References

Kudo, Taku, and John Richardson. 2018 "SentencePiece: A simple and language independent subword tokenizer and detokenizer for Neural Text Processing." In *Proceedings of the 2018 Conference on Empirical Methods in Natural Language Processing: System Demonstrations*.

Marcin Junczys-Dowmunt, Roman Grundkiewicz, Tomasz Dwojak, Hieu Hoang, Kenneth Heafield, Tom Neckermann, Frank Seide, Ulrich Germann, Alham Fikri Aji, Nikolay Bogoychev, André F. T. Martins, Alexandra Birch. 2018. Marian: Fast Neural Machine Translation in C++ http://www.aclweb.org/anthology/P18-4020.

Kishore Papineni, Salim Roukos, Todd Ward, and WeiJing Zhu. 2002. Bleu: a method for automatic evaluation of machine translation. In *Proceedings of the 40th Annual Meeting of the Association for Computational Linguistics*, pages 311–318, Philadelphia, Pennsylvania, USA. Association for Computational Linguistics.

Rico Sennrich, Barry Haddow, and Alexandra Birch. 2016. Improving neural machine translation models with monolingual data. In *Proceedings of the 54th Annual Meeting of the Association for Computational Linguistics (Volume 1: Long Papers)*, pages 86–96, Berlin, Germany. Association for Computational Linguistics.

Ashish Vaswani, Noam Shazeer, Niki Parmar, Jakob Uszkoreit, Llion Jones, Aidan N Gomez, Łukasz Kaiser, and Illia Polosukhin. 2017. Attention is all you need. In *Advances in neural information processing systems*, pages 5998–6008.

# Bering Lab's Submissions on WAT 2021 Shared Task

**Heesoo Park and Dongjun Lee**
Bering Lab, South Korea
{heesoo.park, djlee}@beringlab.com

## Abstract

This paper presents the Bering Lab's submission to the shared tasks of the 8th Workshop on Asian Translation (WAT 2021) on JPC2 and NICT–SAP. We participated in all tasks on JPC2 and IT domain tasks on NICT–SAP. Our approach for all tasks mainly focused on building NMT systems in domain-specific corpora. We crawled patent document pairs for English–Japanese, Chinese–Japanese, and Korean–Japanese. After cleaning noisy data, we built parallel corpus by aligning those sentences with the sentence-level similarity scores. Also, for SAP test data, we collected the OPUS dataset including three IT domain corpora. We then trained transformer on the collected dataset. Our submission ranked $1^{st}$ in eight out of fourteen tasks, achieving up to an improvement of 2.87 for JPC2 and 8.79 for NICT–SAP in BLEU score .

## 1 Introduction

The WAT 2021 Shared Task (Nakazawa et al., 2021) [1] focuses a comprehensive set of machine translations on Asian languages. They gather and share the resources and knowledge about Asian language translation through a variety of tasks on the broad topics such as document-level translation, multi-modal translation, and domain adaptation. Among those tasks, we participated on two tasks: (1) JPO Patent Corpus (JPC2), a translation task on patent corpus of Japanese ↔ English/Korean/Chinese, and (2) NICT-SAP IT domain, a translation task on software documentation corpus of English ↔ Hindi/Indonesian/Malaysian/Thai.

According to the Table 1, both two corpora mostly consist of technical terms. Specifically, jargon such as "acrylic acid" from JPC2 is not commonly used in everyday life. Similarly, terminology "Virus Scan Interface" from NICT-SAP cannot be easily found on the general corpus. Therefore, we focused on domain adaptation for both tasks.

| | JPC2 |
|---|---|
| JP | その中でも、アクリル酸を好適に使用することができる。 |
| EN | Among them, an acrylic acid can be preferably used. |
| | **NICT-SAP IT domain** |
| ID | Spesifikasi Antarmuka Pemindaian Virus (NW-VSI) |
| EN | Virus Scan Interface (NW-VSI) Specification |

Table 1: Sample sentences of JPC2 and NICT-SAP.

Our approach begins with collecting rich and clean sentence pairs from web and public dataset. For JPC2, we crawled the patent documents from web for each language pairs then built parallel corpus by pairing each sentence with the similarity scores between source and target sentence representation vectors. For NICT-SAP IT domain, we collected public dataset, OPUS (Tiedemann, 2012), and weighted the IT corpus among those corpus while training. In addition to the rich and clean additional corpus, we chose transformer (Vaswani et al., 2017), broadly recognized as a strong machine translation system.

Our method obtained the new state-of-the-art results on four out of six JPC2 tasks, especially amounting to 2.87 absolute improvement on BLEU scores for Japanese to Korean translation. To validate the effect of the additional data, we conducted the ablation study on Korean → Japanese data. Furthermore, our models ranked first place on four out of eight NICT-SAP IT domain tasks, achieving 8.79 improvement for Indonesian to English.

[1] https://lotus.kuee.kyoto-u.ac.jp/WAT/WAT2021/index.html



*Proceedings of the 8th Workshop on Asian Translation*, pages 141–145
Bangkok, Thailand (online), August 5-6, 2021. 

| Data | # Sen | Avg. Len |
|---|---|---|
| $\text{Train}_{JP-EN}$ | 1,000,000 | 44.85 |
| $\text{Dev}_{JP-EN}$ | 2,000 | 53.17 |
| $\text{Test}_{JP-EN}$ | 5,668 | 58.63 |
| $\text{Train}_{JP-KO}$ | 1,000,000 | 52.27 |
| $\text{Dev}_{JP-KO}$ | 2,000 | 83.56 |
| $\text{Test}_{JP-KO}$ | 5,230 | 82.67 |
| $\text{Train}_{JP-ZH}$ | 1,000,000 | 53.47 |
| $\text{Dev}_{JP-ZH}$ | 2,000 | 63.14 |
| $\text{Test}_{JP-ZH}$ | 5,204 | 62.37 |

(a) Statistics of JPC2. "Avg. Len" represents the average of the number of characters per Japanese sentence.

| Data | # Sen | Avg. Len |
|---|---|---|
| $\text{Dev}_{EN-HI}$ | 2,016 | 10.25 |
| $\text{Test}_{EN-HI}$ | 2,073 | 8.74 |
| $\text{Dev}_{EN-ID}$ | 2,023 | 10.46 |
| $\text{Test}_{EN-ID}$ | 2,037 | 8.92 |
| $\text{Dev}_{EN-MS}$ | 2,050 | 13.00 |
| $\text{Test}_{EN-MS}$ | 2,050 | 13.05 |
| $\text{Dev}_{EN-TH}$ | 2,049 | 12.57 |
| $\text{Test}_{EN-TH}$ | 2,050 | 12.40 |

(b) Statistics of NICT-SAP (IT domain). "Avg. Len" represents the average of the number of words per English sentence.

Table 2: Data statistics.

## 2 Task Description

We participate JPO Patent Corpus (JPC2) and SAP's IT translation tasks.

### 2.1 Parallel Corpus

**JPO Patent Corpus** JPC2 consists of Chinese-Japanese, Korean-Japanese, and English-Japanese patent description parallel corpus (Nakazawa et al., 2021). Each corpus consists of 1M parallel sentences with four sections (chemistry, electricity, mechanical engineering, and physics).

**SAP's IT Corpus** SAP software documentation corpus (Buschbeck and Exel, 2020) is designed to test the performance of multilingual NMT systems in extremely low-resource conditions (Nakazawa et al., 2021). The dataset consists of Hindi(Hi) / Thai(Th) / Malay(Ms) / Indonesian(Id) $\leftrightarrow$ English software documentation parallel corpus. The number of parallel sentences of each corpus is described in Table 2.

| Language | # Sen | Avg. Len |
|---|---|---|
| JP – EN | 21,254,269 | 215.31 |
| JP – KO | 13,916,372 | 110.29 |
| JP – ZH | 13,881,444 | 144.44 |

Table 3: Statistics of additional parallel sentences. "Avg. Len" represents the average of the number of characters per Japanese sentence.

### 2.2 Evaluation metric

The official evaluation metrics are BLEU (Papineni et al., 2002), RIBES (Isozaki et al., 2010), and AMFM (Banchs et al., 2015).

## 3 System Overview

In this section we introduce our approach for two tasks.

### 3.1 Data crawling and preprocessing

For JPC2 tasks, we trained the models on combination of the given train dataset (Table 2) and web-crawled dataset (Table 3). For NICT-SAP tasks, we trained the models on OPUS dataset with IT domain corpus weighted (Table 4). For both tasks, the models were evaluated on the given test dataset (Table 2).

**Patent crawling data** Additional data for JPC2 was obtained from WIPO [2] through website crawling. The JPC2 data (including the evaluation data) consists only of description section in each document. Since our approach is to collect the data which is very close to the task domain, we filtered out all sections but the description section to avoid the redundant noise while training the model.

To pair each sentence, we first split the whole description into sentences and encoded each sentence to a representation vector. As a sentence encoder, we used LASER [3] for Ko–Ja and Universal Sentence Encoder [4] (Cer et al., 2018) for the other pairs. We then measured the cosine similarity between each sentence pair and filtered out the pairs whose score was under threshold.

**OPUS data** (Tiedemann, 2012) Since the NICT-SAP IT domain translation task does not provide the train dataset, we collected it from public dataset including GNOME, KDE4, Ubuntu,

[2] https://patentscope.wipo.int/search/en/search.jsf

[3] https://github.com/facebookresearch/LASER

[4] https://tfhub.dev/google/universal-sentence-encoder/3

| En–X | GNOME | KDE4 | Ubuntu | ELRC | TANZIL | Opensubtitles | tico-19 | QED | Tatoeba |
|---|---|---|---|---|---|---|---|---|---|
| HI | 145,706 | 97,227 | 11,309 | 245 | 187,080 | 93,016 | 3,071 | 11,314 | 10,900 |
| ID | 47,234 | 14,782 | 96,456 | 2,679 | . | 9,268,181 | 3,071 | 274,581 | 9,967 |
| MS | 299,601 | 87,122 | 120,016 | 1,697 | . | 1,928,345 | 3,071 | 79,697 | . |
| TH | 78 | 70,634 | 3,785 | . | . | 3,281,533 | . | 264,677 | 1,162 |

Table 4: Statistics of additional parallel sentences.

Tateoba, Tanzil, QED (Abdelali et al., 2014), tico-19, OpenSubtitles, ELRC. We downloaded all the dataset from OPUS site. Table 4 shows the statistics of the data obtained from the site.

### 3.2 Model configuration

For the NMT system, we used OpenNMT-py (Klein et al., 2017) [5] to train Transformer (Vaswani et al., 2017) architecture models with several different parameter configurations for each task. Our models have 6 encoder layers, 6 decoder layers, a sequence length of 512 for both source and target side, 8 attention heads with an attention dropout of 0.1. Each model was trained on Nvidia RTX 3090 Ti (24GB). We used an effective batch size of 2048 tokens. We chose Adam (Kingma and Ba, 2014) optimizer with a learning rate of 1, warm-up steps 8000, label smoothing 0.1 and token-level layer normalization. We set the data type to the floating point 32 and applied relative positional encoding (Shaw et al., 2018) to consider the pairwise relationships between the input elements. We changed the hidden layer size from 512 to 2048 and the feed forward networks from 2048 to 4096 for finding the model to perform best. We saved the checkpoint every 20,000 steps and choose the model which performed best on the validation set.

We used google sentencepiece library [6] to train separate SentencePiece models (Kudo and Richardson, 2018) on the source and target sides, for each language. We trained a regularized unigram model (Kudo, 2018). For JPC2, we set a vocabulary size of 32,000 for Japanese and Chinese and 16,000 for Korean and English. We set a character coverage to 0.995. For NICT-SAP, we set a vocabulary size of 8,000 for English and Malaysian and 16,000 for Hindi, Indonesian and Thai. We set a character coverage to 0.995. While training sentence piece models, we used only given train dataset and only IT domain (Ubuntu, GNOME, KDE4) for JPC2 and NICT-SAP, respectively.

[5] `https://github.com/OpenNMT/OpenNMT-py`

[6] `https://github.com/google/sentencepiece`

| Sub-task | Tokenizer | BLEU | Rank |
|---|---|---|---|
| En → Ja | mecab | 47.44 | 3 of 15 |
| Ja → En | moses | 45.13 | 1 of 10 |
| Ko → Ja | mecab | 75.82 | 1 of 15 |
| Ja → Ko | mecab | 76.68 | 1 of 10 |
| Zh → Ja | mecab | 51.28 | 2 of 11 |
| Ja → Zh | kytea | 42.92 | 1 of 10 |

Table 5: Official rank and BLEU scores for JPC2 tasks on Test-n dataset.

| Sub-task | BLEU | AMFM | Rank |
|---|---|---|---|
| En → Hi | 37.23 | 0.81 | 1 of 9 |
| Hi → En | 34.48 | 0.80 | 4 of 9 |
| En → Id | 53.22 | 0.85 | 1 of 9 |
| Id → En | 53.49 | 0.85 | 1 of 9 |
| En → Ms | 45.96 | 0.86 | 1 of 9 |
| Ms → En | 38.42 | 0.81 | 2 of 9 |
| En → Th | 34.52 | 0.70 | 5 of 9 |
| Th → En | 25.07 | 0.73 | 2 of 9 |

Table 6: Rank and BLEU/AMFM scores for NICT-SAP IT tasks on leader-board. The rank is scored by BLEU score.

## 4 Result

We participated in JPC2 and NICT-SAP (IT domain) tasks. JPC2 consists of English–Japanese (En–Ja), Chinese–Japanese (Zh–Ja) and Korean–Japanese (Ko–Ja). NICT-SAP consists of English–Hindi (En–Hi), English–Indonesian (En–Id), English–Malaysian (En–Ms) and English–Thai (En–Th).

### 4.1 JPC2 patent translation task

Table 5 shows overall results on JPC2 dataset. Our models ranked first in all the tasks whose input is Japanese. Across overall process, we weighted the given dataset to the crawled dataset *by oversampling*.

**English – Japanese** We collected the additional

| Subtask | # Sen | Avg. Len | w | wo |
|---|---|---|---|---|
| Test-n | 5,230 | 82.67 | 76.68 | 74.60 |
| Test-n1 | 2,000 | 85.60 | 75.90 | 75.11 |
| Test-n2 | 3,000 | 80.32 | 78.13 | 74.86 |
| Test-n3 | 230 | 87.8 | 64.47 | 66.25 |

Table 7: Ablation studies for JPC2 Ja → Ko sub-task."w" and "wo" represents the BLEU score of the model trained **with** and **without** the additional dataset, repectively. "Avg. Len" represents the average of the number of characters per Japanese sentence.

data 20 times more than the given training dataset. We noticed that the average of the sentence length in the collected dataset is much longer than the given dataset. This represents that the collected dataset is quite different from original data. Therefore, we weighted the given train dataset five times for Ja → En and two times for En → Ja task.

In the inference time, we used the seven independent models ensemble for Ja → En and the six independent models for En → Ja task. We selected each model's checkpoint which performed best in the validation data. We set the beam size to 7. The model ensemble method led to a performance improvement by 1.25 and 0.85 of the BLEU score for Ja → En and En → Ja, respectively. The best performance of our model was a BLEU score of 47.44 in the En → Ja and 45.13 in the Ja → En task.

**Korean – Japanese** Our collected data 13 times more than the given one. Similar to En ↔ Ja, we weighted the original dataset three times for both Ja → Ko and Ko → Ja. In the inference time, we used the five independent models ensemble for both Ja → Ko and for Ko → Ja. We set the beam size to 7. The best performance of our model was a BLEU score of 75.82 for the Ko → Ja task and 76.68 for the Ja → Ko task.

To validate the effect of additional data, we conducted an ablation studies on the Ja → Ko task. Table 7 shows the sub-tasks in the JPC2 dataset. Each test data in JPC2 can be split according to the publish year and the way they were collected. Test-n1 consists of the patent documents published between 2011 and 2013. Test-n2 and test-n3 consist of patent documents between 2016 and 2017, but test-n3 are manually created by translating source sentences. While the model trained with additional data outperforms the other model in test-n1 and test-n2, it shows poor performance on test-n3 which consists of manual translations.

**Chinese – Japanese** Similar to En ↔ Ja and Ko ↔ Ja, we weighted the original dataset two times for both Ja → Zh and three times for Zh → Ja. In the inference time, we used the five independent models ensemble for Ja → Zh and seven models for Zh → Ja. We set the beam size to 7. The best performance of our model was a BLEU score of 51.28 in the Zh → Ja dataset and 42.92 in the Ja → Zh dataset.

### 4.2 NICT-SAP IT domain translation task

Table 6 shows the overall results on NICT-SAP IT domain. While we trained transformer on OPUS dataset from scratch, most of the high-ranked models used the pre-trained mBART (Chipman et al., 2021) and finetuned it. Therefore, others got benefit from the multilingualism and gigantic additional corpus. Even though we used relatively small data, we achieved the state-of-the-art scores on the four out of eight tasks.

For all language pairs, we weighted IT dataset (Ubuntu, GNOME, KDE4) 2.5 times to the general one. We saved the checkpoint at every 20000 step, then submitted the models which showed the best performance for validation set. Except for Thai, our models ranked first on the sub-tasks whose input is English. Furthermore, our models outperformed competitors on En ↔ Id, achieving an improvement of 7.83 for En → Id and 8.79 for Id → En dataset. We used relatively rich amount of dataset in this subtask. In contrast, on the En ↔ Th sub-task, our model performed relatively poor since we used small amount of data to train it.

## 5 Conclusion

In this work, we described the Bering Lab's submission to the WAT 2021 shared tasks. We collected the in-domain dataset for both JPC2 and NICT–SAP tasks and built transformer-based MT systems on those corpora. which were trained on given train dataset and additional crawled patent data. Our models ranked first place in eight out of fourteen tasks, amounting a high improvements for both tasks.

## References

Ahmed Abdelali, Francisco Guzman, Hassan Sajjad, and Stephan Vogel. 2014. The amara corpus: Building parallel language resources for the educational domain. In *LREC*, volume 14, pages 1044–1054.

Rafael E Banchs, Luis F D'Haro, and Haizhou Li. 2015. Adequacy–fluency metrics: Evaluating mt in the continuous space model framework. *IEEE/ACM Transactions on Audio, Speech, and Language Processing*, 23(3):472–482.

Bianka Buschbeck and Miriam Exel. 2020. A parallel evaluation data set of software documentation with document structure annotation. *arXiv preprint arXiv:2008.04550*.

Daniel Cer, Yinfei Yang, Sheng-yi Kong, Nan Hua, Nicole Limtiaco, Rhomni St John, Noah Constant, Mario Guajardo-Céspedes, Steve Yuan, Chris Tar, et al. 2018. Universal sentence encoder. *arXiv preprint arXiv:1803.11175*.

Hugh A Chipman, Edward I George, Robert E McCulloch, and Thomas S Shively. 2021. mbart: Multidimensional monotone bart. *Bayesian Analysis*, 1(1):1–30.

Hideki Isozaki, Tsutomu Hirao, Kevin Duh, Katsuhito Sudoh, and Hajime Tsukada. 2010. Automatic evaluation of translation quality for distant language pairs. In *Proceedings of the 2010 Conference on Empirical Methods in Natural Language Processing*, pages 944–952.

Diederik P Kingma and Jimmy Ba. 2014. Adam: A method for stochastic optimization. *arXiv preprint arXiv:1412.6980*.

Guillaume Klein, Yoon Kim, Yuntian Deng, Jean Senellart, and Alexander Rush. 2017. OpenNMT: Open-source toolkit for neural machine translation. In *Proceedings of ACL 2017, System Demonstrations*, pages 67–72.

Taku Kudo. 2018. Subword regularization: Improving neural network translation models with multiple subword candidates. *arXiv preprint arXiv:1804.10959*.

Taku Kudo and John Richardson. 2018. Sentencepiece: A simple and language independent subword tokenizer and detokenizer for neural text processing. *arXiv preprint arXiv:1808.06226*.

Toshiaki Nakazawa, Hideki Nakayama, Chenchen Ding, Raj Dabre, Shohei Higashiyama, Hideya Mino, Isao Goto, Win Pa Pa, Anoop Kunchukuttan, Shantipriya Parida, Ondřej Bojar, Chenhui Chu, Akiko Eriguchi, Kaori Abe, and Sadao Oda, Yusuke Kurohashi. 2021. Overview of the 8th workshop on Asian translation. In *Proceedings of the 8th Workshop on Asian Translation*, Bangkok, Thailand. Association for Computational Linguistics.

Kishore Papineni, Salim Roukos, Todd Ward, and Wei-Jing Zhu. 2002. Bleu: a method for automatic evaluation of machine translation. In *Proceedings of the 40th annual meeting of the Association for Computational Linguistics*, pages 311–318.

Peter Shaw, Jakob Uszkoreit, and Ashish Vaswani. 2018. Self-attention with relative position representations. *arXiv preprint arXiv:1803.02155*.

Jörg Tiedemann. 2012. Parallel data, tools and interfaces in opus. In *Lrec*, volume 2012, pages 2214–2218.

Ashish Vaswani, Noam Shazeer, Niki Parmar, Jakob Uszkoreit, Llion Jones, Aidan N Gomez, Lukasz Kaiser, and Illia Polosukhin. 2017. Attention is all you need. *arXiv preprint arXiv:1706.03762*.

# NLPHut's Participation at WAT2021

**Shantipriya Parida*, Subhadarshi Panda†, Ketan Kotwal*,
Amulya Ratna Dash♣, Satya Ranjan Dash♠, Yashvardhan Sharma♣,
Petr Motlicek*, Ondřej Bojar◇**

*Idiap Research Institute, Martigny, Switzerland
`{firstname.lastname}@idiap.ch`
†Graduate Center, City University of New York, USA
`spanda@gradcenter.cuny.edu`
♣Birla Institute of Technology and Science, Pilani, India
`{p20200105,yash}@pilani.bits-pilani.ac.in`
♠KIIT University, Bhubaneswar, India
`sdashfca@kiit.ac.in`
◇Charles University, MFF, ÚFAL, Prague, Czech Republic
`bojar@ufal.mff.cuni.cz`

## Abstract

This paper provides the description of shared tasks to the WAT 2021 by our team "NLPHut". We have participated in the English→Hindi Multimodal translation task, English→Malayalam Multimodal translation task, and Indic Multilingual translation task. We have used the state-of-the-art *Transformer* model with language tags in different settings for the translation task and proposed a novel "region-specific" caption generation approach using a combination of image CNN and LSTM for the Hindi and Malayalam image captioning. Our submission tops in English→Malayalam Multimodal translation task (text-only translation, and Malayalam caption), and ranks second-best in English→Hindi Multimodal translation task (text-only translation, and Hindi caption). Our submissions have also performed well in the Indic Multilingual translation tasks.

## 1 Introduction

Machine translation (MT) is considered to be one of the most successful applications of natural language processing (NLP)[1]. It has significantly evolved especially in terms of the accuracy of its output. Though MT performance reached near to human level for several language pairs (see e.g. Popel et al., 2020), it remains challenging for low resource languages or translation effectively utilizing other modalities (e.g. image, Parida et al., 2020).

The Workshop on Asian Translation (WAT) is an open evaluation campaign focusing on Asian languages since 2013 (Nakazawa et al., 2020). In WAT2021 (Nakazawa et al., 2021) Multimodal track, a new Indian language *Malayalam* was introduced for English→Malayalam text, multimodal translation, and Malayalam image captioning task.[2] This year, the MultiIndic[3] task covers 10 Indic languages and English.

In this system description paper, we explain our approach for the tasks (including the subtasks) we participated in:

**Task 1:** English→Hindi (EN-HI) Multimodal Translation
- EN-HI text-only translation
- Hindi-only image captioning

**Task 2:** English→Malayalam (EN-ML) Multimodal Translation
- EN-ML text-only translation
- Malayalam-only image captioning

**Task 3:** Indic Multilingual translation task.

Section 2 describes the datasets used in our experiment. Section 3 presents the model and experimental setups used in our approach. Section 4 provides the official evaluation results of WAT2021[4] followed by the conclusion in Section 5.

[1] `https://morioh.com/p/d596d2d4444d`

[2] `https://ufal.mff.cuni.cz/malayalam-visual-genome/wat2021-english-malayalam-multi`

[3] `http://lotus.kuee.kyoto-u.ac.jp/WAT/indic-multilingual/`

[4] `http://lotus.kuee.kyoto-u.ac.jp/WAT/WAT2021/index.html`



*Proceedings of the 8th Workshop on Asian Translation*, pages 146–154
Bangkok, Thailand (online), August 5-6, 2021. 

## 2 Dataset

We have used the official datasets provided by the WAT2021 organizers for the tasks.

**Task 1: English→Hindi Multimodal Translation** For this task, the organizers provided HindiVisualGenome 1.1 (Parida et al., 2019)[5] dataset (HVG for short). The training part consists of 29k English and Hindi short captions of rectangular areas in photos of various scenes and it is complemented by three test sets: development (D-Test), evaluation (E-Test) and challenge test set (C-Test). Our WAT submissions were for E-Test (denoted "EV" in WAT official tables) and C-Test (denoted "CH" in WAT tables). Additionally, we used the IITB Corpus[6] which is supposedly the largest publicly available English-Hindi parallel corpus (Kunchukuttan et al., 2017). This corpus contains 1.59 million parallel segments and it was found very effective for English-Hindi translation (Parida and Bojar, 2018). The statistics of the datasets are shown in Table 1.

| | | Tokens | | |
|---|---|---|---|---|
| Set | Sentences | English | Hindi | Malayalam |
| Train | 28930 | 143164 | 145448 | 107126 |
| D-Test | 998 | 4922 | 4978 | 3619 |
| E-Test | 1595 | 7853 | 7852 | 5689 |
| C-Test | 1400 | 8186 | 8639 | 6044 |
| IITB Train | 1.5 M | 20.6 M | 22.1 M | – |

Table 1: Statistics of our data used in the English→Hindi and English→Malayalam Multimodal task: the number of sentences and tokens.

**Task 2: English→Malayalam Multimodal Translation** For this task, the organizers provided MalayalamVisualGenome 1.0 dataset[7] (MVG for short). MVG is an extension of the HVG dataset for supporting Malayalam, which belongs to the Dravidian language family (Kumar et al., 2017). The dataset size and images are the same as HVG. While HVG contains bilingual (English and Hindi) segments, MVG contains bilingual (English and Malayalam) segments, with the English shared across HVG and MVG, see Table 1.

[5]https://lindat.mff.cuni.cz/repository/xmlui/handle/11234/1-3267

[6]http://www.cfilt.iitb.ac.in/iitb_parallel/

[7]https://lindat.mff.cuni.cz/repository/xmlui/handle/11234/1-3533

**Task 3: Indic Multilingual Translation** For this task, the organizers provided a training corpus that comprises in total 11 million sentence pairs collected from several corpora. The evaluation (dev and test set) contain filtered data of the PMIndia dataset (Haddow and Kirefu, 2020).[8] We have not used any additional resources in this task. The statistics of the dataset are shown in Table 2.

## 3 Experimental Details

This section describes the experimental details of the tasks we participated in.

### 3.1 EN-HI and EN-ML text-only translation

For the HVG text-only translation track, we train a Transformer model (Vaswani et al., 2017) using the concatenation of IIT-B training data and HVG training data (see Table 1). Similar to the two-phase approach outlined in Section 3.3, we continue the training using only the HVG training data to obtain the final checkpoint. For the MVG text-only translation track, we train a Transformer model using only the MVG training data.

For both EN-HI and EN-ML translation, we trained SentencePiece subword units (Kudo and Richardson, 2018) setting maximum vocabulary size to 8k. The vocabulary was learned jointly on the source and target sentences of HVG and IIT-B for EN-HI and of MVG for EN-ML. The number of encoder and decoder layers was set to 3 each; while the number of heads was set to 8. We have set the hidden size to 128, along with the dropout value of 0.1. We initialized the model parameters using Xavier initialization (Glorot and Bengio, 2010) and used the Adam optimizer (Kingma and Ba, 2014) with a learning rate of $5e-4$ for optimizing model parameters. Gradient clipping was used to clip gradients greater than 1. The training was stopped when the development loss did not improve for 5 consecutive epochs. While EN-HI training using concatenated IIT-B + HVG data and the subsequent training using only HVG data, we used the same HVG dev set for determining early stopping. For generating translations, we used greedy decoding and generated tokens autore-

[8]http://data.statmt.org/pmindia/

| Language pair | en-bn | en-hi | en-gu | en-ml | en-mr | en-ta | en-te | en-pa | en-or | en-kn |
|---|---|---|---|---|---|---|---|---|---|---|
| Train (ALL) | 1756197 | 3534387 | 518015 | 1204503 | 781872 | 1499441 | 686626 | 518508 | 252160 | 396865 |
| Train (PMI) | 23306 | 50349 | 41578 | 26916 | 28974 | 32638 | 33380 | 28294 | 31966 | 28901 |
| Dev | 1000 | | | | | | | | | |
| Test | 2390 | | | | | | | | | |

Table 2: Statistics of the data used for Indic multilingual translation.

gressively till the end-of-sentence token was generated or the maximum translation length was reached, which was set to 100.

We show the training and development perplexities for EN-HI and EN-ML translations during training in Figure 4b. The dev perplexity for EN-HI translation is lower in the beginning (after epoch 1) because the model is trained using more training samples (IIT-B + HVG) in comparison to EN-ML. Overall, EN-HI training takes around twice as much time as EN-ML training, again due to the involvement of the bigger IIT-B training data. The drop in perplexity midway for EN-HI is because of the change of training data from IIT-B + HVG to only HVG after the first phase of the training converges.

Upon evaluating the translations using the development set, we obtained the following scores for Hindi translations. The BLEU score was 46.7 upon using HVG + IIT-B training data. In comparison, we observed that the BLEU score was 39.9 upon using only the HVG training data (without IIT-B training data). For Malayalam translations, the BLEU score on the development set was 31.3. BLEU scores were computed using sacreBLEU (Post, 2018).

### 3.2 Image Caption Generation

This task in WAT 2021 is formulated as generating a caption in Hindi and Malayalam for a specific region in the given image. Most existing research in the area of image captioning refers to generating a textual description for the entire image (Yang and Okazaki, 2020; Yang et al., 2017; Lindh et al., 2018; Staniūtė and Šešok, 2019; Miyazaki and Shimizu, 2016; Wu et al., 2017). However, a naive approach of using only a specified region (as defined by the rectangular bounding box) as an input to the generic image caption generation system often does not yield meaningful results. When a small region of the image with few objects is considered for captioning, it lacks the context

English Text: The snow is white. Hindi Text: बर्फ सफेद है

Malayalam Text: മഞ്ഞ് വെളുത്തതാണ് Gloss: Snow is white

Figure 1: Sample image with specific region and its description for caption generation. Image taken from Hindi Visual Genome (HVG) and Malayalam Visual Genome (MVG) (Parida et al., 2019)

(*i.e.,* overall understanding) around the region that can essentially be captured from the entire image as shown in Figure 1. It is challenging to generate the caption "snow" only considering the specific region (red bounding box).

We propose a region-specific image captioning method through the fusion of encoded features of the region as well as that of the complete image. Our proposed model for this task consists of three modules – an encoder, fusion, and decoder – as shown in Figure 2.

**Image Encoder:** To textually describe an image or a region within, it first needs to be encoded into high-level complex features that capture its visual attributes. Several image captioning works (Yang and Okazaki, 2020; Yang et al., 2017; Lindh et al., 2018; Staniūtė and Šešok, 2019; Miyazaki and Shimizu, 2016; Wu et al., 2017) have demonstrated that the outputs of final or pre-final convolutional (conv) layers of deep CNNs are excellent features for the aforementioned objective. Along with features of the entire image, we propose to extract the features of the subregion as well using the same set of outputs of the conv layer. Let $\mathbf{F} \in \mathbb{R}^{MNC}$ be the features of the final conv

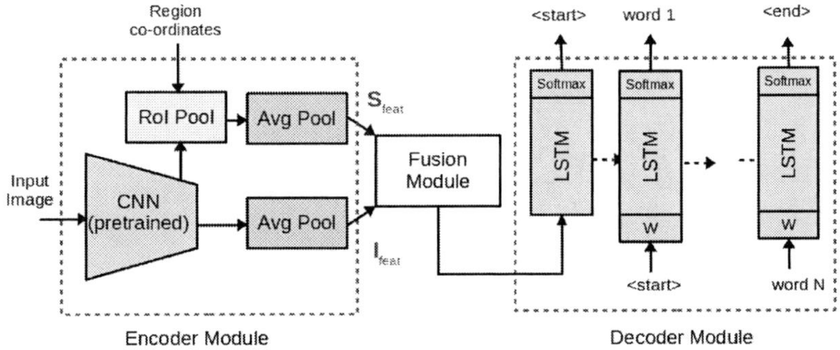


Figure 2: Architecture of the proposed model for region-specific image caption generator. The Encoder module consists of a pre-trained image CNN as feature extractor, while an LSTM-based decoder generates captions. Both modules are connected by a Fusion module.

layer of a pre-trained image CNN where $C$ represents the number of channels or maps, and $M, N$ are the spatial dimensions of each feature map. From the dimensions of the input image and the values of $M, N$, we compute the spatial scaling factor. Through this factor and nominal interpolation, we obtain a corresponding location of the subregion in the conv layer, say with dimensionality $(m,\ n)$. This subset, $\mathbf{F}_s \in \mathbb{R}^{mnC}$, predominantly consists of features from the subregion. The subset $\mathbf{F}_s$ is obtained through the region of interest (RoI) pooling (Girshick, 2015). We do not modify the channel dimensions of $\mathbf{F}_s$. The final features, thus obtained, are linearized to form a single column vector. We denote the region-subset features as $S_{\text{feat}}$. The features of the complete image are nothing but $\mathbf{F}$. We apply spatial pooling on this feature set to reduce their dimensionality, and obtain the linearized vector of full-image features denoted as $I_{\text{feat}}$.

**Fusion Module:** The region-level features capture details of the region (objects) to be described; whereas image-level features provide an overall context. To generate meaningful captions for a region of the image, we consider the features of the region $S_{\text{feat}}$ along with the features of the entire image $I_{\text{feat}}$. This combining of feature vectors is crucial in generating descriptions for the region. In this work, we propose to conduct fusion through the concatenation of weighted features from the region and those from the entire image for region-specific caption generation. The fused feature, $\mathbf{f}$, can be represented as $\mathbf{f} = [\alpha\, S_{\text{feat}}; (1-\alpha)\, I_{\text{feat}}]$, where $\alpha$ is the weightage parameter in $[0.50,\ 1]$ indicating relative importance provided to region-features $S_{\text{feat}}$ over the features of the whole image. For $\alpha = 0.66$, the region-level features are weighted twice as high as the entire image-level features. The weighing of a feature vector scales the magnitude of the corresponding vector without altering its orientation. Unlike the fusion mechanisms based on weighted addition, we do not modify the complex information captured by the features (except for scale); however, its relative importance with respect to the other set of features is adjusted for better caption generation. The fused feature $\mathbf{f}$ with the dimensionality of the sum of both feature vectors are then fed to the LSTM-based decoder.

**LSTM Decoder:** In the proposed approach, the encoder module is not trainable, it only extracts the image features however the LSTM decoder is trainable. We used LSTM decoder using the image features for caption generation using greedy search approach (Soh). We used the cross-entropy loss during decoding (Yu et al., 2019).

### 3.3 Indic Multilingual Translation

Sharing parameters across multiple languages, particularly low-resource Indic languages, results in gains in translation performance (Dabre et al., 2020). Motivated by this finding, we train neural MT models with shared parameters across multiple languages for the Indic multilingual translation task. We additionally apply transfer learning where we train a neural MT model in two phases (Kocmi and Bojar, 2018). The first phase consists of

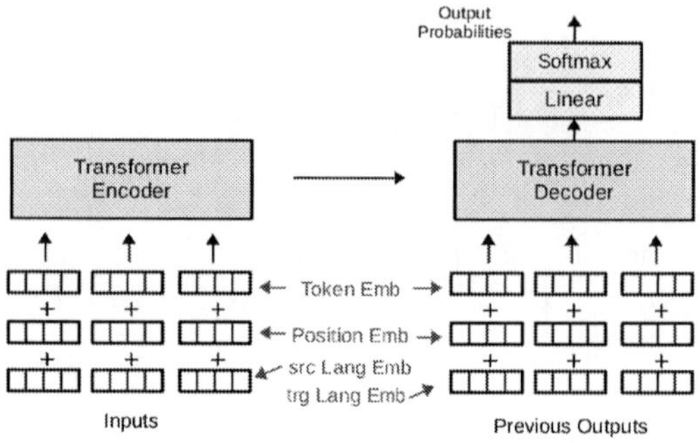


Figure 3: Architecture for Indic Multilingual translation. We show here the setup in which both the source and the target language tags are used.

training a multilingual translation model on training pairs drawn from one of the following options: (a) any Indic language from the dataset as the source and corresponding English target; (b) English as the source and any corresponding Indic language as the target; and (c) combination of (a) and (b), that is, the model is trained to enable translation from any Indic language to English and also English to any Indic language. The second phase involves fine-tuning of the model at the end of phase 1 using pairs from a single language pair. For phase 1, we used the PMI dataset for all the languages combined; whereas, for phase 2, we used either only the PMI portion or all the bilingual data available for the desired language pair. In Table 2, the training data sizes are denoted as *Train (PMI)* for phase 1 of training.

To support multilinguality (*i.e.,* going beyond a bilingual translation setup), we have to either fix the target language (many-to-one setup) or provide a language tag for controlling the generation process. We highlight below the four setups to achieve this:

**Many-to-one setup with no tag** In this setup, we use a transformer model (Vaswani et al., 2017) without any architectural modification that would enable the model to explicitly distinguish between languages. In phase 1 of the training process, we concatenate across all Indic languages the pairs drawn from an Indic language as the source and the corresponding English target and use the resulting data for training.

**Many-to-one setup with source language tag** We use a transformer model where the source language tag explicitly informs the model about the language of the source sentence as in Lample and Conneau (2019). We provide the language information at every position by representing each source token as the sum of token embedding, positional embedding, and language embedding; which is then fed to the encoder (see Figure 3 for the inputs to the encoder). The training data for phase 1 of the training process is the same as in the previous setup.

**One-to-many setup with target language tag** This setup is based on a transformer model where the target language embedding is injected to the decoder at every step and it explicitly informs the model about the desired language of the target sentence (Lample and Conneau, 2019). In this setup, the source is always in English. Similar to the previous setup, we represent each target token as the sum of token embeddings, positional embedding, and language embedding. Figure 3 shows the inputs to the decoder. In phase 1 of the training process, we concatenate across all Indic languages the pairs drawn from English as the source and the corresponding Indic language target and use the resulting data for training.

**Many-to-many setup with both the source and target language tags** In this setup, we use a transformer model where both the encoder and decoder are informed about the source and target languages explicitly through language embedding at every token (Lample and Conneau, 2019). For instance, the same model can be used for *hi-en* translation and also for *en-hi* translation. As shown in the architecture in Figure 3, the source token representation is computed as the sum of the token embedding, positional embedding, and source language embedding. Similarly, the target token representation is computed as the sum of the token embedding, positional embedding, and target language embedding. The source and the target token representations are provided to the encoder and decoder, respectively. The rest of the modules in the transformer model architecture are same as in Vaswani et al. (2017). The training

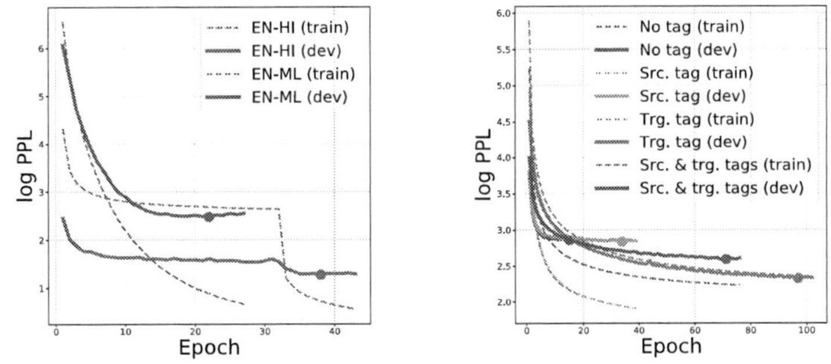


(a) (b)

Figure 4: Training and development perplexity for: (a) EN-HI and EN-ML translation training; and (b) Indic multilingual translation training in various setups (only phase 1 training curves are shown).

data for phase 1 of the training process is the combination of the training datasets for the previous two setups.

In all the four setups described above, the training data for phase 2 is the bilingual data corresponding to the desired language pair. The bilingual data is either the PMI training data or all the available bilingual training data– sizes for which are provided in Table 2.

We now outline the training details for all the setups. We first trained sentencepiece BPE tokenization (Kudo and Richardson, 2018) setting maximum vocabulary size to 32k.[9] The vocabulary was learnt jointly on all the source and target sentence pairs. The number of encoder and decoder layers was set to 3 each, and the number of heads was set to 8. We have considered the hidden size of 128; while the dropout rate was set to 0.1. We initialized the model parameters using Xavier initialization (Glorot and Bengio, 2010). Adam optimizer (Kingma and Ba, 2014) with a learning rate of $5e{-}4$ was used for optimizing model parameters. Gradient clipping was used to clip gradients greater than 1. The training was stopped when the development loss did not improve for 5 consecutive epochs. The same early stopping criterion was followed for both phase 1 and phase 2 of the training process. For phase 1, we used the combination of the development data for all the language pairs in the training data; whereas, for phase 2, we only used the desired language pair's development data. For generating translations, we used greedy decoding where we picked the most likely token at each generation time step. The generation was done token-by-token till the end-of-sentence token is generated or the maximum translation length is reached. The maximum translation length was set to 100.

To compare the training under various setups related to the usage of language tags, we show the perplexity of the training and the development data in Figure 4a. The best (lowest) perplexity is obtained by using the target language tag. However, using the target language tag requires more epochs to converge, where convergence is determined by the early stopping criterion described above.

We show the development BLEU scores, computed using sacreBLEU (Post, 2018) in Table 3 for each language pair. Results indicate that the usage of language tags produces better translation overall. It may also be noted that using both languages' (source and target) tags resulted in the highest development BLEU scores for 8 out of 10 Indic languages while translating to English. For translation from English to Indic languages, the target language tag setup performed the best overall obtaining the highest development BLEU scores in 9 out of 10 languages. We selected the best systems (20 in total) based on the dev BLEU scores for each language pair and used them to generate translations of the test inputs.

The choices related to the hyperparameters that determine the model size and the choice of the training data for phase 1 of the training process were made such that the per epoch

[9]BPE based tokenization performed better in comparison to word-level tokenization using Indic tokenizers (Kunchukuttan, 2020).

| Language pair | No tag | | | Src. tag | | | Trg. tag | | | Src. & trg. tags | | |
|---|---|---|---|---|---|---|---|---|---|---|---|---|
| | Phase 1 | Phase 2 | | Phase 1 | Phase 2 | | Phase 1 | Phase 2 | | Phase 1 | Phase 2 | |
| | | PMI | ALL | | PMI | ALL | | PMI | ALL | | PMI | ALL |
| bn-en | 11.8 | 12.1 | 11.5 | 12.9 | 13.2 | 11.7 | - | - | - | 14.1 | **14.7** | 11.7 |
| gu-en | 17.7 | 17.8 | 24.4 | 19.4 | 19.3 | **24.9** | - | - | - | 22.7 | 23.1 | 23.1 |
| hi-en | 18.7 | 19.6 | 25.6 | 21.3 | 21.6 | 26.0 | - | - | - | 25.1 | 25.7 | **26.2** |
| kn-en | 14.5 | 15.1 | 16.5 | 16.6 | 16.8 | 15.5 | - | - | - | 18.7 | **19.5** | 17.0 |
| ml-en | 12.2 | 12.6 | 12.2 | 13.6 | 13.4 | 12.3 | - | - | - | 15.4 | **15.9** | 12.4 |
| mr-en | 13.3 | 12.9 | 16.1 | 14.9 | 15.1 | 17.0 | - | - | - | 16.6 | 17.2 | **17.3** |
| or-en | 14.0 | 14.1 | 16.9 | 15.5 | 15.6 | 18.7 | - | - | - | 17.5 | 17.8 | **20.3** |
| pa-en | 17.4 | 17.8 | **27.0** | 18.9 | 19.0 | 26.3 | - | - | - | 22.2 | 22.8 | 26.4 |
| ta-en | 13.2 | 13.2 | 15.0 | 14.7 | 14.3 | 14.6 | - | - | - | 15.8 | **16.4** | 15.9 |
| te-en | 14.4 | 14.5 | 16.5 | 15.6 | 16.3 | 16.8 | - | - | - | 16.9 | **17.9** | 16.7 |
| en-bn | - | - | - | - | - | - | 6.2 | **6.5** | 4.6 | 5.6 | 5.9 | 4.4 |
| en-gu | - | - | - | - | - | - | 18.4 | **19.9** | 18.8 | 16.9 | 18.4 | 18.5 |
| en-hi | - | - | - | - | - | - | 22.4 | 24.5 | **24.7** | 20.6 | 23.2 | 24.2 |
| en-kn | - | - | - | - | - | - | 12.6 | **13.4** | 10.6 | 10.9 | 12.6 | 9.8 |
| en-ml | - | - | - | - | - | - | 3.9 | **4.4** | 2.6 | 3.6 | 4.0 | 2.0 |
| en-mr | - | - | - | - | - | - | 10.2 | **11.2** | 10.4 | 8.8 | 10.6 | 10.1 |
| en-or | - | - | - | - | - | - | 12.4 | 13.2 | 14.0 | 11.4 | 12.3 | **14.2** |
| en-pa | - | - | - | - | - | - | 18.8 | 19.7 | **20.9** | 16.5 | 18.8 | 20.5 |
| en-ta | - | - | - | - | - | - | 8.5 | **9.6** | 8.4 | 7.8 | 8.3 | 8.0 |
| en-te | - | - | - | - | - | - | 2.2 | **2.9** | 2.4 | 2.0 | 2.6 | **2.9** |

Table 3: Development BLEU scores for Indic multilingual translations in various setups after phase 1 and phase 2 of the training process. Scores are shown for each language pair separately.

training time is below an hour on a single GPU. We note that there is room for improvement in our results: (a) the model size in any of the setups described earlier can be increased to match the size of the transformer big model (Vaswani et al., 2017), and (b) all the available training data can be used for phase 1 of the training process instead of just the PMI data.

## 4 Results

| System and WAT Task Label | WAT BLEU NLPHut | Best Comp |
|---|---|---|
| **English→Hindi MM Task** | | |
| MMEVTEXT21en-hi | 42.11 | **44.61** |
| MMEVHI21en-hi | **1.30** | - |
| MMCHTEXT21en-hi | 43.29 | **53.54** |
| MMCHHI21en-hi | **1.69** | - |
| **English→Malayalam MM Task** | | |
| MMEVTEXT21en-ml | **34.83*** | 30.49 |
| MMEVHI21en-ml | **0.97** | - |
| MMCHTEXT21en-ml | 12.15 | **12.98** |
| MMCHHI21en-ml | **0.99** | - |

Table 4: WAT2021 Automatic Evaluation Results for English→Hindi and English→Malayalam. Rows containing "TEXT" in the task label name denote text-only translation track, and the rest of the rows represent image-only track. For each task, we show the score of our system (NLPHut) and the score of the best competitor in the respective task. The scores marked with '*' indicate the best performance in its track among all competitors.

We report the official automatic evaluation results of our models for all the participated tasks in Table 4 and Table 5. We have provided the automatic evaluation score (BLEU)

| WAT Task | From English NLPHut | From English Best Comp | Into English NLPHut | Into English Best Comp |
|---|---|---|---|---|
| INDIC21en-bn | 8.13 | **15.97** | 13.88 | **31.87** |
| INDIC21en-hi | 25.37 | **38.65** | 24.55 | **46.93** |
| INDIC21en-gu | 17.76 | **27.80** | 23.10 | **43.98** |
| INDIC21en-ml | 4.57 | **15.49** | 15.47 | **38.38** |
| INDIC21en-mr | 10.41 | **20.42** | 17.07 | **36.64** |
| INDIC21en-ta | 7.68 | **14.43** | 15.40 | **36.13** |
| INDIC21en-te | 4.88 | **16.85** | 16.48 | **39.80** |
| INDIC21en-pa | 22.60 | **33.43** | 24.35 | **46.39** |
| INDIC21en-or | 12.81 | **20.15** | 18.92 | **37.06** |
| INDIC21en-kn | 11.84 | **21.30** | 17.72 | **40.34** |

Table 5: WAT2021 Automatic Evaluation Results for Indic Multilingual Task. For each task, we show the score of our system (NLPHut) and the score of the best competitor ('Best Comp') in the respective task.

for the image captioning task, although it is not apt for evaluating the quality of the generated caption. Thus, we have also provided some sample outputs in Table 6.

## 5 Conclusions

In this system description paper, we presented our systems for three tasks in WAT 2021 in which we participated: (a) English→Hindi Multimodal task, (b) English→Malayalam Multimodal task, and (c) Indic Multilingual translation task. As the next steps, we plan to explore further on the Indic Multilingual translation task by utilizing all given data and using additional resources for training. We are also working on improving the region-specific image captioning by fine-tuning the object detection model.

| | | | |
|---|---|---|---|
|  | Gold: एक लड़की टेनिस खेल रही है<br>Gloss: A girl is playing tennis<br>Output:एक टेनिस रैकेट पकड़े हुए आदमी<br><br>Gloss: A man holding a tennis racket |  | Gold: आदमी समुद्र में सर्फिंग<br>Gloss: man surfing in ocean<br>Output: पानी में एक व्यक्ति<br><br>Gloss: A man in the water |
|  | Gold: एक कुत्ता कूदता है<br>Gloss: A dog is jumping<br>Output: कुत्ता भाग रहा है<br><br>Gloss: A dog is running |  | Gold: हेलमेट पहनना<br>Gloss: Wearing helmet<br>Output: एक आदमी के सिर पर एक काला हेलमेट<br>Gloss: A black helmet on the head of a person |
|  | Gold: തിളക്കമുള്ള പച്ച കൈറ്റ്<br><br>Gloss: Bright green kite<br>Output:ആകാശത്ത് പറക്കുന്ന കൈറ്റ്<br>Gloss: Kite flying in the sky |  | Gold: ഒരു ധ്രുവത്തിലെ ട്രാഫിക് ലൈറ്റ്<br>Gloss: Traffic light at a pole<br>Output: ട്രാഫിക് ലൈറ്റ് ചുവപ്പ് തിളങ്ങുന്നു<br>Gloss: The traffic light glows red |
|  | Gold: തൂങ്ങി കിടക്കുന്ന ഒരു കൂട്ടം വാഴപ്പഴം<br>Gloss: A bunch of hanging bananas<br>Output: ഒരു കൂട്ടം വാഴപ്പഴം<br>Gloss: A bunch of bananas |  | Gold: ചുമരിൽ ഒരു ഘടികാരം വാഴപ്പഴം<br>Gloss: A clock on the wall<br><br>Output: ചുമരിൽ ഒരു ചിത്രം<br>Gloss: A picture on the wall |

Table 6: Sample captions generated for the evaluation test set using the proposed method: the top two rows present results of Hindi captions; and the bottom two rows are results of Malayalam caption.

## Acknowledgments

The authors Shantipriya Parida and Petr Motlicek were supported by the European Union's Horizon 2020 research and innovation program under grant agreement No. 833635 (project ROXANNE: Real-time network, text, and speaker analytics for combating organized crime, 2019-2022). Ondřej Bojar would like to acknowledge the support of the grant 19-26934X (NEUREM3) of the Czech Science Foundation.

The authors do not see any significant ethical or privacy concerns that would prevent the processing of the data used in the study. The datasets do contain personal data, and these are processed in compliance with the GDPR and national law.

## References

Raj Dabre, Chenhui Chu, and Anoop Kunchukuttan. 2020. A survey of multilingual neural machine translation. *ACM Comput. Surv.*, 53(5).

Ross Girshick. 2015. Fast r-cnn. In *Proceedings of the IEEE International Conference on Computer Vision (ICCV)*, pages 1440–1448.

Xavier Glorot and Yoshua Bengio. 2010. Understanding the difficulty of training deep feedforward neural networks. In *Proceedings of the Thirteenth International Conference on Artificial Intelligence and Statistics*, volume 9 of *Proceedings of Machine Learning Research*, pages 249–256, Chia Laguna Resort, Sardinia, Italy. PMLR.

Barry Haddow and Faheem Kirefu. 2020. PMIndia – A Collection of Parallel Corpora of Languages of India. *arXiv e-prints*, page arXiv:2001.09907.

Diederik P. Kingma and Jimmy Ba. 2014. Adam: A method for stochastic optimization. Cite arxiv:1412.6980Comment: Published as a conference paper at the 3rd International Conference for Learning Representations, San Diego, 2015.

Tom Kocmi and Ondřej Bojar. 2018. Trivial transfer learning for low-resource neural machine translation. In *Proceedings of the Third Conference on Machine Translation: Research Papers*, pages 244–252, Brussels, Belgium. Association for Computational Linguistics.

Taku Kudo and John Richardson. 2018. SentencePiece: A simple and language independent subword tokenizer and detokenizer for neural text processing. In *Proceedings of the 2018 Conference on Empirical Methods in Natural Language*

*Processing: System Demonstrations*, pages 66–71, Brussels, Belgium. Association for Computational Linguistics.

Arun Kumar, Ryan Cotterell, Lluís Padró, and Antoni Oliver. 2017. Morphological analysis of the dravidian language family. In *Proceedings of the 15th Conference of the European Chapter of the Association for Computational Linguistics: Volume 2, Short Papers*, pages 217–222.

Anoop Kunchukuttan. 2020. The IndicNLP Library. `https://github.com/anoopkunchukuttan/indic_nlp_library/blob/master/docs/indicnlp.pdf`.

Anoop Kunchukuttan, Pratik Mehta, and Pushpak Bhattacharyya. 2017. The IIT Bombay English-Hindi Parallel Corpus. *arXiv preprint arXiv:1710.02855*.

Guillaume Lample and Alexis Conneau. 2019. Cross-lingual language model pretraining. *CoRR*, abs/1901.07291.

Annika Lindh, Robert J Ross, Abhijit Mahalunkar, Giancarlo Salton, and John D Kelleher. 2018. Generating diverse and meaningful captions. In *International Conference on Artificial Neural Networks*, pages 176–187. Springer.

Takashi Miyazaki and Nobuyuki Shimizu. 2016. Cross-lingual image caption generation. In *Proceedings of the 54th Annual Meeting of the Association for Computational Linguistics (Volume 1: Long Papers)*, pages 1780–1790.

Toshiaki Nakazawa, Hideki Nakayama, Chenchen Ding, Raj Dabre, Shohei Higashiyama, Hideya Mino, Isao Goto, Win Pa Pa, Anoop Kunchukuttan, Shantipriya Parida, Ondřej Bojar, Chenhui Chu, Akiko Eriguchi, Kaori Abe, and Sadao Oda, Yusuke Kurohashi. 2021. Overview of the 8th workshop on Asian translation. In *Proceedings of the 8th Workshop on Asian Translation*, Bangkok, Thailand. Association for Computational Linguistics.

Toshiaki Nakazawa, Hideki Nakayama, Chenchen Ding, Raj Dabre, Shohei Higashiyama, Hideya Mino, Isao Goto, Win Pa Pa, Anoop Kunchukuttan, Shantipriya Parida, et al. 2020. Overview of the 7th workshop on asian translation. In *Proceedings of the 7th Workshop on Asian Translation*, pages 1–44.

Shantipriya Parida and Ondřej Bojar. 2018. Translating short segments with nmt: A case study in english-to-hindi. In *21st Annual Conference of the European Association for Machine Translation*, page 229.

Shantipriya Parida, Ondřej Bojar, and Satya Ranjan Dash. 2019. Hindi visual genome: A dataset for multi-modal english to hindi machine translation. *Computación y Sistemas*, 23(4).

Shantipriya Parida, Petr Motlicek, Amulya Ratna Dash, Satya Ranjan Dash, Debasish Kumar Mallick, Satya Prakash Biswal, Priyanka Pattnaik, Biranchi Narayan Nayak, and Ondřej Bojar. 2020. Odianlp's participation in wat2020. In *Proceedings of the 7th Workshop on Asian Translation*, pages 103–108.

Martin Popel, Marketa Tomkova, Jakub Tomek, Łukasz Kaiser, Jakob Uszkoreit, Ondřej Bojar, and Zdeněk Žabokrtský. 2020. Transforming machine translation: a deep learning system reaches news translation quality comparable to human professionals. *Nature communications*, 11(1):1–15.

Matt Post. 2018. A call for clarity in reporting BLEU scores. In *Proceedings of the Third Conference on Machine Translation: Research Papers*, pages 186–191, Belgium, Brussels. Association for Computational Linguistics.

Moses Soh. Learning cnn-lstm architectures for image caption generation.

Raimonda Staniūtė and Dmitrij Šešok. 2019. A systematic literature review on image captioning. *Applied Sciences*, 9(10):2024.

Ashish Vaswani, Noam Shazeer, Niki Parmar, Jakob Uszkoreit, Llion Jones, Aidan N Gomez, Ł ukasz Kaiser, and Illia Polosukhin. 2017. Attention is all you need. In *Advances in Neural Information Processing Systems*, volume 30. Curran Associates, Inc.

Qi Wu, Chunhua Shen, Peng Wang, Anthony Dick, and Anton Van Den Hengel. 2017. Image captioning and visual question answering based on attributes and external knowledge. *IEEE transactions on pattern analysis and machine intelligence*, 40(6):1367–1381.

Zhishen Yang and Naoaki Okazaki. 2020. Image caption generation for news articles. In *Proceedings of the 28th International Conference on Computational Linguistics*, pages 1941–1951.

Zhongliang Yang, Yu-Jin Zhang, Sadaqat ur Rehman, and Yongfeng Huang. 2017. Image captioning with object detection and localization. In *International Conference on Image and Graphics*, pages 109–118. Springer.

Jun Yu, Jing Li, Zhou Yu, and Qingming Huang. 2019. Multimodal transformer with multi-view visual representation for image captioning. *IEEE transactions on circuits and systems for video technology*, 30(12):4467–4480.

# Improved English to Hindi Multimodal Neural Machine Translation

**Sahinur Rahman Laskar, Abdullah Faiz Ur Rahman Khilji,**
**Darsh Kaushik, Partha Pakray, Sivaji Bandyopadhyay**
Department of Computer Science and Engineering
National Institute of Technology Silchar
Assam, India
{sahinur_rs, abdullah_ug, darsh_ug, partha}@cse.nits.ac.in,
sivaji.cse.ju@gmail.com

## Abstract

Machine translation performs automatic translation from one natural language to another. Neural machine translation attains a state-of-the-art approach in machine translation, but it requires adequate training data, which is a severe problem for low-resource language pairs translation. The concept of multimodal is introduced in neural machine translation (NMT) by merging textual features with visual features to improve low-resource pair translation. WAT2021 (Workshop on Asian Translation 2021) organizes a shared task of multimodal translation for English to Hindi. We have participated the same with team name CNLP-NITS-PP in two submissions: multimodal and text-only translation. This work investigates phrase pairs injection via data augmentation approach and attains improvement over our previous work at WAT2020 on the same task in both text-only and multimodal translation. We have achieved second rank on the challenge test set for English to Hindi multimodal translation where Bilingual Evaluation Understudy (BLEU) score of 39.28, Rank-based Intuitive Bilingual Evaluation Score (RIBES) 0.792097, and Adequacy-Fluency Metrics (AMFM) score 0.830230 respectively.

## 1 Introduction

Multimodal NMT (MNMT) intends to draw insights from the input data through different modalities like text, image, and audio. Combining information from more than one modality attempts to amend the quality of low resource language translation. (Shah et al., 2016) show, combining the visual features of images with corresponding textual features of the input bitext to translate sentences outperform text-only translation. Encoder-decoder architecture is a widely used technique in the MT community for text-only-based NMT as it handles various issues like variable-length phrases using sequence to sequence learning, the problem of long-term dependency using Long Short Term Memory (LSTM) (Sutskever et al., 2014). Nevertheless, the basic encoder-decoder architecture cannot encode all the information when it comes to very long sentences. The attention mechanism is proposed to handle such issues, which pays attention to all source words locally and globally (Bahdanau et al., 2015; Luong et al., 2015). The attention-based NMT yields substantial performance for Indian language translation (Pathak and Pakray, 2018; Pathak et al., 2018; Laskar et al., 2019a,b, 2020a, 2021b,a). Moreover, NMT performance can be enhanced by utilizing monolingual data (Sennrich et al., 2016; Zhang and Zong, 2016; Laskar et al., 2020b) and phrase pair injection (Sen et al., 2020), effective in low resource language pair translation. This paper aims English to Hindi translation using the multimodal concept by taking advantage of monolingual data and phrase pair injections to improve the translation quality at the WAT2021 translation task.

## 2 Related Works

For the English-Hindi language pair, the literature survey revealed minor existing works on translation using multimodal NMT (Dutta Chowdhury et al., 2018; Sanayai Meetei et al., 2019; Laskar et al., 2019c). (Dutta Chowdhury et al., 2018) uses synthetic data, following multimodal NMT settings (Calixto and Liu, 2017), and attains a BLEU score of 24.2 for Hindi to English translation. However, in the WAT 2019 multimodal translation task of English to Hindi, we achieved the highest BLEU score of 20.37 for the challenge test set (Laskar et al., 2019c). This score was improved later in the task of WAT2020 (Laskar et al., 2020c) to obtain the BLEU score of 33.57 on the challenge



*Proceedings of the 8th Workshop on Asian Translation*, pages 155–160
Bangkok, Thailand (online), August 5-6, 2021. 

| Type | Name | Items/Instances | Tokens in millions (En / Hi) |
|---|---|---|---|
| **Train** | Text Data (En - Hi) | 28,927 | 0.143164 / 0.145448 |
| | Image Data | 28,927 | |
| **Test (Evaluation Set)** | Text Data (En - Hi) | 1,595 | 0.007853 / 0.007852 |
| | Image Data | 1,595 | |
| **Test (Challenge Set)** | Text Data (En - Hi) | 1,400 | 0.008186 / 0.008639 |
| | Image Data | 1,400 | |
| **Validation** | Text Data (En - Hi) | 998 | 0.004922 / 0.004978 |
| | Image Data | 998 | |

Table 1: Parallel Data Statistics (Nakazawa et al., 2021; Parida et al., 2019).

| Monolingual Data | Sentences | Tokens in millions |
|---|---|---|
| En | 107,597,494 | 1832.008594 |
| Hi | 44,949,045 | 743.723731 |

Table 2: Monolingual Data Statistics collected from IITB and WMT16.

test set. In (Laskar et al., 2020c), we have used bidirectional RNN (BRNN) at encoder type, and doubly-attentive RNN at decoder type following default settings of (Calixto and Liu, 2017; Calixto et al., 2017) and utilizes pre-train word embeddings of the monolingual corpus and additional parallel data of IITB. This work attempts to utilize phrase pairs (Sen et al., 2020) to enhance the translational performance of the WAT2021: English to Hindi multimodal translation task.

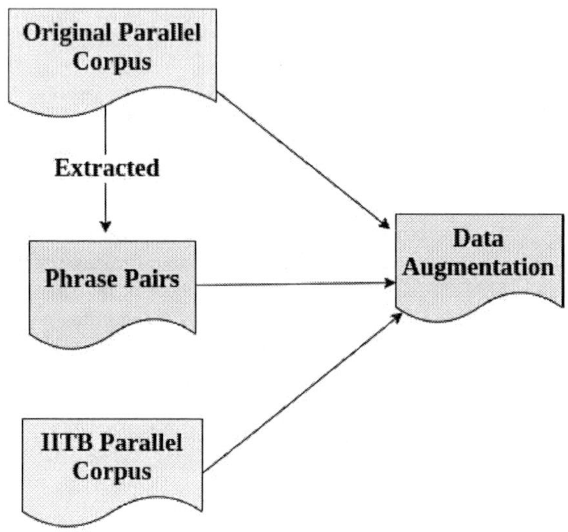


Figure 1: Data augmentation for English-to-Hindi multimodal NMT.

## 3 Dataset Description

We have used the Hindi Visual Genome 1.1 dataset provided by WAT2021 organizers (Nakazawa et al., 2021; Parida et al., 2019). The train data contains English-Hindi 28,930 parallel sentences and 28,928 images. After removing duplicate sentences having ID numbers 2391240, 2385507, 2328549 from parallel data and one image having ID number 2326837 (since corresponding text not present in parallel data), the parallel and image train data reduced to 28,927. Moreover, English-Hindi (En-Hi) parallel and Hindi monolingual corpus[1] (Kunchukuttan et al., 2018) and also, English monolingual data available at WMT16[2] are used. Table 1 and 2 depict the data statistics.

[1]http://www.cfilt.iitb.ac.in/iitb_parallel/

[2]http://www.statmt.org/wmt16/translation-task.html

## 4 System Description

To build multimodal and text-only NMT models, OpenNMT-py (Klein et al., 2017) tool is used. There are four operations which include data augmentation, preprocessing, training and testing. Our multi-model NMT gets advantages from both image and textual features with phrase pairs and word embeddings.

### 4.1 Data Augmentation

In (Sen et al., 2020), authors used SMT-based phrase pairs to augment with the original parallel data to improve low-resource language pairs translation. In SMT[3], Giza++ word alignment tool is used to extract phrase pair. Inspired by the work (Sen et al., 2020), we have extracted phrase

[3]http://www.statmt.org/moses/

Image id: 1159278

| Multi-modal Translation Track<br>Source Language: English<br>Target Language: Hindi | |
|---|---|
| Source Sentence | The top white cross. |
| Predicted Sentence | ऊपर सफेद क्रॉस \|<br>*(Upor shafed cross)* |
| Reference Sentence | शीर्ष पर सफेद क्रॉस।<br>*(Shirse par shafed cross)* |
| Google Translation | शीर्ष सफेद क्रॉस।<br>*(Shirse shafed cross)* |
| **Text-only Translation Track** | |
| Predicted Sentence: | ऊपर सफेद <unk><br>*(Upor shafed <unk>)* |

Figure 2: Examples of our best predicted output on challenge test data.

Image id: 2351980

| Multi-modal Translation Track<br>Source Language: English<br>Target Language: Hindi | |
|---|---|
| Source Sentence | Dirt on the players pants. |
| Predicted Sentence | खिलाड़ी <unk> पर <unk><br>*(khilari <unk> par<unk>)* |
| Reference Sentence | खिलाड़ियों की पैंट पर मिट्टी।<br>*(khilariyo ki pant par mitti)* |
| Google Translation | खिलाड़ियों की पैंट पर गंदगी।<br>*(khilaiyo ki pant par ghandagi)* |
| **Text-only Translation Track** | |
| Predicted Sentence: | खिलाड़ी <unk> पर <unk><br>*(khilari <unk> par <unk>)* |

Figure 3: Examples of our worst predicted output on challenge test data.

pairs using Giza++[4]. Then after removing duplicates and blank lines, the obtained phrase pairs are augmented to the original parallel data. The data statistics of extracted phrase pairs is given in Table 3. Additionally, IITB parallel data is directly augmented with the original parallel to expand the train data. The diagram of data augmentation is presented in Figure 1.

### 4.2 Data Preprocessing

To extract visual features from image data, we have used publicly available[5] pre-trained CNN with VGG19. The visual features are extracted independently for train, validation, and test data. To get the advantage of monolingual data on both multimodal and text-only, GloVe (Pennington et al., 2014) is used to generate vectors of word embeddings. For tokenization of text data, the OpenNMT-py tool is utilized and obtained a vocabulary size of 50004 for source-target sentences. We have not used any word-segmentation technique.

### 4.3 Training

The multimodal and text-only based NMT are trained independently. During the multimodal training process, extracted visual features, pre-trained word vectors are fine-tuned with the augmented parallel data. The bidirectional RNN (BRNN) at encoder type and doubly-attentive RNN at decoder type following default settings of (Calixto and Liu, 2017; Calixto et al., 2017) are used for multimodal NMT. Two different RNNs are used in BRNN, one for backward and another for forwards directions, and two distinct attention mechanisms are utilized over source words and image features at a single decoder. The multimodal NMT is trained up to 40 epochs with 0.3 drop-outs and batch size 32 on a single GPU. During the training process of text-only NMT, we have used only textual data i.e., pre-trained word vectors are fine-tuned with the augmented parallel data, and the model is trained up to 100000 steps using BRNN encoder and RNN decoder following default settings of OpenNMT-py. The primary difference between our previous work (Laskar et al., 2020c) and this work is that the present work uses phrase pairs in augmented parallel data.

### 4.4 Testing

The obtained trained NMT models of both multimodal and text-only are tested on both test data: evaluation and challenge set independently. During testing, the only difference between text-only and multimodal NMT is that multimodal NMT uses

[4] https://github.com/ayushidalmia/Phrase-Based-Model

[5] https://github.com/iacercalixto/MultimodalNMT

| Number of Phrase Pairs | Tokens in millions | |
|---|---|---|
| | En | Hi |
| 158,131 | 0.392966 | 0.410696 |

Table 3: Data Statistics of extracted phrase pairs.

| Our System | Test Set | BLEU | RIBES | AMFM |
|---|---|---|---|---|
| Text-only NMT | Challenge | 37.16 | 0.770621 | 0.798670 |
| | Evaluation | 37.01 | 0.795302 | 0.812190 |
| Multi-modal NMT | Challenge | 39.28 | 0.792097 | 0.830230 |
| | Evaluation | 39.46 | 0.802055 | 0.823270 |

Table 4: Our system's results on English to Hindi multimodal translation Task.

visual features of image test data.

## 5 Result and Analysis

The WAT2021 shared task organizer published the evaluation result[6] of multimodal translation task for English to Hindi and our team stood second position in multimodal submission for challenge test set. Our team name is CNLP-NITS-PP, and we have participated in the multimodal and text-only submission tracks of the same task. In both multimodal and text-only translation submission tracks, a total of three teams participated in both evaluation and challenges test data. The results are evaluated using automatic metrics: BLEU (Papineni et al., 2002), RIBES (Isozaki et al., 2010) and AMFM (Banchs et al., 2015). The results of our system is reported in Table 4, and it is noticed that the multimodal NMT obtains higher than text-only NMT. It is because the combination of textual and visual features outperforms text-only NMT. Furthermore, our system's results are improved as compared to our previous work on the same task (Laskar et al., 2020c). It shows the BLEU, RIBES, AMFM scores of present work show (+5.71, +9.41), (+0.037956, +0.055641), (+0.04291, +0.04835) increments on the challenge test set for multimodal and text-only NMT, where it is realised that phrase pairs augmentation improves translational performance. The sample examples of best and worst outputs, along with Google translation and transliteration of Hindi words, are presented in Figure 2 and 3. In Figure 2 and 3, highlighted the region in the image for the given caption by a red colour rectangular box.

[6]http://lotus.kuee.kyoto-u.ac.jp/WAT/evaluation/index.html

## 6 Conclusion and Future Work

In this work, we have participated in a shared task at WAT2021 multimodal translation task of English to Hindi, where translation submitted at tracks: multimodal and text-only. This work investigates phrase pairs through data augmentation approach in both multimodal and text-only NMT, which shows better performance than our previous work on the same task (Laskar et al., 2020c). In future work, we will investigate a multilingual approach to improve the performance of multimodal NMT.

## Acknowledgement

We want to thank the Center for Natural Language Processing (CNLP), the Artificial Intelligence (AI) Lab, and the Department of Computer Science and Engineering at the National Institute of Technology, Silchar, India, for providing the requisite support and infrastructure to execute this work. We also thank the WAT2021 Translation task organizers.

## References

Dzmitry Bahdanau, Kyunghyun Cho, and Yoshua Bengio. 2015. Neural machine translation by jointly learning to align and translate. In *3rd International Conference on Learning Representations, ICLR 2015, San Diego, CA, USA, May 7-9, 2015, Conference Track Proceedings*.

Rafael E. Banchs, Luis F. D'Haro, and Haizhou Li. 2015. Adequacy-fluency metrics: Evaluating mt in the continuous space model framework. *IEEE/ACM Trans. Audio, Speech and Lang. Proc.*, 23(3):472–482.

Iacer Calixto and Qun Liu. 2017. Incorporating global visual features into attention-based neural machine translation. In *Proceedings of the 2017 Conference on Empirical Methods in Natural Language Processing*, pages 992–1003, Copenhagen, Denmark. Association for Computational Linguistics.

Iacer Calixto, Qun Liu, and Nick Campbell. 2017. Doubly-attentive decoder for multi-modal neural machine translation. In *Proceedings of the 55th Annual Meeting of the Association for Computational Linguistics, ACL 2017, Vancouver, Canada, July 30 - August 4, Volume 1: Long Papers*, pages 1913–1924. Association for Computational Linguistics.

Koel Dutta Chowdhury, Mohammed Hasanuzzaman, and Qun Liu. 2018. Multimodal neural machine translation for low-resource language pairs using synthetic data. In *"."*, pages 33–42.

Hideki Isozaki, Tsutomu Hirao, Kevin Duh, Katsuhito Sudoh, and Hajime Tsukada. 2010. Automatic evaluation of translation quality for distant language pairs. In *Proceedings of the 2010 Conference on Empirical Methods in Natural Language Processing*, pages 944–952, Cambridge, MA. Association for Computational Linguistics.

Guillaume Klein, Yoon Kim, Yuntian Deng, Jean Senellart, and Alexander Rush. 2017. Opennmt: Open-source toolkit for neural machine translation. In *Proceedings of ACL 2017, System Demonstrations*, pages 67–72, Vancouver, Canada. Association for Computational Linguistics.

Anoop Kunchukuttan, Pratik Mehta, and Pushpak Bhattacharyya. 2018. The IIT Bombay English-Hindi parallel corpus. In *Proceedings of the Eleventh International Conference on Language Resources and Evaluation (LREC 2018)*, Miyazaki, Japan. European Language Resources Association (ELRA).

Sahinur Rahman Laskar, Abinash Dutta, Partha Pakray, and Sivaji Bandyopadhyay. 2019a. Neural machine translation: English to hindi. In *2019 IEEE Conference on Information and Communication Technology*, pages 1–6.

Sahinur Rahman Laskar, Abdullah Faiz Ur Rahman Khilji, Partha Pakray, and Sivaji Bandyopadhyay. 2020a. EnAsCorp1.0: English-Assamese corpus. In *Proceedings of the 3rd Workshop on Technologies for MT of Low Resource Languages*, pages 62–68, Suzhou, China. Association for Computational Linguistics.

Sahinur Rahman Laskar, Abdullah Faiz Ur Rahman Khilji, Partha Pakray, and Sivaji Bandyopadhyay. 2020b. Hindi-Marathi cross lingual model. In *Proceedings of the Fifth Conference on Machine Translation*, pages 396–401, Online. Association for Computational Linguistics.

Sahinur Rahman Laskar, Abdullah Faiz Ur Rahman Khilji, Partha Pakray, and Sivaji Bandyopadhyay. 2020c. Multimodal neural machine translation for English to Hindi. In *Proceedings of the 7th Workshop on Asian Translation*, pages 109–113, Suzhou, China. Association for Computational Linguistics.

Sahinur Rahman Laskar, Partha Pakray, and Sivaji Bandyopadhyay. 2019b. Neural machine translation: Hindi-Nepali. In *Proceedings of the Fourth Conference on Machine Translation (Volume 3: Shared Task Papers, Day 2)*, pages 202–207, Florence, Italy. Association for Computational Linguistics.

Sahinur Rahman Laskar, Partha Pakray, and Sivaji Bandyopadhyay. 2021a. Neural machine translation: Assamese–bengali. In *Modeling, Simulation and Optimization: Proceedings of CoMSO 2020*, pages 571–579. Springer Singapore.

Sahinur Rahman Laskar, Partha Pakray, and Sivaji Bandyopadhyay. 2021b. Neural machine translation for low resource assamese–english. In *Proceedings of the International Conference on Computing and Communication Systems: I3CS 2020, NEHU, Shillong, India*, volume 170, page 35. Springer.

Sahinur Rahman Laskar, Rohit Pratap Singh, Partha Pakray, and Sivaji Bandyopadhyay. 2019c. English to Hindi multi-modal neural machine translation and Hindi image captioning. In *Proceedings of the 6th Workshop on Asian Translation*, pages 62–67, Hong Kong, China. Association for Computational Linguistics.

Thang Luong, Hieu Pham, and Christopher D. Manning. 2015. Effective approaches to attention-based neural machine translation. In *Proceedings of the 2015 Conference on Empirical Methods in Natural Language Processing*, pages 1412–1421, Lisbon, Portugal. Association for Computational Linguistics.

Toshiaki Nakazawa, Hideki Nakayama, Chenchen Ding, Raj Dabre, Shohei Higashiyama, Hideya Mino, Isao Goto, Win Pa Pa, Anoop Kunchukuttan, Shantipriya Parida, Ondřej Bojar, Chenhui Chu, Akiko Eriguchi, Kaori Abe, and Sadao Oda, Yusuke Kurohashi. 2021. Overview of the 8th workshop on Asian translation. In *Proceedings of the 8th Workshop on Asian Translation*, Bangkok, Thailand. Association for Computational Linguistics.

Kishore Papineni, Salim Roukos, Todd Ward, and Wei-Jing Zhu. 2002. Bleu: A method for automatic evaluation of machine translation. In *Proceedings of the 40th Annual Meeting on Association for Computational Linguistics*, ACL '02, pages 311–318, Stroudsburg, PA, USA. Association for Computational Linguistics.

Shantipriya Parida, Ondřej Bojar, and Satya Ranjan Dash. 2019. Hindi Visual Genome: A Dataset for Multimodal English-to-Hindi Machine Translation. *Computación y Sistemas*, 23(4):1499–1505.

Amarnath Pathak and Partha Pakray. 2018. Neural machine translation for indian languages. *Journal of Intelligent Systems*, pages 1–13.

Amarnath Pathak, Partha Pakray, and Jereemi Bentham. 2018. English–mizo machine translation using neural and statistical approaches. *Neural Computing and Applications*, 30:1–17.

Jeffrey Pennington, Richard Socher, and Christopher Manning. 2014. GloVe: Global vectors for word representation. In *Proceedings of the 2014 Conference on Empirical Methods in Natural Language Processing (EMNLP)*, pages 1532–1543, Doha, Qatar. Association for Computational Linguistics.

Loitongbam Sanayai Meetei, Thoudam Doren Singh, and Sivaji Bandyopadhyay. 2019. WAT2019: English-Hindi translation on Hindi visual genome dataset. In *Proceedings of the 6th Workshop on Asian Translation*, pages 181–188, Hong Kong, China. Association for Computational Linguistics.

Sukanta Sen, Mohammed Hasanuzzaman, Asif Ekbal, Pushpak Bhattacharyya, and Andy Way. 2020. Neural machine translation of low-resource languages using smt phrase pair injection. *Natural Language Engineering*, page 1–22.

Rico Sennrich, Barry Haddow, and Alexandra Birch. 2016. Improving neural machine translation models with monolingual data. In *Proceedings of the 54th Annual Meeting of the Association for Computational Linguistics (Volume 1: Long Papers)*, pages 86–96, Berlin, Germany. Association for Computational Linguistics.

Kashif Shah, Josiah Wang, and Lucia Specia. 2016. SHEF-multimodal: Grounding machine translation on images. In *Proceedings of the First Conference on Machine Translation: Volume 2, Shared Task Papers*, pages 660–665, Berlin, Germany. Association for Computational Linguistics.

Ilya Sutskever, Oriol Vinyals, and Quoc V. Le. 2014. Sequence to sequence learning with neural networks. In *Proceedings of the 27th International Conference on Neural Information Processing Systems - Volume 2*, NIPS'14, pages 3104–3112, Cambridge, MA, USA. MIT Press.

Jiajun Zhang and Chengqing Zong. 2016. Exploiting source-side monolingual data in neural machine translation. In *Proceedings of the 2016 Conference on Empirical Methods in Natural Language Processing*, pages 1535–1545, Austin, Texas. Association for Computational Linguistics.

# IITP at WAT 2021: System description for English-Hindi Multimodal Translation Task

**Baban Gain***
Indian Institute of Technology Patna
Patna, India
gainbaban@gmail.com

**Dibyanayan Bandyopadhyay***
Indian Institute of Technology Patna
Patna, India
dibyanayan@gmail.com

**Asif Ekbal**
Indian Institute of Technology Patna
Patna, India
asif@iitp.ac.in

## Abstract

Neural Machine Translation (NMT) is a predominant machine translation technology nowadays because of its end-to-end trainable flexibility. However, NMT still struggles to translate properly in low-resource settings specifically on distant language pairs. One way to overcome this is to use the information from other modalities if available. The idea is that despite differences in languages, both the source and target language speakers see the same thing and the visual representation of both the source and target is the same, which can positively assist the system. Multimodal information can help the NMT system to improve the translation by removing ambiguity on some phrases or words. We participate in the 8th Workshop on Asian Translation (WAT - 2021) for English-Hindi multimodal translation task and achieve 42.47 and 37.50 BLEU points for Evaluation and Challenge subset, respectively.

## 1 Introduction

Recent progress in neural machine translation (NMT) focuses on translating a source language into a particular target language. Various methods have been proposed for this task and most of them deal with the textual data. There are certain drawbacks while performing machine translation using only textual datasets.

Human performs translation which is based upon language grounding: our sense of meaning emerges from interacting with the world. NMT methods do not have any mechanism to perform language grounding; thus they are devoid of capturing the true meaning of sentences or phrases while translating them into the other languages. For example, it needs to translate the word "cricket", it can get confused if it is the game cricket or the insect cricket. But the visual information can clear the ambiguity. Multi-modal translation aims to alleviate this issue by training an NMT model on textual data along with associated images to perform language grounding.

This shared task deals with developing multi-modal NMT models for English-Hindi translation. The choice of languages depends on the following issues: *i).* Hindi is the most spoken language in India and the fourth most spoken language in the world with 600 million speakers[1]. Despite the huge amount of speakers, suitable resources in Hindi is limited due to the various factors. *ii)* Automatic translation of texts from one language to the another is a difficult task. Specifically, when one or both of them are resource-poor and distant from each other.

In Multimodal NMT (MNMT), information from the other modalities like audio, image, video, etc. are used along with text to generate the translation. In low-resource languages, this is particularly used to improve the low-quality translations as even though vocabularies, grammar of two languages are different but their visual representation is the same. There are several proposed multi-modal methods for translations that exploit the features of the associated image for better translation. State-of-the-art methods might achieve better accuracy than the models we used. Our main motivation for using simplistic models is to demonstrate a proof-of-concept to be used for multi-modal translation among the resource-poor language pairs. We achieved good results on both Challenge and Evaluation set in different evaluation metrics including BLEU, RIBES, AMFM. In subsequent modifications, we aim to develop our models incorporating

*Equal contribution

[1] https://www.ethnologue.com/guides/ethnologue200



*Proceedings of the 8th Workshop on Asian Translation*, pages 161–165
Bangkok, Thailand (online), August 5-6, 2021. 

several state-of-the-art features. The following sections describe our processes in greater details.

## 2 Related Works

There have been many attempts to use information other than the source for better translation. Uni-modal systems include document-level NMT (Wang et al., 2017), sentence-level NMT with contextual information (Gain et al., 2021), etc. Among multimodal systems, (Huang et al., 2016) used an object detection system and extracted local and global image features. Thereafter, they used those image features as additional inputs to encoder and decoder. (Delbrouck and Dupont, 2017) used attention mechanism on visual inputs for the source hidden states. (Lin et al., 2020) used Dynamic Context-guided Capsule Network (Sabour et al., 2017) (DCCN) for iterative extraction of related visual features.

Multimodal Machine Translation (MMT) for English-Hindi has not been well explored yet. (Dutta Chowdhury et al., 2018) used synthetic data for training. Furthermore they used multi-modal, attention-based MMT which incorporate visual features into different parts of both the encoder and the decoder (Calixto and Liu, 2017). (Sanayai Meetei et al., 2019) used a Recurrent Neural Network (RNN) based approach achieving BLEU score of 28.45 on Evaluation set and 12.58 on Challenge set. (Laskar et al., 2020) exploited monolingual data for better translation. Recent works tried to focus on developing unsupervised model for multi-modal NMT. Su et al. (2018) demonstrated an unsupervised method based on the language translation cycle consistency loss conditional on the image. This is done to learn the bidirectional multi-modal translation simultaneously. Moreover, Su et al. (2021) showed that jointly learning text-image interaction instead of modeling them separately using attentional networks is more useful. This result is in line with several state-of-the-art visual transformer related models, such as VisualBERT (Li et al., 2019), UNITER (Chen et al., 2019) etc.

## 3 Methodology

### 3.1 Dataset Description

We use Hindi Visual Genome 1.1 dataset (Parida et al., 2019)(Nakazawa et al., 2020)(Nakazawa et al., 2021) for our experiments. This dataset consists of 28,929 parallel English-Hindi sentence pairs along with the associated images. Furthermore, we use HindEnCorp dataset for pre-training containing 273K English-Hindi sentence pairs without images. Statistics of the datasets are shown in Table 1.

Figure 1: An example of multimodal dataset

Multimodal dataset consists of an image along with a description of certain rectangular portion of the image. We are given the coordinates of the portion. We aim to translate the description with help of the image. An example of multimodal dataset is given in Figure 1.

### 3.2 Pre-processing

For text data, we lowercase all the utterances. Then, we jointly learn byte-pair-encoding (Sennrich et al., 2016) combining both source and target with a vocabulary of 10,000. We treat the images by cropping a specified rectangular portions. This operation is used to discard the portions that do not contribute much to the translation performance. After we get those cropped-out images, we use the pre-trained VGG19-bn (Simonyan and Zisserman, 2015) to obtain the image representations. We use OpenNMT-py (Klein et al., 2017) framework to perform this step.

### 3.3 Training

We use OpenNMT-py (Klein et al., 2017) for our NMT systems. We use Bidirectional RNN encoder and doubly attentive RNN decoder (Calixto et al., 2017) for our experiments. We train our system in two ways *viz.* With pre-training, and Without pre-training.:

1. **With pre-training** We pre-train one of our models on HindEnCorp dataset. This step does not use any visual features as the dataset used for pre-training is devoid of any visual

| Dataset | Type | Sentences | Avg length source | Avg length target |
|---|---|---|---|---|
| Pre-training | Parallel | 273,885 | 12.33 | 13.36 |
| Train | parallel + multimodal | 28929 | 4.95 | 5.02 |
| Valid | parallel + multimodal | 998 | 4.93 | 4.99 |
| Evaluation | parallel + multimodal | 1595 | 4.92 | 4.92 |
| Challenge | parallel + multimodal | 1400 | 5.85 | 6.17 |

Table 1: Descriptions of datasets used for our experiments

Figure 2: An example of translation generated by the system. Here, the target is *Ek vyakti railgari mein chad raha hai (A man climbing into train.)* The translation by Google NMT system is *Train mein chadta Aadmi (Man climbs into train)*; whereas our NMT system translates it as: *Ek aadmi ek train mein chadta hai (A man climbs into a train.)*

features. After pre-training, we fine-tune the pre-trained model with VisualGenome dataset containing textual and visual features.

2. **Without pre-training** We do not pre-train the model. We directly fine-tune the models on VisualGenome dataset which contains both text and associated image. Consequently, both textual and visual features are used.

Following step is taken into account while doing inference step:
We take the best hypothesis from both the models and filter out any hypothesis containing <unk>token. Then, we pick the hypothesis with best log-likelihood during generation.

### 3.4 Hyper-parameters

We set the word embedding size and size of RNN hidden states to 500. We set the batch size to 40 and train for a maximum 25 epochs. We restrict maximum source and target sequence length to 50. We use the Adam optimizer (Kingma and Ba, 2017) for optimization with $\beta_1 = 0.9$ and $\beta_2 = 0.999$. During training, we use 0.3 as dropout rate to avoid over-fitting. During generation of translation, we use 5 as the beam width.

## 4 Experimental Results

We obtain impressive results on our submissions. There are two sets designed for evaluating our model, *i) Evaluation set*, *ii) Challenge set*. We evaluate our model on both of these test set and tabulate our results in Table 2. We use different evaluation metrics (BLEU, RIBES, AMFM) to test our model. The results shown in the table are sorted according to the obtained BLEU scores. As it can be seen from Table 2, we obtain 42.47 BLEU points and achieve second position in terms of BLEU on Evaluation set on multimodal task. Please refer to Figure 2 for example of translation by our system. We obtain 37.50 BLEU points on Challenge set. One reason for not so good results on Challenge set could be:

- The challenge test set was created by searching for (particularly) ambiguous English words based on the embedding similarity and manually selecting those where the image helps to resolve the ambiguity. Hence, it is difficult to translate compared to the Evaluation set, which was randomly selected.

- Difference between utterance length during training and testing, i.e. while average length

| Team | *Evaluation* | | | *Challenge* | | |
|---|---|---|---|---|---|---|
| | BLEU | RIBES | AMFM | BLEU | RIBES | AMFM |
| Volta | 44.21 | 0.818689 | 0.835480 | 52.02 | 0.854139 | 0.874220 |
| iitp (Ours) | 42.47 | 0.807123 | 0.819720 | 37.50 | 0.790809 | 0.830230 |
| CNLP-NITS | 40.51 | 0.803208 | 0.820980 | 39.28 | 0.792097 | 0.812360 |
| CNLP-NITS | 39.46 | 0.802055 | 0.823270 | 33.57 | 0.754141 | 0.787320 |
| Organizer | 38.63 | 0.767422 | 0.772870 | 20.34 | 0.644230 | 0.669760 |

Table 2: Details of obtained results by different submissions

of Train, Evaluation and Validation set is 5 but average length of Challenge set is 6.

## 5 Conclusion

We participate in WAT-2021 Multimodal Translation Task for English to Hindi. We achieve good results on both the Challenge and Evaluation sets achieving 42.47 and 37.50 BLEU points, respectively. We rank second place on Evaluation set and third place on Challenge set on WAT-2021 Multimodal Translation Task for English to Hindi. In future, we would like to extend our work by training with additional monolingual data and better ways to incorporate multimodal features.

## References


Iacer Calixto and Qun Liu. 2017. Incorporating global visual features into attention-based neural machine translation. In *Proceedings of the 2017 Conference on Empirical Methods in Natural Language Processing*, pages 992–1003, Copenhagen, Denmark. Association for Computational Linguistics.

Iacer Calixto, Qun Liu, and Nick Campbell. 2017. Doubly-attentive decoder for multi-modal neural machine translation. In *Proceedings of the 55th Annual Meeting of the Association for Computational Linguistics (Volume 1: Long Papers)*, pages 1913–1924, Vancouver, Canada. Association for Computational Linguistics.

Yen-Chun Chen, Linjie Li, Licheng Yu, Ahmed El Kholy, Faisal Ahmed, Zhe Gan, Yu Cheng, and Jingjing Liu. 2019. UNITER: learning universal image-text representations. *CoRR*, abs/1909.11740.

Jean-Benoit Delbrouck and Stéphane Dupont. 2017. Modulating and attending the source image during encoding improves multimodal translation.

Koel Dutta Chowdhury, Mohammed Hasanuzzaman, and Qun Liu. 2018. Multimodal neural machine translation for low-resource language pairs using synthetic data. In *Proceedings of the Workshop on Deep Learning Approaches for Low-Resource NLP*, pages 33–42, Melbourne. Association for Computational Linguistics.

Baban Gain, Rejwanul Haque, and Asif Ekbal. 2021. Not all contexts are important: The impact of effective context in conversational neural machine translation. In *2021 International Joint Conference on Neural Networks (IJCNN)*.

Po-Yao Huang, Frederick Liu, Sz-Rung Shiang, Jean Oh, and Chris Dyer. 2016. Attention-based multimodal neural machine translation. In *Proceedings of the First Conference on Machine Translation: Volume 2, Shared Task Papers*, pages 639–645, Berlin, Germany. Association for Computational Linguistics.

Diederik P. Kingma and Jimmy Ba. 2017. Adam: A method for stochastic optimization.

Guillaume Klein, Yoon Kim, Yuntian Deng, Jean Senellart, and Alexander Rush. 2017. OpenNMT: Open-source toolkit for neural machine translation. In *Proceedings of ACL 2017, System Demonstrations*, pages 67–72, Vancouver, Canada. Association for Computational Linguistics.

Sahinur Rahman Laskar, Abdullah Faiz Ur Rahman Khilji, Partha Pakray, and Sivaji Bandyopadhyay. 2020. Multimodal neural machine translation for English to Hindi. In *Proceedings of the 7th Workshop on Asian Translation*, pages 109–113, Suzhou, China. Association for Computational Linguistics.

Liunian Harold Li, Mark Yatskar, Da Yin, Cho-Jui Hsieh, and Kai-Wei Chang. 2019. Visualbert: A simple and performant baseline for vision and language. *CoRR*, abs/1908.03557.

Huan Lin, Fandong Meng, Jinsong Su, Yongjing Yin, Zhengyuan Yang, Yubin Ge, Jie Zhou, and Jiebo Luo. 2020. Dynamic context-guided capsule network for multimodal machine translation. *Proceedings of the 28th ACM International Conference on Multimedia*.

Toshiaki Nakazawa, Hideki Nakayama, Chenchen Ding, Raj Dabre, Shohei Higashiyama, Hideya Mino, Isao Goto, Win Pa Pa, Anoop Kunchukuttan, Shantipriya Parida, Ondřej Bojar, Chenhui

Chu, Akiko Eriguchi, Kaori Abe, and Sadao Oda, Yusuke Kurohashi. 2021. Overview of the 8th workshop on Asian translation. In *Proceedings of the 8th Workshop on Asian Translation*, Bangkok, Thailand. Association for Computational Linguistics.

Toshiaki Nakazawa, Hideki Nakayama, Chenchen Ding, Raj Dabre, Shohei Higashiyama, Hideya Mino, Isao Goto, Win Pa Pa, Anoop Kunchukuttan, Shantipriya Parida, Ondřej Bojar, and Sadao Kurohashi. 2020. Overview of the 7th workshop on Asian translation. In *Proceedings of the 7th Workshop on Asian Translation*, pages 1–44, Suzhou, China. Association for Computational Linguistics.

Shantipriya Parida, Ondřej Bojar, and Satya Ranjan Dash. 2019. Hindi Visual Genome: A Dataset for Multimodal English-to-Hindi Machine Translation. *Computación y Sistemas*, 23(4):1499–1505. Presented at CICLing 2019, La Rochelle, France.

Sara Sabour, Nicholas Frosst, and Geoffrey E Hinton. 2017. Dynamic routing between capsules.

Loitongbam Sanayai Meetei, Thoudam Doren Singh, and Sivaji Bandyopadhyay. 2019. WAT2019: English-Hindi translation on Hindi visual genome dataset. In *Proceedings of the 6th Workshop on Asian Translation*, pages 181–188, Hong Kong, China. Association for Computational Linguistics.

Rico Sennrich, Barry Haddow, and Alexandra Birch. 2016. Neural machine translation of rare words with subword units. In *Proceedings of the 54th Annual Meeting of the Association for Computational Linguistics (Volume 1: Long Papers)*, pages 1715–1725, Berlin, Germany. Association for Computational Linguistics.

Karen Simonyan and Andrew Zisserman. 2015. Very deep convolutional networks for large-scale image recognition.

Jinsong Su, Jinchang Chen, Hui Jiang, Chulun Zhou, Huan Lin, Yubin Ge, Qingqiang Wu, and Yongxuan Lai. 2021. Multi-modal neural machine translation with deep semantic interactions. *Information Sciences*, 554:47–60.

Yuanhang Su, Kai Fan, Nguyen Bach, C.-C. Jay Kuo, and Fei Huang. 2018. Unsupervised multi-modal neural machine translation. *CoRR*, abs/1811.11365.

Longyue Wang, Zhaopeng Tu, Andy Way, and Qun Liu. 2017. Exploiting cross-sentence context for neural machine translation. In *Proceedings of the 2017 Conference on Empirical Methods in Natural Language Processing*, pages 2826–2831, Copenhagen, Denmark. Association for Computational Linguistics.

# ViTA: Visual-Linguistic Translation by Aligning Object Tags

**Kshitij Gupta** **Devansh Gautam** **Radhika Mamidi**
International Institute of Information Technology Hyderabad
{kshitij.gupta,devansh.gautam}@research.iiit.ac.in,
radhika.mamidi@iiit.ac.in

## Abstract

Multimodal Machine Translation (MMT) enriches the source text with visual information for translation. It has gained popularity in recent years, and several pipelines have been proposed in the same direction. Yet, the task lacks quality datasets to illustrate the contribution of visual modality in the translation systems. In this paper, we propose our system under the team name *Volta* for the Multimodal Translation Task of WAT 2021[1] (Nakazawa et al., 2021) from English to Hindi. We also participate in the textual-only subtask of the same language pair for which we use mBART, a pretrained multilingual sequence-to-sequence model. For multimodal translation, we propose to enhance the textual input by bringing the visual information to a textual domain by extracting object tags from the image. We also explore the robustness of our system by systematically degrading the source text. Finally, we achieve a BLEU score of 44.6 and 51.6 on the test set and challenge set of the multimodal task.

## 1 Introduction

Machine Translation deals with the task of translation between language pairs and has been an active area of research in the current stage of globalization. In the task of multimodal machine translation, the problem is further extended to incorporate visual modality in the translations. The visual cues help build a better context for the source text and are expected to help in cases of ambiguity.

With the help of visual grounding, the machine translation system has scope for becoming more robust by mitigating noise from the source text and relying on the visual modality as well.

In the current landscape of multimodal translation, one of the issues is the limited datasets available for the task. Another contributing factor is that often the images add irrelevant information to the sentences, which may act as noise instead of an added feature. The available datasets, like Multi30K (Elliott et al., 2016), are relatively smaller when compared to large-scale text-only datasets (Bahdanau et al., 2015). The scarcity of such datasets hinders building robust systems for multimodal translation.

To address these issues, we propose to bring the visual information to a textual domain and fine-tune a high resource unimodal translation system to incorporate the added information in the input. We add the visual information by extracting the object classes by using an object detector and add them as tags to the source text. Further, we use mBART, a pretrained multilingual sequence-to-sequence model, as the base architecture for our translation system. We fine-tune the model on a textual-only dataset released by Kunchukuttan et al. (2018) consisting of 1,609,682 parallel sentences in English and Hindi. Further, we fine-tune it on the training set enriched with the object tags extracted from the images. We achieve state-of-the-art performance on the given dataset. The code for our proposed system is available at `https://github.com/kshitij98/vita`.

The main contributions of our work are as follows:

- We explore the effectiveness of fine-tuning mBART to translate English sentences to Hindi in the text-only domain.
- We further propose a multimodal system for translation by enriching the input with the object tags extracted from the images using an object detector.
- We explore the robustness of our system by a thorough analysis of the proposed pipelines

[1] `http://lotus.kuee.kyoto-u.ac.jp/WAT/evaluation/index.html`



*Proceedings of the 8th Workshop on Asian Translation*, pages 166–173
Bangkok, Thailand (online), August 5-6, 2021. ©2021 Association for Computational Linguistics

by systematically degrading the source text and finally give a direction for future work.

The rest of the paper is organized as follows. We discuss prior work related to multimodal translation. We describe our systems for the textual-only and multimodal translation tasks. Further, we report and compare the performance of our models with other systems from the leaderboard. Lastly, we conduct a thorough error analysis of our systems and conclude with a direction for future work.

## 2 Related Work

Earlier works in the field of machine translation largely used statistical or rule-based approaches, while neural machine translation has gained popularity in the recent past. Kalchbrenner and Blunsom (2013) released the first deep learning model in this direction, and later works utilize transformer-based approaches (Vaswani et al., 2017; Song et al., 2019; Conneau and Lample, 2019; Edunov et al., 2019; Liu et al., 2020) for the problem.

Multimodal translation aims to use the visual modality with the source text to help create a better context of the source text. Specia et al. (2016) first conducted a shared task on the problem and released the dataset, Multi30K (Elliott et al., 2016). It is an extended German version of Flickr30K (Young et al., 2014), which was further extended to French and Czech (Elliott et al., 2017; Barrault et al., 2018). For multimodal translation between English and Hindi, Parida et al. (2019) propose a subset of Visual Genome dataset (Krishna et al., 2017) and provide parallel sentences for each of the captions.

Although both English and Hindi are spoken by a large number of people around the world, there has been limited research in this direction. Dutta Chowdhury et al. (2018) created a synthetic dataset for multimodal translation of the language pair and further used the system proposed by Calixto and Liu (2017). Later, Sanayai Meetei et al. (2019) work with the same architecture on the multimodal translation task in WAT 2019. Laskar et al. (2019) used a doubly attentive RNN-based encoder and decoder architecture (Calixto and Liu, 2017; Calixto et al., 2017). Laskar et al. (2020) also proposed a similar architecture and pretrained on a large textual parallel dataset (Kunchukuttan et al., 2018) in their system.

| | Train | Valid | Test | Challenge |
|---|---|---|---|---|
| #sentence pairs | 28,930 | 998 | 1,595 | 1,400 |
| Avg. #tokens (source) | 4.95 | 4.93 | 4.92 | 5.85 |
| Avg. #tokens (target) | 5.03 | 4.99 | 4.92 | 6.17 |

Table 1: The statistics of the provided dataset. The average number of tokens in the source and target language are reported for all the sentence pairs.

## 3 System Overview

In this section, we describe the systems we use for the task.

### 3.1 Dataset Description

We use the dataset provided by the shared task organizers (Parida et al., 2019), which consists of images and their associated English captions from Visual Genome (Krishna et al., 2017) along with the Hindi translations of the captions. The dataset also provides a challenge test which consists of sentences where there are ambiguous English words, and the image can help in resolving the ambiguity. The statistics of the dataset are shown in Table 1. We use the provided dataset splits for training our models.

We also use the dataset released by Kunchukuttan et al. (2018) which consists of parallel sentences in English and Hindi. We use the training set, which contains 1,609,682 sentences, for training our systems.

### 3.2 Model

We fine-tune mBART, which is a multilingual sequence-to-sequence denoising auto-encoder that has been pre-trained using the BART (Lewis et al., 2020) objective on large-scale monolingual corpora of 25 languages, including both English and Hindi. The pre-training corpus consists of 55,608 million English tokens (300.8 GB) and 1,715 million Hindi tokens (20.2 GB). Its architecture is a standard sequence-to-sequence Transformer (Vaswani et al., 2017), with 12 encoder and decoder layers each and a model dimension of 1024 on 16 heads resulting in ~680 million parameters. To train our systems efficiently, we prune mBART's vocabulary by removing the tokens which are not present in the provided dataset or the dataset released by Kunchukuttan et al. (2018).

#### 3.2.1 mBART

We fine-tune mBART for text-only translation from English to Hindi and feed the English sentences

| Model | Test Set | | | Challenge Set | | |
|---|---|---|---|---|---|---|
| | BLEU | RIBES | AMFM | BLEU | RIBES | AMFM |
| *Text-only Translation* | | | | | | |
| CNLP-NITS-PP | 37.01 | 0.80 | 0.81 | 37.16 | 0.77 | 0.80 |
| ODIANLP | 40.85 | 0.79 | 0.81 | 38.50 | 0.78 | 0.80 |
| NLPHut | 42.11 | 0.81 | 0.82 | 43.29 | 0.82 | 0.83 |
| mBART (ours) | **44.12** | **0.82** | **0.84** | **51.66** | **0.86** | **0.88** |
| *Multimodal Translation* | | | | | | |
| CNLP-NITS | 40.51 | 0.80 | 0.82 | 33.57 | 0.75 | 0.79 |
| iitp | 42.47 | 0.81 | 0.82 | 37.50 | 0.79 | 0.81 |
| CNLP-NITS-PP | 39.46 | 0.80 | 0.82 | 39.28 | 0.79 | 0.83 |
| ViTA (ours) | **44.64** | **0.82** | **0.84** | **51.60** | **0.86** | **0.88** |

Table 2: Performance of our proposed systems on the test and challenge set.

to the encoder and decode Hindi sentences. We first fine-tune the model on the dataset released by Kunchukuttan et al. (2018) for 30 epochs, and then fine-tune it on the Hindi Visual Genome dataset for 30 epochs.

#### 3.2.2 ViTA

We again fine-tune mBART for multimodal translation from English to Hindi but add the visual information of the image to the text by adding the list of object tags detected from the image. We feed the English sentences along with the list of object tags to the encoder and decode Hindi sentences. For feeding the data to the encoder, we concatenate the English sentence, followed by a separator token '##', followed by the object tags which are separated by ','. We use Faster R-CNN with ResNet-101-C4 backbone[2] (Ren et al., 2015) to detect the list of objects present in the image. We sort the objects by their confidence scores and choose the top ten objects.

For training the model, we first fine-tune the model on the dataset released by Kunchukuttan et al. (2018). Since this is a text-only dataset, we do not add any object tag information. Afterward, we fine-tune the model on Hindi Visual Genome dataset, where each sentence has been concatenated with object tags. Initially, we mask $\sim$15% of the tokens in each sentence to incentivize the model to use the object tags along with the text and fine-tune the model on masked sentences along with object tags for 30 epochs. Finally, we train the model for 30 more epochs on Hindi Visual Genome dataset with unmasked sentences and object tags.

### 3.3 Experimental Setup

We implement our systems using the implementation of mBART available in the fairseq library[3] (Ott et al., 2019). We fine-tune on 4 Nvidia GeForce RTX 2080 Ti GPUs with an effective batch size of 1024 tokens per GPU. We use the Adam optimizer ($\epsilon = 10^{-6}, \beta_1 = 0.9, \beta_2 = 0.98$) (Kingma and Ba, 2015) with 0.1 attention dropout, 0.3 dropout, 0.2 label smoothing and polynomial decay learning rate scheduling. We validate the models every epoch and select the best checkpoint after each training based on the best validation BLEU score. To train our systems efficiently, we prune the vocabulary of our model by removing the tokens which do not appear in any of the datasets mentioned in the previous section. While decoding, we use beam search with a beam size of 5.

## 4 Results and Discussion

The BLEU score (Papineni et al., 2002) is the official metric for evaluating the performance of the models in the leaderboard. The leaderboard further uses RIBES (Isozaki et al., 2010) and AMFM (Banchs and Li, 2011) metrics for the evaluations. We report the performance of our models after tokenizing the Hindi outputs using `indic-tokenizer`[4] in Table 2.

It can be seen that our model is able to generalize well on the challenge set as well and performs better than other systems by a large margin. To

[2] We use the implementation available in Detectron2 (https://github.com/facebookresearch/detectron2).

[3] https://github.com/pytorch/fairseq

[4] https://github.com/ltrc/indic-tokenizer

| | |
|---|---|
| **English Sentence** | A large pipe extending from the wall of the court. |
| **Hindi Translation** | कोर्ट की दीवार से निक्ली हुई एक बड़ी पाइप |
| **Object Tags** | building, man, flowers, shorts, racket, hat, court, shoe, shirt, window |
| **mBART output** | अदालत की दीवार से विस्तारित एक बड़ा पाइप |
| **ViTA output** | कोर्ट की दीवार से विस्तारित एक बड़ा पाइप |

Figure 1: A translation example from the challenge set which illustrates the advantage of using ViTA to resolve ambiguities. mBART is translating the word court to judicial court, while ViTA translates it to tennis court.

| | |
|---|---|
| **English Sentence** | A person riding a motorcycle. |
| **Masked Sentence** | A <mask> riding a <mask>. |
| **Object Tags** | helmet, building, sign, man, shirt, bike, flowers, barrier, tree, wheel |
| **mBART output** | एक आदमी घोड़े की सवारी करता है |
| **ViTA output** | एक आदमी एक बाइक की सवारी कर रहा है |

Figure 2: The effect of object tags on an entity masked input from the test set. ViTA is able to use the context built from the object tags to predict a motorcycle, while mBART is predicting a horse instead.

| | Train | Valid | Test | Challenge |
|---|---|---|---|---|
| #entities in text | 29,583 | 1,028 | 1,631 | 1,592 |
| #objects tags in images | 253,051 | 8,679 | 13,855 | 12,507 |
| #entities in object tags | 13,959 | 498 | 758 | 442 |
| %entities in object tags | 47.18% | 48.44% | 46.47% | 27.76% |

Table 3: We show the overlap between the entities in the text and the object tags detected using Faster R-CNN model. The entities were identified using the `en_core_web_sm` model from the spaCy library[5].

| | No masking | Entity Masking | Degradation % |
|---|---|---|---|
| mBART | 44.2 | 15.1 | 65.8 |
| ViTA | **44.6** | 22.5 | 49.6 |
| ViTA-gt | 43.6 | **25.4** | **41.7** |

Table 4: The effect of entity masking on the BLEU score of the proposed models on the test set.

further analyze the results, we find a few cases in the challenge set wherein ViTA is able to resolve ambiguities, and an example is illustrated in Figure 1. Yet, the performance of the models is very similar across the textual-only and multimodal domains, and there are no significant improvements observed in the multimodal system.

### 4.1 Degradation

Although there is no significant improvement in the multimodal systems over the textual-only models, Caglayan et al. (2019) explore the robustness of multimodal systems by systematically degrading the source text for translations. We employ a similar approach and degrade the source text to compare our systems.

#### 4.1.1 Entity masking

The goal of entity masking is to mask out the visually depictable entities in the source text so that the multimodal systems can make use of the visual cues in the image. To identify such entities, we use the `en_core_web_sm` model in spaCy[5] to predict the nouns in the sentence. The statistics of the tagged entities can be seen in Table 3.

We progressively increase the percentage of masked entities to better compare the degradation of our systems and it can be seen in Figure 3a. The final degraded values are reported in Table 4. Since the masked entities can also be predicted by using only the textual context of the sentence, we similarly add a training step of masking ~15% tokens while training mBART for a valid comparison. An example of the performance of our systems on an entity masked input is illustrated in Figure 2.

As an upper bound to the scope of our system, we propose `ViTA-gt`, which uses the ground-truth object labels from the Visual Genome dataset. Since the number of annotated objects is large, we filter them by removing the objects far from the image region.

[5] `https://spacy.io/`

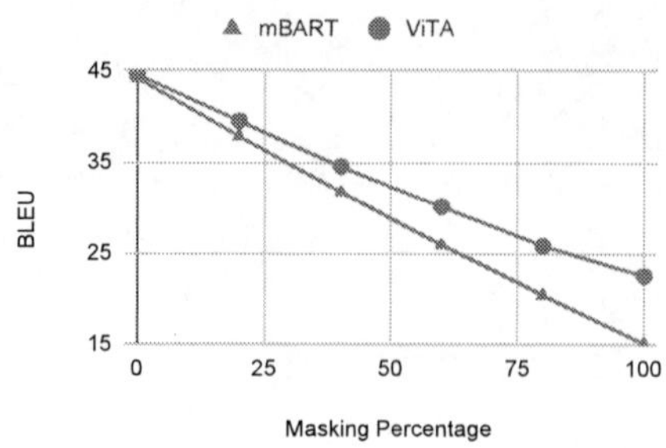


(a) Entity Masking

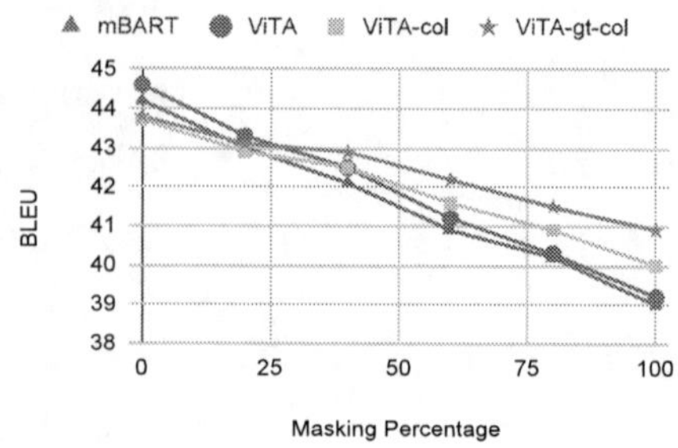


(b) Color Deprivation

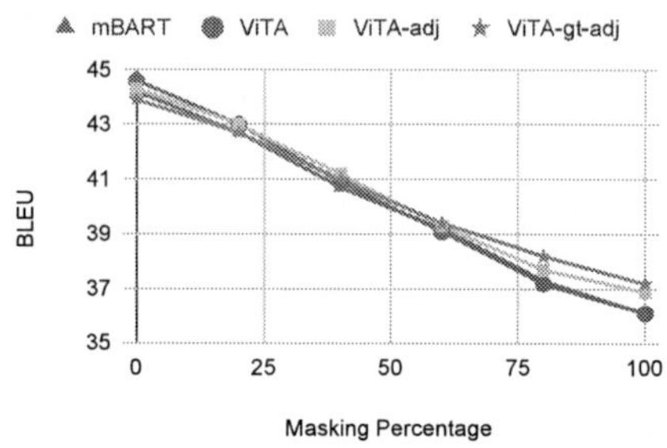


(c) Adjective Masking

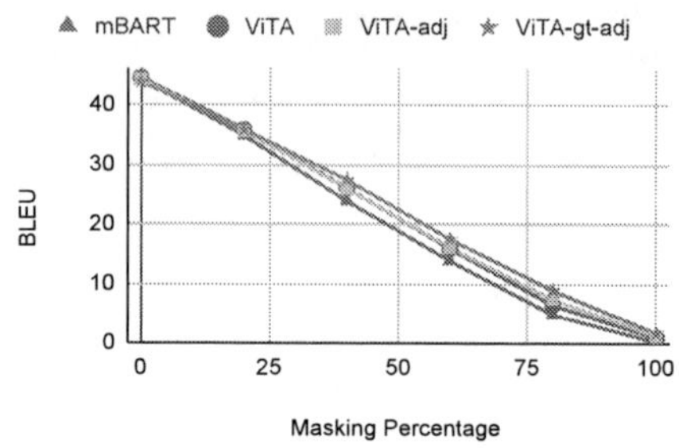


(d) Random Masking

Figure 3: BLEU score comparison of the proposed models by increasing the masking percentage in the source text.

| | No masking | Color Deprivation | Degradation % |
|---|---|---|---|
| mBART | 44.2 | 39.0 | 11.8 |
| ViTA | **44.6** | 39.2 | 12.1 |
| ViTA-col | 43.7 | 40.0 | 8.5 |
| ViTA-gt-col | 43.8 | **40.9** | **6.6** |

Table 5: The effect of color deprivation on the BLEU score of the proposed models on the test set.

| | No masking | Adjective Masking | Degradation % |
|---|---|---|---|
| mBART | 44.2 | 36.1 | 18.3 |
| ViTA | **44.6** | 36.1 | 19.1 |
| ViTA-adj | 44.3 | 36.9 | 16.7 |
| ViTA-gt-adj | 43.9 | **37.2** | **15.3** |

Table 6: The effect of adjective masking on the BLEU score of the proposed models on the test set.

### 4.1.2 Color deprivation

The goal of color deprivation is to similarly mask tokens that are difficult to predict without the visual context of the image. To identify the colors in the source text, we maintain a list of colors and check whether the words in the sentence are present in the list. Similar to entity masking, we progressively increase the percentage of masked colors in the dataset to compare our systems. The comparison of our systems can be seen in Figure 3b. The final values of color deprivation are reported in Table 5.

As an upper bound to the scope of our system, we believe that colors can further be added to the object tags to help build a more robust system. As an added experiment, we propose `ViTA-col` by using the ground-truth annotations from the Visual Genome dataset and adding colors to our predicted object tags, which are present in the ground-truth objects as well. As a part of future work, we would like to extend our system to predict the colors from the image itself. We further experiment with `ViTA-gt-col`, which uses ground-truth objects with added colors in the input.

### 4.1.3 Adjective Masking

Similar to color deprivation, we propose adjective masking as several of the adjectives are visually depictable, and the degradation comparison should not be limited to just entities and colors. We predict the adjectives in the sentence by using the POS tagging model `en_core_web_sm` from spaCy library.

The performance of our models is compared in Figure 3c. The final values are reported in Table 6.

As an upper bound to the scope of our system, we propose to add all the adjectives to their corresponding object tags in the input. We propose

`ViTA-adj` by adding the ground truth adjectives annotated in the Visual Genome dataset to the object tags which are also predicted by our object detector. We also propose `ViTA-gt-adj`, which uses the ground-truth objects with their corresponding adjectives. The objects which are from the image region are removed to mitigate the noise added by the large number of objects in the annotations.

#### 4.1.4 Random Masking

For a general robustness comparison of our models, we remove the limitation of manually masking the source sentences and progressively mask the text by random sampling.

The performance of our models is compared in Figure 3d.

## 5 Conclusion

We propose a multimodal translation system and utilize the textual-only pre-training of a neural machine translation system, mBART, by extracting object tags from the image. Further, we explore the robustness of our proposed multimodal system by systematically degrading the source texts and observe improvements from the textual-only counterpart. We also explore the shortcomings of the currently available object detectors and use ground-truth annotations in our experiments to show the scope of our methodology. The addition of colors and adjectives further adds to the robustness of the system and can be explored further in the future.

## References


Dzmitry Bahdanau, Kyunghyun Cho, and Yoshua Bengio. 2015. Neural machine translation by jointly learning to align and translate. In *3rd International Conference on Learning Representations, ICLR 2015, San Diego, CA, USA, May 7-9, 2015, Conference Track Proceedings*.

Rafael E. Banchs and Haizhou Li. 2011. AM-FM: A semantic framework for translation quality assessment. In *Proceedings of the 49th Annual Meeting of the Association for Computational Linguistics: Human Language Technologies*, pages 153–158, Portland, Oregon, USA. Association for Computational Linguistics.

Loïc Barrault, Fethi Bougares, Lucia Specia, Chiraag Lala, Desmond Elliott, and Stella Frank. 2018. Findings of the third shared task on multimodal machine translation. In *Proceedings of the Third Conference on Machine Translation: Shared Task Papers*, pages 304–323, Belgium, Brussels. Association for Computational Linguistics.

Ozan Caglayan, Pranava Madhyastha, Lucia Specia, and Loïc Barrault. 2019. Probing the need for visual context in multimodal machine translation. In *Proceedings of the 2019 Conference of the North American Chapter of the Association for Computational Linguistics: Human Language Technologies, Volume 1 (Long and Short Papers)*, pages 4159–4170, Minneapolis, Minnesota. Association for Computational Linguistics.

Iacer Calixto and Qun Liu. 2017. Incorporating global visual features into attention-based neural machine translation. In *Proceedings of the 2017 Conference on Empirical Methods in Natural Language Processing*, pages 992–1003, Copenhagen, Denmark. Association for Computational Linguistics.

Iacer Calixto, Qun Liu, and Nick Campbell. 2017. Doubly-attentive decoder for multi-modal neural machine translation. In *Proceedings of the 55th Annual Meeting of the Association for Computational Linguistics (Volume 1: Long Papers)*, pages 1913–1924, Vancouver, Canada. Association for Computational Linguistics.

Alexis Conneau and Guillaume Lample. 2019. Cross-lingual language model pretraining. In *Advances in Neural Information Processing Systems*, volume 32. Curran Associates, Inc.

Koel Dutta Chowdhury, Mohammed Hasanuzzaman, and Qun Liu. 2018. Multimodal neural machine translation for low-resource language pairs using synthetic data. In *Proceedings of the Workshop on Deep Learning Approaches for Low-Resource NLP*, pages 33–42, Melbourne. Association for Computational Linguistics.

Sergey Edunov, Alexei Baevski, and Michael Auli. 2019. Pre-trained language model representations for language generation. In *Proceedings of the 2019 Conference of the North American Chapter of the Association for Computational Linguistics: Human Language Technologies, Volume 1 (Long and Short Papers)*, pages 4052–4059, Minneapolis, Minnesota. Association for Computational Linguistics.

Desmond Elliott, Stella Frank, Loïc Barrault, Fethi Bougares, and Lucia Specia. 2017. Findings of the second shared task on multimodal machine translation and multilingual image description. In *Proceedings of the Second Conference on Machine Translation*, pages 215–233, Copenhagen, Denmark. Association for Computational Linguistics.

Desmond Elliott, Stella Frank, Khalil Sima'an, and Lucia Specia. 2016. Multi30K: Multilingual english-german image descriptions. In *Proceedings of the 5th Workshop on Vision and Language*, pages 70–74. Association for Computational Linguistics.

Hideki Isozaki, Tsutomu Hirao, Kevin Duh, Katsuhito Sudoh, and Hajime Tsukada. 2010. Automatic evaluation of translation quality for distant language pairs. In *Proceedings of the 2010 Conference on*

*Empirical Methods in Natural Language Processing*, pages 944–952, Cambridge, MA. Association for Computational Linguistics.

Nal Kalchbrenner and Phil Blunsom. 2013. Recurrent continuous translation models. In *Proceedings of the 2013 Conference on Empirical Methods in Natural Language Processing*, pages 1700–1709, Seattle, Washington, USA. Association for Computational Linguistics.

Diederik P. Kingma and Jimmy Ba. 2015. Adam: A method for stochastic optimization. In *3rd International Conference on Learning Representations, ICLR 2015, San Diego, CA, USA, May 7-9, 2015, Conference Track Proceedings*.

Ranjay Krishna, Yuke Zhu, Oliver Groth, Justin Johnson, Kenji Hata, Joshua Kravitz, Stephanie Chen, Yannis Kalantidis, Li-Jia Li, David A. Shamma, Michael S. Bernstein, and Li Fei-Fei. 2017. Visual Genome: Connecting language and vision using crowdsourced dense image annotations. *International Journal of Computer Vision*, 123(1):32–73.

Anoop Kunchukuttan, Pratik Mehta, and Pushpak Bhattacharyya. 2018. The IIT Bombay English-Hindi parallel corpus. In *Proceedings of the Eleventh International Conference on Language Resources and Evaluation (LREC 2018)*, Miyazaki, Japan. European Language Resources Association (ELRA).

Sahinur Rahman Laskar, Abdullah Faiz Ur Rahman Khilji, Partha Pakray, and Sivaji Bandyopadhyay. 2020. Multimodal neural machine translation for English to Hindi. In *Proceedings of the 7th Workshop on Asian Translation*, pages 109–113, Suzhou, China. Association for Computational Linguistics.

Sahinur Rahman Laskar, Rohit Pratap Singh, Partha Pakray, and Sivaji Bandyopadhyay. 2019. English to Hindi multi-modal neural machine translation and Hindi image captioning. In *Proceedings of the 6th Workshop on Asian Translation*, pages 62–67, Hong Kong, China. Association for Computational Linguistics.

Mike Lewis, Yinhan Liu, Naman Goyal, Marjan Ghazvininejad, Abdelrahman Mohamed, Omer Levy, Veselin Stoyanov, and Luke Zettlemoyer. 2020. BART: Denoising sequence-to-sequence pre-training for natural language generation, translation, and comprehension. In *Proceedings of the 58th Annual Meeting of the Association for Computational Linguistics*, pages 7871–7880, Online. Association for Computational Linguistics.

Yinhan Liu, Jiatao Gu, Naman Goyal, Xian Li, Sergey Edunov, Marjan Ghazvininejad, Mike Lewis, and Luke Zettlemoyer. 2020. Multilingual denoising pre-training for neural machine translation.

Toshiaki Nakazawa, Hideki Nakayama, Chenchen Ding, Raj Dabre, Shohei Higashiyama, Hideya Mino, Isao Goto, Win Pa Pa, Anoop Kunchukuttan, Shantipriya Parida, Ondřej Bojar, Chenhui Chu, Akiko Eriguchi, Kaori Abe, and Sadao Oda, Yusuke Kurohashi. 2021. Overview of the 8th workshop on Asian translation. In *Proceedings of the 8th Workshop on Asian Translation*, Bangkok, Thailand. Association for Computational Linguistics.

Myle Ott, Sergey Edunov, Alexei Baevski, Angela Fan, Sam Gross, Nathan Ng, David Grangier, and Michael Auli. 2019. fairseq: A fast, extensible toolkit for sequence modeling. In *Proceedings of the 2019 Conference of the North American Chapter of the Association for Computational Linguistics (Demonstrations)*, pages 48–53, Minneapolis, Minnesota. Association for Computational Linguistics.

Kishore Papineni, Salim Roukos, Todd Ward, and Wei-Jing Zhu. 2002. Bleu: a method for automatic evaluation of machine translation. In *Proceedings of the 40th Annual Meeting of the Association for Computational Linguistics*, pages 311–318, Philadelphia, Pennsylvania, USA. Association for Computational Linguistics.

Shantipriya Parida, Ondřej Bojar, and Satya Ranjan Dash. 2019. Hindi Visual Genome: A Dataset for Multimodal English-to-Hindi Machine Translation. *Computación y Sistemas*, 23(4):1499–1505. Presented at CICLing 2019, La Rochelle, France.

Shaoqing Ren, Kaiming He, Ross B. Girshick, and Jian Sun. 2015. Faster R-CNN: towards real-time object detection with region proposal networks. In *Advances in Neural Information Processing Systems 28: Annual Conference on Neural Information Processing Systems 2015, December 7-12, 2015, Montreal, Quebec, Canada*, pages 91–99.

Loitongbam Sanayai Meetei, Thoudam Doren Singh, and Sivaji Bandyopadhyay. 2019. WAT2019: English-Hindi translation on Hindi visual genome dataset. In *Proceedings of the 6th Workshop on Asian Translation*, pages 181–188, Hong Kong, China. Association for Computational Linguistics.

Kaitao Song, Xu Tan, Tao Qin, Jianfeng Lu, and Tie-Yan Liu. 2019. MASS: Masked sequence to sequence pre-training for language generation. In *Proceedings of the 36th International Conference on Machine Learning*, volume 97 of *Proceedings of Machine Learning Research*, pages 5926–5936. PMLR.

Lucia Specia, Stella Frank, Khalil Sima'an, and Desmond Elliott. 2016. A shared task on multimodal machine translation and crosslingual image description. In *Proceedings of the First Conference on Machine Translation: Volume 2, Shared Task Papers*, pages 543–553, Berlin, Germany. Association for Computational Linguistics.

Ashish Vaswani, Noam Shazeer, Niki Parmar, Jakob Uszkoreit, Llion Jones, Aidan N Gomez, Ł ukasz Kaiser, and Illia Polosukhin. 2017. Attention is all you need. In *Advances in Neural Information Processing Systems*, volume 30. Curran Associates, Inc.

Peter Young, Alice Lai, Micah Hodosh, and Julia Hockenmaier. 2014. From image descriptions to visual denotations: New similarity metrics for semantic inference over event descriptions. *Transactions of the Association for Computational Linguistics*, 2:67–78.

# TMEKU System for the WAT2021 Multimodal Translation Task

**Yutiing Zhao[1], Mamoru Komachi[1], Tomoyuki Kajiwara[2], Chenhui Chu[3]**
[1]Tokyo Metropolitan University
[2]Ehime University
[3]Kyoto University
zhao-yuting@ed.tmu.ac.jp, komachi@tmu.ac.jp
kajiwara@cs.ehime-u.ac.jp, chu@i.kyoto-u.ac.jp

## Abstract

We introduce our TMEKU[1] system submitted to the English→Japanese Multimodal Translation Task for WAT 2021. We participated in the Flickr30kEnt-JP task and Ambiguous MSCOCO Multimodal task under the constrained condition using only the officially provided datasets. Our proposed system employs soft alignment of word-region for multimodal neural machine translation (MNMT). The experimental results evaluated on the BLEU metric provided by the WAT 2021 evaluation site show that the TMEKU system has achieved the best performance among all the participated systems. Further analysis of the case study demonstrates that leveraging word-region alignment between the textual and visual modalities is the key to performance enhancement in our TMEKU system, which leads to better visual information use.

## 1 Introduction

Neural machine translation (NMT) (Sutskever et al., 2014; Bahdanau et al., 2015) has achieved state-of-the-art translation performance. However, there remain numerous situations where textual context alone is insufficient for correct translation, such as in the presence of ambiguous words and grammatical gender. Therefore, researchers in this field have established multimodal neural machine translation (MNMT) tasks (Specia et al., 2016; Elliott et al., 2017; Barrault et al., 2018), which translates sentences paired with images into a target language.

Due to the lack of multimodal datasets, multimodal tasks on the English→Japanese (En→Ja) language pair have not been paid attention to. Since the year 2020, as the multimodal dataset on the En→Ja language pair has been made publicly available, the multimodal machine translation (MMT) tasks on the En→Ja were held at the WAT 2020 (Nakazawa et al., 2020) for the first time. Some studies (Tamura et al., 2020) have started to focus on incorporating multimodal contents, particularly images, to improve the translation performance on the En→Ja task.

In this study, we apply our system (Zhao et al., 2021) for the MMT task on the En→Ja language pair, which is called TMEKU system. This system is designed to translate a source word into a target word, focusing on a relevant image region. To guide the model to translate certain words based on certain image regions, explicit alignment over source words and image regions is needed. We propose to generate soft alignment of word-region based on cosine similarity between source words and visual concepts. While encoding, textual and visual modalities are represented interactively by leveraging the word-region alignment, which is associating image regions with respective source words.

The contributions of this study are as follows:

1. Our TMEKU system outperforms baselines and achieves the first place evaluated by BLEU metric among all the submitted systems in the multimodal translation task of WAT 2021[2] (Nakazawa et al., 2021) on the En→Ja.

2. Further analysis demonstrates that our TMEKU system utilizes visual information effectively by relating the textual to visual information.

[1]TMEKU is the abbreviation of the combination of the Tokyo Metropolitan University, the Ehime University and the Kyoto University.

[2]`https://lotus.kuee.kyoto-u.ac.jp/WAT/WAT2021/`



*Proceedings of the 8th Workshop on Asian Translation*, pages 174–180
Bangkok, Thailand (online), August 5-6, 2021. 

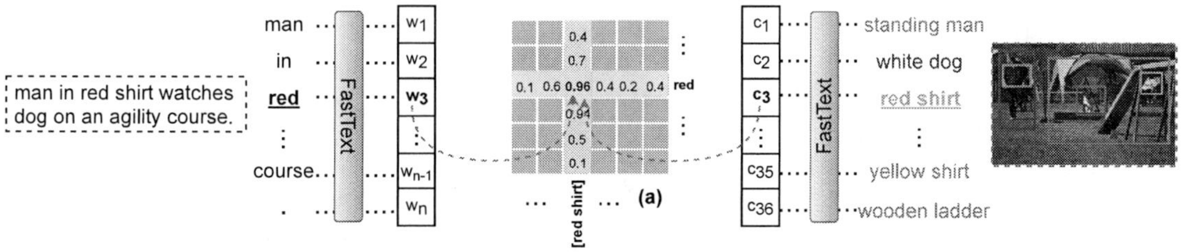


Figure 1: The soft alignment of word-region.

## 2 TMEKU System

### 2.1 Word-Region Alignment

As shown in Figure 1, we propose to create an alignment between semantically relevant source words and image regions.

For the regions, we follow Anderson et al. (2018) in detecting object-level image regions from each image, which are denoted by bounding boxes on the figure. In particular, each bounding box is detected along with a visual concept consisting of an attribute class followed by an object class instead of only the object class. We take these visual concepts to represent the image regions. We set each image labeled with 36 visual concepts of image regions, which are space-separated phrases. For the words, we lowercase and tokenize the source English sentences via the Moses toolkit.[3]

The soft alignment is a similarity matrix filled with the cosine similarity between source words and visual concepts. To avoid unknown words, we convert the words and concepts into subword units using the byte pair encoding (BPE) model (Sennrich et al., 2016). Subsequently, we utilize fastText (Bojanowski et al., 2017) to learn subword embeddings. We use a pre-trained model[4] containing two million word vectors trained with subword information on Common Crawl (600B tokens). The source subword embeddings can be generated directly, whereas the generation of visual concept embeddings should take an average of the embeddings of all constituent subwords because they are phrases. As shown in Figure 1, source subwords are represented by $W = \{\mathbf{w_1}, \mathbf{w_2}, \mathbf{w_3}, \cdots, \mathbf{w_n}\}$, and the visual concepts are represented by $C = \{\mathbf{c_1}, \mathbf{c_2}, \mathbf{c_3}, \cdots, \mathbf{c_{36}}\}$. These embeddings provide a mapping function from a subword to a 300-dim vector, where semantically similar subwords are embedded close to each other. Finally, we calculate a cosine similarity matrix of the word-region as a soft alignment $\mathrm{A_{soft}}$.

[3]https://github.com/moses-smt/mosesdecoder

[4]https://fasttext.cc/docs/en/english-vectors.html

### 2.2 Encoder

#### 2.2.1 Representing Textual Input

In Figure 2, the textual encoder is a bi-directional RNN. Given a source sentence of $n$ source words, the encoder generates the forward annotation vectors $(\overrightarrow{\mathbf{h}_1}, \overrightarrow{\mathbf{h}_2}, \overrightarrow{\mathbf{h}_3}, \cdots, \overrightarrow{\mathbf{h}_n})$, and backward annotation vectors $(\overleftarrow{\mathbf{h}_1}, \overleftarrow{\mathbf{h}_2}, \overleftarrow{\mathbf{h}_3}, \cdots, \overleftarrow{\mathbf{h}_n})$. By concatenating the forward and backward vectors $\mathbf{h}_i = [\overrightarrow{\mathbf{h}_i}; \overleftarrow{\mathbf{h}_i}]$, all words are denoted as $\mathrm{H} = (\mathbf{h}_1, \mathbf{h}_2, \cdots, \mathbf{h}_n)$.

#### 2.2.2 Representing Visual Input

We follow Anderson et al. (2018) in extracting the region-of-interest (RoI) features of detected image regions in each image. There are 36 object-level image region features, each of which is represented as a 2,048-dim vector $\mathbf{r}$, and all features in an image are denoted as $\mathrm{R} = (\mathbf{r}_1, \mathbf{r}_2, \mathbf{r}_3, \cdots, \mathbf{r}_{36})$.

#### 2.2.3 Representations with Word-Region Alignment

As shown in Figure 2, we represent textual annotation of $n$ source words as $\mathrm{A^{txt}} = (\mathbf{a}_1^{\mathrm{txt}}, \mathbf{a}_2^{\mathrm{txt}}, \mathbf{a}_3^{\mathrm{txt}}, \cdots, \mathbf{a}_n^{\mathrm{txt}})$, and visual annotation of 36 regions as $\mathrm{A^{img}} = (\mathbf{a}_1^{\mathrm{img}}, \mathbf{a}_2^{\mathrm{img}}, \mathbf{a}_3^{\mathrm{img}}, \cdots, \mathbf{a}_{36}^{\mathrm{img}})$.

We represented the visual annotation $\mathrm{A^{img}}$ by concatenating R with the aligned textual features $\mathrm{H_{align}}$ and the textual annotation $\mathrm{A^{txt}}$ using textual input representation H directly.

The calculation of the $\mathrm{A^{img}}$ is computed as follows:

$$\mathrm{A^{img}} = \mathrm{CONCAT}(\mathrm{R}, \mathrm{H_{align}})$$

$$\mathrm{H_{align}} = \frac{\mathrm{A_{soft}^{T}} \cdot \mathrm{H}}{|\mathrm{H}|}$$

where the $|\mathrm{R}|$ and $|\mathrm{H}|$ represent the length of source words and the numbers of image regions: $n$ and 36; the CONCAT is a concatenation operator.

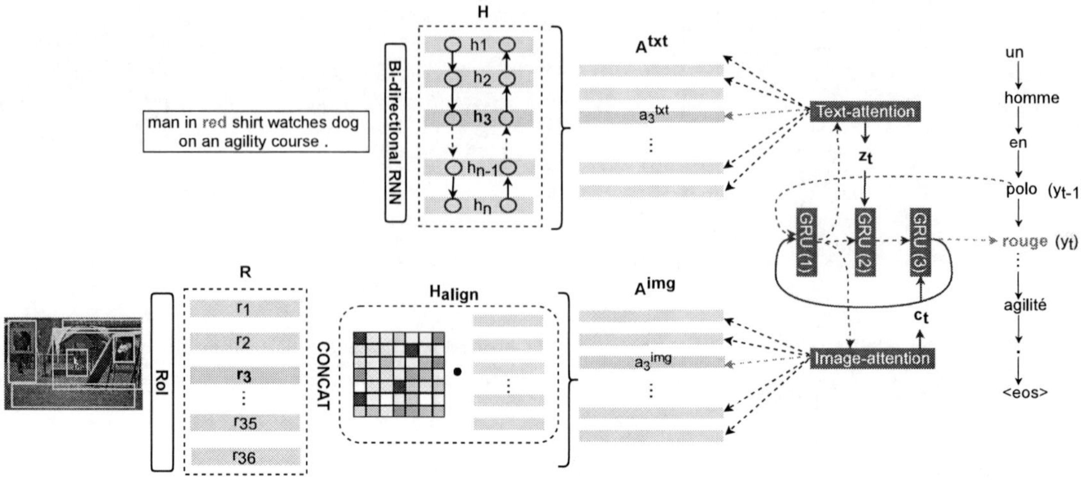


Figure 2: The TMEKU system.

### 2.3 Decoder

To generate target word $y_t$ at time step $t$, a hidden state proposal $\mathbf{s}_t^{(1)}$ is computed in the first cell of deepGRU (Delbrouck and Dupont, 2018) (GRU (1)) by function $\mathrm{f}_{\mathrm{gru}_1}(y_{t-1}, \mathbf{s}_{t-1})$. The function considers the previously emitted target word $y_{t-1}$ and generated hidden state $\mathbf{s}_{t-1}$ as follows.

$$
\begin{aligned}
\mathbf{s}_t^{(1)} &= (1 - \hat{\xi}_t) \odot \dot{\mathbf{s}}_t + \hat{\xi}_t \odot \mathbf{s}_{t-1} \\
\dot{\mathbf{s}}_t &= \tanh(W E_Y[y_{t-1}] + \hat{\gamma}_t \odot (U\mathbf{s}_{t-1})) \\
\hat{\gamma}_t &= \sigma(W_\gamma E_Y[y_{t-1}] + U_\gamma \mathbf{s}_{t-1}) \\
\hat{\xi}_t &= \sigma(W_\xi E_Y[y_{t-1}] + U_\xi \mathbf{s}_{t-1})
\end{aligned}
$$

where $W_\xi, U_\xi, W_\gamma, U_\gamma, W$, and $U$ are training parameters, and $E_Y$ is the target word embedding.

#### 2.3.1 Text-Attention

At time step $t$, the text-attention focuses on every textual annotation $\mathbf{a}_i^{\mathbf{txt}}$ in $\mathrm{A}^{\mathrm{txt}}$ and assigns an attention weight. The textual context vector $\mathbf{z}_t$ is generated as follows.

$$
\begin{aligned}
e_{t,i}^{\mathrm{text}} &= (V^{\mathrm{text}})^{\mathrm{T}} \tanh(U^{\mathrm{text}} \mathbf{s}_t^{(1)} + W^{\mathrm{text}} \mathbf{a}_i^{\mathbf{txt}}), \\
\alpha_{t,i}^{\mathrm{text}} &= \mathrm{softmax}(e_{t,i}^{\mathrm{text}}) \\
\mathbf{z}_t &= \sum_{i=1}^{n} \alpha_{t,i}^{\mathrm{text}} \mathbf{a}_i^{\mathbf{txt}}
\end{aligned}
$$

where $V^{\mathrm{text}}$, $U^{\mathrm{text}}$, and $W^{\mathrm{text}}$ are the training parameters; $e_{t,i}^{\mathrm{text}}$ is the attention energy; and $\alpha_{t,i}^{\mathrm{text}}$ is the attention weight matrix.

#### 2.3.2 Image-Attention

Similarly, the visual context vector $\mathbf{c}_t$ is generated as follows.

$$
\begin{aligned}
e_{t,j}^{\mathrm{img}} &= (V^{\mathrm{img}})^{\mathrm{T}} \tanh(U^{\mathrm{img}} \mathbf{s}_t^{(1)} + W^{\mathrm{img}} \mathbf{a}_{\mathbf{j}}^{\mathbf{img}}), \\
\alpha_{t,j}^{\mathrm{img}} &= \mathrm{softmax}(e_{t,j}^{\mathrm{img}}) \\
\mathbf{c}_t &= \sum_{j=1}^{36} \alpha_{t,j}^{\mathrm{img}} \mathbf{a}_j^{\mathbf{img}}
\end{aligned}
$$

where $V^{\mathrm{img}}$, $U^{\mathrm{img}}$, and $W^{\mathrm{img}}$ are the training parameters; $\alpha_{t,j}^{\mathrm{img}}$ is a weight matrix of each $\mathbf{a}_j^{\mathbf{img}}$; and $e_{t,j}^{\mathrm{img}}$ is the attention energy.

#### 2.3.3 DeepGRU

As shown in Figure 2, deepGRU consists of three layers of GRU cells, which are variants of the conditional gated recurrent unit (cGRU).[5] The hidden state $\mathbf{s}_t$ is computed in GRU (3) as follows. Because the calculation of $\mathrm{f}_{\mathrm{gru}_2}$ and $\mathrm{f}_{\mathrm{gru}_3}$ are similar to function $\mathrm{f}_{\mathrm{gru}_1}$, they are not included in the paper.

$$
\begin{aligned}
\mathbf{s}_t &= \mathrm{f}_{\mathrm{gru}_3}([\mathbf{c}_t, y_{t-1}], \mathbf{s}_t^{(2)}) \\
\mathbf{s}_t^{(2)} &= \mathrm{f}_{\mathrm{gru}_2}(\mathbf{z}_t, \mathbf{s}_t^{(1)})
\end{aligned}
$$

We use a gated hyperbolic tangent activation (Teney et al., 2018) instead of tanh. This nonlinear layer implements function $\mathrm{f}_{\mathrm{ght}} : \mathbf{x} \in \mathbb{R}^m \rightarrow \mathbf{y} \in \mathbb{R}^n$ with parameters defined as follows.

$$
\begin{aligned}
\mathbf{y}' &= \tanh(K\mathbf{x} + \mathbf{b}) \\
\mathbf{g} &= \sigma(K'\mathbf{x} + \mathbf{b}') \\
\mathbf{y} &= \mathbf{y}' \odot \mathbf{g}
\end{aligned}
$$

where $K, K' \in \mathbb{R}^{n \times m}$ and $\mathbf{b}$, $\mathbf{b}' \in \mathbb{R}^n$ are the training parameters.

[5] https://github.com/nyu-dl/dl4mt-tutorial/blob/master/docs/cgru.pdf

To ensure that both representations have their own projections to compute the candidate probabilities, a textual GRU block and visual GRU block (Delbrouck and Dupont, 2018) obtained as below.

$$\mathbf{b}_t^{\mathrm{v}} = \mathrm{f}_{\mathrm{ght}}(W_{\mathrm{b}}^{\mathrm{v}}\mathbf{s}_t)$$
$$\mathbf{b}_t^{\mathrm{t}} = \mathrm{f}_{\mathrm{ght}}(W_{\mathrm{b}}^{\mathrm{t}}\mathbf{s}_t^{(\mathbf{2})})$$
$$y_t \sim p_t = \mathrm{softmax}(W_{\mathrm{proj}}^{\mathrm{t}}\mathbf{b}_t^{\mathrm{t}} + W_{\mathrm{proj}}^{\mathrm{v}}\mathbf{b}_t^{\mathrm{v}}),$$

where $W_{\mathrm{b}}^{\mathrm{v}}, W_{\mathrm{b}}^{\mathrm{t}}, W_{\mathrm{proj}}^{\mathrm{t}}, W_{\mathrm{proj}}^{\mathrm{v}}$ are training parameters.

## 3 Experiments

### 3.1 Dataset

Firstly, we conducted experiments for the En→Ja task using the official Flickr30kEnt-JP dataset (Nakayama et al., 2020), which was extended from the Flickr30k (Young et al., 2014) and Flickr30k Entities (Plummer et al., 2017) datasets, where manual Japanese translations were newly added.

For training and validation, we used the Flickr30kEnt-JP dataset[6] for Japanese sentences, the Flickr30k Entities dataset[7] for English sentences, and the Flickr30k dataset[8] for images. They were sharing the same splits of training and validation data made in Flickr30k Entities. For test data, we used the officially provided data of the Flickr30kEnt-JP task, and their corresponding images were in the Flickr30k dataset.

Note that the Japanese training data size is originally 148,915 sentences, but five sentences are missing. Thus, we used 148,910 sentences for training. In summary, we used 148,910 pairs for training, 5k pairs for validation, and 1k monolingual English sentences for translating test results.

Secondly, we also conducted experiments for the En→Ja task using the official Ambiguous MSCOCO dataset (Merritt et al., 2020),[9] which was extended from the Ambiguous COCO captions and images,[10] where the Japanese translations were newly added. It was including a validation set with 230 pairs and a test set with 231 pairs. For standard training data, the training data from the Flickr30kEnt-JP dataset was officially designated.

[6]https://github.com/nlab-mpg/Flickr30kEnt-JP

[7]http://bryanplummer.com/Flickr30kEntities/

[8]http://shannon.cs.illinois.edu/DenotationGraph/

[9]https://github.com/knccch/JaEnCOCO

[10]http://www.statmt.org/wmt17/multimodal-task.html

### 3.2 Preprocessing

For English sentences, we applied lowercase, punctuation normalization, and the tokenizer in the Moses Toolkit. Then we converted space-separated tokens into subword units using the BPE model with 10k merge operations. For Japanese sentences, we used MeCab[11] for word segmentation with the IPA dictionary. The resulting vocabulary sizes of En→Ja were 9,578→22,274 tokens.

For image regions, we used Faster-RCNN (Ren et al., 2015) in Anderson et al. (2018) to detect up to 36 salient visual objects per image and extracted their corresponding 2,048-dim image region features and attribute-object combined concepts.

### 3.3 Settings

(i) NMT: the baseline NMT system (Bahdanau et al., 2015) is the architecture comprised a 2-layer bidirectional GRU encoder and a 2-layer cGRU decoder with attention mechanism, which only encodes the source sentence as the input.
(ii) MNMT: the baseline MNMT system without word-region alignment (Zhao et al., 2020). This architecture comprised a 2-layer bidirectional GRU encoder and a 2-layer cGRU decoder with double attentions to integrate visual and textual features.
(iii) TMEKU system: our proposed MNMT system with word-region alignment.

We conducted all experiments on Nmtpy toolkit (Caglayan et al., 2017).

#### 3.3.1 Parameters

We ensured that the parameters were consistent in all the settings. We set the encoder and decoder hidden state to 400-dim; word embedding to 200-dim; batch size to 32; beam size to 12; text dropout to 0.3; image region dropout to 0.5; dropout of source RNN hidden states to 0.5; and blocks $\mathbf{b}_t^{\mathrm{t}}$ and $\mathbf{b}_t^{\mathrm{v}}$ to 0.5.

Specifically, the textual annotation $\mathrm{A}^{\mathrm{txt}}$ was 800-dim, which was consistent with H. Further, the visual annotation $\mathrm{A}^{\mathrm{img}}$ was 4,096-dim by a concatenation of R and $\mathrm{H}_{\mathrm{align}}$, where R was 2,048-dim and $\mathrm{H}_{\mathrm{align}}$ was 2,048-dim by a linear transformation from 800-dim.

We trained the model using stochastic gradient descent with ADAM (Kingma and Ba, 2015) and a learning rate of 0.0004. We stopped training when the BLEU (Papineni et al., 2002) score did not improve for 20 evaluations on the validation set,

[11]https://taku910.github.io/mecab/

| Model | Test | Score |
|---|---|---|
| Baseline NMT | 46.16 | |
| Baseline MNMT | 46.33 | |
| TMEKU System | **47.02** | |
| v.s. baseline NMT | ↑ 0.86 | |
| v.s. baseline MNMT | ↑ 0.69 | |
| Ensemble (top 10 models) | **48.57** | 4.7225 |

Table 1: Flickr30kEnt-JP task: BLEU scores and human evaluation score (full score is 5) on the En→Ja.

| Model | Test | Score |
|---|---|---|
| TMEKU System | 30.23 | |
| Ensemble (8 models) | 31.04 | 4.4825 |

Table 2: Ambiguous MSCOCO task: BLEU scores and human evaluation score (full score is 5) on the En→Ja.

and one validation evaluation was performed after every epoch.

#### 3.3.2 Ensembling Models

For the Flickr30kEnt-JP task on the En→Ja, each experiment is repeated with 12 different seeds to mitigate the variance of BLEU. At last, we choose the top 10 trained models that evaluated by BLEU scores on the validation set for ensembling.

For the Ambiguous MSCOCO task on the En→Ja, each experiment is repeated with 8 different seeds to mitigate the variance of BLEU and benefit from ensembling these 8 trained models for the final testing.

### 3.4 Evaluation

We evaluated the quality of the translation results using the official evaluation system provided by WAT 2021. We submitted the final translation results in Japanese, which was translated from the official test data in English. On the WAT 2021 evaluation site, an automatic evaluation server was prepared and the BLEU was the main metric to evaluate our submitted translation results.

### 3.5 Results

In Table 1, we presented the results of the baselines and our TMEKU system on the Flickr30kEnt-JP task. We compared all the results based on BLEU scores evaluated by WAT 2021 evaluation site. For instance, the TMEKU system outperformed the NMT baseline by BLEU scores of 0.86 and outperformed the MNMT baseline by BLEU scores of 0.69 on the official test set. Our TMEKU system achieved significant improvement over both the NMT and MNMT baselines. Moreover, the result of ensembling the top 10 models has achieved the first place in the ranking of this task.

We also participated in the Ambiguous MSCOCO task on the En→Ja translation using our TMEKU system. Our reported BLEU scores are shown in Table 2, and the result of ensembling 8 models has ranked the first among all the submissions in this task.

### 3.6 Human Evaluation

To further validate the translation performance, a human evaluation was done by the organizers.

There are two native speakers of Japanese to rate the translation results with a score of 1 to 5 (1 is the worst and 5 is the best), who are informed to focus more on semantic meaning than grammatical correctness. There are 200 randomly selected examples for evaluation on the En→Ja language pair of Flickr30kEnt-JP task and Ambiguous MSCOCO task, respectively.

The human evaluation scores provided by the organizers are added in Table 1 and Table 2, which have achieved the best scores among the participated systems in their respective tasks.

## 4 Case Study

We show two cases in Figure 3, and improvement is highlighted in green.

We perform two types of visualization for each case: (1) We visualize the source-target word alignment of the text-attention. (2) We visualize the region-target alignment of the image-attention at a time step that generates a certain target word along with attending to the most heavily weighted image region feature.

In the case shown on the left, our TMEKU system translates "entering" to "entrant," but the baselines under-translate. By visualization, the text-attention and image-attention assign the highest weights to the word and region that are semantically relevant at that time step of generating "entrant." This example shows that translation quality improvement is due to the simultaneous attentions of semantically related image regions and words.

In the case shown on the right, our TMEKU system correctly translates "backyard" to a com-

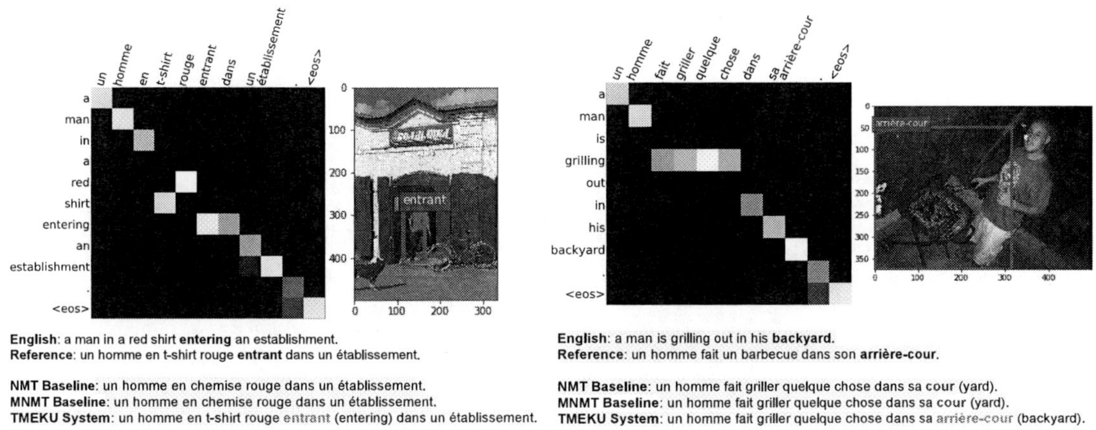


Figure 3: Examples for case study. The improved translation is highlighted in green.

pound noun of "arrière-cour." But the baselines mistranslates it to "cour," which means "yard" in English. Through visualization, we find that the text-attention and image-attention focus on the features that are semantically relevant at that time step. This example shows that the image region feature associated with its semantically relevant textual feature can overcome the deficiency, where the object attribute cannot be specifically represented by only the image region feature.

## 5 Conclusion

We presented our TMEKU system to the English→Japanese MMT tasks for WAT 2021, which is designed to simultaneously consider relevant textual and visual features during translation. By integrating the explicit word-region alignment, the object-level regional features can be further specified with respective source textual features. This leads the two attention mechanisms to understand the semantic relationships between textual objects and visual concepts.

Experimental results show that our TMEKU system exceeded baselines by a large margin and achieved the best performance among all the participated systems. We also performed analysis of case study to demonstrate the specific improvements resulting from related modalities.

In the future, we plan to propose a more efficient integration method to make modalities interactive with each other.

## Acknowledgments

This work was supported by Grant-in-Aid for Young Scientists #19K20343, JSPS. We are immensely grateful to Mr. Tosho Hirasawa, who provided coding support, and comments that significantly help the implementation of our system.

## References

Peter Anderson, Xiaodong He, Chris Buehler, Damien Teney, Mark Johnson, Stephen Gould, and Lei Zhang. 2018. Bottom-up and top-down attention for image captioning and visual question answering. In *CVPR*, pages 6077–6086.

Dzmitry Bahdanau, Kyunghyun Cho, and Yoshua Bengio. 2015. Neural machine translation by jointly learning to align and translate. *ICLR*, abs/1409.0473.

Loïc Barrault, Fethi Bougares, Lucia Specia, Chiraag Lala, Desmond Elliott, and Stella Frank. 2018. Findings of the third shared task on multimodal machine translation. In *WMT*, pages 304–323.

Piotr Bojanowski, Edouard Grave, Armand Joulin, and Tomas Mikolov. 2017. Enriching word vectors with subword information. *TACL*, 5:135–146.

Ozan Caglayan, Mercedes García-Martínez, Adrien Bardet, Walid Aransa, Fethi Bougares, and Loïc Barrault. 2017. NMTPY: A flexible toolkit for advanced neural machine translation systems. *Prague Bull. Math. Linguistics*, 109:15–28.

Jean-Benoit Delbrouck and Stéphane Dupont. 2018. UMONS submission for WMT18 multimodal translation task. In *WMT*, pages 643–647.

Desmond Elliott, Stella Frank, Loïc Barrault, Fethi Bougares, and Lucia Specia. 2017. Findings of the second shared task on multimodal machine translation and multilingual image description. In *WMT*, pages 215–233.

Diederik P. Kingma and Jimmy Ba. 2015. Adam: A method for stochastic optimization. In *ICLR*, pages 1–15.

Andrew Merritt, Chenhui Chu, and Yuki Arase. 2020. A corpus for english-japanese multimodal neural machine translation with comparable sentences. *CoRR*, abs/2010.08725.

Hideki Nakayama, Akihiro Tamura, and Takashi Ninomiya. 2020. A visually-grounded parallel corpus with phrase-to-region linking. In *LREC*, pages 4204–4210.

Toshiaki Nakazawa, Hideki Nakayama, Chenchen Ding, Raj Dabre, Shohei Higashiyama, Hideya Mino, Isao Goto, Win Pa Pa, Anoop Kunchukuttan, Shantipriya Parida, Ondřej Bojar, Chenhui Chu, Akiko Eriguchi, Kaori Abe, and Sadao Oda, Yusuke Kurohashi. 2021. Overview of the 8th workshop on Asian translation. In *WAT*.

Toshiaki Nakazawa, Hideki Nakayama, Chenchen Ding, Raj Dabre, Shohei Higashiyama, Hideya Mino, Isao Goto, Win Pa Pa, Anoop Kunchukuttan, Shantipriya Parida, Ondřej Bojar, and Sadao Kurohashi. 2020. Overview of the 7th workshop on Asian translation. In *WAT*, pages 1–44.

Kishore Papineni, Salim Roukos, Todd Ward, and Wei-Jing Zhu. 2002. BLEU: a method for automatic evaluation of machine translation. In *ACL*, pages 311–318.

Bryan A. Plummer, Liwei Wang, Christopher M. Cervantes, Juan C. Caicedo, Julia Hockenmaier, and Svetlana Lazebnik. 2017. Flickr30k entities: Collecting region-to-phrase correspondences for richer image-to-sentence models. *IJCV*, pages 74–93.

Shaoqing Ren, Kaiming He, Ross Girshick, and Jian Sun. 2015. Faster R-CNN: Towards real-time object detection with region proposal networks. In *NIPS*, pages 91–99.

Rico Sennrich, Barry Haddow, and Alexandra Birch. 2016. Neural machine translation of rare words with subword units. In *ACL*, pages 1715–1725.

Lucia Specia, Stella Frank, Khalil Sima'an, and Desmond Elliott. 2016. A shared task on multimodal machine translation and crosslingual image description. In *WMT*, pages 543–553.

Ilya Sutskever, Oriol Vinyals, and Quoc V Le. 2014. Sequence to sequence learning with neural networks. In *NIPS*, pages 3104–3112.

Hiroto Tamura, Tosho Hirasawa, Masahiro Kaneko, and Mamoru Komachi. 2020. TMU Japanese-English multimodal machine translation system for WAT 2020. In *WAT*, pages 80–91.

D. Teney, P. Anderson, X. He, and A. v. d. Hengel. 2018. Tips and tricks for visual question answering: Learnings from the 2017 challenge. In *CVPR*, pages 4223–4232.

Peter Young, Alice Lai, Micah Hodosh, and Julia Hockenmaier. 2014. From image descriptions to visual denotations: New similarity metrics for semantic inference over event descriptions. *TACL*, 2:67–78.

Yuting Zhao, Mamoru Komachi, Tomoyuki Kajiwara, and Chenhui Chu. 2020. Double attention-based multimodal neural machine translation with semantic image regions. In *EAMT*, pages 105–114.

Yuting Zhao, Mamoru Komachi, Tomoyuki Kajiwara, and Chenhui Chu. 2021. Neural machine translation with semantically relevant image regions. In *NLP*.

# Optimal Word Segmentation for Neural Machine Translation into Dravidian Languages

**Prajit Dhar** **Arianna Bisazza** **Gertjan van Noord**
University of Groningen
{p.dhar, a.bisazza, g.j.m.van.noord}@rug.nl

## Abstract

Dravidian languages, such as Kannada and Tamil, are notoriously difficult to translate by state-of-the-art neural models. This stems from the fact that these languages are morphologically very rich as well as being low-resourced. In this paper, we focus on subword segmentation and evaluate Linguistically Motivated Vocabulary Reduction (LMVR) against the more commonly used SentencePiece (SP) for the task of translating from English into four different Dravidian languages. Additionally we investigate the optimal subword vocabulary size for each language. We find that SP is the overall best choice for segmentation, and that larger subword vocabulary sizes lead to higher translation quality.

## 1 Introduction

Dravidian languages are an important family of languages spoken by about 250 million of people primarily located in Southern India and Sri Lanka (Steever, 2019). Kannada (KN), Malayalam (MA), Tamil (TA) and Telugu (TE) are the four most spoken Dravidian languages with approximately 47, 34, 71 and 79 million native speakers, respectively. Together, they account for 93% of all Dravidian language speakers. While Kannada, Malayalam and Tamil are classified as South Dravidian languages, Telugu is a part of South-Central Dravidian languages. All four languages are SOV (Subject-Object-Verb) languages with free word order. They are highly agglutinative and inflectionally rich languages. Additionally, each language has a different writing system. Table 1 presents an English sentence example and its Dravidian-language translations.

The highly complex morphology of the Dravidian languages under study is illustrated if we compare translated sentence pairs. The analysis of our parallel datasets (section 4.1, Table 3) shows for instance that an average English sentence contains almost ten times as many words as its Kannada equivalent. For the other three languages, the ratio is a bit smaller but the difference with English remains considerable. This indicates why it is important to consider word segmentation algorithms as part of the translation system.

In this paper we describe our work on Neural Machine Translation (NMT) from English into the Dravidian languages Kannada, Malayalam, Tamil and Telugu. We investigated the optimal translation settings for the pairs and in particular looked at the effect of word segmentation. The aim of the paper is to answer the following research questions:

- Does LMVR, a linguistically motivated word segmentation algorithm, outperform the purely data-driven SentencePiece?
- What is the optimal subword dictionary size for translating from English into these Dravidian languages?

In what follows, we review the relevant previous work (Sect. 2), introduce the two segmenters (Sect. 3), describe the experimental setup (Sect. 4), and present our answers to the above research questions (Sect. 5).

## 2 Previous Work

### 2.1 Translation Systems

**Statistical Machine Translation** One of the earliest automatic translation systems for English into a Dravidian language was the English→Tamil system by Germann (2001). They trained a hybrid rule-based/statistical machine translation system that was trained on only 5k English-Tamil parallel sentences. Ramasamy et al. (2012) created SMT systems (phrase-based and hierarchical) which were trained on a dataset of 190k parallel



*Proceedings of the 8th Workshop on Asian Translation*, pages 181–190
Bangkok, Thailand (online), August 5-6, 2021. 

| | |
|---|---|
| EN | He was born in Thirukkuvalai village in Nagapattinam District on 3rd June, 1924. |
| KN | ಅವರು ನಾಗಪಟ್ಟಣಂ ಜಿಲ್ಲೆಯ ತಿರುಕ್ಕುವಲಯ್ ಗ್ರಾಮದಲ್ಲಿ 1924ರ ಜೂನ್ 3ರಂದು ಜನಿಸಿದ್ದರು.<br>avaru nāgapaṭṭaṇam jilleya tirukkuvalay grāmadalli 1924ra jūn 3randu janisiddaru. |
| ML | 1924ല് നാഗപട്ടണം ജില്ലയിലെ തിരുക്കുവളൈ ഗ്രാമത്തിലാണ് അദ്ദേഹം ജനിച്ചത്<br>1924l nāgapaṭṭaṇam jillayile tirukkuvaḷai grāmattilāṇ addēham janiccat. |
| TA | நாகப்பட்டினம் மாவட்டம் திருக்குவளைக் கிராமத்தில் அவர் 1924-ஆம் ஆண்டு ஜூன் மாதம் 3-ஆம் தேதி பிறந்தார்.<br>nāgappaṭṭinam māvaṭṭam tirukkuvaḷaik kirāmattil avar 1924-ām āṇṭu jūn mātam 3-ām tēti pirantār. |
| TE | ఆయన నాగపట్టణం జిల్లా తిరుక్కువాలై గ్రామంలో 1924 జూన్ 3న జన్మించారు.<br>āyana nāgapaṭṭaṇam jillā tirukkuvālai grāmanlō 1924 jūn 3na janmincāru. |

Table 1: Example sentence in English along with its translation and transliteration in the four Dravidian languages.

sentences (henceforth referred to as UFAL). They also reported that applying pre-processing steps involving morphological rules based on Tamil suffixes improved the BLEU score of the baseline model to a small extent (from 9.42 to 9.77). For the Indic languages multilingual tasks of WAT-2018, the Phrasal-based SMT system of Ojha et al. (2018) with a BLEU score of 30.53.

Subsequent papers also focused on SMT systems for Malayalam and Telugu with some notable work including: (Anto and Nisha, 2016; Sreelekha and Bhattacharyya, 2017, 2018) for Malayalam and (Lingam et al., 2014; Yadav and Lingam, 2017) for Telugu.

**Neural Machine Translation** On the neural machine translation (NMT) side, there have been a handful of NMT systems trained on English→Tamil. On the aforementioned Indic languages multilingual tasks of WAT-2018, Sen et al. (2018), Dabre et al. (2018) reported only 11.88 and 18.60 BLEU scores, respectively, for English→Tamil. The poor performance of these systems compared to the 30.53 BLEU score of the SMT system (Ojha et al., 2018) showed that those NMT systems were not yet suitable for translating into the morphologically rich Tamil.

However, the following year, Philip et al. (2019) outperformed Ramasamy et al. (2012) on the UFAL dataset with a BLEU score of 13.05 (the previous best score on this test set was 9.77). They report that techniques such as domain adaptation and back-translation can make training NMT systems on low-resource languages possible. Similar findings was also reported by Ramesh et al. (2020) for Tamil and Dandapat and Federmann (2018) for Telugu .

To the best of our knowledge and as of 2021, there has not been any scientific publication involving translation to and from Kannada, except for Chakravarthi et al. (2019). One possible reason for this could be the fact that sizeable corpora involving Kannada (i.e. in the order of magnitude of at least thousand sentences) have been readily available only since 2019, with the release of the JW300 Corpus (Agić and Vulić, 2019).

**Multilingual NMT** Since 2018 several studies have presented multilingual NMT systems that can handle English → Malayalam, Tamil and Telugu translation (Dabre et al., 2018; Choudhary et al., 2020; Ojha et al., 2018; Sen et al., 2018; Yu et al., 2020; Dabre and Chakrabarty, 2020). In particular, Sen et al. (2018) presented results where the BLEU score improved when comparing monolingual and multilingual models. Conversely, Yu et al. (2020) found that NMT systems that were multi-way (Indic ↔ Indic) performed worse than English ↔ Indic systems.

To our knowledge, no work so far has explored the effect of the segmentation algorithm and dictionary size on the four languages: Kannada, Malayalam, Tamil and Telugu.

## 3 Subword Segmentation Techniques

Prior to the emergence of subword segmenters, translation systems were plagued with the issue of

| Name | Domain | Available in: | | | |
|---|---|---|---|---|---|
| | | Kannada | Malayalam | Tamil | Telugu |
| Bible | Religion | 18 | 1 | | 14 |
| ELRC | COVID-19 | | <1 | <1 | <1 |
| GNOME | Technical | <1 | <1 | <1 | <1 |
| JW300 | Religion | 70 | 45 | 52 | 45 |
| KDE | Technical | 1 | <1 | <1 | <1 |
| NLPC | General | | | <1 | |
| OpenSubtitles | Cinema | | 26 | 3 | 3 |
| CVIT-PIB | Press | | 5 | 10 | 10 |
| PMIndia | Politics | 10 | 4 | 3 | 8 |
| Tanzil | Religion | | 18 | 9 | |
| Tatoeba | General | <1 | <1 | <1 | <1 |
| Ted2020 | General | <1 | <1 | <1 | 1 |
| TICO-19 | COVID-19 | | | <1 | |
| Ubuntu | Technical | <1 | <1 | <1 | <1 |
| UFAL | Mixed | | | 11 | |
| Wikimatrix | General | | <1 | 10 | 18 |
| Wikititles | General | | | 1 | |

Table 2: Composition of training corpora. The numbers indicate the relative size (in percentages) of the corresponding part for that language.

out-of-vocabulary (OOV) tokens. This was particularly an issue for translations involving agglutinative languages such as Turkish (Ataman and Federico, 2018) or Malayalam (Manohar et al., 2020). Various segmentation algorithms were brought forward to circumvent this issue and in turn, improve translation quality.

Perhaps the most widely used algorithm in NMT to date is the language-agnostic Byte Pair Encoding (BPE) by Sennrich et al. (2016). Initially proposed by Gage (1994), BPE was repurposed by Sennrich et al. (2016) for the task of subword segmentation, and is based on a simple principle whereby pairs of character sequences that are frequently observed in a corpus get *merged* iteratively until a predetermined dictionary size is attained. In this paper we use a popular implementation of BPE, called **SentencePiece (SP)** (Kudo and Richardson, 2018).

While purely statistical algorithms are able to segment any token into smaller segments, there is no guarantee that the generated tokens will be linguistically sensible. Unsupervised morphological induction is a rich area of research that also aims at learning a segmentation from data, but in a linguistically motivated way. The most well-known example is Morphessor with its different variants (Creutz and Lagus, 2002; Kohonen et al., 2010; Grönroos et al., 2014). An important obstacle to applying Morfessor to the task of NMT is the lack of a mechanism to determine the dictionary size. To address this, Ataman et al. (2017) proposed a modification of Morfessor FlatCat (Grönroos et al., 2014), called **Linguistically Motivated Vocabulary Reduction (LMVR)**. Specifically, LMVR imposes an extra condition on the cost function of Morfessor Flatcat so as to favour vocabularies of the desired size. In a comparison of LMVR to BPE, Ataman et al. (2017) reported a +2.3 BLEU improvement on the English-Turkish translation task of WMT18.

Given the encouraging results reported on the agglutinative Turkish language, we hypothesise that translation into Dravidian languages may also benefit from a linguistically motivated segmenter, and evaluate LMVR against SP across varying vocabulary sizes.

## 4 Experimental Setup

### 4.1 Training Corpora

The parallel training data is mostly taken from the datasets available for the MultiIndicMT task from WAT 2021. If a certain dataset is not available from the MultiIndicMT training repository, we resorted to extract that dataset from OPUS (Tiedemann, 2012) or WMT20. Table 2 reports on the datasets that we used along with their domain and their source.

After extracting and cleaning the data (see below), approximately 8 million English tokens and their corresponding target language tokens are selected as our training corpora. We fixed the number of source tokens across language pairs in or-

| Target Language | Tokens(k) | EN Tokens(k) | Sentences(k) | Source/Target Token Ratio |
|---|---|---|---|---|
| Kannada | 817 | 7791 | 361 | 9.53 |
| Malayalam | 1153 | 7973 | 458 | 6.91 |
| Tamil | 1171 | 7854 | 345 | 6.71 |
| Telugu | 1027 | 7872 | 385 | 7.67 |

Table 3: Approximate sizes (in thousands) of the parallel training corpora

der to compare the efficacy of a segmentation technique across the languages without a size bias. Table 3 presents the statistics on the corpora for all language pairs. One takeaway from the table is that there is a very large difference in the token sizes between English and the Dravidian languages. On average, there are 6 to 9 times more tokens on the English side of a corpus than on its Dravidian language translation. This shows that all our Dravidian languages are morphologically *very* complex, but there are also important differences among them, with Kannada having the highest source/target ratio, considerably higher than the more widely studied Tamil language.

### 4.2 Pre-Processing

Sentence pairs with identical source and target sides, or with more than 150 tokens are removed. The target language texts are then normalized using the Indic NLP Library[1]. Afterwards, either SP[2] or LMVR[3] is used to segment both source and target sentences. To further reduce noise in the datasets, we discard sentences pairs with either (i) a target to source length ratio above 0.7 or (ii) a language match threshold below 85% according to the lang-id tool (Lui and Baldwin, 2011), and (iii) duplicate sentence pairs.

### 4.3 NMT Training

We developed our NMT systems using Fairseq (Ott et al., 2019). We adopt the Transformer-Base implementation (BASE) with a few modifications following the architecture setup of Philip et al. (2019) and Dhar et al. (2020). These modifications include: setting both encoder and decoder layers to 6, embedding dimensions to size 1024 and number of attention heads to 8. Training is performed using batches of 4k tokens, using a label-smoothed cross entropy loss. The hidden layers are of 1024 dimensions and layer normalization is applied before each encoder and decoder layer. Dropout is set to 0.001 and weight decay to 0.2. Our loss function is cross-entropy with label smoothing of 0.3. The models are trained for a maximum of 100 epochs with early stopping criterion set to 5.

### 4.4 Dictionary Size

The segmentation algorithms are trained on the training data described in Section 4.1. We experiment with the following subword dictionary sizes: 1k, 5k, 10k, 15k, 20k, 30k, 40k and 50k. In all experiments, we learn separate subword dictionaries for the source and target languages, for two reasons: (i) LMVR is a linguistically motivated morphology learning algorithm that models the composition of a word based on the transitions between different morphemes and their categories. Therefore, training jointly on two languages would not be a principled choice. (ii) Prior studies such as (Dhar et al., 2020) have reported better translation scores for English-Tamil using SP models that were separately trained on the source and target sides.

## 5 Results

The NMT systems are evaluated and tested on the official development and test sets, respectively from WAT21. These evaluation sets are sourced from the PMIndia dataset (Haddow and Kirefu, 2020). During validation, models are evaluated by BLEU on the segmented data, whereas final test scores are computed on the un-segmented and de-tokenized sentences (de-tokenization is performed with the Indic NLP library tool). In addition to BLEU (Papineni et al., 2002), we also report on CHRF score (Popović, 2015), which is based on character n-grams and is therefore more suitable to assess translation quality in morphologically complex languages.[4] We report the macro-averaged

[1] http://anoopkunchukuttan.github.io/indic_nlp_library/

[2] https://github.com/google/sentencepiece

[3] https://github.com/d-ataman/lmvr

[4] We compute BLEU scores with SacreBLEU (Post, 2018), and CHRF scores with chrF++.py https://github.com/

| Target Language | Dictionary Size | BLEU | | CHRF | | Jaccard Similarity (%) | |
|---|---|---|---|---|---|---|---|
| | | SP | LMVR | SP | LMVR | Types | Tokens |
| Kannada | 1k | 10.4 | 6.2 | 48.3 | 40.6 | 17.0 | 2.5 |
| | 5k | 13.0 | 5.9 | **50.2** | 40.7 | 14.8 | 0.6 |
| | 10k | **13.9** | 6.8 | 49.6 | 42.8 | 13.1 | 0.4 |
| | 15k | 13.4 | 6.4 | 48.8 | 41.8 | 10.7 | 0.3 |
| | 20k | 13.0 | 7.3 | 48.3 | 43.4 | 10.6 | 0.3 |
| | 30k | 12.6 | 6.6 | 47.4 | 42.4 | 10.1 | 0.2 |
| | 40k | 12.3 | 7.4 | 46.5 | 43.9 | 9.5 | 0.2 |
| | 50k | 12.0 | 6.8 | 46.0 | 42.7 | 9.0 | 0.2 |
| Malayalam | 1k | 8.1 | 8.8 | 47.4 | 46.1 | 15.6 | 3.3 |
| | 5k | 11.2 | 12.6 | 52.3 | 50.5 | 16.6 | 1.3 |
| | 10k | 14.6 | 15.9 | 55.3 | 50.5 | 14.2 | 0.8 |
| | 15k | 17.0 | 18.6 | 57.9 | 54.9 | 14.2 | 0.7 |
| | 20k | 19.2 | 19.7 | 60.1 | 55.2 | 12.0 | 0.6 |
| | 30k | 23.4 | 23.8 | 63.6 | 58.3 | 11.8 | 0.5 |
| | 40k | 24.5 | 27.3 | **63.7** | 60.2 | 11.3 | 0.5 |
| | 50k | 24.4 | **28.5** | 63.6 | 60.9 | 11.3 | 0.5 |
| Tamil | 1k | 10.4 | 8.1 | 48.3 | 45.7 | 16.7 | 2.4 |
| | 5k | 13.2 | 8.2 | 50.6 | 46.2 | 15.7 | 0.6 |
| | 10k | 15.6 | 10.0 | 51.8 | 48.7 | 14.2 | 0.3 |
| | 15k | 20.1 | 10.9 | 53.6 | 49.1 | 11.7 | 0.2 |
| | 20k | 21.8 | 12.4 | 54.5 | 50.0 | 11.8 | 0.2 |
| | 30k | 23.8 | 11.3 | 55.3 | 49.2 | 11.6 | 0.2 |
| | 40k | 22.8 | 10.5 | 54.0 | 48.8 | 11.2 | 0.2 |
| | 50k | **27.3** | 9.1 | **55.9** | 47.3 | 10.8 | 0.2 |
| Telugu | 1k | 5.3 | 11.8 | 40.7 | 45.9 | 16.8 | 4.5 |
| | 5k | 5.6 | 10.8 | 44.6 | 43.5 | 17.8 | 1.6 |
| | 10k | 6.2 | 12.8 | 45.4 | 45.6 | 15.3 | 1.1 |
| | 15k | 10.4 | 14.1 | 50.1 | 47.6 | 15.7 | 1.0 |
| | 20k | 11.1 | 23.7 | 50.8 | 54.7 | 13.7 | 0.7 |
| | 30k | 14.1 | 23.8 | 54.0 | 58.3 | 14.2 | 0.7 |
| | 40k | 18.6 | 18.8 | 58.1 | 50.7 | 14.2 | 0.7 |
| | 50k | 19.3 | **24.5** | **59.4** | 54.6 | 14.1 | 0.6 |

Table 4: BLEU and CHRF scores for English-to-X NMT, using different segmenters and varying subword vocabulary size. SP refers to the purely statistical SentencePiece segmenter, LMVR to Linguistically Motivated Vocabulary Reduction. Dictionary size refers to the size of both the source and target subword dictionaries. Rightmost columns show the Jaccard similarity (percentage) for the types and tokens from the segmenter outputs.

document level F3-score.Results are presented in Table 4.

**SP clear winner for Kannada and Tamil:** SP presented the highest BLEU and CHRF scores for Kannada and Tamil. When we compare the best systems for both SP and LMVR, large differences are observed. For Kannada differences of +6 BLEU and +7.4 are observed and for Tamil the differences are +14.9 for BLEU and +5.9 for CHRF.

**Mixed results for Telugu and Malayalam:** However, we find no clear winner for the other two languages. When observing only BLEU scores, LMVR appears to have the upper hand, with an improvement of +2.8 BLEU and +4.5 BLEU for Malayalam and Telugu, respectively. However the results are flipped when we look at the CHRF scores. SP systems here report higher scores, with

m-popovic/chrF

+3.5 improvement in Malayalam and +1.1 for Telugu. Given the morphological richness of our target languages, we take CHRF as the more reliable score, and conclude that the purely statistical segmenter SP is a better choice for translation into Dravidian languages in our setup.

**Larger dictionary sizes better:** When observing the effect of the dictionary size, we find that the size 50k gives the highest BLEU scores for Malayalam, Tamil and Telugu. This is in contrast with studies such as (Philip et al., 2019; Sennrich and Zhang, 2019) who suggest to use a smaller dictionary size for low-resource settings. For these language pairs, we see a steady increase in BLEU and CHRF as we increase the dictionary size. For Kannada, the best results are obtained for much smaller dictionary sizes, but in contrast with the other three languages, the differences between the scores for other dictionary sizes is much smaller. For instance, looking at the CHRF scores of SP, the numbers decrease from 48.3 to 46.0, whereas for instance for Malayalam, these numbers range from 47.4 to 63.6.

**Kannada hardest to translate:** When comparing more in general translation difficulty across target languages, Kannada appears to be the most challenging language by far. A possible explanation for this difference is the genre distribution of our datasets (cf. Table 2): While the test sets are from PMIndia (a mixture of background information, news and speeches), the majority of our Kannada training data consists of religion related texts. Another possible confounding factor is that we based our NMT configuration on prior work that focused only on English-Tamil (Philip et al., 2019; Dhar et al., 2020), and this may be sub-optimal for the other Dravidian languages despite the similar training data size.

## 6 Analysis

### 6.1 Different Subtokens generated

Table 4 presents the Jaccard similarity (JS) between the segmenter outputs between LMVR and SP. The outputs are either the types (dictionaries) or the tokens in the training sentences. A JS of 0 denotes that none of the subwords were the same in the sentences being compared, while a score of 100 denotes a complete match (i.e, they are identical). As visible from the scores, though there is some sharing of types between the segmenters (ranging from 9-17%), there is no such sharing of subwords in the training data, with a maximum JS score of only around 4% for the smallest dictionary sizes. In fact, these values reduce even further as the dictionary size are increased. For the largest dictionary size (50k), almost no subtoken sharing occurs.

### 6.2 Effect of Unknown Subwords

We carried out an analysis on the effect of unknown subwords found in the development set after the application of a given segmentation algorithm.We present these statistics in Figure 1. Few details stand out:

**High percentage of unknown subwords in Kannada with LMVR** While development sets encoded with SP reported the lowest percentage of unknowns, it is the complete opposite for the ones encoded with LMVR (0.2% vs 15% on average). This could have played a role in the lowest CHRF scores achieved by the LMVR systems on Kannada.

**LMVR sensitive to dictionary size** This is observed in particular for Kannada and Malayalam, where the increase in dictionary size leads to higher numbers of unknown subwords. Conversely for SP, increasing the dictionary size causes no major change in the number of unknowns found for these two languages. On the other hand, SP is more susceptible to the dictionary size for Tamil while Telugu, in general, does not present any such trends.

Overall we find no strong correlation between system performance and percentage of unknown subwords. By contrast, and quite surprisingly so, our best NMT systems for Malayalam, Tamil and Telugu are those with larger dictionary sizes and higher percentage of unknowns in the development set.

### 6.3 Effect of subword lengths

We also looked at the effect of the segmenter on the subword length. Given a language and segmenter, we calculate the average length of a subword (in characters) for the training sets. In Figure 2 we plot the distribution of the average subword lengths for all our settings. Few observations are apparent,

- For every language and dictionary size, LMVR results in shorter subwords. Taking dictionary size of 50k as an example, the dif-

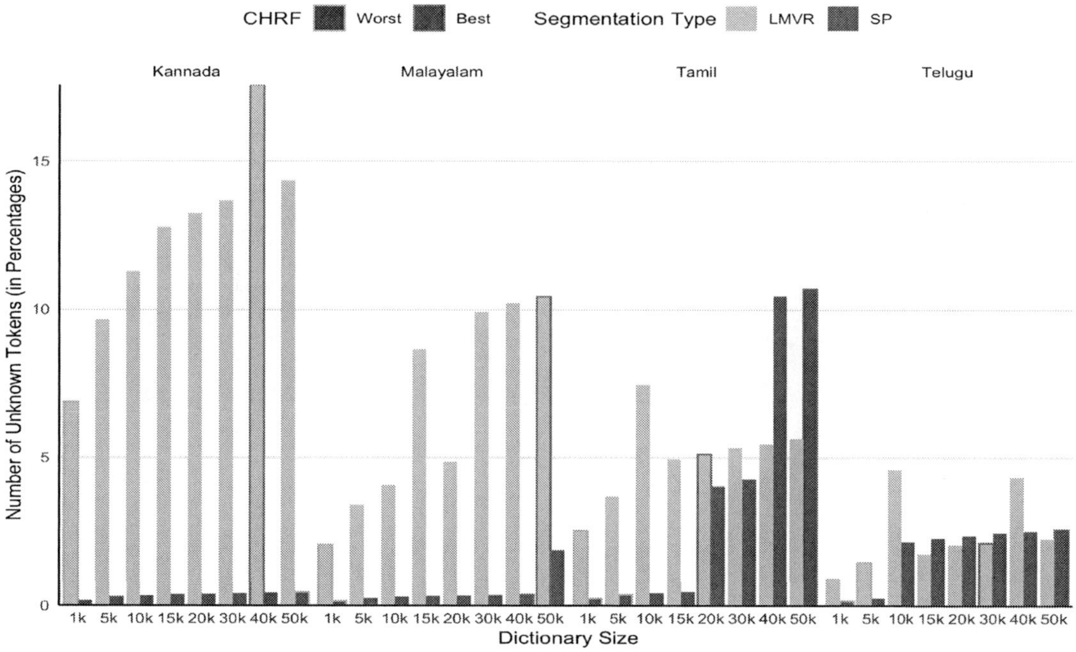


Figure 1: Number of unknown tokens (in percentages) in the development set vs Dictionary size for each language and segmentation type. Also systems that reported the lowest and highest CHRF scores (on the development set) for each language and segmentation are marked.

ference between LMVR and SP ranges from 1.2 for Malayalam to 1.7 for Tamil.

- As the dictionary size increases, we see the distributions spreading out. As the dictionary size decreases, the distributions become more centered. This is particularly seen for LMVR. As the dictionary size increases, the distributions of the SP systems spread out more than their LMVR counterparts.

- While it makes sense that the average subword length increases as we increase the dictionary size (from 3 to 5), the apparent widening in the difference between SP and LMVR is not so easily explained.

In the end however, we find no discernible connection between the subword length and the performance of a segmenter. Across all languages, we see similar trends of how the distrubtions change, but this does not seem to affect the translation quality, as seen in the difference in the CHRF scores.

## 7 Conclusion

We presented our work on Neural Machine Translation from English into four Dravidian languages (Kannada, Malayalam, Tamil and Telugu). Several experiments were carried out to find out whether a linguistically motivated subword segmenter (LMVR) is more suitable than a purely statistical one (SentencePiece) for translating into the morphologically complex Dravidian languages, while using a Transformer architecture. While BLEU results were mixed on Malayalam and Telugu, CHRF scores clearly suggest that SentencePiece remains the best option for all of our tested language pairs.

We also found interesting differences among the four target languages. Though they all belong to the same language family and share various linguistic phenomena, they are different with respect to source/target token ratio (Table 3), and the rate of unknown subwords in the development set (Figure 1). Whether this is due to linguistic characteristics or to genre differences in the training corpora remains hard to gauge.

Finally, we invite future researchers to carry out research on Dravidian languages, especially Kannada. Compared to the plethora of work found for other languages, the work on Dravidian languages is lagging behind. As our results show, there remains a large space for improvements, particularly

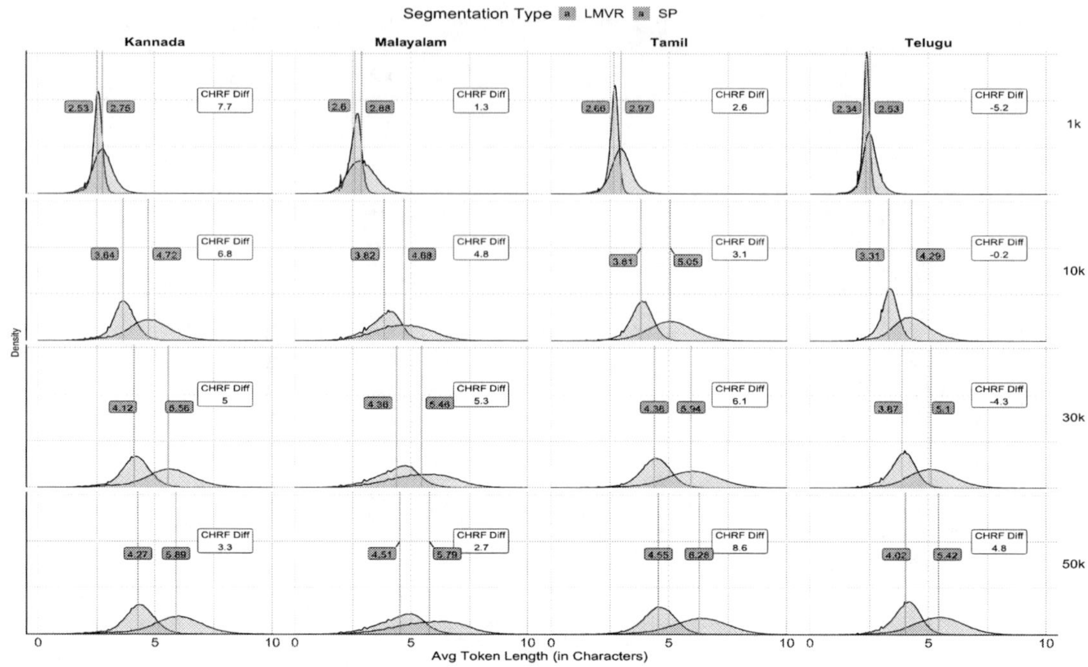


Figure 2: The Probability density function plot showing the distribution of the average subword length for a given segmenter and language on the training sets. The colored boxes denote the mean of the respective distributions. Also included are the differences in the CHRF scores between SP and LMVR.

when translating *into* these languages.

## References


Željko Agić and Ivan Vulić. 2019. JW300: A wide-coverage parallel corpus for low-resource languages. In *Proceedings of the 57th Annual Meeting of the Association for Computational Linguistics*, pages 3204–3210, Florence, Italy. Association for Computational Linguistics.

Ancy Anto and K. Nisha. 2016. Text to speech synthesis system for english to malayalam translation. *2016 International Conference on Emerging Technological Trends (ICETT)*, pages 1–6.

Duygu Ataman and Marcello Federico. 2018. Compositional representation of morphologically-rich input for neural machine translation. In *Proceedings of the 56th Annual Meeting of the Association for Computational Linguistics (Volume 2: Short Papers)*, pages 305–311, Melbourne, Australia. Association for Computational Linguistics.

Duygu Ataman, Matteo Negri, Marco Turchi, and Marcello Federico. 2017. Linguistically motivated vocabulary reduction for neural machine translation from turkish to english. *The Prague Bulletin of Mathematical Linguistics*, 108(1):331 – 342.

Bharathi Raja Chakravarthi, Mihael Arcan, and John P. McCrae. 2019. Comparison of Different Orthographies for Machine Translation of Under-Resourced Dravidian Languages. In *2nd Conference on Language, Data and Knowledge (LDK 2019)*, volume 70 of *OpenAccess Series in Informatics (OASIcs)*, pages 6:1–6:14, Dagstuhl, Germany. Schloss Dagstuhl–Leibniz-Zentrum fuer Informatik.

Himanshu Choudhary, Shivansh Rao, and Rajesh Rohilla. 2020. Neural machine translation for low-resourced Indian languages. In *Proceedings of the 12th Language Resources and Evaluation Conference*, pages 3610–3615, Marseille, France. European Language Resources Association.

Mathias Creutz and Krista Lagus. 2002. Unsupervised discovery of morphemes. In *Proceedings of the ACL-02 Workshop on Morphological and Phonological Learning*, pages 21–30. Association for Computational Linguistics.

Raj Dabre and Abhisek Chakrabarty. 2020. NICT's submission to WAT 2020: How effective are simple many-to-many neural machine translation models? In *Proceedings of the 7th Workshop on Asian Translation*, pages 98–102, Suzhou, China. Association for Computational Linguistics.

Raj Dabre, Anoop Kunchukuttan, Atsushi Fujita, and Eiichiro Sumita. 2018. NICT's participation in WAT 2018: Approaches using multilingualism and recurrently stacked layers. In *Proceedings of the 32nd Pacific Asia Conference on Language, Information and Computation: 5th Workshop on Asian Translation:*

*5th Workshop on Asian Translation*, Hong Kong. Association for Computational Linguistics.

Sandipan Dandapat and Christian Federmann. 2018. Iterative data augmentation for neural machine translation: a low resource case study for english–telugu. In *Proceedings of the 21st Annual Conference of the European Association for Machine Translation*, pages 287–292, Alacant, Spain.

Prajit Dhar, Arianna Bisazza, and Gertjan van Noord. 2020. Linguistically motivated subwords for English-Tamil translation: University of Groningen's submission to WMT-2020. In *Proceedings of the Fifth Conference on Machine Translation*, pages 126–133, Online. Association for Computational Linguistics.

Philip Gage. 1994. A new algorithm for data compression. *C Users J.*, 12(2):23–38.

Ulrich Germann. 2001. Building a statistical machine translation system from scratch: How much bang for the buck can we expect? In *Proceedings of the ACL 2001 Workshop on Data-Driven Methods in Machine Translation*.

Stig-Arne Grönroos, Sami Virpioja, Peter Smit, and Mikko Kurimo. 2014. Morfessor FlatCat: An HMM-based method for unsupervised and semi-supervised learning of morphology. In *Proceedings of COLING 2014, the 25th International Conference on Computational Linguistics: Technical Papers*, pages 1177–1185, Dublin, Ireland.

Barry Haddow and Faheem Kirefu. 2020. Pmindia – a collection of parallel corpora of languages of india.

Oskar Kohonen, Sami Virpioja, and Krista Lagus. 2010. Semi-supervised learning of concatenative morphology. In *Proceedings of the 11th Meeting of the ACL Special Interest Group on Computational Morphology and Phonology*, pages 78–86, Uppsala, Sweden. Association for Computational Linguistics.

Taku Kudo and John Richardson. 2018. SentencePiece: A simple and language independent subword tokenizer and detokenizer for neural text processing. In *Proceedings of the 2018 Conference on Empirical Methods in Natural Language Processing: System Demonstrations*, pages 66–71, Brussels, Belgium. Association for Computational Linguistics.

Keerthi Lingam, E. Ramalakshmi, and Srujana Inturi. 2014. English to telugu rule based machine translation system: A hybrid approach. *International Journal of Computer Applications*, 101(2):19–24. Full text available.

Marco Lui and Timothy Baldwin. 2011. Cross-domain feature selection for language identification. In *Proceedings of 5th International Joint Conference on Natural Language Processing*, pages 553–561, Chiang Mai, Thailand. Asian Federation of Natural Language Processing.

Kavya Manohar, A. R. Jayan, and Rajeev Rajan. 2020. Quantitative analysis of the morphological complexity of malayalam language. In *Text, Speech, and Dialogue*, pages 71–78, Cham. Springer International Publishing.

Atul Kr. Ojha, Koel Dutta Chowdhury, Chao-Hong Liu, and Karan Saxena. 2018. The RGNLP machine translation systems for WAT 2018. In *Proceedings of the 32nd Pacific Asia Conference on Language, Information and Computation: 5th Workshop on Asian Translation: 5th Workshop on Asian Translation*, Hong Kong. Association for Computational Linguistics.

Myle Ott, Sergey Edunov, Alexei Baevski, Angela Fan, Sam Gross, Nathan Ng, David Grangier, and Michael Auli. 2019. fairseq: A fast, extensible toolkit for sequence modeling. In *Proceedings of NAACL-HLT 2019: Demonstrations*.

Kishore Papineni, S. Roukos, T. Ward, and Wei-Jing Zhu. 2002. Bleu: a method for automatic evaluation of machine translation. In *ACL*.

Jerin Philip, Shashank Siripragada, Upendra Kumar, Vinay Namboodiri, and C V Jawahar. 2019. Cvit's submissions to wat-2019. In *Proceedings of the 6th Workshop on Asian Translation*, pages 131–136, Hong Kong, China. Association for Computational Linguistics.

Maja Popović. 2015. chrF: character n-gram F-score for automatic MT evaluation. In *Proceedings of the Tenth Workshop on Statistical Machine Translation*, pages 392–395, Lisbon, Portugal. Association for Computational Linguistics.

Matt Post. 2018. A call for clarity in reporting BLEU scores. In *Proceedings of the Third Conference on Machine Translation: Research Papers*, pages 186–191, Brussels, Belgium. Association for Computational Linguistics.

Loganathan Ramasamy, Ondřej Bojar, and Zdeněk Žabokrtský. 2012. Morphological processing for english-tamil statistical machine translation. In *Proceedings of the Workshop on Machine Translation and Parsing in Indian Languages (MTPIL-2012)*, pages 113–122.

Akshai Ramesh, Venkatesh Balavadhani Parthasa, Rejwanul Haque, and Andy Way. 2020. An error-based investigation of statistical and neural machine translation performance on Hindi-to-Tamil and English-to-Tamil. In *Proceedings of the 7th Workshop on Asian Translation*, pages 178–188, Suzhou, China. Association for Computational Linguistics.

Sukanta Sen, Kamal Kumar Gupta, Asif Ekbal, and Pushpak Bhattacharyya. 2018. IITP-MT at WAT2018: Transformer-based multilingual indic-English neural machine translation system. In *Proceedings of the 32nd Pacific Asia Conference on Language, Information and Computation: 5th Workshop on Asian Translation: 5th Workshop on Asian Translation*, Hong Kong. Association for Computational Linguistics.

Rico Sennrich, Barry Haddow, and Alexandra Birch. 2016. Neural machine translation of rare words with subword units. In *Proceedings of the 54th Annual Meeting of the Association for Computational Linguistics (Volume 1: Long Papers)*, pages 1715–1725, Berlin, Germany. Association for Computational Linguistics.

Rico Sennrich and Biao Zhang. 2019. Revisiting low-resource neural machine translation: A case study. In *Proceedings of the 57th Annual Meeting of the Association for Computational Linguistics*, pages 211–221, Florence, Italy. Association for Computational Linguistics.

S Sreelekha and P Bhattacharyya. 2017. A case study on english-malayalam machine translation. *ArXiv*, abs/1702.08217.

S Sreelekha and P Bhattacharyya. 2018. Morphology injection for English-Malayalam statistical machine translation. In *Proceedings of the Eleventh International Conference on Language Resources and Evaluation (LREC 2018)*, Miyazaki, Japan. European Language Resources Association (ELRA).

Sanford B Steever. 2019. *The Dravidian Languages*. Routledge.

Jörg Tiedemann. 2012. Parallel data, tools and interfaces in opus. In *Proceedings of the Eight International Conference on Language Resources and Evaluation (LREC'12)*, Istanbul, Turkey. European Language Resources Association (ELRA).

K Deepthi Yadav and L Lingam. 2017. Rule based machine translation of complex sentences from english to telugu. *International Journal of Research*, 4(9):790–800.

Zhengzhe Yu, Zhanglin Wu, Xiaoyu Chen, Daimeng Wei, Hengchao Shang, Jiaxin Guo, Zongyao Li, Minghan Wang, Liangyou Li, Lizhi Lei, Hao Yang, and Ying Qin. 2020. HW-TSC's participation in the WAT 2020 indic languages multilingual task. In *Proceedings of the 7th Workshop on Asian Translation*, pages 92–97, Suzhou, China. Association for Computational Linguistics.

# Itihāsa: A large-scale corpus for Sanskrit to English translation

**Rahul Aralikatte**[1] **Miryam de Lhoneux**[1] **Anoop Kunchukuttan**[2] **Anders Søgaard**[1]
[1]University of Copenhgagen [2]Microsoft AI and Research
[1]{rahul,ml,soegaard}@di.ku.dk
[2]ankunchu@microsoft.com

## Abstract

This work introduces Itihāsa, a large-scale translation dataset containing 93,000 pairs of Sanskrit *shloka*s and their English translations. The *shloka*s are extracted from two Indian epics viz., The Rāmāyana and The Mahābhārata. We first describe the motivation behind the curation of such a dataset and follow up with empirical analysis to bring out its nuances. We then benchmark the performance of standard translation models on this corpus and show that even state-of-the-art transformer architectures perform poorly, emphasizing the complexity of the dataset.[1]

## 1 Introduction

Sanskrit is one of the oldest languages in the world and most Indo-European languages are influenced by it (Beekes, 1995). There are about 30 million pieces of Sanskrit literature available to us today (Goyal et al., 2012), most of which have not been digitized. Among those that have been, few have been translated. The main reason for this is the lack of expertise and funding. An automatic translation system would not only aid and accelerate this process, but it would also help in democratizing the knowledge, history, and culture present in this literature. In this work, we present Itihāsa, a large-scale Sanskrit-English translation corpus consisting of more than 93,000 *shlokas* and their translations.

Itihāsa, literally meaning 'it happened this way' is a collection of historical records of important events in Indian history. These bodies of work are mostly composed in the form of verses or *shloka*s, a poetic form which usually consists of four parts containing eight syllables each (Fig. 1). The most important among these works are The Rāmāyana and The Mahābhārata. The Rāmāyana, which describes the events in the life of Lord Rāma, consists of 24,000 verses. The Mahābhārata details the war between cousins of the Kuru dynasty, in 100,000 verses. The Mahābhārata is the longest poem ever written with about 1.8 million words in total and is roughly ten times the length of the Iliad and the Odyssey combined.

**मा निषाद प्रतिष्ठां त्वमगमश्शाश्वतीस्समाः।**
**यत्क्रौञ्चमिथुनादेकमवधीः काममोहितम्॥**

**O fowler, since you have slain one of a pair of Krauñcas, you shall never attain prosperity (respect)!**

Figure 1: An introductory *shloka* from The Rāmāyana. The four parts with eight syllables each are highlighted with different shades of gray.

Only two authors have attempted to translate the unabridged versions of both The Rāmāyana and The Mahābhārata to English: Manmatha Nāth Dutt in the 1890s and Bibek Debroy in the 2010s. M. N. Dutt was a prolific translator whose works are now in the public domain. These works are published in a *shloka*-wise format as shown in Fig. 1 which makes it easy to automatically align *shloka*s with their translations. Though many of M. N. Dutt's works are freely available, we choose to extract data from The Rāmāyana (Vālmiki and Dutt, 1891), and The Mahābhārata (Dwaipāyana and Dutt, 1895), mainly due to its size and popularity. As per our knowledge, this is the biggest Sanskrit-English translation dataset to be released in the public domain.

We also train and evaluate standard translation systems on this dataset. In both translation directions, we use Moses as an SMT baseline, and Transformer-based seq2seq models as NMT baselines (see §4). We find that models which are generally on-par with human performance on other

[1]The processed and split dataset can be found at https://github.com/rahular/itihasa and a human-readable version can be found at http://rahular.com/itihasa.



*Proceedings of the 8th Workshop on Asian Translation*, pages 191–197
Bangkok, Thailand (online), August 5-6, 2021. 

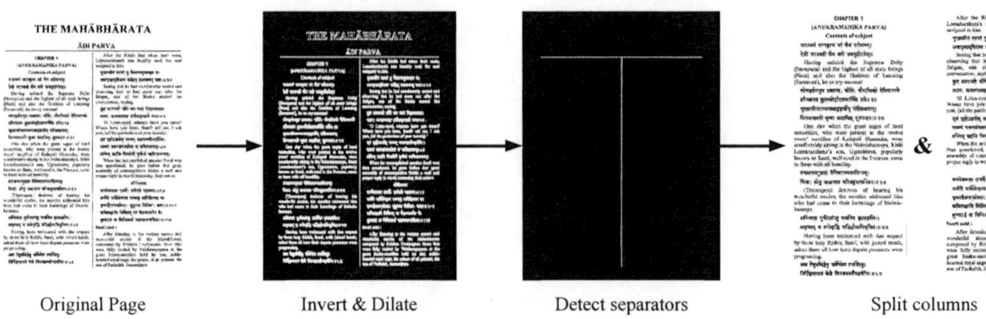

Figure 2: Pre-processing Pipeline: The three steps shown here are: (i) invert the colour scheme of the PDF and dilate every detectable edge, (ii) find the indices of the longest vertical and horizontal lines in the page, and (iii) split the original PDF along the found separator lines.

translation tasks, perform poorly on Itihāsa, with the best models scoring between 7-8 BLEU points. This indicates the complex nature of the dataset (see §3 for a detailed analysis of the dataset and its vocabulary).

**Motivation** The main motivation behind this work is to provide an impetus for the Indic NLP community to build better translation systems for Sanskrit. Additionally, since The Rāmāyana and The Mahābhārata are so pervasive in Indian culture, and have been translated to all major Indian languages, there is a possibility of creating an $n$-way parallel corpus with Sanskrit as the pivot language, similar to Europarl (Koehn, 2005) and PMIndia (Haddow and Kirefu, 2020) datasets.

The existence of Sanskrit-English parallel data has other advantages as well. Due to Sanskrit being a morphologically rich, agglutinative, and highly inflexive, complex concepts can be expressed in compact forms by combining individual words through *Sandhi* and *Samasa*.[2] This also enables a speaker to potentially create an infinite number of unique words in Sanskrit. Having a parallel corpus can help us induce word translations through bilingual dictionary induction (Søgaard et al., 2018). It also allows us to use English as a surrogate language for tasks like knowledge base population. Constituency or dependency parsing, NER, and word sense disambiguation can be improved using indirect supervision (Täckström, 2013). Essentially, a parallel corpus allows us to apply a plethora of transfer learning techniques to improve NLP tools for Sanskrit.

## 2 Data Preparation

The translated works of The Rāmāyana and The Mahābhārata were published in four and nine volumes respectively.[3] All volumes have a standard two-column format as shown in Fig. 2. Each page has a header with the chapter name and page number separated from the main text by a horizontal line. The two columns of text are separated by a vertical line. The process of data preparation can be divided into (i) automatic OCR extraction, and (ii) manual inspection for alignment errors.

**Automatic Extraction** The OCR systems we experimented with performed poorly on digitized documents due to their two-column format. They often fail to recognize line breaks which result in the concatenation of text present in different columns. To mitigate this issue, we use an edge detector[4] to find the largest horizontal and vertical lines, and using the indices of the detected lines, split the original page horizontally and vertically to remove the header and separate the columns (see Fig. 2). We then input the single-column documents to Google Cloud's OCR API[5] to extract text from them. To verify the accuracy of the extracted text, one chapter from each volume (13 chapters in total) is manually checked for mistakes. We find that the extracted text is more than 99% and 97% accurate in Sanskrit and English respectively. The surprising accuracy of Devanagari OCR can be attributed to

[2] *Sandhi* refers to the concatenation of words, where the edge characters combine to form a new one. *Samasa* can be thought of as being similar to elliptic constructions in English where certain phrases are elided since their meaning is obvious from the context.

[3] The digitized (scanned) PDF versions of these books are available at https://hinduscriptures.in

[4] We invert the color scheme and apply a small dilation for better edge detection using OpenCV (Bradski, 2000).

[5] More information can be found at https://cloud.google.com/vision/docs/pdf

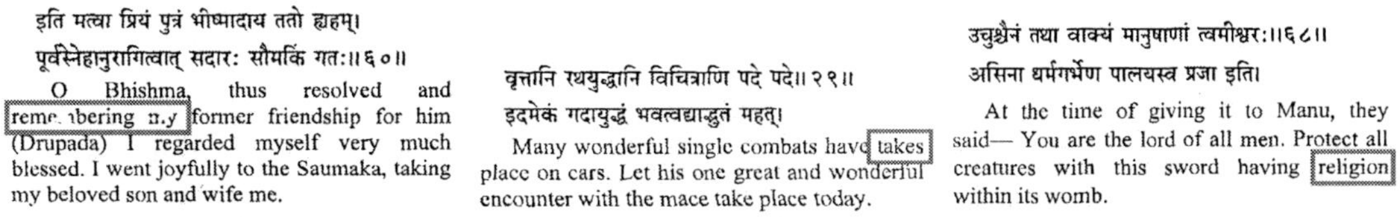

इति मत्वा प्रियं पुत्रं भीष्मादाय ततो ह्यहम्।
पूर्वस्नेहानुरागित्वात् सदार: सौमकिं गत:॥६०॥
O Bhishma, thus resolved and reme. ıbering n.y former friendship for him (Drupada) I regarded myself very much blessed. I went joyfully to the Saumaka, taking my beloved son and wife me.

(a) Print error.

वृत्तानि रथयुद्धानि विचित्राणि पदे पदे॥२९॥
इदमेकं गदायुद्धं भवत्वद्याद्भुतं महत्।
Many wonderful single combats have takes place on cars. Let his one great and wonderful encounter with the mace take place today.

(b) Input error.

उचुश्चैनं तथा वाक्यं मानुषाणां त्वमीश्वर:॥६८॥
असिना धर्मगर्भेण पालयस्व प्रजा इति।
At the time of giving it to Manu, they said— You are the lord of all men. Protect all creatures with this sword having religion within its womb.

(c) Subjective error.

Figure 3: Different types of errors found in the original text while performing manual inspection.

the distinctness of its alphabet. For English, this number decreases as the OCR system often misclassifies similar-looking characters (viz., *e* and *c*, *i* and *l*, etc.).

**Manual Inspection** An important limitation of the OCR system is its misclassification of alignment spaces and line breaks. It sometimes wrongly treats large gaps between words as line breaks and the rest of the text on the line is moved to the end of the paragraph which results in translations being misaligned with its *shloka*s. Therefore, the output of all 13 volumes was manually inspected and such misalignments were corrected.[6]

Upon manual inspection, other kinds of errors were discovered and corrected where possible.[7] These errors can be categorized as follows: (i) *print errors*: this type of error is caused by occluded or faded text, smudged ink, etc. An example can be seen in Fig. 3a, (ii) *input errors*: these are human errors during typesetting the volumes which include typos (Fig, 3b), exclusion of words, inclusion of spurious words, etc., (iii) *subjective errors*: these are contextual errors in the translation itself. For example, in Fig. 3c, the word *dharma* is incorrectly translated as 'religion' instead of 'righteousness', and (iv) *OCR errors*: these errors arise from the underlying OCR system. An example of such errors is the improper handling of split words across lines in the Devanagari script. If the OCR system encounters a hyphen as the last character of a line, the entire line is ignored. In general, print errors are corrected as much as possible, subjective errors are retained for originality, and other types of errors are corrected when encountered.

[6]This was a time-consuming process and the first author inspected the output manually over the course of one year.

[7]It was not feasible for the authors to correct every error, especially the lexical ones. The most common error that exists in the corpus is the swapping of *e* and *c*. For example, 'thcir' instead of 'their'. Though these errors can easily be corrected using automated tools like the one proposed in (Boyd, 2018), it is out-of-scope of this paper and is left for future work.

| | Train | Dev. | Test | Total |
|---|---|---|---|---|
| Rāmayana | | | | |
| Chapters | 514 | 42 | 86 | 642 |
| Shlokas | 15,834 | 1,115 | 2,422 | 19,371 |
| Mahābhārata | | | | |
| Chapters | 1,688 | 139 | 283 | 2,110 |
| Shlokas | 59,327 | 5,033 | 9,299 | 73,659 |
| Overall | | | | |
| Chapters | 2202 | 181 | 369 | 2,752 |
| Shlokas | 75,161 | 6,148 | 11,721 | 93,030 |

Table 1: Size of training, development, and test sets.

## 3 Analysis

In total, we extract 19,371 translation pairs from 642 chapters of The Rāmāyana and 73,659 translation pairs from 2,110 chapters of The Mahābhārata. It should be noted that these numbers do not correspond to the number of *shloka*s because, in the original volumes, *shloka*s are sometimes split and often combined to make the English translations flow better. We reserve 80% of the data from each text for training MT systems and use the rest for evaluation. From the evaluation set, 33% is used for development and 67% for testing. The absolute sizes of the split data are shown in Tab. 1.

Due to Sanskrit's agglutinative nature, the dataset is asymmetric in the sense that, the number of words required to convey the same information, is less in Sanskrit when compared with English. The Rāmāyana's English translations, on average, have 2.54 words for every word in its *shloka*. This value is even larger in The Mahābhārata with 2.82 translated words per *shloka* word.

This effect is clearly seen when we consider the vocabulary sizes and the percentage of common tokens between the texts. For this, we tokenize the data with two different tokenization schemes: word-level and byte-pair encoding (Sennrich et al., 2016, BPE). For word-level tokenization, the translations of The Rāmāyana (The Mahābhārata) have 16,820 (31,055) unique word tokens, and the *shloka*s have 66,072 (184,407) tokens. The English vocabularies

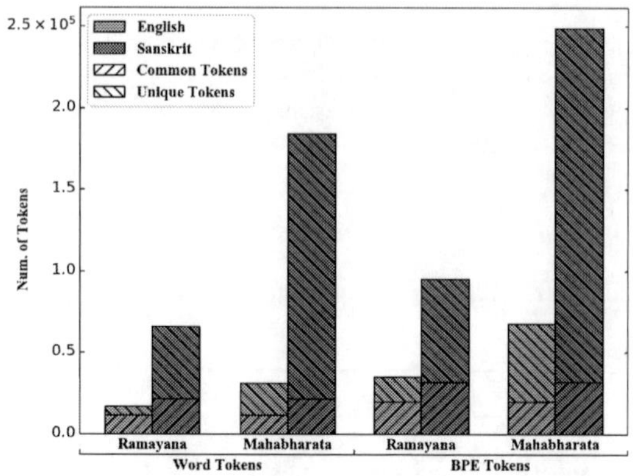


Figure 4: Comparison of vocabulary sizes. Sanskrit's morphological and agglutinative nature accounts for the large number of unique tokens in the vocabularies.

| Model | chrF | Tok. Acc. | BLEU | TER (↓) |
|---|---|---|---|---|
| English to Sanskrit | | | | |
| Moses | 25.9 | 5.48 | 0.21 | 1.53 |
| B2B-Tiny | 15.1 | 8.07 | 2.85 | 1.04 |
| B2B-Mini | 21.6 | 8.52 | 5.66 | 1.03 |
| B2B-Small | 23.4 | 8.75 | 6.93 | 1.03 |
| B2B-Medium | 23.7 | 8.67 | 6.94 | **1.02** |
| B2B-Base | **24.3** | **8.89** | **7.59** | 1.04 |
| Sanskrit to English | | | | |
| Moses | 29.3 | 8.03 | 5.67 | **0.91** |
| B2B-Tiny | 24.5 | **8.61** | 5.64 | 0.98 |
| B2B-Mini | 29.3 | 8.58 | 7.28 | 0.95 |
| B2B-Small | 30.1 | 8.55 | **7.49** | 0.95 |
| B2B-Medium | 30.4 | 8.49 | 7.48 | 0.94 |
| B2B-Base | **30.5** | 8.38 | 7.09 | 0.93 |

Table 2: Character F1, Token accuracy, BLEU, and TER scores for Moses and Transformer models. Scores marked with (↓) are better if they are lower.

have 11,579 common tokens which is 68.8% of The Rāmāyana's and 37.3% of The Mahābhārata's. But the overlap percentages drop significantly for the Sanskrit vocabularies. In this case, we find 21,635 common tokens which amount to an overlap of 32.7% and 11.7% respectively. As shown in Fig. 4, this trend holds for BPE tokenization as well.

## 4 Experiments

We train one SMT and five NMT systems in both directions and report the (i) character $n$-gram F-score, (ii) token accuracy, (iii) BLEU (Papineni et al., 2002), and (iv) Translation Edit Ratio (Snover et al., 2006, TER) scores in Tab. 2. For SMT, we use Moses (Koehn et al., 2007) and for NMT, we use sequence-to-sequence (seq2seq) Transformers (Vaswani et al., 2017). We train the seq2seq models from scratch by initializing the encoders and decoders with standard BERT (B2B) architectures. These `Tiny`, `Mini`, `Small`, `Medium`, and `Base` models have 2/128, 4/256, 4/512, 8/512, and 12/768 layers/dimensions respectively. See Turc et al. (2019) for more details. In our early experiments, we also tried initializing the encoders and decoders with weights from pre-trained Indic language models like MuRIL (Khanuja et al., 2021), but they showed poor performance and thus are not reported here.

**Implementation Details** All models are trained using HuggingFace Transformers (Wolf et al., 2020). Both source and target sequences are truncated at 128 tokens. We train WordPiece tokenizers on our dataset and use them for all models. Adam optimizer (Kingma and Ba, 2014) with weight-decay of 0.01, and learning rate of $5 \times 10^{-5}$ is used. All models are trained for 100 epochs. The learning rate is warmed up over 8,000 steps and decayed later with a linear scheduler. We use a batch size of 128, and use standard cross-entropy loss with no label smoothing. We run into memory errors on bigger models (`medium` and `base`), but maintain the effective batch-size and optimization steps by introducing gradient accumulation and increasing the number of epochs, respectively. Also, to reduce the total training time of bigger models, we stop training if the BLEU score does not improve over 10 epochs. During generation, we use a beam size of 5 and compute all metrics against truncated references.

**Discussion** We see that all models perform poorly, with low token accuracy and high TER. While the English to Sanskrit (E2S) models get better with size, this pattern is not clearly seen in Sanskrit to English (S2E) models. Surprisingly for S2E models, the token accuracy progressively decreases as their size increases. Also, Moses has the best TER among S2E models which suggests that the seq2seq models have not been able to learn even simple co-occurrences between source and target tokens. This leads us to hypothesize that the Sanskrit encoders produce sub-optimal representations. One way to improve them would be to add a *Sandhi-splitting* step to the tokenization pipeline, thereby decreasing the Sanskrit vocabulary size. Another natural extension to improve the quality of representations would be to initialize the encoders with a pre-trained language model.

| | |
|---|---|
| **EN** | **Hearing the words of Viśvāmitra, Rāghava, together with Laksmana, was struck with amazement, and spoke to Viśvāmitra, saying,** |
| **SN** | **विश्वामित्रवचः श्रुत्वा राघवः सहलक्ष्मणः।**<br>**विस्मयं परमं गत्वा विश्वामित्रमथाब्रवीत्॥** |
| **Pred.** | **विश्वामित्रवचः श्रुत्वा लक्ष्मणः सहलक्ष्मणः।**<br>**विश्वामित्रवचः श्रुत्वा विश्वामित्रोऽब्रवीदिदम्॥** |

Figure 5: A gold sentence and *shloka* from the test set, and its corresponding `small` model prediction.

Though it is clear that there is a large scope for improvement, the models are able to learn some interesting features of the dataset. Fig. 5 shows a random gold translation pair and the `small` model's prediction. Though we see repetitions of phrases and semantic errors, the prediction follows the meter in which the original *shloka*s are written, i.e. it also consists of 4 parts containing 8 syllables each.

## 5 Related Work

Early translation efforts from Sanskrit to English were limited to the construction of dictionaries by Western Indologists (Müller, 1866; Monier-Williams, 1899). Over the years, though notable translation works like Ganguli (1883) have been published, the lack of digitization has been a bottleneck hindering any meaningful progress towards automatic translation systems. This has changed recently, at least for monolingual data, with the curation of digital libraries like GRETIL[8] and DCS[9]. Currently, the largest freely available repository of translations are for The Bhagavadgita (Prabhakar et al., 2000) and The Rāmāyana (Geervani et al., 1989).

However, labeled datasets for other tasks, like the ones proposed in (Kulkarni, 2013; Bhardwaj et al., 2018; Krishnan et al., 2020) have resulted in parsers (Krishna et al., 2020, 2021) and sandhi splitters (Aralikatte et al., 2018; Krishnan and Kulkarni, 2020) which are pre-cursors to modular translation systems. Though there have been attempts at building Sanskrit translation tools (Bharati and Kulkarni, 2009), they are mostly rule-based and rely on manual intervention. We hope that the availability of the Itihāsa corpus pushes the domain towards end-to-end systems.

[8]`http://gretil.sub.uni-goettingen.de/gretil.html`

[9]`http://www.sanskrit-linguistics.org/dcs/index.php`

## 6 Conclusion

In this work, we introduce Itihāsa, a large-scale dataset containing more than 93,000 pairs of Sanskrit *shlokas* and their English translations from The Rāmāyana and The Mahābhārata. First, we detail the extraction process which includes an automated OCR phase and a manual alignment phase. Next, we analyze the dataset to give an intuition of its asymmetric nature and to showcase its complexities. Lastly, we train state-of-the-art translation models which perform poorly, proving the necessity for more work in this area.

## Acknowledgements

We thank the reviewers for their valuable feedback. Rahul Aralikatte and Anders Søgaard are funded by a Google Focused Research Award.

## References

Rahul Aralikatte, Neelamadhav Gantayat, Naveen Panwar, Anush Sankaran, and Senthil Mani. 2018. Sanskrit sandhi splitting using seq2(seq)2. In *Proceedings of the 2018 Conference on Empirical Methods in Natural Language Processing*, pages 4909–4914, Brussels, Belgium. Association for Computational Linguistics.

Robert Stephen Paul Beekes. 1995. *Comparative Indo-European Linguistics*. Benjamins Amsterdam.

Akshar Bharati and Amba Kulkarni. 2009. Anusaaraka: an accessor cum machine translator. *Department of Sanskrit Studies, University of Hyderabad, Hyderabad*, pages 1–75.

Shubham Bhardwaj, Neelamadhav Gantayat, Nikhil Chaturvedi, Rahul Garg, and Sumeet Agarwal. 2018. SandhiKosh: A benchmark corpus for evaluating Sanskrit sandhi tools. In *Proceedings of the Eleventh International Conference on Language Resources and Evaluation (LREC 2018)*, Miyazaki, Japan. European Language Resources Association (ELRA).

Adriane Boyd. 2018. Using Wikipedia edits in low resource grammatical error correction. In *Proceedings of the 2018 EMNLP Workshop W-NUT: The 4th Workshop on Noisy User-generated Text*, pages 79–84, Brussels, Belgium. Association for Computational Linguistics.

G. Bradski. 2000. The OpenCV Library. *Dr. Dobb's Journal of Software Tools*.

Krishna Dwaipāyana and Manmatha Nāth Dutt. 1895. *Mahabharata*. Elysium Press, Calcutta.

Kisari Mohan Ganguli. 1883. *The Mahabharata*.

P Geervani, K Kamala, and V. V. Subba Rao. 1989. Valmiki ramayana.

Pawan Goyal, Gérard Huet, Amba Kulkarni, Peter Scharf, and Ralph Bunker. 2012. A distributed platform for Sanskrit processing. In *Proceedings of COLING 2012*, pages 1011–1028, Mumbai, India. The COLING 2012 Organizing Committee.

Barry Haddow and Faheem Kirefu. 2020. Pmindia – a collection of parallel corpora of languages of india.

Simran Khanuja, Diksha Bansal, Sarvesh Mehtani, Savya Khosla, Atreyee Dey, Balaji Gopalan, Dilip Kumar Margam, Pooja Aggarwal, Rajiv Teja Nagipogu, Shachi Dave, Shruti Gupta, Subhash Chandra Bose Gali, Vish Subramanian, and Partha Talukdar. 2021. Muril: Multilingual representations for indian languages.

Diederik P Kingma and Jimmy Ba. 2014. Adam: A method for stochastic optimization. *arXiv preprint arXiv:1412.6980*.

Philipp Koehn. 2005. Europarl: A Parallel Corpus for Statistical Machine Translation. In *Conference Proceedings: the tenth Machine Translation Summit*, pages 79–86, Phuket, Thailand. AAMT, AAMT.

Philipp Koehn, Hieu Hoang, Alexandra Birch, Chris Callison-Burch, Marcello Federico, Nicola Bertoldi, Brooke Cowan, Wade Shen, Christine Moran, Richard Zens, Chris Dyer, Ondřej Bojar, Alexandra Constantin, and Evan Herbst. 2007. Moses: Open source toolkit for statistical machine translation. In *Proceedings of the 45th Annual Meeting of the Association for Computational Linguistics Companion Volume Proceedings of the Demo and Poster Sessions*, pages 177–180, Prague, Czech Republic. Association for Computational Linguistics.

Amrith Krishna, Ashim Gupta, Deepak Garasangi, Pavankumar Satuluri, and Pawan Goyal. 2020. Keep it surprisingly simple: A simple first order graph based parsing model for joint morphosyntactic parsing in Sanskrit. In *Proceedings of the 2020 Conference on Empirical Methods in Natural Language Processing (EMNLP)*, pages 4791–4797, Online. Association for Computational Linguistics.

Amrith Krishna, Bishal Santra, Ashim Gupta, Pavankumar Satuluri, and Pawan Goyal. 2021. A Graph-Based Framework for Structured Prediction Tasks in Sanskrit. *Computational Linguistics*, 46(4):785–845.

Sriram Krishnan and Amba Kulkarni. 2020. Sanskrit segmentation revisited.

Sriram Krishnan, Amba Kulkarni, and Gérard Huet. 2020. Validation and normalization of dcs corpus using sanskrit heritage tools to build a tagged gold corpus.

Amba Kulkarni. 2013. A deterministic dependency parser with dynamic programming for Sanskrit. In *Proceedings of the Second International Conference on Dependency Linguistics (DepLing 2013)*, pages 157–166, Prague, Czech Republic. Charles University in Prague, Matfyzpress, Prague, Czech Republic.

Monier Monier-Williams. 1899. *A Sanskrit-English dictionary : etymologically and philologically arranged with special reference to cognate Indo-European languages*. Clarendon Press.

F.M. Müller. 1866. *A Sanskrit Grammar for Beginners: In Devanâgarî and Roman Letters Throughout*. Handbooks for the study of Sanskrit. Longmans, Green, and Company.

Kishore Papineni, Salim Roukos, Todd Ward, and Wei-Jing Zhu. 2002. Bleu: a method for automatic evaluation of machine translation. In *Proceedings of the 40th Annual Meeting of the Association for Computational Linguistics*, pages 311–318, Philadelphia, Pennsylvania, USA. Association for Computational Linguistics.

T. V Prabhakar, Ravi Mula, T Archana, Harish Karnick, Nitin Gautam, Murat Dhwaj Singh, Madhu Kumar Dhavala, Rajeev Bhatia, and Saurabh Kumar. 2000. Gita supersite.

Rico Sennrich, Barry Haddow, and Alexandra Birch. 2016. Neural machine translation of rare words with subword units. In *Proceedings of the 54th Annual Meeting of the Association for Computational Linguistics (Volume 1: Long Papers)*, pages 1715–1725, Berlin, Germany. Association for Computational Linguistics.

Matthew Snover, Bonnie Dorr, Richard Schwartz, Linnea Micciulla, and Ralph Weischedel. 2006. A study of translation error rate with targeted human annotation. In *In Proceedings of the Association for Machine Transaltion in the Americas (AMTA 2006*.

Anders Søgaard, Sebastian Ruder, and Ivan Vulić. 2018. On the limitations of unsupervised bilingual dictionary induction. In *Proceedings of the 56th Annual Meeting of the Association for Computational Linguistics (Volume 1: Long Papers)*, pages 778–788, Melbourne, Australia. Association for Computational Linguistics.

Oscar Täckström. 2013. *Predicting Linguistic Structure with Incomplete and Cross-Lingual Supervision*. Ph.D. thesis, Uppsala University.

Iulia Turc, Ming-Wei Chang, Kenton Lee, and Kristina Toutanova. 2019. Well-read students learn better: On the importance of pre-training compact models. *arXiv preprint arXiv:1908.08962v2*.

Ashish Vaswani, Noam Shazeer, Niki Parmar, Jakob Uszkoreit, Llion Jones, Aidan N. Gomez, undefinedukasz Kaiser, and Illia Polosukhin. 2017. Attention is all you need. In *Proceedings of the 31st International Conference on Neural Information Processing Systems*, NIPS'17, page 6000–6010, Red Hook, NY, USA. Curran Associates Inc.

Vālmiki and Manmatha Nāth Dutt. 1891. *Ramayana*. Deva Press, Calcutta.

Thomas Wolf, Lysandre Debut, Victor Sanh, Julien Chaumond, Clement Delangue, Anthony Moi, Pierric Cistac, Tim Rault, Remi Louf, Morgan Funtowicz, Joe Davison, Sam Shleifer, Patrick von Platen, Clara Ma, Yacine Jernite, Julien Plu, Canwen Xu, Teven Le Scao, Sylvain Gugger, Mariama Drame, Quentin Lhoest, and Alexander Rush. 2020. Transformers: State-of-the-art natural language processing. In *Proceedings of the 2020 Conference on Empirical Methods in Natural Language Processing: System Demonstrations*, pages 38–45, Online. Association for Computational Linguistics.

# NICT-5's Submission To WAT 2021: MBART Pre-training And In-Domain Fine Tuning For Indic Languages

**Raj Dabre**[‡] **Abhisek Chakrabarty**[‡]
[‡]National Institute of Information and Communications Technology, Kyoto, Japan
{raj.dabre, abhisek.chakra}@nict.go.jp

## Abstract

In this paper we describe our submission to the multilingual Indic language translation task "MultiIndicMT" under the team name "NICT-5". This task involves translation from 10 Indic languages into English and vice-versa. The objective of the task was to explore the utility of multilingual approaches using a variety of in-domain and out-of-domain parallel and monolingual corpora. Given the recent success of multilingual NMT pre-training we decided to explore pre-training an MBART model on a large monolingual corpus collection covering all languages in this task followed by multilingual fine-tuning on small in-domain corpora. Firstly, we observed that a small amount of pre-training followed by fine-tuning on small bilingual corpora can yield large gains over when pre-training is not used. Furthermore, multilingual fine-tuning leads to further gains in translation quality which significantly outperforms a very strong multilingual baseline that does not rely on any pre-training.

## 1 Introduction

Neural machine translation (NMT) (Bahdanau et al., 2014) is known to give state-of-the-art translations for a variety of language pairs. NMT is known to perform poorly for language pairs for which parallel corpora are scarce. This happens due to lack of translation knowledge as well as due to overfitting which is inevitable in a low-resource setting. Fortunately, transfer learning via cross-lingual transfer (Zoph et al., 2016; Dabre et al., 2019), multilingualism (Firat et al., 2016; Dabre et al., 2020), back-translation (Sennrich et al., 2016) or monolingual pre-training (Liu et al., 2020; Lewis et al., 2020; Mao et al., 2020) can significantly improve translation quality in a low-resource situation.

Cross-lingual transfer learning involves pre-training a model using a parallel corpus for a resource-rich language pair $XX - YY$ and then fine-tuning on a parallel corpus for a resource-poor language pair $AA - BB$. Naturally the improvements in translation quality will be impacted by if $XX = AA$ or $YY = BB$[1] and it is often better to have a shared target language. Cross-lingual transfer despite its simplicity and effectiveness relies on shared source or target languages for effective transfer and thus depending on methods that use monolingual corpora are preferable. This also applies to vanilla multilingual training which does not rely on monolingual corpora. Another reason for focusing on utilizing monolingual corpora is that they are extremely abundant when compared to parallel corpora and they contain a large amount of language modeling information. In this regard, back-translation and multilingual pre-training are two of the most reliable methods.

While back-translation is easy to use, it involves the translation of millions of monolingual sentences and quite often it is necessary to perform multiple iterations of the back-translation process to yield the best results (Hoang et al., 2018) which means that it is quite resource intensive. This leaves us with multilingual pre-training using methods such as BART/MBART (Liu et al., 2020; Lewis et al., 2020) which we use for developing our translation system. The advantage of BART/MBART is that we need to pre-train these models once and then fine-tune not only for machine translation but also for any natural language generation task such as summarization (Shi et al., 2021). These models can be upgraded to include additional language pairs in the future by simply resuming pre-training (Tang et al., 2020).

In this paper, we describe our simple approach involving MBART pre-training and fine-tuning. First, we use the official monolingual corpora to train an MBART model spanning all 11 languages in

[1] If $XX - YY$ and $AA - BB$ are the same pairs then it is known as domain adaptation.



*Proceedings of the 8th Workshop on Asian Translation*, pages 198–204
Bangkok, Thailand (online), August 5-6, 2021. 

the shared task. Following this we fine-tune the MBART model using the officially provided in-domain corpora in two different ways: bilingual fine-tuning and multilingual fine-tuning. Additionally we also train multilingual models without any pre-training. The multilingual models are one-to-many (English to Indic) and many-to-one (Indic to English) in nature. The bilingual fine-tuning and non pre-trained multilingual model serve as strong baselines which significantly outperform the organizers weak bilingual baselines. Our multilingual fine-tuning models exhibit the best translation quality out of all our models which shows the power of effectively combining monolingual corpora with multilingualism.

We refer readers to the workshop overview paper (Nakazawa et al., 2021) for a better understanding of the task and the comparison of our results with those of other participants.

## 2 Related Work

The techniques used in this paper revolve around multilingualism, sequence-to-sequence pre-training and transfer learning.

Firat et al. (2016) proposed multilingual neural translation using multiple encoders and decoders which was then simplified by Johnson et al. (2017) to require a single encoder and decoder to be shared among multiple language pairs. Due to the simplicity of the latter approach, most modern multilingual models are based on it and in this paper we also use the same approach. Multilingualism involves implicit transfer learning but a more explicit way to do the same is to use fine-tuning (Zoph et al., 2016). However all these aforementioned approaches rely on bilingual data which is not always readily available. This can be remedied by the use of monolingual corpora for backtranslation (Sennrich et al., 2016) or for pre-training (Lewis et al., 2020; Liu et al., 2020; Mao et al., 2020). As backtranslation is resource intensive, given that it involves translation of a large amount of monolingual corpora, pre-training is more attractive as a pre-trained model can be used for a variety of natural language generation tasks. In this paper we combine sequence-to-sequence pre-training followed by multilingual fine-tuning. For an overview of multilingual NMT we refer readers to a survey paper on multilingualism and low-resource NMT in general (Dabre et al., 2020).

## 3 Our Approaches

For our submissions we focused on combining multilingual denoising pre-training (MBART) and multilingual fine tuning.

### 3.1 Multilingual NMT Training

We follow the multilingual NMT training approach proposed by Johnson et al. (2017). Consider a multilingual parallel corpora collection spanning corpora for $N$ language pairs $L^i_{src} - L^i_{tgt}$ for $i \in [1, N]$. The sizes of the parallel corpora are typically different, often radically different, in which case it is important to balance corpora sizes to prevent the model from focusing too much on some language pairs. Johnson et al. (2017) showed that training by oversampling smaller corpora to match the size of the largest corpus is the best approach. However, since then newer corpora balancing approaches have been proposed and the most recent effective method is known as the temperature based sampling approach (Aharoni et al., 2019). Suppose that the size of the $i^{th}$ corpus is $s_i$ which means the probability of sampling a sentence pair from each corpus is $p_i = \frac{s_i}{S}$ where $S = \sum_i s_i$. Using this default sampling probability is biased towards larger corpora so first the probability values are tempered using a temperature $T$. The resultant probabilities $p^t_i$ are obtained as follows:

$$p^t_i = \frac{p_i^{\frac{1}{T}}}{\sum_j p_j^{\frac{1}{T}}} \quad (1)$$

When $T = 1$, $p^t_i = p_i$ and when $T = \infty$, $p^t_i = \frac{1}{N}$. Aharoni et al. (2019) showed that a value of $T = 5$ works well in practice which is what we use in our experiments. During training, sentence pairs are sampled from each corpus following which the source sentence is prepended with a token $< 2L^i_{tgt} >$ which indicates that the source sentence should be translated into $L^i_{tgt}$. Thereafter, the pre-processed source sentence and target sentence are fed to the NMT model which learns how to translate between multiple language pairs.

### 3.2 MBART Pre-training and Fine-Tuning

Liu et al. (2020) extended the BART model (Lewis et al., 2020) by denoising pre-training the BART model on 25 languages instead of 2 which leads to an MBART model. The main advantage of an MBART model is that it can be fine-tuned with corpora for a variety of language pairs which naturally

| Language | #Lines |
|---|---|
| as | 1.39M |
| bn | 39.9M |
| en | 54.3M |
| gu | 41.1M |
| hi | 63.1M |
| kn | 53.3M |
| ml | 50.2M |
| mr | 34.0M |
| or | 6.94M |
| pa | 29.2M |
| ta | 31.5M |
| te | 47.9M |

Table 1: Monolingual corpora statistics.

| Language Pair | #Lines |
|---|---|
| bn-en | 23,306 |
| gu-en | 41,578 |
| hi-en | 50,349 |
| kn-en | 28,901 |
| ml-en | 26,916 |
| mr-en | 28,974 |
| or-en | 31,966 |
| pa-en | 28,294 |
| ta-en | 32,638 |
| te-en | 33,380 |

Table 2: Bilingual corpora statistics for the PMI dataset only.

includes many zero-shot pairs. The way to train an MBART model is by "corrupting" an input sentence, feeding it to the encoder and then training the model to predict the original sentence. Corruption can be done in a variety of ways and in this paper we use 'text infilling' approach which finds random spans of the source tokens and replaces them with a token such as $< MASK >$ till a certain percentage of the sentence is masked. The length of the span is sampled from a Poisson distribution with a mean of $\lambda$. Liu et al. (2020) determined an optimal value of $\lambda = 3.5$ which we also use. The denoising objective helps the MBART model learn about using context to translate and also helps it acquire language modeling information.

After an MBART model is trained it is fine-tuned on a bilingual or multilingual parallel corpus which is then used for translation. The language modeling priors help account for missing translation knowledge in low-resource settings which leads to large improvements in translation quality over baselines which only use parallel corpora.

## 4 Experimental Setup

Our goal was to study how far the translation quality can be pushed via MBART pre-training and multilingual fine-tuning. To do so, we describe the datasets, implementation details, evaluation metrics and the models trained.

### 4.1 Datasets and Preprocessing

The languages involved in the task are: Bengali, Gujarati, Hindi, Kannada, Malayalam, Marathi, Oriya, Punjabi, Tamil, Telugu and English. We used the official parallel corpora[2] provided by the organizers. The 11-way evaluation development and test sets come from the PMI dataset[3]. Although the organizers provided corpora from other sources as well, we decided to restrict ourselves to the PMI part of the parallel corpora to avoid the need for data selection. Instead we relied on pre-training to compensate for using smaller amount of parallel corpora. For MBART pre-training we used the AI4Bharat's monolingual corpora known as IndicCorp [4] (Kunchukuttan et al., 2020). Note that MBART pre-training supposes the monolingual data is available as documents however since we only use the masking denoising approach, sentence level corpora[5] are sufficient. The IndicCorp covers an additional language Assamese which is not in this shared task. Nevertheless, we use the monolingual corpus for this language as well because it can potentially improve translation involving Bengali given their similarity. However, the small size of Assamese data (1.39M lines) relative to the Bengali data (39.9M lines) should not significantly affect the final outcome for translation involving Benglai[6]. The monolingual corpora stats are given in Table 1 and the bilingual corpora stats are given in Table 2.

Regarding pre-processing, we do not perform anything specific and instead let our implementation handle everything via its internal mechanisms.

[2]https://lotus.kuee.kyoto-u.ac.jp/WAT/indic-multilingual/index.html

[3]http://data.statmt.org/pmindia

[4]https://indicnlp.ai4bharat.org/corpora

[5]The IndicCorp is supposed to be document level but the downloadable version is sentence level.

[6]However, this may significantly improve translation involving Assamese thanks to the Bengali data.

### 4.2 Implementation Details

We implement the methods mentioned in Section 3 in our in-house toolkit which we make publicly available[7]. This toolkit is based on the HuggingFace transformers library (Wolf et al., 2020) v4.3.2. Note that the MBART implementation in the library shares the encoder embedding, decoder embedding and decoder softmax projection layers. We implement denoising, temperature based data sampling and multilingual training ourselves. We also use the HuggingFace transformer tokenizer library to train tokenizers. These tokenizers are wrappers around Byte Pair Encoding (BPE) (Gage, 1994) or SentencePiece (SPM) (Kudo and Richardson, 2018) models and we choose[8] the latter as opposed to the former which is used by the original MBART implementation.

### 4.3 Training and Evaluation

We first trained a tokenizer with a joint vocabulary size of 64,000 sub-words which is learned on the IndicCorp monolingual data. We consider this vocabulary size to be sufficient for all languages. For pre-training, we use hyperparameters corresponding to the "transformer_big" (Vaswani et al., 2017) with a few exceptions such as dropout of 0.1, positional embeddings instead of positional encodings and a maximum learning rate of 0.001. When performing batching we truncate all sequences longer than 256 subwords. Our MBART model is pre-trained on 48 NVIDIA V-100 GPUs using the distributed data parallel mechanism in PyTorch. Due to lack of time we only trained for 150,000 batches which corresponded to roughly 1 epoch over the entire monolingual data. After pre-training we train unidirectional models using the bilingual data on a single GPU. We train the one-to-many (English to Indic) and many-to-one (Indic to English) models on the multilingual data on 8 GPUs. For both cases we use a dropout of 0.3 and train till convergence on the development BLEU score and choose the model with the best development set BLEU score for decoding the test set. In our initial experiments we did additional exploration to choose the particular checkpoint which yields best average development BLEU score over all language pairs for decoding the test set. We found that the results are inferior compared to when the best model is chosen language pairwise. We use beam search for decoding with a beam size of 4 and a length penalty of 0.8[9]. For unidirectional models this is strightforward but for multilingual models train till convergence on the global development set BLEU score, an average of BLEU scores for each language pair. Different from most previous works, instead of decoding a single final model, we choose a particular model for a language pair with the highest development set BLEU score for that pair. Therefore, we treat multilingualism as a way get a (potentially) different model per language pair leading to the best BLEU scores for that pair and not as a way to get a single model that gives the best performance for each language pair.

For evaluation, as we have mentioned before, we use BLEU (Papineni et al., 2002) as the primary evaluation metric. WAT also uses metrics such as RIBES (Isozaki et al., 2010), AM-FM (Zhang et al., 2021) and human evaluation (Nakazawa et al., 2019, 2020, 2021). All these metrics focus on different aspects of translations and may lead to different rankings for submissions, however this multi-metric evaluation helps us understand that there may not be one perfect model. To avoid confusing the reader with a clutter of scores, we only show BLEU scores and we refer the reader to the evaluation page where all scores and rankings[10] can be seen[11].

### 4.4 Models Trained

We trained the following models:

- A pre-trained MBART model.
- Unidirectional models for each language pair trained from scratch or via fine-tuning the MBART model.
- One-to-many (English to Indic) and many-to-one (Indic to English) multilingual models trained from scratch or via fine-tuning the MBART model.

[7] https://github.com/prajdabre/yanmtt

[8] We choose SPM because SPM can work with unsegmented, untokenized raw text for any language. Inside the transformers library, the AlbertTokenizer acts as a wrapper for the SPM model. Our implementation also allows the usage of the BPE model but we do not use it in this paper.

[9] We have not tuned these decoding hyperparameters and our BLEU scores may improve.

[10] As can be seen, the rankings of translation can change depending on the metric which indicates that multi-metric ranking is important

[11] http://lotus.kuee.kyoto-u.ac.jp/WAT/evaluation/index.html

| Model | Source Language | | | | | | | | | |
|---|---|---|---|---|---|---|---|---|---|---|
| | Bn | Gu | Hi | Kn | Ml | Mr | Or | Pa | Ta | Te |
| Unidirectional | 11.27 | 26.21 | 28.21 | 20.33 | 13.64 | 15.10 | 16.35 | 23.66 | 16.07 | 14.70 |
| Many-to-one | 20.06 | 27.72 | 30.86 | 24.66 | 21.79 | 22.66 | 23.04 | 27.61 | 21.90 | 23.39 |
| MBART+ Unidirectional | 21.37 | **33.65** | 35.80 | 29.29 | 26.55 | 25.45 | 25.81 | 34.34 | 24.72 | 27.76 |
| MBART+ Many-to-one | **23.89** | 33.53 | **36.20** | **30.87** | **28.23** | **27.88** | **27.93** | **35.81** | **26.90** | **28.77** |
| Official Best Submission | 31.87 | 43.98 | 46.93 | 40.34 | 38.38 | 36.64 | 37.06 | 46.39 | 36.13 | 39.80 |
| Model | Target Language | | | | | | | | | |
| | Bn | Gu | Hi | Kn | Ml | Mr | Or | Pa | Ta | Te |
| Unidirectional | 5.58 | 16.38 | 23.31 | 10.11 | 3.34 | 8.82 | 9.08 | 21.77 | 6.38 | 2.80 |
| One-to-many | 11.56 | 23.49 | 29.12 | 17.53 | 6.22 | 15.01 | 16.43 | 28.37 | 10.82 | 3.81 |
| MBART+ Unidirectional | 10.59 | 23.04 | 29.59 | 16.13 | 5.98 | 14.69 | 15.01 | 26.94 | 10.33 | **4.59** |
| MBART+ One-to-many | **12.84** | **24.26** | **30.18** | **18.22** | **6.51** | **16.38** | **16.69** | **29.15** | **11.42** | 4.20 |
| Official Best Submission | 15.97 | 27.80 | 38.65 | 21.30 | 15.49 | 20.42 | 20.15 | 33.43 | 14.43 | 16.85 |

Table 3: Evaluation results of all language pairs. All scores are taken from the leaderboard. Our best results are in bold. Differences in BLEU smaller than 0.5 are not significant in most cases.

## 5 Results and Observations

Table 3 contains the results of the unidirectional[12], and multilingual models. We also show the the best submissions for reference.

### 5.1 Without Fine-tuning

It is clear from the results that multilingual models are vastly superior than unidirectional models which shows that multilingualism is very helpful in a low-resource setting. Secondly, comparing with corpora sizes (see Table 2), it can be seen that the gains in BLEU are (roughly) inversely proportional to the size of the parallel corpora.

### 5.2 Non Fine-Tuned Multilingual Models vs Fine-Tuned Unidirectional Models

In the case of Indic to English translation, MBART+unidirectional models are significantly better than many-to-one models. We can attribute this phenomenon to the fact that the PMI corpus has a limited number of English sentences and even though combining all corpora might seem to increase the number of English sentences, most of them are redundant which causes some form of overfitting. This is remedied by the MBART model with incorporates additional language modeling information through the monolingual corpora.

On the other hand, for English to Indic translation, the one-to-many models are often comparable if not better than the fine-tuned unidirectional models. Fine-tuning significantly outperforms non fine-tuned unidirectional models which means pre-training is useful. However, given that multilingual training is better, this indicates that it may not be necessary to perform pre-training for one-to-many translation. Remember that the English side of the text contains a large number of redundant sentences and this may be one of the reasons for this kind of behavior. We think that this deserves some future investigation.

### 5.3 Multilingual Fine-tuning

Ultimately, multilingual fine-tuning of an MBART model leads to the best translation quality for all language pairs, except two (Gujarati to English and English to Telugu). This approach combines the best of both worlds and the outcome is not surprising. Our MBART models consisted of only 6 layers and was trained for only 1 epoch and this may not be enough to incorporate knowledge from the full monolingual corpus. We also did not perform any hyperparameter tuning with parameters such as dropout and learning rate[13] We expect that a larger model with more careful hyperparameter tuning should lead to even better results. However, we are

[12]The unidirectional scores without fine-tuning are actually organizer baselines but we were the ones who actually developed them so we use the scores as is.

[13]We used a high learning rate which may not have been a good idea in retrospect.

confident that a multilingual fine-tuned model will reign supreme.

### 5.4 Comparison With Other Submissions

For Indic to English translation the several submissions outperformed ours and we think that this is because the other participants have indicated that they have performed data selection, backtranslation and script mapping. In our case we only performed pre-training and fine-tuning with PMI data. Although MBART pre-training is helpful, it can never compare with the power of a large parallel corpus obtained via careful data selection and script manipulation. While for PMI, the largest parallel corpus, Hindi-English, contains roughly 50,000 lines, the full Hindi-English corpus is larger than 2M lines and most pairs have more than 500,000 lines. In the future we will try training with larger parallel corpora and script mapping to see what kind of results we get.

On the other hand for English to Indic translation, the gap between the the best submissions and ours is much smaller than for the reverse direction. This also shows that, at least for this task, multilingualism benefits translation into English a lot more than it benefits translation from English.

## 6 Conclusion

In this paper we have described our NMT systems and results for the MultiIndicMT task in WAT 2021. We worked on MBART pre-training and multilingual fine-tuning which we found to significantly outperform unidirectional models with and without pre-training and multilingual models without pre-training. We did not train our MBART models for more than 1 epoch and used only the PMI data for fine-tuning instead of the whole parallel corpus. We did not try any additional methods such as back-translation either. Despite this, our results are competitive and despite the simplicity of our methods our results do not lag far behind those of the best systems that use advanced methods such as data selection, domain adaptation, back-translation etc. This also means that we have a lot of room for improvement in the future.

## References

Roee Aharoni, Melvin Johnson, and Orhan Firat. 2019. Massively multilingual neural machine translation. In *Proceedings of the 2019 Conference of the North American Chapter of the Association for Computational Linguistics: Human Language Technologies, Volume 1 (Long and Short Papers)*, pages 3874–3884, Minneapolis, Minnesota. Association for Computational Linguistics.

Dzmitry Bahdanau, Kyunghyun Cho, and Yoshua Bengio. 2014. Neural Machine Translation by Jointly Learning to Align and Translate. *arXiv e-prints*, page arXiv:1409.0473.

Raj Dabre, Chenhui Chu, and Anoop Kunchukuttan. 2020. A survey of multilingual neural machine translation. *ACM Comput. Surv.*, 53(5).

Raj Dabre, Atsushi Fujita, and Chenhui Chu. 2019. Exploiting multilingualism through multistage fine-tuning for low-resource neural machine translation. In *Proceedings of the 2019 Conference on Empirical Methods in Natural Language Processing and the 9th International Joint Conference on Natural Language Processing (EMNLP-IJCNLP)*, pages 1410–1416, Hong Kong, China. Association for Computational Linguistics.

Orhan Firat, Kyunghyun Cho, and Yoshua Bengio. 2016. Multi-way, multilingual neural machine translation with a shared attention mechanism. In *NAACL HLT 2016, The 2016 Conference of the North American Chapter of the Association for Computational Linguistics: Human Language Technologies, San Diego California, USA, June 12-17, 2016*, pages 866–875. The Association for Computational Linguistics.

Philip Gage. 1994. A new algorithm for data compression. *C Users J.*, 12(2):23–38.

Vu Cong Duy Hoang, Philipp Koehn, Gholamreza Haffari, and Trevor Cohn. 2018. Iterative back-translation for neural machine translation. In *Proceedings of the 2nd Workshop on Neural Machine Translation and Generation*, pages 18–24, Melbourne, Australia. Association for Computational Linguistics.

Hideki Isozaki, Tsutomu Hirao, Kevin Duh, Katsuhito Sudoh, and Hajime Tsukada. 2010. Automatic evaluation of translation quality for distant language pairs. In *Proceedings of the 2010 Conference on Empirical Methods in Natural Language Processing*, pages 944–952, Cambridge, MA. Association for Computational Linguistics.

Melvin Johnson, Mike Schuster, Quoc V. Le, Maxim Krikun, Yonghui Wu, Zhifeng Chen, Nikhil Thorat, Fernanda Viégas, Martin Wattenberg, Greg Corrado, Macduff Hughes, and Jeffrey Dean. 2017. Google's multilingual neural machine translation system: Enabling zero-shot translation. *Transactions of the Association for Computational Linguistics*, 5:339–351.

Taku Kudo and John Richardson. 2018. SentencePiece: A simple and language independent subword tokenizer and detokenizer for neural text processing. In

*Proceedings of the 2018 Conference on Empirical Methods in Natural Language Processing: System Demonstrations*, pages 66–71, Brussels, Belgium. Association for Computational Linguistics.

Anoop Kunchukuttan, Divyanshu Kakwani, Satish Golla, Gokul N. C., Avik Bhattacharyya, Mitesh M. Khapra, and Pratyush Kumar. 2020. Ai4bharat-indicnlp corpus: Monolingual corpora and word embeddings for indic languages. *CoRR*, abs/2005.00085.

Mike Lewis, Yinhan Liu, Naman Goyal, Marjan Ghazvininejad, Abdelrahman Mohamed, Omer Levy, Veselin Stoyanov, and Luke Zettlemoyer. 2020. BART: Denoising sequence-to-sequence pre-training for natural language generation, translation, and comprehension. In *Proceedings of the 58th Annual Meeting of the Association for Computational Linguistics*, pages 7871–7880, Online. Association for Computational Linguistics.

Yinhan Liu, Jiatao Gu, Naman Goyal, Xian Li, Sergey Edunov, Marjan Ghazvininejad, Mike Lewis, and Luke Zettlemoyer. 2020. Multilingual denoising pre-training for neural machine translation. *Transactions of the Association for Computational Linguistics*, 8:726–742.

Zhuoyuan Mao, Fabien Cromieres, Raj Dabre, Haiyue Song, and Sadao Kurohashi. 2020. Jass: Japanese-specific sequence to sequence pre-training for neural machine translation. In *Proceedings of The 12th Language Resources and Evaluation Conference*, pages 3683–3691, Marseille, France. European Language Resources Association.

Toshiaki Nakazawa, Chenchen Ding, Raj Dabre, Anoop Kunchukuttan, Nobushige Doi, Yusuke Oda, Ondřej Bojar, Shantipriya Parida, Isao Goto, and Hidaya Mino, editors. 2019. *Proceedings of the 6th Workshop on Asian Translation*. Association for Computational Linguistics, Hong Kong, China.

Toshiaki Nakazawa, Hideki Nakayama, Chenchen Ding, Raj Dabre, Shohei Higashiyama, Hideya Mino, Isao Goto, Win Pa Pa, Anoop Kunchukuttan, Shantipriya Parida, Ondřej Bojar, Chenhui Chu, Akiko Eriguchi, Kaori Abe, and Sadao Oda, Yusuke Kurohashi. 2021. Overview of the 8th workshop on Asian translation. In *Proceedings of the 8th Workshop on Asian Translation*, Bangkok, Thailand. Association for Computational Linguistics.

Toshiaki Nakazawa, Hideki Nakayama, Chenchen Ding, Raj Dabre, Shohei Higashiyama, Hideya Mino, Isao Goto, Win Pa Pa, Anoop Kunchukuttan, Shantipriya Parida, Ondřej Bojar, and Sadao Kurohashi. 2020. Overview of the 7th workshop on Asian translation. In *Proceedings of the 7th Workshop on Asian Translation*, pages 1–44, Suzhou, China. Association for Computational Linguistics.

Kishore Papineni, Salim Roukos, Todd Ward, and Wei-Jing Zhu. 2002. Bleu: a method for automatic evaluation of machine translation. In *Proceedings of the 40th Annual Meeting of the Association for Computational Linguistics*, pages 311–318, Philadelphia, Pennsylvania, USA. Association for Computational Linguistics.

Rico Sennrich, Barry Haddow, and Alexandra Birch. 2016. Neural machine translation of rare words with subword units. In *Proceedings of the 54th Annual Meeting of the Association for Computational Linguistics (Volume 1: Long Papers)*, pages 1715–1725, Berlin, Germany. Association for Computational Linguistics.

Tian Shi, Yaser Keneshloo, Naren Ramakrishnan, and Chandan K. Reddy. 2021. Neural abstractive text summarization with sequence-to-sequence models. *ACM/IMS Trans. Data Sci.*, 2(1).

Yuqing Tang, Chau Tran, Xian Li, Peng-Jen Chen, Naman Goyal, Vishrav Chaudhary, Jiatao Gu, and Angela Fan. 2020. Multilingual translation with extensible multilingual pretraining and finetuning. *CoRR*, abs/2008.00401.

Ashish Vaswani, Noam Shazeer, Niki Parmar, Jakob Uszkoreit, Llion Jones, Aidan N Gomez, Ł ukasz Kaiser, and Illia Polosukhin. 2017. Attention is all you need. In I. Guyon, U. V. Luxburg, S. Bengio, H. Wallach, R. Fergus, S. Vishwanathan, and R. Garnett, editors, *Advances in Neural Information Processing Systems 30*, pages 5998–6008. Curran Associates, Inc.

Thomas Wolf, Lysandre Debut, Victor Sanh, Julien Chaumond, Clement Delangue, Anthony Moi, Pierric Cistac, Tim Rault, Remi Louf, Morgan Funtowicz, Joe Davison, Sam Shleifer, Patrick von Platen, Clara Ma, Yacine Jernite, Julien Plu, Canwen Xu, Teven Le Scao, Sylvain Gugger, Mariama Drame, Quentin Lhoest, and Alexander Rush. 2020. Transformers: State-of-the-art natural language processing. In *Proceedings of the 2020 Conference on Empirical Methods in Natural Language Processing: System Demonstrations*, pages 38–45, Online. Association for Computational Linguistics.

Chen Zhang, Luis Fernando D'Haro, Rafael E. Banchs, Thomas Friedrichs, and Haizhou Li. 2021. *Deep AM-FM: Toolkit for Automatic Dialogue Evaluation*, pages 53–69. Springer Singapore, Singapore.

Barret Zoph, Deniz Yuret, Jonathan May, and Kevin Knight. 2016. Transfer learning for low-resource neural machine translation. In *Proceedings of the 2016 Conference on Empirical Methods in Natural Language Processing*, pages 1568–1575, Austin, Texas. Association for Computational Linguistics.

# How far can we get with one GPU in 100 hours? CoAStaL at MultiIndicMT Shared Task

**Rahul Aralikatte** **Héctor Ricardo Murrieta Bello** **Miryam de Lhoneux**
**Daniel Hershcovich** **Marcel Bollmann** **Anders Søgaard**
Department of Computer Science
University of Copenhagen
{rahul,ml,dh,marcel,soegaard}@di.ku.dk xhd160@alumni.ku.dk

## Abstract

This work shows that competitive translation results can be obtained in a constrained setting by incorporating the latest advances in memory and compute optimization. We train and evaluate large multilingual translation models using a single GPU for a maximum of 100 hours and get within 4-5 BLEU points of the top submission on the WAT 2021 leaderboard. We also benchmark standard baselines on the PMI corpus and re-discover well-known shortcomings of current translation metrics.

## 1 Introduction

Machine Translation is one of the few tasks in NLP which has the luxury of data. Due to the efforts of the community over the last two decades (Koehn, 2005; Tiedemann, 2012, 2020), most major languages of the world have millions of translated sentence pairs with English. With the introduction of sequence to sequence models (Sutskever et al., 2014; Cho et al., 2014), transformers (Vaswani et al., 2017), and large pre-trained language models (Devlin et al., 2019; Radford et al., 2019; Yang et al., 2019; Liu et al., 2019), the accuracy of machine translation models has almost risen to that of humans (Wu et al., 2016). Yet, the ability to train such models is limited by the availability of compute. Today's state-of-the-art models are trained by industry research labs, using large compute infrastructure which is usually unavailable or unaffordable to others. Such training is also shown to have large carbon footprints (Strubell et al., 2019).

In this work, we show that competitive translation performance can be achieved even with limited resources. We first train a statistical MT system that does not require GPUs, as a baseline. Next, we run inference on the best publicly available pre-trained models to benchmark their performance. Finally, we train graph2seq, seq2seq, and text2text models, which progressively perform better. All our experiments are constrained both in compute[1] and training time: we use one NVIDIA Titan RTX GPU for a maximum of 100 hours. Our main findings are: (i) pre-trained seq2seq and text2text models perform the best, especially when trained only on the PMI corpus, (ii) the benefits of pre-trained multilingual language models diminish for Indic language decoding due to their under-representation in pre-training data, and (iii) a small empirical evaluation on 2 languages shows that the prediction fluency and faithfulness start plateauing at 100 hours.

| Source | Language(s) |
|---|---|
| CVIT-PIB (2020) | BN,GU,HI,ML,MR,OR,PA,TA,TE |
| JW (2019) | BN,GU,HI,KN,ML,MR,PA,TA,TE |
| TED (2012) | BN,GU,HI,KN,ML,MR,PA,TA,TE |
| PMIndia (2020) | BN,GU,HI,KN,ML,MR, OR,PA,TA,TE |
| Bible-uedin (2014) | GU,HI,KN,ML,MR,TE |
| OpenSubtitles (2016) | BN,HI,ML,TA,TE |
| WikiMatrix (2019) | HI,ML,MR,TA,TE |
| Wiki Titles (2021) | GU,TA |
| ALT (2016) | BN,HI |
| IITB 3.0 (2018) | HI |
| NLPC (2020) | TA |
| UFAL EnTam (2012) | TA |
| Uka Tarsadia (2019) | GU |
| MTEnglish2Odia (2018) | OR |
| OdiEnCorp 2.0 (2020) | OR |

Table 1: Sources of MultiIndicMT data.

## 2 Data

The MultiIndicMT data is a combination of parallel corpora from different sources as shown in Tab. 1. It contains translations from 10 Indic languages to English. The Indic languages included are Bengali (BN), Gujarati (GU), Hindi (HI), Kannada (KN), Malayalam (ML), Marathi (MR), Oriya (OR), Punjabi (PA), Tamil (TA), and Telugu (TE). The training split contains about 11 million translation pairs

[1]which in turn constrains the number of model parameters



*Proceedings of the 8th Workshop on Asian Translation*, pages 205–211
Bangkok, Thailand (online), August 5-6, 2021. 

| Sentence | Translation | Fluency | Faithfulness | Comment |
|---|---|---|---|---|
| Big Business! | बड़ा व्यवसाय ! | 5 | 5 | - |
| It affects all of us . It helps us — and it harms us . | हम सब पर इसका प्रभाव पड़ता है । | 5 | 3 | Translation of second sentence missing |
| And there are things we can do about it . A giant , or " big , " corporation may have assets worth $ 1,500,000,000 . | यह हमारी सहायता करता है — और हमें हानि भी पहुँचाता है । | 5 | 0 | Translation of the previous line's second sentence |
| Many have far more . That kind of money represents power . | और कुछ ऐसी बातें हैं जो हम उसके बारे में कर सकते हैं । | 5 | 0 | Misalignment |
| Giant corporations have tussled with countries — and won . No wonder so many are suspicious of them ! | एक विशाल , या " बड़े " निगम के पास शायद १,५०,००,००,००० डॉलर की सम्पत्ति हो । | 5 | 0 | Misalignment |

Figure 1: A sample from the JW corpus which shows misalignments between the translation pairs.

from these languages. The development and test splits contain 1000 and 2390 11-way parallel sentences taken from the PMIndia corpus (Haddow and Kirefu, 2020), respectively.

**Analysis** To understand the data better, a small analysis is performed by randomly sampling 100 sentences from each language the authors can read (HI and KN). Overall, the translations are of high quality, except in a few sources where the parallel sentences are automatically extracted. For example, we found that JW (Agić and Vulić, 2019) has alignment issues, where a part of the translation is moved to the next line, thereby starting a chain of misalignments, as shown in Fig. 1. We manually annotate 100 translations for fluency and faithfulness on a scale of 0-5 and get a score of 4.01 for fluency and 3.54 for faithfulness.

## 3 Models

We train four types of models: (i) a phrase-based statistical model, (ii) a graph-to-text model, (iii) a sequence-to-sequence model, and (iv) a text-to-text model. Brief descriptions of the models are given below.

### 3.1 Moses

We train a statistical phrase-based model with Moses (Koehn et al., 2007) using default settings, following the guidelines for training a baseline.[2] We prune words that occur less than three times in the corpus and use the same tokenizer as for the other models and de-tokenize predictions before evaluating. We train a separate model for each language pair and use the respective development set for tuning before translating the test set.

### 3.2 GRAPH-TO-TEXT model

We also train a graph2seq model with a GCN (Kipf and Welling, 2016) encoder and LSTM decoder. In addition to text, we input the source syntax trees obtained from a parser trained on Universal Dependencies (Nivre et al., 2016). We borrow hyperparameter settings from Bastings et al. (2017) and input a bag of source words to the encoder and expect subword units from the decoder. We train separate models for each language pair.

### 3.3 SEQ2SEQ model

For training multilingual models, we use pre-trained transformer-based language models to initialize the encoder and decoder of our seq2seq models. For English, we use standard uncased BERT-Base (Devlin et al., 2019) and for Indic languages, we use MuRIL (Khanuja et al., 2021). MuRIL's architecture is similar to BERT and is pre-trained on 17 Indic languages including all ten required for our translation task. It is pre-trained on publicly available corpora from Wikipedia and Common Crawl. It also uses automatically translated and transliterated data for pre-training. We add cross-attention between the encoder and decoder following Rothe et al. (2020).

The model has 375M trainable parameters. When the decoder is multilingual, we follow previous works and force a language identifier as the BOS token. We use a learning rate of $5 \times 10^{-5}$ and a batch size of 12. We truncate sequences to a maximum length of 128 and use a cosine learning rate scheduler with a warmup of 10,000 steps. We denote our models as BERT2MURIL and MURIL2BERT when translating from and to En-

[2]http://www.statmt.org/moses/?n=Moses.Baseline

| Model | Bn | | Gu | | Hi | | Kn | | Ml | | Mr | | Or | | Pa | | Ta | | Te | |
|---|---|---|---|---|---|---|---|---|---|---|---|---|---|---|---|---|---|---|---|---|
| | **chrF** | **bleu** | **chrF** | **bleu** | **chrF** | **bleu** | **chrF** | **bleu** | **chrF** | **bleu** | **chrF** | **bleu** | **chrF** | **bleu** | **chrF** | **bleu** | **chrF** | **bleu** | **chrF** | **bleu** |
| m2m100 (418M) | 0.30 | 2.98 | 0.11 | 0.40 | 0.48 | 21.21 | 0.15 | 0.05 | 0.21 | 0.69 | 0.31 | 3.96 | 0.05 | 0.06 | 0.11 | 0.66 | 0.20 | 1.43 | - | - |
| m2m100 (1.2B) | 0.35 | 4.48 | 0.16 | 1.35 | 0.49 | 22.22 | 0.18 | 0.15 | 0.28 | 1.29 | 0.35 | 6.19 | 0.05 | 0.04 | 0.16 | 1.84 | 0.23 | 1.26 | - | - |
| Moses (PMI) | 0.40 | 4.90 | 0.46 | 12.4 | 0.48 | 15.7 | 0.44 | 8.00 | 0.39 | 2.60 | 0.41 | 7.50 | 0.42 | 8.40 | 0.44 | 14.1 | 0.42 | 5.20 | 0.35 | 3.40 |
| Moses (all) | 0.38 | 5.00 | 0.47 | 13.0 | 0.51 | 18.0 | 0.43 | 7.90 | 0.41 | 3.50 | 0.45 | 9.50 | 0.44 | 10.5 | 0.44 | 14.5 | 0.42 | 7.00 | 0.36 | 3.60 |
| GCN (PMI) | 0.40 | 5.20 | 0.48 | 14.3 | 0.50 | 17.1 | 0.44 | 9.10 | 0.36 | 2.10 | 0.41 | 7.30 | 0.40 | 8.90 | 0.46 | 16.7 | 0.48 | 8.20 | 0.35 | 4.90 |
| mT5-large (PMI) | 0.40 | 7.14 | **0.52** | **20.8** | **0.55** | **26.5** | **0.52** | 15.0 | **0.46** | 5.37 | 0.46 | 12.6 | - | - | 0.48 | 20.8 | **0.49** | **10.1** | 0.39 | 3.89 |
| mT5-large (all) | 0.36 | 5.52 | 0.46 | 16.0 | 0.54 | **26.5** | 0.45 | 9.18 | 0.42 | 3.83 | 0.41 | 9.40 | - | - | 0.43 | 16.9 | 0.47 | 8.46 | 0.35 | 3.79 |
| bert2muril (PMI) | 0.42 | 7.68 | 0.51 | 19.6 | 0.53 | 23.5 | 0.49 | 14.0 | 0.43 | 5.62 | 0.46 | 12.8 | 0.46 | 13.6 | 0.49 | 21.8 | 0.46 | 8.30 | 0.39 | 6.04 |
| bert2muril (all) | 0.37 | 5.09 | 0.50 | 18.9 | 0.53 | 23.3 | 0.45 | 11.0 | 0.38 | 3.95 | 0.46 | 12.3 | 0.48 | 14.8 | 0.48 | 19.4 | 0.43 | 7.03 | 0.36 | 4.68 |
| +FT on PMI | **0.44** | **8.89** | **0.52** | 20.2 | **0.55** | 25.5 | **0.52** | **16.0** | **0.46** | **5.91** | **0.48** | **14.3** | **0.49** | **15.3** | **0.52** | **24.1** | **0.49** | 9.83 | **0.41** | **6.54** |

Table 2: Character F1 and BLEU scores of English to Indic translations.

| Model | Bn | | Gu | | Hi | | Kn | | Ml | | Mr | | Or | | Pa | | Ta | | Te | |
|---|---|---|---|---|---|---|---|---|---|---|---|---|---|---|---|---|---|---|---|---|
| | **chrF** | **bleu** | **chrF** | **bleu** | **chrF** | **bleu** | **chrF** | **bleu** | **chrF** | **bleu** | **chrF** | **bleu** | **chrF** | **bleu** | **chrF** | **bleu** | **chrF** | **bleu** | **chrF** | **bleu** |
| m2m100 (418M) | 0.43 | 13.8 | 0.10 | 0.18 | 0.55 | 26.0 | 0.10 | 0.08 | 0.32 | 7.45 | 0.40 | 13.4 | 0.15 | 0.75 | 0.36 | 9.65 | 0.25 | 2.44 | - | - |
| m2m100 (1.2B) | 0.44 | 14.7 | 0.10 | 0.16 | 0.55 | 26.7 | 0.09 | 0.16 | 0.36 | 11.0 | 0.41 | 14.1 | 0.15 | 0.42 | 0.36 | 9.08 | 0.21 | 2.91 | - | - |
| Moses (PMI) | 0.37 | 6.00 | 0.46 | 10.6 | 0.49 | 12.6 | 0.42 | 8.30 | 0.39 | 5.90 | 0.41 | 7.50 | 0.41 | 7.60 | 0.44 | 10.0 | 0.38 | 6.20 | 0.41 | 7.00 |
| Moses (all) | 0.40 | 8.00 | 0.48 | 12.5 | 0.52 | 16.1 | 0.43 | 8.80 | 0.43 | 8.50 | 0.44 | 10.4 | 0.43 | 10.6 | 0.48 | 13.0 | 0.42 | 9.60 | 0.43 | 8.80 |
| GCN (PMI) | 0.40 | 8.30 | 0.49 | 12.8 | 0.54 | 14.8 | 0.44 | 10.9 | 0.48 | 11.5 | 0.48 | 13.5 | 0.46 | 7.20 | 0.45 | 12.6 | 0.43 | 14.3 | 0.45 | 14.7 |
| mT5-large (PMI) | **0.51** | **24.2** | **0.60** | **34.5** | **0.62** | **36.3** | **0.57** | **30.9** | **0.55** | **28.4** | **0.54** | **27.5** | - | - | **0.61** | **35.7** | **0.53** | **26.6** | **0.57** | **30.4** |
| mT5-large (all) | 0.49 | 21.5 | 0.59 | 31.9 | **0.62** | 35.2 | 0.55 | 27.9 | 0.53 | 25.7 | 0.52 | 25.3 | - | - | 0.59 | 33.4 | 0.51 | 24.4 | 0.54 | 26.5 |
| muril2bert (PMI) | 0.48 | 16.6 | 0.56 | 24.3 | 0.59 | 26.9 | 0.54 | 22.1 | 0.52 | 20.5 | 0.51 | 19.8 | **0.51** | **20.1** | 0.57 | 26.1 | 0.50 | 19.2 | 0.53 | 21.3 |
| muril2bert (all) | 0.37 | 11.0 | 0.41 | 13.8 | 0.46 | 17.1 | 0.41 | 13.3 | 0.40 | 13.0 | 0.39 | 12.0 | 0.38 | 11.8 | 0.42 | 14.6 | 0.39 | 12.1 | 0.41 | 13.1 |
| +FT on PMI | 0.47 | 16.6 | 0.55 | 24.0 | 0.58 | 26.5 | 0.53 | 21.7 | 0.52 | 20.5 | 0.51 | 19.6 | 0.50 | 19.7 | 0.57 | 25.5 | 0.50 | 19.1 | 0.52 | 21.2 |

Table 3: Character F1 and BLEU scores of Indic to English translations.

glish, respectively.[3]

### 3.4 TEXT2TEXT model

To push the extent to which a single GPU can be utilized, we also train the large multilingual-T5 (mT5-large; Xue et al., 2020) model on our translation task. This model is pre-trained on mC4, a multilingual version of the Common Crawl consisting of text from 101 languages. It contains 1.2B trainable parameters which do not fit on our 24GB GPU, even if trained with mixed-precision and a batch size of one. Therefore, we resort to optimizer state and gradient partitioning with ZeRO (Rajbhandari et al., 2020). ZeRO is a zero-redundancy optimizer that offloads some computations and memory to the host's CPU and provides a better GPU management system that uses smart allocation methods to reduce memory fragmentation. For more details, see Rasley et al. (2020). With these modifications, we train the model with a learning rate of $3 \times 10^{-5}$. All other hyper-parameters remain unchanged.

## 4 Results

We report results in both English to Indic, and Indic to English directions. We use character F1 and BLEU (Papineni et al., 2002), which are standard metrics to evaluate translations. We train two variants of all models: (i) only on the PMI corpus, and (ii) on the full training data. The English to Indic results are shown in Tab. 2 and the Indic to English results, in Tab. 3.[4]

**m2m100** We first benchmark the performance of the Many-to-Many multilingual model (m2m100; Fan et al., 2020) which is trained on non-English centric translation. It can translate to and from all Indic languages in our task, except Telugu. As expected, with no finetuning, both the small (418M parameters) and large (1.2B parameters) models perform poorly, on all languages except Hindi. This is expected as the other languages are underrepresented in the mC4 dataset.

**Moses** We see that simple phrase-based translation works relatively well. Though significantly worse than the best model, Moses produces results comparable to that of mT5-large (all) in both directions. Although this can be attributed to mT5-large being under-trained, it gives us an insight into

[3]This is the largest model we could train on our GPU without using optimization tricks.

[4]Note that we report local evaluation metrics which do not exactly match with the leaderboard numbers because of the differences in tokenization. We do this to avoid uploading multiple prediction files and overloading the evaluation server.

| Language | En→* | | *→En | |
|---|---|---|---|---|
| | Loc. | Off. | Loc. | Off. |
| Bengali | 8.89 | 11.1 | 24.2 | 24.4 |
| Gujarati | 20.8 | 20.4 | 34.5 | 34.6 |
| Hindi | 26.5 | 31.7 | 36.3 | 36.5 |
| Kannada | 16.0 | 16.1 | 30.9 | 31.0 |
| Malayalam | 5.91 | 6.27 | 28.4 | 28.5 |
| Marathi | 14.3 | 14.5 | 27.5 | 27.7 |
| Oriya | 15.3 | 15.7 | 20.1 | 19.6 |
| Punjabi | 24.1 | 27.2 | 35.7 | 35.9 |
| Tamil | 10.1 | 10.0 | 26.6 | 26.7 |
| Telugu | 6.54 | 12.9 | 30.4 | 30.5 |

Table 4: Comparison of BLEU scores obtained during local and official evaluations.

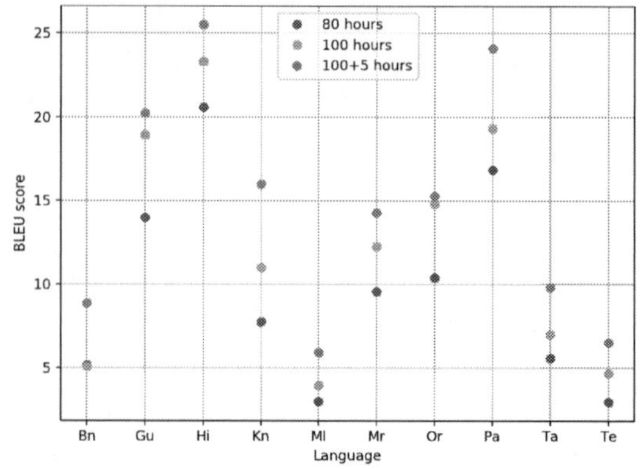


Figure 2: Increase in BLEU score across languages when trained on the full training data, at different intervals of time.

the ability of simpler models to learn quickly in constrained environments. We also note that just training on the PMI corpus gives a result that is almost on par with the results obtained by training on the entire training split. The model trained on PMI even surpasses the other model, on Kannada indicating a strong in-domain training bias.

**GCN** In this setup, we only train on the PMI corpus due to time constraints. We find that while it comfortably surpasses Moses, it also comes close to the much bigger models, especially when translating to Indic languages. It is to be noted that, this small gap in results can be mainly attributed to the lack of convergence of the bigger models, as discussed next.

**mT5** mT5 can translate to and from all Indic languages required by our task, except Oriya. We note that the model trained only on the PMI corpus is always better than the model trained on the complete data. We postulate that 100 hours is not enough time for the model to converge on the full data. We also see that mT5's performance is far superior compared to all other models for Indic to English translation. This may be expected as the model is pre-trained to generate fluent English text. For English to Indic translation, mT5 performs on-par or slightly worse than bert2muril finetuned on PMI data, except for Hindi and Tamil, where it is better.

**MuRIL and BERT** Following the mT5 models, these models also perform better when trained only on the PMI corpus as it fails to converge on the larger data in the given time. As an additional step, we finetune these under-fit models on the PMI data for 5 hours and see a significant performance gain in the English to Indic direction (bert2muril). The model outperforms the much bigger mT5 on 7 languages with Gujarati, Hindi, and Tamil being the exceptions. However, finetuning does not seem to have a major effect in the other direction (muril2bert). As in the case of mT5, we believe that the BERT decoder's pre-training subsumes any gains from extra finetuning.

**Official Evaluation** Since Tab. 2 and 3 show BLEU scores obtained by evaluating the generated predictions locally, they do not exactly match the official scores on the leaderboard.[5] For a fair comparison, we present both local and official BLEU scores of our best submissions in Tab. 4. We see that the scores are similar when translating from Indic languages to English. But when translating from English, the official scores are often significantly higher. This is a result of our use of minimal tokenization (mteval-v13a) before computing BLEU, while the official evaluation uses the Indic-tokenizer (Kunchukuttan, 2020).

## 5 Discussion

As reported in §4, the text2text and seq2seq models perform better when trained only on the PMI corpus when compared to them being trained on the entire train split. Though it can be argued that they perform better since the test set also comes from the same domain,[6] we hypothesize that 100

[5] `http://lotus.kuee.kyoto-u.ac.jp/WAT/evaluation/index.html`

[6] The development and test sets are taken from the PMI corpus.

hours is not enough time for the models to converge when trained on the full training set. Fig 2 shows the BLEU scores of BERT2MuRIL model after 80 and 100 hours of training, respectively. We see that the model gets significantly better in the last 20 hours. A 5 hour finetuning with the PMI corpus, further increases its performance. This clearly shows that the model would become more accurate if it is trained for a longer period or with more compute.

To establish whether an increase in BLEU scores corresponds to an increase in the fluency and faithfulness of the translations, we manually annotate 50 Hindi and Kannada test predictions from the best model to find that the increase in both cases is marginal. In the 20 additional training hours, the fluency and faithfulness increased by 0.005 and 0.01 respectively which suggests that BLEU may not be the best metric to quantify the goodness of translation systems, as shown in works like Zhang et al. (2004); Callison-Burch et al. (2006).

## 6 Conclusion

In this work, we show that it is possible to get competitive translation results using a single GPU for a limited amount of time by carefully selecting and training large pre-trained encoder-decoder models. We also show that we can train models which have more than $10^9$ trainable parameters using the latest advances in GPU resource optimization. Finally, through a small empirical study, we find that while longer training can increase BLEU scores, it may not increase their fluency and faithfulness.

## Acknowledgements

We thank the reviewers for their valuable feedback. Rahul Aralikatte and Anders Søgaard were funded by a Google Focused Research Award. Miryam de Lhoneux was funded by the Swedish Research Council (grant 2020-00437). Marcel Bollmann was funded from the European Union's Horizon 2020 research and innovation programme under the Marie Skłodowska-Curie grant agreement No. 845995.

## References

2018. MTEnglish2Odia. `https://odianlp.github.io/`. Accessed: 2021-05-20.

2021. Wiki Titles. `http://data.statmt.org/wikititles/v3/`. Accessed: 2021-05-20.

Željko Agić and Ivan Vulić. 2019. JW300: A wide-coverage parallel corpus for low-resource languages. In *Proceedings of the 57th Annual Meeting of the Association for Computational Linguistics*, pages 3204–3210, Florence, Italy. Association for Computational Linguistics.

Jasmijn Bastings, Ivan Titov, Wilker Aziz, Diego Marcheggiani, and Khalil Sima'an. 2017. Graph convolutional encoders for syntax-aware neural machine translation. In *Proceedings of the 2017 Conference on Empirical Methods in Natural Language Processing*, pages 1957–1967, Copenhagen, Denmark. Association for Computational Linguistics.

Chris Callison-Burch, Miles Osborne, and Philipp Koehn. 2006. Re-evaluating the role of Bleu in machine translation research. In *11th Conference of the European Chapter of the Association for Computational Linguistics*, Trento, Italy. Association for Computational Linguistics.

Kyunghyun Cho, Bart van Merriënboer, Caglar Gulcehre, Dzmitry Bahdanau, Fethi Bougares, Holger Schwenk, and Yoshua Bengio. 2014. Learning phrase representations using RNN encoder–decoder for statistical machine translation. In *Proceedings of the 2014 Conference on Empirical Methods in Natural Language Processing (EMNLP)*, pages 1724–1734, Doha, Qatar. Association for Computational Linguistics.

Christos Christodoulopoulos and Mark Steedman. 2014. A massively parallel corpus: the bible in 100 languages. *Language Resources and Evaluation*, 49:1–21.

Jacob Devlin, Ming-Wei Chang, Kenton Lee, and Kristina Toutanova. 2019. BERT: Pre-training of deep bidirectional transformers for language understanding. In *Proceedings of the 2019 Conference of the North American Chapter of the Association for Computational Linguistics: Human Language Technologies, Volume 1 (Long and Short Papers)*, pages 4171–4186, Minneapolis, Minnesota. Association for Computational Linguistics.

Angela Fan, Shruti Bhosale, Holger Schwenk, Zhiyi Ma, Ahmed El-Kishky, Siddharth Goyal, Mandeep Baines, Onur Celebi, Guillaume Wenzek, Vishrav Chaudhary, Naman Goyal, Tom Birch, Vitaliy Liptchinsky, Sergey Edunov, Edouard Grave, Michael Auli, and Armand Joulin. 2020. Beyond english-centric multilingual machine translation. *CoRR*, abs/2010.11125.

Aloka Fernando, Surangika Ranathunga, and Gihan Dias. 2020. Data augmentation and terminology integration for domain-specific sinhala-english-tamil statistical machine translation. *CoRR*, abs/2011.02821.

Barry Haddow and Faheem Kirefu. 2020. Pmindia - A collection of parallel corpora of languages of india. *CoRR*, abs/2001.09907.

Simran Khanuja, Diksha Bansal, Sarvesh Mehtani, Savya Khosla, Atreyee Dey, Balaji Gopalan, Dilip Kumar Margam, Pooja Aggarwal, Rajiv Teja Nagipogu, Shachi Dave, Shruti Gupta, Subhash Chandra Bose Gali, Vish Subramanian, and Partha Talukdar. 2021. Muril: Multilingual representations for indian languages.

Thomas N Kipf and Max Welling. 2016. Semi-supervised classification with graph convolutional networks. *arXiv preprint arXiv:1609.02907*.

Philipp Koehn. 2005. Europarl: A Parallel Corpus for Statistical Machine Translation. In *Conference Proceedings: the tenth Machine Translation Summit*, pages 79–86, Phuket, Thailand. AAMT, AAMT.

Philipp Koehn, Hieu Hoang, Alexandra Birch, Chris Callison-Burch, Marcello Federico, Nicola Bertoldi, Brooke Cowan, Wade Shen, Christine Moran, Richard Zens, Chris Dyer, Ondřej Bojar, Alexandra Constantin, and Evan Herbst. 2007. Moses: Open source toolkit for statistical machine translation. In *Proceedings of the 45th Annual Meeting of the Association for Computational Linguistics Companion Volume Proceedings of the Demo and Poster Sessions*, pages 177–180, Prague, Czech Republic. Association for Computational Linguistics.

Anoop Kunchukuttan. 2020. The IndicNLP Library. `https://github.com/anoopkunchukuttan/indic_nlp_library/blob/master/docs/indicnlp.pdf`.

Anoop Kunchukuttan, Pratik Mehta, and Pushpak Bhattacharyya. 2018. The IIT Bombay English-Hindi parallel corpus. In *Proceedings of the Eleventh International Conference on Language Resources and Evaluation (LREC 2018)*, Miyazaki, Japan. European Language Resources Association (ELRA).

Yinhan Liu, Myle Ott, Naman Goyal, Jingfei Du, Mandar Joshi, Danqi Chen, Omer Levy, Mike Lewis, Luke Zettlemoyer, and Veselin Stoyanov. 2019. Roberta: A robustly optimized bert pretraining approach. *arXiv preprint arXiv:1907.11692*.

Joakim Nivre, Marie-Catherine de Marneffe, Filip Ginter, Yoav Goldberg, Jan Hajic, Christopher D. Manning, Ryan McDonald, Slav Petrov, Sampo Pyysalo, Natalia Silveira, Reut Tsarfaty, and Daniel Zeman. 2016. Universal dependencies v1: A multilingual treebank collection. In *Proceedings of the Tenth International Conference on Language Resources and Evaluation (LREC 2016)*, Paris, France. European Language Resources Association (ELRA).

Kishore Papineni, Salim Roukos, Todd Ward, and Wei-Jing Zhu. 2002. Bleu: A method for automatic evaluation of machine translation. In *Proceedings of the 40th Annual Meeting on Association for Computational Linguistics*, ACL '02, page 311–318, USA. Association for Computational Linguistics.

Shantipriya Parida, Satya Ranjan Dash, Ondřej Bojar, Petr Motlicek, Priyanka Pattnaik, and Debasish Kumar Mallick. 2020. OdiEnCorp 2.0: Odia-English parallel corpus for machine translation. In *Proceedings of the WILDRE5– 5th Workshop on Indian Language Data: Resources and Evaluation*, pages 14–19, Marseille, France. European Language Resources Association (ELRA).

Jerin Philip, Shashank Siripragada, Vinay P. Namboodiri, and C. V. Jawahar. 2020. Revisiting low resource status of indian languages in machine translation. *CoRR*, abs/2008.04860.

Alec Radford, Jeff Wu, Rewon Child, David Luan, Dario Amodei, and Ilya Sutskever. 2019. Language models are unsupervised multitask learners.

Samyam Rajbhandari, Jeff Rasley, Olatunji Ruwase, and Yuxiong He. 2020. Zero: Memory optimizations toward training trillion parameter models. In *Proceedings of the International Conference for High Performance Computing, Networking, Storage and Analysis*, SC '20. IEEE Press.

Loganathan Ramasamy, Ondřej Bojar, and Zdeněk Žabokrtský. 2012. Morphological processing for english-tamil statistical machine translation. In *Proceedings of the Workshop on Machine Translation and Parsing in Indian Languages (MTPIL-2012)*, pages 113–122.

Jeff Rasley, Samyam Rajbhandari, Olatunji Ruwase, and Yuxiong He. 2020. Deepspeed: System optimizations enable training deep learning models with over 100 billion parameters. In *Proceedings of the 26th ACM SIGKDD International Conference on Knowledge Discovery and Data Mining*, KDD '20, page 3505–3506, New York, NY, USA. Association for Computing Machinery.

Sascha Rothe, Shashi Narayan, and Aliaksei Severyn. 2020. Leveraging pre-trained checkpoints for sequence generation tasks. *Transactions of the Association for Computational Linguistics*, 8:264–280.

Holger Schwenk, Vishrav Chaudhary, Shuo Sun, Hongyu Gong, and Francisco Guzmán. 2019. Wikimatrix: Mining 135m parallel sentences in 1620 language pairs from wikipedia. *CoRR*, abs/1907.05791.

Parth Shah and Vishvajit Bakrola. 2019. Neural machine translation system of indic languages - an attention based approach. In *2019 Second International Conference on Advanced Computational and Communication Paradigms (ICACCP)*, pages 1–5.

Emma Strubell, Ananya Ganesh, and Andrew McCallum. 2019. Energy and policy considerations for deep learning in NLP. In *Proceedings of the 57th Annual Meeting of the Association for Computational Linguistics*, pages 3645–3650, Florence, Italy. Association for Computational Linguistics.

Ilya Sutskever, Oriol Vinyals, and Quoc V. Le. 2014. Sequence to sequence learning with neural networks. In *Proceedings of the 27th International Conference on Neural Information Processing Systems - Volume 2*, NIPS'14, page 3104–3112, Cambridge, MA, USA. MIT Press.

Ye Kyaw Thu, Win Pa Pa, Masao Utiyama, Andrew Finch, and Eiichiro Sumita. 2016. Introducing the Asian language treebank (ALT). In *Proceedings of the Tenth International Conference on Language Resources and Evaluation (LREC'16)*, pages 1574–1578, Portorož, Slovenia. European Language Resources Association (ELRA).

Jörg Tiedemann. 2012. Parallel data, tools and interfaces in opus. In *Lrec*, volume 2012, pages 2214–2218.

Jörg Tiedemann. 2016. Finding alternative translations in a large corpus of movie subtitle. In *Proceedings of the Tenth International Conference on Language Resources and Evaluation (LREC'16)*, pages 3518–3522, Portorož, Slovenia. European Language Resources Association (ELRA).

Jörg Tiedemann. 2020. The Tatoeba Translation Challenge – Realistic data sets for low resource and multilingual MT. In *Proceedings of the Fifth Conference on Machine Translation*, pages 1174–1182, Online. Association for Computational Linguistics.

Ashish Vaswani, Noam Shazeer, Niki Parmar, Jakob Uszkoreit, Llion Jones, Aidan N Gomez, Ł ukasz Kaiser, and Illia Polosukhin. 2017. Attention is all you need. In *Advances in Neural Information Processing Systems*, volume 30. Curran Associates, Inc.

Yonghui Wu, Mike Schuster, Zhifeng Chen, Quoc V. Le, Mohammad Norouzi, Wolfgang Macherey, Maxim Krikun, Yuan Cao, Qin Gao, Klaus Macherey, Jeff Klingner, Apurva Shah, Melvin Johnson, Xiaobing Liu, Łukasz Kaiser, Stephan Gouws, Yoshikiyo Kato, Taku Kudo, Hideto Kazawa, Keith Stevens, George Kurian, Nishant Patil, Wei Wang, Cliff Young, Jason Smith, Jason Riesa, Alex Rudnick, Oriol Vinyals, Greg Corrado, Macduff Hughes, and Jeffrey Dean. 2016. Google's neural machine translation system: Bridging the gap between human and machine translation.

Linting Xue, Noah Constant, Adam Roberts, Mihir Kale, Rami Al-Rfou, Aditya Siddhant, Aditya Barua, and Colin Raffel. 2020. mt5: A massively multilingual pre-trained text-to-text transformer. *CoRR*, abs/2010.11934.

Zhilin Yang, Zihang Dai, Yiming Yang, Jaime Carbonell, Ruslan Salakhutdinov, and Quoc V Le. 2019. Xlnet: Generalized autoregressive pretraining for language understanding. *arXiv preprint arXiv:1906.08237*.

Ying Zhang, Stephan Vogel, and Alex Waibel. 2004. Interpreting bleu/nist scores: How much improvement do we need to have a better system? In *LREC*.

# IIIT Hyderabad Submission To WAT 2021: Efficient Multilingual NMT systems for Indian languages

**Sourav Kumar, Salil Aggarwal, Dipti Misra Sharma**
LTRC, IIIT-Hyderabad
sourav.kumar@research.iiit.ac.in
salil.aggarwal@research.iiit.ac.in
dipti@iiit.ac.in

## Abstract

This paper describes the work and the systems submitted by the IIIT-Hyderbad team (Id: IIIT-H) in the WAT 2021 (Nakazawa et al., 2021) MultiIndicMT shared task. The task covers 10 major languages of the Indian subcontinent. For the scope of this task, we have built multilingual systems for 20 translation directions namely English-Indic (one-to-many) and Indic-English (many-to-one). Individually, Indian languages are resource poor which hampers translation quality but by leveraging multilingualism and abundant monolingual corpora, the translation quality can be substantially boosted. But the multilingual systems are highly complex in terms of time as well as computational resources. Therefore, we are training our systems by efficiently selecting data that will actually contribute to most of the learning process. Furthermore, we are also exploiting the language relatedness found in between Indian languages. All the comparisons were made using BLEU score and we found that our final multilingual system significantly outperforms the baselines by an average of **11.3** and **19.6** BLEU points for English-Indic (en-xx) and Indic-English (xx-en) directions, respectively.

## 1 Introduction

Good translation systems are an important requirement due to substantial government, business and social communication among people speaking different languages. Neural machine translation (Sutskever et al., 2014; Bahdanau et al., 2014; Vaswani et al., 2017) is the current state-of-the-art approach for Machine Translation in both academia and industry. The success of NMT heavily relies on substantial amounts of parallel sentences as training data (Koehn and Knowles, 2017) which is again an arduous task for low resource languages like Indian languages (Philip et al., 2021). Many techniques have been devised to improve the translation quality of low resource languages like back translation (Sennrich et al., 2015), dual learning (Xia et al., 2016), transfer learning (Zoph et al., 2016; Kocmi and Bojar, 2018), etc. Also, using the traditional approaches, one would still need to train a separate model for each translation direction. So, building multilingual neural machine translation models by means of sharing parameters with high-resource languages is a common practice to improve the performance of low-resource language pairs (Firat et al., 2017; Johnson et al., 2017; Ha et al., 2016). Low resource language pairs perform better when combined opposed to the case where the models are trained separately due to sharing of parameters. It also enables training a single model that supports translation from multiple source languages to a single target language or from a single source language to multiple target languages. This approach mainly works by combining all the parallel data in hand which makes the training process quite complex in terms of both time and computational resources (Arivazhagan et al., 2019). Therefore, we are training our systems by efficiently selecting data that will actually contribute to most of the learning process. Sometimes, this learning is hindered in case of language pairs that do not show any kind of relatedness among themselves. But on the other hand, Indian languages exhibit a lot of lexical and structural similarities on account of sharing a common ancestry (Kunchukuttan and Bhattacharyya, 2020). Therefore, in this work, we have exploited the lexical similarity of these related languages to build efficient multilingual NMT systems.

This paper describes our work in the WAT 2021 MultiIndicMT shared task (cite). The task



*Proceedings of the 8th Workshop on Asian Translation*, pages 212–216
Bangkok, Thailand (online), August 5-6, 2021. ©2021 Association for Computational Linguistics

| Domain | PMI | Cvit | IITB | ocor | m2o | ufal | Wmat | ALT | JW | Osub | Ted | Wtile | nlpc | Tanz | urst | Bible |
|---|---|---|---|---|---|---|---|---|---|---|---|---|---|---|---|---|
| Vocab Overlap | 100 | 74.14 | 72.04 | 70.60 | 65.30 | 47.47 | 42.93 | 31.12 | 29.99 | 22.44 | 22.15 | 16.70 | 16.28 | 14.86 | 10.58 | 10.09 |

Table 1: Vocab Overlap of domains with PMI

covers 10 Indic Languages (Bengali, Gujarati, Hindi, Kannada, Malayalam, Marathi, Oriya, Punjabi, Tamil and Telugu) and English. The objective of this shared task is to build translation models for 20 translation directions (English-Indic and Indic-English). This paper is further organized as follows. Section 2 describes the methodology behind our experiments. Section 3 talks about the experimental details like dataset pre-processing and training details. Results and analysis have been discussed in Section 4, followed by conclusion in Section 5.

## 2 Methodology

### 2.1 Exploiting Language Relatedness

India is one of the most linguistically diverse countries of the world but underlying this vast diversity in Indian languages are many commonalities. These languages exhibit lexical and structural similarities on account of sharing a common ancestry or being in contact for a long period of time (Bhattacharyya et al., 2016). These languages share many common cognates and therefore, it is very important to utilize the lexical similarity of these languages to build good quality multilingual NMT systems. To do this, we are using the two different approaches namely **Unified Transliteration** and **Sub-word Segmentation** proposed by (Goyal et al., 2020).

#### 2.1.1 Unified Transliteration

The major Indian languages have a long written tradition and use a variety of scripts but correspondences can be established between equivalent characters across scripts. These scripts are derived from the ancient Brahmi script. In order to achieve this, we transliterated all the Indian languages into a common Devanagari script (which in our case is the script for Hindi) to share the same surface form. This unified transliteration is a string homomorphism, replacing characters in all the languages to a single desired script.

#### 2.1.2 Subword Segmentation

Despite sharing a lot of cognates, Indian languages do not share many words at their non-root level. Therefore, the more efficient approach is to exploit Indian languages at their sub-word level which will ensure more vocabulary overlap. Therefore, we are converting every word to sub-word level using the very well known technique **Byte Pair Encoding (BPE)** (Sennrich et al., 2015). This technique is applied after the unified transliteration in order to ensure that languages share same surface form (script). BPE units are variable length units which provide appropriate context for translation systems involving related languages. Since their vocabularies are much smaller than the morpheme and word-level models, data sparsity is also not a problem. In a multilingual scenario, learning BPE merge rules will not only find the common sub-words between multiple languages but it also ensures consistency of segmentation among each considered language pair.

### 2.2 Data Selection Strategy

Since the traditional approaches of training a multilingual system simply work by combining all the parallel dataset in hand, making it infeasible in terms of both time as well as computational resources. Therefore, in order to select only the relevant domains, we are incrementally adding all the domains in decreasing order of their vocab overlap with the PMI domain (Haddow and Kirefu, 2020). Detection of dip in the BLEU score (Papineni et al., 2002) is considered as the stopping criteria for our strategy. The vocab overlap between any two domains is calculated using the formula shown below:

$$\text{Vocab Overlap} = \frac{|Vocab_{d1} \cap Vocab_{d2}|}{max(|Vocab_{d1}|, |Vocab_{d2}|)} * 100$$

Here, $Vocab_{d1}$ & $Vocab_{d2}$ represents vocabulary of domain 1 and domain 2 respectively. Vocab overlap of each domain with PMI is shown in **Table 1**.

### 2.3 Back Translation

Back translation (Sennrich et al., 2015)is a widely used data augmentation method where the reverse direction is used to translate sentences from target side monolingual data into the source language. This synthetic parallel data is combined with the actual parallel data to re-train the model leading to better language modelling on the target side, regularization and target domain adaptation. Back

| Dataset | **En-hi** | **En-pa** | **En-gu** | **En-mr** | **En-bn** | **En-or** | **En-kn** | **En-ml** | **En-ta** | **En-te** | |
|---|---|---|---|---|---|---|---|---|---|---|---|
| Parallel corpus | | | | | | | | | | | |
| PMI | 50349 | 28294 | 41578 | 28974 | 23306 | 31966 | 28901 | 26916 | 32638 | 33380 | |
| CVIT | 266545 | 101092 | 58264 | 114220 | 91985 | 94494 | - | 43087 | 115968 | 44720 | |
| IITB | 1603080 | - | - | - | - | - | - | - | - | - | |
| Monolingual corpus | | | | | | | | | | | |
| | **En** | **Hi** | **Pa** | **Gu** | **Mr** | **Bn** | **Or** | **Kn** | **Ml** | **Ta** | **Te** |
| PMI | 89269 | 151792 | 87804 | 123008 | 118848 | 116835 | 103331 | 79024 | 81786 | 90912 | 111325 |

Table 2: Training dataset statistics

translation is particularly useful for low resource languages. We use back translation to augment our multilingual models. The back translation data is generated by multilingual models in the reverse direction, hence some implicit multilingual transfer is incorporated in the back translated data also. For the scope of this paper, we have used monolingual data of the PMI given on the WAT website.

### 2.4 Multilingual NMT and Fine-tuning

Multilingual model enables us to translate to and from multiple languages using a shared word piece vocabulary, which is significantly simpler than training a different model for each language pair. We used the technique proposed by Johnson et al. (2017) where he introduced a "language flag" based approach that shares the attention mechanism and a single encoder-decoder network to enable multilingual models. A language flag or token is part of the input sequence to indicate which direction to translate to. The decoder learns to generate the target given this input. This approach has been shown to be simple, effective and forces the model to generalize across language boundaries during training. It is also observed that when language pairs with little available data and language pairs with abundant data are mixed into a single model, translation quality on the low resource language pair is significantly improved. Furthermore, We are also fine tuning our multilingual system on PMI (multilingual) domain by the means of transfer learning b/w the parent and the child model.

## 3 Experimental Details

### 3.1 Dataset and Preprocessing

We are using the dataset provided in WAT 2021 shared task. Our experiments mainly use PMI (Haddow and Kirefu, 2020), CVIT (Siripragada et al., 2020) and IIT-B (Kunchukuttan et al., 2017) parallel dataset, along with monolingual data of PMI for further improvements **Table 2**. We used Moses (Koehn et al., 2007) toolkit for tokenization and cleaning of English and Indic NLP library (Kunchukuttan, 2020) for normalizing, tokenization and transliteration of all Indian languages. For our bilingual model we used BPE segmentation with 16K merge operation and for multilingual models we learned the Joint-BPE on source and target side with 16K merges (Sennrich et al., 2015).

### 3.2 Training

For all of our experiments, we use the **OpenNMT-py** (Klein et al., 2017) toolkit for training the NMT systems. We used the Transformer model with 6 layers in both the encoder and decoder, each with 512 hidden units. The word embedding size is set to 512 with 8 heads. The training is done in batches of maximum 4096 tokens at a time with dropout set to 0.3. We use Adam (Kingma and Ba, 2014) optimizer to optimize model parameters. We validate the model every 5,000 steps via BLEU (Papineni et al., 2002) and perplexity on the development set. We are training all of our models with early stopping criteria based on validation set accuracy. During testing, we rejoin translated BPE segments and convert the translated sentences back to their original language scripts. Finally, we evaluate the accuracy of our translation models using BLEU.

## 4 Results and Analysis

We report the Bleu score on the test set provided in the WAT 2021 MultiIndic shared task. **Table 3** and **Table 4** represents the results for different experiments we have performed for En-XX and XX-En directions respectively. The rows corresponding to *PMI + CVIT + Back Translation + Fine tuning on PMI multilingual* is our final system submitted for this shared task (Bleu scores shown in the table for this task are from automatic evaluation system). We observe that Multilingual system of PMI outperforms the bilingual baseline model of PMI by significant margins. The reason for this is the abil-

| En-XX | en-hi | en-pa | en-gu | en-mr | en-bn | en-or | en-kn | en-ml | en-ta | en-te |
|---|---|---|---|---|---|---|---|---|---|---|
| PMI Baselines | 23.21 | 18.26 | 15.46 | 7.07 | 5.25 | 8.32 | 8.67 | 4.63 | 5.32 | 6.12 |
| PMI Multilingual | 28.22 | 26.00 | 21.19 | 13.37 | 10.53 | 14.78 | 15.39 | 8.99 | 9.38 | 8.57 |
| PMI + CVIT Multilingual | 32.86 | 28.29 | 23.85 | 16.74 | 11.71 | 16.79 | 15.63 | 10.71 | 11.85 | 9.18 |
| PMI + CVIT + IITB Multilingual | 32.68 | 23.55 | 22.36 | 15.74 | 8.66 | 13.88 | 13.71 | 8.03 | 9.23 | 7.31 |
| PMI + CVIT + Back Translation | 35.81 | 30.15 | 25.84 | 18.47 | 12.50 | 18.52 | 17.98 | 11.99 | 12.31 | 12.89 |
| PMI + CVIT + Back Translation + Fine Tuning on PMI Multilingual | **38.25** | **33.35** | **26.97** | **19.48** | **14.73** | **20.15** | **19.57** | **12.76** | **14.43** | **15.61** |

Table 3: Results for En-XX direction

| XX-En | hi-en | pa-en | gu-en | mr-en | bn-en | or-en | kn-en | ml-en | ta-en | te-en |
|---|---|---|---|---|---|---|---|---|---|---|
| PMI Baselines | 24.69 | 19.80 | 20.16 | 11.70 | 10.25 | 13.80 | 13.32 | 11.30 | 9.82 | 13.39 |
| PMI Multilingual | 26.91 | 24.26 | 23.91 | 19.66 | 17.44 | 19.65 | 21.08 | 18.99 | 18.95 | 19.94 |
| PMI + CVIT Multilingual | 39.40 | 37.35 | 35.12 | 29.59 | 25.35 | 30.38 | 29.56 | 27.69 | 28.12 | 28.97 |
| PMI + CVIT + IITB Multilingual | 37.93 | 36.08 | 35.03 | 28.71 | 24.18 | 29.04 | 28.95 | 27.24 | 27.61 | 28.41 |
| PMI + CVIT + Back Translation | 41.41 | 39.15 | 37.84 | 32.17 | 26.90 | 32.52 | 32.58 | 28.99 | 29.31 | 30.29 |
| PMI + CVIT + Back Translation+ Fine Tuning on PMI Multilingual | **43.23** | **41.24** | **39.39** | **34.02** | **28.28** | **34.11** | **34.69** | **29.19** | **29.61** | **30.44** |

Table 4: Results for XX-En direction

ity to induce learning from multiple languages; also there is increase in vocab overlap using our technique of exploiting language relatedness. Further we tried to improve the performance of system using the relevant domains by incrementally adding different domains based on vocab overlap to the already existing system. We observed a decrease in Bleu score after adding the IIT-B corpus and therefore we stopped our incremental training at that point. Further we can see that our final multilingual model using back translation and fine tuning outperforms all other systems. Our submission also got evaluated with AMFM scores which can be found in the WAT 2021 evaluation website.

## 5 Conclusion

This paper presents the submissions by IIIT Hyderabd on the WAT 2021 MultiIndicMT shared Task. We performed experiments by combining different pre-processing and training techniques in series to achieve competitive results. The effectiveness of each technique is demonstrated. Our final submission able to achieve the second rank in this task according to automatic evaluation.

## References


Naveen Arivazhagan, Ankur Bapna, Orhan Firat, Dmitry Lepikhin, Melvin Johnson, Maxim Krikun, Mia Xu Chen, Yuan Cao, George Foster, Colin Cherry, et al. 2019. Massively multilingual neural machine translation in the wild: Findings and challenges. *arXiv preprint arXiv:1907.05019*.

Dzmitry Bahdanau, Kyunghyun Cho, and Yoshua Bengio. 2014. Neural machine translation by jointly learning to align and translate. *arXiv preprint arXiv:1409.0473*.

Pushpak Bhattacharyya, Mitesh M Khapra, and Anoop Kunchukuttan. 2016. Statistical machine translation between related languages. In *Proceedings of the 2016 Conference of the North American Chapter of the Association for Computational Linguistics: Tutorial Abstracts*, pages 17–20.

Orhan Firat, Kyunghyun Cho, Baskaran Sankaran, Fatos T Yarman Vural, and Yoshua Bengio. 2017. Multi-way, multilingual neural machine translation. *Computer Speech & Language*, 45:236–252.

Vikrant Goyal, Sourav Kumar, and Dipti Misra Sharma. 2020. Efficient neural machine translation for low-resource languages via exploiting related languages. In *Proceedings of the 58th Annual Meeting of the Association for Computational Linguistics: Student Research Workshop*, pages 162–168.

Thanh-Le Ha, Jan Niehues, and Alexander Waibel. 2016. Toward multilingual neural machine translation with universal encoder and decoder. *arXiv preprint arXiv:1611.04798*.

Barry Haddow and Faheem Kirefu. 2020. Pmindia–a collection of parallel corpora of languages of india. *arXiv preprint arXiv:2001.09907*.

Melvin Johnson, Mike Schuster, Quoc V Le, Maxim Krikun, Yonghui Wu, Zhifeng Chen, Nikhil Thorat, Fernanda Viégas, Martin Wattenberg, Greg Corrado, et al. 2017. Google's multilingual neural machine translation system: Enabling zero-shot translation. *Transactions of the Association for Computational Linguistics*, 5:339–351.

Diederik P Kingma and Jimmy Ba. 2014. Adam: A method for stochastic optimization. *arXiv preprint arXiv:1412.6980*.

Guillaume Klein, Yoon Kim, Yuntian Deng, Jean Senellart, and Alexander Rush. 2017. OpenNMT: Open-source toolkit for neural machine translation. In *Proceedings of ACL 2017, System Demonstrations*, pages 67–72, Vancouver, Canada. Association for Computational Linguistics.

Tom Kocmi and Ondřej Bojar. 2018. Trivial transfer learning for low-resource neural machine translation. *arXiv preprint arXiv:1809.00357*.

Philipp Koehn, Hieu Hoang, Alexandra Birch, Chris Callison-Burch, Marcello Federico, Nicola Bertoldi, Brooke Cowan, Wade Shen, Christine Moran, Richard Zens, et al. 2007. Moses: Open source toolkit for statistical machine translation. In *Proceedings of the 45th annual meeting of the association for computational linguistics companion volume proceedings of the demo and poster sessions*, pages 177–180.

Philipp Koehn and Rebecca Knowles. 2017. Six challenges for neural machine translation. *arXiv preprint arXiv:1706.03872*.

Anoop Kunchukuttan. 2020. The IndicNLP Library. `https://github.com/anoopkunchukuttan/indic_nlp_library/blob/master/docs/indicnlp.pdf`.

Anoop Kunchukuttan and Pushpak Bhattacharyya. 2020. Utilizing language relatedness to improve machine translation: A case study on languages of the indian subcontinent. *arXiv preprint arXiv:2003.08925*.

Anoop Kunchukuttan, Pratik Mehta, and Pushpak Bhattacharyya. 2017. The iit bombay english-hindi parallel corpus. *arXiv preprint arXiv:1710.02855*.

Toshiaki Nakazawa, Hideki Nakayama, Chenchen Ding, Raj Dabre, Shohei Higashiyama, Hideya Mino, Isao Goto, Win Pa Pa, Anoop Kunchukuttan, Shantipriya Parida, Ondřej Bojar, Chenhui Chu, Akiko Eriguchi, Kaori Abe, and Sadao Oda, Yusuke Kurohashi. 2021. Overview of the 8th workshop on Asian translation. In *Proceedings of the 8th Workshop on Asian Translation*, Bangkok, Thailand. Association for Computational Linguistics.

Kishore Papineni, Salim Roukos, Todd Ward, and Wei-Jing Zhu. 2002. Bleu: a method for automatic evaluation of machine translation. In *Proceedings of the 40th annual meeting of the Association for Computational Linguistics*, pages 311–318.

Jerin Philip, Shashank Siripragada, Vinay P Namboodiri, and CV Jawahar. 2021. Revisiting low resource status of indian languages in machine translation. In *8th ACM IKDD CODS and 26th COMAD*, pages 178–187.

Rico Sennrich, Barry Haddow, and Alexandra Birch. 2015. Improving neural machine translation models with monolingual data. *arXiv preprint arXiv:1511.06709*.

Shashank Siripragada, Jerin Philip, Vinay P Namboodiri, and CV Jawahar. 2020. A multilingual parallel corpora collection effort for indian languages. *arXiv preprint arXiv:2007.07691*.

Ilya Sutskever, Oriol Vinyals, and Quoc V Le. 2014. Sequence to sequence learning with neural networks. *arXiv preprint arXiv:1409.3215*.

Ashish Vaswani, Noam Shazeer, Niki Parmar, Jakob Uszkoreit, Llion Jones, Aidan N Gomez, Lukasz Kaiser, and Illia Polosukhin. 2017. Attention is all you need. *arXiv preprint arXiv:1706.03762*.

Yingce Xia, Di He, Tao Qin, Liwei Wang, Nenghai Yu, Tie-Yan Liu, and Wei-Ying Ma. 2016. Dual learning for machine translation. *arXiv preprint arXiv:1611.00179*.

Barret Zoph, Deniz Yuret, Jonathan May, and Kevin Knight. 2016. Transfer learning for low-resource neural machine translation. *arXiv preprint arXiv:1604.02201*.

# Language Relatedness and Lexical Closeness can help Improve Multilingual NMT: IITBombay@MultiIndicNMT WAT2021

**Jyotsana Khatri, Nikhil Saini, Pushpak Bhattacharyya**
Department of Computer Science and Engineering
Indian Institute of Technology Bombay
Mumbai, India
{jyotsanak, nikhilra, pb}@cse.iitb.ac.in

## Abstract

Multilingual Neural Machine Translation has achieved remarkable performance by training a single translation model for multiple languages. This paper describes our submission (Team ID: CFILT-IITB) for the MultiIndicMT: An Indic Language Multilingual Task at WAT 2021. We train multilingual NMT systems by sharing encoder and decoder parameters with language embedding associated with each token in both encoder and decoder. Furthermore, we demonstrate the use of transliteration (script conversion) for Indic languages in reducing the lexical gap for training a multilingual NMT system. Further, we show improvement in performance by training a multilingual NMT system using languages of the same family, i.e., related languages.

## 1 Introduction

Neural Machine Translation (Sutskever et al., 2014; Bahdanau et al., 2015; Wu et al., 2016) has become a de-facto for automatic translation of language pairs. NMT systems with Transformer (Vaswani et al., 2017) based architectures have achieved competitive accuracy on data-rich language pairs like English-French. However, NMT systems are data-hungry, and only a few pairs of languages have abundant parallel data. For low resource setting, techniques like transfer learning (Zoph et al., 2016) and utilization of monolingual data in an unsupervised setting (Artetxe et al., 2018; Lample et al., 2017, 2018) have shown support for increasing the translation accuracy. Multilingual Neural Machine Translation is an ideal setting for low resource MT (Lakew et al., 2018) since it allows sharing of encoder-decoder parameters, word embeddings, and joint or separate vocabularies. It also enables zero-shot translations, i.e., translating between language pairs that were not seen during training (Johnson et al., 2017a).

In this paper, we present our system for MultiIndicMT: An Indic Language Multilingual Task at WAT 2021 (Nakazawa et al., 2021). The task covers 10 Indic Languages (Bengali, Gujarati, Hindi, Kannada, Malayalam, Marathi, Oriya, Punjabi, Tamil, and Telugu) and English.

To summarize our approach and contributions, we **(i)** present a multilingual NMT system with shared encoder-decoder framework, **(ii)** show results on many-to-one translation, **(iii)** use transliteration to a common script to handle the lexical gap between languages, **(iv)** show how grouping of languages in regard to their language family helps multilingual NMT and **(v)** use language embeddings with each token in both encoder and decoder.

## 2 Related work

### 2.1 Neural Machine Translation

Neural Machine Translation architectures consist of encoder layers, attention layers, and decoder layers. NMT framework takes a sequence of words as an input; the encoder generates an intermediate representation, conditioned on which, the decoder generates an output sequence. The decoder also attends to the encoder states. Bahdanau et al. (2015) introduced the encoder-decoder attention to allow the decoder to soft-search the parts of the source sentence to predict the next token. The encoder-decoder can be a LSTM framework (Sutskever et al., 2014; Wu et al., 2016), CNN (Gehring et al., 2017), or Transformer layers (Vaswani et al., 2017). A Transformer layer comprises of self-attention that bakes the understanding of input sequence with positional encoding and passes on to the next component, feed-forward neural network, layer normalization, and residual connections. The decoder in the transformer has an additional encoder-attention layer that attends to the output states of the transformer encoder.



*Proceedings of the 8th Workshop on Asian Translation*, pages 217–223
Bangkok, Thailand (online), August 5-6, 2021. ©2021 Association for Computational Linguistics

NMT is data-hungry, and only a few pairs of languages have abundant parallel data. In recent years, NMT has been accompanied by several techniques to improve the performance of both low & high resource language pairs. Back-translation (Sennrich et al., 2016b) is used to augment the parallel data with synthetically generated parallel data by passing monolingual datasets to the previously trained models. Currently, NMT systems also perform on-the-fly back-translation to train the model simultaneously. Tokenization methods like Byte Pair Encoding (Sennrich et al., 2016a) are used in almost all NMT models. Pivoting (Cheng et al., 2017) and Transfer Learning (Zoph et al., 2016) have leveraged the language relatedness by indirectly providing the model with more parallel data from related language pairs.

### 2.2 Multilingual Neural Machine Translation

Multilingual NMT trains a single model utilizing data from multiple language-pairs to improve the performance. There are different approaches to incorporate multiple language pairs in a single system, like multi-way NMT, pivot-based NMT, transfer learning, multi-source NMT and, multilingual NMT (Dabre et al., 2020). Multilingual NMT came into picture because many languages share certain amount of vocabulary and share some structural similarity. These languages together can be utilized to improve the performance of NMT systems. In this paper, our focus is to analyze the performance of multi-source NMT. The simplest approach is to share the parameters of NMT model across multiple language pairs. These kinds of systems work better if languages are related to each other. In Johnson et al. (2017b), the encoder, decoder, and attention are shared for the training of multiple language pairs and a target language token is added at the beginning of target sentence while decoding. Firat et al. (2016) utilizes a shared attention mechanism to train multilingual models. Recently many approaches have been proposed, where monolingual data of multiple languages is utilized to pre-train a single model using different objectives like masked language modeling and denoising (Lample and Conneau, 2019; Song et al., 2019; Lewis et al., 2020; Liu et al., 2020). Multilingual pre-training followed by multilingual finetuning has also proven to be beneficial (Tang et al., 2020).

### 2.3 Language Relatedness

Telugu, Tamil, Kannada, and Malayalam are Dravidian languages whose speakers are predominantly found in South India, with some speakers in Sri Lanka and a few pockets of speakers in North India. The speakers of these languages constitute around 20% of the Indian population (Kunchukuttan and Bhattacharyya, 2020). Dravidian languages are agglutinative, i.e., long and complex words are formed by stringing together morphemes without changing them in spelling or phonetics. Most Dravidian languages have clusivity distinction. Hindi, Bengali, Marathi, Gujarati, Oriya, Punjabi are Indo-Aryan languages and are primarily spoken in North and Central India and the neighboring countries of Pakistan, Nepal, and Bangladesh. The speakers of these languages constitute around 75% of the Indian population. Both Dravidian and Indo-Aryan language families follow the Subject(S)-Object(O)-Verb(V) order.

Grouping languages concerning their families have inherent advantages because they form a closely related group with several linguistic phenomenons shared amongst them. Indo-Aryan languages are morphologically rich and have huge similarities when compared to English. A language group also share vocabularies at both word and character level. They contain similarly spelled words that are derived from the same root. ‘

### 2.4 Transliteration

Indic languages share a lot of vocabulary, but most languages utilize different scripts. Nevertheless, these scripts have phoneme overlap and can be converted easily from one to another using a simple rule-based system. To convert all Indic language data into the same script, we use IndicNLP[1] which maps different Unicode range for the conversion. The conversion of all Indic language scripts to the same script helps with better shared vocabulary and leads to smaller subword vocabulary (Ramesh et al., 2021).

## 3 System overview

In this section, we describe the details of the submitted systems to MultiIndicMT task at WAT2021. We report results for four types of models:

- **Bilingual**: Trained only using parallel data for a particular language pair (bilingual models).

[1]https://github.com/anoopkunchukuttan/indic_nlp_library

- **All-En**: Multilingual many-to-one system trained using all available parallel data of all language pairs.
- **IA-En**: Multilingual many-to-one system trained using Indo-Aryan languages from the provided parallel data.
- **DR-En**: Multilingual many-to-one system trained using Dravidian languages from the provided parallel data.

To train our multilingual models, we use shared encoder-decoder transformer architecture. To handle the lexical gap between Indic languages in multilingual models, we convert the data of all Indic languages to a common script. We choose the common script as Devanagari (arbitrary choice). We also perform a comparative study of systems when the encoder and decoder are shared only between related languages. To perform this comparative study, we group the provided set of languages in two parts based on the language families they belong to, i.e, the system is trained from Indo-Aryan (group) to English, and Dravidian (group) to English. Indo-Aryan-to-English contains Bengali, Gujarati, Hindi, Marathi, Oriya, Punjabi to English, and Dravidian-to-English contains Kannada, Malayalam, Tamil, Telugu to English. We use shared subword vocabulary of the languages involved while training multilingual models, and a common vocabulary of source and target languages to train bilingual models.

## 4 Experimental details

### 4.1 Dataset

Our models are trained using only the parallel data provided for the task. The size of the parallel data available and its source of origin are summarized in Table 1. The validation and test data provided in the task is n-way and contains 1000 sentences for validation and 2390 sentences in test set.

### 4.2 Data preprocessing

We tokenize English language data using moses tokenizer (Koehn et al., 2007), and Indian language data using IndicNLP[2] library. For multilingual models, we transliterate (script mapping) all Indic language data into Devanagari script using the IndicNLP library. Our aim here is to convert data of all languages into the same script, hence the choice of Devnagari as a common script is arbitrary. We use fastBPE[3] to learn BPE (Byte pair encoding) (Bojanowski et al., 2017). For bilingual models, we use 60000 BPE codes over the combined tokenized data of both languages. The number of BPE codes is set to 100000 for All-En, and 80000 for DR-En and IA-En.

### 4.3 Experimental Setup

We use six layers in the encoder, six layers in the decoder, 8 attention heads in both encoder and decoder, and 1024 embedding dimension. The encoder and decoder are trained using Adam (Kingma and Ba, 2015) optimizer with inverse square root learning rate schedule. We use the same setting as used in Song et al. (2019) for warmup phase, in which the learning rate is increased linearly for some initial steps starting from $1e^{-}7$ to 0.0001, warmup phase is set to 4000 steps. We use mini-batches of size 2000 tokens and set the dropout to 0.1 (Gal and Ghahramani, 2016). Maximum sentence length is set to 100 after applying BPE. At decoding time, we use greedy decoding. For experiments, we are using mt_steps from MASS[4] codebase. Our models are trained using only parallel data provided in the task, we are not training the model using any kind of pretraining objective. We train bilingual models for 100 epochs and multilingual models for 150 epochs. The epoch size is set to 200000 sentences. Due to resource constraints, we train our model for fixed number of epochs, it does not guarantee convergence. Similar to MASS (Song et al., 2019), language embeddings are added to each token in the encoder and decoder to distinguish between languages. These language embeddings are learnt during training.

### 4.4 Results and Discussion

We report BLEU scores for our four settings: bilingual, All-En (multilingual many-to-one), IA-En (multilingual many-to-one Indo-Aryan to English), and DR-En (multilingual many-to-one Dravidian to English) in Table 2. We use multi-bleu.perl [5] to calculate BLEU scores of baseline models. BLEU score is calculated using the tokenized reference and hypothesis files as followed by organizers in

[2]https://github.com/anoopkunchukuttan/indic_nlp_library

[3]https://github.com/glample/fastBPE

[4]https://github.com/microsoft/MASS

[5]https://github.com/moses-smt/mosesdecoder/blob/RELEASE-2.1.1/scripts/generic/multi-bleu.perl

| Lang Pair | Size | Data sources |
|---|---|---|
| **bn-en** | 1.70M | alt, cvit-pib, jw, opensubtitles, pmi, tanzil, ted2020, wikimatrix |
| **gu-en** | 0.51M | bibleuedin, cvit, jw, pmi, ted2020, urst, wikititles |
| **hi-en** | 3.50M | alt, bibleuedin, cvit-pib, iitb, jw, opensubtitles, pmi, tanzil, ted2020, wikimatrix |
| **kn-en** | 0.39M | bibleuedin, jw, pmi, ted2020 |
| **ml-en** | 1.20M | bibleudein, cvit-pib, jw, opensubtitles, pmi, tanzil, ted2020, wikimatrix |
| **mr-en** | 0.78M | bibleuedin, cvit-pib, jw, pmi, ted2020, wikimatrix |
| **or-en** | 0.25M | cvit, mtenglish2odia, odiencorp, pmi |
| **pa-en** | 0.51M | cvit-pib, jw, pmi, ted2020 |
| **ta-en** | 1.40M | cvit-pib, jw, nlpc, opensubtitles, pmi, tanzil, ted2020, ufal, wikimatrix, wikititles |
| **te-en** | 0.68M | cvit-pib, jw, opensubtitles, pmi, ted2020, wikimatrix |

Table 1: Parallel Dataset amongst 10 Indic-English language pairs. *Size* is the number of parallel sentences (in millions). (bn, gu, hi, kn, ml, mr, or, pa, ta, te and en: Bengali, Gujarati, Hindi, Kannada, Malayalam, Marathi, Oriya, Punjabi, Tamil, Telugu and English respectively

| | BLEU | | | | AMFM | | |
|---|---|---|---|---|---|---|---|
| **Lang Pair** | **Bilingual** | **IA-En** | **DR-En** | **All-En** | **IA-En** | **DR-En** | **All-En** |
| **bn-en** | 18.52 | **20.18** | - | 18.48 | **0.734491** | - | 0.730379 |
| **gu-en** | 26.51 | **31.02** | - | 28.79 | **0.776935** | - | 0.765441 |
| **hi-en** | 33.53 | **33.7** | - | 30.9 | **0.791408** | - | 0.775032 |
| **mr-en** | 21.28 | **25.5** | - | 23.57 | **0.767347** | - | 0.751917 |
| **or-en** | 22.6 | **26.34** | - | 25.05 | **0.780009** | - | 0.770941 |
| **pa-en** | 29.92 | **32.34** | - | 29.87 | **0.782112** | - | 0.772655 |
| **kn-en** | 17.93 | - | **24.18** | 24.01 | - | 0.744802 | **0.751223** |
| **ml-en** | 19.52 | - | **22.84** | 22.1 | - | **0.745908** | 0.744459 |
| **ta-en** | **23.62** | - | 22.75 | 21.37 | - | **0.74509** | 0.742311 |
| **te-en** | 19.89 | - | **24.02** | 22.37 | - | **0.745885** | 0.743435 |

Table 2: Results: *XX-en* is the translation direction. *IA, DR, All* are Indo-Aryan, Dravidian and All Indic languages respectively. The numbers under BLEU and AMFM headings represent BLEU score and AMFM score respectively.

the evaluation of MultiIndicMT task[6]. Tokenization is performed using moses-tokenizer (Koehn et al., 2007). For IA-En, DR-En, and All-En, we report results provided by the organizers. Table 2 also reports the Adequacy-Fluency Metrics (AM-FM) for Machine Translation (MT) Evaluation (Banchs et al., 2015) provided by organizers.

[6]http://lotus.kuee.kyoto-u.ac.jp/WAT/evaluation/automatic_evaluation_systems/automaticEvaluationEN.html

The BLEU score in table 2 highlights that the multilingual model outperforms the simpler bilingual models. Although we did not submit bilingual models in the shared task submission, we use it here as a baseline to compare with multilingual models. Moreover, upon grouping languages based on their language families, significant improvement in BLEU scores is observed due to less confusion and better learning of the language representations in shared encoder-decoder architecture. We ob-

| lang1 \ lang2 | bn | gu | hi | mr | or | pa | kn | ml | ta | te |
|---|---|---|---|---|---|---|---|---|---|---|
| **bn** | - | 37.86 | 80.63 | 55.1 | 34.81 | 35.93 | 24.69 | 54.83 | 61.79 | 60.89 |
| **gu** | 70.47 | - | 93.51 | 83.52 | 51.02 | 54.09 | 49.22 | 61.21 | 46.85 | 71.74 |
| **hi** | 68.96 | 42.97 | - | 59.62 | 30.79 | 38.29 | 27.66 | 52.68 | 55.77 | 60.5 |
| **mr** | 72.35 | 58.91 | 91.53 | - | 40.36 | 45.2 | 38.04 | 60.91 | 53.59 | 69.23 |
| **or** | 83.6 | 65.83 | 86.47 | 73.82 | - | 48.94 | 48.1 | 61.66 | 44.71 | 68.7 |
| **pa** | 72.39 | 58.54 | 90.19 | 69.36 | 41.05 | - | 36.64 | 60.16 | 59.18 | 68.58 |
| **kn** | 63.08 | 67.57 | 82.64 | 74.04 | 51.17 | 46.48 | - | 74.39 | 50.34 | 84.07 |
| **ml** | 67.37 | 40.4 | 75.68 | 56.99 | 31.54 | 36.69 | 35.77 | - | 66.00 | 68.86 |
| **ta** | 63.49 | 25.86 | 67.00 | 41.94 | 19.13 | 30.19 | 20.24 | 55.19 | - | 56.59 |
| **te** | 71.66 | 45.36 | 83.26 | 62.05 | 33.67 | 40.07 | 38.72 | 65.96 | 64.82 | - |

Table 3: Shared Vocabulary: Percentage of vocabulary (after applying BPE) of lang1 present in lang2 (rows: lang1, columns: lang2) after transliteration to a common script (devnagari)

serve that the BLEU score increases by 14 percent on average when the languages are grouped based on their families *(IA-En & DR-En)* and by 7 percent when all languages are combined in a single multilingual model *(All-En)* as compared to the bilingual models. The *IA-En* and *DR-En* BLEU scores being better than both bilingual and multilingual *(All-En)* models encourage the exploitation of linguistic insights like languages relatedness and lexical closeness among language families.

Table 3 shows the percentage of vocabulary overlap in two languages. We get the vocabulary of each language using the source language part of the BPE processed parallel train set files as used in *All-En* experiment. The vocabulary size for each language is different. Equation 1 states how the value in each cell is calculated. $V1$, $V2$ are the vocabularies of lang1 & lang2 respectively. The numerator is the count of intersection of the two vocabularies and denominator is the count of the vocabulary of lang1.

$$\frac{|V1 \cap V2|}{|V1|} * 100 \qquad (1)$$

Almost all indic languages provided in the task *bn, gu, (hi,mr), or, pa, kn, ml, ta, te,* use different scripts except *hi* and *mr*. Both *hi* and *mr* utilize the same script (devnagari). It is clear from Table 3 that transliteration to a common script helps in increasing the shared vocabulary and helps the model to leverage the benefit of the lexical similarity between languages.

## 5 Conclusion

In this paper, we study the influence of sharing encoder-decoder parameters between related languages in multilingual NMT by performing experiments with the grouping of languages based on language family. Furthermore, we also perform experiments of multilingual NMT with all Indic language data converted to the same script, which helps the model in learning better translation by utilizing the benefit of better shared vocabulary. In the future, we plan to utilize monolingual data from (Kakwani et al., 2020) to improve multilingual NMT further.

## References

Mikel Artetxe, Gorka Labaka, Eneko Agirre, and Kyunghyun Cho. 2018. Unsupervised neural machine translation. *ArXiv*, abs/1710.11041.

Dzmitry Bahdanau, Kyunghyun Cho, and Yoshua Bengio. 2015. Neural machine translation by jointly learning to align and translate. In *International Conference on Learning Representations.*

Rafael E. Banchs, Luis F. D'Haro, and Haizhou Li. 2015. Adequacy–fluency metrics: Evaluating mt in the continuous space model framework. *IEEE/ACM Transactions on Audio, Speech, and Language Processing*, 23(3):472–482.

Piotr Bojanowski, Edouard Grave, Armand Joulin, and Tomas Mikolov. 2017. Enriching word vectors with subword information. *Transactions of the Association for Computational Linguistics*, 5:135–146.

Yong Cheng, Qian Yang, Yang Liu, Maosong Sun, and Wei Xu. 2017. Joint training for pivot-based neural machine translation. In *IJCAI*, pages 3974–3980.

Raj Dabre, Chenhui Chu, and Anoop Kunchukuttan. 2020. A survey of multilingual neural machine translation. *ACM Computing Surveys (CSUR)*, 53(5):1–38.

Orhan Firat, Kyunghyun Cho, and Yoshua Bengio. 2016. Multi-way, multilingual neural machine translation with a shared attention mechanism. In *Proceedings of the 2016 Conference of the North American Chapter of the Association for Computational Linguistics: Human Language Technologies*, pages 866–875.

Yarin Gal and Zoubin Ghahramani. 2016. A theoretically grounded application of dropout in recurrent neural networks. In *Proceedings of the 30th International Conference on Neural Information Processing Systems*, NIPS, pages 1027–1035, Red Hook, NY, USA. Curran Associates Inc.

Jonas Gehring, Michael Auli, David Grangier, Denis Yarats, and Yann N. Dauphin. 2017. Convolutional sequence to sequence learning.

Melvin Johnson, Mike Schuster, Quoc V. Le, Maxim Krikun, Yonghui Wu, Zhifeng Chen, Nikhil Thorat, Fernanda Viégas, Martin Wattenberg, Greg Corrado, Macduff Hughes, and Jeffrey Dean. 2017a. Google's multilingual neural machine translation system: Enabling zero-shot translation. *Transactions of the Association for Computational Linguistics*, 5:339–351.

Melvin Johnson, Mike Schuster, Quoc V Le, Maxim Krikun, Yonghui Wu, Zhifeng Chen, Nikhil Thorat, Fernanda Viégas, Martin Wattenberg, Greg Corrado, et al. 2017b. Google's multilingual neural machine translation system: Enabling zero-shot translation. *Transactions of the Association for Computational Linguistics*, 5:339–351.

Divyanshu Kakwani, Anoop Kunchukuttan, Satish Golla, NC Gokul, Avik Bhattacharyya, Mitesh M Khapra, and Pratyush Kumar. 2020. inlpsuite: Monolingual corpora, evaluation benchmarks and pre-trained multilingual language models for indian languages. In *Proceedings of the 2020 Conference on Empirical Methods in Natural Language Processing: Findings*, pages 4948–4961.

Diederik P. Kingma and Jimmy Ba. 2015. Adam: A method for stochastic optimization. *CoRR*, abs/1412.6980.

Philipp Koehn, Hieu Hoang, Alexandra Birch, Chris Callison-Burch, Marcello Federico, Nicola Bertoldi, Brooke Cowan, Wade Shen, Christine Moran, Richard Zens, et al. 2007. Moses: Open source toolkit for statistical machine translation. In *Proceedings of the 45th annual meeting of the association for computational linguistics companion volume proceedings of the demo and poster sessions*, pages 177–180.

Anoop Kunchukuttan and Pushpak Bhattacharyya. 2020. Utilizing language relatedness to improve machine translation: A case study on languages of the indian subcontinent. *CoRR*, abs/2003.08925.

Surafel M. Lakew, Quintino F. Lotito, Matteo Negri, Marco Turchi, and Marcello Federico. 2018. Improving zero-shot translation of low-resource languages.

Guillaume Lample and Alexis Conneau. 2019. Cross-lingual language model pretraining. *Advances in Neural Information Processing Systems (NeurIPS)*.

Guillaume Lample, Ludovic Denoyer, and Marc'Aurelio Ranzato. 2017. Unsupervised machine translation using monolingual corpora only. In *International Conference on Learning Representations*.

Guillaume Lample, Myle Ott, Alexis Conneau, Ludovic Denoyer, and Marc'Aurelio Ranzato. 2018. Phrase-based & neural unsupervised machine translation. In *Proceedings of the 2018 Conference on Empirical Methods in Natural Language Processing*, pages 5039–5049, Brussels, Belgium. Association for Computational Linguistics.

Mike Lewis, Yinhan Liu, Naman Goyal, Marjan Ghazvininejad, Abdelrahman Mohamed, Omer Levy, Veselin Stoyanov, and Luke Zettlemoyer. 2020. BART: Denoising sequence-to-sequence pre-training for natural language generation, translation, and comprehension. In *Proceedings of the 58th Annual Meeting of the Association for Computational Linguistics*, pages 7871–7880, Online. Association for Computational Linguistics.

Yinhan Liu, Jiatao Gu, Naman Goyal, Xian Li, Sergey Edunov, Marjan Ghazvininejad, Mike Lewis, and Luke Zettlemoyer. 2020. Multilingual denoising pre-training for neural machine translation. *Transactions of the Association for Computational Linguistics*, 8:726–742.

Toshiaki Nakazawa, Hideki Nakayama, Chenchen Ding, Raj Dabre, Shohei Higashiyama, Hideya Mino, Isao Goto, Win Pa Pa, Anoop Kunchukuttan, Shantipriya Parida, Ondřej Bojar, Chenhui Chu, Akiko Eriguchi, Kaori Abe, and Sadao Oda, Yusuke Kurohashi. 2021. Overview of the 8th workshop on Asian translation. In *Proceedings of the 8th Workshop on Asian Translation*, Bangkok, Thailand. Association for Computational Linguistics.

Gowtham Ramesh, Sumanth Doddapaneni, Aravinth Bheemaraj, Mayank Jobanputra, Raghavan AK, Ajitesh Sharma, Sujit Sahoo, Harshita Diddee, Divyanshu Kakwani, Navneet Kumar, et al. 2021.

Samanantar: The largest publicly available parallel corpora collection for 11 indic languages. *arXiv preprint arXiv:2104.05596*.

Rico Sennrich, B. Haddow, and Alexandra Birch. 2016a. Neural machine translation of rare words with subword units. *ArXiv*, abs/1508.07909.

Rico Sennrich, Barry Haddow, and Alexandra Birch. 2016b. Improving neural machine translation models with monolingual data. In *Proceedings of the 54th Annual Meeting of the Association for Computational Linguistics (Volume 1: Long Papers)*, pages 86–96.

Kaitao Song, Xu Tan, Tao Qin, Jianfeng Lu, and Tie-Yan Liu. 2019. Mass: Masked sequence to sequence pre-training for language generation. In *International Conference on Machine Learning*, pages 5926–5936.

Ilya Sutskever, Oriol Vinyals, and Quoc V. Le. 2014. Sequence to sequence learning with neural networks. In *NIPS*.

Yuqing Tang, Chau Tran, Xian Li, Peng-Jen Chen, Naman Goyal, Vishrav Chaudhary, Jiatao Gu, and Angela Fan. 2020. Multilingual translation with extensible multilingual pretraining and finetuning. *arXiv preprint arXiv:2008.00401*.

Ashish Vaswani, Noam Shazeer, Niki Parmar, Jakob Uszkoreit, Llion Jones, Aidan N Gomez, Łukasz Kaiser, and Illia Polosukhin. 2017. Attention is all you need. In *Advances in neural information processing systems*, pages 5998–6008.

Y. Wu, M. Schuster, Z. Chen, Quoc V. Le, Mohammad Norouzi, Wolfgang Macherey, M. Krikun, Yuan Cao, Q. Gao, Klaus Macherey, J. Klingner, Apurva Shah, M. Johnson, X. Liu, Lukasz Kaiser, Stephan Gouws, Y. Kato, Taku Kudo, H. Kazawa, K. Stevens, George Kurian, Nishant Patil, W. Wang, C. Young, J. Smith, Jason Riesa, Alex Rudnick, Oriol Vinyals, G. Corrado, Macduff Hughes, and J. Dean. 2016. Google's neural machine translation system: Bridging the gap between human and machine translation. *ArXiv*, abs/1609.08144.

Barret Zoph, Deniz Yuret, Jonathan May, and Kevin Knight. 2016. Transfer learning for low-resource neural machine translation. *ArXiv*, abs/1604.02201.

# Samsung R&D Institute Poland submission to WAT 2021 Indic Language Multilingual Task

**Adam Dobrowolski, Marcin Szymański, Marcin Chochowski, Paweł Przybysz**
Samsung R&D Institute, Warsaw, Poland
{a.dobrowols2, m.szymanski, m.chochowski, p.przybysz} @samsung.com

MultiIndicMT: An Indic Language Multilingual Task
Team ID: SRPOL

## Abstract

This paper describes the submission to the WAT 2021 Indic Language Multilingual Task by Samsung R&D Institute Poland. The task covered translation between 10 Indic Languages (Bengali, Gujarati, Hindi, Kannada, Malayalam, Marathi, Oriya, Punjabi, Tamil and Telugu) and English.

We combined a variety of techniques: transliteration, filtering, backtranslation, domain adaptation, knowledge-distillation and finally ensembling of NMT models. We applied an effective approach to low-resource training that consist of pretraining on backtranslations and tuning on parallel corpora.

We experimented with two different domain-adaptation techniques which significantly improved translation quality when applied to monolingual corpora. We researched and applied a novel approach for finding the best hyperparameters for ensembling a number of translation models.

All techniques combined gave significant improvement - up to +8 BLEU over baseline results. The quality of the models has been confirmed by the human evaluation where SRPOL models scored best for all 5 manually evaluated languages.

## 1 Introduction

Samsung R&D Poland Team researched effective techniques that worked especially well for low-resource languages: transliteration, iterative back-translation followed by tuning on parallel corpora. We successfully applied these techniques during the WAT2021 competition (Nakazawa et al., 2021). Especially for the competition we also applied custom domain-adaptation techniques which substantially improved the final results.

Most of the applied techniques and ideas are commonly used for works on Indian languages machine translation (Chu and Wang, 2018) (Dabre et al., 2020).

This document is structured as follows. In section 2 we describe the sources and techniques of corpora preparation used for the training. In sections 3 and 4 we describe the model architecture and techniques used in training, tuning and ensembling and finally Section 5 presents the results we gained on every stage of the training.

All trainings were performed on Transformer models. We used standard Marian NMT [1] v.1.9 framework.

## 2 Data

### 2.1 Multilingual trainings

Multilingual models trained for the competition use a target language tag at the beginning of sentence to select the direction of the translation.

### 2.2 Transliteration

Indian languages use a variety of scripts. Using transliteration between scripts of similar languages may improve the quality of multilingual models as described in (Bawden et al., 2019) (Goyal and Sharma, 2019). The transliteration we applied was to replace Indian letters of various scripts to their equivalents in Devanagari script. We used indic-NLP [2] library to perform the transliteration.

In our previous experiments with Indian languages we noticed an overall improvement of the quality for multi-indian models, so we used transliteration in all trainings. However, additional experiments on transliteration during the competition were not conclusive. The results for trainings on raw corpora, without transliteration were similar (see Table 1).

[1] github.com/marian-nmt/marian
[2] https://github.com/anoopkunchukuttan/indic_nlp_library



*Proceedings of the 8th Workshop on Asian Translation*, pages 224–232
Bangkok, Thailand (online), August 5-6, 2021. 

### 2.3 Parallel Corpora Filtering

The base corpus for all trainings was the concatentaion of complete bilingual corpora provided by the organizers (further referenced as *bitext*) (11M lines in total). No filtering or preprocessing (but the transliteration) were performed on this corpus. The corpus included parallel data from: CVIT-PIB, PMIndia, IITB 3.0, JW, NLPC, UFAL EnTam, Uka Tarsadia, Wiki Titles, ALT, OpenSubtitles, Bibleuedin, MTEnglish2Odia, OdiEnCorp 2.0, TED, WikiMatrix. During the competition we performed several experiments to enrich/filter this parallel corpora:

- Inclusion of CCAligned corpus
- Removing *far from domain* sentence pairs like religious corpora
- Removing sentence pairs of low probability (according to e.g. sentence lengths, detected language etc.)
- Domain adaptation by fastText
- Domain adaptation by language model

None of these techniques applied on parallel corpora had led to quality improvement which is why we decided to continue with the basic non-filtered corpora as the base for future trainings.

### 2.4 Backtranslation

Backtranslation of monolingual corpora is a commonly used technique for improving machine translation. Especially for low-resource languages where only small bilingual corpora are available (Edunov et al., 2018). Training on backtranslations enriches the target language model, which improves the overall translation quality. The synthetic backtranslated corpus was joined with the original bilingual corpus for the trainings.

Using backtranslations of the full monolingual corpuses led to the improvement of results on translation on Indian to English directions by 1.2 BLEU on average. There was no improvement in the opposite directions. See Tables 5 and 6.

### 2.5 Domain adaptation

We enriched the parallel training corpora with backtranslated monolingual data selecting only sentences similar to PMI domain to increase the rate of in-domain data in the training corpus. We used two different techniques to select the in domain sentences for backtranslation. With these techniques we trained two separate families of MT models.

**Domain adaptation by fastText (FT)** - We applied the domain adaptation described in (Yu et al., 2020). Following the hints from the paper, we trained the fastText (Joulin et al., 2017) model using balanced corpus containing sentences from PMIndia labelled as in-domain and CCAligned sentences labelled as out-domain. Using the trained model we filtered the parallel as well as monolingual corpora.

**Domain adaptation by language model (LM)** As the second approach to select a subset of best PMI-like sentences from monolingual general-domain AI4Bharat (Kunchukuttan et al., 2020) corpora available for the task, we used the approach described in (Axelrod et al., 2011). For each of 10 Indian languages two RNN language models were constructed using Marian toolkit: in-domain trained with a particular part of PMI corpus and out-of-domain created using a similar number of lines from a mix of all other corpora available for that language respectively. All these models were regularized with exponential smoothing of 0.0001, dropout of 0.2 along with source and target word token dropout of 0.1. For the AI4Bharat mono corpus sentence ranking, we used a cross-entropy difference between scores of previously mentioned models as suggested in (Axelrod et al., 2011), normalized by the line length. Only sentences with a score above arbitrarily chosen threshold were selected for further processing. We noticed a significant influence of domain adaptation while selecting mono corpora used for backtranslation (see Table 3).

### 2.6 Multi-Agent Dual Learning

For some of trainings, we used the simplified version of Multi-Agent Dual Learning (MADL) (Wang et al., 2019), proposed in Kim et al. (2019), to generate additional training data from the parallel corpus. We generated $n$-best translations of both the source and the target sides of the parallel data, with strong ensembles of, respectively, the forward and the backward models. Next, we picked the best translation from among $n$ candidates w.r.t. the sentence-level BLEU score. Thanks to these steps, we tripled the number of sentences by combining three types of datasets:

1. original source – original target,
2. original source – synthetic target,
3. synthetic source – original target,

where the synthetic target is the translation of the original source with the forward model, and the synthetic source is the translation of the original target with the backward model.

### 2.7 Postprocessing

In comparison to our competitors we noticed significantly weaker performance on the En-Or direction. After the analysis we found out that the generated corpora contain sequences of characters (U+0B2F-U+0B3C, U+0B5F) not present in the devset corpora. Replacing these sequences with sequence (U+0B5F-U+0B3E) gave a significant improvement for En-Or of about +4 BLEU.

| Parallel | En-In | In-En |
|---|---|---|
| bitext | 18.03 | 31.41 |
| CCAligned | 6.82 | 12.15 |
| PMIndia | 5.59 | 11.94 |
| bitext+CC | 17.62 | 30.56 |
| bitext, no religious | 15.33 | 29.02 |
| bitext, filtered FT | 17.84 | 29.38 |
| bitext, most likely | 17.98 | 31.00 |
| bitext, no transliteration | 18.36 | 31.27 |
| **With backtranslation** | | |
| bitext+BT filtered LM | 18.22 | 31.38 |
| bitext+BT filtered FT | 18.71 | 32.77 |
| bitext+CC+BT flitered FT | 18.21 | 30.64 |
| **MADL** | | |
| MADL | 18.87 | 31.94 |
| MADL+BT filtered FT | 18.83 | 33.25 |

Table 1: Average BLEU for preliminary trainings (4.1) on different corpora.

## 3 NMT System Overview

All of our systems are trained with the Marian NMT[3] (Junczys-Dowmunt et al., 2018) framework.

### 3.1 Baseline systems for preliminary experiments

First experiments were performed with transformer models (Vaswani et al., 2017), which we will now refer to as *transformer-base*. The only difference is that we used 8 encoder layers and 4 decoder layers instead of default configuration 6-6. The model has default embedding dimension of 512 and a feed-forward layer dimension of 2048.

We also used layer normalization (Ba et al., 2016) and tied the weights of the target-side embedding and the transpose of the output weight matrix, as well as source- and target-side embeddings (Press and Wolf, 2017). Optimizer delay was used to simulate batches of size up to 200GB, Adam (Kingma and Ba, 2017) was used as an optimizer, with a learning rate of 0.0003 and linear warm-up for the initial $48,000$ updates with subsequent inverted squared decay. No dropout was applied.

### 3.2 Final configuration

After the first experiments further trainings were performed on a *transformer-big* model. It has bigger dimensions than the *transformer-base*: an embedding dimension of 1024 and a feed-forward layer dimension of 4096. The *transformer-big* trainings were regularized with a dropout between transformer layers of 0.1 and a label smoothing of 0.1 unlike the *transformer-base* which was trained without a dropout.

## 4 Trainings

### 4.1 Preliminary trainings

During preliminary trainings, we tested which techniques of filtering/backtranslation/MADL work best for the task. Preliminary trainings were performed for all 20 directions on a single *transformer-base* model with no dropout.

There was no clear answer, which of the techniques work best. Generally, adding CCAligned corpus worsened the results. Training only on a big CCAligned corpus (15M lines) gave similar results to training on small PMIndia corpus (300k lines). For further trainings we decided to use the most promising techniques: filtered backtranslation (both methods fastText and Language Model) and MADL.

The preliminary training for one *transformer-base* model lasted 50 hours on two V100 GPUs - 13 epochs. A summary of the preliminary results are gathered in Table 1

### 4.2 Pretraining with backtranslations

For the final trainings we prepared various corpora with backtranslations filtered with a domain-transfer. We applied two methods of domain-

[3] `github.com/marian-nmt/marian`

| fastText filtering | Source | Selected |
|---|---|---|
| backtranslations | 400M | 86M |
| bitext filtered FT | 11M | 1,5M |
| CCAligned | 15M | 400k |
| PMIndia | 300k | 300k |
| bitext full | 11M | 11M |
| **Language Model filtering** | **Source** | **Selected** |
| backtranslations | 400M | 58M |
| bitext full | 11M | 11M |
| bitext distilled forward | 11M | 11M |
| bitext distilled backward | 11M | 11M |

Table 2: Components of mixed corpora used for pretrainings with backtranslation (4.2) using fastText filtering and language model filtering of monolingual corpora.

| | BLEU | | Improvement | |
|---|---|---|---|---|
| **No filtering** | **2In** | **2En** | **2In** | **2En** |
| Bitext only | 18.81 | 31.80 | | |
| Full BT | 18.77 | 33.02 | -0.04 | 1.22 |
| **LM filtering** | | | | |
| Filtered BT | 20.06 | 35.43 | 1.25 | 3.63 |
| Tuned Bitext | 21.03 | 36.95 | 0.97 | 1.52 |
| FT PMIndia | 21.39 | 37.26 | 0.36 | 0.31 |
| **fastText filtering** | | | | |
| Filtered BT | 19.77 | 36.62 | 0.96 | 4.86 |
| Tuned BT-PMI | 21.01 | 37.64 | 1.24 | 1.02 |
| Tuned Bitext | 21.31 | 38.47 | 1.54 | 1.85 |
| FT PMIndia | **21.91** | **38.72** | 0.60 | 0.25 |
| FT BT-PMI | 21.81 | 38.42 | 0.50 | -0.05 |
| FT MADL | | 38.67 | | 0.20 |

Table 3: Comparison of domain-adaptation techniques - Average BLEU over 10 directions for subsequent stages of final training: pretraining with backtranslation, tuning with bitext, tuning with mono PMIndia backtranslated, finetuning with bitext PMIndia, finetuning with backtranslated mono PMIndia, finetuning with MADL.

transfer described in previous sections: fastText and language model. Trainings were performed on separate *transformer-big* models. One *many-to-one* model for 10 directions to-English and second *one-to-many* for 10 directions from-English.

The whole pretraining for one *transformer-big* model lasted 200 hours on four V100 GPUs - 8 epochs. Further tunings took additional 20 hours of processing.

### 4.3 Tuning with bitext

The best two pretrained models with domain-transfer (LM filtered and FT filtered) were the baselines to start the tuning with the parallel corpora. During the bitext tuning we used all bilingual data provided by organizers except CCAligned corpus - 11M sentences in total. Tuning of baselines with the original parallel corpora improved the average BLEU of pretrained models by 0.97-1.85 BLEU (see Table 3)

### 4.4 Finetuning with PMIndia

We performed several attempts to finetune the final results with different corpora:

1. PMIndia parallel corpus (300k lines)
2. Baktranslated PMIndia mono corpus (1,1M lines)
3. MADL on PMIndia parallel corpus (3 * 300k lines)

First of these attempts, finetuning with bilingual PMIndia, gave the best improvement of final result - 0.25-0.6 BLEU on average. All 3 finetuned models were taken into process of mixing the best ensemble.

### 4.5 Ensembling

To further boost the translation quality, we used ensembles of models during decoding. Two separate ensembles were formed and tuned, one for transliterated Indian to English, the other in the opposite direction. Each ensemble consisted of: a number of Neural Translation Models, derived from various stages of training and model tuning – up to as much as 9 NMT were used during weight-optimization; and a single Neural Language Model, either English or common Indian (based on all languages, transliterated into Hindi), depending on the direction.

The tuning of ensemble weights was performed on the Development set and consisted of the following stages:

- Expectation-Maximization of posterior emission probability for a mixture of models(Kneser and Steinbiss, 1993), based on NMT log-scores of Development sentence-pairs, obtained using `marian-score`; this procedure, as well as being fast due to *not* requiring actual decoding, also worked well in practice, despite being based on interpolation

| Set<br>Technique | Indian-En<br>Dev | <br>Test | En-Indian<br>Dev | <br>Test |
|---|---|---|---|---|
| Best sng | 41.39 | 38.52 | 22.32 | 20.50 |
| Unif w/o LM | 42.33 | 39.6 | 22.57 | 20.79 |
| Unif. w/ LM | 40.69 | 37.88 | 21.51 | 20.01 |
| Expert sel. | 42.11 | 39.24 | 22.62 | 20.94 |
| E-M* | 42.35 | 39.71 | 22.64 | 20.99 |
| + ind. wgts | 42.49 | 39.65 | 22.74 | 20.99 |
| + norm-fact. | 42.50 | 39.58 | n/a | n/a |

Table 4: BLEU scores for different techniques of determining ensemble weights.
* Expectation-Maximization of likelihoods optimized weights of translation models only; Language Model was then added with small arbitrary weight of ca. 0.3%, and the presented scores were obtained using such an ensemble.

in the linear probability domain, as opposed to log-domain interpolation used in Marian;

- tuning single weights of the ensemble (bisectioning procedure, performed for a limited number of iterations; weights were tuned in the arbitrary order), based on BLEU scores of translated Development set (before normalization and tokenization);
- (only for Indian-to-English) a sweep of normalization-factor, also on BLEU. [4]

Individual tuning for target languages of English-to-Indian directions was originally planned, but wasn't eventually used for submission, mostly due to lack of time, however visual inspection of the partial results also showed that some weights varied wildly, so devset over-fitting could be suspected at this point; normalization-factor optimization was planned to be performed after the aforementioned optimization, so consequently it was also skipped for English-to-Indian directions. Post-submission tests showed an average improvement of ca. 0.2 BLEU, when using tuning for individual Indian target languages, but the gain was strongly dominated by the improvement on a single direction (En→Hi).

We experimented with several beam sizes increasing it up to 40. For the final submission we chose the size of 16. The larger beam gave little or no improvement at a cost of slowing down the decoding. For very large ensembles of 10 big models the decoding of the whole devset for 10 directions (10k lines) lasts about 25 minutes on a single V100 GPU.

[4]Translation score of each hypothesis is divided by $length^{factor}$, this value is then used to select the final translation, default is 1.

Table 4 presents the impact of tuning on BLEU scores on both devset and testset, in relation to a few manually selected setups, namely best-single-model, uniform and expert-selected "50-25-25%" ensemble. The final weight selection improved translation of the Indian-to-En directions by ca. 0.5 BLEU, compared to the expert ensemble or ca. 1.2 BLEU compared to best single model; on En-to-Indian directions, the improvement was <0.1 BLEU or ca. 0.5 BLEU, respectively. The results on the testset differ slightly from our final submissions as, during the ensemble tuning, we used simplified BLEU calculations algorithm (before normalization and tokenization)

## 5 Final Results

The detailed results of each stage of the best branch of trainings are gathered in Tables 5 and 6. The ensemble values are the submission evaluation results provided by the organizers.

Tables 7 and 8 contain the results of the models submitted by SRPOL compared with best results of competitors. The tables present values provided by WAT2021 organizers, calculated by 3 different metrics: BLEU (Papineni et al., 2002), RIBES (Isozaki et al., 2010), AMFM (Banchs and Li, 2011)

Figure 1 shows the results of the human evaluation. The figure presents the values provided by WAT2021 organizers showing significant advance over the competitors. Especially amount of bad translations (scored 1-2) has been significantly reduced.

### 5.1 English → Indian

Application of all techniques for En→In directions gave the overall improvement of 3.6 BLEU from baseline average 18.8 to final 22.4 BLEU. Adding non-filtered backtranslations gave no improvement, probably because general Indian monocorpus is too different from specific language used in PMIndia. However, after domain adaptation of the training corpus we gained improvement of 1 BLEU. Most of the improvement was gained by finetuning on parallel corpora (1.5 BLEU) and PMI corpora (0.6 BLEU). Final ensembling process gave the average improvement of 0.5 BLEU.

| Stage | Bn | Gu | Hi | Kn | Ml | Mr | Or | Pa | Ta | Te | AVG | Boost |
|---|---|---|---|---|---|---|---|---|---|---|---|---|
| Baseline - bitext | 13.1 | 23.7 | 35.8 | 15.8 | 12.2 | 16.7 | 17.0 | 29.8 | 12.0 | 11.9 | 18.81 | |
| Backtranslations | 12.5 | 23.5 | 36.1 | 16.6 | 12.4 | 17.1 | 17.0 | 29.8 | 11.8 | 11.0 | 18.77 | -0.04 |
| Domain adapt. | 13.4 | 23.8 | 36.8 | 17.2 | 13.8 | 18.7 | 18.3 | 30.6 | 12.9 | 12.2 | 19.77 | 1.00 |
| Tuning bitext | 14.6 | 25.9 | 38.1 | 19.5 | 14.9 | 19.6 | 19.5 | 32.3 | 13.6 | 14.9 | 21.31 | 1.54 |
| Tuning PMIndia | 15.5 | 27.2 | 38.1 | 20.8 | 15.1 | 19.8 | 19.1 | 32.9 | 13.7 | 16.8 | 21.91 | 0.60 |
| Ensemble | 16.0 | 27.8 | 38.7 | 21.3 | 15.5 | 20.4 | 19.9 | 33.4 | 14.2 | 16.9 | 22.40 | 0.49 |

Table 5: Final results - BLEU for 10 directions from-English in subsequent stages of final training

| Stage | Bn | Gu | Hi | Kn | Ml | Mr | Or | Pa | Ta | Te | AVG | Boost |
|---|---|---|---|---|---|---|---|---|---|---|---|---|
| Baseline - bitext | 25.2 | 36.4 | 39.9 | 31.0 | 29.5 | 29.8 | 30.2 | 38.0 | 28.5 | 29.5 | 31.80 | |
| Backtranslations | 25.3 | 37.8 | 40.6 | 33.6 | 30.8 | 30.6 | 31.8 | 39.2 | 29.3 | 31.2 | 33.02 | 1.22 |
| Domain adapt. | 29.4 | 40.6 | 44.5 | 36.9 | 35.1 | 33.6 | 35.2 | 42.7 | 33.0 | 35.0 | 36.62 | 3.60 |
| Tuning bitext | 31.1 | 42.7 | 45.3 | 38.9 | 37.2 | 35.2 | 36.2 | 44.8 | 34.9 | 38.3 | 38.47 | 1.85 |
| Tuning PMIndia | 31.8 | 43.3 | 45.6 | 39.1 | 37.1 | 35.7 | 36.2 | 44.8 | 35.0 | 38.6 | 38.72 | 0.25 |
| Ensemble | 31.9 | 44.0 | 46.9 | 40.3 | 38.4 | 36.6 | 37.1 | 46.4 | 36.1 | 39.8 | 39.75 | 1.03 |

Table 6: Final results - BLEU for 10 directions to-English in subsequent stages of final training

### 5.2 Indian $\rightarrow$ English

Application of all techniques for In$\rightarrow$En directions gave the overall improvement of 8 BLEU from baseline average 31.8 to final 39.8 BLEU. Adding non-filtered backtranslations gave 1.2 BLEU improvement but most of the improvement had been gained by domain adaptation which gave surprisingly high improvement of 3.6 BLEU. Further improvement was gained by finetuning on parallel corpora (1.9 BLEU) and PMI corpora (0.3 BLEU). The final ensembling process gave additional improvement of 1.0 BLEU.

## 6 Conclusions

We presented an effective approach to low-resource training consisting of pretraining on backtranslations and tuning on parallel corpora. We successfully applied domain-adaptation techniques which significantly improved translation quality measured by BLEU. We presented an effective approach for finding best hyperparameters for the ensembling number of single translation models.

We applied transliteration, but the final results did not confirm that this approach is effective, at least for that particular task.

We tried several filtering techniques for parallel corpora but the results showed no improvement. This may be a confirmation that the parallel corpora provided by the competition organizers are of high quality which is hard to improve.

Probably for the same reason domain-adaptation on parallel corpora didn't improve the results. However domain-adaptation worked surprisingly well for monolingual corpora.

## References


Amittai Axelrod, Xiaodong He, and Jianfeng Gao. 2011. Domain adaptation via pseudo in-domain data selection. In *Proceedings of the 2011 Conference on Empirical Methods in Natural Language Processing*, pages 355–362, Edinburgh, Scotland, UK. Association for Computational Linguistics.

Jimmy Lei Ba, Jamie Ryan Kiros, and Geoffrey E. Hinton. 2016. Layer normalization.

Rafael E. Banchs and Haizhou Li. 2011. AM-FM: A semantic framework for translation quality assessment. In *Proceedings of the 49th Annual Meeting of the Association for Computational Linguistics: Human Language Technologies*, pages 153–158, Portland, Oregon, USA. Association for Computational Linguistics.

Rachel Bawden, Nikolay Bogoychev, Ulrich Germann, Roman Grundkiewicz, Faheem Kirefu, Antonio Valerio Miceli Barone, and Alexandra Birch. 2019. The university of edinburgh's submissions to the wmt19 news translation task.

Chenhui Chu and Rui Wang. 2018. A survey of domain adaptation for neural machine translation. In *Proceedings of the 27th International Conference on Computational Linguistics*, pages 1304–1319, Santa Fe, New Mexico, USA. Association for Computational Linguistics.

Raj Dabre, Chenhui Chu, and Anoop Kunchukuttan. 2020. A brief survey of multilingual neural machine translation.

| Model | Bn | Gu | Hi | Kn | Ml | Mr | Or | Pa | Ta | Te | AVG |
|---|---|---|---|---|---|---|---|---|---|---|---|
| BLEU | | | | | | | | | | | |
| Baseline | 12.03 | 22.99 | 35.25 | 14.72 | 11.93 | 16.07 | 12.33 | 28.65 | 11.44 | 10.65 | 17.61 |
| Competitor | 14.73 | 26.97 | 38.25 | 19.57 | 12.79 | 19.48 | **20.15** | 33.35 | **14.43** | 15.61 | 21.53 |
| Best single | 15.58 | 27.31 | 38.04 | 20.91 | 15.43 | 19.93 | 19.15 | 32.88 | 13.89 | 16.82 | 21.99 |
| Ensemble | **15.97** | **27.80** | **38.65** | **21.30** | **15.49** | **20.42** | 19.94 | **33.43** | 14.15 | **16.85** | **22.40** |
| RIBES | | | | | | | | | | | |
| Baseline | 0.7072 | 0.8020 | 0.8438 | 0.7281 | 0.6874 | 0.7388 | 0.7146 | 0.8203 | 0.6971 | 0.6924 | 0.7432 |
| Competitor | 0.7242 | 0.8202 | 0.8542 | 0.7601 | 0.7074 | 0.7600 | 0.7503 | **0.8376** | 0.7215 | 0.7284 | 0.7664 |
| Best single | 0.7328 | 0.8223 | 0.8525 | 0.7701 | 0.7341 | 0.7669 | 0.7497 | 0.8355 | 0.7288 | 0.7345 | 0.7727 |
| Ensemble | **0.7336** | **0.8249** | **0.8559** | **0.7712** | **0.7369** | **0.7718** | **0.7511** | 0.8375 | **0.7307** | **0.7398** | **0.7753** |
| AMFM | | | | | | | | | | | |
| Baseline | 0.7675 | 0.8166 | 0.8224 | 0.8091 | 0.7986 | 0.8050 | 0.7146 | 0.7733 | 0.7957 | 0.7633 | 0.7866 |
| Competitor | **0.7796** | 0.8201 | 0.8228 | 0.8178 | 0.8053 | 0.8115 | 0.7699 | 0.8137 | **0.8029** | 0.7898 | **0.8033** |
| Best single | 0.7723 | 0.8199 | 0.8224 | 0.8213 | 0.8080 | **0.8108** | 0.7715 | 0.8132 | 0.7994 | **0.7930** | 0.8032 |
| Ensemble | 0.7710 | **0.8212** | **0.8246** | **0.8219** | **0.8081** | 0.8097 | **0.7718** | **0.8141** | 0.7988 | 0.7911 | 0.8032 |

Table 7: Official results of translations from-English by 3 metrics for submitted results of: baseline model, best competitor's result, submitted single SRPOL's model and submitted best SRPOL's ensemble

| Model | Bn | Gu | Hi | Kn | Ml | Mr | Or | Pa | Ta | Te | AVG |
|---|---|---|---|---|---|---|---|---|---|---|---|
| BLEU | | | | | | | | | | | |
| Baseline | 25.39 | 35.86 | 39.49 | 30.67 | 28.69 | 29.10 | 30.07 | 37.61 | 28.01 | 29.05 | 31.39 |
| Competitor | 29.96 | 39.39 | 43.23 | 35.46 | 33.21 | 34.02 | 34.11 | 41.24 | 31.94 | 35.44 | 35.80 |
| Best single | 31.82 | 42.87 | 45.61 | 39.01 | 37.04 | 35.68 | 36.04 | 44.87 | 35.06 | 38.57 | 38.66 |
| Ensemble | **31.87** | **43.98** | **46.93** | **40.34** | **38.38** | **36.64** | **37.06** | **46.39** | **36.13** | **39.80** | **39.75** |
| RIBES | | | | | | | | | | | |
| Baseline | 0.7649 | 0.8186 | 0.8448 | 0.7984 | 0.7927 | 0.7879 | 0.7895 | 0.8335 | 0.7881 | 0.7803 | 0.7999 |
| Competitor | 0.7983 | 0.8394 | 0.8591 | 0.8209 | 0.8132 | 0.8103 | 0.8017 | 0.8495 | 0.8070 | 0.8168 | 0.8216 |
| Best single | 0.8001 | 0.8497 | 0.8677 | 0.8373 | 0.8304 | 0.8212 | 0.8128 | 0.8614 | 0.8160 | 0.8315 | 0.8328 |
| Ensemble | **0.8005** | **0.8533** | **0.8729** | **0.8405** | **0.8354** | **0.8248** | **0.8170** | **0.8658** | **0.8223** | **0.8364** | **0.8369** |
| AMFM | | | | | | | | | | | |
| Baseline | 0.7699 | 0.8129 | 0.8250 | 0.7927 | 0.7936 | 0.7916 | 0.7940 | 0.8151 | 0.7884 | 0.7872 | 0.7970 |
| Competitor | 0.7786 | 0.8207 | 0.8345 | 0.8097 | 0.8068 | 0.7958 | 0.8082 | 0.8235 | 0.7961 | 0.8040 | 0.8078 |
| Best single | **0.7924** | 0.8331 | 0.8435 | 0.8204 | 0.8207 | 0.8103 | 0.8149 | 0.8364 | 0.8036 | 0.8204 | 0.8196 |
| Ensemble | 0.7897 | **0.8358** | **0.8471** | **0.8237** | **0.8230** | **0.8123** | **0.8173** | **0.8416** | **0.8065** | **0.8209** | **0.8218** |

Table 8: Official results of translations to-English by 3 metrics for submitted results of: baseline model, best competitor's result, submitted single SRPOL's model and submitted best SRPOL's ensemble

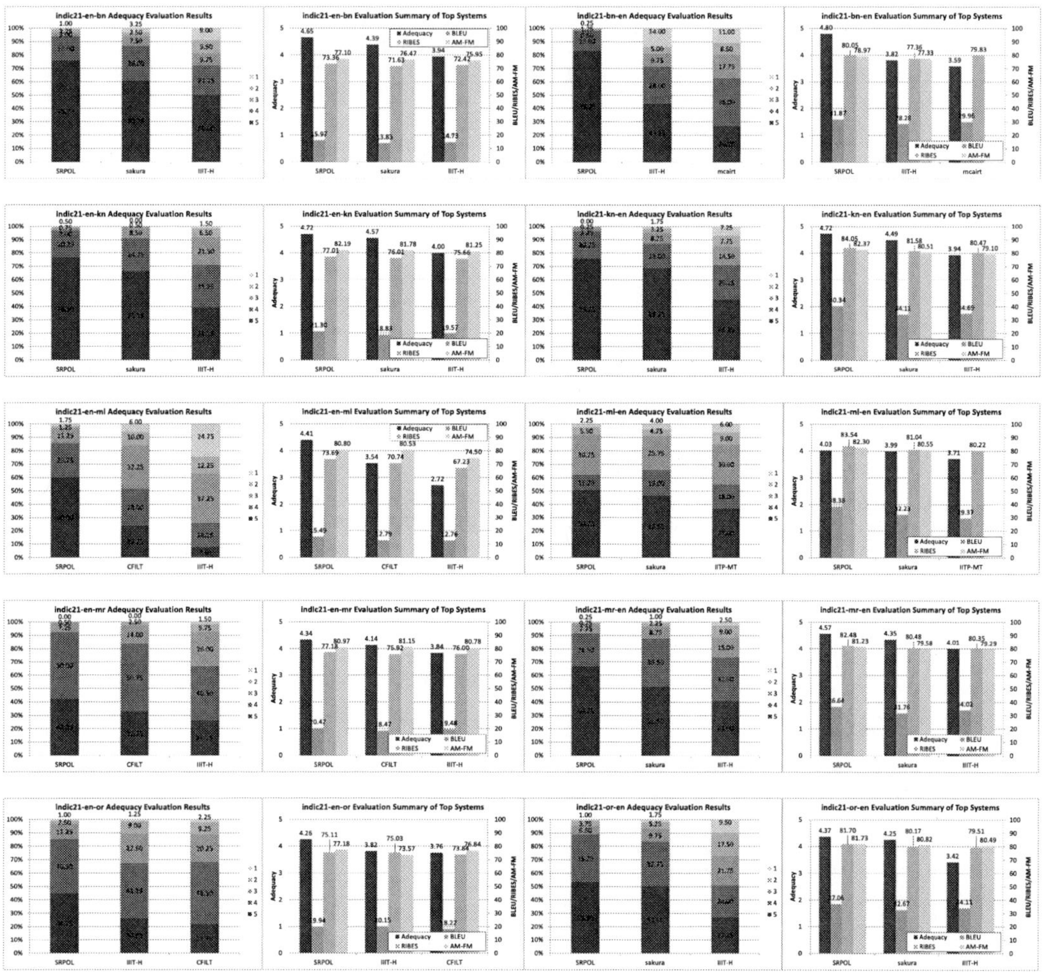

Figure 1: Summary results for all 5 manually evaluated languages - Bengali, Kannada, Malayalam, Marathi, Oriya

Sergey Edunov, Myle Ott, Michael Auli, and David Grangier. 2018. Understanding back-translation at scale. In *Proceedings of the 2018 Conference on Empirical Methods in Natural Language Processing*, pages 489–500, Brussels, Belgium. Association for Computational Linguistics.

Vikrant Goyal and Dipti Misra Sharma. 2019. The IIIT-H Gujarati-English machine translation system for WMT19. In *Proceedings of the Fourth Conference on Machine Translation (Volume 2: Shared Task Papers, Day 1)*, pages 191–195, Florence, Italy. Association for Computational Linguistics.

Hideki Isozaki, Tsutomu Hirao, Kevin Duh, Katsuhito Sudoh, and Hajime Tsukada. 2010. Automatic evaluation of translation quality for distant language pairs. In *Proceedings of the 2010 Conference on Empirical Methods in Natural Language Processing*, pages 944–952, Cambridge, MA. Association for Computational Linguistics.

Armand Joulin, Edouard Grave, Piotr Bojanowski, and Tomas Mikolov. 2017. Bag of tricks for efficient text classification. In *Proceedings of the 15th Conference of the European Chapter of the Association for Computational Linguistics: Volume 2, Short Papers*, pages 427–431. Association for Computational Linguistics.

Marcin Junczys-Dowmunt, Roman Grundkiewicz, Tomasz Dwojak, Hieu Hoang, Kenneth Heafield, Tom Neckermann, Frank Seide, Ulrich Germann, Alham Fikri Aji, Nikolay Bogoychev, André F. T. Martins, and Alexandra Birch. 2018. Marian: Fast neural machine translation in C++. In *Proceedings of ACL 2018, System Demonstrations*, pages 116–121, Melbourne, Australia. Association for Computational Linguistics.

Young Jin Kim, Marcin Junczys-Dowmunt, Hany Hassan, Alham Fikri Aji, Kenneth Heafield, Roman Grundkiewicz, and Nikolay Bogoychev. 2019. From research to production and back: Ludicrously fast neural machine translation. In *Proceedings of the 3rd Workshop on Neural Generation and Translation*, pages 280–288, Hong Kong. Association for Computational Linguistics.

Diederik P. Kingma and Jimmy Ba. 2017. Adam: A method for stochastic optimization.

Reinhard Kneser and Volker Steinbiss. 1993. On the dynamic adaptation of stochastic language models. In *1993 IEEE International Conference on Acoustics, Speech, and Signal Processing*, volume 2, pages 586–589 vol.2.

Anoop Kunchukuttan, Divyanshu Kakwani, Satish Golla, Gokul N. C., Avik Bhattacharyya, Mitesh M. Khapra, and Pratyush Kumar. 2020. Ai4bharat-indicnlp corpus: Monolingual corpora and word embeddings for indic languages.

Toshiaki Nakazawa, Hideki Nakayama, Chenchen Ding, Raj Dabre, Shohei Higashiyama, Hideya Mino, Isao Goto, Win Pa Pa, Anoop Kunchukuttan, Shantipriya Parida, Ondřej Bojar, Chenhui Chu, Akiko Eriguchi, Kaori Abe, and Sadao Oda, Yusuke Kurohashi. 2021. Overview of the 8th workshop on Asian translation. In *Proceedings of the 8th Workshop on Asian Translation*, Bangkok, Thailand. Association for Computational Linguistics.

Kishore Papineni, Salim Roukos, Todd Ward, and Wei-Jing Zhu. 2002. Bleu: a method for automatic evaluation of machine translation. In *Proceedings of the 40th Annual Meeting of the Association for Computational Linguistics*, pages 311–318, Philadelphia, Pennsylvania, USA. Association for Computational Linguistics.

Ofir Press and Lior Wolf. 2017. Using the output embedding to improve language models.

Ashish Vaswani, Noam Shazeer, Niki Parmar, Jakob Uszkoreit, Llion Jones, Aidan N. Gomez, Lukasz Kaiser, and Illia Polosukhin. 2017. Attention is all you need.

Yiren Wang, Yingce Xia, Tianyu He, Fei Tian, Tao Qin, ChengXiang Zhai, and Tie-Yan Liu. 2019. Multi-agent dual learning. In *International Conference on Learning Representations*.

Zhengzhe Yu, Zhanglin Wu, Xiaoyu Chen, Daimeng Wei, Hengchao Shang, Jiaxin Guo, Zongyao Li, Minghan Wang, Liangyou Li, Lizhi Lei, Hao Yang, and Ying Qin. 2020. HW-TSC's participation in the WAT 2020 indic languages multilingual task. In *Proceedings of the 7th Workshop on Asian Translation*, pages 92–97, Suzhou, China. Association for Computational Linguistics.

# Multilingual Machine Translation Systems at WAT 2021: One-to-Many and Many-to-One Transformer based NMT

**Shivam Mhaskar, Aditya Jain, Aakash Banerjee, Pushpak Bhattacharyya**
Department of Computer Science and Engineering
Indian Institute of Technology Bombay
Mumbai, India
{shivammhaskar, adityajainiitb, abanerjee, pb}@cse.iitb.ac.in

## Abstract

In this paper, we present the details of the systems that we have submitted for the WAT 2021 MultiIndicMT: An Indic Language Multilingual Task. We have submitted two separate multilingual NMT models: one for English to 10 Indic languages and another for 10 Indic languages to English. We discuss the implementation details of two separate multilingual NMT approaches, namely one-to-many and many-to-one, that makes use of a shared decoder and a shared encoder, respectively. From our experiments, we observe that the multilingual NMT systems outperforms the bilingual baseline MT systems for each of the language pairs under consideration.

## 1 Introduction

In recent years, the Neural Machine Translation (NMT) systems (Vaswani et al., 2017; Bahdanau et al., 2014; Sutskever et al., 2014; Cho et al., 2014) have consistently outperformed the Statistical Machine Translation (SMT) (Koehn, 2009) systems. One of the major problems with NMT systems is that they are ***data hungry***, which means that they require a large amount of parallel data to give better performance. This becomes a very challenging task while working with low-resource language pairs for which a very less amount of parallel corpora is available. Multilingual NMT (MNMT) systems (Dong et al., 2015; Johnson et al., 2017) alleviate this issue by using the phenomenon of transfer learning among related languages, which are the languages that are related by genetic and contact relationships. (Kunchukuttan and Bhattacharyya, 2020) have shown that the lexical and orthographic similarity among languages can be utilized to improve translation quality between Indic languages when limited parallel corpora is available. Another advantage of using MNMT systems is that they support zero-shot translation, that is, translation among two languages for which no parallel corpora is available during training.

A MNMT system can also drastically reduce the total number of models required for a large scale translation system by making use of a single many-to-many MNMT model instead of having to train a separate translation system for each of the language pairs. This reduces the amount of computation and time required for training. Among various MNMT approaches, using a single shared encoder and decoder will further reduce the number of parameters and allow related languages to share vocabulary. In this paper, we describe the two MNMT systems that we have submitted for the WAT 2021 MultiIndicMT: An Indic Language Multilingual Task (Nakazawa et al., 2021) as team 'CFILT', namely one-to-many for English to Indic languages and many-to-one for Indic languages to English. This task covers 10 Indic languages which are Bengali, Gujarati, Hindi, Kannada, Malayalam, Marathi, Oriya, Punjabi, Tamil and Telugu.

## 2 Related Work

Dong et al. (2015) was the first to introduce MNMT. The authors used a one-to-many model where a separate decoder and an attention mechanism was used for each target language. Firat et al. (2016) extended this to a many-to-many setting using a shared attention mechanism. In Zoph and Knight (2016) a multi-source translation approach was proposed where multiple encoders were used, each having a separate attention mechanism. Lee et al. (2017) proposed a CNN-based character level approach where a single encoder was shared across all the source languages.

A second line of work on MNMT uses a single shared encoder and decoder (Ha et al., 2016; Johnson et al., 2017) irrespective of the number of languages on the source or the target side. An



*Proceedings of the 8th Workshop on Asian Translation*, pages 233–237
Bangkok, Thailand (online), August 5-6, 2021. ©2021 Association for Computational Linguistics

| | en-bn | en-gu | en-hi | en-kn | en-ml | en-mr | en-or | en-pa | en-ta | en-te |
|---|---|---|---|---|---|---|---|---|---|---|
| **ALT** | 20 | - | 20 | - | - | - | - | - | - | - |
| **Bible-uedin** | - | 16 | 62 | 61 | 61 | 61 | - | - | - | 62 |
| **CVIT-PIB** | 92 | 58 | 267 | - | 43 | 114 | 94 | 101 | 116 | 45 |
| **IITB 3.0** | - | - | 1603 | - | - | - | - | - | - | - |
| **MTEnglish2Odia** | - | - | - | - | - | - | 35 | - | - | - |
| **NLPC** | - | - | - | - | - | - | - | - | 31 | - |
| **OdiEnCorp 2.0** | - | - | - | - | - | - | 91 | - | - | - |
| **OpenSubtitles** | 411 | - | 92 | - | 383 | - | - | - | 32 | 27 |
| **PMIndia** | 23 | 41 | 50 | 29 | 27 | 29 | 32 | 28 | 33 | 33 |
| **TED2020** | - | - | - | 2 | - | - | - | 0.7 | - | - |
| **Total** | 546 | 115 | 2094 | 92 | 514 | 204 | 252 | 130 | 212 | 167 |

Table 1: Statistics of number of parallel sentences for each of the English-Indic language pairs across different datasets used for **training**. All the numbers are in thousands. (bn:Bengali, gu:Gujarati, hi:Hindi, kn:Kannada, ml:Malayalam, mr:Marathi, or:Oriya, pa:Punjabi, ta:Tamil, te:Telugu)

advantage of this approach is that the number of parameters are drastically reduced. Dabre et al. (2019) gives a summary of various techniques that can be used to implement MNMT systems. The MNMT systems that we have implemented are based on Johnson et al. (2017)'s approach where in one-to-many and many-to-many models a language specific token is prepended to the input sentence to indicate the target language that the model should translate to. We use transformer (Vaswani et al., 2017) architecture which has proven to give superior performance over the RNN based models (Bahdanau et al., 2014; Sutskever et al., 2014; Cho et al., 2014).

## 3 Our Approach

The various types of multilingual models that we have implemented are one-to-many and many-to-one, each of which are discussed below.

### 3.1 One-to-Many

In a one-to-many multilingual model, the translation task involves a single source language and two or more target languages. One of the ways to achieve this is by making use of a single encoder for the source language and separate decoders for each of the target languages. The disadvantage of this method is that, as there are multiple decoders, the size of the model increases. Another way to achieve this is to use a single encoder and a single shared decoder. An advantage of this method is that the representations learnt by some language pair can further be utilized by the some other language pair. For example, the representations learnt during the training of the English-Hindi language pair can help training the English-Marathi language pair. Also, in this approach, a language specific token is prepended to the input sentence to indicate the model to which target language the input sentence should be translated.

### 3.2 Many-to-One

This approach is similar to the one-to-many approach. The major point of difference is that there are multiple source languages and a single target language. As a result, here we use a single shared encoder and a single decoder. Also, as the target language is same for all the source languages, it is optional to prepend a token to the input sentence unlike in the one-to-many approach which has multiple target languages for a given source language.

## 4 Experiments

In this section, we discuss the details of the system architecture, dataset, preprocessing, models and the training setup.

### 4.1 System Architecture

Table 4 lists the details of the transformer architecture used for all the experiments.

### 4.2 Data

The dataset provided for the shared task by WAT 2021 was used for all the experiments. We did not use any additional data to train the models. Table 1 lists the datasets used for each of the English-Indic

|  | Baseline |  | One-to-Many |  |  |
|---|---|---|---|---|---|
|  | BLEU | RIBES | BLEU | RIBES | AMFM |
| **en → bn** | 12.14 | 0.691941 | 13.24 | 0.710664 | 0.777074 |
| **en → gu** | 18.26 | 0.745845 | 24.56 | 0.806649 | 0.817681 |
| **en → hi** | 33.06 | 0.836683 | 35.39 | 0.843969 | 0.821713 |
| **en → kn** | 11.43 | 0.666605 | 17.98 | 0.747233 | 0.816981 |
| **en → ml** | 10.56 | 0.668024 | 12.79 | 0.707437 | 0.805291 |
| **en → mr** | - | - | 18.47 | 0.759182 | 0.811499 |
| **en → or** | 11.19 | 0.644931 | 18.22 | 0.738397 | 0.768399 |
| **en → pa** | 29.00 | 0.810395 | 31.16 | 0.826367 | 0.813658 |
| **en → ta** | 10.97 | 0.662236 | 12.99 | 0.715699 | 0.802920 |
| **en → te** | - | - | 15.52 | 0.725496 | 0.789820 |

Table 2: Results for the one-to-many MNMT model. To obtain the baseline results, we performed the same automatic evaluation procedures as those performed in WAT 2021. The one-to-many results are the official evaluation results provided by the organizers of WAT 2021. (bn:Bengali, gu:Gujarati, hi:Hindi, kn:Kannada, ml:Malayalam, mr:Marathi, or:Oriya, pa:Punjabi, ta:Tamil, te:Telugu)

|  | Baseline |  | Many-to-One |  |  |
|---|---|---|---|---|---|
|  | BLEU | RIBES | BLEU | RIBES | AMFM |
| **bn → en** | 24.38 | 0.772800 | 25.98 | 0.760268 | 0.766461 |
| **gu → en** | 31.92 | 0.799512 | 35.31 | 0.807849 | 0.797069 |
| **hi → en** | 37.72 | 0.847265 | 39.71 | 0.837668 | 0.822034 |
| **kn → en** | 21.30 | 0.738755 | 30.23 | 0.772913 | 0.778602 |
| **ml → en** | 26.80 | 0.786290 | 29.28 | 0.784424 | 0.789095 |
| **mr → en** | - | - | 29.71 | 0.786570 | 0.789075 |
| **or → en** | - | - | 30.46 | 0.772850 | 0.793769 |
| **pa → en** | 37.89 | 0.827826 | 38.01 | 0.818396 | 0.804561 |
| **ta → en** | - | - | 29.34 | 0.784291 | 0.785098 |
| **te → en** | - | - | 30.10 | 0.778981 | 0.783349 |

Table 3: Results for the many-to-one MNMT model. To obtain the baseline results, we performed the same automatic evaluation procedures as those performed in WAT 2021. The many-to-one results are the official evaluation results provided by the organizers of WAT 2021.(bn:Bengali, gu:Gujarati, hi:Hindi, kn:Kannada, ml:Malayalam, mr:Marathi, or:Oriya, pa:Punjabi, ta:Tamil, te:Telugu)

language pairs along with the number of parallel sentences. The validation and test sets have 1,000 and 2,390 sentences, respectively and are 11-way parallel.

### 4.3 Preprocessing

We used Byte Pair Encoding (BPE) (Sennrich et al., 2016) technique for data segmentation, that is, break up the words into sub-words. This technique is especially helpful for Indic languages as they are morphologically rich. Separate vocabularies are used for the source and target side languages. For training the one-to-many and many-to-one models, the data of all the 10 Indic languages is combined before learning the BPE codes. 48000, 48000 and 8000 merge operations are used for learning the BPE codes of the one-to-many, many-to-one and bilingual baseline models, respectively.

### 4.4 Baseline Models

The baseline MT models are bilingual MT models based on the vanilla transformer architecture. We have trained 20 separate bilingual MT models, 10 for English to each Indic language and 10 for each Indic language to English.

### 4.5 Models and Training

For this task, we built two separate MNMT systems, a one (English) to many (10 Indic languages) model and a many (10 Indic languages) to one (English)

| | Encoder | Decoder |
|---|---|---|
| **No. of layers** | 6 | 6 |
| **No. of attention heads** | 8 | 8 |
| **Embedding dimensions** | 512 | 512 |
| **FFNN hidden layer dim** | 2048 | 2048 |

Table 4: System architecture details

model. In our one-to-many model, we used the transformer architecture with a single encoder and a single shared decoder. The encoder used the English vocabulary and the decoder used a shared vocabulary of all the Indic languages. In our many-to-one model, we used the transformer architecture with a single shared encoder and a single decoder. Here the encoder used a shared vocabulary of all the Indic languages and English vocabulary is used for the decoder. In both of these MNMT models, we prepended a language specific token to the input sentence.

We used the fairseq (Ott et al., 2019) library for implementing the multilingual systems. For training, we used Adam optimizer with betas '(0.9,0.98)'. The initial learning rate used was 0.0005 and the inverse square root learning rate scheduler was used with 4000 warm-up updates. The dropout probability value used was 0.3 and the criterion used was label smoothed cross entropy with label smoothing of 0.1. We used an update frequency, that is, after how many batches the backward pass is performed, of 8 for the multilingual models and 4 for the bilingual baseline models.

During decoding we used the beam search algorithm with a beam length of 5 and length penalty of 1. The many-to-one model was trained for 160 epochs and the one-to-many model was trained for 145 epochs. The model with the best average BLEU score was chosen as the best model. The average BLEU score for a MNMT model was calculated by taking the average of the BLEU scores obtained across all the language pairs.

## 5 Results and Analysis

The Bilingual Evaluation Understudy (BLEU) (Papineni et al., 2002) metric, the Rank-based Intuitive Bilingual Evaluation Score (RIBES) (Isozaki et al., 2010) metric and Adequacy-Fluency Metrics (AMFM) (Banchs et al., 2015) are used to report the results. Table 2 and 3 lists the results for all our experiments.

The baseline results are obtained by training bilingual models and then we have used automatic evaluation procedures same as those performed in WAT 2021. The one-to-many and many-to-one results are those reported by WAT 2021 on our submitted translation files.

We observe that for all language pairs in both the translation directions, the MNMT models give superior performance as compared to the bilingual NMT models. For relatively high resource language pairs like English-Hindi and English-Bengali the increase in BLEU score is less while for relatively low resource language pairs like English-Kannada and English-Oriya the increase in BLEU score is substantial. From the above observation it follows that low resource language pairs benefit much more from multilingual training than high resource language pairs. An increase of up to 8.93 BLEU scores (for Kannada to English) is observed using MNMT systems over the bilingual baseline NMT systems.

## 6 Conclusion

In this paper, we have discussed our submission to the WAT 2021 MultiIndicMT: An Indic Language Multilingual Task. We have submitted two separate MNMT models: a one-to-many (English to 10 Indic languages) model and a many-to-one (10 Indic languages to English) model. We evaluated our models using BLEU and RIBES scores and observed that the MNMT models outperform the separately trained bilingual NMT models across all the language pairs. We also observe that for the lower resource language pairs the improvement in performance is much more as compared to that for the higher resource language pairs.

## References


Dzmitry Bahdanau, Kyunghyun Cho, and Yoshua Bengio. 2014. Neural machine translation by jointly learning to align and translate. *arXiv preprint arXiv:1409.0473*.

Rafael E. Banchs, Luis F. D'Haro, and Haizhou Li. 2015. Adequacy–fluency metrics: Evaluating mt in the continuous space model framework. *IEEE/ACM Transactions on Audio, Speech, and Language Processing*, 23(3):472–482.

KyungHyun Cho, Bart van Merrienboer, Dzmitry Bahdanau, and Yoshua Bengio. 2014. On the properties of neural machine translation: Encoder-decoder approaches. *CoRR*, abs/1409.1259.

Raj Dabre, Chenhui Chu, and Anoop Kunchukuttan. 2019. A survey of multilingual neural machine translation. *CoRR*, abs/1905.05395.

Daxiang Dong, Hua Wu, Wei He, Dianhai Yu, and Haifeng Wang. 2015. Multi-task learning for multiple language translation. In *Proceedings of the 53rd Annual Meeting of the Association for Computational Linguistics and the 7th International Joint Conference on Natural Language Processing (Volume 1: Long Papers)*, pages 1723–1732, Beijing, China. Association for Computational Linguistics.

Orhan Firat, Kyunghyun Cho, and Yoshua Bengio. 2016. Multi-way, multilingual neural machine translation with a shared attention mechanism. In *Proceedings of the 2016 Conference of the North American Chapter of the Association for Computational Linguistics: Human Language Technologies*, pages 866–875, San Diego, California. Association for Computational Linguistics.

Thanh-Le Ha, Jan Niehues, and Alexander H. Waibel. 2016. Toward multilingual neural machine translation with universal encoder and decoder. *CoRR*, abs/1611.04798.

Hideki Isozaki, Tsutomu Hirao, Kevin Duh, Katsuhito Sudoh, and Hajime Tsukada. 2010. Automatic evaluation of translation quality for distant language pairs. In *Proceedings of the 2010 Conference on Empirical Methods in Natural Language Processing*, pages 944–952, Cambridge, MA. Association for Computational Linguistics.

Melvin Johnson, Mike Schuster, Quoc V. Le, Maxim Krikun, Yonghui Wu, Zhifeng Chen, Nikhil Thorat, Fernanda Viégas, Martin Wattenberg, Greg Corrado, Macduff Hughes, and Jeffrey Dean. 2017. Google's multilingual neural machine translation system: Enabling zero-shot translation. *Transactions of the Association for Computational Linguistics*, 5:339–351.

Philipp Koehn. 2009. *Statistical machine translation*. Cambridge University Press.

Anoop Kunchukuttan and Pushpak Bhattacharyya. 2020. Utilizing language relatedness to improve machine translation: A case study on languages of the indian subcontinent. *arXiv preprint arXiv:2003.08925*.

Jason Lee, Kyunghyun Cho, and Thomas Hofmann. 2017. Fully character-level neural machine translation without explicit segmentation. *Transactions of the Association for Computational Linguistics*, 5:365–378.

Toshiaki Nakazawa, Hideki Nakayama, Chenchen Ding, Raj Dabre, Shohei Higashiyama, Hideya Mino, Isao Goto, Win Pa Pa, Anoop Kunchukuttan, Shantipriya Parida, Ondřej Bojar, Chenhui Chu, Akiko Eriguchi, Kaori Abe, and Sadao Oda, Yusuke Kurohashi. 2021. Overview of the 8th workshop on Asian translation. In *Proceedings of the 8th Workshop on Asian Translation*, Bangkok, Thailand. Association for Computational Linguistics.

Myle Ott, Sergey Edunov, Alexei Baevski, Angela Fan, Sam Gross, Nathan Ng, David Grangier, and Michael Auli. 2019. fairseq: A fast, extensible toolkit for sequence modeling. In *Proceedings of NAACL-HLT 2019: Demonstrations*.

Kishore Papineni, Salim Roukos, Todd Ward, and Wei-Jing Zhu. 2002. Bleu: a method for automatic evaluation of machine translation. In *Proceedings of the 40th Annual Meeting of the Association for Computational Linguistics*, pages 311–318, Philadelphia, Pennsylvania, USA. Association for Computational Linguistics.

Rico Sennrich, Barry Haddow, and Alexandra Birch. 2016. Neural machine translation of rare words with subword units. In *Proceedings of the 54th Annual Meeting of the Association for Computational Linguistics (Volume 1: Long Papers)*, pages 1715–1725, Berlin, Germany. Association for Computational Linguistics.

Ilya Sutskever, Oriol Vinyals, and Quoc V. Le. 2014. Sequence to sequence learning with neural networks. *CoRR*, abs/1409.3215.

Ashish Vaswani, Noam Shazeer, Niki Parmar, Jakob Uszkoreit, Llion Jones, Aidan N. Gomez, Lukasz Kaiser, and Illia Polosukhin. 2017. Attention is all you need. *CoRR*, abs/1706.03762.

Barret Zoph and Kevin Knight. 2016. Multi-source neural translation. In *Proceedings of the 2016 Conference of the North American Chapter of the Association for Computational Linguistics: Human Language Technologies*, pages 30–34, San Diego, California. Association for Computational Linguistics.

# IITP-MT at WAT2021: Indic-English Multilingual Neural Machine Translation using Romanized Vocabulary

**Ramakrishna Appicharla*, Kamal Kumar Gupta*, Asif Ekbal, Pushpak Bhattacharyya**
Department of Computer Science and Engineering
Indian Institute of Technology Patna
Patna, Bihar, India
{appicharla_2021cs01,kamal.pcs17,asif,pb}@iitp.ac.in

## Abstract

This paper describes the systems submitted to WAT 2021 MultiIndicMT shared task by IITP-MT team. We submit two multilingual Neural Machine Translation (NMT) systems (Indic-to-English and English-to-Indic). We romanize all Indic data and create subword vocabulary which is shared between all Indic languages. We use back-translation approach to generate synthetic data which is appended to parallel corpus and used to train our models. The models are evaluated using BLEU, RIBES and AMFM scores with Indic-to-English model achieving 40.08 BLEU for Hindi-English pair and English-to-Indic model achieving 34.48 BLEU for English-Hindi pair. However, we observe that the shared romanized subword vocabulary is not helping English-to-Indic model at the time of generation, leading it to produce poor quality translations for Tamil, Telugu and Malayalam to English pairs with BLEU score of 8.51, 6.25 and 3.79 respectively.

## 1 Introduction

In this paper, we describe our submission to the MultiIndicMT shared task at the 8th Workshop on Asian Translation [1] (WAT 2021) (Nakazawa et al., 2021). The objective of this shared task is to build Machine Translation (MT) models between 10 Indic languages (Bengali, Gujarati, Hindi, Kannada, Malayalam, Marathi, Odia, Punjabi, Tamil, Telugu) and English. We submit two Multilingual Neural Machine Translation models (MNMT): one for XX $\rightarrow$ EN and one for EN $\rightarrow$ XX (here XX denotes a set of all 10 Indic languages).

Multilingual Machine Translation (Dong et al., 2015; Firat et al., 2016; Johnson et al., 2017; Aharoni et al., 2019; Freitag and Firat, 2020) has gained popularity in recent times due to the ability to train a single model which is capable of translating between multiple language pairs. The main benefit of multilingual model is transfer learning. When a low resource language pair is trained together with a high resource pair, the translation quality of a low resource pair may improve (Zoph et al., 2016; Nguyen and Chiang, 2017). This method of training is more suitable for Indic languages as they are similar to each other (Dabre et al., 2017, 2020) and relatively under-resourced when compared with European languages (Sen et al., 2018).

Romanization is the process of converting characters that are written in various scripts into Latin script. Amrhein and Sennrich (2020) showed that in a transfer learning setting, romanization improves the transfer between related languages that use different scripts. We train two MNMT models, which translate between Indic languages and English with all Indic data romanized. The models are evaluated using the BLEU (Papineni et al., 2002), RIBES (Isozaki et al., 2010) and AMFM (Banchs et al., 2015) metrics.

The paper is organized as follows. In section 2, we briefly mention some notable works on multilingual NMT and romanized NMT. In section 3, we describe the systems submitted along with preprocessing and romanization of Indic data. Results are described in section 4. Finally, the work is concluded in section 5.

## 2 Related Works

Multilingual Machine Translation enabled the ability to deploy a single model for multiple language pairs without training multiple models. Dong et al. (2015) proposes a multi-task learning framework to translate one source language into multiple target languages by adding language specific decoders. Their method has shown improvements over base-

*Equal contribution
[1] Our Team ID: IITP-MT



*Proceedings of the 8th Workshop on Asian Translation*, pages 238–243
Bangkok, Thailand (online), August 5-6, 2021. 

line models which are trained for individual language pairs. Firat et al. (2016) proposes a many-to-many model for multi-way, multilingual translation using shared attention and language specific encoders and decoders. However, with this setting, model parameters will increase as the number of languages increases.

Johnson et al. (2017) use shared encoder-decoder model in which multiple languages share both encoder and decoder also the attention module. This is achieved by combining multiple language pairs data into a single corpus and adding a language tag to every source sentence to specify its target language. This method enables the zero-shot translation, in which the model can generate sentences belonging to a language pair that is not seen at training time. Aharoni et al. (2019) show that multilingual NMT models are capable of handling large number of language pairs. Freitag and Firat (2020) proposes that the use of multi-way alignment information will improve the translation quality of language pairs for which training data is scarce in multilingual settings.

Improving the quality of NMT models with monolingual data is a common approach nowadays, especially in low resource settings. Back-translation Sennrich et al. (2016) is an effective approach to make use of target monolingual data. In this approach, with the help of existing target-to-source MT system target is translated into source and resulting synthetic parallel corpus is combined with clean corpus and used to train source-to-target NMT system. Multi-task learning framework (Zhang and Zong, 2016; Domhan and Hieber, 2017) is another way to utilize monolingual data to improve the performance of NMT.

Recent studies (Du and Way, 2017; Gheini and May, 2019; Briakou and Carpuat, 2019) show that the romanization will improve the performance of NMT system. However these approaches apply romanization at source side only. Amrhein and Sennrich (2020) showed that romanization can be applied on the target side also followed by an additional, learned deromanization step.

In this work, we follow Johnson et al. (2017) method to train multilingual NMT models. We romanize Indic data and use it to train our models. We also follow back-translation approach (Sennrich et al., 2016) to create synthetic parallel data. We report the results of the models which are trained on combined synthetic and clean parallel corpus.

## 3 System Description

This section describes datasets, preprocessing and experimental setup of our models.

### 3.1 Datasets

We use MultiIndicMT parallel corpus [2] consisting of following languages: Bengali, Gujarati, Hindi, Kannada, Malayalam, Marathi, Odia, Punjabi, Tamil, Telugu and English. It contains the parallel corpora for 10 Indic languages which are translated into English. We also use PMI monolingual corpus [3] to generate synthetic data with back-translation (Sennrich et al., 2016) approach. Table 1 shows the data sizes of corpora used in the experiments. Development and Test sets contain 1,000 and 2,390 sentences respectively for each language pair.

| Language | Parallel | Monolingual |
|---|---|---|
| Bengali (BN) | 1,341,284 | 117,757 |
| Gujarati (GU) | 518,015 | 125,647 |
| Hindi (HI) | 3,069,725 | 156,605 |
| Kannada (KN) | 396,865 | 79,433 |
| Malayalam (ML) | 1,142,053 | 82,026 |
| Marathi (MR) | 621,481 | 120,362 |
| Odia (OR) | 252,160 | 103,876 |
| Punjabi (PA) | 518,508 | 90,916 |
| Tamil (TA) | 1,354,247 | 91,324 |
| Telugu (TE) | 457,453 | 111,749 |
| English (EN) | - | 109,480 |

Table 1: Language wise training set sizes in terms of number of sentences. **Parallel**: Parallel corpus size of Indic-EN language pair. **Monolingual**: PMI monolingual corpora sizes of all languages.

### 3.2 Preprocessing and Romanization

We use a Python based transliteration tool [4] to romanize all Indic language data. This tool supports all Indic language scripts that are used in the experiments. It also has deromanization support which maps Latin script into various Indic scripts. We romanize all Indic language data (Amrhein and Sennrich, 2020) (both parallel and monolingual corpora are romanized) and merge all parallel corpora into single corpus. This combined parallel corpus used to train baseline models.

[2] http://lotus.kuee.kyoto-u.ac.jp/WAT/indic-multilingual/indic_wat_2021.tar.gz

[3] http://lotus.kuee.kyoto-u.ac.jp/WAT/indic-multilingual/filteredmono.tar.gz

[4] https://github.com/sanskrit-coders/indic_transliteration

We follow back-translation (Sennrich et al., 2016) approach to generate synthetic parallel corpora. We merge monolingual corpora of all Indic languages and generate synthetic English data using baseline XX $\rightarrow$ EN model. The resulting synthetic English - Clean Indic parallel corpus is merged with clean English-Indic parallel corpus and used to further train baseline EN $\rightarrow$ XX model. We also generate synthetic Indic languages data using monolingual English data. We duplicate the monolingual English data 10 times and the baseline EN $\rightarrow$ XX model is used to generate synthetic Indic data. The reason to duplicate English data is to get equal size synthetic parallel corpus for all Indic languages. The resulting synthetic Indic - Clean English parallel corpus is merged with clean Indic-English parallel corpus and used to further train baseline XX $\rightarrow$ EN model.

For the training of EN $\rightarrow$ XX model, we add language tag to start of every source sentence (Johnson et al., 2017) to denote to which language [5] the source should be translated to. We do not use language tags for XX $\rightarrow$ EN model as the target is English always. All the training data is shuffled before feeding to the models. The training corpus statistics are shown in Table 2. The combined Development set contains 10,000 sentences and is the same for all models. Table 3 shows the contribution of each language pair in the combined training corpus. Hindi-English pair being the most contributing pair with almost 30% and Odia-English pair being least contributing pair with 3.3%, in both directions.

| Model | Train |
|---|---|
| XX $\rightarrow$ EN | 9,671,791 |
| XX $\rightarrow$ EN + BT | 10,766,591 |
| EN $\rightarrow$ XX | 9,671,791 |
| EN $\rightarrow$ XX + BT | 10,751,486 |

Table 2: Training data sizes of combined corpora. {XX, EN} $\rightarrow$ {EN, XX} denotes training data sizes of Baseline models. BT denotes total training data sizes after adding synthetic back-translated parallel corpora.

### 3.3 Experimental Setup

We train two multilingual models namely XX $\rightarrow$ EN (Indic languages to English) and EN $\rightarrow$ XX (English to Indic languages). All the models are trained on the Transformer architecture (Vaswani et al., 2017). We use 6 layered Encoder-Decoder stacks with 8 attention heads. Embedding size and hidden sizes are set to 512, dropout rate is set to 0.1. Feed-forward layer consists of 2048 cells. Adam optimizer (Kingma and Ba, 2015) is used for training with 8,000 warm up steps with initial learning rate of 2. We split the training data of baseline models into subwords with the unigram language model (Kudo, 2018) using SentencePiece (Kudo and Richardson, 2018) implementation. We create two subword vocabularies, one for English and one for all romanized Indic data [6]. The size of English subword vocabulary is 60K and of Indic languages is 100K, for both the models. We use OpenNMT toolkit (Klein et al., 2017)[7] to train our models with batch size of 2048 tokens. Models are evaluated on development sets after every 10,000 steps and checkpoints are created. The baseline models are trained for 100,000 steps and the last checkpoint is used to create a synthetic corpus with the back-translation approach as described in Section 3.2. After creating synthetic parallel corpora, baseline models are further trained for another 200,000 steps [8] on combined synthetic and clean parallel corpora (see Table 2). Finally, all checkpoints that are created by the model using the combined corpora are averaged [9] and considered as the best parameters for each model and used to test our models. We

| Language Pair | XX $\rightarrow$ EN | EN $\rightarrow$ XX |
|---|---|---|
| HI-EN | 29.53 | 30.0 |
| TA-EN | 13.60 | 13.45 |
| BN-EN | 13.47 | 13.57 |
| ML-EN | 11.62 | 11.38 |
| MR-EN | 6.79 | 6.90 |
| GU-EN | 5.83 | 6.0 |
| PA-EN | 5.83 | 5.67 |
| TE-EN | 5.27 | 5.29 |
| KN-EN | 4.70 | 4.43 |
| OR-EN | 3.36 | 3.31 |

Table 3: Contribution of each language pair (in %) in the training set after merging clean corpus with synthetic back-translated corpus. **XX $\rightarrow$ EN**: Indic-to-English model. **EN $\rightarrow$ XX**: English-to-Indic model.

[5] We use following tags: ##2BN, ##2GU, ##2HI, ##2KN, ##2ML, ##2MR, ##2OR, ##2PA, ##2TA, ##2TE

[6] All Indic languages data is merged after romanization and created subword vocabulary on combined corpus.

[7] https://github.com/OpenNMT/OpenNMT-py/tree/1.2.0

[8] We stop the training as there is no improvement in terms of perplexity of models on training data.

[9] OpenNMT-py provides script to average model weights.

| Language Pair | XX → EN | | | EN → XX | | |
|---|---|---|---|---|---|---|
| | **BLEU** | **RIBES** | **AMFM** | **BLEU** | **RIBES** | **AMFM** |
| BN-EN | 25.77 | 0.77 | 0.78 | 11.04 | 0.70 | 0.73 |
| GU-EN | 36.49 | 0.83 | 0.81 | 20.46 | 0.75 | 0.81 |
| HI-EN | 40.08 | 0.85 | 0.83 | 34.48 | 0.84 | 0.82 |
| KN-EN | 31.24 | 0.81 | 0.80 | 13.22 | 0.64 | 0.79 |
| ML-EN | 29.37 | 0.80 | 0.80 | 3.79 | 0.44 | 0.76 |
| MR-EN | 29.96 | 0.80 | 0.80 | 13.95 | 0.67 | 0.80 |
| OR-EN | 31.19 | 0.79 | 0.80 | 12.57 | 0.71 | 0.74 |
| PA-EN | 38.41 | 0.84 | 0.82 | 16.81 | 0.79 | 0.66 |
| TA-EN | 27.76 | 0.79 | 0.79 | 8.51 | 0.58 | 0.76 |
| TE-EN | 28.13 | 0.78 | 0.78 | 6.25 | 0.53 | 0.76 |

Table 4: Official BLEU, RIBES and AMFM scores of multilingual models for each language pair. **XX → EN** denotes score of Indic-to-English model. **EN → XX** denotes score of English-to-Indic model.

keep OpenNMT-py's default beam size of 5 during back-translation and inference. For the EN → XX model, after getting the model predictions on the test set, we deromanize these predictions and convert them into respective language scripts.

## 4 Results and Analysis

The official BLEU (Papineni et al., 2002), RIBES (Isozaki et al., 2010) and AMFM (Banchs et al., 2015) scores of the multilingual models are shown in Table 4. We observe that the XX → EN model performance is consistent across all language pairs in terms of all the three scores. HI-EN being the most contributing pair (see Table 3), achieves the BLEU score of 40.08 points. Even the language pair with the least amount of data (OR-EN) yield a BLEU score of 31.19 points. However, we do not observe the same with EN → XX model. The performance of EN → XX model is inconsistent with achieving a high BLEU score of 34.48 points (EN-HI) and least BLEU score of 3.79 (ML-EN). We observe same in terms of RIBES score also. However, AMFM scores of EN → XX model are quite consistent despite having less BLEU and RIBES scores for some language pairs.

Sen et al. (2018) observe that, in the multilingual setting where a single decoder has to handle information about more languages (7 in their case), the performance of the model is limited because of different vocabulary and different linguistic features. In our case, we romanize all data and feed it to the model. Still the EN → XX model is unable to produce good quality translations. We believe that the main reason for such low quality translations is the romanized subword vocabulary, which is shared across 10 different languages, is not helping decoder at the time of generation. There can be two possible ways to fix this issue. One is, using a larger target vocabulary size as 100K subword vocabulary is not giving good results in our case. Another is, creating separate vocabularies for each language instead of combining them together and creating a joint vocabulary, while the data being romanized.

## 5 Conclusion

In this paper, we describe our submission to the MultiIndicMT shared task to WAT 2021. We submit two multilingual NMT models: many-to-one (10 Indic languages to English) and one-to-many (English to 10 Indic languages). We romanize all Indic language data to convert all languages' tokens in roman script. We also generate synthetic data using the back-translation approach. We train our models on the romanized data sets which is a combination of clean corpora and synthetic back-translated corpora. We evaluate our models using BLEU, RIBES and AMFM scores and observed that many-to-one model achieves highest BLEU score of 40.08 for Hindi-English pair and one-to-many model achieves highest BLEU score of 34.48 for English-Hindi pair. However, the shared subword vocabulary at target side for the one-to-many model lead to the poor performance of the one-to-many model especially in Tamil, Telugu and Malayalam to English pairs by achieving BLEU score of 8.51, 6.25 and 3.79 respectively.

## References


Roee Aharoni, Melvin Johnson, and Orhan Firat. 2019. Massively multilingual neural machine translation. In *Proceedings of the 2019 Conference of the North American Chapter of the Association for Computational Linguistics: Human Language Technologies, Volume 1 (Long and Short Papers)*, pages 3874–3884, Minneapolis, Minnesota. Association for Computational Linguistics.

Chantal Amrhein and Rico Sennrich. 2020. On Romanization for model transfer between scripts in neural machine translation. In *Findings of the Association for Computational Linguistics: EMNLP 2020*, pages 2461–2469, Online. Association for Computational Linguistics.

Rafael E. Banchs, Luis F. D'Haro, and Haizhou Li. 2015. Adequacy–fluency metrics: Evaluating mt in the continuous space model framework. *IEEE/ACM Transactions on Audio, Speech, and Language Processing*, 23(3):472–482.

Eleftheria Briakou and Marine Carpuat. 2019. The University of Maryland's Kazakh-English neural machine translation system at WMT19. In *Proceedings of the Fourth Conference on Machine Translation (Volume 2: Shared Task Papers, Day 1)*, pages 134–140, Florence, Italy. Association for Computational Linguistics.

Raj Dabre, Chenhui Chu, and Anoop Kunchukuttan. 2020. A survey of multilingual neural machine translation. *ACM Comput. Surv.*, 53(5).

Raj Dabre, Fabien Cromierès, and Sadao Kurohashi. 2017. Enabling multi-source neural machine translation by concatenating source sentences in multiple languages. *CoRR*, abs/1702.06135.

Tobias Domhan and Felix Hieber. 2017. Using target-side monolingual data for neural machine translation through multi-task learning. In *Proceedings of the 2017 Conference on Empirical Methods in Natural Language Processing*, pages 1500–1505, Copenhagen, Denmark. Association for Computational Linguistics.

Daxiang Dong, Hua Wu, Wei He, Dianhai Yu, and Haifeng Wang. 2015. Multi-task learning for multiple language translation. In *Proceedings of the 53rd Annual Meeting of the Association for Computational Linguistics and the 7th International Joint Conference on Natural Language Processing (Volume 1: Long Papers)*, pages 1723–1732, Beijing, China. Association for Computational Linguistics.

Jinhua Du and Andy Way. 2017. Pinyin as subword unit for chinese-sourced neural machine translation. In *Proceedings of the 25th Irish Conference on Artificial Intelligence and Cognitive Science, Dublin, Ireland, December 7 - 8, 2017, volume 2086 of CEUR Workshop Proceedings*, page 89–101. CEUR-WS.org.

Orhan Firat, Kyunghyun Cho, and Yoshua Bengio. 2016. Multi-way, multilingual neural machine translation with a shared attention mechanism. In *Proceedings of the 2016 Conference of the North American Chapter of the Association for Computational Linguistics: Human Language Technologies*, pages 866–875, San Diego, California. Association for Computational Linguistics.

Markus Freitag and Orhan Firat. 2020. Complete multilingual neural machine translation. In *Proceedings of the Fifth Conference on Machine Translation*, pages 550–560, Online. Association for Computational Linguistics.

Mozhdeh Gheini and Jonathan May. 2019. A universal parent model for low-resource neural machine translation transfer. *arXiv preprint arXiv:1909.06516*.

Hideki Isozaki, Tsutomu Hirao, Kevin Duh, Katsuhito Sudoh, and Hajime Tsukada. 2010. Automatic evaluation of translation quality for distant language pairs. In *Proceedings of the 2010 Conference on Empirical Methods in Natural Language Processing*, pages 944–952, Cambridge, MA. Association for Computational Linguistics.

Melvin Johnson, Mike Schuster, Quoc V. Le, Maxim Krikun, Yonghui Wu, Zhifeng Chen, Nikhil Thorat, Fernanda Viégas, Martin Wattenberg, Greg Corrado, Macduff Hughes, and Jeffrey Dean. 2017. Google's multilingual neural machine translation system: Enabling zero-shot translation. *Transactions of the Association for Computational Linguistics*, 5:339–351.

Diederik P. Kingma and Jimmy Ba. 2015. Adam: A method for stochastic optimization. In *3rd International Conference on Learning Representations, ICLR 2015, San Diego, CA, USA, May 7-9, 2015, Conference Track Proceedings*.

Guillaume Klein, Yoon Kim, Yuntian Deng, Jean Senellart, and Alexander Rush. 2017. OpenNMT: Open-source toolkit for neural machine translation. In *Proceedings of ACL 2017, System Demonstrations*, pages 67–72, Vancouver, Canada. Association for Computational Linguistics.

Taku Kudo. 2018. Subword regularization: Improving neural network translation models with multiple subword candidates. In *Proceedings of the 56th Annual Meeting of the Association for Computational Linguistics (Volume 1: Long Papers)*, pages 66–75, Melbourne, Australia. Association for Computational Linguistics.

Taku Kudo and John Richardson. 2018. SentencePiece: A simple and language independent subword tokenizer and detokenizer for neural text processing. In *Proceedings of the 2018 Conference on Empirical Methods in Natural Language Processing: System Demonstrations*, pages 66–71, Brussels, Belgium. Association for Computational Linguistics.

Toshiaki Nakazawa, Hideki Nakayama, Chenchen Ding, Raj Dabre, Shohei Higashiyama, Hideya Mino, Isao Goto, Win Pa Pa, Anoop Kunchukuttan, Shantipriya Parida, Ondřej Bojar, Chenhui Chu, Akiko Eriguchi, Kaori Abe, and Sadao Oda, Yusuke Kurohashi. 2021. Overview of the 8th workshop on Asian translation. In *Proceedings of the 8th Workshop on Asian Translation*, Bangkok, Thailand. Association for Computational Linguistics.

Toan Q. Nguyen and David Chiang. 2017. Transfer learning across low-resource, related languages for neural machine translation. In *Proceedings of the Eighth International Joint Conference on Natural Language Processing (Volume 2: Short Papers)*, pages 296–301, Taipei, Taiwan. Asian Federation of Natural Language Processing.

Kishore Papineni, Salim Roukos, Todd Ward, and Wei-Jing Zhu. 2002. Bleu: a method for automatic evaluation of machine translation. In *Proceedings of the 40th Annual Meeting of the Association for Computational Linguistics*, pages 311–318, Philadelphia, Pennsylvania, USA. Association for Computational Linguistics.

Sukanta Sen, Kamal Kumar Gupta, Asif Ekbal, and Pushpak Bhattacharyya. 2018. IITP-MT at WAT2018: Transformer-based multilingual indic-English neural machine translation system. In *Proceedings of the 32nd Pacific Asia Conference on Language, Information and Computation: 5th Workshop on Asian Translation: 5th Workshop on Asian Translation*, Hong Kong. Association for Computational Linguistics.

Rico Sennrich, Barry Haddow, and Alexandra Birch. 2016. Improving neural machine translation models with monolingual data. In *Proceedings of the 54th Annual Meeting of the Association for Computational Linguistics (Volume 1: Long Papers)*, pages 86–96, Berlin, Germany. Association for Computational Linguistics.

Ashish Vaswani, Noam Shazeer, Niki Parmar, Jakob Uszkoreit, Llion Jones, Aidan N Gomez, Łukasz Kaiser, and Illia Polosukhin. 2017. Attention is all you need. In *Advances in neural information processing systems*, pages 5998–6008.

Jiajun Zhang and Chengqing Zong. 2016. Exploiting source-side monolingual data in neural machine translation. In *Proceedings of the 2016 Conference on Empirical Methods in Natural Language Processing*, pages 1535–1545, Austin, Texas. Association for Computational Linguistics.

Barret Zoph, Deniz Yuret, Jonathan May, and Kevin Knight. 2016. Transfer learning for low-resource neural machine translation. In *Proceedings of the 2016 Conference on Empirical Methods in Natural Language Processing*, pages 1568–1575, Austin, Texas. Association for Computational Linguistics.

# ANVITA Machine Translation System for WAT 2021 MultiIndicMT Shared Task

**Pavanpankaj Vegi, Sivabhavani J, Biswajit Paul,**
**Chitra Viswanathan, Prasanna Kumar K R**
Centre for Artificial Intelligence and Robotics
CV Raman Nagar, Bangalore
{pavanpankaj333@gmail.com, jsbhavani@cair.drdo.in, biswajit@cair.drdo.in,
chitrav@cair.drdo.in, prasanna@cair.drdo.in }

## Abstract

This paper describes ANVITA-1.0 MT system, architected for submission to WAT 2021 MultiIndicMT shared task by mcairt team, where the team participated in 20 translation directions: English→Indic and Indic→English; Indic set comprised of 10 Indian languages. ANVITA-1.0 MT system comprised of two multi-lingual NMT models one for the English→Indic directions and other for the Indic→English directions with shared encoder-decoder, catering 10 language pairs and twenty translation directions. The base models were built based on Transformer architecture and trained over MultiIndicMT WAT 2021 corpora and further employed back-translation and transliteration for selective data augmentation, and model ensemble for better generalization. Additionally, MultiIndicMT WAT 2021 corpora was distilled using a series of filtering operations before putting up for training. ANVITA-1.0 achieved highest AM-FM score for English→Bengali, 2nd for English→Tamil and 3rd for English→Hindi, Bengali→English directions on official test set. In general, performance achieved by ANVITA for the Indic→English directions are relatively better than that of English→Indic directions for all the 10 language pairs when evaluated using BLEU and RIBES, although the same trend is not observed consistently when AM-FM based evaluation was carried out. As compared to BLEU, RIBES and AM-FM based scoring placed ANVITA relatively better among all the task participants.

## 1 Introduction

This paper presents ANVITA-1.0 (A Neural Version of Indic Translation Assistance) MT system, architected for submission to WAT 2021 MultiIndicMT shared task by mcairt team. WAT 2021 MultiIndicMT shared task (Nakazawa et al., 2021) comprised of translation of 10 Indian languages Bengali(bn), Gujarati(gu), Hindi(hi), Kannada(kn), Marathi(mr), Malayalam(ml), Oriya(or), Punjabi(pa), Tamil(ta), Telugu(te) and Engish(en) in 20 translation directions (English→Indic and Indic→English) and our team participated in all 20 translation directions.

Developing quality machine translation system for the Indian languages still remains a major challenge, as large number of Indian languages are individually resource poor which greatly impacts translation quality. However some of the recent developments do show that careful utilization of multilingualism and/or monolingual corpora, translation quality can be boosted (Johnson et al., 2017; Sennrich et al., 2015).The purpose of WAT 2021 MultiIndicMT shared task is to validate the utility of MT techniques that focus on multilingualism and/or monolingual data in the context of Indian languages.

Our ANVITA-1.0 is realized as a Multilingual Neural Machine Translation(MNMT) system based on Transformer architecture (Vaswani et al., 2017). As transformer is sensitive to training noise (Liu et al., 2018), we have rigorously cleaned up the training corpus by applying set of heuristics. For better transfer of translation knowledge among the language pairs, ANVITA-1.0 used multilingual NMT approach and trained two models, one for the English→Indic and one for the Indic→English with shared encoder-decoder similar to MNMT models described by Johnson et.al (Johnson et al., 2017). Additionally, we employed back-translation (Sennrich et al., 2015) and transliteration techniques between related languages (Li et al., 2019) for selective data augmentation followed by model ensemble for better generalization. As Indian languages are morphologically rich, instead of word level tokenization, ANVITA-1.0 employed sub-word level tokenization, sentence piece (Kudo and Richardson, 2018) before putting up for training.



*Proceedings of the 8th Workshop on Asian Translation*, pages 244–249
Bangkok, Thailand (online), August 5-6, 2021. 

Details are mentioned in the subsequent sections.

ANVITA-1.0 achieved highest AM-FM score for English→Bengali, 2nd for English→Tamil and 3rd for English→Hindi, Bengali→English directions on the official WAT 2021 MultiIndicMT test set. Overall, as compared to BLEU, RIBES and Adequacy-Fluency based scoring relatively placed us better in the ranking chart.

## 2 Related Work

A comprehensive survey covering challenges, design choices and other aspects related to Multilingual Neural Machine Translation(MNMT) was presented by Dabre et.al (Dabre et al., 2020). Siripragada et al. (2020) published a low resource Indian language dataset and trained a Multilingual NMT model on it. Aharoni et al. (2019) presented a massive multilingual neural translation model with 102 languages. Li et al. (2019) has done rigorous filtering of parallel corpora. Liu et al. (2018) and Pinnis (2018) have proposed some heuristics for rigorous filtering of noise from parallel corpora. Li et al. (2019) have proposed combining parallel corpora by transliteration of related languages(grammar similarity) which improves performance. Back translation (Sennrich et al., 2015) is considered by many as one of the effective mechanism for enhancing MT performance.

## 3 Data sets

ANVITA-1.0 was primarily trained using MultiIndicMT WAT 2021[1] corpora. Additionally AI4Bharat[2] monolingual corpora was used for generating synthetic parallel data by back translation. No other additional corpora or linguistic resources were used in ANVITA-1.0.

MultiIndicMT WAT 2021 corpora (Nakazawa et al., 2021) as shared by the organizer comprises of approximately 10 million parallel sentences covering 10 language pairs (Indic, English) and sourced from the following multiple datasets. CVIT-PIB, PMIndia, IITB 3.0, JW, NLPC, UFAL EnTam, Uka Tarsadia, Wikititles, ALT, OpenSubtitles, Bible-uedin, MTEnglish2Odia, OdiaEncorp2.0, TED, WikiMatrix. MultiIndicMT WAT 2021 training corpora is summarised in Table-1. Hindi↔English has the highest number of sentence pair and Oriya↔English lowest.

[1]http://lotus.kuee.kyoto-u.ac.jp/WAT/indic-multilingual/

[2]https://indicnlp.ai4bharat.org/corpora/

| Sl. No. | Indic↔En | # Sentences | %Share |
|---|---|---|---|
| 1 | bn-en | 1302940 | 13.52% |
| 2 | gu-en | 518179 | 5.37% |
| 3 | hi-en | 3070239 | 31.86% |
| 4 | kn-en | 396882 | 4.11% |
| 5 | ml-en | 1142115 | 11.85% |
| 6 | mr-en | 621725 | 6.45% |
| 7 | or-en | 252160 | 2.62% |
| 8 | pa-en | 518520 | 5.38% |
| 9 | ta-en | 1354374 | 14.05% |
| 10 | te-en | 457523 | 4.75% |

Table 1: Statistics of MultiIndicMT WAT 2021 training corpora (before filtering)

## 4 System Overview

This section describes ANVITA-1.0 MT system and its subsystems with reasonable details.

### 4.1 Data Preprocessing

This section presents set of preprocessing steps employed by ANVITA-1.0.

#### 4.1.1 Data Filtering

Like most automatically curated corpora and corpora compiled from such curated corpus, MultiIndicMT WAT 2021 corpora is also not free from noises. A quick glance through the corpora provided with a rough assessment of noises present and aided in employing set of heuristics to filter out many of those noisy sentence pairs. This is all the more critical as transformer based models are sensitive to noises (Liu et al., 2018). Rigorous distillation of training corpora was carried by employing set of heuristics similar to as described by Bei Li (Li et al., 2019). The heuristics applied for filtering out noises from MultiIndicMT WAT 2021 corpora are as given below.

- Filter out sentence pair, in which either source or target sentence is empty.
- Filter out sentence pair, in which either source or target sentence length greater than 800 characters.
- Filter out sentence pair in which length of source and target sentence ratio is greater than 2.5.
- Filter out sentence pair in which length of source and target sentence ratio is less than 0.4.

| Indic↔En | # Sentences | %Share | %Filtered |
|---|---|---|---|
| bn-en | 1198915 | 13.73% | 7.98% |
| gu-en | 491036 | 5.62% | 5.23% |
| hi-en | 2885632 | 33.05% | 6.01% |
| kn-en | 336967 | 3.85% | 15.09% |
| ml-en | 967909 | 11.08% | 15.25% |
| mr-en | 587576 | 6.72% | 5.49% |
| or-en | 245077 | 2.80% | 2.81% |
| pa-en | 493337 | 5.65% | 4.85% |
| ta-en | 1123269 | 12.85% | 17.06% |
| te-en | 401318 | 4.60% | 12.28% |

Table 2: Statistics of MultiIndicMT WAT 2021 training corpora after filtering noisy sentence pairs

- Filter out sentence pair , if source or target sentence contains word having length greater than 10.
- Filter out sentence pair, if source sentence has at least 10 characters of other language.
- Filter out sentence pair, if source sentence has at least 60% characters of other language (used utf-8 ranges for other language character identification).

Approximately 15% of the total sentence pairs, amounting to 1.5 million sentence pairs were tagged as noisy after applying the above heuristics and were filtered out from the MultiIndicMT WAT 2021 training corpora. Detailed corpus statistics after filtering operation is given in Table-2. Final training data size after filtering turned out to be 8731036 sentence pairs. Data filtering improved both translation performance and convergence rate.

#### 4.1.2 Tokenization at Sub-word Level

To effectively make use of the morphological richness property of Indian languages, sub-word level tokenization is employed instead of word or character level tokenization.

**English→Indic:** Sentence piece tokenizer (Kudo and Richardson, 2018) was used with 80K joint vocabulary of 10 target Indic languages, 16K vocabulary of English and character coverage of 1.0.

**Indic→English:** Sentence piece tokenizer (Kudo and Richardson, 2018) was used with 48K joint vocabulary of 10 Indic source languages, 16K vocabulary of English and character coverage of 1.0.

| Indic↔English | Special Token |
|---|---|
| bn-en | @%+@ |
| gu-en | {%-} |
| hi-en | —_^ |
| kn-en | &*—& |
| ml-en | ?:/? |
| mr-en | #_+# |
| or-en | =&-= |
| pa-en | ~&[~ |
| ta-en | :*&: |
| te-en | *]̂* |

Table 3: Special tokens used for tagging language pairs at the source side

#### 4.1.3 Tagging of Source Sentences

To guide the input-output sequence mapping task better under multilingual setting, all sentences at the source side were tagged with language pair information using special tokens and placed at the beginning of each source sentence (Johnson et al., 2017). Special language tokens consisted of 4 characters and all having special symbols. Special symbols were used to avoid overlapping of language tokens with data tokens and token lengths were decided based on minimum number of characters required to tag 10 language pairs distinctly. Language tokens were used only at the source side during training of both the models i.e Indic→English and English→Indic models. Table-3 lists out the language tokens used.

### 4.2 Data Augmentation

Data augmentation has become a de-facto step for low resource MT. Following strategies were applied for augmenting data in ANVITA-1.0.

#### 4.2.1 Related Language Transliteration

As most of the languages fall under low resource category, we employed related-language transliteration strategy for the top three low resource languages. Relatedness is decided based on similarities between languages (Li et al., 2019). Top three low resource languages as found in MultiIndicMT WAT 2021 corpora are Oriya(or), Kannada(kn), and Gujarati(gu). To the best of our knowledge, related languages of these three low resource Indian languages are listed in Table-4. Relatively high resource related language training data were transliterated into low resource language using transliterated method as described by Ahmad Bhat et

| Low Resource Language | Related Language |
|---|---|
| Oriya | Bengali |
| Kannada | Telugu |
| Gujarati | Hindi |

Table 4: Related languages of top three low resource languages

| Language Pair Indic↔English | # Sentence (%Share) Indic→En | En→Indic |
|---|---|---|
| bn-en | 1198915 (7.67%) | 1198915 (9.07%) |
| gu-en | 3976668 (25.46%) | 3376668 (25.54%) |
| hi-en | 2885632 (18.47%) | 2885632 (21.83%) |
| kn-en | 1338285 (8.56%) | 738285 (5.58%) |
| ml-en | 967909 (6.19%) | 967909 (7.32%) |
| mr-en | 587576 (3.76%) | 587576 (4.44%) |
| or-en | 2043992 (13.08%) | 1443992 (10.92%) |
| pa-en | 1093337 (7.00%) | 493337 (3.73%) |
| ta-en | 1123269 (7.19%) | 1123269 (8.49%) |
| te-en | 401318 (2.56%) | 401318 (3.03%) |

Table 5: Statistics of final training data after applying transliteration and back translation

al. (Bhat et al., 2014) and added to the low resource language training data. For instance, Bengali sentences were transliterated into Oriya and augmented with Oriya training data.

As Marathi and Hindi languages both share the same script, so in order to avoid script overlapping, we mapped characters of Marathi sentences to Unicode Block 0D80- 0DFF. This seems to have reduced sharing of translation knowledge and impacted results. However this needs to be verified further through experimentation.

#### 4.2.2 Back Translation

Back translation (Sennrich et al., 2015) is considered as one of the effective mechanism for enhancing MT performance, specially involving low resource languages. As most of languages in the task involved are low resource, back translation was applied for the top four low resource languages observed in the MultiIndicMT WAT 2021 corpora namely Oriya, Kannada, Punjabi, and Gujarati. We extracted monolingual corpora of 6 lakh sentences for each of the four low resource language pair from the AI4Bharat (Kakwani et al., 2020) corpora for the purpose. Statistics of the final training corpora after data augmentation is shown in Table-5.

### 4.3 Model Training

ANVITA-1.0 was trained based on Transformer architecture and for better sharing of knowledge among Indian languages, specially for resource poor languages, two multilingual models were trained in (a) One-to-Many fashion for English→Indic and (b) Many-to-One fashion for Indic→English with shared encoder-decoder, similar to as described by Johnson et.al (Johnson et al., 2017).

Ensembling of multiple models, which are diverse in nature, have shown improvement of translation performance and better generalization (Li et al., 2019). Due to time and resource limitations, we could not work out on diverse models. However, we ensemble last 5 checkpoints i.e (560000-600000 iterations).

## 5 Experimental Details

ANVITA-1.0 used OpenNMT-py 2.0 (Klein et al., 2017) toolkit for training. Training configuration are 600000 steps for Indic→English, 440000 steps for English→Indic, with batch size of 4096, dropout 0.1, batch type tokens, adam optimizer, warmup steps 8000, word embedding size 512, encoder layers 6, decoder layers 6, heads 8,feed forward dimension of 2048, rnn size 512 and noam as learning rate decay method. ANVITA-1.0 was trained on NVIDIA DGX machine having 4 V100 GPU cards, each having 32GB of GPU memory. Training of Indic→English took approximately 96 hours and English→Indic took approximately 72 hours.

## 6 Evaluation and Results

Translation quality of ANVITA-1.0 was assessed by the organizer (Nakazawa et al., 2021) on the official WAT 2021 MultiIndicMT test set using BLEU, RIBES(Isozaki et al., 2010) and Adequacy-Frequency(Banchs et al., 2015) based metrics. The official evaluation results as declared by the organizer for all the 20 translation directions are shown in Table-6 and Table-7.

Performance of Indic→English 10 translation directions ranges from 27.29 to 40.05 BLEU points, where Marathi→English happens to be the lowest and Hindi→English highest scorers respectively. For English→Indic 10 translation directions performance ranges from 35.85 to 6.17 BLEU points, in which English→Malayalam scored lowest and English→Hindi highest. We believe that, because of the relatively high resource nature of Hindi↔English language pair, this particular pair outperformed all other pairs.

| Indic→English | BLEU | RIBES | AM-FM |
|---|---|---|---|
| bn→en | 29.96 | 0.798326 | 0.786717 |
| gu→en | 36.77 | 0.829389 | 0.819546 |
| hi→en | 40.05 | 0.850322 | 0.832119 |
| kn→en | 31.16 | 0.803525 | 0.799216 |
| ml→en | 28.07 | 0.792884 | 0.794932 |
| mr→en | 27.29 | 0.785579 | 0.780231 |
| or→en | 29.96 | 0.798326 | 0.795586 |
| pa→en | 38.42 | 0.840360 | 0.818332 |
| ta→en | 28.04 | 0.793839 | 0.790184 |
| te→en | 29.26 | 0.790319 | 0.786396 |

Table 6: Performance of ANVITA-1.0 for Indic→English directions on the official WAT 2021 MultiIndicMT test set.

| English→Indic | BLEU | RIBES | AM-FM |
|---|---|---|---|
| en→bn | 13.02 | 0.715490 | 0.779592 |
| en→gu | 23.21 | 0.809389 | 0.816739 |
| en→hi | 35.85 | 0.846656 | 0.822626 |
| en→kn | 14.58 | 0.726259 | 0.805963 |
| en→ml | 6.17 | 0.622598 | 0.793308 |
| en→mr | 14.90 | 0.740079 | 0.791850 |
| en→or | 17.71 | 0.743984 | 0.763064 |
| en→pa | 30.56 | 0.830405 | 0.810106 |
| en→ta | 11.98 | 0.707054 | 0.801632 |
| en→te | 11.17 | 0.702337 | 0.783647 |

Table 7: Performance of ANVITA-1.0 for English→Indic directions on the official WAT 2021 MultiIndicMT test set

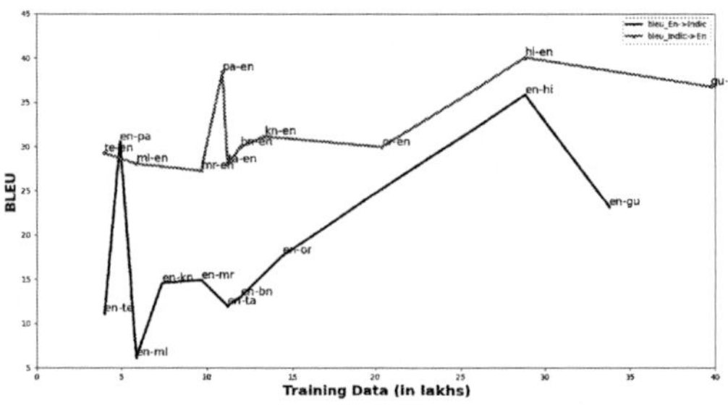


Figure 1: Performance of ANVITA-1.0 wrt size of training data, when evaluated using BLEU for Indic→English and English→Indic directions on the official WAT 2021 MultiIndicMT test set.

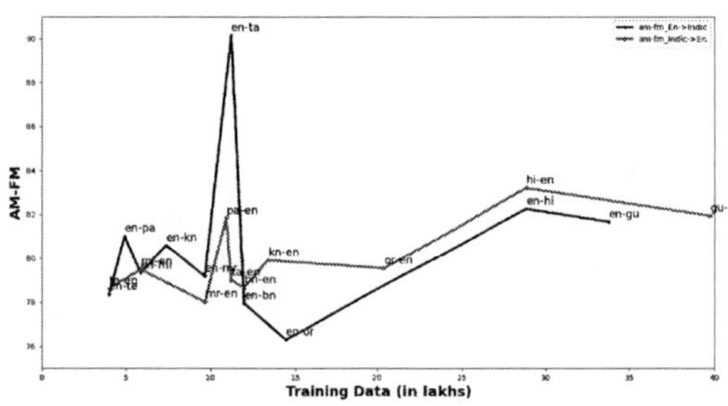


Figure 2: Performance of ANVITA-1.0 wrt size of training data, when evaluated using AM-FM scores for Indic→English and English→Indic directions on the official WAT 2021 MultiIndicMT test set.

Figure-1 and Figure-2 show how performance of ANVITA-1.0 changes as a parameter of training data size. This evaluated was carried out on the official WAT 2021 MultiIndicMT test set using BLEU and AM-FM metrics. Barring few exceptions, training data size seems to be positively correlated with the translation performance. The exceptions are possibly due to implicit transfer of translation knowledge among the related languages.

## 7 Conclusion and Future Directions

The overall translation performance achieved by ANVITA-1.0 for the Indic→English directions are encouraging. Data augmentation largely aided the relatively lower resource languages well. Transfer of translation knowledge through shared encoder-decoder seems to be aided the related language better and data filtering improved the overall performance. RIBES and AM-FM based scoring placed us relatively better than BLEU.

Translation performance figures for the Indic→English directions achieved by ANVITA-1.0 are relatively better than that of English→Indic directions for all language pairs, when evaluated using BLEU and RIBES, though the same trend is not observed consistently when AM-FM based evaluation was carried out. Potential reasons could be One to Many mapping is relatively harder to learn as compared to Many to One mapping with shared decoder. One of the future direction would be to closely investigate whether having shared encoder but separate decoders helps for One-to-Many models in the Indic context. Though we have applied a large number of data filtering heuristics, we noticed that training data was still not free from noises. So another potential future direction would be to explore more effective data filtering techniques and its impacts on MT performance. Exploration of additional data augmentation strategies and effective transfer of translation knowledge, their shares in improving MT performance would be a critical direction when it comes to handling low resource languages. Having more diverse parallel corpora for the Indian languages will help Indic MT tasks and automated methods for compilation of large and diverse Indic corpus is a much needed one.

## 8 Acknowledgments

The authors would like to thank Director, CAIR for his constant encouragement, guidance and enablement.

## References

Roee Aharoni, Melvin Johnson, and Orhan Firat. 2019. Massively multilingual neural machine translation. *arXiv preprint arXiv:1903.00089*.

Rafael E. Banchs, Luis F. DHaro, and Haizhou Li. 2015. Adequacyfluency metrics: Evaluating mt in the continuous space model framework. *IEEE/ACM Transactions on Audio, Speech, and Language Processing*, 23(3):472–482.

Irshad Ahmad Bhat, Vandan Mujadia, Aniruddha Tammewar, Riyaz Ahmad Bhat, and Manish Shrivastava. 2014. Iiit-h system submission for fire2014 shared task on transliterated search. In *Proceedings of the Forum for Information Retrieval Evaluation*, pages 48–53.

Raj Dabre, Chenhui Chu, and Anoop Kunchukuttan. 2020. A comprehensive survey of multilingual neural machine translation. *arXiv preprint arXiv:2001.01115*.

Hideki Isozaki, Tsutomu Hirao, Kevin Duh, Katsuhito Sudoh, and Hajime Tsukada. 2010. Automatic evaluation of translation quality for distant language pairs. In *Proceedings of the 2010 Conference on Empirical Methods in Natural Language Processing*, pages 944–952, Cambridge, MA. Association for Computational Linguistics.

Melvin Johnson, Mike Schuster, Quoc V Le, Maxim Krikun, Yonghui Wu, Zhifeng Chen, Nikhil Thorat, Fernanda Viégas, Martin Wattenberg, Greg Corrado, et al. 2017. Googles multilingual neural machine translation system: Enabling zero-shot translation. *Transactions of the Association for Computational Linguistics*, 5:339–351.

Divyanshu Kakwani, Anoop Kunchukuttan, Satish Golla, NC Gokul, Avik Bhattacharyya, Mitesh M Khapra, and Pratyush Kumar. 2020. inlpsuite: Monolingual corpora, evaluation benchmarks and pre-trained multilingual language models for indian languages. In *Proceedings of the 2020 Conference on Empirical Methods in Natural Language Processing: Findings*, pages 4948–4961.

Guillaume Klein, Yoon Kim, Yuntian Deng, Jean Senellart, and Alexander M. Rush. 2017. Opennmt: Open-source toolkit for neural machine translation. In *Proc. ACL*.

Taku Kudo and John Richardson. 2018. Sentencepiece: A simple and language independent subword tokenizer and detokenizer for neural text processing. *arXiv preprint arXiv:1808.06226*.

Bei Li, Yinqiao Li, Chen Xu, Ye Lin, Jiqiang Liu, Hui Liu, Ziyang Wang, Yuhao Zhang, Nuo Xu, Zeyang Wang, et al. 2019. The niutrans machine translation systems for wmt19. In *Proceedings of the Fourth Conference on Machine Translation (Volume 2: Shared Task Papers, Day 1)*, pages 257–266.

Hairong Liu, Mingbo Ma, Liang Huang, Hao Xiong, and Zhongjun He. 2018. Robust neural machine translation with joint textual and phonetic embedding. *arXiv preprint arXiv:1810.06729*.

Toshiaki Nakazawa, Hideki Nakayama, Chenchen Ding, Raj Dabre, Shohei Higashiyama, Hideya Mino, Isao Goto, Win Pa Pa, Anoop Kunchukuttan, Shantipriya Parida, Ondej Bojar, Chenhui Chu, Akiko Eriguchi, Kaori Abe, and Sadao Oda, Yusuke Kurohashi. 2021. Overview of the 8th workshop on Asian translation. In *Proceedings of the 8th Workshop on Asian Translation*, Bangkok, Thailand. Association for Computational Linguistics.

Mārcis Pinnis. 2018. Tildes parallel corpus filtering methods for wmt 2018. In *Proceedings of the Third Conference on Machine Translation: Shared Task Papers*, pages 939–945.

Rico Sennrich, Barry Haddow, and Alexandra Birch. 2015. Improving neural machine translation models with monolingual data. *arXiv preprint arXiv:1511.06709*.

Shashank Siripragada, Jerin Philip, Vinay P Namboodiri, and CV Jawahar. 2020. A multilingual parallel corpora collection effort for indian languages. *arXiv preprint arXiv:2007.07691*.

Ashish Vaswani, Noam Shazeer, Niki Parmar, Jakob Uszkoreit, Llion Jones, Aidan N Gomez, Lukasz Kaiser, and Illia Polosukhin. 2017. Attention is all you need. *arXiv preprint arXiv:1706.03762*.

# Author Index

**Association for Computational Linguistics**
209 N. Eighth Street
Stroudsburg, Pennsylvania 18360

ISBN 978-1-7138-3390-1

CURRAN ASSOCIATES INC.
proceedings.com